FOCUSED INQUIRY

True Stories | Narrative & Understanding

2015–2016 Edition

Department of Focused Inquiry
University College | Virginia Commonwealth University

HAYDEN McNEIL

Pree

Focused Inquiry Textbook Committee, eds.

Photos provided by Hayden-McNeil, LLC are owned or used under license

Cover design by Ivan Witteborg

Printed in the United States of America

10 9 8 7 6 5 4 3 2 1

ISBN 978-0-7380-7460-3

Hayden-McNeil Publishing
14903 Pilot Drive
Plymouth, MI 48170
www.hmpublishing.com

Reed 7460-3 F15

Acknowledgments

Chinua Achebe—"Africa's Tarnished Name." Reprinted by Permission of the Publisher of *Multiculturalism and Hybridity in African Literatures*, edited by Hal Wylie, Bernth Lindfors © 2000 Africa World Press.

Acknowledgements and copyrights are continued at the back of the book on pages 435–438, which constitute an extension of the copyright page.

TABLE OF CONTENTS

Preface

Readings

Student Essays

Narrative

Analysis

Argument

PREFACE

PREFACE

You Are Here

By Gardner Campbell

I hope you had a good high school experience. There are many wonderful, kind, thoughtful teachers in high school, teachers who can stimulate young minds and help to mentor students through the particularly difficult time called adolescence. Perhaps you were fortunate to have one of those teachers—perhaps even more than one. I hope so. It seems to get harder every year for those teachers to flourish and do their best work within a system that's increasingly test-driven, monitored, scheduled, regulated, and regimented. I imagine you felt those pressures too, especially as you tried to make sense of your own place in the world of your peers, and then in the world of adults—a quest that for some of us has never ended. (Perhaps I'm just projecting here.) You may have wondered whether college would be more of the same, grades 13–16, but away from home and your family's support…and their surveillance as well.

Now you've come through the anxious, exciting moments as you waited to find out which college or university you'd be going to after you graduated. You've been oriented, welcomed, enrolled. Now you are in your first-year seminar, Focused Inquiry. You hold the textbook in your hand. Now what?

That's the question, all right, and there are many ways to approach it, including the one in which the university turns the question around and asks it of *you*. That's actually not a bad way to approach the question. It's both a challenge and a compliment, for it assumes that you are capable of self-authorship, and that the university exists to help that capability grow and become strong, strong enough to last through all the surprises of a lifetime, whether those surprises are good or bad or simply baffling.

Yet even the attractive (and very teacherly) strategy of taking your "Now what?" and returning it to you for an answer leaves out a crucial part of the story. If you were very, very lucky in high school, you may know something about that crucial part. I wasn't lucky that way. Most folks aren't. No one in high school told me that "now what?" is a question human beings have been asking about school itself ever since the idea of school emerged in human history. What is school for? Why do we do it? What do we suppose will happen as a result? Do we find that our expectations are met? Is there a place for odd, quirky, even defiant minds in a school? If so, how would you grade their work?

Lately, even more intense questions have been added to the growing list, especially those related to the phase of schooling you're beginning right now. How does the life of the mind lead to or empower a life of work and gainful employment? Why has state support for public higher education declined so dramatically? Why is tuition so expensive, and student debt so high? What is the real value of a college degree? Should everyone go to college? If not, who'll decide who gets to go and who doesn't? And for crying out loud, what role should computers, the Internet, the World Wide Web, Twitter and Facebook and YouTube and Vine and Instagram and Snapchat and Reddit and Yik Yak and [insert latest app, gadget, or social media start-up here] play in a university education?

Forget crying out loud. Try sobbing out loud. What does school have to do with education? What does education have to do with learning? What does learning look like when it leads not just to memorized knowledge or practiced skills, but to *understanding*? If thinking and understanding involve "going beyond the information given," as one cognitive psychologist has argued (Bruner 34), how on earth can school teach thinking and understanding without making those very concepts just another piece of information that you've been given?

These are urgent questions. They concern what it means to be human, and how (or even whether) we can build a better world together. By being here, you're not just preparing to be part of that conversation. You're taking your place in that conversation. There's much to learn, but there's also much you already know, and years of experience in your own efforts to make sense of the world. We long to hear your voices. We need them, for we all have more questions than answers.

It is true and important that your professors have learned a great deal, and that they have distinguished themselves in their own education by their ability to work within these vast questions, to create new knowledge, and to imagine new modes of understanding. When I encountered my best professors in college, whether they were in English, statistics, psychology, or musicology, I knew I was in the presence of very special human beings, people who had devoted their lives to the kind of understanding I wanted for my own life. At the same time, though, my best professors assumed from the very start that I had something to contribute to their understanding, something they could learn from, too. This intensely reciprocal learning is why most of us joined this profession. It's where the magic happens. It's one of the great rewards of school at its best.

One of my favorite books about college is Robert Pirsig's *Zen and the Art of Motorcycle Maintenance*. It's an honest book, which means that many of the descriptions of school are pretty grim. What gives those moments their weight, however, isn't the pain or ironies so much as the great love Pirsig's characters have for the big questions and for the people who ask them. Can school be an aspect of love? *Zen and the Art of Motorcycle Maintenance* asks that question in a number of ways, many of them involving, yes, real motorcycle maintenance. Throughout the book, though, the bike is a metaphor for humanity's relation to the things it builds—and one of those things is school. In the excerpt below, Pirsig's narrator is writing about bad motorcycle mechanics, but he could just as well be writing about a danger we all face in this university we build together:

> But the biggest clue seemed to be their expressions. They were hard to explain. Good-natured, friendly, easygoing—and uninvolved. They were like spectators. You had the feeling they had just wandered in there themselves and somebody had handed them a wrench. There was no identification with the job. No saying, "I am a mechanic." At 5 P.M. or whenever their eight hours were in, you knew they would cut it off and not have another thought about their work. They were already trying not to have any thoughts about their work on the job.... Or rather, they had something to do with it, but their own selves were outside of it, detached, removed. (Pirsig 25)

One of the bad things school can teach is how to be "good-natured, friendly, easygoing—and uninvolved." Sometimes it seems as if that's the only way to get through all the assignments, grades, expectations, distractions, judgments, and uncertainties. Commitment, passion, involvement: these can seem recipes for disappointment, especially when we see how much we have to learn and how hard we have to work to get there. But there's no magic unless we are intensely involved—unless we're all in.

All in. Pirsig has a word for this commitment to the very idea of commitment. He calls it gumption.

> Gumption is the psychic gasoline that keeps the whole thing going. If you haven't got it there's no way the motorcycle can possibly be fixed. But if you have got it and know how to keep it there's absolutely no way in this whole world that motorcycle can keep from getting fixed. It's bound to happen. Therefore the thing that must be monitored at all times and preserved before anything else is the gumption. (Pirsig 286)

Gumption is what I dig for as I write these very words. Gumption is the only thing that kept the writers, thinkers, and dreamers in this anthology from giving up on the essays they eventually finished, and now offer to you. Gumption is what your professors need every time they think, write, create, or teach. Gumption is what you will need to become your best self: you, a thinker and writer and creator and a teacher, too. Gumption is the gift we give each other as we make our way on the journey we share.

I wish for you this gumption, this commitment to commitment itself. I look forward to the school we will bring into being together, and the understanding we will gain as a result. Caravanistas, I salute you!

Appreciatively,

"Dr. C."
Gardner Campbell, PhD
Vice Provost for Learning Innovation and Student Success
Dean, University College

Works Cited

Bruner, Jerome. *In Search of Pedagogy Volume I: The Selected Works of Jerome Bruner, 1957–1978*. New York, NY: Routledge, 2006.

Pirsig, Robert. *Zen and the Art of Motorcycle Maintenance*. 25th Anniversary Edition. New York, NY: HarperCollins, 1999. Rpt. 2009.

A Message from the Writing Center Director

By Brian McTague

Welcome to VCU and the beginning of an exciting new chapter in your life! VCU has a ton of wonderful resources, including the Writing Center, to help you develop the tools you need to succeed in college and your professional life. Writing is one of the most important of these tools, but it is often undervalued and misunderstood. At the Writing Center, we can help you think about your writing in more meaningful and exciting ways. By having conversations about your ideas and how to best articulate them, we will help you to see the potential you have to make a difference in your life and learning through your writing. As scholar R.D. Walshe says in the article, "The Learning Power of Writing," "I am about to use humanity's second greatest invention, writing, with which I will take language from the invisible mind and make it visible on paper where I can work on it with full attention until it becomes the best thinking, the best learning, of which I am capable" (22). At the Writing Center, we will help you reach new levels of capability.

Writing is special in that it is both a transformative learning experience for you, as well as a way to share your thoughts and ideas with others. It has limitless potential to profoundly influence both the writer and reader. Emily Dickinson, the American poet, famously said, "I know nothing in the world that has as much power as a word." Yet, many people still say they do not enjoy writing. This is understandable—after all, writing is hard work. There are various reasons why this might be true: not knowing how to get started on a piece, exploring the unknown alone, or memories of stressful essay exams. Regardless of the source of any writing anxiety you have, or even if you love to write and have been succeeding at it for years, the Writing Center is here to help you make the transition to successful academic writing. Along the way, we may help debunk some myths about writing: that it has to be done in isolation, that it's only about surface correctness, and that using a resource like the Center means you cannot manage on your own. Overall, we strive to make more confident writers who are able to best articulate their ideas. That's something *everyone* can benefit from.

As you become a more confident writer, you will see that writing is so much more than many people realize. Especially at the university level, writing becomes more than just a way to show what you have learned. It is about thinking critically, discovering new things, making meaning out of what you find, and guiding your reader to understand and value that meaning. In the best writing, you continue to think and learn *as you write* and as you get feedback from others. That might all sound challenging, and it is, but in the best way possible. Your collegiate experience will be that much more profound if you fully engage on all levels, discovering new things about yourself and the world you live in. Writing is one of the best ways you can do this, and the Writing Center is here to help you accomplish it.

Our consultants are going to ask you a lot of questions—to get to know about you and your interests, to understand your ideas as they pertain to your assignment, and to help you figure out how you can best articulate those ideas. We're going to ask you to read your work aloud. This is not meant to embarrass you or make you feel self-conscious, but to get you to fully engage with your work. Reading your written words out loud is a powerful way for you to truly gain ownership over your work. You will also be surprised how much proofreading and editing you can get done while reading out loud ("Oh, that comma shouldn't be there!" "That's not the word I meant to use!"), so we can then concentrate on the bigger picture with you. Students are often surprised to find out we do not just read and "correct" papers. It is not that editing and proofreading are not important—they are—but they do not represent the meaningful learning opportunities that, as a learning support service, the Writing Center is dedicated to.

It is this "bigger picture" we are dedicated to helping you understand and learn from. What does this mean? Well, again, it is your ideas and how you are articulating them. As writers, we usually know what we want to say, but finding the best, most academic way of saying it can be more difficult. This is especially true when writing is viewed as an isolated activity, which is something most of us have been taught through our elementary and high school experiences. Through research and experience, however, we have found that dialogue with others is an integral part of the writing process. What better way to figure out how to best represent your ideas than by sharing them with someone else—someone who is not your professor. You never want your instructor to be the first person to read your work. By meeting with a consultant at the Writing Center *before* you turn in a paper, you're sharing and talking about your work with another person—someone who will give you honest feedback to help you revise and strengthen your work.

As I mentioned, we are here to help you evolve into a more self-assured writer who can best articulate the complicated ideas we engage with in college. The more you talk to us, the more confidence you will gain about your work. It makes sense, because you need to talk and think things through in order to make sense of them and figure out what you want to say—and *how* to say it. Academic writing is often different from the school writing you've done in the past. Professors expect a more nuanced, higher level of engagement and critical thinking. Consultants at the Writing Center are all experienced in excelling at that type of writing. We also participate in ongoing training and development so we can best help all students with all types of writing. We are not just here for you while you are in Focused Inquiry, but also for all other classes you are taking, be it Biology, Psychology, Business, or English. We are also here for other writing projects you may have, such as creative work or personal statements. We will continue to be here for your entire time at VCU. Join us and start your journey to becoming the most confident and capable writer you can be!

Works Cited

Walshe, R.D. "The Learning Power of Writing." *The English Journal* 76.6 (1987): 22–27. Print.

What Is Focused Inquiry?

By Jessica Shim

Dear Focused Inquiry student,

Congratulations on making it to VCU! You are, according to research, on your way to being a part of the 7% of people in the world who have college degrees. As a former Focused Inquiry student, I have no doubt in my mind that if you do it right, this class will take your college experience to a whole new level of meaningful.

Every FI experience is different. It depends on your personality, your passions, your classmates, your professor, your past experiences...I could go on and on. I hope I can somewhat articulately share with you what my experiences in this class have brought me, and in turn you can get a better understanding of the course as well as decide where you want your experiences to go. This could be the first "focused inquiry" task of your textbook!

My love for Focused Inquiry began when my professor held a class on the top of the Broad Street parking deck for a lesson on Richmond. She pointed out all these buildings and talked to us about the historical moments that happened in them, and the individual people who were involved in these moments. She showed us where Anna Whitehead Bodeker organized the first Virginia State Woman Suffrage Association meeting in 1870, and pointed out the less-than-handful of women who went to this meeting. After several decades of dedication and change from hundreds of women, the movement grew all around Richmond and in Virginia, and by 1916, the Equal Suffrage League had opened 115 chapters across the state. This all started in the mind of a human being who decided it was not fair that women didn't have the right to vote, and wanted to educate people on this issue and convince them that the community needed a significant shift in thought and culture. I fell in love with the idea that one brave person could be all that is necessary to inspire and ignite progress.

This is what you will be doing in Focused Inquiry. You will hone your power to perceive, evaluate, and act on a problem you wish to change. Through your research and assessments, you may notice some changes in your personal and academic life. You may start catching yourself having deeper, more meaningful conversations with your friends and family, perhaps about how frustrating it is that apathy seems like an engrained stitch in our society. You may start noticing situations and observing your surroundings in ways you never really have before—general things like how a person's experiences can shape perspective in a million different ways, and specific things like how a popular Chinese chain restaurant opened on a street with four other family-owned Asian restaurants. You may start questioning why Richmond is one of the largest food deserts in the States and how you can rally your peers to discuss and act upon helping those who are marginalized because of this issue.

These changes are good; opening up your mind to the seemingly endless problems in the world may seem a little depressing, but FI helps you see the plethora of inspiring solutions, as well. You will obtain the tools you need to act on problems you are passionate about, and that is the beauty of this class. The power you gain from learning how to research, connect, and come up with a viable solution, the sense of identity and self-awareness you obtain from learning how to convince people to do the right thing, is the priceless consequence of taking this mandatory class.

It took me a while to realize the full effects of FI. When I took UNIV111 freshman year, I didn't realize how practical every single moment in that class would be in the long run. FI came back to me when I was drafting my first petitions and writing my first cover letters. It came back to me when I was promoting the importance of local businesses through the annual Earth Day market I organize. It came back to me when I was fundraising and educating for cleaner water flow in the James River. It came back to me when I started noticing all of the world's problems, and when I started wondering why someone wasn't doing anything about it. It came back to me when I realized I was "someone," just like everyone else.

We are living in our generation, right now. Through this class, I hope you realize the power you have as an individual to make changes in the community while it is our time, so that our collective can work towards a better society for ourselves and for those who come after us. Remember, it's your world—we're all just living in it.

Sincerely,

Jessica Shim
Class of 2016

READINGS

Africa's Tarnished Name

By Chinua Achebe

It is a great irony of history and geography that Africa, whose landmass is closer than any other to the mainland of Europe, should come to occupy in the European psychological disposition the farthest point of otherness, should indeed become Europe's very antithesis. The French-African poet and statesman Léopold Sédar Senghor, in full awareness of this paradox, chose to celebrate that problematic proximity in a poem, "Prayer to Masks," with the startling imagery of one of nature's most profound instances of closeness: "joined together at the navel." And why not? After all, the shores of northern Africa and southern Europe enclose, like two cupped hands, the waters of the world's most famous sea, perceived by the ancients as the very heart and center of the world. Senghor's metaphor would have been better appreciated in the days of ancient Egypt and Greece than today.

History aside, geography has its own brand of lesson in the paradox of proximity for us. This lesson, which was probably lost on everyone else except those of us living in West Africa in the last days of the British Raj, was the ridiculous fact of longitudinal equality between London, mighty imperial metropolis, and Accra, rude rebel camp of colonial insurrection; so that, their unequal stations in life notwithstanding, they were named by the same Greenwich meridian and consequently doomed together to the same time of day!

But longitude is only half the story. There is also latitude, and latitude gives London and Accra very different experiences of midday temperature, for example, and perhaps gave their inhabitants over past eons of time radically different complexions. So differences are there, if those are what one is looking for. But there is no way in which such differences as do exist could satisfactorily explain the profound perception of alienness which Africa has come to represent for Europe.

This perception problem is not in its origin the result of ignorance, as we are sometimes inclined to think. At least, it is not ignorance entirely, or even primarily. It was in general a deliberate *invention* devised to facilitate two gigantic historical events: the Atlantic slave trade and the colonization of Africa by Europe, the second event following closely on the heels of the first, and the two together stretching across almost half a millennium from about A.D. 1500. In an important and authoritative study of this invention, two American scholars, Dorothy Hammond and Alta Jablow, show how a dramatic change in the content of British writing about Africa coincided with an increase in the volume of the slave trade to its highest level in the eighteenth century. That content shifted from almost indifferent and matter-of-fact reports of what the voyagers had seen to judgmental evaluation of the Africans.... The shift to such a pejorative comment was due in large measure to the effects of the slave trade. A vested interest in the slave trade produced a literature of devaluation, and since the slave trade was under attack, the most derogatory writing about Africa came from its literary defenders. [Scottish slave trader Archibald] Dalzel, for instance, prefaced his work [*The History of Dahomy*] with an apologia for slavery: "Whatever evils the slave trade may be attended with…it is mercy…to poor wretches, who…would otherwise suffer from the butcher's knife." Numerous proslavery tracts appeared, all intent upon showing the immorality and degradation of Africans.…Enslavement of such a degraded people was thus not only justifiable but even desirable. The character of Africans could change only for the better through contact with their European masters. Slavery, in effect, became the means of the Africans' salvation, for it introduced them to Christianity and civilization.

The vast arsenal of derogatory images of Africa amassed to defend the slave trade and, later, colonization gave the world a literary tradition that is now, happily, defunct, but also a particular way of looking (or, rather, not looking) at Africa and Africans that endures, alas, into our own day. And so, although those sensational "African" novels which were so popular in the nineteenth century and the early part of the twentieth have trickled to a virtual stop, their centuries-old obsession with lurid and degrading stereotypes of Africa has been bequeathed to the cinema, to journalism, to certain varieties of anthropology, even to humanitarianism and missionary work itself.

A few years ago, there was an extraordinary program on television about the children of the major Nazi war criminals, whose lives had been devastated by the burden of the guilt of their fathers. I remember how I felt quite sorry for them in the beginning. But then, out of nowhere, came the information that one of them had gone into the church and would go as a missionary to the Congo. I sat up.

"What has the Congo got to do with it?" I asked my television screen. Then I remembered the motley parade of adventurers, of saints and sinners that had been drawn from Europe to that region since it was first discovered by Europe in 1482—Franciscan monks, Jesuit priests, envoys from the kings of Portugal, explorers and missionaries, agents of King Leopold of the Belgians, H. M. Stanley, Roger Casement, Joseph Conrad, Albert Schweitzer, ivory hunters and rubber merchants, slave traders and humanitarians. They all made their visit and left their mark, for good or ill. And the Congo, like the ancient tree by the much used farm road, bears on its bark countless scars of the machete.

Paradoxically, a saint like Schweitzer can give one a lot more trouble than a King Leopold II, villain of unmitigated guilt, because along with doing good and saving African lives Schweitzer also managed to announce that the African was indeed his brother, but only his *junior* brother.

But of all the hundreds and thousands of European visitors to the Congo region in the last five hundred years, there were few who had the deftness and sleight of hand of Joseph Conrad, or who left as deep a signature on that roadside tree. In his Congo novella, *Heart of Darkness*, Conrad managed to transform elements from centuries of transparently crude and fanciful writing about Africans into a piece of "serious" and permanent literature.

Halfway through his story, Conrad describes a journey up the River Congo in the 1890s as though it were the very first encounter between conscious humanity, coming from Europe, and an unconscious, primeval hegemony that had apparently gone nowhere and seen nobody since the world was created. Naturally, it is the conscious party that tells the story:

> We were wanderers on a prehistoric earth, on the earth that wore the aspect of an unknown planet. We could have fancied ourselves the first of men taking possession of an accursed inheritance.

"Prehistoric earth...unknown planet...fancied ourselves the first of men."

This passage, which is Conrad at his best, or his worst, according to the reader's predilection, goes on at some length through "a burst of yells," "a whirl of black limbs," "of hands clapping," "feet stamping," "bodies swaying," "eyes rolling," "black incomprehensible frenzy," "the prehistoric man himself," "the night of first ages." And then Conrad delivers his famous coup de grâce. Were these creatures really human? And he answers the question with the most sophisticated ambivalence of double negatives:

> No they were not inhuman. Well, you know that was the worst of it—this suspicion of their not being inhuman.

But to return to the word "fancied," which Conrad's genius had lit upon:

> We could have fancied ourselves the first of men taking possession of an accursed inheritance.

I suggest that "fancied" is the alarm word insinuated into Conrad's dangerously highfalutin delirium by his genius as well as simple reason and sanity, but almost immediately crowded out, alas, by the emotional and psychological spell cast on him by the long-established and well-heeled tradition of writing about Africa. Conrad was at once a prisoner of this tradition and its most influential promoter, for he, more than anyone else, secured its admission into the hall of fame of "canonical" literature. Fancy, sometimes called Imagination, is not inimical to Fiction. On the contrary, they are bosom friends. But they also observe careful protocol around each other's property and around the homestead of their droll and difficult neighbor, Fact.

Conrad was a writer who kept much of his fiction fairly close to the facts of his life as a sailor. He had no obligation to do so, but that was what he chose to do—to write about places that actually exist and about people who live in them. He confessed in his 1917 author's note that

> *Heart of Darkness* is experience too, but it is experience pushed a little (and only a very little) beyond the actual facts of the case for the perfectly legitimate, I believe, purpose of bringing it home to the minds and bosoms of the readers.

One fact of the case which Conrad may not have known was how much traffic the River Congo had already seen before it saw him in the 1890s. Even if one discounts the Africans who lived on its banks, there had been many Europeans on the river before Conrad. There was a European sailing ship on the Congo four hundred years before he made his journey, and fancied himself the first of men to do it. That degree of fancying needs a good dose of fact to go with it.

The Portuguese captain, Diogo Cão, who discovered the river for Europe in 1482 was actually looking for something else when he stumbled on it; he was looking for a passage around Africa into the Indian Ocean. On his second voyage, he went beyond his first stop up the river and heard from the inhabitants of the area about a powerful ruler whose capital was still farther up. Cão left four Franciscan monks to study the situation and resumed the primary purpose of his expedition. On his way back, he once more detoured into the Congo to pick up his monks; but they were gone! He seized, in retaliation, a number of African hostages, carried them off to Lisbon, and delivered them to King Manuel of Portugal. This unpropitious beginning of Europe's adventure in the heart of Africa was quickly mended when Cão returned to the Congo for the third time in 1487, bringing back his African hostages, who had meanwhile learned the Portuguese language and Christian religion. Cão was taken to see the king, the Mweni-Congo, seated on an ivory throne surrounded by his courtiers. Cão's monks were returned to him, and all was well. An extraordinary period ensued in which the king of Congo became a Christian with the title of Dom Afonso I. Before very long,

> the royal brothers of Portugal and Congo were writing letters to each other that were couched in terms of complete equality of status. Emissaries went back and forth between them. Relations were established between Mbanza and the Vatican. A son of the Mweni-Congo was appointed in Rome itself as bishop of his country.

This bishop, Dom Henrique, had studied in Lisbon, and when he led a delegation of Congo noblemen to Rome for his consecration, he addressed the pope in Latin.

Nzinga Mbemba, baptized as Dom Afonso, was a truly extraordinary man. I have written of him elsewhere, but want to emphasize that he learned in middle life to read and speak Portuguese. It was said that when he examined the legal code of Portugal he was surprised by its excessive harshness. In jest he asked the Portuguese envoy what the penalty was in his country for a citizen who dared to put his foot on the ground! This criticism was probably reported back to the king of Portugal, for in a 1511 letter to his "royal brother," Dom Afonso, he made defensive reference to differing notions of severity between their two nations. Can we today imagine a situation in which an African ruler is giving, rather than receiving, admonition on law and civilization?

The Christian kingdom of Dom Afonso I in Congo did not fare well and was finally destroyed two centuries later after a long and protracted struggle with the Portuguese. A major source of the problem was the determination of the Portuguese to take out of Congo as many slaves as their vast new colony in Brazil demanded, and the Congo kings' desire to limit or end the traffic. There was also a dispute over mining rights. In the war that finally ended the independence of the kingdom of Congo and established Portuguese control over it, the armies of both nations marched under Christian banners.

If this story reads like a fairy tale, that is not because it did not happen but because we have become all too familiar with the Africa created by Conrad's *Heart of Darkness*, its long line of predecessors going back to the sixteenth century, and its successors today, in print and the electronic media. This tradition has invented an Africa where nothing good happens or ever happened, an Africa that has not been discovered yet and is waiting for the first European visitor to explore it and explain it and straighten it up, or, more likely, perish in the attempt.

In Conrad's boyhood, explorers were the equivalent of today's Hollywood superstars. As a child of nine, Conrad had pointed at the center of Africa on a map and said: When I grow up I shall go there! Among his heroes were Mungo Park, who drowned exploring the River Niger; David Livingstone, who died looking for the source of the Nile; Dr. Barth, the first white man to approach the gates of the walled city of Kano. Conrad tells a memorable story of Barth "approaching Kano which no European eye had seen till then," and an excited population of Africans streaming out of the gates "to behold the wonder."

And Conrad also tells us how much better he liked Dr. Barth's first-white-man story than the account of Sir Hugh Clifford, British governor of Nigeria, traveling in state to open a college in Kano, forty years later. Even though Conrad and Hugh Clifford were friends, the story and pictures of this second Kano event left Conrad "without any particular elation. Education is a great thing, but Doctor Barth gets in the way."

That is neatly and honestly put. The Africa of colleges is understandably of little interest to avid lovers of unexplored Africa. In one of his last essays, "Geography and Some Explorers," Conrad describes the explorers he admired as "fathers of militant geography," or even more reverentially as "the blessed of militant geography." Too late on the scene himself to join their ranks, did he become merely a militant conjurer of geography, and history? Let it be said right away that it is not a crime to prefer the Africa of explorers to the Africa of colleges. There were some good people who did. When I was a young radio producer in Lagos in the early 1960s, a legendary figure from the first decade of British colonial rule in Nigeria returned for a final visit in her eighties. Sylvia Leith-Ross had made a very important study of Igbo women in her pioneering work *African Women*, in which she established from masses of personal interviews of Igbo women that they did not fit European stereotypes of downtrodden slaves and beasts of burden. She graciously agreed to do a radio program for me about Nigeria at the turn of the twentieth century. It was a wonderful program. What has stuck in my mind was when she conceded the many good, new things in the country, like Ibadan University College, and asked wistfully: "But where is my beloved bush?"

Was this the same hankering for the exotic which lay behind Conrad's preference for a lone European explorer over African education? I could hear a difference in tone. Sylvia Leith-Ross was gentle, almost self-mocking in her choice, and without the slightest hint of hostility. At worst, you might call her a starry-eyed conservationist! Conrad is different. At best, you are uncertain about the meaning of his choice. Until, that is, you encounter his portrait, in *Heart of Darkness*, of an African who has received the rudiments of education:

> And between whiles I had to look after the savage who was fireman. He was an improved specimen; he could fire up a vertical boiler. He was there below me and, upon my word, to look at him was as edifying as seeing a dog in a parody of breeches and a feather hat walking on his hind legs. A few months of training had done for that really fine chap. He squinted at the steam-gauge and at the water-gauge with an evident effort of intrepidity—and he had filed teeth too, the poor devil, and the wool of his pate shaved into queer patterns, and three ornamental scars on each of his cheeks. He ought to have been clapping his hands and stamping his feet on the bank, instead of which he was hard at work, a thrall to strange witchcraft, full of improving knowledge.

This is poisonous writing, in full consonance with the tenets of the slave trade-inspired tradition of European portrayal of Africa. There are endless variations in that tradition of the "problem" of education for Africa; for example, a highly educated African might be shown sloughing off his veneer of civilization along with his Oxford blazer when the tom-tom begins to beat. The moral: Africa and education do not mix. Or: Africa will revert to type. And what is this type? Something dark and ominous and different. At the center of all the problems Europe has had in its perception of Africa lies the simple question of African humanity: are they or are they not like us?

Conrad devised a simple hierarchical order of souls for the characters in *Heart of Darkness*. At the bottom are the Africans, whom he calls "rudimentary souls." Above them are the defective Europeans, obsessed with ivory, petty, vicious, morally obtuse; he calls them "tainted souls" or "small souls." At the top are regular Europeans, and their souls don't seem to have the need for an adjective. The gauge for measuring a soul turns out to be the evil character Mr. Kurtz:

> He had the power to charm or frighten rudimentary souls into an aggravated witch-dance in his honor, he could also fill the small souls of the pilgrims with bitter misgivings—he had one devoted friend at least and he had conquered one soul in the world that was neither rudimentary nor tainted with self-seeking.

The alleged tendency of Africans to offer worship to any European who comes along is another favorite theme in European writing about Africa. Variations on it include the veneration by Africans of an empty Coca-Cola bottle that falls out of an airplane. Even children's stories are not free of this insult, as I once learned from foolishly buying an expensive, colorful book for my little girl without first checking it out.

The aggravated witch-dance for a mad white man by hordes of African natives may accord with the needs and desires of the fabulists of the Africa that never was, but the experience of Congo was different. Far from falling over themselves to worship their invaders, the people of this region of Africa have a long history of resistance to European control. In 1687, an exasperated Italian priest, Father Cavazzi, complained:

> These nations think themselves the foremost men in the world. They imagine that Africa is not only the greatest part of the world, but also the happiest and most agreeable....[Their king] is persuaded that there is no other monarch in the world who is his equal.

Between Father Cavazzi's words and Joseph Conrad's images of gyrating and babbling savages there was indeed a hiatus of two harsh centuries. But that would not explain the difference.

People are wrong when they tell you that Conrad was on the side of the Africans because his story showed great compassion towards them. Africans are not really served by his compassion, whatever it means; they ask for one thing alone—to be seen for what they are: human beings. Conrad pulls back from granting them this favor in *Heart of Darkness*. Apparently, some people can read it without seeing any problem. We simply have to be patient. But a word may be in order for those last-ditch defenders who fall back on the excuse that the racial insensitivity of Conrad was normal in his time. Even if that were so, it would still be a flaw in a serious writer—a flaw which responsible criticism today could not gloss over. But it is not even true that everybody in Conrad's day was like him. David Livingstone, an older contemporary and by no means a saint, was different. Ironically, he was also Conrad's great hero, whom he placed

> among the blessed of militant geography...a notable European figure and the most venerated perhaps of all the objects of my early geographical enthusiasm.

And yet his hero's wise, inclusive humanity eluded Conrad. What did he think of Livingstone's famous judgment of Africans?

> I have found it difficult to come to a conclusion on their [Africans'] character. They sometimes perform actions remarkably good, and sometimes as strangely the opposite....After long observation, I came to the conclusion that they are just a strange mixture of good and evil as men are everywhere else.

Joseph Conrad was forty-four years *younger* than David Livingstone. If his times were responsible for his racial attitude, we should expect him to be more advanced than Livingstone, not more backward. Without doubt, the times in which we live influence our behavior, but the best or merely the better among us, like Livingstone, are never held hostage by their times.

An interesting analogy may be drawn here with the visual arts imagery of Africans in eighteenth-century Britain. I refer to a 1997 exhibition at the National Portrait Gallery in London on the subject of Ignatius Sancho, an eighteenth-century African man of letters, and his contemporaries. The centerpiece of the exhibition was the famous painting of Ignatius Sancho by Thomas Gainsborough in 1786. The art historian Reyahn King describes the painting in these words:

> Gainsborough's skill is clearest in his treatment of Sancho's skin colour. Unlike Hogarth, whose use of violet pigments when painting black faces results in a greyish skin tone, the brick-red of Sancho's waistcoat in Gainsborough's portrait, combined with the rich brown background and Sancho's own skin colour, makes the painting unusually warm in tone as well as feeling. Gainsborough has painted thinly over a reddish base with shading in a chocolate tone and minimal colder lights on Sancho's nose, chin and lips. The resulting face seems to glow and contrasts strongly with the vanishing effect so often suffered by the faces of black servants in the shadows of 18th-century portraits of their masters.

Evidently Gainsborough put care and respect into his painting; and he produced a magnificent portrait of an African who had been born on a slave ship and, at the time of his sitting, was still a servant in an English aristocratic household. But neither of these facts was allowed to take away from him his human dignity in Gainsborough's portrait.

There were other portraits of Africans in Britain painted at the same time. One of them provides a study in contrasts with Gainsborough's rendering of Ignatius Sancho. The African portrayed in this other picture was one Francis Williams, a graduate of Cambridge, a poet, and a founder of a school in Jamaica: an amazing phenomenon in those days. A portrait of Williams by an anonymous artist shows a man with a big, flat face lacking any distinctiveness, standing in a cluttered library on tiny broomstick legs. It was clearly an exercise in mockery. Perhaps Francis Williams aroused resentment because of his rare accomplishments. Certainly the anonymous scarecrow portrait was intended to put him in his place, in much the same way as the philosopher David Hume was said to have dismissed Williams's accomplishments by comparing the admiration people had for him to the praise they might give "a parrot who speaks a few words plainly." It is clear, then, that in eighteenth-century Britain there were Britons, like the painter Gainsborough, who were ready to accord respect to an African, even an African who was a servant; and there were other Britons, like the anonymous painter of Francis Williams, or the eminent philosopher Hume, who would sneer at a black man's achievement. And it was not so much a question of the times in which they lived as the kind of people they were. It was the same in the times of Joseph Conrad a century later, and it is the same today!

Things have not gone well in Africa for quite a while. The era of colonial freedom which began so optimistically with Ghana in 1957 would soon be captured by Cold War manipulators and skewed into a deadly season of ostensible ideological conflicts which encouraged the emergence of all kinds of evil rulers able to count on limitless supplies of military hardware from their overseas patrons, no matter how atrociously they ruled their peoples.

With the sudden end of the Cold War, these rulers or their successor regimes lost their value to their sponsors and were cast on the rubbish heap and forgotten, along with their nations. Disaster parades today with impunity through the length and breadth of much of Africa: war, genocide, military and civilian dictatorships, corruption, collapsed economies, poverty, disease, and every ill attendant upon political and social chaos! It is necessary for these sad conditions to be reported, because evil thrives best in quiet, untidy corners. In many African countries, however, the local news media cannot report these events without unleashing serious and even deadly consequences. And so the foreign correspondent is frequently the only means of getting an important story told, or of drawing the world's attention to disasters in the making or being covered up. Such an important role is risky in more ways than one. It can expose the correspondent to actual physical danger; but there is also the moral danger of indulging in sensationalism and dehumanizing the sufferer. This danger immediately raises the question of the character and attitude of the correspondent, because the same qualities of mind which in the past separated a Conrad from a Livingstone, or a Gainsborough from an anonymous painter of Francis Williams, are still present and active in the world today. Perhaps this difference can best be put in one phrase: the presence or absence of respect for the human person.

In a 1997 calendar issued by Amnesty International USA in a joint effort with the International Center of Photography, a brief but important editorial message criticizes some current journalistic practices:

> The apocalyptic vision of the newsmakers [does not] accurately document the world community. Nor are they particularly helpful in forming a picture of our common humanity.

And the text goes on to set down the principles which guided the selection of the twelve photographs in the calendar, as follows:

> [They] document an authentic humanity. They also communicate the fact that every person, everywhere, possesses an inalienable rightness and an imperishable dignity—two qualities that must be respected and protected.

There is a documentary film which I have seen more than once on PBS which is not troubled by Amnesty's concern. It is about sex and reproduction through the entire range of living things, from the simplest single-cell creatures in the water to complex organisms like fishes and birds and mammals. It is a very skillful, scientific production that pulls no punches with respect to where babies come from. It is all there in its starkness. Was it necessary to conclude this graphic reproductive odyssey with man (or rather woman)? I did not think so. The point had already been more than well made with apes, including, I believe, those that invented the "missionary position."

But the producers of the documentary were quite uncompromising in their exhaustiveness. And so a woman in labor *was* exposed to show the baby coming out of her. But the real shock for me was that everybody in that labor room was white except the Ghanaian (by her accent) mother in childbirth. Why were all the rest white? you may ask. Because this was all happening in a hospital in London, not in Accra.

I am sure that the producers of that program would reject with indignation any suggestion that their choice of candidate was influenced in any way by race. And they might even be right, to the extent that they would not have had a meeting of their production team to decide that a white woman would not be an appropriate subject. But then, such deliberations do not happen except perhaps in the crude caucuses of the lunatic fringe. Race is no longer a visible presence in the boardroom. But it may lie, unseen, in our subconscious. The lesson for that production team, for those who broadcast their product, and for the rest of us is that when we are comfortable and inattentive, we run the risk of committing grave injustices absentmindedly. ■

1998

AUTHOR PROFILE

Chinua Achebe (1930–2013) was a novelist, poet, and professor. Born in Ogidi, Nigeria, during British colonial rule, Achebe was part of an ethnically Ibo family, but he was educated in colonial schools that emphasized British literature and culture. This continued during his education at the University College of Ibidan, where his professors were all Europeans. Achebe's writing directly challenged colonial rule: he wrote about Nigeria from the point of view of the colonized, not the colonizer, and he portrayed the African continent as a place of humanity and struggle, not the savage space of the colonial imagination. Achebe's first novel, *Things Fall Apart* (1958), uses his own family story to tell the larger story of the Ibo nation, oppressed first under racist British rule and then under military dictators from other African ethnicities. Published in 1958, the book has sold more than 10 million copies and is translated into more than 45 languages. Achebe's work struggled with the complexity of colonial subjectivities: he drew on the oral tradition of the Ibo people (using proverbs, folk tales, and songs) but framed that in the Western tradition of the English-language novel. Of *Things Fall Apart*, he wrote, "In the end, I began to understand. There is such a thing as absolute power over narrative. Those who secure this privilege for themselves can arrange stories about others pretty much where, and as, they like." Through writing, Achebe reclaimed this power.

The Lockdown

From *The New Jim Crow*

By Michelle Alexander

We may think we know how the criminal justice system works. Television is overloaded with fictional dramas about police, crime, and prosecutors—shows such as *Law & Order*. These fictional dramas, like the evening news, tend to focus on individual stories of crime, victimization, and punishment, and the stories are typically told from the point of view of law enforcement. A charismatic police officer, investigator, or prosecutor struggles with his own demons while heroically trying to solve a horrible crime. He ultimate achieves a personal and moral victory by finding the bad guy and throwing him in jail. That is the made-for-TV version of the criminal justice system. It perpetuates the myth that the primary function of the system is to keep our streets safe and our homes secure by rooting out dangerous criminals and punishing them. These television shows, especially those that romanticize drug-law enforcement, are the modern-day equivalent of the old movies portraying happy slaves, the fictional gloss placed on a brutal system of racialized oppression and control.

Those who have been swept within the criminal justice system know that the way the system actually works bears little resemblance to what happens on television or in movies. Full-blown trials of guilt or innocence rarely occur; many people never even meet with an attorney; witnesses are routinely paid and coerced by the government; police regularly stop and search people for no reason whatsoever; penalties for many crimes are so severe that innocent people plead guilty, accepting plea bargains to avoid harsh mandatory sentences; and children, even as young as fourteen, are sent to adult prisons. Rules of law and procedure, such as "guilt beyond a reasonable doubt" or "probable cause" or "reasonable suspicion," can easily be found in court cases and law-school textbooks but are much harder to find in real life.

In this chapter, we shall see how the system of mass incarceration actually works. Our focus is the War on Drugs. The reason is simple: Convictions for drug offenses are the single most important cause of the explosion in incarceration rates in the United States. Drug offenses alone account for two-thirds of the rise in the federal inmate population and more than half of the rise in state prisoners between 1985 and 2000.[1] Approximately a half-million people are in prison or jail for a drug offense today, compared to an estimated 41,100 in 1980—an increase of 1,100 percent.[2] Drug arrests have tripled since 1980. As a result, more than 31 million people have been arrested for drug offenses since the drug war began.[3] To put the matter in perspective, consider this: there are more people in prisons and

---

1 See Marc Mauer, *Race to Incarcerate*, rev. ed. (New York: The New Press, 2006), 33.

2 Marc Mauer and Ryan King, *A 25-Year Quagmire: The "War on Drugs" and Its Impact on American Society* (Washington, DC: Sentencing Project, 2007), 2.

3 Ibid., 3.

jails today just for drug offenses than were incarcerated for *all* reasons in 1980.[4] Nothing has contributed more to the systematic mass incarceration of people of color in the United States than the War on Drugs.

Before we begin our tour of the drug war, it is worthwhile to get a couple of myths out of the way. The first is that the war is aimed at ridding the nation of drug "kingpins" or big-time dealers. Nothing could be further from the truth. The vast majority of those arrested are *not* charged with serious offenses. In 2005, for example, four out of five drug arrests were for possession, and only one out of five was for sales. Moreover, most people in state prison for drug offenses have *no* history of violence or significant selling activity.[5]

The second myth is that the drug war is principally concerned with dangerous drugs. Quite to the contrary, arrests for marijuana possession—a drug less harmful than tobacco or alcohol—accounted for nearly 80 percent of the growth in drug arrests in the 1990s.[6] Despite the fact that most drug arrests are for nonviolent minor offenses, the War on Drugs has ushered in an era of unprecedented punitiveness.

The percentage of drug arrests that result in prison sentences (rather than dismissal, community service, or probation) has quadrupled, resulting in a prison-building boom the likes of which the world has never seen. In two short decades, between 1980 and 2000, the number of people incarcerated in our nation's prisons and jails soared from roughly 300,000 to more than 2 million. By the end of 2007, more than 7 million Americans—or one in every 31 adults—were behind bars, on probation, or on parole.[7]

We begin our exploration of the drug war at the point of entry—arrest by the police—and then consider how the system of mass incarceration is structured to reward mass drug arrests and facilitate the conviction and imprisonment of an unprecedented number of Americans, whether guilty or innocent. In subsequent chapters, we will consider how the system specifically targets people of color and

---

4 Testimony of Marc Mauer, Executive Director of the Sentencing Project, Prepared for the House Judiciary Subcommittee on Crime, Terrorism, and Homeland Security, 111th Cong., *Hearing on Unfairness in Federal Cocaine Sentencing: Is It Time to Crack the 100 to 1 Disparity?* May 21, 2009, 2.

5 Mauer and King, *A 25-Year Quagmire*, 2–3.

6 Ibid.; and Ryan King and Marc Mauer, *The War on Marijuana: The Transformation of the War on Drugs in the 1990s* (New York: Sentencing Project, 2005), documenting the dramatic increase in marijuana arrests. Marijuana is a relatively harmless drug. The 1988 surgeon general's report lists tobacco as a more dangerous drug than marijuana, and Francis Young, an administrative law judge for the Drug Enforcement Administration found there are no credible medical reports to suggest that consuming marijuana, in any dose, has ever caused a single death. U.S. Department of Justice, Drug Enforcement Administration, Opinion and Recommended Ruling, Findings of Fact, Conclusions of Law and Decision of Administrative Law Judge Francis L. Young, in the *Matter of Marijuana Rescheduling Petition*, Docket no. 86-22, Sept. 6, 1988, 56–57. By comparison, tobacco kills roughly 390,000 Americans annually, and alcohol is responsible for some 150,000 U.S. deaths a year. See Doug Bandow, "War on Drugs or War on America?" *Stanford Law and Policy Review* 3: 242, 245 (1991).

7 Pew Center on the States, *One in 31: The Long Reach of American Corrections* (Washington, DC: Pew Charitable Trusts, 2009).

then relegates them to a second-class status analogous to Jim Crow. At this point, we simply take stock of the means by which the War on Drugs facilitates the roundup and lockdown of an extraordinary percentage of the U.S. population.

Rules of the Game

Few legal rules meaningfully constrain the police in the War on Drugs. This may sound like an overstatement, but upon examination it proves accurate. The absence of significant constraints on the exercise of police discretion is a key feature of the drug war's design. It has made the roundup of millions of Americans for nonviolent drug offenses relatively easy.

With only a few exceptions, the Supreme Court has seized every opportunity to facilitate the drug war, primarily by eviscerating Fourth Amendment protections against unreasonable searches and seizures by the police. The rollback has been so pronounced that some commentators charge that a virtual "drug exception" now exists to the Bill of Rights. Shortly before his death, Justice Thurgood Marshall felt compelled to remind his colleagues that there is, in fact, "no drug exception" written into the text of the Constitution.[8]

Most Americans do not know what the Fourth Amendment of the U.S. Constitution actually says or what it requires of the police. It states, in its entirety:

> The right of the people to be secure in their persons, houses, papers, and effects, against unreasonable searches and seizures, shall not be violated, and no warrants shall issue, but upon probable cause, supported by oath or affirmation, and particularly describing the place to be searched, and the person or things to be seized.

Courts and scholars agree that the Fourth Amendment governs all searches and seizures by the police and that the amendment was adopted in response to the English practice of conducting arbitrary searches under general warrants to uncover seditious libels. The routine police harassment, arbitrary searches, and widespread police intimidation of those subject to English rule helped to inspire the American Revolution. Not surprisingly, then, preventing arbitrary searches and seizures by the police was deemed by the Founding Fathers an essential element of the U.S. Constitution. Until the War on Drugs, courts had been fairly stringent about enforcing the Fourth Amendment's requirements.

Within a few years after the drug war was declared, however, many legal scholars noted a sharp turn in the Supreme Court's Fourth Amendment jurisprudence. By the close of the Supreme Court's 1990–91 term, it had become clear that a major shift in the relationship between the citizens of this country and the police was under way. Justice Stevens noted the trend in a powerful dissent issued in *California v. Acevedo*, a case upholding the warrantless search of a bag locked in a motorist's trunk:

---

[8] *Skinner v. Railway Labor Executive Association*, 489 U.S. 602, 641 (1980), Marshall, J., dissenting.

> In the years [from 1982 to 1991], the Court has heard argument in 30 Fourth Amendment cases involving narcotics. In all but one, the government was the petitioner. All save two involved a search or seizure without a warrant or with a defective warrant. And, in all except three, the Court upheld the constitutionality of the search or seizure. In the meantime, the flow of narcotics cases through the courts has steadily and dramatically increased. No impartial observer could criticize this Court for hindering the progress of the war on drugs. On the contrary, decisions like the one the Court makes today will support the conclusion that this Court has become a loyal foot soldier in the Executive's fight against crime.[9]

The Fourth Amendment is but one example. Virtually all constitutionally protected civil liberties have been undermined by the drug war. The Court has been busy in recent years approving mandatory drug testing of employees and students, upholding random searches and sweeps of public schools and students, permitting police to obtain search warrants based on an anonymous informant's tip, expanding the government's wiretapping authority, legitimating the use of paid, unidentified informants by police and prosecutors, approving the use of helicopter surveillance of homes without a warrant, and allowing the forfeiture of cash, homes, and other property based on unproven allegations of illegal drug activity.

For our purposes here, we limit our focus to the legal rules crafted by the Supreme Court that grant law enforcement a pecuniary interest in the drug war and make it relatively easy for the police to seize people virtually anywhere—on public streets and sidewalks, on buses, airplanes and trains, or any other public place—and usher them behind bars. These new legal rules have ensured that anyone, virtually anywhere, for any reason, can become a target of drug-law enforcement activity.

• • • • • • • • • • • • • • •

Just Say No

The first major sign that the Supreme Court would not allow the Fourth Amendment to interfere with the prosecution of the War on Drugs came in *Florida v. Bostick*. In that case, Terrance Bostick, a twenty-eight-year-old African American, had been sleeping in the back seat of a Greyhound bus on his way from Miami to Atlanta. Two police officers, wearing bright green "raid" jackets and displaying their badges and a gun, woke him with a start. The bus was stopped for a brief layover in Fort Lauderdale, and the officers were "working the bus," looking for persons who might be carrying drugs. Bostick provided them with his identification and ticket, as requested. The officers then asked to search his bag. Bostick complied, even though he knew his bag contained a pound of cocaine. The officers had no basis for suspecting Bostick of any criminal activity, but they got lucky. They arrested Bostick, and he was charged and convicted of trafficking cocaine.

---

9 *California v. Acevedo*, 500 U.S. 565, 600 (1991), Stevens, J., dissenting.

Bostick's search and seizure reflected what had become an increasingly common tactic in the War on Drugs: suspicionless police sweeps of buses in interstate or intrastate travel. The resulting "interviews" of passengers in these dragnet operations usually culminate in a request for "consent" to search the passenger's luggage.[10] Never do the officers inform passengers that they are free to remain silent or to refuse to answer questions. By proceeding systematically in this manner, the police are able to engage in an extremely high volume of searches. One officer was able to search over three thousand bags in a nine-month period employing these techniques.[11] By and large, however, the hit rates are low. For example, in one case, a sweep of one hundred buses resulted in only seven arrests.[12]

On appeal, the Florida Supreme Court ruled in Bostick's case that the police officer's conduct violated the Fourth Amendment's prohibition of unreasonable searches and seizures. The Fourth Amendment, the court reasoned, forbids the police from seizing people and searching them without some individualized suspicion that they have committed or are committing a crime. The court thus overturned Bostick's conviction, ruling that the cocaine, having been obtained illegally, was inadmissible. It also broadly condemned "bus sweeps" in the drug war, comparing them to methods employed by totalitarian regimes:

> The evidence in this case has evoked images of other days, under other flags, when no man traveled his nation's roads or railways without fear of unwarranted interruption, by individuals who had temporary power in Government... This is not Hitler's Berlin, nor Stalin's Moscow, nor is it white supremacist South Africa. Yet in Broward County, Florida, these police officers approach every person on board buses and trains ("that time permits") and check identification, tickets, ask to search luggage—all in the name of "voluntary cooperation" with law enforcement.[13]

The U.S. Supreme Court reversed. The Court ruled that Bostick's encounter with the police was purely voluntary, and therefore he was not "seized" within the meaning of the Fourth Amendment. Even if Bostick did not feel free to leave when confronted by police at the back of the bus, the proper question, according to the Court, was whether "a reasonable person" in Bostick's shoes would have felt free to terminate the encounter. A reasonable person, the Court concluded, would have felt free to sit there and refuse to answer the police officer's questions, and would have felt free to tell the officer "No, you can't search my bag." Accordingly, Bostick was not really "seized" within the meaning of the Fourth Amendment, and the subsequent search was purely consensual. The Court made clear that its decision was to govern all future drug sweeps, no matter what the circumstances

[10] See generally *United States v. Lewis*, 921 F.2d 1294, 1296 (1990); *United States v. Flowers*, 912 F.2d 707, 708 (4th Cir. 1990); and *Florida v. Bostick*, 501 U.S. 429, 441 (1991).

[11] See, e.g., *Florida v. Kerwick*, 512 So.2d 347, 349 (Fla. App. 4 Dist. 1987).

[12] See *United States v. Flowers*, 912 F.2d 707, 710 (4th Cir. 1990).

[13] *Bostick v. State*, 554 So.2d 1153, 1158 (Fla. 1989), quoting *State v. Kerwick*, 512 So.2d 347, 348–349 (Fla. 4th DCA 1987).

A

of the targeted individual. Given the blanket nature of the ruling, courts have found police encounters to be consensual in truly preposterous situations. For example, a few years after Bostick, the District of Columbia Court of Appeals applied the ruling to a case involving a fourteen-year-old girl interrogated by the police, concluding that she must be held to the same reasonable-person standard.[14]

Prior to the *Bostick* decision, a number of lower courts had found absurd the notion that "reasonable people" would feel empowered to refuse to answer questions when confronted by the police. As federal judge Prentiss Marshall explained, "The average person encountered will feel obliged to stop and respond. Few will feel that they can walk away or refuse to answer."[15] Professor Tracey Maclin put it this way, "Common sense teaches that most of us do not have the chutzpah or stupidity to tell a police officer to 'get lost' after he has stopped us and asked us for identification or questioned us about possible criminal conduct."[16] Other courts emphasized that granting police the freedom to stop, interrogate, and search anyone who consented would likely lead to racial and ethnic discrimination. Young black men would be the likely targets, rather than older white women. Justice Thurgood Marshall acknowledged as much in his dissent in *Bostick*, noting "the basis of the decision to single out particular passengers during a suspicionless sweep is less likely to be inarticulable than unspeakable."[17]

Studies have shown that Maclin's common sense is correct: the overwhelming majority of people who are confronted by police and asked questions respond, and when asked to be searched, they comply.[18] This is the case even among those, like Bostick, who have every reason to resist these tactics because they actually have something to hide. This is no secret to the Supreme Court. The Court long ago acknowledged that effective use of consent searches by the police depends on the ignorance (and powerlessness) of those who are targeted. In *Schneckloth v. Bustamonte*, decided in 1973, the Court admitted that if waiver of one's right to refuse consent were truly "knowing, intelligent, and voluntary," it would "in practice create serious doubt whether consent searches would continue to be conducted."[19] In other words, consent searches are valuable tools for the police only because hardly anyone dares to say no.

• • • • • • • • • • • • • • •

[14] *In re J.M.* 619 A.2d 497, 501 (D.C. App. 1992).

[15] *Illinois Migrant Council v. Pilliod*, 398 F. Supp. 882, 899 (N.D. Ill. 1975).

[16] Tracy Maclin, "Black and Blue Encounters—Some Preliminary Thoughts About Fourth Amendment Seizures: Should Race Matter?" *Valparaiso University Law Review* 26 (1991): 249–50.

[17] *Florida v. Bostick*, 501 U.S. 429, 441 n. 1 (1991), Marshall, J., dissenting.

[18] Maclin, "Black and Blue Encounters."

[19] *Schneckloth v. Bustamonte*, 412 U.S. 218, 229 (1973).

Kissing Frogs

Court cases involving drug-law enforcement almost always involve guilty people. Police usually release the innocent on the street—often without a ticket, citation, or even an apology—so their stories are rarely heard in court. Hardly anyone files a complaint, because the last thing most people want to do after experiencing a frightening and intrusive encounter with the police is show up at the police station where the officer works and attract more attention to themselves. For good reason, many people—especially poor people of color—fear police harassment, retaliation, and abuse. After having your car torn apart by the police in a futile search for drugs, or being forced to lie spread-eagled on the pavement while the police search you and interrogate you for no reason at all, how much confidence do you have in law enforcement? Do you expect to get a fair hearing? Those who try to find an attorney to represent them in a lawsuit often learn that unless they have broken bones (and no criminal record), private attorneys are unlikely to be interested in their case. Many people are shocked to discover that what happened to them on the side of the road was not, in fact, against the law.

The inevitable result is that the people who wind up in front of a judge are usually guilty of some crime. The parade of guilty people through America's courtrooms gives the false impression to the public—as well as to judges—that when the police have a "hunch," it makes sense to let them act on it. Judges tend to imagine the police have a sixth sense—or some kind of special police training—that qualifies them to identify drug criminals in the absence of any evidence. After all, they seem to be right so much of the time, don't they?

The truth, however, is that most people stopped and searched in the War on Drugs are perfectly innocent of any crime. The police have received no training that enhances the likelihood they will spot the drug criminals as they drive by and leave everyone else alone. To the contrary, tens of thousands of law enforcement officers have received training that guarantees precisely the opposite. The Drug Enforcement Agency (DEA) trains police to conduct utterly unreasonable and discriminatory stops and searches throughout the United States.

Perhaps the best known of these training programs is Operation Pipeline. The DEA launched Operation Pipeline in 1984 as part of the Reagan administration's rollout of the War on Drugs. The federal program, administered by over three hundred state and local law enforcement agencies, trains state and local law enforcement officers to use pretextual traffic stops and consent searches on a large scale for drug interdiction. Officers learn, among other things, how to use a minor traffic violation as a pretext to stop someone, how to lengthen a routine traffic stop and leverage it into a search for drugs, how to obtain consent from a reluctant motorist, and how to use drug-sniffing dogs to obtain probable cause.[20] By 2000, the DEA had directly trained more than 25,000 officers in forty-eight states in Pipeline tactics and helped to develop training programs for countless municipal and state law enforcement agencies. In legal scholar Ricardo Bascuas's words, "Operation Pipeline is exactly what the Framers meant to prohibit: a federally-run

[20] See U.S. Department of Justice, Drug Enforcement Administration, *Operations Pipeline and Convoy* (Washington, DC, n.d.), www.usdoj.gov/dea/programs/pipecon.htm.

general search program that targets people without cause for suspicion, particularly those who belong to disfavored groups."[21]

The program's success requires police to stop "staggering" numbers of people in shotgun fashion.[22] This "volume" approach to drug enforcement sweeps up extraordinary numbers of innocent people. As one California Highway Patrol Officer said, "It's sheer numbers.... You've got to kiss a lot of frogs before you find a prince."[23] Accordingly, every year, tens of thousands of motorists find themselves stopped on the side of the road, fielding questions about imaginary drug activity, and then succumbing to a request for their vehicle to be searched—sometimes torn apart—in the search for drugs. Most of these stops and searches are futile. It has been estimated that 95 percent of Pipeline stops yield no illegal drugs.[24] One study found that up to 99 percent of traffic stops made by federally funded narcotics task forces result in no citation and that 98 percent of task-force searches during traffic stops are discretionary searches in which the officer searches the car with the driver's verbal "consent" but has no other legal authority to do so.[25]

The "drug-courier profiles" utilized by the DEA and other law enforcement agencies for drug sweeps on highways, as well as in airports and train stations, are notoriously unreliable. In theory, a drug-courier profile reflects the collective wisdom and judgment of a law enforcement agency's officials. Instead of allowing each officer to rely on his or her own limited experience and biases in detecting suspicious behavior, a drug-courier profile affords every officer the advantage of the agency's collective experience and expertise. However, as legal scholar David Cole has observed, "in practice, the drug-courier profile is a scattershot hodgepodge of traits and characteristics so expansive that it potentially justifies stopping anybody and everybody."[26] The profile can include traveling with luggage, traveling without luggage, driving an expensive car, driving a car that needs repairs, driving with out-of- state license plates, driving a rental car, driving with "mismatched occupants," acting too calm, acting too nervous, dressing casually, wearing expensive clothing or jewelry, being one of the first to deplane, being one of the last to deplane, deplaning in the middle, paying for a ticket in cash, using large-denomination currency, using small-denomination currency, traveling alone, traveling with a companion, and so on. Even striving to obey the law fits the profile! The Florida Highway Patrol Drug Courier Profile cautioned troopers to be

---

[21] Ricardo J. Bascuas, "Fourth Amendment Lessons from the Highway and the Subway: A Principled Approach to Suspicionless Searches," *Rutgers Law Journal* 38 (2007): 719, 763.

[22] *State v. Rutherford*, 93 Ohio App.3d 586, 593–95, 639 N.E. 2d 498, 503–4, n. 3 (Ohio Ct. App. 1994).

[23] Gary Webb, "Driving While Black," *Esquire*, Apr. 1, 1999, 122.

[24] Ibid.

[25] Scott Henson, *Flawed Enforcement: Why Drug Task Force Highway Interdiction Violates Rights, Wastes Tax Dollars, and Fails to Limit the Availability of Drugs in Texas* (Austin: American Civil Liberties Union—Texas Chapters, 2004), 9, www.aclu.org/racialjusttice/racialprofiling/15897pub20040519.html.

[26] David Cole, *No Equal Justice: Race and Class in the American Criminal Justice System* (New York: The New Press, 1999), 47.

suspicious of "scrupulous obedience to traffic laws."[27] As Cole points out, "such profiles do not so much focus an investigation as provide law enforcement officials a ready-made excuse for stopping whomever they please."[28]

The Supreme Court has allowed use of drug-courier profiles as guides for the exercise of police discretion. Although it has indicated that the mere fact that someone fits a profile does not automatically constitute reasonable suspicion justifying a stop, courts routinely defer to these profiles, and the Court has yet to object. As one judge said after conducting a review of drug courier profile decisions: "Many courts have accepted the profile, as well as the Drug Enforcement Agency's scattershot enforcement efforts, unquestioningly, mechanistically, and dispositively."[29]

It Pays to Play

Clearly, the rules of the game are designed to allow for the roundup of an unprecedented number of Americans for minor nonviolent drug offenses. The number of annual drug arrests more than tripled between 1980 and 2005, as drug sweeps and suspicionless stops and searches proceeded in record numbers.[30]

Still, it is fair to wonder why the police would choose to arrest such an astonishing percentage of the American public for minor drug crimes. The fact that police are legally *allowed* to engage in a wholesale roundup of nonviolent drug offenders does not answer the question *why* they would choose to do so, particularly when most police departments have far more serious crimes to prevent and solve. Why would police prioritize drug-law enforcement? Drug use and abuse is nothing new; in fact, it was on the decline, not on the rise, when the War on Drugs began. So why make drug-law enforcement a priority now?

Once again, the answer lies in the system's design. Every system of control depends for its survival on the tangible and intangible benefits that are provided to those who are responsible for the system's maintenance and administration. This system is no exception.

At the time the drug war was declared, illegal drug use and abuse was not a pressing concern in most communities. The announcement of a War on Drugs was therefore met with some confusion and resistance within law enforcement, as well as among some conservative commentators.[31] The federalization of drug crime violated the conservative tenet of states' rights and local control, as street crime was typically the responsibility of local law enforcement. Many state and local law enforcement officials were less than pleased with the attempt by the federal government to assert itself in local crime fighting, viewing the new drug war as an unwelcome distraction. Participation in the drug war required a diversion of

[27] Florida Department of Highway Safety and Motor Vehicles, Office of General Counsel, *Common Characteristics of Drug Couriers* (1984), sec. I.A.4.

[28] Cole, *No Equal Justice*, 49.

[29] "Fluid Drug Courier Profiles See Everyone As Suspicious," *Criminal Practice Manual* 5 (Bureau of National Affairs: July 10, 1991): 334–35.

[30] Mauer and King, *25-Year Quagmire*, 3.

[31] Katherine Beckett, *Making Crime Pay: Law and Order in Contemporary American Politics* (New York: Oxford University Press, 1997), 45; and Mauer, Race to Incarcerate, 49.

resources away from more serious crimes, such as murder, rape, grand theft, and violent assault—all of which were of far greater concern to most communities than illegal drug use.

The resistance within law enforcement to the drug war created something of a dilemma for the Reagan administration. In order for the war to actually work—that is, in order for it to succeed in achieving its political goals—it was necessary to build a consensus among state and local law enforcement agencies that the drug war should be a top priority in their hometowns. The solution: cash. Huge cash grants were made to those law enforcement agencies that were willing to make drug-law enforcement a top priority. The new system of control is traceable, to a significant degree, to a massive bribe offered to state and local law enforcement by the federal government.

In 1988, at the behest of the Reagan administration, Congress revised the program that provides federal aid to law enforcement, renaming it the Edward Byrne Memorial State and Local Law Enforcement Assistance Program after a New York City police officer who was shot to death while guarding the home of a drug-case witness. The Byrne program was designed to encourage every federal grant recipient to help fight the War on Drugs. Millions of dollars in federal aid have been offered to state and local law enforcement agencies willing to wage the war. This federal grant money has resulted in the proliferation of narcotics task forces, including those responsible for highway drug interdiction. Nationally, narcotics task forces make up about 40 percent of all Byrne grant funding, but in some states as much as 90 percent of all Byrne grant funds go toward specialized narcotics task forces.[32] In fact, it is questionable whether any specialized drug enforcement activity would exist in some states without the Byrne program.

Other forms of valuable aid have been offered as well. The DEA has offered free training, intelligence, and technical support to state highway patrol agencies that are willing to commit their officers to highway drug interdiction. The Pentagon, for its part, has given away military intelligence and millions of dollars in firepower to state and local agencies willing to make the rhetorical war a literal one.

Almost immediately after the federal dollars began to flow, law enforcement agencies across the country began to compete for funding, equipment, and training. By the late 1990s, the overwhelming majority of state and local police forces in the country had availed themselves of the newly available resources and added a significant military component to buttress their drug-war operations. According to the Cato Institute, in 1997 alone, the Pentagon handed over more than 1.2 million pieces of military equipment to local police departments.[33] Similarly, the *National Journal* reported that between January 1997 and October 1999, the agency handled 3.4 million orders of Pentagon equipment from over eleven thousand domestic police agencies in all fifty states. Included in the bounty were "253 aircraft (including six- and seven-passenger airplanes, UH-60 Blackhawk

---

[32] U.S. Department of Justice, *Department of Justice Drug Demand Reduction Activities, Report No. 3-12* (Washington, DC: Office of the Inspector General, Feb. 2003), 35, www.usdoj.gov/oig/reports/plus/a0312.

[33] Radley Balko, *Overkill: The Rise of Paramilitary Police Raids in America* (Washington, DC: Cato Institute, July 17, 2006), 8.

and UH-1 Huey helicopters, 7,856 M-16 rifles, 181 grenade launchers, 8,131 bulletproof helmets, and 1,161 pairs of night-vision goggles."[34] A retired police chief in New Haven, Connecticut, told the *New York Times*, "I was offered tanks, bazookas, anything I wanted."[35]

• • • • • • • • • • • • • • •

Finders Keepers

As if the free military equipment, training, and cash grants were not enough, the Reagan administration provided law enforcement with yet another financial incentive to devote extraordinary resources to drug law enforcement, rather than more serious crimes: state and local law enforcement agencies were granted the authority to keep, for their own use, the vast majority of cash and assets they seize when waging the drug war. This dramatic change in policy gave state and local police an enormous stake in the War on Drugs—not in its success, but in its perpetual existence. Law enforcement gained a pecuniary interest not only in the forfeited property, but in the profitability of the drug market itself.

Modern drug forfeiture laws date back to 1970, when Congress passed the Comprehensive Drug Abuse Prevention and Control Act. The Act included a civil forfeiture provision authorizing the government to seize and forfeit drugs, drug manufacturing and storage equipment, and conveyances used to transport drugs. As legal scholars Eric Blumenson and Eva Nilsen have explained, the provision was justified as an effort "to forestall the spread of drugs in a way criminal penalties could not—by striking at its economic roots."[36] When a drug dealer is sent to jail, there are many others ready and willing to take his place, but seizing the means of production, some legislators reasoned, may shut down the trafficking business for good. Over the years, the list of properties subject to forfeiture expanded greatly, and the required connection to illegal drug activity became increasingly remote, leading to many instances of abuse. But it was not until 1984, when Congress amended the federal law to allow federal law enforcement agencies to retain and use any and all proceeds from asset forfeitures, and to allow state and local police agencies to retain up to 80 percent of the assets' value, that a true revolution occurred.

Suddenly, police departments were capable of increasing the size of their budgets, quite substantially, simply by taking the cash, cars, and homes of people suspected of drug use or sales. At the time the new rules were adopted, the law governing civil forfeiture was so heavily weighted in favor of the government that fully 80 percent of forfeitures went uncontested. Property or cash could be seized based on mere suspicion of illegal drug activity, and the seizure could occur without notice or hearing, upon an ex parte showing of mere probable cause to believe that the property had somehow been "involved" in a crime. The probable cause showing could be based on nothing more than hearsay, innuendo, or

---

[34] Megan Twohey, "SWATs Under Fire," *National Journal*, Jan. 1, 2000, 37; Balko, Overkill, 8.

[35] Timothy Egan, "Soldiers of the Drug War Remain on Duty," *New York Times*, Mar. 1, 1999.

[36] Eric Blumenson and Eva Nilsen, "Policing for Profit: The Drug War's Hidden Economic Agenda," *University of Chicago Law Review* 65 (1998): 35, 45.

even the paid, self-serving testimony of someone with interests clearly adverse to the property owner. Neither the owner of the property nor anyone else need be charged with a crime, much less found guilty of one. Indeed, a person could be found innocent of any criminal conduct and the property could still be subject to forfeiture. Once the property was seized, the owner had no right of counsel, and the burden was placed on him to prove the property's "innocence." Because those who were targeted were typically poor or of moderate means, they often lacked the resources to hire an attorney or pay the considerable court costs. As a result, most people who had their cash or property seized did not challenge the government's action, especially because the government could retaliate by filing criminal charges—baseless or not.

Not surprisingly, this drug forfeiture regime proved highly lucrative for law enforcement, offering more than enough incentive to wage the War on Drugs. According to a report commissioned by the Department of Justice, between 1988 and 1992 alone, Byrne-funded drug task forces seized over $1 billion in assets.[37] Remarkably, this figure does not include drug task forces funded by the DEA or other federal agencies.

The actual operation of drug forfeiture laws seriously undermines the usual rhetoric offered in support of the War on Drugs, namely that it is the big "kingpins" that are the target of the war. Drug-war forfeiture laws are frequently used to allow those with assets to buy their freedom, while drug users and small-time dealers with few assets to trade are subjected to lengthy prison terms. In Massachusetts, for example, an investigation by journalists found that on average a "payment of $50,000 in drug profits won a 6.3 year reduction in a sentence for dealers," while agreements of $10,000 or more bought elimination or reduction of trafficking charges in almost three-fourths of such cases.[38] Federal drug forfeiture laws are one reason, Blumenson and Nilsen note, "why state and federal prisons now confine large numbers of men and women who had relatively minor roles in drug distribution networks, but few of their bosses."[39]

The Shakedown

Quite predictably, the enormous economic rewards created by both the drug-war forfeiture and Byrne-grant laws has created an environment in which a very fine line exists between the lawful and the unlawful taking of other people's money and property—a line so thin that some officers disregard the formalities of search warrants, probable cause, and reasonable suspicion altogether. In *United States v. Reese*, for example, the Ninth Circuit Court of Appeals described a drug task force completely corrupted by its dependence on federal drug money. Operating as a separate unit within the Oakland Housing Authority, the task force behaved, in the words of one officer, "more or less like a wolfpack," driving up in police vehicles and taking "anything and everything we saw on the street corner."[40] The officers were under tremendous pressure from their commander to keep their arrest numbers up, and all of the officers were aware that their jobs depended on

[37] Ibid., 64.

[38] Blumenson and Nilsen, "Policing for Profit," 72.

[39] Ibid., 71.

[40] Ibid., 82.

the renewal of a federal grant. The task force commander emphasized that they would need statistics to show that the grant money was well spent and sent the task force out to begin a shift with comments like, "Let's go out and kick ass," and "Everybody goes to jail tonight for everything, right?"[41]

Journalists and investigators have documented numerous other instances in which police departments have engaged in illegal shakedowns, searches, and threats in search of forfeitable property and cash. In Florida, reporters reviewed nearly one thousand videotapes of highway traffic stops and found that police had used traffic violations as an excuse—or pretext—to confiscate "tens of thousands of dollars from motorists against whom there [was] no evidence of wrongdoing," frequently taking the money without filing any criminal charges.[42] Similarly, in Louisiana, journalists reported that Louisiana police engaged in massive pretextual stops in an effort to seize cash, with the money diverted to police department ski trips and other unauthorized uses.[43] And in Southern California, a Los Angeles Sheriff's Department employee reported that deputies routinely planted drugs and falsified police reports to establish probable cause for cash seizures.[44]

Lots of small seizures can be nearly as profitable, and require the expenditure of fewer investigative resources, than a few large busts. The Western Area Narcotics Task Force (WANT) became the focus of a major investigation in 1996 when almost $66,000 was discovered hidden in its headquarters. The investigation revealed that the task force seized large amounts of money, but also small amounts, and then dispensed it freely, unconstrained by reporting requirements or the task force's mission. Some seizures were as small as eight cents. Another seizure of ninety-three cents prompted the local newspaper to observe that "once again the officers were taking whatever the suspects were carrying, even though by no stretch could pocket change be construed to be drug money."[45]

In 2000, Congress passed the Civil Asset Forfeiture Reform Act which was meant to address many of the egregious examples of abuse of civil forfeiture. Some of the most widely cited examples involved wealthy whites whose property was seized. One highly publicized case involved a reclusive millionaire, Donald Scott, who was shot and killed when a multiagency task force raided his two-hundred-acre Malibu ranch purportedly in search of marijuana plants. They never found a single marijuana plant in the course of the search. A subsequent investigation revealed that the primary motivation for the raid was the possibility of forfeiting Scott's property. If the forfeiture had been successful, it would have netted the law enforcement agencies about $5 million in assets.[46] In another case, William Munnerlynn had his Learjet seized by the DEA after he inadvertently used it to

---

[41] Ibid.

[42] Ibid., 83.

[43] Ibid.

[44] Ibid.

[45] Ibid., 98.

[46] Michael Fessier Jr., "Trail's End Deep in a Wild Canyon West of Malibu, a Controversial Law Brought Together a Zealous Sheriff's Deputy and an Eccentric Recluse; a Few Seconds Later, Donald Scott Was Dead," *Los Angeles Times Magazine*, Aug. 1, 1993; and Office of the District Attorney of Ventura, California, "Report on the Death of Donald Scott," (Mar. 30, 1993), available at www.fear.org/chron/scott.txt.

transport a drug dealer. Though charges were dropped against him within seventy-two hours, the DEA refused to return his Learjet. Only after five years of litigation and tens of thousands of dollars in legal fees was he able to secure return of his jet. When the jet was returned, it had sustained $100,000 worth of damage.[47] Such cases were atypical but got the attention of Congress.

The Reform Act resulted in a number of significant due-process changes, such as shifting the burden of proof onto the government, eliminating the requirement that an owner post a cost bond, and providing some minimal hardship protections for innocent parties who stand to lose their homes. These reforms, however, do not go nearly far enough.

Arguably the most significant reform is the creation of an "innocent owner" defense. Prior to the Reform Act, the Supreme Court had ruled that the guilt or innocence of the property's owner was irrelevant to the *property's* guilt—a ruling based on the archaic legal fiction that a piece of property could be "guilty" of a crime. The act remedied this insanity to some extent; it provides an "innocent owner" defense to those whose property has been seized. However, the defense is seriously undermined by the fact that the government's burden of proof is so low—the government need only establish by a "preponderance of the evidence" that the property was involved in the commission of a drug crime. This standard of proof is significantly lower than the "clear and convincing evidence" standard contained in an earlier version of the legislation, and it is far lower than the "proof beyond a reasonable doubt" standard for criminal convictions.

Once the government meets this minimal burden, the burden then shifts to the owner to prove that she "did not know of the conduct giving rise to the forfeiture" or that she did "all that reasonably could be expected under the circumstances to terminate such use of the property." This means, for example, that a woman who knew that her husband occasionally smoked pot could have her car forfeited to the government because she allowed him to use her car. Because the "car" was guilty of transporting someone who had broken a drug law at some time, she could legally lose her only form of transportation, even though she herself committed no crime. Indeed, women who are involved in some relationship with men accused of drug crimes, typically husbands or boyfriends, are among the most frequent claimants in forfeiture proceedings.[48] Courts have not been forgiving of women in these circumstances, frequently concluding that "the nature and circumstances of the marital relationship may give rise to an inference of knowledge by the spouse claiming innocent ownership."[49]

There are other problems with this framework, not the least of which being that the owner of the property is not entitled to the appointment of counsel in the forfeiture proceeding, unless he or she has been charged with a crime. The overwhelming majority of forfeiture cases do not involve any criminal charges, so

---

[47] Peter D. Lepsch, "Wanted: Civil Forfeiture Reform," *Drug Policy Letter*, Summer 1997, 12.

[48] James Massey, Susan Miller, and Anna Wilhelmi, "Civil Forfeiture of Property: The Victimization of Women as Innocent Owners and Third Parties," in *Crime Control and Women*, ed. Susan Miller (Thousand Oaks, CA: Sage Publications, 1998), 17.

[49] *United States v. One Parcel of Real Estate Located at 9818 S.W. 94 Terrace*, 788 F. Supp. 561, 565 (S.D. Fla. 1992).

the vast majority of people who have their cash, cars, or homes seized must represent themselves in court, against the federal government. Oddly, someone who has actually been charged with a crime is entitled to the appointment of counsel in civil forfeiture proceedings, but those whose property has been forfeited but whose conduct did not merit criminal charges are on their own. This helps to explain why up to 90 percent of forfeiture cases in some jurisdictions are not challenged. Most people simply cannot afford the considerable cost of hiring an attorney. Even if the cost is not an issue, the incentives are all wrong. If the police seized your car worth $5,000, or took $500 cash from your home, would you be willing to pay an attorney more than your assets are worth to get them back? If you haven't been charged with a crime, are you willing to risk the possibility that fighting the forfeiture might prompt the government to file criminal charges against you?

The greatest failure of the Reform Act, however, has nothing to do with one's due process rights once property has been seized in a drug investigation. Despite all of the new procedural rules and formal protections, the law does not address the single most serious problem associated with drug-war forfeiture laws: the profit motive in drug-law enforcement. Under the new law, drug busts motivated by the desire to seize cash, cars, homes, and other property are still perfectly legal. Law enforcement agencies are still allowed, through revenue-sharing agreements with the federal government, to keep seized assets for their own use. Clearly, so long as law enforcement is free to seize assets allegedly associated with illegal drug activity—without ever charging anyone with a crime—local police departments, as well as state and federal law enforcement agencies, will continue to have a direct pecuniary interest in the profitability and longevity of the drug war. The basic structure of the system remains intact.

None of this is to suggest that the financial rewards offered for police participation in the drug war are the only reason that law enforcement decided to embrace the war with zeal. Undoubtedly, the political and cultural context of the drug war—particularly in the early years—encouraged the roundup. When politicians declare a drug war, the police (our domestic warriors) undoubtedly feel some pressure to wage it. But it is doubtful that the drug war would have been launched with such intensity on the ground but for the bribes offered for law enforcement's cooperation.

Today the bribes may no longer be necessary. Now that the SWAT teams, the multiagency drug task forces, and the drug enforcement agenda have become a regular part of federal, state, and local law enforcement, it appears the drug war is here to stay. Funding for the Byrne-sponsored drug task forces had begun to dwindle during President Bush's tenure, but Barack Obama, as a presidential candidate, promised to revive the Byrne grant program, claiming that it is "critical to creating the anti-drug task forces our communities need."[50] Obama honored his word following the election, drastically increasing funding for the Byrne grant program despite its abysmal track record. The Economic Recovery Act of 2009 included more than $2 billion in new Byrne funding and an additional $600

[50] David Hunt, "Obama Fields Questions on Jacksonville Crime," *Florida Times-Union*, Sept. 22, 2008.

million to increase state and local law enforcement across the country.[51] Relatively little organized opposition to the drug war currently exists, and any dramatic effort to scale back the war may be publicly condemned as "soft" on crime. The war has become institutionalized. It is no longer a special program or politicized project; it is simply the way things are done.

Legal Misrepresentation

So far, we have seen that the legal rules governing the drug war ensure that extraordinary numbers of people will be swept into the criminal justice system—arrested on drug charges, often for very minor offenses. But what happens after arrest? How does the design of the system help to ensure the creation of a massive undercaste?

Once arrested, one's chances of ever being truly free of the system of control are slim, often to the vanishing point. Defendants are typically denied meaningful legal representation, pressured by the threat of a lengthy sentence into a plea bargain, and then placed under formal control—in prison or jail, on probation or parole. Most Americans probably have no idea how common it is for people to be convicted without ever having the benefit of legal representation, or how many people plead guilty to crimes they did not commit because of fear of mandatory sentences.

Tens of thousands of poor people go to jail every year without ever talking to a lawyer, and those who do meet with a lawyer for a drug offense often spend only a few minutes discussing their case and options before making a decision that will profoundly affect the rest of their lives. As one public defender explained to the *Los Angeles Times*, "They are herded like cattle [into the courtroom lockup], up at 3 or 4 in the morning. Then they have to make decisions that affect the rest of their lives. You can imagine how stressful it is."[52]

More than forty years ago, in *Gideon v. Wainwright*, the Supreme Court ruled that poor people accused of serious crimes were entitled to counsel. Yet thousands of people are processed through America's courts annually either with no lawyer at all or with a lawyer who does not have the time, resources or, in some cases, the inclination to provide effective representation. In *Gideon*, the Supreme Court left it to state and local governments to decide how legal services should be funded. However, in the midst of a drug war, when politicians compete with each other to prove how "tough" they can be on crime and criminals, funding public defender offices and paying private attorneys to represent those accused of crimes has been a low priority.

Approximately 80 percent of criminal defendants are indigent and thus unable to hire a lawyer.[53] Yet our nation's public defender system is woefully inadequate. The most visible sign of the failed system is the astonishingly large caseloads public

---

[51] See Phillip Smith, "Federal Budget: Economic Stimulus Bill Stimulates Drug War, Too," Drug War Chronicle, no. 573 (Feb. 20, 2009). See also Michelle Alexander, "Obama's Drug War," *The Nation*, Dec. 9, 2010 (noting that the 2009 economic stimulus package included a twelvefold increase in financing for Byrne programs).

[52] John Balzar, "The System: Deals, Deadlines, Few Trials," *Los Angeles Times*, Sept. 4, 2006.

[53] Marc Mauer and Ryan S. King, *Schools and Prisons: Fifty Years After Brown v. Board of Education* (Washington, DC: Sentencing Project, 2004), 4.

defenders routinely carry, making it impossible for them to provide meaningful representation to their clients. Sometimes defenders have well over one hundred clients at a time; many of these clients are facing decades behind bars or life imprisonment. Too often the quality of court-appointed counsel is poor because the miserable working conditions and low pay discourage good attorneys from participating in the system. And some states deny representation to impoverished defendants on the theory that somehow they should be able to pay for a lawyer, even though they are scarcely able to pay for food or rent. In Virginia, for example, fees paid to court-appointed attorneys for representing someone charged with a felony that carries a sentence of less than twenty years are capped at $428. And in Wisconsin, more than 11,000 poor people go to court without representation every year because anyone who earns more than $3,000 per year is considered able to afford a lawyer.[54] In Lake Charles, Louisiana, the public defender office has only two investigators for the 2,500 new felony cases and 4,000 new misdemeanor cases assigned to the office each year.[55] The NAACP Legal Defense Fund and the Southern Center for Human Rights in Atlanta sued the city of Gulfport, Mississippi, alleging that the city operated a "modern day debtor's prison" by jailing poor people who are unable to pay their fines and denying them the right to lawyers.

In 2004, the American Bar Association released a report on the status of indigent defense, concluding that, "All too often, defendants plead guilty, even if they are innocent, without really understanding their legal rights or what is occurring. Sometimes the proceedings reflect little or no recognition that the accused is mentally ill or does not adequately understand English. The fundamental right to a lawyer that Americans assume applies to everyone accused of criminal conduct effectively does not exist in practice for countless people across the United States."[56]

Even when people are charged with extremely serious crimes, such as murder, they may find themselves languishing in jail for years without meeting with an attorney, much less getting a trial. One extreme example is the experience of James Thomas, an impoverished day laborer in Baton Rouge, Louisiana, who was charged with murder in 1996, and waited eight and a half years for his case to go to trial. It never did. His mother finally succeeded in getting his case dismissed, after scraping together $500 to hire an attorney, who demonstrated to the court that, in the time Thomas spent waiting for his case to go to trial, his alibi witness had died of kidney disease. Another Louisiana man, Johnny Lee Ball, was convicted of second-degree murder and sentenced to life in prison without the possibility of parole after meeting with a public defender for just eleven minutes before trial. If indicted murderers have a hard time getting meaningful representation, what are the odds that small-time drug dealers find themselves represented by a zealous advocate? As

---

[54] Laura Parker, "8 Years in a Louisiana Jail but He Never Went to Trial," *USA Today*, Aug. 29, 2005.

[55] Mauer and King, *Schools and Prisons*, 4.

[56] American Bar Association, Standing Committee on Legal Aid and Indigent Defendants, *Gideon's Broken Promise: American's Continuing Quest for Equal Justice* (Washington, DC: American Bar Association, Dec. 2004), Executive Summary IV; adopted by American Bar Association House of Delegates, Aug. 9, 2005, www.abanet.org/leadership/2005/annual/dailyjournal/107.doc.

David Carroll, the research director for the National Legal Aid & Defender Association explained to *USA Today*, "There's a real disconnect in this country between what people perceive is the state of indigent defense and what it is. I attribute that to shows like *Law & Order*, where the defendant says, 'I want a lawyer,' and all of a sudden Legal Aid appears in the cell. That's what people think."[57]

Children caught up in this system are the most vulnerable and yet are the least likely to be represented by counsel. In 1967, the U.S. Supreme Court ruled in *In re Gault* that children under the age of eighteen have the right to legal assistance with any criminal charges filed against them. In practice, however, children routinely "waive" their right to counsel in juvenile proceedings. In some states, such as Ohio, as many as 90 percent of children charged with criminal wrongdoing are not represented by a lawyer. As one public defender explained, "The kids come in with their parents, who want to get this dealt with as quickly as possible, and they say, 'You did it, admit it.' If people were informed about what could be done, they might actually ask for help."[58]

Bad Deal

Almost no one ever goes to trial. Nearly all criminal cases are resolved through plea bargaining—a guilty plea by the defendant in exchange for some form of leniency by the prosecutor. Though it is not widely known, the prosecutor is the most powerful law enforcement official in the criminal justice system. One might think that judges are the most powerful, or even the police, but in reality the prosecutor holds the cards. It is the prosecutor, far more than any other criminal justice official, who holds the keys to the jailhouse door.

After the police arrest someone, the prosecutor is in charge. Few rules constrain the exercise of his or her discretion. The prosecutor is free to dismiss a case for any reason or no reason at all. The prosecutor is also free to file more charges against a defendant than can realistically be proven in court, so long as probable cause arguably exists—a practice known as overcharging.

The practice of encouraging defendants to plead guilty to crimes, rather than affording them the benefit of a full trial, has always carried its risks and downsides. Never before in our history, though, have such an extraordinary number of people felt compelled to plead guilty, even if they are innocent, simply because the punishment for the minor, nonviolent offense with which they have been charged is so unbelievably severe. When prosecutors offer "only" three years in prison when the penalties defendants could receive if they took their case to trial would be five, ten, or twenty years—or life imprisonment—only extremely courageous (or foolish) defendants turn the offer down.

The pressure to plead guilty to crimes has increased exponentially since the advent of the War on Drugs. In 1986, Congress passed The Anti-Drug Abuse Act, which established extremely long mandatory minimum prison terms for low-level drug dealing and possession of crack cocaine. The typical mandatory sentence

---

[57] Parker, "8 Years in a Louisiana Jail."

[58] Kim Brooks and Darlene Kamine, eds., *Justice Cut Short: An Assessment of Access to Counsel and Quality of Representation in Delinquency Proceedings In Ohio* (Columbus: Ohio State Bar Foundation, 2003), 28.

for a first-time drug offense in federal court is five or ten years. By contrast, in other developed countries around the world, a first-time drug offense would merit no more than six months in jail, if jail time is imposed at all.[59] State legislatures were eager to jump on the "get tough" bandwagon, passing harsh drug laws, as well as "three strikes" laws mandating a life sentence for those convicted of any third offense. These mandatory minimum statutory schemes have transferred an enormous amount of power from judges to prosecutors. Now, simply by charging someone with an offense carrying a mandatory sentence of ten to fifteen years or life, prosecutors are able to force people to plead guilty rather than risk a decade or more in prison. Prosecutors admit that they routinely charge people with crimes for which they technically have probable cause but which they seriously doubt they could ever win in court.[60] They "load up" defendants with charges that carry extremely harsh sentences in order to force them to plead guilty to lesser offenses and—here's the kicker—to obtain testimony for a related case. Harsh sentencing laws encourage people to snitch.

The number of snitches in drug cases has soared in recent years, partly because the government has tempted people to "cooperate" with law enforcement by offering cash, putting them "on payroll," and promising cuts of seized drug assets, but also because ratting out co-defendants, friends, family, or acquaintances is often the only way to avoid a lengthy mandatory minimum sentence.[61] In fact, under the federal sentencing guidelines, providing "substantial assistance" is often the only way defendants can hope to obtain a sentence below the mandatory minimum. The "assistance" provided by snitches is notoriously unreliable, as studies have documented countless informants who have fabricated stories about drug-related and other criminal activity in exchange for money or leniency in their pending criminal cases.[62] While such conduct is deplorable, it is not difficult to understand. Who among us would not be tempted to lie if it was the only way to avoid a forty-year sentence for a minor drug crime?

The pressure to plea-bargain and thereby "convict yourself" in exchange for some kind of leniency is not an accidental by-product of the mandatory-sentencing regime. The U.S. Sentencing Commission itself has noted that "the value of a mandatory minimum sentence lies not in its imposition, but in its value as a bargaining chip to be given away in return for the resource-saving plea from the

---

59 Mauer, *Race to Incarcerate*, 3537.

60 See Angela J. Davis, *Arbitrary Justice: The Power of the American Prosecutor* (New York: Oxford University Press, 2007), 3133.

61 See Alexandra Natapoff, "Snitching: The Institutional and Communal Consequences," *University of Cincinnati Law Review* 645 (2004); and Emily Jane Dodds, "I'll Make You a Deal: How Repeat Informants Are Corrupting the Criminal Justice System and What to Do About It," *William and Mary Law Review* 50 (2008): 1063.

62 See "Riverside Drug Cases Under Review Over Use of Secret Informant," Associated Press, Aug. 20, 2004; Ruben Narvette Jr., "Blame Stretches Far and Wide in Drug Scandal," *Dallas Morning News*, Nov. 14, 2003; Rob Warden, *How Snitch Testimony Sent Randy Steidl and Other Innocent Americans to Death Row* (Chicago: Northwestern University School of Law, Center for Wrongful Convictions, 2004–5); "The Informant Trap," *National Law Journal*, Mar. 6, 1995; Steven Mills and Ken Armstrong, "The Jailhouse Informant," *Chicago Tribune*, Nov. 16, 1999; and Ted Rohrlich and Robert Stewart, "Jailhouse Snitches: Trading Lies for Freedom," *Los Angeles Times*, Apr. 16, 1989.

defendant to a more leniently sanctioned charge." Describing severe mandatory sentences as a bargaining chip is a major understatement, given its potential for extracting guilty pleas from people who are innocent of any crime.

It is impossible to know for certain how many innocent drug defendants convict themselves every year by accepting a plea bargain out of fear of mandatory sentences, or how many are convicted due to lying informants and paid witnesses, but reliable estimates of the number of innocent people currently in prison tend to range from 2 percent to 5 percent.[63] While those numbers may sound small (and probably are underestimates), they translate into thousands of innocent people who are locked up, some of whom will die in prison. In fact, if only 1 percent of America's prisoners are actually innocent of the crimes for which they have been convicted, that would mean tens of thousands of innocent people are currently languishing behind bars in the United States.

The real point here, however, is not that innocent people are locked up. That has been true since penitentiaries first opened in America. The critical point is that thousands of people are swept into the criminal justice system every year pursuant to the drug war without much regard for their guilt or innocence. The police are allowed by the courts to conduct fishing expeditions for drugs on streets and freeways based on nothing more than a hunch. Homes may be searched for drugs based on a tip from an unreliable, confidential informant who is trading the information for money or to escape prison time. And once swept inside the system, people are often denied attorneys or meaningful representation and pressured into plea bargains by the threat of unbelievably harsh sentences—sentences for minor drug crimes that are higher than many countries impose on convicted murderers. This is the way the roundup works, and it works this way in virtually every major city in the United States.

Time Served

Once convicted of felony drug charges, one's chances of being released from the system in short order are slim, at best. The elimination of judicial discretion through mandatory sentencing laws has forced judges to impose sentences for drug crimes that are often longer than those violent criminals receive. When judges have discretion, they may consider a defendant's background and impose a lighter penalty if the defendant's personal circumstances—extreme poverty or experience of abuse, for example—warrant it. This flexibility—which is important in all criminal cases—is especially important in drug cases, as studies have indicated that many drug defendants are using or selling to support an addiction.[64] Referring a defendant to treatment, rather than sending him or her to prison, may well be the most prudent choice—saving government resources and potentially saving the defendant from a lifetime of addiction. Likewise, imposing a short prison

63 See Adam Liptak, "Consensus on Counting the Innocent: We Can't," *New York Times*, Mar. 25, 2008; and Adam Liptak, "Study Suspects Thousands of False Confessions," *New York Times*, Apr. 19, 2004.

64 Christopher J. Mumola and Jennifer C. Karberg, *Drug Use and Dependence, State and Federal Prisoners*, 2004 (Washington, DC: U.S. Department of Justice, Bureau of Justice Statistics, 2006); and Ashley Nellis, Judy Greene, and Marc Mauer, *Reducing Racial Disparity in the Criminal Justice System: A Manual for Practitioners and Policymakers*, 2d ed. (Washington, DC: Sentencing Project, 2008), 8.

sentence (or none at all) may increase the chances that the defendant will experience successful re-entry. A lengthy prison term may increase the odds that re-entry will be extremely difficult, leading to relapse, and re-imprisonment. Mandatory drug sentencing laws strip judges of their traditional role of considering all relevant circumstances in an effort to do justice in the individual case.

Nevertheless, harsh mandatory minimum sentences for drug offenders have been consistently upheld by the U.S. Supreme Court. In 1982, the Supreme Court upheld forty years of imprisonment for possession and an attempt to sell 9 ounces of marijuana.[65] Several years later, in *Harmelin v. Michigan*, the Court upheld a sentence of *life imprisonment* for a defendant with no prior convictions who attempted to sell 672 grams (approximately 23 ounces) of crack cocaine.[66] The Court found the sentences imposed in those cases "reasonably proportionate" to the offenses committed—and not "cruel and unusual" in violation of the Eighth Amendment. This ruling was remarkable given that, prior to the Drug Reform Act of 1986, the longest sentence Congress had ever imposed for possession of any drug in any amount was one year. A life sentence for a first-time drug offense is unheard of in the rest of the developed world. Even for high-end drug crimes, most countries impose sentences that are measured in months, rather than years. For example, a conviction for selling a kilogram of heroin yields a mandatory ten-year sentence in U.S. federal court, compared with six months in prison in England.[67] Remarkably, in the United States, a life sentence is deemed perfectly appropriate for a first-time drug offender.

The most famous Supreme Court decision upholding mandatory minimum sentences is *Lockyer v. Andrade*.[68] In that case, the Court rejected constitutional challenges to sentences of twenty-five years without parole for a man who stole three golf clubs from a pro shop, and fifty years without parole for another man for stealing children's videotapes from a Kmart store. These sentences were imposed pursuant to California's controversial three strikes law, which mandates a sentence of twenty-five years to life for recidivists convicted of a third felony, no matter how minor. Writing for the Court's majority, Justice Sandra Day O'Connor acknowledged that the sentences were severe but concluded that they are not grossly disproportionate to the offense, and therefore do not violate the Eighth Amendment's ban on "cruel and unusual" punishments. In dissent, Justice David H. Souter retorted, "If Andrade's sentence [for stealing videotapes] is not grossly disproportionate, the principle has no meaning." Similarly, counsel for one of the defendants, University of Southern California law professor Erwin Chemerinsky, noted that the Court's reasoning makes it extremely difficult if not impossible to challenge any recidivist sentencing law: "If these sentences aren't cruel and unusual punishment, what would be?"[69]

---

[65] *Hutto v. Davis*, 454 U.S. 370 (1982).

[66] *Harmelin v. Michigan*, 501 U.S. 967 (1991).

[67] Marc Mauer, "The Hidden Problem of Time Served in Prison," *Social Research* 74, no. 2 (Summer 2007): 701, 703.

[68] *Lockyer v. Andrade*, 538 U.S. 63 (2003).

[69] Anne Gearam, "Supreme Court Upholds 'Three Strikes Law,'" Associated Press, Mar. 5, 2003.

Mandatory sentencing laws are frequently justified as necessary to keep "violent criminals" off the streets, yet those penalties are imposed most often against drug offenders and those who are guilty of nonviolent crimes. In fact, under the three-strikes regime in California, a "repeat offender" could be someone who had only a single prior case decades ago, and one arrest can result in multiple strikes. For example, imagine a young man, eighteen years old, who is arrested as part of an undercover operation and charged with two counts of dealing cocaine to minors. He had been selling to friends to earn extra money for shoes and basic things his mother could not afford. The prosecutor offers him probation if he agrees to plead guilty to both charges and to snitch on a bigger dealer. Terrified of doing prison time, he takes the deal. Several years later, he finds his punishment will never end. Branded a felon, he is struggling to survive and to support his children. One night he burglarizes a corner store and steals food, toothpaste, Pepsi, and diapers for his baby boy. He is arrested almost immediately a few blocks away. That's it for him. He now has three strikes. His burglary can be charged as a third strike because of his two prior felony convictions. He is eligible for life imprisonment. His children will be raised without a father.

Or imagine a woman struggling with drug addiction, unable to obtain treatment, and desperate for money so she can feed her habit. Together with her boyfriend, she burglarizes two homes, stealing televisions they hope to sell. After her arrest, she takes a plea deal, spends several years in prison, and is released with two strikes on her record, one for each burglary. Two decades later, she relapses—after being clean for fifteen years—and is arrested for selling crack. She made the sale to support her relapse. That's it for her. She can be locked up for the rest of her life.

These examples may sound extreme, but real life can be worse. Sentences for each charge can run consecutively, so a defendant can easily face a sentence of fifty, seventy-five, or one hundred years to life arising from a single case. It is not uncommon for people to receive prison sentences of more than fifty years for minor crimes. In fact, fifty years to life was the actual sentence given to Leandro Andrade for stealing videotapes, a sentence upheld by the Supreme Court.

The clear majority of those subject to harsh mandatory minimum sentences in the federal system are drug offenders. Most are low-level, minor drug dealers—not "drug kingpins." The stories are legion. Marcus Boyd was arrested after selling 3.9 grams of crack cocaine to a confidential informant working with a regional drug task force. At the time of his arrest, Marcus was twenty-four years old and had been addicted to drugs for six years, beginning shortly after his mother's death and escalating throughout his early twenties. He met the informant through a close family friend, someone he trusted. At sentencing, the judge based the drug quantity calculation on testimony from the informant and another witness, who both claimed they bought crack from Marcus on other occasions. As a result, Marcus was held accountable for 37.4 grams (the equivalent of 1.3 ounces) based on the statements made by the informant and the other witness. He was sentenced to more than fourteen years in prison. His two children were six and seven years old at the time of his sentencing. They will be adults when he is released.[70]

[70] See Families Against Mandatory Minimums, "Profiles of Injustice," at www.famm.org/ProfilesofInjustice/FederalProfiles/MarcusBoyd.aspx.

Weldon Angelos is another casualty of the drug war. He will spend the rest of his life in prison for three marijuana sales. Angelos, a twenty-four-year-old record producer, possessed a weapon—which he did not use or threaten to use—at the time of the sales. Under federal sentencing guidelines, however, the sentencing judge was obligated to impose a fifty-five-year mandatory minimum sentence. Upon doing so, the judge noted his reluctance to send the young man away for life for three marijuana sales. He said from the bench, "The Court believes that to sentence Mr. Angelos to prison for the rest of his life is unjust, cruel, and even irrational."[71]

Some federal judges, including conservative judges, have quit in protest of federal drug laws and sentencing guidelines. Face-to-face with those whose lives hang in the balance, they are far closer to the human tragedy occasioned by the drug war than the legislators who write the laws from afar. Judge Lawrence Irving, a Reagan appointee, noted upon his retirement: "If I remain on the bench, I have no choice but to follow the law. I just can't, in good conscience, continue to do this."[72] Other judges, such as Judge Jack Weinstein, publicly refused to take any more drug cases, describing "a sense of depression about much of the cruelty I have been a party to in connection with the 'war on drugs.'"[73] Another Reagan appointee, Judge Stanley Marshall, told a reporter, "I've always been considered a fairly harsh sentencer, but it's killing me that I'm sending so many low-level offenders away for all this time."[74] He made the statement after imposing a five-year sentence on a mother in Washington, D.C., who was convicted of "possession" of crack found by police in a locked box that her son had hidden in her attic. In California, reporters described a similar event:

> U.S. District Judge William W. Schwarzer, a Republican appointee, is not known as a light sentencer. Thus it was that everyone in his San Francisco courtroom watched in stunned silence as Schwarzer, known for his stoic demeanor, choked with tears as he anguished over sentencing Richard Anderson, a first offender Oakland longshoreman, to ten years in prison without parole for what appeared to be a minor mistake in judgment in having given a ride to a drug dealer for a meeting with an undercover agent.[75]

Even Supreme Court Justice Anthony Kennedy has condemned the harsh mandatory minimum sentences imposed on drug offenders. He told attorneys gathered for the American Bar Association's 2003 annual conference: "Our [prison] resources are misspent, our punishments too severe, our sentences too

---

[71] Marc Mauer, "Hidden Problem," 701–2.

[72] Special to the *New York Times*, "Criticizing Sentencing Rules, US Judge Resigns," *New York Times*, Sept. 30, 1990.

[73] Joseph Treaster, "Two Federal Judges, in Protest, Refuse to Accept Drug Cases," *New York Times*, Apr. 17, 1993.

[74] Chris Carmody, "Revolt to Sentencing is Gaining Momentum," *National Law Journal*, May 17, 1993, 10.

[75] Stuart Taylor Jr., "Ten Years for Two Ounces," *American Lawyer*, Mar. 1990, 65–66.

loaded." He then added, "I can accept neither the necessity nor the wisdom of federal mandatory minimum sentences. In all too many cases, mandatory minimum sentences are unjust."[76]

The Prison Label

Most people imagine that the explosion in the U.S. prison population during the past twenty-five years reflects changes in crime rates. Few would guess that our prison population leaped from approximately 350,000 to 2.3 million in such a short period of time due to changes in laws and policies, not changes in crime rates. Yet it has been changes in our laws—particularly the dramatic increases in the length of prison sentences—that have been responsible for the growth of our prison system, not increases in crime. One study suggests that the entire increase in the prison population from 1980 to 2001 can be explained by sentencing policy changes.[77]

Because harsh sentencing is a major cause of the prison explosion, one might reasonably assume that substantially reducing the length of prison sentences would effectively dismantle this new system of control. That view, however, is mistaken. This system depends on the prison label, not prison time.

Once a person is labeled a felon, he or she is ushered into a parallel universe in which discrimination, stigma, and exclusion are perfectly legal, and privileges of citizenship such as voting and jury service are off-limits. It does not matter whether you have actually spent time in prison; your second-class citizenship begins the moment you are branded a felon. Most people branded felons, in fact, are not sentenced to prison. As of 2008, there were approximately 2.3 million people in prisons and jails, and a staggering 5.1 million people under "community correctional supervision"—i.e., on probation or parole.[78] Merely reducing prison terms does not have a major impact on the majority of people in the system. It is the badge of inferiority—the felony record—that relegates people for their entire lives, to second-class status. As described in chapter 4, for drug felons, there is little hope of escape. Barred from public housing by law, discriminated against by private landlords, ineligible for food stamps, forced to "check the box" indicating a felony conviction on employment applications for nearly every job, and denied licenses for a wide range of professions, people whose only crime is drug addiction or possession of a small amount of drugs for recreational use find themselves locked out of the mainstream society and economy—permanently.

No wonder, then, that most people labeled felons find their way back into prison. According to a Bureau of Justice Statistics study, about 30 percent of released prisoners in its sample were rearrested within six months of release.[79] Within three years, nearly 68 percent were rearrested at least once for a new offense.[80] Only

---

76 Michael Jacobson, *Downsizing Prisons: How to Reduce Crime and End Mass Incarceration* (New York: New York University Press, 2005), 215.

77 See Mauer, *Race to Incarcerate*, 33, 36–38, citing Warren Young and Mark Brown.

78 PEW Center for the States, *One in 31*.

79 Jeremy Travis, *But They All Come Back: Facing the Challenges of Prisoner Reentry* (Washington, DC: Urban Institute Press, 2002), 32, citing Bureau of Justice Statistics.

80 Ibid., 94, citing Bureau of Justice Statistics.

a small minority are rearrested for violent crimes; the vast majority are rearrested for property offenses, drug offenses, and offenses against the public order.[81]

For those released on probation or parole, the risks are especially high. They are subject to regular surveillance and monitoring by the police and may be stopped and searched (with or without their consent) for any reason or no reason at all. As a result, they are far more likely to be arrested (again) than those whose behavior is not subject to constant scrutiny by law enforcement. Probationers and parolees are at increased risk of arrest because their lives are governed by additional rules that do not apply to everyone else. Myriad restrictions on their travel and behavior (such as a prohibition on associating with other felons), as well as various requirements of probation and parole (such as paying fines and meeting with probation officers), create opportunities for arrest. Violation of these special rules can land someone right back in prison. In fact, that is what happens a good deal of the time.

The extraordinary increase in prison admissions due to parole and probation violations is due almost entirely to the War on Drugs. With respect to parole, in 1980, only 1 percent of all prison admissions were parole violators. Twenty years later, more than one third (35 percent) of prison admissions resulted from parole violations.[82] To put the matter more starkly: *About as many people were returned to prison for parole violations in 2000 as were admitted to prison in 1980 for all reasons.*[83] Of all parole violators returned to prison in 2000, only one-third were returned for a new conviction; two-thirds were returned for a technical violation such as missing appointments with a parole officer, failing to maintain employment, or failing a drug test.[84] In this system of control, failing to cope well with one's exile status is treated like a crime. If you fail, after being released from prison with a criminal record—your personal badge of inferiority—to remain drug free, or if you fail to get a job against all the odds, or if you get depressed and miss an appointment with your parole officer (or if you cannot afford the bus fare to take you there), you can be sent right back to prison—where society apparently thinks millions of Americans belong.

This disturbing phenomenon of people cycling in and out of prison, trapped by their second-class status, has been described by Loïc Wacquant as a "closed circuit of perpetual marginality."[85] Hundreds of thousands of people are released from prison every year, only to find themselves locked out of the mainstream society and economy. Most ultimately return to prison, sometimes for the rest of their lives. Others are released again, only to find themselves in precisely the circumstances they occupied before, unable to cope with the stigma of the prison label and their permanent pariah status.

---

[81] Ibid.

[82] Ibid., 32.

[83] Ibid.

[84] Ibid., 49, citing Bureau of Justice Statistics.

[85] Loïc Wacquant, "The New 'Peculiar Institution': On the Prison as Surrogate Ghetto," *Theoretical Criminology* 4, no. 3 (2000): 377–89.

Reducing the amount of time people spend behind bars—by eliminating harsh mandatory minimums—will alleviate some of the unnecessary suffering caused by this system, but it will not disturb the closed circuit. Those labeled felons will continue to cycle in and out of prison, subject to perpetual surveillance by the police, and unable to integrate into the mainstream society and economy. Unless the number of people who are labeled felons is dramatically reduced, and unless the laws and policies that keep ex-offenders marginalized from the mainstream society and economy are eliminated, the system will continue to create and maintain an enormous undercaste. ■

AUTHOR PROFILE

Michelle Alexander (born 1967) is a civil rights lawyer, social activist, legal scholar, and writer. Alexander current serves as an associate professor of law at the Ohio State University. "The Lockdown" is the second chapter of Alexander's book, *The New Jim Crow: Mass Incarceration in the Age of Colorblindness.* The book argues that the U.S. Criminal Justice System functions to inflict great harm to communities of color by relegating them second-class status in society, while creating the illusion that it adheres to principles of colorblindness. Her book, which has been widely praised, has brought national attention to the complex problems created by the criminal justice system and led to the development of a number of grassroots social advocacy campaigns.

Defending Walt Whitman

By Sherman Alexie

Basketball is like this for young Indian boys, all arms and legs
and serious stomach muscles. Every body is brown!
These are the twentieth-century warriors who will never kill,
although a few sat quietly in the deserts of Kuwait,
waiting for orders to do something, to do something.

God, there is nothing as beautiful as a jumpshot
on a reservation summer basketball court
where the ball is moist with sweat,
and makes a sound when it swishes through the net
that causes Walt Whitman to weep because it is so perfect.

There are veterans of foreign wars here
although their bodies are still dominated
by collarbones and knees, although their bodies still respond
in the ways that bodies are supposed to respond when we are young.
Every body is brown! Look there, that boy can run
up and down this court forever. He can leap for a rebound
with his back arched like a salmon, all meat and bone
synchronized, magnetic, as if the court were a river,
as if the rim were a dam, as if the air were a ladder
leading the Indian boy toward home.

Some of the Indian boys still wear their military hair cuts
while a few have let their hair grow back.
It will never be the same as it was before!
One Indian boy has never cut his hair, not once, and he braids it
into wild patterns that do not measure anything.
He is just a boy with too much time on his hands.
Look at him. He wants to play this game in bare feet.

God, the sun is so bright! There is no place like this.
Walt Whitman stretches his calf muscles
on the sidelines. He has the next game.
His huge beard is ridiculous on the reservation.
Some body throws a crazy pass and Walt Whitman catches it
with quick hands. He brings the ball close to his nose
and breathes in all of its smells: leather, brown skin, sweat,
black hair, burning oil, twisted ankle, long drink of warm water,
gunpowder, pine tree. Walt Whitman squeezes the ball tightly.
He wants to run. He hardly has the patience to wait for his turn.
"What's the score?" he asks. He asks, "What's the score?"

Basketball is like this for Walt Whitman. He watches these Indian boys
as if they were the last bodies on earth. Every body is brown!
Walt Whitman shakes because he believes in God.
Walt Whitman dreams of the Indian boy who will defend him,
trapping him in the corner, all flailing arms and legs
and legendary stomach muscles. Walt Whitman shakes
because he believes in God. Walt Whitman dreams
of the first jumpshot he will take, the ball arcing clumsily
from his fingers, striking the rim so hard that it sparks.
Walt Whitman shakes because he believes in God.
Walt Whitman closes his eyes. He is a small man and his beard
is ludicrous on the reservation, absolutely insane.
His beard makes the Indian boys righteously laugh. His beard
frightens the smallest Indian boys. His beard tickles the skin
of the Indian boys who dribble past him. His beard, his beard!

God, there is beauty in every body. Walt Whitman stands
at center court while the Indian boys run from basket to basket.
Walt Whitman cannot tell the difference between
offense and defense. He does not care if he touches the ball.
Half of the Indian boys wear t-shirts damp with sweat
and the other half are bareback, skin slick and shiny.
There is no place like this. Walt Whitman smiles.
Walt Whitman shakes. This game belongs to him. ■

AUTHOR PROFILE

Sherman Alexie (born October 7, 1966) is a prolific writer in many genres, producing novels, volumes of poetry and short stories, and the screenplay for the first all-Native American movie, *Smoke Signals* (1998). Alexie describes himself as a Spokane/Coeur d'Alene Indian who grew up on the Spokane Indian Reservation. His writing puts experiences of reservation life in the larger context of American culture, exploring themes ranging from racism and substance abuse to blues music and basketball. "Defending Walt Whitman" was first published in the fall of 1995 by *Beloit Poetry Journal*. The poem explores a complex problem that often appears in his work: what does it mean for a Native American writer, whose language and culture were so disrupted by colonization, to adopt the language, form, and culture of his colonizers?

Wrong Answer

In an era of high-stakes testing, a struggling high school made a shocking choice.

By Rachel Aviv

One afternoon in the spring of 2006, Damany Lewis, a math teacher at Parks Middle School, in Atlanta, unlocked the room where standardized tests were kept. It was the week before his students took the Criterion-Referenced Competency Test, which determined whether schools in Georgia had met federal standards of achievement. The tests were wrapped in cellophane and stacked in cardboard boxes. Lewis, a slim twenty-nine-year-old with dreadlocks, contemplated opening the test with scissors, but he thought his cut marks would be too obvious. Instead, he left the school, walked to the corner store, and bought a razor blade. When he returned, he slit open the cellophane and gently pulled a test book from its wrapping. Then he used a lighter to warm the razor, which he wedged under the adhesive sealing the booklet, and peeled back the tab.

He photocopied the math, reading, and language-arts sections—the subjects that would determine, under the No Child Left Behind guidelines, whether Parks would be classified as a "school in need of improvement" for the sixth year in a row. Unless fifty-eight per cent of students passed the math portion of the test and sixty-seven per cent passed in language arts, the state could shut down the school. Lewis put on gloves, to prevent oil from his hands from leaving a residue on the plastic, and then used his lighter to melt the edges of the cellophane together, so that it appeared as if the package had never been opened. He gave the reading and language-arts sections to two teachers he trusted and took the math section home.

Flipping through its pages, he felt proud of how much material he had covered that year. "Without even reading the question, I could tell you just by the shape of the graph, 'Oh, my kids know that,' " he told me. He put the test in his fireplace once he'd confirmed that he had taught the necessary concepts. But he worried that his students would struggle with questions that were delivered in paragraph form. Some of his seventh-grade students were still reading by sounding out the letters. It seemed unfair that the concepts were "buried in words." Lewis felt that he had pushed them to work harder than they ever had in their lives. "I'm not going to let the state slap them in the face and say they're failures," he told me. "I'm going to do everything I can to prevent the why-try spirit."

The principal of Parks, Christopher Waller, knew that he had seen the questions before the test. Waller told me that Lewis was a "star teacher," a "very hard worker, who will go the extra mile." When the math portion of the test had been completed, Lewis said that Waller asked him how his students had done. Since Lewis had looked at the questions, it no longer seemed like a big deal to review the answers. Lewis returned to the testing office and opened up the answer sheets of a few students in his class who got average grades. He looked for a hard question and, when he saw that they'd solved it, he moved on, assuming that they had done fine. Then he said that he "piddled" in the room, wasting time. When he felt that he had been in there long enough, he told Waller that it looked as if his students had done O.K. But Waller told him to check the answers of students who weren't in his class. This time, when he looked, Lewis saw that some of the smartest students at Parks had the wrong answers.

At the end of the testing week, Lewis went back to the testing office with Crystal Draper, a language-arts teacher. For about an hour, they erased wrong answers and bubbled in the right ones. They exchanged no words. Lewis couldn't even look at her. "I couldn't believe what we'd been reduced to," he said. He tried to stay focussed on the mechanics of the work: he took care to change, at most, one or two answers for every ten questions. "I had a minor in statistics, and it's not that hard to figure out windows of probability," he told me. Many students were on the cusp of passing, and he gave them a little nudge, so that they would pass by one or two points.

A month later, when the scores came back, Waller told the students to gather in the hallway outside the cafeteria, where there was a spread of ice cream, pizza, and hot wings. A teacher announced, "You did it! You finally made it!" For the first time since the passage of No Child Left Behind, Parks had met its annual goals: the percentage of eighth graders who passed rose thirty-one points in reading and sixty-two points in math. "Everyone was jumping up and down," Neekisia Jackson, a student, said. "It was like our World Series, our Olympics." She went on, "We had heard what everyone was saying: *Y'all aren't good enough*. Now we could finally go to school with our heads held high."

Parks Middle School is three miles south of downtown Atlanta, in Pittsburgh, a neighborhood bordered by a run-down trucking lot and railway tracks fallen into disuse. Founded after the Civil War, Pittsburgh was a black working-class area until the nineteen-sixties and seventies, when residents began leaving for the suburbs. Half the homes in the neighborhood are now vacant. Lewis's students called the area Little Vietnam and Jack City, because of all the armed robberies. Once, when Lewis stopped at a convenience store to tell his students to go home and do their homework, a prostitute approached him. "I'm, like, 'Whoa, whoa, I'm a teacher!' " he said. "And she's, like, 'I don't care. Teachers get down.' "

Lewis grew up in a violent neighborhood in East Oakland, California, in a house built by Habitat for Humanity. His father was a crack addict, and his mother supported four children by working as a bank teller; she later opened a safe house for ex-prostitutes. "She's a real underdog-lover," Lewis told me. On the weekends, she took Lewis to picnics hosted by the Black Panther Party. She worked so much that the neighbors helped raise Lewis: they often told him to wash his face or tuck in his shirt or put Vaseline on his chapped lips. His football coach became a father figure and encouraged Lewis to go to college in Atlanta so that he could have a "historical black experience."

Lewis received a scholarship to attend Clark Atlanta University, which is less than three miles from Parks. He was homeless for several months and got arrested for possessing marijuana, but he still earned good grades. He was a "lightweight nerd," as he put it. When he graduated with degrees in math and philosophy, his mother urged him to try teaching, since he'd always had a talent for simplifying complex ideas. In 2000, he started working at Parks and was immediately moved by his students' despair. "Being born in the seventies, coming out of the civil-rights movement, amidst the Black Panther meetings in Oakland, I didn't have limitations," he told me. "I was raised in the generation that lost the shame of being black."

His students, who came to school with bad breath and parkas that smelled of urine, seemed to lack the conviction that they would ever leave the neighborhood. Parks was run by an older woman who was not inclined to innovate. Homework was a joke. There was litter in the hallways, and students urinated in trash cans. A veteran teacher told Lewis that only twenty per cent of his students would grasp what he was teaching, so he should go over each lesson five times. "Please—I'm a better teacher than that," he remembered thinking. "She was just making excuses for why she spiralled in circles."

Atlanta's school superintendent, Beverly Hall, who was hired in 1999, quickly became aware of the problems at Parks. A neighborhood minister repeatedly called to complain about drug dealing in front of the school. Hall, who was born in Jamaica, had spent her career in underperforming urban districts: she began as a teacher in Fort Greene, Brooklyn, in the seventies, and moved on to become a superintendent in Newark. At one of her first meetings in Atlanta, she said, someone "got up and was literally screaming, 'Just tell us what to do. We've got to do something about education in Atlanta.' " Three-quarters of the students in the district were living near or below the poverty line—ninety per cent were black or Latino—and fewer than forty per cent graduated from high school.

Hall belonged to a movement of reformers who believed that the values of the marketplace could resuscitate public education. She approached the job like a business executive: she courted philanthropists, set accountability measures, and created performance objectives that were more rigorous than those required by No Child Left Behind, which became law in 2002. When a school met its targets, all employees, including bus drivers and cafeteria staff, received up to two thousand dollars. She linked teacher evaluations to test scores and warned principals that they'd be fired if they didn't meet targets within three years. Eventually, ninety per cent were replaced. She repeated the mantra "No exceptions and no excuses."

In 2001, she hired a new principal for Parks, a former college-football player named Michael Sims, whom Lewis described as the "father I never had." Sims focussed nearly as much on building a sense of community as he did on academics: he renovated the school, hired guidance counsellors, and replaced the "P" that had fallen off the sign at Parks's entryway. He told students that they were representing their school even when they were off campus. If they got into a fight over the weekend, they would be suspended on Monday. The school provided computer classes to parents, who had been so removed from their children's academic lives that it was a struggle to get them to sign progress reports. "We had to trick the parents and give away this, that, and the third in order to get them into the building," Lewis said. "Some of them looked like they were on drugs—not fun drugs but ruin-your-life drugs."

Parks started to feel like a place where both teachers and students, nearly all of them black, could expose their vulnerabilities. "All our little problems that we grew up hiding from the rest of the world—it became our line of communication," Lewis said. He told students to dump their laundry into the back of his pickup truck, so that he could wash it for them, and encouraged them to sleep at his house when their mothers were absent or high. (Few had fathers in their lives.) He became the football coach, and if practice ran late he dropped students off at their homes. Several ended up calling him Dad. He told them, "I don't know how you feel about me, but I, at least, feel like I made it. If you want to know if you can make it, look at me." He married a language-arts teacher at Parks, who was similarly devoted to the students. "She was a great model of what an adult woman is supposed to act like, talk like," Lewis said.

With the help of a college-prep program called Project Grad, which Beverly Hall implemented after securing millions of dollars from donors, Parks set up after-school programs and hired tutors. A 2004 documentary called "Expect the Best" explained that Parks, which had previously functioned like "day care," had become a "model of what a good school can and should be." The video shows Lewis on his porch, playing chess with a student who had moved in with him. The narrator of the video explains that the student, Antonio, was living with his math teacher "because his mother is in no shape to support or care for him. This arrangement, though temporary and unusual, has done a lot to stabilize Antonio's life."

The school steadily improved, but students' test scores were never high enough for Parks to make "adequate yearly progress," a measurement defined by No Child Left Behind, a nearly utopian statute that required all public-school students to become proficient in math and reading by 2014, as judged by their test scores. The reform model, which drew on an accountability system used in Texas in the nineties, ignored less quantifiable signs of intellectual development. Schools that didn't progress at an appropriate pace were eligible for federally funded support. They also received a series of escalating sanctions, including state monitoring, a revised curriculum, replacement of staff, and restructuring or closure of the school. LaShawn Hoffman, the head of the Pittsburgh Community Improvement Association, told me that when Parks opened, in 1966, it was a source of pride for the community, the neighborhood's "jewel." Now he worried about the burden of another large abandoned building in the neighborhood.

When Lewis showed up for the new school year in 2004, Parks's principal was absent. Lewis knew that Sims would never miss the first day of school and assumed that he must have been in some sort of accident. Then a district administrator called a meeting and explained that Sims would not be returning; he had resigned after being accused of sexual misconduct in a previous job.

After a few months, Christopher Waller, a Methodist pastor who had worked in public schools for nine years, became the new leader of Parks. Waller was burly and freckled, and, at thirty-one, he was the youngest principal in the district. After a week of introductory meetings, he saw that the district prioritized testing results more than any other place he'd ever worked did. "All decisions have to be made by data—you have to be baptized in it," he told me. "I lived it, slept it, ate it."

He held a meeting with the faculty and explained that teachers needed to use data to drive every aspect of instruction. Lewis raised his hand and said, "I need to be excused from this meeting." He left the room. Another administrator followed him into the hallway and tried to appease him, but he told her, "You all come in here trying to change every goddam thing we've been doing for years. We've been making step-by-step progress, and it's working."

The next day, Lewis said that Waller asked him to come to his office. "I hear you're the man around here," he told Lewis. At that point, Lewis was the football, soccer, and softball coach, the athletic director, and the founder of the chess club. As they talked, Lewis found himself impressed by Waller's intellect and social awareness. When Waller asked him what changes he should make, Lewis told him to bide his time. "It's like if you get a new stepmom in the house," he said. "If she immediately comes in and changes everything, she'll be hated forever."

Every fall, the district held a convocation ceremony, which was usually in the Georgia Dome, where the Atlanta Falcons play. Schools that met their performance targets were seated on the field, while schools that fell short were relegated to the bleachers. Teachers spoke nervously all year about whether they would "make the floor." At Waller's first convocation, in 2005, he was humiliated by his seat in the bleachers. "It's almost like having leprosy in the Bible," he told me. "No one wants to associate with failure."

Waller quickly learned that principals in the district insured loyalty by working with teachers whom they had personally selected. At one of his first meetings with Beverly Hall, Waller said that he was willing to work with the school's current teachers. Hall laughed and told him, "You will need your own team." Waller began encouraging veteran teachers to retire early. Lewis soon found himself one of the most senior teachers at Parks. He worried that the new faculty were being deprived of the "ethical guidance that comes from listening to older teachers."

Under Hall, four sub-superintendents oversaw different regions within the district, making sure that schools advanced toward their targets. After Waller had been at the school for a year, he received a stern memo, titled "Mid-year Review," from Michael Pitts, the sub-superintendent who was responsible for Parks. "Please understand that no excuse can or will be accepted for any results that are less than 70% of school-based target acquisition," Pitts wrote.

Waller told Pitts that the targets—set by the district's Department of Research, Planning, and Accountability—were unrealistic. It took a quarter of the year just to gain students' trust. Two students, he said, were raped in the neighborhood that year. Others lived alone, with neither parent at home, or were on the verge of being placed in juvenile detention. When a student was arrested for stealing cars, Waller went to court and asked the judge not to send him to jail. Waller told me, "The administration wanted to move kids out of poverty—I do believe that. But test scores could not be the only means." When Waller expressed his concerns, Pitts reiterated that Hall accepted no excuses, and told him, "The way principals keep their jobs in Atlanta is they make targets."

Waller struggled to understand his students' success in elementary school. They had passed the Criterion-Referenced Competency Test in fifth grade, and yet when they arrived at Parks they were reading at a first-grade level. "The students and the data aren't matching," he told Pitts. "They've got to be cheating at the elementary schools. There's no way those scores are real." One day, when he and Pitts were walking through Parks, Waller pointed out a disruptive sixth grader who had excelled on the test the year before, even though his academic skills were dismal. He recalled that Pitts laughed and said, "Sometimes children just test well." Then Pitts told him, "You need to keep your mouth shut." He urged Waller to "forge stronger relationships" with the principals at the elementary schools, which Waller interpreted as a message to learn how they'd artificially boosted their scores.

Waller concluded that the school couldn't meet its targets that year. More than half of the students were performing below grade level. The reading coördinator, Sandra Ward, told Waller that she had heard about an elementary school where teachers changed students' answers under the pretense of erasing stray pencil marks. According to Waller and Ward, the vice-principal, Gregory Reid, informed them that he knew of another school where teachers were obtaining test questions in advance. (Reid has denied this.) Waller decided to adopt both strategies by recruiting a "team" of teachers who could be trusted. He told himself, "We're helping them. They'll catch up by eighth grade."

The first teacher he approached was Lewis, who was resistant. Lewis told him, "Fuck the test. Our students are doing hot. We know they are learning." But after several months, Lewis said, Waller "chewed away at me." Waller reminded him that Parks was a "sanctuary," a "safe haven" for the community. If the school didn't meet its targets, Waller explained, the students would be separated and sent to different schools, outside Pittsburgh. Lewis said he felt that "it was my sole obligation to never let that happen."

In 2006, Tameka Grant, a sixth-grade teacher at Parks, sent a letter to Beverly Hall. She wrote that Waller was attempting to persuade teachers to cheat by describing how the teachers at elementary schools did it. "If you can't beat them, join them," she heard him say. She also noted that he often asked teachers how many of their students would pass the test, and when they equivocated he said, "Are you a team player? Are you on my team?"

The president of the Atlanta Federation of Teachers sent a letter to the district's central office, reporting that "Mr. Waller frequently intimidates the staff by telling them that the school will either be closing, or will be taken over." The letter described an "us/them mentality among staff where Mr. Waller works with new staff and not old and is trying to divide and conquer the seasoned staff." Lewis and other favored teachers were part of what became known as "Waller's circle." Some had their own reserved parking spaces.

After learning of the complaints, Pitts, the sub-superintendent, attended a faculty meeting at Parks. Teachers remember him saying, "Stop writing letters about Waller, because he is not going anywhere. There is nothing you can do to make us think negatively of Principal Waller." Lewis said he admired Tameka Grant for writing the letter, and he found it confusing that Pitts seemed to view her complaints as a low form of snitching. "I was, like, Damn, I thought that was kind of our obligation," he said.

At the request of the district's Office of Internal Resolution, a private investigator, Reginal Dukes, looked into the reported problems and, in March of 2006, concluded that teachers at Parks had cheated on the Georgia Middle Grades Writing Assessment, leaking the essay prompt to students. Dukes presented his preliminary findings to Hall at a lunch meeting with her senior staff and was shocked by her apparent lack of interest. "I expected her to take definite action," he told me. Instead, he was informed that he couldn't hire any additional investigators. Hall asked few questions. The only one he remembered was "Is there any more evidence?" "That question floored me," Dukes said. "I'd just gone through this litany of violations."

Waller was never reprimanded, and he said he never heard anything about the outcome of the investigation. The next year, Tameka Grant was transferred against her will to Long Middle School, known at the time as one of the most dangerous schools in the district.

In 2007, Parks had to score even higher to surpass its falsely achieved scores from the previous year. According to statements later made by teachers and administrators (obtained through Georgia's open-records act), the cheating process began to take the form of a routine. During testing week, after students had completed the day's section, Waller distracted the testing coördinator, Alfred Kiel, by taking him out for leisurely lunches in downtown Atlanta. On their way, Waller called the reading coördinator to let her know that it was safe to enter Kiel's office. She then paged up to six teachers and told them to report to the room. While their students were at recess, the teachers erased wrong answers and filled in the right ones. Lewis took photographs of the office with his cell phone so that he could make sure he left every object, even the pencils on Kiel's desk, exactly as he'd found them.

Lewis dreaded the process. It felt to him like "a bad date where you've had too much to drink." He woke up the morning after erasing answers and thought, I shouldn't have gone that far. He worried that, because of the cheating, students wouldn't develop "the feeling you get when you take a test and know whether you did all right or whether you knocked that shit out of the park," he said. He also felt guilty that other teachers were deprived of feedback. Lewis never told his wife that other teachers were correcting her students' answers. One year, she got the highest scores in the building. Lewis said, "I wasn't going to burst her bubble. I was, like, 'Good job. Keep going strong.' "

At happy-hour drinks, he and other teachers complained that the legislators who wrote No Child Left Behind must never have been near a school like Parks. He felt as if he and his colleagues were part of a nationwide "biological experiment" in which the variables—the fact that so many children were hungry and transient, and witnessing violence—hadn't been controlled. David Berliner, the former dean of the school of education at Arizona State University, told me that, with the passage of the law, teachers were asked to compensate for factors outside their control. He said, "The people who say poverty is no excuse for low performance are now using teacher accountability as an excuse for doing nothing about poverty."

Hall's targets required that the number of students who met standards rise by nearly three per cent annually; in addition, a group of students had to "exceed" standards each year. Later, when asked by a state investigator how she had arrived at those figures, she acknowledged that there were no studies supporting that rate of improvement. According to Waller, the district became increasingly "corporate," with every school focussed on the "bottom line." He wrote teachers' targets in marker on the floor of the entryway to their classrooms, in view of the students. He instructed the teachers, "I need those numbers," and, "You need to teach to the test. Do what you've got to do."

A 2007 report by the Annie E. Casey Foundation, titled "Beating the Odds at Atlanta's Parks Middle School," attributed its unlikely progress, in part, to its "relentless focus on data." The report noted that Waller kept an index card in his pocket listing all the school's achievements, which he read aloud to parents and students. "Even the kids know their data," Waller said. Kiel, the testing coördinator, told the foundation that data is a "passion, it's a love, because it tells the truth: it's not what I think—and what I feel, and what ought to be, and how I perceive it—but how it actually *is*."

Lewis was initially enthusiastic about judging teaching by what appeared to be an objective metric. Since college, he had found himself devising mathematical equations to make sense of events in his own life. He was no longer as disappointed when his father, who was in and out of rehab, didn't return his calls, because he saw the situation in terms of mathematical probability: if he assigned a zero to every day that his father hadn't called and a one to every day that he had and added all the digits and divided them by three hundred and sixty-five, he saw that the probability that his father would call on any given day was about zero. His calculations "gave me back my sense of control," he said.

But Lewis began to worry that mathematics had assumed an unhealthy role in the district. "Data" and "accountability" had become almost magic words: if administrators repeated them enough, it seemed they believed that scores should rise, even if there hadn't been significant enhancements in instruction. Lewis welcomed the district's new emphasis on reading—teachers got specialized training and taught reading more intensively—but many of the other reforms were oriented around deadlines and time frames. Lewis said, "We had two weeks to teach percentages, and if you're still on percentages at week three, because your kids don't get it yet, they'll say, 'You don't teach well enough!' Well, come, now, we are dealing with human brains." He continued, "I sincerely believe that demographics does not determine destiny. But you have to be patient."

Lewis felt pressure not only to make testing targets but to meet more ambitious attendance goals. After two years of improvement, teachers began taking attendance later in the day so that students had more time to get to school. Eventually, Lewis recalled, the teachers ceased marking absences altogether. In a letter of complaint, the school secretary, who refused to delete absences from the records, informed the district's central office that her attendance duties had been taken away and "given to someone whom my principal calls a team player." "I am lying low because I feel my job is on the line," she wrote. "I am so overwhelmed by what I'm seeing."

Waller said that he had never experienced so much pressure in his life. Although administrators throughout the district knew that there was cheating, he said that "nobody wanted to talk about it." "We'd been cultivated in so many untruths throughout the years," he told me. In 2008, he decided to resign, but Hall worked with the Casey Foundation to give him an "incentive award grant" of fifteen thousand dollars. He agreed to stay, believing that soon he would have the strength to tell the district that its targets couldn't continue to rise.

By 2008, there were nine teachers on Waller's team, and cheating had become a "well-oiled machine," as he put it. A principal at an elementary school in southeast Atlanta e-mailed Waller charts detailing the number of questions students in each grade needed to answer correctly in order to get a passing score—information that the state's Department of Education does not publish. The teachers now changed answers in the chorus room, because they didn't want to raise the suspicions of the testing coördinator, who noticed that someone had been in his office and had changed the lock. (A day later, Lewis found a copy of the new key in his school mailbox.) The room was so crowded that two teachers placed test booklets in a cooler and took them to another room. "It went from a two-man show to out of control," Lewis said. A sixth-grade teacher, who asked that his name not be used, told me that he got involved only because he respected Lewis, whom he described as the "alpha male of the building" and a "humanitarian." "I don't think Waller could have run the school without him," he said. "It's kind of like every king has to have a general, and the general gets his hands way dirtier than the king does."

When teachers panicked about what they'd done, Lewis reminded them that the school had already gone through three principals in five years. "Calm down," he told them. "Waller's going to be gone in a minute. Let's just survive until he's gone." He tried not to reflect on the cheating process at all. "Cheating was just something we did in April, when the tests were in the building," he said.

In the spring of 2008, Parks's scores were almost as high as those of a middle school in Inman Park, a gentrified neighborhood with yoga studios, bike paths, and million-dollar houses. Waller thought the results seemed obviously false, and he called his supervisor, Michael Pitts, to warn him. Pitts gave Waller the cellphone number for Lester McKee, the executive director of the district's Department of Research, Planning, and Accountability. When Waller explained that Parks's results were unusually high, he said that McKee responded, "Shit happens, and sometimes when it happens it's not always bad. Let's see if anyone else says something." The district took no action to investigate the improbable scores. (McKee, who could not be reached for comment, was not charged with any wrongdoing.)

Morris Johnson, the president of the parent-teacher association at Parks in 2009, told me that he never "questioned those test scores—not for one minute." He was in the school nearly every day, and he saw administrators and teachers giving "a hundred per cent plus" and instilling in students a "winning attitude." Both the football and the basketball teams were nearly undefeated. Using money from fund-raisers and donations, students took field trips to Washington, D.C., New Orleans, and New York. "I was so impressed," Johnson said. "Mr. Waller wanted to expose these kids to other parts of life. They were finally escaping their Zip Code."

Waller was lauded by the district, and became a minor celebrity of the reform movement. Hall invited him to attend the Harvard Leadership Conference with her, and she arranged a "Tour of Georgia" bus ride for civic leaders which made a stop at Parks, where Hall gave a speech. Once, at a meeting, when the principal of a middle school said that the targets were out of his students' reach, Hall responded, "You have to make your targets," and then pointed to a chart with data from

Parks, explaining, "Parks did it." Waller thought it would have been "evident even to a blind man that the scores were not legitimate."

Parks attracted so many visitors who were eager to understand the school's turnaround that teachers had to come up with ways to explain it. At Waller's direction, they began maintaining what they called "standard-based mastery folders," an index of all the objectives that each student needed to grasp in order to comprehend a given lesson. Lewis, who was taking night classes at the School of Education at Clark Atlanta University, wrote his master's thesis on the technique. "It was a wonderful system," he said. "But we only put it in place to hide the fact that we were cheating."

Lewis took pride in the attention that Parks was receiving, and he liked the fact that his students had developed egos about their education. A few tattooed the number of the school zone on their arms. The only time an accolade made him uncomfortable was when Parks won a 2009 Dispelling the Myth Award. He and other teachers were sent to Arlington, Virginia, for a ceremony in the ballroom of a Marriott hotel. Arne Duncan, the Secretary of Education, gave the keynote speech. "I swear to God, I need to write that man, Duncan, a letter of apology," Lewis told me. "I stood in his court and acted like I was doing something I wasn't. He held us at the tip-top of education."

On September 8, 2009, the Atlanta city council declared that the date should be known as Dr. Beverly L. Hall Day. Hall had just been named Superintendent of the Year by the American Association of School Administrators, and the city held a ceremony to honor her for making the district one of the highest-performing urban school systems in the nation. Under her leadership, the district had received more than forty million dollars from the G. E. Foundation and the Bill and Melinda Gates Foundation. When she began as superintendent, fewer than fifty per cent of eighth graders met the state's standards in language arts. By 2009, ninety per cent of eighth graders had passed the exam.

A month after the dedication, Heather Vogell and John Perry, of the Atlanta *Journal-Constitution*, reported that there were statistically improbable testing gains at several schools in Atlanta. Hall's deputy superintendent told the paper, "I don't have any reason to look at that." The paper's reporting prompted the Governor's Office of Student Achievement to conduct its own analysis of testing improprieties, not only in Atlanta but throughout the state. In early 2010, the office found that one in five schools exhibited an abnormal pattern of erasure marks, in which a wrong answer had been corrected. At Parks and at one of its feeder schools, there were suspicious erasure marks on tests from more than seventy-five per cent of the classrooms.

At the instruction of the governor, Sonny Perdue, Atlanta's Board of Education formed a panel to investigate the erasures. Although the investigation was supposed to be independent, it was run by civic leaders who had invested in the district and touted its success, and Hall's administrators sat in on interviews. The panel concluded that there had been no coördinated effort to manipulate test scores, a finding that Perdue called "woefully inadequate." He decided that Atlanta was incapable of investigating itself. In August, 2010, he issued an executive order that granted authority to the former state attorney general, along with a prosecutor and a special investigator, to conduct a more thorough investigation.

There have been accounts of widespread cheating in dozens of cities, including Philadelphia, Toledo, El Paso, Baltimore, Cincinnati, Houston, and St. Louis. According to a 2013 report by the Government Accountability Office, forty states detected instances of cheating by educators in the previous two years. But Atlanta is one of the few districts in which educators have been subpoenaed. "It's hard to find anyone in the system who wants to look under the rock and see what's there," Jennifer Jennings, a sociology professor at N.Y.U. who studies standardized tests, said. She noted that even in Texas, whose reform model inspired No Child Left Behind, scholars doubted whether students had progressed as rapidly as the data suggested—administrators exempted low-performing students from taking the test and underreported dropouts. Jennings worries that one consequence of cheating and other forms of gaming the system is that it interferes with the "policy-feedback loop," the conclusions we draw about student learning and the narratives we tell about reform. Given what happened in Texas, she said, the cheating in Atlanta "should have been very easy to anticipate."

In October, 2010, fifty agents with the Georgia Bureau of Investigation visited Parks and other Atlanta schools. They ate in school cafeterias, handed out their business cards, and befriended teachers in the doorways of their classrooms. As soon as Lewis learned of the investigation, he was ready to confess. Occasionally, in the middle of teaching a lesson, he had to step outside the classroom and lean silently against the wall, closing his eyes. He and his wife had separated—they shared custody of a young daughter—and he found himself lying in bed, startled awake by nightmares. In one, he heard a knock at his door, and when he opened it one of his former students shot him.

His first meeting with investigators was in Waller's office. He wondered if Waller was clever enough to bug the room and told the agents, "I'd feel a lot more comfortable at your office." A few weeks later, he and several other teachers met at the downtown law office of Balch & Bingham, which was assisting with the investigation. The agents told the teachers that anyone who coöperated would be granted immunity from criminal prosecution. A social-studies teacher asked, "Can we all huddle for a minute?" When the agents left the room, Lewis told everyone, "The jig is up. I'm not letting this shit drive me crazy." He urged his colleagues to blame the cheating on him, but they refused.

They all decided to tell the truth. Righton Johnson, a lawyer with Balch & Bingham who sat in on interviews, told me that it became clear that most teachers thought they were committing a victimless crime. "They didn't see the value in the test, so they didn't see that they were devaluing the kids by cheating," she said. Unlike recent cheating scandals at Harvard and at Stuyvesant High School, where privileged students were concerned with their own advancement, those who cheated at Parks were never convinced of the importance of the tests; they viewed the cheating as a door they had to pass through in order to focus on issues that seemed more relevant to their students' lives.

Waller initially refused to acknowledge to the agents that he'd cheated. He told himself that, since he hadn't physically handled the tests himself, he hadn't committed the act. Hoping to extract more information, the agents asked Latasha Smiley, a teacher who had already confessed, to surreptitiously record a meeting with Waller at a Panera Bread. Waller seemed flustered and suspicious when he spoke with her. "It's messy—it's messy," he said. "We've worked too hard...all kids can learn...I don't have—a lot of people kick a dog when they down." When Smiley, who had transferred to a different school, told Waller that she missed Parks, he responded, "That school is going to hell."

After more than two thousand interviews, the investigators concluded that forty-four schools had cheated and that a "culture of fear, intimidation and retaliation has infested the district, allowing cheating—at all levels—to go unchecked for years." They wrote that data had been "used as an abusive and cruel weapon to embarrass and punish." Several teachers had been told that they had a choice: either make targets or be placed on a Performance Development Plan, which was often a precursor to termination. At one elementary school, during a faculty meeting, a principal forced a teacher whose students had tested poorly to crawl under the table.

The investigators' report didn't conclude that Hall had directed anyone to cheat, but it did recount a number of episodes in which she ignored or minimized evidence that scores had been falsely achieved. In one instance, her staff had ordered an administrator to shred a draft of a report that described cheating at an elementary school. But in an eight-hour interview with investigators Hall insisted that there was no reason to doubt students' scores, because other metrics showed the same trajectory. During her tenure, the graduation rate in Atlanta rose by thirty percentage points. On the National Assessment of Educational Progress test, which is less susceptible to tampering, Atlanta's reading scores rose more rapidly than those of the other nine cities where students took the test. (Critics have suggested that the gains may be partly the result of a demographic shift, but it appears that there was also authentic improvement.)

To explain the improvement in scores, Hall told the investigators that "an effective teacher three years in a row will completely close the gap between a child born in poverty and a child born to a middle-income family." This theory, in its earliest form, derives from a study by William L. Sanders, a statistician formerly at the University of Tennessee, but the findings, which have contributed to a nationwide effort to rate teachers rigorously, have been overstated to the point of becoming a myth. According to a recent statement by the American Statistical Association, most studies show that teachers account for between one and fourteen per cent of variability in test scores.

John Ewing, who served as the executive director of the American Mathematical Society for fifteen years, told me that he is perplexed by educators' "infatuation with data," their faith that it is more authoritative than using their own judgment. He explains the problem in terms of Campbell's law, a principle that describes the risks of using a single indicator to measure complex social phenomena: the greater the value placed on a quantitative measure, like test scores, the more likely it is that the people using it and the process it measures will be corrupted. "The end goal of education isn't to get students to answer the right number of questions," he said. "The goal is to have curious and creative students who can function in life." In a 2011 paper in *Notices of the American Mathematical Society*, he warned that policymakers were using mathematics "to intimidate—to preëmpt debate about the goals of education and measures of success."

In July, 2011, the district placed a hundred and ten teachers who had either confessed to having cheated or been accused of it on administrative leave. Lewis received a letter that read, "Your actions and inactions brought embarrassment, suspicion, scorn, and disrepute upon APS"—Atlanta Public Schools. The district intended to fire him unless he could prove at a hearing that he was innocent of the charges. His colleagues at Parks got similar letters and wanted to resign, but Lewis felt that they should express their devotion to Parks by "standing arm in arm before the firing squad."

A woman from Oakland who had dated Lewis on and off since middle school saw his name in the news and called him, and said, "Tell me you didn't cheat. You were the smartest guy I knew. Tell me that guy didn't change." He invited her to Atlanta so that he could explain himself in person. In the fall of 2011, they were married. Lewis was comforted by the fact that "she knew me as a child and could hold me to the character that my mom instilled in me." To his mother, his decision to cheat was an act of civil disobedience. She told him that as soon as she heard about cheating in Atlanta she thought, "I bet my son was part of that."

His termination hearing was held in March, 2012, at the district's headquarters. It was the first hearing to arise from the cheating investigation; many of the other teachers in the district who had been implicated resigned. Three former educators, appointed by the school board, served as the jury. Lewis wore a gray striped button-up shirt, untucked, and sat with his chin resting on his hand, looking down. He waived his right to an attorney, thinking, he said, "I did this shit—I brought it onto myself—and I'm going to take it in the face." When the hearing officer asked him to give an opening statement, he said, "I think the evidence will prove that there was a systemic problem in the Atlanta public schools. That's my statement." An agent from the Georgia Bureau of Investigation served as a witness for the district, and, after detailing Lewis's wrongdoing, explained that he "seemed to be well liked by the school and the teachers that were there. They kind of looked up to him."

When Lewis was questioned by the district's lawyer, he repeatedly invoked the Fifth Amendment, taking care not to incriminate anyone else. He didn't speak at length until his closing statement, at which point he stood up and began reading, through tears, from a long speech that he had written about his eleven years at Parks. He described how Parks had made incremental progress each year, but its test scores "cast a cloud of doubt over whether Parks Middle School even deserved to exist at all." Soon, data became the "underlying force behind everything we did." He described the resilience of the students, who were "down but never out, losing but never lost." He told the panel, "You may wonder why I haven't resigned. It's because the morality that resides within me are the same morals I taught my students for years; that is, whenever you are persecuted or face challenges or circumstances rise against you, you must see things through to the end."

Of a hundred and seventy-eight educators named in the cheating investigation, Lewis was the first to be fired. "I felt like someone had hit me with the butt end of an axe," he said. He shaved off his dreadlocks, which, in Rastafarian tradition—a culture with which he sporadically associated—signalled the loss of a child. What troubled him most, he said, was that "I was fired for doing something that I didn't even believe in."

He applied for jobs at charter and alternative schools, community centers, and jails, but he didn't get any of them. "Education let me go," he finally concluded. He broadened his search, applying for positions that required manual labor. In interviews, he promised employers that he had the "persistence and tough skin of a middle-school teacher to bring to the workforce." He applied for a job installing cable, and, after getting a nearly perfect score on the applicant test, he daydreamed about how he would use his teaching skills to help employees streamline the process. But a few days later the company told him that he didn't have enough experience.

His house was foreclosed on and his car was repossessed. Old friends came to him with alternative methods of earning money. "They had some of the most illegal propositions," he said. "They were, like, 'Man, remember when we used to take that trip to St. Louis? Don't you want to take over that run?' " He supported his wife, their newborn son, and his daughter from his previous marriage by working as an auto mechanic.

At first, he was glad to see the district attorney bring charges against Christopher Waller, Beverly Hall, and thirty-three administrators and teachers, but he became troubled by the portrayal of their crimes as mercenary. On April 2, 2013, on the evening news, he watched his colleagues, nearly all of them black, report to the Fulton County Jail in an event that was described in the media as a "perp walk." They were charged under the Racketeer Influenced and Corrupt Organizations statute—used to apprehend criminal organizations like the Mafia—and accused of conspiring in order to receive the bonuses tied to high test scores. Hall, who earned more than five hundred thousand dollars in bonuses, faces up to forty-five years in prison.

More than half of the defendants, including Christopher Waller, pleaded guilty to lesser charges. Now the senior pastor at a church three miles from Parks, Waller agreed to serve five years of probation, pay forty thousand dollars in restitution, and testify as a witness for the prosecution. He told me that he was offended by the idea that he would cheat in order to get what amounted to five thousand dollars in bonuses. He and other teachers at Parks spent their own money to buy groceries, H.I.V. medications, furniture, and clothes for students and their mothers, and this continued even after he was fired. "It wasn't because of the money—I can promise you that," he said.

In lengthy plea statements, Waller and the other defendants provided a miniature history of the past twelve years in education policy, describing how No Child Left Behind, in conjunction with the district's targets, created an atmosphere in which cheating came to seem like a reasonable option. One principal described a "toxic culture throughout APS where all that mattered was test scores, even if ill-gotten." Another said that the district's "primary focus...became meeting targets instead of focusing on the needs of the students."

In statements sent to me through their respective lawyers, Hall and Michael Pitts both denied wrongdoing and said they were confident that a jury would find them innocent of the charges. Hall wrote, "I did not order, request, or condone cheating to meet targets nor did I have knowledge of cheating." She explained that in setting targets she had "relied on APS educators to behave with integrity." She also said that, compared with the objectives set by No Child Left Behind, Atlanta's targets were "decidedly more incremental in nature," and the sanctions less "draconian." (Many of her employees disagree; the district was unusual in that it required a certain percentage of students to exceed targets each year.)

Since the investigation, the stakes for testing in Georgia have escalated. Although the state is replacing the Criterion-Referenced Competency Test with a more comprehensive method of evaluation, this fall Georgia is implementing a new teacher-evaluation program that bases fifty per cent of a teacher's assessment on test scores. The program, along with a merit-pay system, is required as a condition for receiving a four-hundred-million-dollar grant from President Obama's Race to the Top program. Tim Callahan, the spokesman for the Professional Association of Georgia Educators, which represents eighty-four thousand teachers, told me, "The state is going down the same path as Atlanta, and we are not exactly enthused." He said that many teachers have become so demoralized that they're retiring early or transferring to private schools. He told me, "Our teachers' best qualities—their sense of humor, their love for the subject, their excitement, their interest in students as individuals—are not being honored or valued, because those qualities aren't measurable."

This spring, Lewis was hired as a database developer at a mortgage company. He was thrilled by the job, to such a degree that his energy level was out of synch with that of his colleagues. When I met him at his home, a small ranch house in East Point, Georgia, he said that he found his co-workers surprisingly detached and unemotional. He often dreamed about his students. "I miss having a classroom full of Energizer bunnies," he told me. In his dreams, Waller occasionally apologized or offered him a new job.

Lewis was looking forward to hearing Beverly Hall explain herself at the cheating trial, which is scheduled to begin in August. It had been delayed several months, because Hall is undergoing treatment for cancer. She's now bedridden and may not be able to attend her trial. For years, Lewis had assumed that Hall instructed people to cheat, but now he began to wonder if she'd been so idealistic that she didn't understand the environment she had created and, when it became clear, didn't want to undermine her cause—the idea that educational reform could swiftly lift children out of poverty—by acknowledging the evidence that was in front of her. Lewis said, "I know that sometimes when you're in the fight, and you're swinging, you want to win so badly that you don't recognize where your blows land."

Last year, Parks merged with Sylvan Hills Middle School, which Lewis called "our archrival." The students were still in the Parks building, which had been renamed, but in a year they would move into a renovated building outside

Pittsburgh. No one in the community knew what would become of the vacated building. Lewis blamed himself for the fact that Parks had ceased to exist. According to the district, the school closed because of low enrollment, but Pittsburgh residents believed that it was because Parks's reputation had been ruined. After the cheating investigation, and the departure of nine teachers and administrators, students' scores dropped each year.

Lewis told me that in a week one of his most ambitious students, Neekisia Jackson, who graduated from Parks in 2006, would receive her diploma from Emory University. She had asked Lewis and two other former teachers from Parks to come to her graduation. Lewis found himself, almost against his will, plotting out Jackson's future. She would go to law school, become a judge—no matter what kind of defendant was in her courtroom, she would be able to "empathetically go there"—and then become a model for kids in Pittsburgh, just as he'd been. For the past year, he'd been putting away a small percentage of his paycheck so that he could give Jackson some cash. "This is a real drop in the bucket for what life has in store for you," he planned to tell her at graduation. "Just spread your wings—the wind is coming." ■

AUTHOR PROFILE

Rachel Aviv is a non-fiction writer, a staff contributor for *The New Yorker* magazine, and a teacher specializing in narrative and medical writing at several New York medical schools, including the Columbia University Medical Center. Aviv writes about a wide range of topics centered on public welfare, including mental health, criminal justice, homelessness, and education. For her writing on mental health Aviv has received a Rona Jaffe Foundation Writers' Award and a Rosalynn Carter fellowship. Aviv has been published in *Poetry Magazine, The Believer, Harper's,* and *The New York Times Magazine.* "Wrong Answer" was published in *The New Yorker* in July 2014.

Making Moral Arguments

From the introduction to *Today's Moral Issues*

By Daniel A. Bonevac

This is a book about moral issues. What are moral issues? To answer this question, we need to consider the definition of philosophy. If the word itself is any guide, philosophy is the love of wisdom. A simple definition of wisdom, in turn, is good judgment. Philosophy, then, is the love or pursuit of good judgment. Moral philosophy, or ethics, is the pursuit of good judgment about character and action—about what kind of person to be and about what to do. Ethics addresses questions about virtue and vice, good and bad, right and wrong.

Such questions, clearly, have varied answers; they are often the subject of controversy and debate. The moral issues considered in this book—abortion, euthanasia, pornography, capital punishment, affirmative action, and many others—are among the most controversial our society faces. Most of this book consists of moral arguments, in which a moral issue is considered and a particular position is supported or a particular conclusion is reached through reasoning.

How can we think through moral issues carefully and systematically? How do we develop arguments for ethical conclusions? These are questions that I attempt to answer in this introduction.

Arguments

Arguments are bits of reasoning in language. Frequently, we think of arguments as conflicts. In that sense, this book presents a series of arguments about issues such as abortion, euthanasia, and affirmative action. But philosophers and logicians primarily use "argument'" in the sense that one argues for a conclusion. An argument starts with some assertions and tries to justify a thesis.

Components of Arguments

The initial assertions of an argument are its *premises*; the thesis that the argument tries to justify is its *conclusion*. Arguments consist of *statements*, sentences that can be true or false. Almost every sentence in this book falls into this category. Statements are declarative, in the indicative mood; they say something about the way the world is, correctly or incorrectly. Here, for example, is a simple argument:

(1) Stealing is wrong.

∴ Stealing this book is wrong.

(This format lists the premises in the order in which they are given and then gives the conclusion. The symbol ∴ means "therefore.")

How can we recognize arguments? The premises of an argument are meant to support the conclusion. We can recognize arguments, then, by recognizing when some statements are offered in support of others. We can do this most easily, in turn, if we can distinguish premises from conclusions. But how can we pick out the conclusion of an argument? In English, various words and phrases can signal the premises or the conclusion of an argument.

- *Conclusion Indicators:* therefore, thus, hence, consequently, it follows that, in conclusion, as a result, then, must, accordingly, this implies that, this entails that, we may infer that
- *Premise Indicators:* because, as, for, since, given that, for the reason that

Beware: These words and phrases have other uses as well.

Extended or *complex* arguments contain other arguments. *Simple* arguments do not. Because extended arguments are good only if the simple arguments within them are good, it is best to break extended arguments down into their simple components and analyze them separately.

Validity and Soundness

To evaluate arguments, we need to ask, What distinguishes good from bad arguments? What makes a good argument good?

A good argument links its premises to its conclusion in the right way. In a (deductively) *valid* argument, the truth of the premises guarantees the truth of the conclusion. If the premises are all true, then the conclusion has to be true. Or, equivalently, if the conclusion of a valid argument is false, at least one premise must also be false. Consider, for example, the argument

(2) All promises ought to be kept.

Your promise to Joe is a promise.

∴ You ought to keep your promise to Joe.

In any circumstance in which the premises of this argument are true, the conclusion must be true as well. It is impossible to conceive of a state of affairs in which, while all promises ought to be kept, and your promise to Joe is a promise, you nevertheless should not keep your promise to Joe. If it is false that you should keep your promise to Joe, then either there are promises that shouldn't be kept, or your "promise" wasn't a real promise.

Valid arguments are only one species of good argument. Others are *inductively strong* (or *reliable*). The truth of the premises of such an argument does not guarantee the truth of its conclusion, but it does make the truth of the conclusion probable. Consider, for example, this argument,

(3) Every generous person I've ever known has also been kind.

∴ All generous people are kind.

It is possible for the premise to be true while the conclusion is false. There may be generous but nasty people I've never met. So the argument is invalid. Nevertheless, the premise lends some support to the conclusion. The argument is inductively strong; how strong depends on how many generous people I've known, among other things.

In general, good arguments not only are valid or inductively strong but also have true premises. A *sound* argument is a valid argument with true premises. In any valid argument, the truth of the premises guarantees the truth of the conclusion, so a sound argument also has a true conclusion. A *cogent* argument is an inductively strong argument with true premises. In a cogent argument, the truth of the conclusion is likely but not guaranteed.

Logic develops precise ways of determining whether arguments are valid (although the most powerful ways of evaluating arguments are intuitive). An argument is valid if the truth of the premises guarantees the truth of the conclusion. To show that an argument is invalid, therefore, one needs to show that the premises could all be true while the conclusion is false.

There are two ways of showing that an argument is invalid. The first, the *direct* method, is simply to describe such a situation; that is, we can show an argument to be invalid by depicting a possible circumstance in which the premises were all true but the conclusion was false.

The second way to show that an argument is invalid, devised by Aristotle, is based on the idea of *form* and is known as the method of *counterexamples*. To show that an argument is invalid using this method, we must produce another argument of the same form with true premises and a false conclusion. This introduction is too short to present a detailed discussion of form. But Aristotle's insight was that validity is *formal* in the sense that arguments can be classified into certain general patterns, or forms, of which individual arguments are instances. An argument form is valid if and only if every instance of it is valid. More to the point, an argument form is invalid if and only if some instance of it is invalid. To show that an argument form is invalid, then, find an instance with true premises and a false conclusion. To show that an *individual argument* is invalid, find an argument with true premises and a false conclusion that shares the *specific form* of the original argument: the most explicit form we can devise, displaying the most structure.

Making Moral Arguments

As we have seen, it is possible to attack an argument by showing that one of its premises is false. Even if the argument is valid or strong, such an attack shows that it is not sound or cogent and undercuts its conclusion.

Moral arguments typically have both moral and factual premises. Some statements are *factual* or *descriptive*. They say how the world is. Other statements are *evaluative*, *prescriptive*, or *normative*. They say how the world ought to be; more generally, they evaluate how the world is, characterizing it as right or wrong, acceptable or unacceptable, delightful or dismal. They include specifically evaluative terms. A *moral argument* is an argument with an evaluative conclusion. People who reach opposite conclusions may differ in moral principles, but they may also differ in factual assumptions. One of the chief purposes of a contemporary moral problems course is to teach people how to disentangle moral from factual issues. The distinction matters, because factual and moral conclusions require different kinds of support

Consider a simple example.

(4) You promised to sublet the apartment.

You should keep your promises.

∴ You should sublet the apartment.

The first premise is factual. Whether you promised to sublet the apartment is a matter of fact. If it is disputed, we may ask about the facts: What exactly did you say? Is there any agreement in writing? Did you sign anything? Was it really this apartment? The second premise, in contrast, is evaluative. It speaks of how things ought to be, not how they are. Consequently, no amount of inquiry into the facts can help us determine its truth or falsehood. To justify it, we must appeal to more general moral principles.

The general pattern of moral arguments for particular conclusions is thus:

(5) Factual premise(s)

Moral premise(s)

∴ Moral conclusion

This is utterly familiar. You ought to return those books to the library. Why? You borrowed them (factual premise), they are due (factual premise), and you ought to return what you borrow when it is due (moral premise). Or, you may take vacation the last week of April. Why? It won't cause your coworkers any inconvenience (factual premise), and you may take vacation whenever it won't cause your coworkers any inconvenience (moral premise).

Arguing for a Moral Principle

(5) is a pattern for arguing to a particular moral conclusion. But how can one argue for general moral conclusions, such as the moral principles on which such arguments rely? How, in other words, does one support moral premises such as You ought to keep your promises, You ought to return what you borrow when it's due, or You may take vacation whenever it won't cause your coworkers any inconvenience?

In essence, there are two ways to argue for a moral generalization: from above and from below. To argue from above, appeal to a more general moral principle. John Stuart Mill, for example, would argue as follows for the generalization, You ought to keep your promises:

(6) You ought to follow the rules that will maximize human happiness.

Following the rule: You ought to keep your promises will maximize human happiness.

∴ You ought to keep your promises.

Immanuel Kant would justify it differently:

(7) You ought to treat others as ends, not merely as means.

Keeping a promise to someone treats that person as an end, but breaking one treats him or her as a means to your ends.

∴ You ought to keep your promises.

Philosophers who prefer justifications from above tend, like Mill and Kant, to search for a single, very general moral principle that can justify other principles.

Moral principles may also be justified from below, by appeal to their instances. One could try to argue that it is wrong to break promises, for example, by generalizing from examples of particular situations.

(8) Say someone promises to marry you but doesn't show up at the altar; that would be wrong.

Say Frank borrows money from you, promising insincerely to repay it, and then absconds; that would be wrong.

Say the doctor makes an appointment to see you and then goes to play golf instead; that would be wrong.

Say Joan agrees to pay you $1,000 for landscaping her yard, you do the work, and she refuses to pay; that would be wrong.

∴ Breaking promises is wrong.

Or more specific kinds of situations:

(9) Someone who agrees to marry someone on a particular day should show up for the wedding.

Someone who borrows money ought to repay it.

Someone who makes an appointment ought to keep it.

Someone who signs a contract ought to fulfill it.

∴ Breaking promises is wrong.

These arguments are not valid, but they are inductively strong if the examples are numerous and diverse enough.

The readings in this book contain many arguments for moral principles, some from above, some from below. Arguments from above are important, for they say something about *why* the moral principle holds. Kant's argument for promise keeping, for example, not only concludes that promises should be kept but also indicates that they should be kept because breaking them treats others as means to your own ends. Mill's argument, similarly, indicates that promise keeping is obligatory because it maximizes human happiness. Arguments from below are also important, for they link principles to particular cases about which we have strong moral intuitions. The more abstract and general a moral principle is, the fewer intuitions we have about whether it is correct. Moral theories therefore rely on both kinds of arguments.

Arguing against a Moral Principle

How does one argue *against* a moral principle? One tries to find a counter-example: an instance in which the principle seems to give the wrong result. Is it always right to keep promises, for instance? One can try to find examples of promises that should not be kept. Recall that, in a valid argument, the truth of the premises guarantees the truth of the conclusion, or, equivalently, the falsehood of the conclusion guarantees the falsehood of at least one premise. One can construct a valid argument from the principle to a false conclusion:

(10) One should always keep one's promises.

∴ If Herman promised to murder the entire city council, he should do it.

The absurdity of the conclusion shows that there is something wrong with the premise.

Many philosophers have objected to Kant's opinion that lying is always wrong by constructing a similar argument. Suppose that a distraught child runs to you begging for help. A homicidal maniac is chasing her. You hide her in a closet. The maniac bangs on your door and asks whether you know where she is. Surely you should not tell the truth.

Exceptions to Moral Principles

This example illustrates that most moral principles have exceptions. Most moral principles are true *other things being equal* (in Latin, *ceteris paribus*), but not universally. Plato recognized this about promise keeping and telling the truth:

> ...are we to say that justice or right is simply to speak the truth and to pay back any debt one may have contracted? Or are these same actions sometimes right and sometimes wrong? I mean this sort of thing, for example, everyone would surely agree that if a friend has deposited weapons with you when he was sane, and he asks for them when he is out of his mind, you should not return them. The man who returns them is not doing right, nor is one who is willing to tell the whole truth to a man in such a state (*Republic*, 331c).[1]

Although "Keep your promises" and "Tell the truth" are good moral rules in general, they can be overridden or defeated by other moral considerations. For that reason, they are called *defeasible*. Normally, you ought to keep your promises. Normally, you ought to tell the truth. But sometimes there are good reasons to break a promise or to lie, and then you have a moral conflict.

Philosophers often analyze such situations of moral conflict in terms of *prima facie* duties. W. D. Ross defined "prima facie duty" as a "characteristic (quite distinct from that of being a duty proper) which an act has, in virtue of being of a certain kind (e.g., the keeping of a promise), of being an act which would be a duty proper if it were not at the same time of another kind which is morally

[1] *Plato the Republic*, translated by Paul Shorey (Cambridge, Mass.: Loeb Classical Library, 1930).

significant."[2] A prima facie obligation, that is, holds under normal circumstances; it holds all other things being equal, becoming *actual*—an obligation all things considered, or, in Ross's terms, "a duty proper"—unless some other moral consideration intervenes.

Prima facie obligations offer a way to explain the force of rules while allowing for exceptions. The idea, in essence, is that a prima facie rule applies unless some other rule conflicts with it. John Stuart Mill's secondary principles are paradigms of prima facie principles: They dictate obligations unless they come into conflict. In that case, Mill stipulates, the principle of utility, the sole rule in his system that has an absolute rather than prima facie character, resolves the conflict. This indicates a key difference between actual and prima facie obligation: Prima facie obligations can conflict, whereas actual obligations cannot. If a homicidal maniac asks whether you know where an innocent child is hiding, there is a moral conflict: You have a prima facie obligation to tell the truth and another to tell a lie. Only one can be actual—what you ought actually to do in that situation, all things considered. Saving a life is more important than never telling a lie, so your obligation to lie is actual, over-riding your obligation to tell the truth.

Let's revisit Plato's puzzle about returning weapons to a friend who is out of his mind. Because unconditional statements of actual obligation *cannot* conflict, this pair is inconsistent:

(11) You have an actual obligation to return the weapons.

You have an actual obligation not to return the weapons.

You cannot be obliged, actually, all things considered, both to return the weapons and not to return them.

Because conditional prima facie obligations *can* conflict, this pair of statements is consistent:

(12) You have a prima facie obligation to return the weapons.

You have a prima facie obligation not to return the weapons.

In general, you have a prima facie obligation to do something whenever the circumstances trigger a defeasible moral rule. In Plato's case, there are defeasible rules that you ought to keep your promises and that you ought to prevent harm. Your promise gives rise to the prima facie obligation to return the weapons; your friend's madness gives rise to the prima facie obligation not to return them.

Here are some basic reasoning patterns involving prima facie obligation and defeasible rules:

Default Modus Ponens. Inferences such as (13) count as acceptable if no other moral considerations apply:

(13) If you make a promise, you should keep it. You promised you would go.

∴ You should go.

---

[2] W.D. Ross, *The Right and the Good* (Oxford: Oxford University Press, 1930). 19.

They are not deductively valid, but they are reasonable. They are legitimate default inferences; we may draw the conclusion if no other rules intervene. We may infer actual obligations from prima facie obligations in the absence of moral complications.

Conditional Conflict. In cases where conditional prima facie principles conflict, we can generally draw no conclusions. Consider Plato's puzzle:

(14) If you promised to return the weapons, you should return them.

If returning them will cause mayhem, you should not return them.

You did promise.

Returning the weapons will cause mayhem. ∴??

Should you return the weapons? This is a substantive moral question; no obligation follows as a matter of logic. We must look at the situation and the importance of the conflicting considerations.

Specificity. More specific prima facie obligations take precedence over less specific ones. To return to Plato's puzzle: Add the premise that results from reflecting on the competing values at stake in the situation. Lives are more important than promises. It follows that you should not return the weapons.

(15) If you promised to return the weapons, you should return them.

If returning them will cause mayhem, you should not return them.

You did promise.

Returning the weapons will cause mayhem. If you promised to return the weapons but doing so will cause mayhem, you should not return them.

∴ You should not return the weapons.

But it is important that the last premise requires independent moral reflection. We cannot infer it from the other premises. Indeed, moral conflicts such as those Plato describes have spurred philosophers to devise moral theories to help us compare different kinds of moral considerations and resolve conflicts generated by them.

Seeing that moral considerations can come into conflict helps to dissolve some of the motivation for relativism. In morality, it is often true that one person or culture sees things one way and another sees them quite differently. But even within the view of a single person and culture, there are many different perspectives, which it is the task of morality to relate, evaluate, and, in particular situations, reconcile. Reasonable people can differ on how to reconcile them. That is what makes a book like this both possible and important. ■

B

AUTHOR PROFILE

Daniel A. Bonevac (born 1955) is a Professor of Philosophy at the University of Texas at Austin. His research focuses on philosophical logic and moral and ethical reasoning. He has authored five books, *Reduction in the Abstract Sciences* (1982), *The Art and Science of Logic* (1990), *Simple Logic* (1999), *Wordly Wisdom* (2001), and *Deduction* (2003), and has edited several volumes. "Making Moral Arguments" is selected from one of Bonevac's edited volumes, *Today's Moral Issues*, published in 2010.

Six Provocations for Big Data

By danah boyd and Kate Crawford

Technology is neither good nor bad; nor is it neutral...technology's interaction with the social ecology is such that technical developments frequently have environmental, social, and human consequences that go far beyond the immediate purposes of the technical devices and practices themselves.

—Melvin Kranzberg (1986, p. 545)

We need to open a discourse—where there is no effective discourse now—about the varying temporalities, spatialities and materialities that we might represent in our databases, with a view to designing for maximum flexibility and allowing as possible for an emergent polyphony and polychrony. Raw data is both an oxymoron and a bad idea; to the contrary, data should be cooked with care.

—Geoffrey Bowker (2005, p. 183–184)

The era of Big Data has begun. Computer scientists, physicists, economists, mathematicians, political scientists, bio-informaticists, sociologists, and many others are clamoring for access to the massive quantities of information produced by and about people, things, and their interactions. Diverse groups argue about the potential benefits and costs of analyzing information from Twitter, Google, Verizon, 23andMe, Facebook, Wikipedia, and every space where large groups of people leave digital traces and deposit data. Significant questions emerge. Will large-scale analysis of DNA help cure diseases? Or will it usher in a new wave of medical inequality? Will data analytics help make people's access to information more efficient and effective? Or will it be used to track protesters in the streets of major cities? Will it transform how we study human communication and culture, or narrow the palette of research options and alter what 'research' means? Some or all of the above?

Big Data is, in many ways, a poor term. As Lev Manovich (2011) observes, it has been used in the sciences to refer to data sets large enough to require supercomputers, although now vast sets of data can be analyzed on desktop computers with standard software. There is little doubt that the quantities of data now available are indeed large, but that's not the most relevant characteristic of this new data ecosystem. Big Data is notable not because of its size, but because of its relationality to other data. Due to efforts to mine and aggregate data, Big Data is fundamentally networked. Its value comes from the patterns that can be derived by making connections between pieces of data, about an individual, about individuals in relation to others, about groups of people, or simply about the structure of information itself.

Furthermore, Big Data is important because it refers to an analytic phenomenon playing out in academia and industry. Rather than suggesting a new term, we are using Big Data here because of its popular salience and because it is the phenomenon around Big Data that we want to address. Big Data tempts some researchers to believe that they can see everything at a 30,000-foot view. It is the kind of data that encourages the practice of apophenia: seeing patterns where none actually exist, simply because massive quantities of data can offer connections that radiate in all directions. Due to this, it is crucial to begin asking questions about the analytic assumptions, methodological frameworks, and underlying biases embedded in the Big Data phenomenon.

While databases have been aggregating data for over a century, Big Data is no longer just the domain of actuaries and scientists. New technologies have made it possible for a wide range of people—including humanities and social science academics, marketers, governmental organizations, educational institutions, and motivated individuals—to produce, share, interact with, and organize data. Massive data sets that were once obscure and distinct are being aggregated and made easily accessible. Data is increasingly digital air: the oxygen we breathe and the carbon dioxide that we exhale. It can be a source of both sustenance and pollution.

How we handle the emergence of an era of Big Data is critical: while it is taking place in an environment of uncertainty and rapid change, current decisions will have considerable impact in the future. With the increased automation of data collection and analysis—as well as algorithms that can extract and inform us of massive patterns in human behavior—it is necessary to ask which systems are driving these practices, and which are regulating them. In *Code*, Lawrence Lessig (1999) argues that systems are regulated by four forces: the market, the law, social norms, and architecture—or, in the case of technology, code. When it comes to Big Data, these four forces are at work and, frequently, at odds. The market sees Big Data as pure opportunity: marketers use it to target advertising, insurance providers want to optimize their offerings, and Wall Street bankers use it to read better readings on market temperament. Legislation has already been proposed to curb the collection and retention of data, usually over concerns about privacy (for example, the Do Not Track Online Act of 2011 in the United States). Features like personalization allow rapid access to more relevant information, but they present difficult ethical questions and fragment the public in problematic ways (Pariser, 2011).

There are some significant and insightful studies currently being done that draw on Big Data methodologies, particularly studies of practices in social network sites like Facebook and Twitter. Yet, it is imperative that we begin asking critical questions about what all this data means, who gets access to it, how it is deployed, and to what ends. With Big Data come big responsibilities. In this essay, we are offering six provocations that we hope can spark conversations about the issues of Big Data. Social and cultural researchers have a stake in the computational culture of Big Data precisely because many of its central questions are fundamental to our disciplines. Thus, we believe that it is time to start critically interrogating this phenomenon, its assumptions, and its biases.

1. Automating Research Changes the Definition of Knowledge

In the early decades of the 20th century, Henry Ford devised a manufacturing system of mass production, using specialized machinery and standardized products. Simultaneously, it became the dominant vision of technological progress. Fordism meant automation and assembly lines, and for decades onward, this became the orthodoxy of manufacturing: out with skilled craftspeople and slow work, in with a new machine-made era (Baca, 2004). But it was more than just a new set of tools. The 20th century was marked by Fordism at a cellular level: it produced a new understanding of labor, the human relationship to work, and society at large.

Big Data not only refers to very large data sets and the tools and procedures used to manipulate and analyze them, but also to a *computational turn* in thought and research (Burkholder, 1992). Just as Ford changed the way we made cars—and then transformed work itself—Big Data has emerged a system of knowledge that is already changing the objects of knowledge, while also having the power to inform how we understand human networks and community. 'Change the instruments, and you will change the entire social theory that goes with them,' Latour reminds us (2009, p. 9).

We would argue that Bit Data creates a radical shift in how we think about research. Commenting on computational social science, Lazer *et al.* argue that it offers 'the capacity to collect and analyze data with an unprecedented breadth and depth and scale' (2009, p. 722). But it is not just a matter of scale. Neither is enough to consider it in terms of proximity, or what Moretti (2007) refers to as distant or close analysis of texts. Rather, it is a profound change at the levels of epistemology and ethics. It reframes key questions about the constitution of knowledge, the processes of research, how we should engage with information, and the nature and the categorization of reality. Just as du Gay and Pryke note that 'accounting tools...do not simply aid the measurement of economic activity, they shape the reality they measure' (2002, pp. 12–13), so Big Data stakes out new terrains of objects, methods of knowing, and definitions of social life.

Speaking in praise of what he terms 'The Petabyte Age', Chris Anderson, Editor-in-Chief of *Wired*, writes:

> This is a world where massive amounts of data and applied mathematics replace every other tool that might be brought to bear. Out with every theory of human behavior, from linguistics to sociology. Forget taxonomy, ontology, and psychology. Who knows why people do what they do? The point is they do it, and we can track and measure it with unprecedented fidelity. With enough data, the numbers speak for themselves. (2008)

Do numbers speak for themselves? The answer, we think, is a resounding 'no'. Significantly, Anderson's sweeping dismissal of all other theories and disciplines is a tell: it reveals an arrogant undercurrent in many Big Data debates where all other forms of analysis can be sidelined by production lines of numbers, privileged as having a direct line to raw knowledge. Why people do things, write things, or make things is erased by the sheer volume of numerical repetition and large patterns. This is not a space for reflection or the older forms of intellectual craft. As David Berry (2011, p. 8) writes, Big Data provides 'destablising amounts of knowledge and information that lack the regulating force of philosophy.' Instead of philosophy—which Kant saw as the rational basis for all institutions—'computationality might then be understood as an ontotheology, creating a new ontological "epoch" as a new historical constellation of intelligibility' (Berry 2011, p. 12).

We must ask difficult questions of Big Data's models of intelligibility before they crystallize into new orthodoxies. If we return to Ford, his innovation was using the assembly line to break down interconnected, holistic tasks into simple, atomized, mechanistic ones. He did this by designing specialized tools that strongly predetermined and limited the action of the worker. Similarly, the specialized tools of Big Data also have their own inbuilt limitations and restrictions. One is the issue of time. 'Big Data is about exactly right now, with no historical context that is predictive,' observes Joi Ito, the director of the MIT Media Lab (Bollier 2010, p. 19). For example, Twitter and Facebook are examples of Big Data sources that offer very poor archiving and search functions, where researchers are much more likely to focus on something in the present or immediate past—tracking reactions to an election, TV finale or natural disaster—because of the sheer difficulty or impossibility of accessing older data.

If we are observing the automation of particular kinds of research functions, then we must consider the inbuilt flaws of the machine tools. It is not enough to simply ask, as Anderson suggests 'what can science learn from Google?', but to ask how Google and the other harvesters of Big Data might change the *meaning* of learning, and what new possibilities and new limitations may come with these systems of knowing.

2. Claims to Objectivity and Accuracy Are Misleading

'Numbers, numbers, numbers,' writes Latour (2010). 'Sociology has been obsessed by the goal of becoming a quantitative science.' Yet sociology has never reached this goal, in Latour's view, because of where it draws the line between what is and is not quantifiable knowledge in the social domain.

Big Data offers the humanistic disciplines a new way to claim the status of quantitative science and objective method. It makes many more social spaces quantifiable. In reality, working with Big Data is still subjective, and what it quantifies does not necessarily have a closer claim on objective truth—particularly when considering messages from social media sites. But there remains a mistaken belief that qualitative researchers are in the business of interpreting stories and quantitative researchers are in the business of producing facts. In this way, Big Data risks reinscribing established divisions in the long running debates about scientific method.

The notion of objectivity has been a central question for the philosophy of science and early debates about the scientific method (Durkheim, 1895). Claims to objectivity suggest an adherence to the sphere of objects, to things as they exist in and for themselves. Subjectivity, on the other hand, is viewed with suspicion, colored as it is with various forms of individual and social conditioning. The scientific method attempts to remove itself from the subjective domain through the application of a dispassionate process whereby hypotheses are proposed and tested, eventually resulting in improvements in knowledge. Nonetheless, claims to objectivity are necessarily made by subjects and are based on subjective observations and choices.

All researchers are interpreters of data. As Lisa Gitelman (2011) observes, data needs to be imagined as data in the first instance, and this process of the imagination of data entails an interpretative base: 'every discipline and disciplinary institution has its own norms and standards for the imagination of data.' As computational scientists have started engaging in acts of social science, there is a tendency to claim their work as the business of facts and not interpretation. A model may be mathematically sound, an experiment may seem valid, but as soon as a researcher seeks to understand what it means, the process of interpretation has begun. The design decisions that determine what will be measured also stem from interpretation.

For example, in the case of social media data, there is a 'data cleaning' process: making decisions about what attributes and variables will be counted, and which will be ignored. This process is inherently subjective. As Bollier explains,

> As a large mass of raw information, Big Data is not self-explanatory. And yet the specific methodologies for interpreting the data are open to all sorts of philosophical debate. Can the data represent an 'objective truth' or is any interpretation necessarily biased by some subjective filter or the way that data is 'cleaned?' (2010, p. 13)

In addition to this question, there is the issue of data errors. Large data sets from Internet sources are often unreliable, prone to outages and losses, and these errors and gaps are magnified when multiple data sets are used together. Social scientists have a long history of asking critical questions about the collection of data and trying to account for any biases in their data (Cain & Finch, 1981; Clifford & Marcus, 1986). This requires understanding the properties and limits of a dataset, regardless of its size. A dataset may have many millions of pieces of data, but this does not mean it is random or representative. To make statistical claims about a dataset, we need to know where data is coming from; it is similarly important to know and account for the weaknesses in that data. Furthermore, researchers must be able to account for the biases in their interpretation of the data. To do so requires recognizing that one's identity and perspective informs one's analysis (Behar & Gordon, 1996).

Spectacular errors can emerge when researchers try to build social science findings into technological systems. A classic example arose when Friendster chose to implement Robin Dunbar's (1998) work. Analyzing gossip practices in humans and grooming habits in monkeys, Dunbar found that people could only actively maintain 150 relationships at any time and argued that this number represented the maximum size of a person's personal network. Unfortunately, Friendster believed that people were replicating their pre-existing personal networks on the site, so they inferred that no one should have a friend list greater than 150. Thus, they capped the number of 'Friends' people could have on the system (boyd, 2006).

Interpretation is at the center of data analysis. Regardless of the size of a data set, it is subject to limitation and bias. Without those biases and limitations being understood and outlined, misinterpretation is the result. Big Data is at its most effective when researchers take account of the complex methodological processes that underlie the analysis of social data.

3. Bigger Data Are Not Always Better Data

Social scientists have long argued that what makes their work rigorous is rooted in their systematic approach to data collection and analysis (McClosky, 1985). Ethnographers focus on reflexively accounting for bias in their interpretations. Experimentalists control and standardize the design of their experiment. Survey researchers drill down on sampling mechanisms and question bias. Quantitative researchers weigh up statistical significance. These are but a few of the ways in which social scientists try to assess the validity of each other's work. Unfortunately, some who are embracing Big Data presume the core methodological issues in the social sciences are no longer relevant. There is a problematic underlying ethos that bigger is better, that quantity necessarily means quality.

Twitter provides an example in the context of a statistical analysis. First, Twitter does not represent 'all people', although many journalists and researchers refer to 'people' and 'Twitter users' as synonymous. Neither is the population using Twitter representative of the global population. Nor can we assume that accounts and users are equivalent. Some users have multiple accounts. Some accounts are used by multiple people. Some people never establish an account, and simply access Twitter via the web. Some accounts are 'bots' that produce automated content without involving a person. Furthermore, the notion of an 'active' account is problematic. While some users post content frequently through Twitter, others participate as 'listeners' (Crawford 2009, p. 532). Twitter Inc. has revealed that 40 percent of active users sign in just to listen (Twitter, 2011). The very meanings of 'user' and 'participation' and 'active' need to be critically examined.

Due to uncertainties about what an account represents and what engagement looks like, it is standing on precarious ground to sample Twitter accounts and make claims about people and users. Twitter Inc. can make claims about all accounts or all tweets or a random sample thereof as they have access to the central database. Even so, they cannot easily account for lurkers, people who have multiple accounts or groups of people who all access one account. Additionally, the central database is also prone to outages, and tweets are frequently lost and deleted.

Twitter Inc. makes a fraction of its material available to the public through its APIs.[1] The 'firehose' theoretically contains all public tweets ever posted and explicitly excludes any tweet that a user chose to make private or 'protected.' Yet, some publicly accessible tweets are also missing from the firehose. Although a handful of companies and startups have access to the firehose, very few researchers have this level of access. Most either have access to a 'gardenhose' (roughly 10% of public tweets), a 'spritzer' (roughly 1% of public tweets), or have used 'white-listed' accounts where they could use the APIs to get access to different subsets of content from the public stream.[2] It is not clear what tweets are included in these different data streams or sampling them represents. It could be that the API pulls

---

1 API stands for application programming interface; this refers to a set of tools that developers can use to access structured data.

2 Details of what Twitter provides can be found at https://dev.twitter.com/docs/streaming-api/methods. White-listed accounts were a common mechanism of acquiring access early on, but they are no longer available.

a random sample of tweets or that it pulls the first few thousand tweets per hour or that it only pulls tweets from a particular segment of the network graph. Given uncertainty, it is difficult for researchers to make claims about the quality of the data that they are analyzing. Is the data representative of all tweets? No, because it excludes tweets from protected accounts.[3] Is the data representative of all public tweets? Perhaps, but not necessarily.

These are just a few of the unknowns that researchers face when they work with Twitter data, yet these limitations are rarely acknowledged. Even those who provide a mechanism for how they sample from the firehose or the gardenhose rarely reveal what might be missing or how their algorithms or the architecture of Twitter's system introduces biases into the dataset. Some scholars simply focus on the raw number of tweets: but big data and whole data are not the same. Without taking into account the sample of a dataset, the size of the dataset is meaningless. For example, a researcher may seek to understand the topical frequency of tweets, yet if Twitter removes all tweets that contain problematic words or content—such as references to pornography—from the stream, the topical frequency would be wholly inaccurate. Regardless of the number of tweets, it is not a representative sample as the data is skewed from the beginning.

Twitter has become a popular source for mining Big Data, but working with Twitter data has serious methodological challenges that are rarely addressed by those who embrace it. When researchers approach a dataset, they need to understand—and publicly account for—not only the limits of the dataset, but also the limits of which questions they can ask of a dataset and what interpretations are appropriate.

This is especially true when researchers combine multiple large datasets. Jesper Anderson, co-founder of open financial data store FreeRisk, explains that combining data from multiple sources creates unique challenges: 'Every one of those sources is errorprone…I think we are just magnifying that problem [when we combine multiple data sets]' (Bollier 2010, p. 13). This does not mean that combining data doesn't have value—studies like those by Alessandro Acquisti and Ralph Gross (2009), which reveal how databases can be combined to reveal serious privacy violations are crucial. Yet, it is imperative that such combinations are not without methodological rigor and transparency.

Finally, in the era of the computational turn, it is increasingly important to recognize the value of 'small data'. Research insights can be found at any level, including at very modest scales. In some cases, focusing just on a single individual can be extraordinarily valuable. Take, for example, the work of Tiffany Veinot (2007), who followed one worker—a vault inspector at a hydroelectric utility company—in order to understand the information practices of blue-collar worker. In doing this unusual study, Veinot reframed the definition of 'information practices' away from the usual focus on early-adopter, white-collar workers, to spaces outside of the offices and urban context. Her work tells a story that could not be discovered by farming millions of Facebook or Twitter accounts, and contributes

---

3 The percentage of protected accounts is unknown. In a study of Twitter where they attempted to locate both protected and public Twitter accounts, Meeder *et al.* (2010) found that 8.4% of the accounts they identified were protected.

to the research field in a significant way, despite the smallest possible participant count. The size of data being sampled should fit the research question being asked: in some cases, small is best.

4. Not All Data Are Equivalent

Some researchers assume that analyses done with small data can be done better with Big Data. This argument also presumes that data is interchangeable. Yet, taken out of context, data lose meaning and value. Context matters. When two datasets can be modeled in a similar way, this does not mean that they are equivalent or can be analyzed in the same way. Consider, for example, the rise of interest in social network analysis that has emerged alongside the rise of social network sites (boyd & Ellison, 2007) and the industry-driven obsession with the 'social graph'. Countless researchers have flocked to Twitter and Facebook and other social media to analyze the resultant social graphs, making claims about social networks.

The study of social networks dates back to early sociology and anthropology (e.g., Radcliffe-Brown, 1940), with the notion of a 'social network' emerging in 1954 (Barnes) and the field of 'social network analysis' emerging shortly thereafter (Freeman, 2006). Since then, scholars from diverse disciplines have been trying to understand people's relationships to one another using diverse methodological and analytical approaches. As researchers began interrogating the connections between people on public social media, there was a surge of interest in social network analysis. Now, network analysts are turning to study networks produced through mediated communication, geographical movement, and other data traces.

However, the networks produced through social media and resulting from communication traces are not necessarily interchangeable with other social network data. Just because two people are physically co-present—which may be made visible to cell towers or captured through photographs—does not mean that they know one another. Furthermore, rather than indicating the presence of predictable objective patterns, social network sites facilitate connectedness across structural boundaries and act as a dynamic source of change: taking a snapshot, or even witnessing a set of traces over time does not capture the complexity of all social relations. As Kilduff and Tsai (2003, p. 117) note, 'network research tends to proceed from a naive ontology that takes as unproblematic the objective existence and persistence of patterns, elementary parts and social systems.' This approach can yield a particular kind of result when analysis is conducted only at a fixed point in time, but quickly unravels as soon as broader questions are asked (Meyer *et al.* 2005).

Historically speaking, when sociologists and anthropologists were the primary scholars interested in social networks, data about people's relationships was collected through surveys, interviews, observations, and experiments. Using this data, social scientists focused on describing one's 'personal networks'—the set of relationships that individuals develop and maintain (Fischer, 1982). These connections were evaluated based on a series of measures developed over time to identify personal connections. Big Data introduces two new popular types of social networks derived from data traces: 'articulated networks' and 'behavioral networks.'

Articulated networks are those that result from people specifying their contacts through a mediating technology (boyd, 2004). There are three common reasons in which people articulate their connections: to have a list of contacts for personal use; to publicly display their connections to others; and to filter content on social media. These articulated networks take the form of email or cell phone address books, instant messaging buddy lists, 'Friends' lists on social network sites, and 'Follower' lists on other social media genres. The motivations that people have for adding someone to each of these lists vary widely, but the result is that these lists can include friends, colleagues, acquaintances, celebrities, friends-of-friends, public figures, and interesting strangers.

Behavioral networks are derived from communication patterns, cell coordinates, and social media interactions (Meiss *et al.*, 2008; Onnela *et al.*, 2007). These might include people who text message one another, those who are tagged in photos together on Facebook, people who email one another, and people who are physically in the same space, at least according to their cell phone.

Both behavioral and articulated networks have great value to researchers, but they are not equivalent to personal networks. For example, although often contested, the concept of 'tie strength' is understood to indicate the importance of individual relationships (Granovetter, 1973). When a person chooses to list someone as their 'Top Friend' on MySpace, this may or may not be their closest friend; there are all sorts of social reasons to not list one's most intimate connections first (boyd, 2006). Likewise, when mobile phones recognize that a worker spends more time with colleagues than their spouse, this does not necessarily mean that they have stronger ties with their colleagues than their spouse. Measuring tie strength through frequency or public articulation is a common mistake: tie strength—and many of the theories built around it—is a subtle reckoning in how people understand and value their relationships with other people.

Fascinating network analysis can be done with behavioral and articulated networks. But there is a risk in an era of Big Data of treating every connection as equivalent to every other connection, of assuming frequency of contact is equivalent to strength of relationship, and of believing that an absence of connection indicates a relationship should be made. Data is not generic. There is value to analyzing data abstractions, yet the context remains critical.

5. Just Because It Is Accessible Doesn't Make It Ethical

In 2006, a Harvard-based research project started gathering the profiles of 1,700 college-based Facebook users to study how their interests and friendships changed over time (Lewis *et al.*, 2008). This supposedly anonymous data was released to the world, allowing other researchers to explore and analyze it. What other researchers quickly discovered was that it was possible to de-anonymize parts of the dataset: compromising the privacy of students, none of whom were aware their data was being collected (Zimmer, 2008).

The case made headlines, and raised a difficult issue for scholars: what is the status of so-called 'public' data on social media sites? Can it simply be used, without requesting permission? What constitutes best ethical practice for researchers? Privacy campaigners already see this as a key battleground where better privacy protections are needed. The difficulty is that privacy breaches are hard to make specific—is there damage done at the time? What about twenty years hence? 'Any data on human subjects inevitably raise privacy issues, and the real risks of abuse of such data are difficult to quantify' (*Nature*, cited in Berry, 2010).

Even when researchers try to be cautious about their procedures, they are not always aware of the harm they might be causing in their research. For example, a group of researchers noticed that there was a correlation between self-injury ('cutting') and suicide. They prepared an educational intervention seeking to discourage people from engaging in acts of self-injury, only to learn that their intervention prompted an increase in suicide attempts. For some, self-injury was a safety valve that kept the desire to attempt suicide at bay. They immediately ceased their intervention (Emmens & Phippen, 2010).

Institutional Review Boards (IRBs)—and other research ethics committees—emerged in the 1970s to oversee research on human subjects. While unquestionably problematic in implementation (Schrag, 2010), the goal of IRBs is to provide a framework for evaluating the ethics of a particular line of research inquiry and to make certain that checks and balances are put into place to protect subjects. Practices like 'informed consent' and protecting the privacy of informants are intended to empower participants in light of earlier abuses in the medical and social sciences (Blass, 2004; Reverby, 2009). Although IRBs cannot always predict the harm of a particular study—and, all too often, prevent researchers from doing research on grounds other than ethics—their value is in prompting scholars to think critically about the ethics of their research.

With Big Data emerging as a research field, little is understood about the ethical implications of the research being done. Should someone be included as a part of a large aggregate of data? What if someone's 'public' blog post is taken out of context and analyzed in a way that the author never imagined? What does it mean for someone to be spotlighted or to be analyzed without knowing it? Who is responsible for making certain that individuals and communities are not hurt by the research process? What does consent look like?

It may be unreasonable to ask researchers to obtain consent from every person who posts a tweet, but it is unethical for researchers to justify their actions as ethical simply because the data is accessible. Just because content is publicly accessible doesn't mean that it was meant to be consumed by just anyone (boyd & Marwick, 2011). There are serious issues involved in the ethics of online data collection and analysis (Ess, 2002). The process of evaluating the research ethics cannot be ignored simply because the data is seemingly accessible. Researchers must keep asking themselves—and their colleagues—about the ethics of their data collection, analysis, and publication.

In order to act in an ethical manner, it is important that scholars reflect on the importance of accountability. In the case of Big Data, this means both accountability to the field of research, and accountability to the research subjects. Academic researchers are held to specific professional standards when working with human participants in order to protect their rights and well-being. However, many ethics boards do not understand the processes of mining and anonymizing Big Data, let alone the errors that can cause data to become personally identifiable. Accountability to the field and to human subjects required rigorous thinking about the ramifications of Big Data, rather than assuming that ethics boards will necessarily do the work of ensuring people are protected. Accountability here is used as a broader concept that privacy, as Troshynski *et al.* (2008) have outlined, where the concept of accountability can apply even when conventional expectations of privacy aren't in question. Instead, accountability is a multi-directional relationship: there may be accountability to superiors, to colleagues, to participants and to the public (Dourish & Bell, 2011).

There are significant questions of truth, control and power in Big Data studies: researchers have the tools and the access, while social media users as a whole do not. Their data was created in highly context-sensitive spaces, and it is entirely possible that some social media users would not give permission for their data to be used elsewhere. Many are not aware of the multiplicity of agents and algorithms currently gathering and storing their data for future use. Researchers are rarely in a user's imagined audience, neither are users necessarily aware of all the multiple uses, profits and other gains that come from information they have posted. Data may be public (or semi-public) but this does not simplistically equate with full permission being given for all uses. There is a considerable difference between being in public and being public, which is rarely acknowledged by Big Data researchers.

6. Limited Access to Big Data Creates New Digital Divides

In an essay on Big Data, Scott Golder (2010) quotes sociologist George Homans (1974): 'The methods of social science are dear in time and money and getting dearer every day.' Historically speaking, collecting data has been hard, time consuming, and resource intensive. Much of the enthusiasm surrounding Big Data stems from the perception that it offers easy access to massive amounts of data.

But who gets access? For what purposes? In what contexts? And with what constraints? While the explosion of research using data sets from social media sources would suggest that access is straightforward, it is anything but. As Lev Manovich (2011) points out, 'only social media companies have access to really large social data—especially transactional data. An anthropologist working for Facebook or a sociologist working for Google will have access to data that the rest of the scholarly community will not.' Some companies restrict access to their data entirely; others sell the privilege of access for a high fee; and others offer small data sets to university-based researchers. This produces considerable unevenness in the system: those with money—or those inside the company—can produce a different type of research than those outside. Those without access can neither reproduce nor evaluate the methodological claims of those who have privileged access.

It is also important to recognize that the class of the Big Data rich is reinforced through the university system: top-tier, well-resourced universities will be able to buy access to data, and students from the top universities are the ones most likely to be invited to work within large social media companies. Those from the periphery are less likely to get those invitations and develop their skills. The result is that the divisions between those who went to the top universities and the rest will widen significantly.

In addition to questions of access, there are questions of skills. Wrangling APIs, scraping and analyzing big swathes of data is a skill set generally restricted to those with a computational background. When computational skills are positioned as the most valuable, questions emerge over who is advantaged and who is disadvantaged in such a context. This, in its own way, sets up new hierarchies around 'who can read the numbers', rather than recognizing that computer scientists and social scientists both have valuable perspectives to offer. Significantly, this is also a gendered division. Most researchers who have computational skills at the present moment are male and, as feminist historians and philosophers of science have demonstrated, who is asking the questions determines which questions are asked (Forsythe, 2001; Harding, 1989). There are complex questions about what kinds of research skills are valued in the future and how those skills are taught. How can students be educated so that they are equally comfortable with algorithms and data analysis as well as with social analysis and theory?

Finally, the difficulty and expense of gaining access to Big Data produces a restricted culture of research findings. Large data companies have no responsibility to make their data available, and they have total control over who gets to see it. Big Data researchers with access to proprietary data sets are less likely to choose questions that are contentious to a social media company, for example, if they think it may result in their access being cut. The chilling effects on the kinds of research questions that can be asked—in public or private—are something we all need to consider when assessing the future of Big Data.

The current ecosystem around Big Data creates a new kind of digital divide: the Big Data rich and the Big Data poor. Some company researchers have even gone so far as to suggest that academics shouldn't bother studying social media—as in-house people can do it so much better.[4] Such explicit efforts to demarcate research 'insiders' and 'outsiders'—while by no means new—undermine the utopian rhetoric of those who evangelize about the values of Big Data. 'Effective democratisation can always be measured by this essential criterion,' Derrida claimed, 'the participation in and access to the archive, its constitution, and its interpretation' (1996, p. 4). Whenever inequalities are explicitly written into the system, they produce class-based structures. Manovich writes of three classes of people in the realm of Big Data: 'those who create data (both consciously and by leaving digital footprints), those who have the means to collect it, and those who have expertise to analyze it' (2011). We know that the last group is the smallest, and the most privileged: they are also the ones who get to determine the rules about how Big Data will be used, and who gets to participate. While institutional inequalities may be a forgone conclusion in academia, they should nevertheless be examined and questioned. They produce a bias in the data and the types of research that emerge.

By arguing that the Big Data phenomenon is implicated in some much broader historical and philosophical shifts is not to suggest it is solely accountable; the academy is by no means the sole driver behind the computational turn. There

---

[4] During his keynote talk at the International Conference on Weblogs and Social Media (ICWSM) in Barcelona on July 19, 2011, Jimmy Lin—a researcher at Twitter—discouraged researchers from pursuing lines of inquiry that internal Twitter researchers could do better given their preferential access to Twitter data.

is a deep government and industrial drive toward gathering and extracting maximal value from data, be it information that will lead to more targeted advertising, product design, traffic planning or criminal policing. But we do think there are serious and wide-ranging implications for the operationalization of Big Data, and what it will mean for future research agendas. As Lucy Suchman (2011) observes, via Levi Strauss, 'we are our tools.' We should consider how they participate in shaping the world with us as we use them. The era of Big Data has only just begun, but it is already important that we start questioning the assumptions, values, and biases of this new wave of research. As scholars who are invested in the production of knowledge, such interrogations are an essential component of what we do.

Acknowledgements

We wish to thank Heather Casteel for her help in preparing this article. We are also deeply grateful to Eytan Adar, Tarleton Gillespie, and Christian Sandvig for inspiring conversations, suggestions, and feedback. ■

References

Acquisti, A. & Gross, R. (2009) 'Predicting Social Security Numbers from Public Data', *Proceedings of the National Academy of Science*, vol. 106, no. 27, pp. 10975–10980.

Anderson, C. (2008) 'The End of Theory, Will the Data Deluge Makes the Scientific Method Obsolete?', *Edge*, <http://www.edge.org/3rd_culture/anderson08/ anderson08_index.html>. [25 July 2011]

Baca, G. (2004) 'Legends of Fordism: Between Myth, History, and Foregone Conclusions', *Social Analysis*, vol. 48, no. 3, pp. 169–178.

Barnes, J. A. (1954) 'Class and Committees in a Norwegian Island Parish', *Human Relations*, vol. 7, no. 1, pp. 39–58.

Barry, A. and Born, G. (2012) *Interdisciplinarity: reconfigurations of the Social and Natural Sciences*. Taylor and Francis, London.

Behar, R. and Gordon, D. A., eds. (1996) *Women Writing Culture*. University of California Press, Berkeley, California.

Berry, D. (2011) 'The Computational Turn: Thinking About the Digital Humanities', *Culture Machine*. vol 12. <http://www.culturemachine.net/index.php/cm/article/view/440/470>. [11 July 2011].

Blass, T. (2004) *The Man Who Shocked the World: The Life and Legacy of Stanley Milgram*. Basic Books, New York, New York.

Bollier, D. (2010) 'The Promise and Peril of Big Data', <http:// www.aspeninstitute.org/sites/default/files/content/docs/pubs/The_Promise_and_Peril_of_Big_Data.pdf>. [11 July 2011].

boyd, d. (2004) 'Friendster and Publicly Articulated Social Networks', Conference on Human Factors and Computing Systems (CHI 2004). ACM, April 24-2, Vienna.

boyd, d. (2006) 'Friends, Friendsters, and Top 8: Writing community into being on social network sites', *First Monday* vol. 11, no. 12, article 2.

boyd, d. and Ellison, N. (2007) 'Social Network Sites: Definition, History, and Scholarship', *Journal of Computer-Mediated Communication*, vol. 13, no. 1, article 11.

boyd, d. and Marwick, A. (2011) 'Social Privacy in Networked Publics: Teens' Attitudes, Practices, and Strategies,' paper given at Oxford Internet Institute Decade in Time Conference. Oxford, England.

Bowker, G. C. (2005) *Memory Practices in the Sciences*. MIT Press, Cambridge, Massachusetts.

Burkholder, L, ed. (1992) *Philosophy and the Computer*, Boulder, San Francisco, and Oxford: Westview Press.

Cain, M. and Finch, J. (1981) Towards a Rehabilitation of Data. In: P. Abrams, R. Deem, J. Finch, & P. Rock (eds.), *Practice and Progress: British Sociology 1950–1980*, George Allen and Unwin, London.

Clifford, J. and Marcus, G. E., eds. (1986) *Writing Culture: The Poetics and Politics of Ethnography*. University of California Press, Berkeley, California.

Crawford, K. (2009) 'Following you: Disciplines of listening in social media', *Continuum: Journal of Media & Cultural Studies* vol. 23, no. 4, 532–33.

Du Gay, P. and Pryke, M. (2002) *Cultural Economy: Cultural Analysis and Commercial Life*, Sage, London.

Dunbar, R. (1998) *Grooming, Gossip, and the Evolution of Language*, Harvard University Press, Cambridge.

Derrida, J. (1996) *Archive Fever: A Freudian Impression*. Trans. Eric Prenowitz, University of Chicago Press, Chicago & London.

Emmens, T. and Phippen, A. (2010) 'Evaluating Online Safety Programs', Harvard Berkman Center for Internet and Society, <http://cyber.law.harvard.edu/sites/cyber.law.harvard.edu/files/Emmens_Phippen_Evaluating-Online-Safety-Programs_2010.pdf>. [23 July 2011].

Ess, C. (2002) 'Ethical decision-making and Internet research: Recommendations from the aoir ethics working committee,' Association of Internet Researchers, <http://aoir.org/reports/ethics.pdf >. [12 September 2011].

Fischer, C. (1982) *To Dwell Among Friends: Personal Networks in Town and City*. University of Chicago, Chicago.

Forsythe, D. (2001) *Studying Those Who Study Us: An Anthropologist in the World of Artificial Intelligence*, Stanford University Press, Stanford.

Freeman, L. (2006) *The Development of Social Network Analysis*, Empirical Press, Vancouver.

Gitelman, L. (2011) Notes for the upcoming collection 'Raw Data' is an Oxymoron, <https://files.nyu.edu/lg91/public/>. [23 July 2011].

Golder, S. (2010) 'Scaling Social Science with Hadoop', Cloudera Blog, <http://www.cloudera.com/blog/2010/04/scaling-social-science-with-hadoop/>. [June 18 2011].

Granovetter, M. S. (1973) 'The Strength of Weak Ties,' *American Journal of Sociology* vol. 78, issue 6, pp. 1360–80.

Harding, S. (2010) 'Feminism, science and the anti-Enlightenment critiques', in *Women, knowledge and reality: explorations in feminist philosophy*, eds A. Garry and M. Pearsall, Boston: Unwin Hyman, 298–320.

Homans, G.C. (1974) *Social Behavior: Its Elementary Forms*, Harvard University Press, Cambridge, MA.
Isbell, C., Kearns, M., Kormann, D., Singh, S. & Stone, P. (2000) 'Cobot in LambdaMOO: A Social Statistics Agent', paper given at the 17th National Conference on Artificial Intelligence (AAAI-00). Austin, Texas.
Kilduff, M. and Tsai, W. (2003) *Social Networks and Organizations*, Sage, London.
Kranzberg, M. (1986) 'Technology and History: Kranzberg's Laws', *Technology and Culture* vol. 27, no. 3, pp. 544–560.
Latour, B. (2009). 'Tarde's idea of quantification', in *The Social After Gabriel Tarde: Debates and Assessments*, ed M. Candea, London: Routledge, pp. 145–162. <http://www.brunolatour.fr/articles/article/116-TARDE-CANDEA.pdf>. [19 June 2011].
Lazer, D., Pentland, A., Adamic, L., Aral, S., Barabási, A., Brewer, D., Christakis, N., Contractor, N., Fowler, J., Gutmann, M., Jebara, T., King, G., Macy, M., Roy, D., & Van Alstyne, M. (2009). 'Computational Social Science'. *Science* vol. 323, pp. 721–3.
Lewis, K., Kaufman, J., Gonzalez, M.,Wimmer, A., & Christakis, N. (2008) 'Tastes, ties, and time: A new social network dataset using Facebook.com', *Social Networks* vol. 30, pp. 330–342.
Manovich, L. (2011) 'Trending: The Promises and the Challenges of Big Social Data', *Debates in the Digital Humanities*, ed. M.K. Gold. The University of Minnesota Press, Minneapolis, MN <http://www.manovich.net/DOCS/Manovich_trending_paper.pdf>. [15 July 2011].
McCloskey, D. N. (1985) 'From Methodology to Rhetoric', In *The Rhetoric of Economics* au D. N. McCloskey, University of Wisconsin Press, Madison, pp. 20–35.
Meeder, B., Tam, J., Gage Kelley, P., & Faith Cranor, L. (2010) 'RT @IWantPrivacy: Widespread Violation of Privacy Settings in the Twitter Social Network', Paper presented at Web 2.0 Security and Privacy, W2SP 2011, Oakland, CA.
Meiss, M.R., Menczer, F., and A. Vespignani. (2008) 'Structural analysis of behavioral networks from the Internet', *Journal of Physics A: Mathematical and Theoretical*, vol. 41, no. 22, pp. 220–224.
Meyer, D., Gaba, V., Colwell, K.A., (2005) 'Organizing Far from Equilibrium: Nonlinear Change in Organizational Fields', *Organization Science*, vol. 16, no. 5, pp. 456–473.
Moretti, F. (2007) *Graphs, Maps, Trees: Abstract Models for a Literary History*. Verso, London.
Onnela, J. P., Saramäki, J., Hyvönen, J., Szabó, G., Lazer, D., Kaski, K., & Kertész, J., Barabási, A.L. (2007) 'Structure and tie strengths in mobile communication networks', Proceedings from the National Academy of Sciences, vol. 104, no. 18, pp. 7332–7336.
Pariser, E. (2011) *The Filter Bubble: What the Internet is Hiding from You*. Penguin Press, New York, NY.
Radcliffe-Brown, A.R. (1940) 'On Social Structure', *The Journal of the Royal Anthropological Institute of Great Britain and Ireland* vol. 70, no. 1, pp. 1–12.

B

Reverby, S. M. (2009) *Examining Tuskegee: The Infamous Syphilis Study and Its Legacy*. University of North Carolina Press.

Schrag, Z. M. (2010) *Ethical Imperialism: Institutional Review Boards and the Social Sciences, 1965–2009*. Johns Hopkins University Press, Baltimore, Maryland.

Suchman, L. (2011) 'Consuming Anthropology', in *Interdisicpinarity: Reconfigurations of the social and natural sciences*, eds. Andrew Barry and Georgina Born, Routledge, London and New York.

Twitter. (2011) 'One hundred million voices', Twitter blog, <http://blog.twitter.com/2011/09/one-hundred-million-voices.html>. [12 September 2011]

Veinot, T. (2007) 'The Eyes of the Power Company: Workplace Information Practices of a Vault Inspector', *The Library Quarterly*, vol. 77, no. 2, pp. 157–180.

Zimmer, M. (2008) 'More on the 'Anonymity' of the Facebook Dataset—It's Harvard College', MichaelZimmer.org Blog, <http://www.michaelzimmer.org/2008/01/03/more-on-the-anonymity-of-the-facebook-dataset-its-harvard-college/>. [20 June 2011].

AUTHOR PROFILE

danah boyd is a scholar and researcher whose work focuses on the intersection of technology and society, especially for young people. boyd earned her masters degree at the MIT Media Lab's Sociable Media Group and her PhD at Berkeley's School of Information. She is the author of two books: *It's Complicated: The Social Lives of Networked Teens* (2014) and *Hanging Out, Messing Around, and Geeking Out: Kids Living and Learning With New Media* (2009). She is also a Visiting Professor in NYU's Interactive Telecommunications Program and a faculty affiliate at Harvard's Berkman Center. As a young teen, boyd struggled with her identity and sexuality, and boyd credits the internet as offering an outlet and resources during this period of self-discovery. Today boyd serves on the board of directors for Crisis Text Line, an organization that employs volunteers to use texting to help young people at moments of struggle. boyd's name is not capitalized, she notes, "to satisfy [her] own political irritation at the importance of capitalization."

Kate Crawford is a scholar, researcher, and author of numerous works on the intersections of data, ethics, and power. Her book, *Adult Themes: Rewriting the Rules about Adulthood* (Macmillan 2006), argues that cultural definitions of adulthood (such as homeownership, parenthood, and marriage) are changing in the 21st century to allow individuals more freedom. In 2014, she co-edited *Big Data, Big Questions*, a special section of the *International Journal of Communication*. Crawford grew up in Australia, and, along with Nicole Skeltys, she formed B(if)tek, an electronic music duo that recorded 3 albums between 1998 and 2003. She is Visiting Professor at MIT's Center for Civic Media, Senior Fellow at NYU's Information Law Insitute, and Associate Professor at the University of South Wales.

Both boyd and Crawford are Principle Researchers at Microsoft Research, a collaboration between Microsoft and university scholars for innovation in computing and networking.

Bloodchild

By Octavia E. Butler

My last night of childhood began with a visit home. T'Gatoi's sister had given us two sterile eggs. T'Gatoi gave one to my mother, brother, and sisters. She insisted that I eat the other one alone. It didn't matter. There was still enough to leave everyone feeling good. Almost everyone. My mother wouldn't take any. She sat, watching everyone drifting and dreaming without her. Most of the time she watched me.

I lay against T'Gatoi's long, velvet underside, sipping from my egg now and then, wondering why my mother denied herself such a harmless pleasure. Less of her hair would be gray if she indulged now and then. The eggs prolonged life, prolonged vigor. My father, who had never refused one in his life, had lived more than twice as long as he should have. And toward the end of his life, when he should have been slowing down, he had married my mother and fathered four children.

But my mother seemed content to age before she had to. I saw her turn away as several of T'Gatoi's limbs secured me closer. T'Gatoi liked our body heat and took advantage of it whenever she could. When I was little and at home more, my mother used to try to tell me how to behave with T'Gatoi—how to be respectful and always obedient because T'Gatoi was the Tlic government official in charge of the Preserve, and thus the most important of her kind to deal directly with Terrans. It was an honor, my mother said, that such a person had chosen to come into the family. My mother was at her most formal and severe when she was lying.

I had no idea why she was lying, or even what she was lying about. It *was* an honor to have T'Gatoi in the family, but it was hardly a novelty. T'Gatoi and my mother had been friends all my mother's life, and T'Gatoi was not interested in being honored in the house she considered her second home. She simply came in, climbed onto one of her special couches, and called me over to keep her warm. It was impossible to be formal with her while lying against her and hearing her complain as usual that I was too skinny.

"You're better," she said this time, probing me with six or seven of her limbs. "You're gaining weight finally. Thinness is dangerous." The probing changed subtly, became a series of caresses.

"He's still too thin," my mother said sharply.

T'Gatoi lifted her head and perhaps a meter of her body off the couch as though she were sitting up. She looked at my mother, and my mother, her face lined and old looking, turned away.

"Lien, I would like you to have what's left of Gan's egg."

"The eggs are for the children," my mother said.

"They are for the family. Please take it."

Unwillingly obedient, my mother took it from me and put it to her mouth. There were only a few drops left in the now-shrunken, elastic shell, but she squeezed them out, swallowed them, and after a few moments some of the lines of tension began to smooth from her face.

"It's good," she whispered. "Sometimes I forget how good it is."

"You should take more," T'Gatoi said. "Why are you in such a hurry to be old?"

My mother said nothing.

"I like being able to come here," T'Gatoi said. "This place is a refuge because of you, yet you won't take care of yourself."

T'Gatoi was hounded on the outside. Her people wanted more of us made available. Only she and her political faction stood between us and the hordes who did not understand why there was a Preserve—why any Terran could not be courted, paid, drafted, in some way made available to them. Or they did understand, but in their desperation, they did not care. She parceled us out to the desperate and sold us to the rich and powerful for their political support. Thus, we were necessities, status symbols, and an independent people. She oversaw the joining of families, putting an end to the final remnants of the earlier system of breaking up Terran families to suit impatient Tlic. I had lived outside with her. I had seen the desperate eagerness in the way some people looked at me. It was a little frightening to know that only she stood between us and that desperation that could so easily swallow us. My mother would look at her sometimes and say to me, "Take care of her." And I would remember that she too had been outside, had seen.

Now T'Gatoi used four of her limbs to push me away from her onto the floor. "Go on, Gan," she said. "Sit down there with your sisters and enjoy not being sober. You had most of the egg. Lien, come warm me."

My mother hesitated for no reason that I could see. One of my earliest memories is of my mother stretched alongside T'Gatoi, talking about things I could not understand, picking me up from the floor and laughing as she sat me on one of T'Gatoi's segments. She ate her share of eggs then. I wondered when she had stopped, and why.

She lay down now against T'Gatoi, and the whole left row of T'Gatoi's limbs closed around her, holding her loosely, but securely. I had always found it comfortable to lie that way, but except for my older sister, no one else in the family liked it. They said it made them feel caged.

T'Gatoi meant to cage my mother. Once she had, she moved her tail slightly, then spoke. "Not enough egg, Lien. You should have taken it when it was passed to you. You need it badly now."

T'Gatoi's tail moved once more, its whip motion so swift I wouldn't have seen it if I hadn't been watching for it. Her sting drew only a single drop of blood from my mother's bare leg.

My mother cried out—probably in surprise. Being stung doesn't hurt. Then she sighed and I could see her body relax. She moved languidly into a more comfortable position within the cage of T'Gatoi's limbs. "Why did you do that?" she asked, sounding half asleep.

"I could not watch you sitting and suffering any longer."

My mother managed to move her shoulders in a small shrug. "Tomorrow," she said.

"Yes. Tomorrow you will resume your suffering—if you must. But just now, just for now, lie here and warm me and let me ease your way a little."

"He's still mine, you know," my mother said suddenly.

"Nothing can buy him from me." Sober, she would not have permitted herself to refer to such things.

"Nothing," T'Gatoi agreed, humoring her.

"Did you think I would sell him for eggs? For long life? My son?"

"Not for anything," T'Gatoi said, stroking my mother's shoulders, toying with her long, graying hair.

I would like to have touched my mother, shared that moment with her. She would take my hand if I touched her now. Freed by the egg and the sting, she would smile and perhaps say things long held in. But tomorrow, she would remember all this as a humiliation. I did not want to be part of a remembered humiliation. Best just be still and know she loved me under all the duty and pride and pain.

"Xuan Hoa, take off her shoes," T'Gatoi said. "In a little while I'll sting her again and she can sleep."

My older sister obeyed, swaying drunkenly as she stood up. When she had finished, she sat down beside me and took my hand. We had always been a unit, she and I.

My mother put the back of her head against T'Gatoi's underside and tried from that impossible angle to look up into the broad, round face. "You're going to sting me again?"

"Yes, Lien."

"I'll sleep until tomorrow noon."

"Good. You need it. When did you sleep last?"

My mother made a wordless sound of annoyance. "I should have stepped on you when you were small enough," she muttered.

It was an old joke between them. They had grown up together, sort of, though T'Gatoi had not, in my mother's lifetime, been small enough for any Terran to step on. She was nearly three times my mother's present age, yet would still be young when my mother died of age. But T'Gatoi and my mother had met as T'Gatoi was coming into a period of rapid development—a kind of Tlic adolescence. My mother was only a child, but for a while they developed at the same rate and had no better friends than each other.

T'Gatoi had even introduced my mother to the man who became my father. My parents, pleased with each other in spite of their different ages, married as T'Gatoi was going into her family's business—politics. She and my mother saw each other less. But sometime before my older sister was born, my mother promised T'Gatoi one of her children. She would have to give one of us to someone, and she preferred T'Gatoi to some stranger.

Years passed. T'Gatoi traveled and increased her influence. The Preserve was hers by the time she came back to my mother to collect what she probably saw as her just reward for her hard work. My older sister took an instant liking to her and wanted to be chosen, but my mother was just coming to term with me and T'Gatoi liked the idea of choosing an infant and watching and taking part in all the phases of development. I'm told I was first caged within T'Gatoi's many limbs only three minutes after my birth. A few days later, I was given my first taste of egg. I tell Terrans that when they ask whether I was ever afraid of her. And I tell it to Tlic when T'Gatoi suggests a young Terran child for them and they, anxious and ignorant, demand an adolescent. Even my brother who had somehow grown up to fear and distrust the Tlic could probably have gone smoothly into one of their families if he had been adopted early enough. Sometimes, I think for his sake he should have been. I looked at him, stretched out on the floor across the room, his eyes open, but glazed as he dreamed his egg dream. No matter what he felt toward the Tlic, he always demanded his share of egg.

"Lien, can you stand up?" T'Gatoi asked suddenly.

"Stand?" my mother said. "I thought I was going to sleep."

"Later. Something sounds wrong outside." The cage was abruptly gone.

"What?"

"Up, Lien!"

My mother recognized her tone and got up just in time to avoid being dumped on the floor. T'Gatoi whipped her three meters of body off her couch, toward the door, and out at full speed. She had bones—ribs, a long spine, a skull, four sets of limb bones per segment. But when she moved that way, twisting, hurling herself into controlled falls, landing running, she seemed not only boneless, but aquatic—something swimming through the air as though it were water. I loved watching her move.

I left my sister and started to follow her out the door, though I wasn't very steady on my own feet. It would have been better to sit and dream, better yet to find a girl and share a waking dream with her. Back when the Tlic saw us as not much more than convenient, big, warm-blooded animals, they would pen several of us together, male and female, and feed us only eggs. That way they could be sure of getting another generation of us no matter how we tried to hold out. We were lucky that didn't go on long. A few generations of it and we would have *been* little more than convenient, big animals.

"Hold the door open, Gan," T'Gatoi said. "And tell the family to stay back."

"What is it?" I asked.

"N'Tlic."

I shrank back against the door. "Here? Alone?"

"He was trying to reach a call box, I suppose." She carried the man past me, unconscious, folded like a coat over some of her limbs. He looked young—my brother's age perhaps—and he was thinner than he should have been. What T'Gatoi would have called dangerously thin.

"Gan, go to the call box," she said. She put the man on the floor and began stripping off his clothing.

I did not move.

After a moment, she looked up at me, her sudden stillness a sign of deep impatience.

"Send Qui," I told her. "I'll stay here. Maybe I can help."

She let her limbs begin to move again, lifting the man and pulling his shirt over his head. “You don’t want to see this,” she said. “It will be hard. I can’t help this man the way his Tlic could.”

“I know. But send Qui. He won’t want to be of any help here. I’m at least willing to try.”

She looked at my brother—older, bigger, stronger, certainly more able to help her here. He was sitting up now, braced against the wall, staring at the man on the floor with undisguised fear and revulsion. Even she could see that he would be useless.

“Qui, go!” she said.

He didn’t argue. He stood up, swayed briefly, then steadied, frightened sober.

“This man’s name is Bram Lomas,” she told him, reading from the man’s armband. I fingered my own armband in sympathy. “He needs T’Khotgif Teh. Do you hear?”

“Bram Lomas, T’Khotgif Teh,” my brother said. “I’m going.” He edged around Lomas and ran out the door.

Lomas began to regain consciousness. He only moaned at first and clutched spasmodically at a pair of T’Gatoi’s limbs. My younger sister, finally awake from her egg dream, came close to look at him, until my mother pulled her back.

T’Gatoi removed the man’s shoes, then his pants, all the while leaving him two of her limbs to grip. Except for the final few, all her limbs were equally dexterous. “I want no argument from you this time, Gan,” she said.

I straightened. “What shall I do?”

“Go out and slaughter an animal that is at least half your size.”

“Slaughter? But I’ve never—”

She knocked me across the room. Her tail was an efficient weapon whether she exposed the sting or not.

I got up, feeling stupid for having ignored her warning, and went into the kitchen. Maybe I could kill something with a knife or an ax. My mother raised a few Terran animals for the table and several thousand local ones for their fur. T’Gatoi would probably prefer something local. An achti, perhaps. Some of those were the right size, though they had about three times as many teeth as I did and a real love of using them. My mother, Hoa, and Qui could kill them with knives. I had never killed one at all, had never slaughtered any animal. I had spent most of my time with T’Gatoi while my brother and sisters were learning the family business. T’Gatoi had been right. I should have been the one to go to the call box. At least I could do that.

I went to the corner cabinet where my mother kept her large house and garden tools. At the back of the cabinet there was a pipe that carried off waste water from the kitchen—except that it didn’t anymore. My father had rerouted the waste water below before I was born. Now the pipe could be turned so that one half slid around the other and a rifle could be stored inside. This wasn’t our only gun, but it was our most easily accessible one. I would have to use it to shoot one of the biggest of the achti. Then T’Gatoi would probably confiscate it. Firearms were illegal in the Preserve. There had been incidents right after the Preserve was established—Terrans shooting Tlic, shooting N’Tlic. This was before the joining of families began, before everyone had a personal stake in keeping the peace. No one had shot a Tlic in my lifetime or my mother's, but the law still stood—for our protection, we were told. There were stories of whole Terran families wiped out in reprisal back during the assassinations.

I went out to the cages and shot the biggest achti I could find. It was a handsome breeding male, and my mother would not be pleased to see me bring it in. But it was the right size, and I was in a hurry.

I put the achti's long, warm body over my shoulder—glad that some of the weight I'd gained was muscle—and took it to the kitchen. There, I put the gun back in its hiding place. If T'Gatoi noticed the achti's wounds and demanded the gun, I would give it to her. Otherwise, let it stay where my father wanted it.

I turned to take the achti to her, then hesitated. For several seconds, I stood in front of the closed door wondering why I was suddenly afraid. I knew what was going to happen. I hadn't seen it before but T'Gatoi had shown me diagrams and drawings. She had made sure I knew the truth as soon as I was old enough to understand it.

Yet I did not want to go into that room. I wasted a little time choosing a knife from the carved, wooden box in which my mother kept them. T'Gatoi might want one, I told myself, for the tough, heavily furred hide of the achti.

"Gan!" T'Gatoi called, her voice harsh with urgency.

I swallowed. I had not imagined a single moving of the feet could be so difficult. I realized I was trembling and that shamed me. Shame impelled me through the door.

I put the achti down near T'Gatoi and saw that Lomas was unconscious again. She, Lomas, and I were alone in the room—my mother and sisters probably sent out so they would not have to watch. I envied them.

But my mother came back into the room as T'Gatoi seized the achti. Ignoring the knife I offered her, she extended claws from several of her limbs and slit the achti from throat to anus. She looked at me, her yellow eyes intent. "Hold this man's shoulders, Gan."

I stared at Lomas in panic, realizing that I did not want to touch him, let alone hold him. This would not be like shooting an animal. Not as quick, not as merciful, and, I hoped, not as final, but there was nothing I wanted less than to be part of it.

My mother came forward. "Gan, you hold his right side," she said. "I'll hold his left." And if he came to, he would throw her off without realizing he had done it. She was a tiny woman. She often wondered aloud how she had produced, as she said, such "huge" children.

"Never mind," I told her, taking the man's shoulders. "I'll do it." She hovered nearby.

"Don't worry," I said. "I won't shame you. You don't have to stay and watch."

She looked at me uncertainly, then touched my face in a rare caress. Finally, she went back to her bedroom.

T'Gatoi lowered her head in relief. "Thank you, Gan," she said with courtesy more Terran than Tlic. "That one…she is always finding new ways for me to make her suffer."

Lomas began to groan and make choked sounds. I had hoped he would stay unconscious. T'Gatoi put her face near his so that he focused on her.

"I've stung you as much as I dare for now," she told him. "When this is over, I'll sting you to sleep and you won't hurt anymore."

"Please," the man begged. "Wait..."

"There's no more time, Bram. I'll sting you as soon as it's over. When T'Khotgif arrives she'll give you eggs to help you heal. It will be over soon."

"T'Khotgif!" the man shouted, straining against my hands.

"Soon, Bram." T'Gatoi glanced at me, then placed a claw against his abdomen slightly to the right of the middle, just below the left rib. There was movement on the right side—tiny, seemingly random pulsations moving his brown flesh, creating a concavity here, a convexity there, over and over until I could see the rhythm of it and knew where the next pulse would be.

Lomas's entire body stiffened under T'Gatoi's claw, though she merely rested it against him as she wound the rear section of her body around his legs. He might break my grip, but he would not break hers. He wept helplessly as she used his pants to tie his hands, then pushed his hands above his head so that I could kneel on the cloth between them and pin them in place. She rolled up his shirt and gave it to him to bite down on.

And she opened him.

His body convulsed with the first cut. He almost tore himself away from me. The sound he made...I had never heard such sounds come from anything human. T'Gatoi seemed to pay no attention as she lengthened and deepened the cut, now and then pausing to lick away blood. His blood vessels contracted, reacting to the chemistry of her saliva, and the bleeding slowed.

I felt as though I were helping her torture him, helping her consume him. I knew I would vomit soon, didn't know why I hadn't already. I couldn't possibly last until she was finished.

She found the first grub. It was fat and deep red with his blood—both inside and out. It had already eaten its own egg case but apparently had not yet begun to eat its host. At this stage, it would eat any flesh except its mother's. Let alone, it would have gone on excreting the poisons that had both sickened and alerted Lomas. Eventually it would have begun to eat. By the time it ate its way out of Lomas's flesh, Lomas would be dead or dying—and unable to take revenge on the thing that was killing him. There was always a grace period between the time the host sickened and the time the grubs began to eat him.

T'Gatoi picked up the writhing grub carefully and looked at it, somehow ignoring the terrible groans of the man.

Abruptly, the man lost consciousness.

"Good," T'Gatoi looked down at him. "I wish you Terrans could do that at will." She felt nothing. And the thing she held . . .

It was limbless and boneless at this stage, perhaps fifteen centimeters long and two thick, blind and slimy with blood. It was like a large worm. T'Gatoi put it into the belly of the achti, and it began at once to burrow. It would stay there and eat as long as there was anything to eat.

Probing through Lomas's flesh, she found two more, one of them smaller and more vigorous. "A male!" she said happily. He would be dead before I would. He would be through his metamorphosis and screwing everything that would hold still before his sisters even had limbs. He was the only one to make a serious effort to bite T'Gatoi as she placed him in the achti.

Paler worms oozed to visibility in Lomas's flesh. I closed my eyes. It was worse than finding something dead, rotting, and filled with tiny animal grubs. And it was far worse than any drawing or diagram.

"Ah, there are more," T'Gatoi said, plucking out two long, thick grubs. "You may have to kill another animal, Gan. Everything lives inside you Terrans."

I had been told all my life that this was a good and necessary thing Tlic and Terran did together—a kind of birth. I had believed it until now. I knew birth was painful and bloody, no matter what. But this was something else, something worse. And I wasn't ready to see it. Maybe I never would be. Yet I couldn't not see it. Closing my eyes didn't help.

T'Gatoi found a grub still eating its egg case. The remains of the case were still wired into a blood vessel by their own little tube or hook or whatever. That was the way the grubs were anchored and the way they fed. They took only blood until they were ready to emerge. Then they ate their stretched, elastic egg cases. Then they ate their hosts.

T'Gatoi bit away the egg case, licked away the blood. Did she like the taste? Did childhood habits die hard—or not die at all?

The whole procedure was wrong, alien. I wouldn't have thought anything about her could seem alien to me.

"One more, I think," she said. "Perhaps two. A good family. In a host animal these days, we would be happy to find one or two alive." She glanced at me. "Go outside, Gan, and empty your stomach. Go now while the man is unconscious."

I staggered out, barely made it. Beneath the tree just beyond the front door, I vomited until there was nothing left to bring up. Finally, I stood shaking, tears streaming down my face. I did not know why I was crying, but I could not stop. I went further from the house to avoid being seen. Every time I closed my eyes I saw red worms crawling over redder human flesh.

There was a car coming toward the house. Since Terrans were forbidden motorized vehicles except for certain farm equipment, I knew this must be Lomas's Tlic with Qui and perhaps a Terran doctor. I wiped my face on my shirt, struggled for control.

"Gan," Qui called as the car stopped. "What happened?" He crawled out of the low, round, Tlic-convenient car door. Another Terran crawled out the other side and went into the house without speaking to me. The doctor. With his help and a few eggs, Lomas might make it.

"T'Khotgif Teh?" I said. The Tlic driver surged out of her car, reared up half her length before me. She was paler and smaller than T'Gatoi—probably born from the body of an animal. Tlic from Terran bodies were always larger as well as more numerous.

"Six young," I told her. "Maybe seven, all alive. At least one male."

"Lomas?" she said harshly. I liked her for the question and the concern in her voice when she asked it. The last coherent thing he had said was her name.

"He's alive," I said.

She surged away to the house without another word.

"She's been sick," my brother said, watching her go. "When I called, I could hear people telling her she wasn't well enough to go out even for this."

I said nothing. I had extended courtesy to the Tlic. Now I didn't want to talk to anyone. I hoped he would go in—out of curiosity if nothing else.

"Finally found out more than you wanted to know, eh?"

I looked at him.

"Don't give me one of *her* looks," he said. "You're not her. You're just her property."

One of her looks. Had I picked up even an ability to imitate her expressions?

"What'd you do, puke?" He sniffed the air. "So now you know what you're in for."

I walked away from him. He and I had been close when we were kids. He would let me follow him around when I was home, and sometimes T'Gatoi would let me bring him along when she took me into the city. But something had happened when he reached adolescence. I never knew what. He began keeping out of T'Gatoi's way. Then he began running away—until he realized there was no "away." Not in the Preserve. Certainly not outside. After that he concentrated on getting his share of every egg that came into the house and on looking out for me in a way that made me all but hate him—a way that clearly said, as long as I was all right, he was safe from the Tlic.

"How was it, really?" he demanded, following me.

"I killed an achti. The young ate it."

"You didn't run out of the house and puke because they ate an achti."

"I had…never seen a person cut open before." That was true, and enough for him to know. I couldn't talk about the other. Not with him.

"Oh," he said. He glanced at me as though he wanted to say more, but he kept quiet.

We walked, not really headed anywhere. Toward the back, toward the cages, toward the fields.

"Did he say anything?" Qui asked. "Lomas, I mean."

Who else would he mean? "He said 'T'Khotgif.'"

Qui shuddered. "If she had done that to me, she'd be the last person I'd call for."

"You'd call for her. Her sting would ease your pain without killing the grubs in you."

"You think I'd care if they died?"

No. Of course he wouldn't. Would I?

"Shit!" He drew a deep breath. "I've seen what they do. You think this thing with Lomas was bad? It was nothing."

I didn't argue. He didn't know what he was talking about.

"I saw them eat a man," he said.

I turned to face him. "You're lying!"

"*I saw them eat a man.*" He paused. "It was when I was little. I had been to the Hartmund house and I was on my way home. Halfway here, I saw a man and a Tlic, and the man was N'Tlic. The ground was hilly. I was able to hide from them and watch. The Tlic wouldn't open the man because she had nothing to feed the grubs. The man couldn't go any further and there were no houses around. He was in so much pain, he told her to kill him. He begged her to kill him. Finally, she did. She cut his throat. One swipe of one claw. I saw the grubs eat their way out, then burrow in again, still eating."

His words made me see Lomas's flesh again, parasitized, crawling. "Why didn't you tell me that?" I whispered.

He looked startled as though he'd forgotten I was listening. "I don't know."

"You started to run away not long after that, didn't you?"

"Yeah. Stupid. Running inside the Preserve. Running in a cage."

I shook my head, said what I should have said to him long ago. "She wouldn't take you, Qui. You don't have to worry."

"She would…if anything happened to you."

"No. She'd take Xuan Hoa. Hoa…wants it." She wouldn't if she had stayed to watch Lomas.

"They don't take women," he said with contempt.

"They do sometimes." I glanced at him. "Actually, they prefer women. You should be around them when they talk among themselves. They say women have more body fat to protect the grubs. But they usually take men to leave the women free to bear their own young."

"To provide the next generation of host animals," he said, switching from contempt to bitterness.

"It's more than that!" I countered. Was it?

"If it were going to happen to me, I'd want to believe it was more, too."

"It *is* more!" I felt like a kid. Stupid argument.

"Did you think so while T'Gatoi was picking worms out of that guy's guts?"

"It's not supposed to happen that way."

"Sure it is. You weren't supposed to see it, that's all. And his Tlic was supposed to do it. She could sting him unconscious and the operation wouldn't have been as painful. But she'd still open him, pick out the grubs, and if she missed even one, it would poison him and eat him from the inside out."

There was actually a time when my mother told me to show respect for Qui because he was my older brother. I walked away, hating him. In his way, he was gloating. He was safe and I wasn't. I could have hit him, but I didn't think I would be able to stand it when he refused to hit back, when he looked at me with contempt and pity.

He wouldn't let me get away. Longer legged, he swung ahead of me and made me feel as though I were following him.

"I'm sorry," he said.

I strode on, sick and furious.

"Look, it probably won't be that bad with you. T'Gatoi likes you. She'll be careful."

I turned back toward the house, almost running from him.

"Has she done it to you yet?" he asked, keeping up easily. "I mean, you're about the right age for implantation. Has she—"

I hit him. I didn't know I was going to do it, but I think I meant to kill him. If he hadn't been bigger and stronger, I think I would have.

He tried to hold me off, but in the end, had to defend himself. He only hit me a couple of times. That was plenty. I don't remember going down, but when I came to, he was gone. It was worth the pain to be rid of him.

I got up and walked slowly toward the house. The back was dark. No one was in the kitchen. My mother and sisters were sleeping in their bedrooms—or pretending to.

Once I was in the kitchen, I could hear voices—Tlic and Terran from the next room. I couldn't make out what they were saying—didn't want to make it out.

I sat down at my mother's table, waiting for quiet. The table was smooth and worn, heavy and well crafted. My father had made it for her just before he died. I remembered hanging around underfoot when he built it. He didn't mind. Now I sat leaning on it, missing him. I could have talked to him. He had done it three times in his long life. Three clutches of eggs, three times being opened up and sewed up. How had he done it? How did anyone do it?

I got up, took the rifle from its hiding place, and sat down again with it. It needed cleaning, oiling.

All I did was load it.

"Gan?"

She made a lot of little clicking sounds when she walked on bare floor, each limb clicking in succession as it touched down. Waves of little clicks.

She came to the table, raised the front half of her body above it, and surged onto it. Sometimes she moved so smoothly she seemed to flow like water itself. She coiled herself into a small hill in the middle of the table and looked at me.

"That was bad," she said softly. "You should not have seen it. It need not be that way."

"I know."

"T'Khotgif—Ch'Khotgif now—she will die of her disease. She will not live to raise her children. But her sister will provide for them, and for Bram Lomas." Sterile sister. One fertile female in every lot: One to keep the family going. That sister owed Lomas more than she could ever repay.

"He'll live then?"

"Yes."

"I wonder if he would do it again."

"No one would ask him to do that again."

I looked into the yellow eyes, wondering how much I saw and understood there, and how much I only imagined. "No one ever asks us," I said. "You never asked me."

She moved her head slightly. "What's the matter with your face?"

"Nothing. Nothing important." Human eyes probably wouldn't have noticed the swelling in the darkness. The only light was from one of the moons, shining through a window across the room.

"Did you use the rifle to shoot the achti?"

"Yes."

"And do you mean to use it to shoot me?"

I stared at her, outlined in the moonlight—coiled, graceful body. "What does Terran blood taste like to you?"

She said nothing.

"What are you?" I whispered. "What are we to you?"

She lay still, rested her head on her topmost coil. "You know me as no other does," she said softly. "You must decide."

"That's what happened to my face," I told her.

"What?"

"Qui goaded me into deciding to do something. It didn't turn out very well." I moved the gun slightly, brought the barrel up diagonally under my own chin. "At least it was a decision I made."

"As this will be."

"Ask me, Gatoi."

"For my children's lives?"

She would say something like that. She knew how to manipulate people, Terran and Tlic. But not this time.

"I don't want to be a host animal," I said. "Not even yours."

It took her a long time to answer. "We use almost no host animals these days," she said. "You know that."

"You use us."

"We do. We wait long years for you and teach you and join our families to yours." She moved restlessly. "You know you aren't animals to us."

I stared at her, saying nothing.

"The animals we once used began killing most of our eggs after implantation long before your ancestors arrived," she said softly. "You know these things, Gan. Because your people arrived, we are relearning what it means to be a healthy, thriving people. And your ancestors, fleeing from their home-world, from their own kind who would have killed or enslaved them—they survived because of us. We saw them as people and gave them the Preserve when they still tried to kill us as worms."

At the word "worms," I jumped. I couldn't help it, and she couldn't help noticing it.

"I see," she said quietly. "Would you really rather die than bear my young, Gan?"

I didn't answer.

"Shall I go to Xuan Hoa?"

"Yes!" Hoa wanted it. Let her have it. She hadn't had to watch Lomas. She'd be proud....Not terrified.

T'Gatoi flowed off the table onto the floor, startling me almost too much.

"I'll sleep in Hoa's room tonight," she said. "And sometime tonight or in the morning, I'll tell her."

This was going too fast. My sister Hoa had had almost as much to do with raising me as my mother. I was still close to her—not like Qui. She could want T'Gatoi and still love me.

"Wait! Gatoi!" She looked back, then raised nearly half her length off the floor and turned to face me. "These are adult things, Gan. This is my life, my family!"

"But she's...my sister."

"I have done what you demanded. I have asked you!"

"But—"

"It will be easier for Hoa. She has always expected to carry other lives inside her."

Human lives. Human young who should someday drink at her breasts, not at her veins.

I shook my head. "Don't do it to her, Gatoi." I was not Qui. It seemed I could become him, though, with no effort at all. I could make Xuan Hoa my shield. Would it be easier to know that red worms were growing in her flesh instead of mine?

"Don't do it to Hoa," I repeated. She stared at me, utterly still.

I looked away, then back at her. "Do it to me."

I lowered the gun from my throat and she leaned forward to take it.

"No," I told her.

"It's the law," she said.

"Leave it for the family. One of them might use it to save my life someday."

She grasped the rifle barrel, but I wouldn't let go. I was pulled into a standing position over her.

"Leave it here!" I repeated. "If we're not your animals, if these are adult things, accept the risk. There is risk, Gatoi, in dealing with a partner."

It was clearly hard for her to let go of the rifle. A shudder went through her and she made a hissing sound of distress. It occurred to me that she was afraid. She was old enough to have seen what guns could do to people. Now her young and this gun would be together in the same house. She did not know about the other guns. In this dispute, they did not matter.

"I will implant the first egg tonight," she said as I put the gun away. "Do you hear, Gan?"

Why else had I been given a whole egg to eat while the rest of the family was left to share one? Why else had my mother kept looking at me as though I were going away from her, going where she could not follow? Did T'Gatoi imagine I hadn't known?

"I hear."

"Now!" I let her push me out of the kitchen, then walked ahead of her toward my bedroom. The sudden urgency in her voice sounded real.

"You would have done it to Hoa tonight!" I accused.

"I must do it to someone tonight."

I stopped in spite of her urgency and stood in her way. "Don't you care who?"

She flowed around me and into my bedroom. I found her waiting on the couch we shared. There was nothing in Hoa's room that she could have used. She would have done it to Hoa on the floor. The thought of her doing it to Hoa at all disturbed me in a different way now, and I was suddenly angry.

Yet I undressed and lay down beside her. I knew what to do, what to expect. I had been told all my life. I felt the familiar sting, narcotic, mildly pleasant. Then the blind probing of her ovipositor. The puncture was painless, easy. So easy going in. She undulated slowly against me, her muscles forcing the egg from her body into mine. I held on to a pair of her limbs until I remembered Lomas holding her that way. Then I let go, moved inadvertently, and hurt her. She gave a low cry of pain and I expected to be caged at once within her limbs. When I wasn't, I held on to her again, feeling oddly ashamed.

"I'm sorry," I whispered.

She rubbed my shoulders with four of her limbs.

"Do you care?" I asked. "Do you care that it's me?"

She did not answer for some time. Finally, "You were the one making the choices tonight, Gan. I made mine long ago."

"Would you have gone to Hoa?"

"Yes. How could I put my children into the care of one who hates them?"

"It wasn't…hate."

"I know what it was."

"I was afraid."

Silence.

"I still am." I could admit it to her here, now.

"But you came to me…to save Hoa."

"Yes." I leaned my forehead against her. She was cool velvet, deceptively soft. "And to keep you for myself," I said. It was so. I didn't understand it, but it was so.

She made a soft hum of contentment. "I couldn't believe I had made such a mistake with you," she said. "I chose you. I believed you had grown to choose me."

"I had, but…"

"Lomas."

"Yes."

"I had never known a Terran to see a birth and take it well. Qui has seen one, hasn't he?"

"Yes."

"Terrans should be protected from seeing."

I didn't like the sound of that—and I doubted that it was possible. "Not protected," I said. "Shown. Shown when we're young kids, and shown more than once. Gatoi, no Terran ever sees a birth that goes right. All we see is N'Tlic—pain and terror and maybe death."

She looked down at me. "It is a private thing. It has always been a private thing."

Her tone kept me from insisting—that and the knowledge that if she changed her mind, I might be the first public example. But I had planted the thought in her mind. Chances were it would grow, and eventually she would experiment.

"You won't see it again," she said. "I don't want you thinking any more about shooting me."

The small amount of fluid that came into me with her egg relaxed me as completely as a sterile egg would have, so that I could remember the rifle in my hands and my feelings of fear and revulsion, anger and despair. I could remember the feelings without reviving them. I could talk about them.

"I wouldn't have shot you," I said. "Not you." She had been taken from my father's flesh when he was my age.

"You could have," she insisted.

"Not you." She stood between us and her own people, protecting, interweaving.

"Would you have destroyed yourself?"

I moved carefully, uncomfortable. "I could have done that. I nearly did. That's Qui's 'away.' I wonder if he knows."

"What?"

I did not answer.

"You will live now."

"Yes." *Take care of her*, my mother used to say. Yes.

"I'm healthy and young," she said. "I won't leave you as Lomas was left—alone, N'Tlic. I'll take care of you." ■

AUTHOR PROFILE

Octavia Butler (1947–2006) was a writer who expanded the realms of the possible in an already wide-ranging genre: speculative fiction. She began her writing career in the early 1970s, when SF was still a genre largely represented by white men. Butler, who describes herself as a black feminist, challenged readers' expectations with stories that transgressed social norms. "Bloodchild" is the story that first won her wide acclaim, winning SF's biggest awards, the Hugo Award and the Nebula Award in 1985. This story, which Butler describes as a coming-of-age love story, explores gender roles, sexuality, and personhood in ways that are still challenging to readers today. Butler's novels, the most widely read of which are *Kindred* (1979) and *Fledgling* (2005), continue to explore issues of race and sexuality. Butler died in 2006, leaving her final trilogy, the *Parable* series, unfinished.

Acting French

It's hard to learn a new language. But it's way harder to learn a new culture.

By Ta-Nehisi Coates

I spent the majority of this summer at Middlebury College, studying at l'École Française. I had never been to Vermont. I have not been many places at all. I did not have an adult passport until I was 37 years old. Sometimes I regret this. And then sometimes not. Learning to travel when you're older allows you to be young again, to touch the childlike amazement that is so often dulled away by adult things. In the past year, I have seen more of the world than at any point before, and thus, I have been filled with that juvenile feeling more times then I can count—at a train station in Strasbourg, in an old Parisian bookstore, on a wide avenue in Lawndale. It was no different in Vermont where the green mountains loomed like giants. I would stare at these mountains out of the back window of the Davis Family Library. I would watch the clouds, which, before the rain, drooped over the mountains like lampshades, and I would wonder what, precisely, I had been doing with my life.

I was there to improve my French. My study consisted of four hours of class work and four hours of homework. I was forbidden from reading, writing, speaking, or hearing English. I watched films in French, tried to read a story in *Le Monde* each day, listened to RFI and a lot of Barbara and Karim Oeullet. At every meal I spoke French, and over the course of the seven weeks I felt myself gradually losing touch with the broader world. This was not a wholly unpleasant feeling. In the moments I had to speak English (calling my wife, interacting with folks in town or at the book store), my mouth felt alien and my ear slightly off.

And there were the latest developments, the likes of which I perceived faintly through the French media. I had some vague sense that King James had done something grand, that the police were killing black men over cigarette sales, that a passenger plane had been shot out the sky, and that powerful people in the world still believed that great problems could be ultimately solved with great armaments. In sum, I knew that very little had changed. And I knew this even with my feeble French eyes, which turned the news of the world into an exercise in impressionism. Everything felt distorted. I understood that things were happening out there, but their size and scope mostly eluded me.

Acquiring a second language is hard. I have been told that it is easier for children, but I am not so sure if this is for reasons of biology or because adults have so much more to learn. Still, it remains true that the vast majority of students at Middlebury were younger than me, and not just younger, but fiercer. My classmates were, in the main, the kind of high-achieving college students who elect to spend their summer vacation taking on eight hours a day of schoolwork. There was no difference in work ethic between us. If I spent more time studying than my classmates, that fact should not be taken as an accolade but as a marker of my inefficiency.

They had something over me, and that something was a culture, which is to say a suite of practices so ingrained as to be ritualistic. The scholastic achievers knew how to quickly memorize a poem in a language they did not understand. They knew that recopying a handout a few days before an exam helped them digest the information. They knew to bring a pencil, not a pen, to that exam. They knew that you could (with the professor's permission) record lectures and take pictures of the blackboard.

This culture of scholastic achievement had not been acquired yesterday. The same set of practices had allowed my classmates to succeed in high school, and had likely been reinforced by other scholastic achievers around them. I am sure many of them had parents who were scholastic high-achievers. This is how social capital reinforces itself and compounds. It is not merely one high achieving child, but a flock of high achieving children, each backed by high-achieving parents. I once talked to a woman who spoke German, English and French and had done so since she was a child. How did this happen, I asked? "Everyone in my world spoke multiple languages," she explained. "It was just what you did."

There were five tiers of French students, starting with those who could barely speak a word and scaling upward to those who were pursuing a master's degree. I was in the second tier, meaning I could order a coffee, recount a story with some difficulty, write a short note (sans verb and gender agreement), and generally understand a French speaker provided he or she talked to me really slowly. The majority of people I interacted with spoke better, wrote better, read better, and heard better than me. There was no escape from my ineptitude. At every waking hour, someone said something to me that I did not understand. At every waking-hour, I mangled some poor Frenchman's lovely language. For the entire summer, I lived by two words: "Désolé, encore."

Compared with my classmates on the second tier, my test scores were on the lower end. Each week, in my literature class, we were responsible for the recitation of some French poems (Baudelaire, Verlaine, Lamartine) from memory, and each day we had to recite a stanza. This sort of exercise may well be familiar to readers of *The Atlantic*, but the rituals required to master it were totally new to me. I had never been a high-achieving student. Indeed, during my 15 or so years in school, I was a remarkably low-achieving student.

There were years when I failed the majority of my classes. This was not a matter of my being better suited for the liberal arts than sciences. I was an English minor in college. I failed American Literature, British Literature, Humanities, and (voilà) French. The record of failure did not end until I quit college to become a writer. My explanation for this record is unsatisfactory: I simply never saw the point of school. I loved the long process of understanding. In school, I often felt like I was doing something else.

Like many black children in this country, I did not have a culture of scholastic high achievement around me. There were very few adults around me who'd been great students and were subsequently rewarded for their studiousness. The phrase "Ivy League" was an empty abstraction to me. I mostly thought of school as a place one goes so as not to be eventually killed, drugged, or jailed. These observations cannot be disconnected from the country I call home, nor from the government to which I swear fealty.

For most of American history, it has been national policy to plunder the capital accumulated by black people—social or otherwise. It began with the prohibition against reading, proceeded to separate and wholly unequal schools, and continues to this very day in our tacit acceptance of segregation. When building capital, it helps to know the right people. One aim of American policy, historically, has been to insure that the "right people" are rarely black. Segregation then ensures that these rare exceptions are spread thin, and that the rest of us have no access to other "right people."

And so a white family born into the lower middle class can expect to live around a critical mass of people who are more affluent or worldly and thus see other things, be exposed to other practices and other cultures. A black family with a middle class salary can expect to live around a critical mass of poor people, and mostly see the same things they (and the poor people around them) are working hard to escape. This too compounds.

Now, in America, invocations of culture are mostly an exercise in awarding power an air of legitimacy. You can see this in the recent remarks by the president, where he turned a question about preserving Native American culture into a lecture on how we (blacks and Native Americans) should be more like the Jews and Asian Americans, who refrain from criticizing the intellectuals in their midst of "acting white." The entire charge rests on shaky social science and the obliteration of history. When Asian Americans and Jewish Americans—on American soil—endure the full brunt of white supremacist assault, perhaps a comparison might be in order.

But probably not. That is because fences are an essential element of human communities. The people who patrol these fences are generally unkind to those they find in violation. The phrase "getting above your raising" is little more than anxious working-class border patrolling. The term "white trash" is little more than anxious ruling-class border patrolling. I am neither an expert in the culture of Jewish Americans nor Asian Americans, but I would be shocked if they too were immune. Some years ago I profiled the rapper Jin. As the first Asian-American rapper to secure a major label contract, he often found himself enduring racist cracks from black rappers abroad and the prodding of fence-patrollers at home. "'Yo, what is this? You really think you're black, Jin?" he recalled his parents saying. "Bottom line—you're not black, Jin.'"

Pretending that black people are unique—or more ardent—in their fence-patrolling, and thus more parochial and anti-intellectual, serves to justify the current uses of American power. The American citizen is free to say, "Look at them, they criticize each other *for reading*!" and then go about his business. In that sense it is little different than raising the myth of "black on black crime" when asked about Ferguson.

I will confess to having very little experience with fence-patrolling, and virtually none with the idea that if you are holding a book, you are "acting white." The Baltimore of my youth was a place where white people rarely ventured. It would not have occurred to anyone I knew to associate reading with white people because very few of us knew any. And I read everything I could find: *A Wrinkle In Time, David Walker's Appeal, Dragon's of Autumn Twilight, Seize The Time, Deadly Bugs and Killer Insects, The Web of Spider-Man.* I had a full set of Childcraft. I loved the volume *Make and Do*. I had a full set of World Book encyclopedias. I used to pick up the fat "P" edition, flip to a random page, and read for hours. When I was just 6 years old, my mother took me to the Enoch Pratt Free Library on Garrison Boulevard and enrolled me in a competition to see which child could read the most books. I read 24 that summer, far outdistancing the competition. My mother smiled. The librarian gave me candy. I was very proud.

For carrying books in black neighborhoods, in black schools, around black people, I was called many things—nerd, bright, doofus, Malcolm, Farrakhan, Mandela, sharp, smart, airhead. I was told that my "head was too far in the clouds." I was told that I was "going to do something one day." But I was never called white. The people who called me a nerd were black. The people who said I was going to "do something one day" were also black. There was no one else around me, and no one else in America then cared. This was not just true of me, it was true of most black children of that era who were then, and are now, the most segregated group in this country. Segregation meant many of us had to rely on traditions closer to home.

And at home I found a separate culture of intellectual achievement. This is the tradition of Carter G. Woodson, Frederick Douglass, and Malcolm X. It argues for education not simply as credentialism or certification, but as a profound act of auto-liberation. This was the culture of my childhood and it gave me some of the greatest thrills of my youth.

I was a boy haunted by questions: Why do the lilies close at night? Why does my father always say, "I can dig it"? And who really killed the dinosaurs? And why is my life so unlike everything I see on TV? That feeling—the not knowing, the longing for knowing, and the eventual answer—is love and youth to me. And I have always preferred libraries to classrooms because the wide open library is the ultimate venue for this theater. This culture was reinforced by my parents, and the politically conscious parents around me, and their politically conscious children. The culture was so strong that it could be regarded as a kind of social capital. It was so old that it could also be regarded as a legacy. This legacy is more responsible for my presence in these august pages than any other. That is because a good writer must ultimately be an autodidact and take a dim view of credentials. My culture failed to make me into a high-achieving student. It succeeded at making me into a writer.

I have never had much of an urge to brag about this. I have always known that in failing to become a scholastic achiever, I forfeited knowledge of certain things. (A mastery of Augustine comes to mind.) But what I did not understand was that I had also forfeited a culture, which is to say a tool kit, a set of pins and tumblers that might have unlocked the language which I so presently adore.

Scholastic achievement is sometimes demeaned as the useless memorization of facts. I suspect that it has more to offer than this. If you woke my French literature professor at 2 a.m., she could recite the deuxième strophe of Verlaine's

"Il Pleure Dans Mon Coeur." I suspect this memorization, this holding of the work in her head, allowed her to analyze it and turn it over in ways I could only do with the text in front of me. More directly, there is no real way for an adult to learn French without some amount of memorization. French is a language that obeys its rules when it feels like it. There is no unwavering rule to tell you which nouns are masculine, or which verbs require a preposition. Memory is the only way through.

At Middlebury, I spent as much time as I could with the master's students, hovering right at the edge of overbearing. On average, I understood 30 percent of what was being said. This was, of course, the point. I wanted to be reminded of who I was. I wanted to be young again, to feel that old thrill of not knowing. It is the same feeling I had as a boy, wondering about the lilies and dinosaurs, listening to "The Bridge Is Over," wondering where in the world was Queens.

And I was ignorant. I felt as if someone had carried me off at night, taken me out to sea, and set me adrift in a life-raft. And the night was beautiful because it held all the things I would never know, and in that I saw my doom—the time when I could learn no more. Morning, noon, and evening, I sat on the terrace listening to the young master's students talk. They would recount their days, share their jokes, or pass on their complaints. They came from everywhere—San Francisco, Atlanta, Seattle, Boulder, Hackensack, Philadelphia, Kiev. And they loved all the things I so wanted to love, but had not made time to love—Baudelaire, Balzac, Rimbaud. I would listen and feel the night folding around me, and the ice-water of youth surging through me.

One afternoon, I was walking from lunch feeling battered by the language. I started talking with a young master in training. I told her I was having a tough time. She gave me some encouraging words in French from a famous author. I told her I didn't understand. She repeated them. I still didn't understand. She repeated them again. I shook my head, smiled, and walked away mildly frustrated because I understood every word she was saying but could not understand how it fit. It was as though someone had said, "He her walks swim plus that yesterday the fight." (This is how French often sounds to me.)

The next day, I sat at lunch with her and another young woman. I asked her to spell the quote out for me. I wrote the phrase down. I did not understand. The other young lady explained the function of the pronouns in the sentence. Suddenly I understood—and not just the meaning of the phrase. I understood something about the function of language, why being able to diagram sentences was important, why understanding partitives and collective nouns was important.

In my long voyage through this sea of language, that was my first sighting of land. I now knew how much I didn't know. The feeling of discovery and understanding that came from this was incredible. It was the first moment when I thought I might survive the sea.

My personal road to this great feeling, to these discoveries, to Middlebury, was not the normal one. I was raised among people skeptical of a canon that had long been skeptical of them. I needed some independent sense of myself, of my cultures and traditions, before I could take a mature look at the West. I wanted nothing to do with Locke because I knew that he wanted little to do with me. I saw no reason to learn French because it was the language of the plunderers of Haiti.

I had to be a nationalist before I could be a humanist. I had to come to understand that black people are not merely the victims of the West, but its architects. The philosophes started the sentence and Martin Luther King finished it. The greatest renditions of this country's greatest anthems are all sung by black people—Ray, Marvin, Whitney. That is neither biology nor a mistake. It is the necessary cosmopolitanism of a people, viewing America from the basement and thus forced to take their lessons when they get them—absorbing, reinterpreting, refining, creating.

Now it must never be concluded that an urge toward the cosmopolitan, toward true education, will make people stop hitting you. The inverse is more likely. In the early 19th century, the Cherokee Nation was told by the new Americans that if its members adopted their "civilized" ways, they would soon be respected as equals. This promise was deeply embedded in the early 19th century approach to this continents indigenous nations.

"We will never do an unjust act towards you. on the contrary we wish you to live in peace, to increase in numbers, to learn to labor, as we do," Thomas Jefferson said. "In time you will be as we are; you will become one people with us; your blood will mix with ours; & will spread, with ours, over this great Island. Hold fast then, my Children, the Chain of friendship, which binds us together; & join us in keeping it forever bright & unbroken."

The Cherokee Nation—likely for their own reasons—embraced mission schools. Some of them converted to Christianity. Other intermarried. Others still enslaved blacks. They adopted a written Constitution, created a script for their language and published a newspaper, *The Cherokee Phoenix*, in English and Cherokee. Thus the Native Americans of that time showed themselves to be as able to to integrate elements of the West with their own culture as any group of Asian or Jewish American. But the wolf has never much cared whether the sheep were cultured or not.

"The problem, from a white point of view," writes historian Daniel Walker Howe, "was that the success of these efforts to 'civilize the Indians' had not yielded the expected dividend in land sales. On the contrary, the more literate, prosperous, and politically organized the Cherokees made themselves, the more resolved they became to keep what remained of their land and improve it for their own benefit."

Cosmopolitanism, openness to other cultures, openness to education did not make the Cherokee pliant to American power; it gave them tools to resist. Realizing this, the United States dropped the veneer of "culture" and "civilization" and resorted to "Indian Removal," or The Trail of Tears. The plunder was celebrated in a popular song:

All I want in this creation
Is a pretty little wife and a big plantation
Away up yonder in the Cherokee nation.

The Native Americans of this period found that America's talk of trading culture for rights was just a cover. In our time, it is common to urge young black children toward education so that they may be respectable or impress the "right people." But the "right people" remain unimpressed, and the credentials of black people, in a country rooted in white supremacy, must necessarily be less. That great powers are in the business of using "respectability" and "education" to ignore these discomfiting facts does not close the book. You can never fully know. But you can walk in the right direction.

The citizen is lost in the labyrinth constructed by his country, when in fact straight is the gate, and narrow must always be the way. When I left for Middlebury, I had just published an article arguing for reparations. People would often ask me what change I expected to come from it. But change had already come. I had gone further down the unending path of knowing, deeper into the night. I was rejecting mental enslavement. I was rejecting the lie.

I came to Middlebury in the spirit of the autodidactic, of auto-liberation, of writing, of Douglass and Malcolm X. I came in ignorance, and found I was more ignorant than I knew. Even there, I was much more comfortable in the library, thumbing through random histories in French, than I was in the classroom. It was not enough. It will not be enough. Sometimes you do need the master's tools to dismantle his house. ■

C

AUTHOR PROFILE

Ta-Nehisi Coates (born 1975) is one of the country's foremost living writers and thinkers on race, culture, and politics. His debut memoir, *The Beautiful Struggle: A Father, Two Sons, and an Unlikely Road to Manhood* (2008) tells his story of growing up in a "black hippie" family in Baltimore. Coates' work on topics as varied as politics, comic books, hip hop, and history, has been published in myriad places, including *The Village Voice*, *The New Yorker*, and *The New York Times Magazine*. He is now senior editor at *The Atlantic*. His blog at *TheAtlantic.com* has been named one of the world's 25 best by *Time* magazine, in part because of Coates' active moderation and participation in the blog's comment section. Best known for his insightful work on race and racism in American culture, Coates wrote on Twitter (@tanehisicoates) that being a black intellectual "is not about comforting yourself" but about a nuanced understanding of struggle and power. He wrote, "It's a privilege for me to be black. It's imposed rigor on me."

The Trouble with Wilderness; or, Getting Back to the Wrong Nature

By William Cronon

The time has come to rethink wilderness.

This will seem a heretical claim to many environmentalists, since the idea of wilderness has for decades been a fundamental tenet—indeed, a passion—of the environmental movement, especially in the United States. For many Americans wilderness stands as the last remaining place where civilization, that all too human disease, has not fully infected the earth. It is an island in the polluted sea of urban-industrial modernity, the one place we can turn for escape from our own too-muchness. Seen in this way, wilderness presents itself as the best antidote to our human selves, a refuge we must somehow recover if we hope to save the planet. As Henry David Thoreau once famously declared, "In Wildness is the preservation of the World." (1)

But is it? The more one knows of its peculiar history, the more one realizes that wilderness is not quite what it seems. Far from being the one place on earth that stands apart from humanity, it is quite profoundly a human creation—indeed, the creation of very particular human cultures at very particular moments in human history. It is not a pristine sanctuary where the last remnant of an untouched, endangered, but still transcendent nature can for at least a little while longer be encountered without the contaminating taint of civilization. Instead, it's a product of that civilization, and could hardly be contaminated by the very stuff of which it is made. Wilderness hides its unnaturalness behind a mask that is all the more beguiling because it seems so natural. As we gaze into the mirror it holds up for us, we too easily imagine that what we behold is Nature when in fact we see the reflection of our own unexamined longings and desires. For this reason, we mistake ourselves when we suppose that wilderness can be the solution to our culture's problematic relationships with the nonhuman world, for wilderness is itself no small part of the problem.

To assert the unnaturalness of so natural a place will no doubt seem absurd or even perverse to many readers, so let me hasten to add that the nonhuman world we encounter in wilderness is far from being merely our own invention. I celebrate with others who love wilderness the beauty and power of the things it contains. Each of us who has spent time there can conjure images and sensations that seem all the more hauntingly real for having engraved themselves so indelibly on our memories. Such memories may be uniquely our own, but they are also familiar enough be to be instantly recognizable to others. Remember this? The torrents of mist shoot out from the base of a great waterfall in the depths of a Sierra canyon, the tiny droplets cooling your face as you listen to the roar of the water and gaze up toward the sky through a rainbow that hovers just out of reach.

Remember this too: looking out across a desert canyon in the evening air, the only sound a lone raven calling in the distance, the rock walls dropping away into a chasm so deep that its bottom all but vanishes as you squint into the amber light of the setting sun. And this: the moment beside the trail as you sit on a sandstone ledge, your boots damp with the morning dew while you take in the rich smell of the pines, and the small red fox—or maybe for you it was a raccoon or a coyote or a deer—that suddenly ambles across your path, stopping for a long moment to gaze in your direction with cautious indifference before continuing on its way. Remember the feelings of such moments, and you will know as well as I do that you were in the presence of something irreducibly nonhuman, something profoundly Other than yourself Wilderness is made of that too.

And yet: what brought each of us to the places where such memories became possible is entirely a cultural invention. Go back 250 years in American and European history, and you do not find nearly so many people wandering around remote corners of the planet looking for what today we would call "the wilderness experience." As late as the eighteenth century, the most common usage of the word "wilderness" in the English language referred to landscapes that generally carried adjectives far different from the ones they attract today. To be a wilderness then was to be "deserted," "savage," "desolate," "barren"—in short, a "waste," the word's nearest synonym. Its connotations were anything but positive, and the emotion one was most likely to feel in its presence was "bewilderment" or terror. (2)

Many of the word's strongest associations then were biblical, for it is used over and over again in the King James Version to refer to places on the margins of civilization where it is all too easy to lose oneself in moral confusion and despair. The wilderness was where Moses had wandered with his people for forty years, and where they had nearly abandoned their God to worship a golden idol. (3) "For Pharaoh will say of the Children of Israel," we read in Exodus, "They are entangled in the land, the wilderness hath shut them in." (4) The wilderness was where Christ had struggled with the devil and endured his temptations: "And immediately the Spirit driveth him into the wilderness. And he was there in the wilderness for forty days tempted of Satan; and was with the wild beasts; and the angels ministered unto him." (5) The "delicious Paradise" of John Milton's Eden was surrounded by "a steep wilderness, whose hairy sides /Access denied" to all who sought entry." When Adam and Eve were driven from that garden, the world they entered was a wilderness that only their labor and pain could redeem. Wilderness, in short, was a place to which one came only against one's will, and always in fear and trembling. Whatever value it might have arose solely from the possibility that it might be "reclaimed" and turned toward human ends—planted as a garden, say, or a city upon a hill. (7) In its raw state, it had little or nothing to offer civilized men and women.

But by the end of the nineteenth century, all this had changed. The wastelands that had once seemed worthless had for some people come to seem almost beyond price. That Thoreau in 1862 could declare wildness to be the preservation of the world suggests the sea change that was going on. Wilderness had once been the antithesis of all that was orderly and good—it had been the darkness, one might say, on the far side of the garden wall—and yet now it was frequently likened to Eden itself. When John Muir arrived in the Sierra Nevada in 1869, he would declare, "No description of Heaven that I have ever heard or read of seems half so fine." (8) He was hardly alone in expressing such emotions. One by one, various corners of the American map came to be designated as sites whose wild beauty was so spectacular that a growing number of citizens had to visit and see them for themselves. Niagara Falls was the first to undergo this transformation, but it was soon followed by the Catskills, the Adirondacks, Yosemite, Yellowstone, and others. Yosemite was deeded by the U.S. government to the state of California in 1864 as the nation's first wildland park, and Yellowstone became the first true national park in 1872. (9)

By the first decade of the twentieth century, in the single most famous episode in American conservation history, a national debate had exploded over whether the city of San Francisco should be permitted to augment its water supply by damming the Tuolumne River in Hetch Hetchy valley, well within the boundaries of Yosemite National Park. The dam was eventually built, but what today seems no less significant is that so many people fought to prevent its completion. Even as the fight was being lost, Hetch Hetchy became the battle cry of an emerging movement to preserve wilderness. Fifty years earlier, such opposition would have been unthinkable. Few would have questioned the merits of "reclaiming" a wasteland like this in order to put it to human use. Now the defenders of Hetch Hetchy attracted widespread national attention by portraying such an act not as improvement or progress but as desecration and vandalism. Lest one doubt that the old biblical metaphors had been turned completely on their heads, listen to John Muir attack the dam's defenders. "Their arguments," he wrote, "are curiously like those of the devil, devised for the destruction of the first garden—so much of the very best Eden fruit going to waste; so much of the best Tuolumne water and Tuolumne scenery going to waste." (10) For Muir and the growing number of Americans who shared his views, Satan's home had become God's Own Temple.

The sources of this rather astonishing transformation were many, but for the purposes of this essay they can be gathered under two broad headings: the sublime and the frontier. Of the two, the sublime is the older and more pervasive cultural construct, being one of the most important expressions of that broad transatlantic movement we today label as romanticism; the frontier is more peculiarly American, though it too had its European antecedents and parallels. The two converged to remake wilderness in their own image, freighting it with moral values and cultural symbols that it carries to this day. Indeed, it is not too much to say that the modern environmental movement is itself a grandchild of romanticism and post-frontier ideology, which is why it is no accident that so much environmentalist discourse takes its bearings from the wilderness these intellectual movements helped create. Although wilderness may today seem to be just one environmental concern among many, it in fact serves as the foundation for a long list of other such concerns that on their face seem quite remote from it. That is why its influence is so pervasive and, potentially, so insidious.

To gain such remarkable influence, the concept of wilderness had to become loaded with some of the deepest core values of the culture that created and idealized it: it had to become sacred. This possibility had been present in wilderness even in the days when it had been a place of spiritual danger and moral temptation. If Satan was there, then so was Christ, who had found angels as well as wild beasts during His sojourn in the desert. In the wilderness the boundaries between human and nonhuman, between natural and supernatural, had always seemed less certain than elsewhere. This was why the early Christian saints and mystics had often emulated Christ's desert retreat as they sought to experience for themselves the visions and spiritual testing He had endured. One might meet devils and run the risk of losing one's soul in such a place, but one might also meet God. For some that possibility was worth almost any price.

By the eighteenth century this sense of the wilderness as a landscape where the supernatural lay just beneath the surface was expressed in the doctrine of the sublime, a word whose modern usage has been so watered down by commercial hype and tourist advertising that it retains only a dim echo of its former power. (11) In the theories of Edmund Burke, Immanuel Kant, William Gilpin, and others, sublime landscapes were those rare places on earth where one had more chance than elsewhere to glimpse the face of God. (12) Romantics had a clear notion of where one could be most sure of having this experience. Although God might, of course, choose to show Himself anywhere, He would most often be found in those vast, powerful landscapes where one could not help feeling insignificant and being reminded of one's own mortality. Where were these sublime places? The eighteenth century catalog of their locations feels very familiar, for we still see and value landscapes as it taught us to do. God was on the mountaintop, in the chasm, in the waterfall, in the thundercloud, in the rainbow, in the sunset. One has only to think of the sites that Americans chose for their first national parks—Yellowstone, Yosemite, Grand Canyon, Rainier, Zion—to realize that virtually all of them fit one or more of these categories. Less sublime landscapes simply did not appear worthy of such protection; not until the 1940s, for instance, would the first swamp be honored, in Everglades National Park, and to this day there is no national park in the grasslands. (13)

Among the best proofs that one had entered a sublime landscape was the emotion it evoked. For the early romantic writers and artists who first began to celebrate it, the sublime was far from being a pleasurable experience. The classic description is that of William Wordsworth as he recounted climbing the Alps and crossing the Simplon Pass in his autobiographical poem "The Prelude." There, surrounded by crags and waterfalls, the poet felt himself literally to be in the presence of the divine—and experienced an emotion remarkably close to terror:

> The immeasurable height
> Of woods decaying, never to be decayed,
> The stationary blasts of waterfalls,
> And in the narrow rent at every turn
> Winds thwarting winds, bewildered and forlorn,
> The torrents shooting from the clear blue sky,
> The rocks that muttered close upon our ears,
> Black drizzling crags that spake by the way-side

> As if a voice were in them, the sick sight
> And giddy prospect of the raving stream,
> The unfettered clouds and region of the Heavens,
> Tumult and peace, the darkness and the light
> Were all like workings of one mind, the features
> Of the same face, blossoms upon one tree;
> Characters of the great Apocalypse,
> The types and symbols of Eternity,
> Of first, and last, and midst, and without end. (14)

This was no casual stroll in the mountains, no simple sojourn in the gentle lap of nonhuman nature. What Wordsworth described was nothing less than a religious experience, akin to that of the Old Testament prophets as they conversed with their wrathful God. The symbols he detected in this wilderness landscape were more supernatural than natural, and they inspired more awe and dismay than joy or pleasure. No mere mortal was meant to linger long in such a place, so it was with considerable relief that Wordsworth and his companion made their way back down from the peaks to the sheltering valleys. Lest you suspect that this view of the sublime was limited to timid Europeans who lacked the American know-how for feeling at home in the wilderness, remember Henry David Thoreau's 1846 climb of Mount Katahdin, in Maine. Although Thoreau is regarded by many today as one of the great American celebrators of wilderness, his emotions about Katahdin were no less ambivalent than Wordsworth's about the Alps.

> It was vast, Titanic, and such as man never inhabits. Some part of the beholder, even some vital part, seems to escape through the loose grating of his ribs as he ascends. He is more lone than you can imagine...Vast, Titanic, inhuman Nature has got him at disadvantage, caught him alone, and pilfers him of some of his divine faculty. She does not smile on him as in the plains. She seems to say sternly, why came ye here before your time? This ground is not prepared for you. Is it not enough that I smile in the valleys? I have never made this soil for thy feet, this air for thy breathing, these rocks for thy neighbors. I cannot pity nor fondle thee here, but forever relentlessly drive thee hence to where I am kind. Why seek me where I have not called thee, and then complain because you find me but a stepmother? (15)

This is surely not the way a modern backpacker or nature lover would describe Maine's most famous mountain, but that is because Thoreau's description owes as much to Wordsworth and other romantic contemporaries as to the rocks and clouds of Katahdin itself. His words took the physical mountain on which he stood and transmuted it into an icon of the sublime: a symbol of God's presence on earth. The power and the glory of that icon were such that only a prophet might gaze on it for long. In effect, romantics like Thoreau joined Moses and the children of Israel in Exodus when "they looked toward the wilderness, and behold, the glory of the Lord appeared in the cloud." (16)

But even as it came to embody the awesome power of the sublime, wilderness was also being tamed—not just by those who were building settlements in its midst but also by those who most celebrated its inhuman beauty. By the second half of the nineteenth century, the terrible awe that Wordsworth and Thoreau regarded as the appropriately pious stance to adopt in the presence of their mountaintop God was giving way to a much more comfortable, almost sentimental demeanor. As more and more tourists sought out the wilderness as a spectacle to be looked at and enjoyed for its great beauty, the sublime in effect became domesticated. The wilderness was still sacred, but the religious sentiments it evoked were more those of a pleasant parish church than those of a grand cathedral or a harsh desert retreat. The writer who best captures this late romantic sense of a domesticated sublime is undoubtedly John Muir, whose descriptions of Yosemite and the Sierra Nevada reflect none of the anxiety or terror one finds in earlier writers. Here he is, for instance, sketching on North Dome in Yosemite Valley:

> No pain here, no dull empty hours, no fear of the past, no fear of the future. These blessed mountains are so compactly filled with God's beauty, no petty personal hope or experience has room to be. Drinking this champagne water is pure pleasure, so is breathing the living air, and every movement of limbs is pleasure, while the body seems to feel beauty when exposed to it as it feels the campfire or sunshine, entering not by the eyes alone, but equally through all one's flesh like radiant heat, making a passionate ecstatic pleasure glow not explainable.

The emotions Muir describes in Yosemite could hardly be more different from Thoreau's on Katahdin or Wordsworth's on the Simplon Pass. Yet all three men are participating in the same cultural tradition and contributing to the same myth—the mountain as cathedral. The three may differ in the way they choose to express their piety—Wordsworth favoring an awe-filled bewilderment, Thoreau a stern loneliness, Muir a welcome ecstasy—but they agree completely about the church in which they prefer to worship. Muir's closing words on North Dome diverge from his older contemporaries only in mood, not in their ultimate content:

> Perched like a fly on this Yosemite dome, I gaze and sketch and bask, oftentimes settling down into dumb admiration without definite hope of ever learning much, yet with the longing, unresting effort that lies at the door of hope, humbly prostrate before the vast display of God's power, and eager to offer self-denial and renunciation with eternal toil to learn any lesson in the divine manuscript. (17)

Muir's "divine manuscript" and Wordsworth's "Characters of the great Apocalypse" are in fact pages from the same holy book. The sublime wilderness had ceased to be place of satanic temptation and become instead a sacred temple, much as it continues to be for those who love it today.

C

But the romantic sublime was not the only cultural movement that helped transform wilderness into a sacred American icon during the nineteenth century. No less important was the powerful romantic attraction of primitivism, dating back at least to of that the best antidote to the ills of an overly refined and civilized modern world was a return to simpler, more primitive living. In the United States, this was embodied most strikingly in the national myth of the frontier. The historian Frederick Jackson Turner wrote in 1893 the classic academic statement of this myth, but it had been part of American cultural traditions for well over a century. As Turner described the process, easterners and European immigrants, in moving to the wild unsettled lands of the frontier, shed the trappings of civilization, rediscovered their primitive racial energies, reinvented direct democratic institutions, and by reinfused themselves with a vigor, an independence, and a creativity that the source of American democracy and national character. Seen in this way, wild country became a place not just of religious redemption but of national renewal, the quintessential location for experiencing what it meant to be an American.

One of Turner's most provocative claims was that by the 1890s the frontier was passing away. Never again would "such gifts of free land offer themselves" to the American people. "The frontier has gone," he declared, "and with its going has closed the first period of American history." (18) Built into the frontier myth from its very beginning was the notion that this crucible of American identity was temporary and would pass away. Those who have celebrated the frontier have almost always looked backward as they did so, mourning an older, simpler, truer world that is about to disappear, forever. That world and all of its attractions, Turner said, depended on free land—on wilderness. Thus, in the myth of the vanishing frontier lay the seeds of wilderness preservation in the United States, for if wild land had been so crucial in the making of the nation, then surely one must save its last remnants as monuments to the American past—and as an insurance policy to protect its future. It is no accident that the movement to set aside national parks and wilderness areas began to gain real momentum at precisely the time that laments about the passing frontier reached their peak. To protect wilderness was in a very real sense to protect the nation's most sacred myth of origin.

Among the core elements of the frontier myth was the powerful sense among certain groups of Americans that wilderness was the last bastion of rugged individualism. Turner tended to stress communitarian themes when writing frontier history, asserting that Americans in primitive conditions had been forced to band together with their neighbors to form communities and democratic institutions. For other writers, however, frontier democracy for communities was less compelling than frontier freedom for individuals. (19) By fleeing to the outer margins of settled land and society—so the story ran—an individual could escape the confining strictures of civilized life. The mood among writers who celebrated frontier individualism was almost always nostalgic; they lamented not just a lost way of life but the passing of the heroic men who had embodied that life. Thus Owen Wister in the introduction to his classic 1902 novel *The Virginian* could write of "a vanished world" in which "the horseman, the cow-puncher, the last romantic figure upon our soil" rode only "in his historic yesterday" and would "never come again." For Wister, the cowboy was a man who gave his word and kept it ("Wall

Street would have found him behind the times"), who did not talk lewdly to women ("Newport would have thought him old-fashioned"), who worked and played hard, and whose "ungoverned hours did not unman him." (20) Theodore Roosevelt wrote with much the same nostalgic fervor about the "fine, manly qualities" of the "wild rough-rider of the plains." No one could be more heroically masculine, thought Roosevelt, or more at home in the western wilderness:

> There he passes his days, there he does his life-work, there, when he meets death, he faces it as he has faced many other evils, with quiet, uncomplaining fortitude. Brave, hospitable, hardy, and adventurous, he is the grim pioneer of our race; he prepares the way for the civilization from before whose face he must himself disappear. Hard and dangerous though his existence is, it has yet a wild attraction that strongly draws to it his bold, free spirit. (21)

This nostalgia for a passing frontier way of life inevitably implied ambivalence, if not downright hostility, toward modernity and all that it represented. If one saw the wild lands of the frontier as freer, truer, and more natural than other, more modern places, then one was also inclined to see the cities and factories of urban-industrial civilization as confining, false, and artificial. Owen Wister looked at the post-frontier "transition" that had followed "the horseman of the plains," and did not like what he saw: "a shapeless state, a condition of men and manners as unlovely as is that moment in the year when winter is gone and spring not come, and the face of Nature is ugly." (22) In the eyes of writers who shared Wister's distaste for modernity, civilization contaminated its inhabitants and absorbed them into the faceless, collective, contemptible life of the crowd. For all of its troubles and dangers, and despite the fact that it must pass away, the frontier had been a better place. If civilization was to be redeemed, it would be by men like the Virginian who could retain their frontier virtues even as they made the transition to post-frontier life.

The mythic frontier individualist was almost always masculine in gender: here, in the wilderness, a man could be a real man, the rugged individual he was meant to be before civilization sapped his energy and threatened his masculinity. Wister's contemptuous remarks about Wall Street and Newport suggest what he and many others of his generation believed—that the comforts and seductions of civilized life were especially insidious for men, who all too easily became emasculated by the feminizing tendencies of civilization. More often than not, men who felt this way came, like Wister and Roosevelt, from elite class backgrounds. The curious result was that frontier nostalgia became an important vehicle for expressing a peculiarly bourgeois form of antimodernism. The very men who most benefited from urban-industrial capitalism were among those who believed they must escape its debilitating effects. If the frontier was passing, then men who had the means to do so should preserve for themselves some remnant of its wild landscape so that they might enjoy the regeneration and renewal that came from sleeping under the stars, participating in blood sports, and living off the land. The frontier might be gone, but the frontier experience could still be had if only wilderness were preserved.

Thus the decades following the Civil War saw more and more of the nation's wealthiest citizens seeking out wilderness for themselves. The elite passion for wild land took many forms: enormous estates in the Adirondacks and elsewhere (disingenuously called "camps" despite their many servants and amenities), cattle ranches for would-be rough riders on the Great Plains, guided big-game hunting trips in the Rockies, and luxurious resort hotels wherever railroads pushed their way into sublime landscapes. Wilderness suddenly emerged as the landscape of choice for elite tourists, who brought with them strikingly urban ideas of the countryside through which they traveled. For them, wild land was not a site for productive labor and not a permanent home; rather, it was a place of recreation. One went to the wilderness not as a producer but as a consumer, hiring guides and other backcountry residents who could serve as romantic surrogates for the rough riders and hunters of the frontier if one was willing to overlook their new status as employees and servants of the rich. In just this way, wilderness came to embody the national frontier myth, standing for the wild freedom of America's past and seeming to represent a highly attractive natural alternative to the ugly artificiality of modern civilization. The irony, of course, was that in the process wilderness came to reflect the very civilization its devotees sought to escape. Ever since the nineteenth century, celebrating wilderness has been an activity mainly for well-to-do city folks. Country people generally know far too much about working the land to regard unworked land as their ideal. In contrast, elite urban tourists and wealthy sportsmen projected their leisure-time frontier fantasies onto the American landscape and so created wilderness in their own image.

There were other ironies as well. The movement to set aside national parks and wilderness areas followed hard on the heels of the final Indian wars, in which the prior human inhabitants of these areas were rounded up and moved onto reservations. The myth of the wilderness as "virgin " uninhabited land had always been especially cruel when seen from the perspective of the Indians who had once called that land home. Now they were forced to move elsewhere, with the result that tourists could safely enjoy the illusion that they were seeing their nation in its pristine, original state, in the new morning of God's own creation. (23) Among the things that most marked the new national parks as reflecting a post-frontier consciousness was the relative absence of human violence within their boundaries. The actual frontier had often been a place of conflict, in which invaders and invaded fought for control of land and resources. Once set aside within the fixed and carefully policed boundaries of the modern bureaucratic state, the wilderness lost its savage image and became safe: a place more of reverie than of revulsion or fear. Meanwhile, its original inhabitants were kept out by dint of force, their earlier uses of the land redefined as inappropriate or even illegal. To this day, for instance, the Blackfeet continue to be accused of "poaching" on the lands of Glacier National Park that originally belonged to them and that were ceded by treaty only with the proviso that they be permitted to hunt there. (24)

The removal of Indians to create an "uninhabited wilderness"—uninhabited as never before in the human history of the place—reminds us just how invented, just how constructed, the American wilderness really is. To return to my opening argument: there is nothing natural about the concept of wilderness. It is entirely a creation of the culture that holds it dear, a product of the very history it seeks to deny. Indeed, one of the most striking proofs of the cultural invention of wilderness is its thoroughgoing erasure of the history from which it sprang. In virtually all of its manifestations, wilderness represents a flight from history. Seen as the original garden, it is a place outside of time, from which human beings had to be ejected before the fallen world of history could properly begin. Seen as the frontier, it is a savage world at the dawn of civilization, whose transformation represents the very beginning of the national historical epic. Seen as the bold landscape of frontier heroism, it is the place of youth and childhood, into which men escape by abandoning their pasts and entering a world of freedom where the constraints of civilization fade into memory. Seen as the sacred sublime, it is the home of a God who transcends history by standing as the One who remains untouched and unchanged by time's arrow. No matter what the angle from which we regard it, wilderness offers us the illusion that we can escape the cares and troubles of the world in which our past has ensnared us. (25)

This escape from history is one reason why the language we use to talk about wilderness is often permeated with spiritual and religious values that reflect human ideals far more than the material world of physical nature. Wilderness fulfills the old romantic project of secularizing Judeo-Christian values so as to make a new cathedral not in some petty human building but in God's own creation, Nature itself. Many environmentalists who reject traditional notions of the Godhead and who regard themselves as agnostics or even atheists nonetheless express feelings tantamount to religious awe when in the presence of wilderness—a fact that testifies to the success of the romantic project. Those who have no difficulty seeing God as the expression of our human dreams and desires nonetheless have trouble recognizing that in a secular age Nature can offer precisely the same sort of mirror.

Thus it is that wilderness serves as the unexamined foundation on which so many of the quasi-religious values of modern environmentalism rest. The critique of modernity that is one of environmentalism's most important contributions to the moral and political discourse of our time more often than not appeals, explicitly or implicitly, to wilderness as the standard against which to measure the failings of our human world. Wilderness is the natural, unfallen antithesis of an unnatural civilization that has lost its soul. It is a place of freedom in which we can recover the true selves we have lost to the corrupting influences of our artificial lives. Most of all, it is the ultimate landscape of authenticity. Combining the sacred grandeur of the sublime with the primitive simplicity of the frontier, it is the place where we can see the world as it really is, and so know ourselves as we really are—or ought to be.

But the trouble with wilderness is that it quietly expresses and reproduces the very values its devotees seek to reject. The flight from history that is very nearly the core of wilderness represents the false hope of an escape from responsibility, the illusion that we can somehow wipe clean the slate of our past and return to the tabula rasa that supposedly existed before we began to leave our marks on the world. The dream of an unworked natural landscape is very much the fantasy of people who have never themselves had to work the land to make a living— urban folk for whom food comes from a supermarket or a restaurant instead of a field, and for whom the wooden houses in which they live and work apparently have no meaningful connection to the forests in which trees grow and die. Only people whose relation to the land was already alienated could hold up wilderness as a model for human life in nature, for the romantic ideology of wilderness leaves precisely nowhere for human beings actually to make their living from the land.

This, then, is the central paradox: wilderness embodies a dualistic vision in which the human is entirely outside the natural. If we allow ourselves to believe that nature, to be true, must also be wild, then our very presence in nature represents its fall. The place where we are is the place where nature is not. If this is so—if by definition wilderness leaves no place for human beings, save perhaps as contemplative sojourners enjoying their leisurely reverie in God's natural cathedral—then also by definition it can offer no solution to the environmental and other problems that confront us. To the extent that we celebrate wilderness as the measure with which we judge civilization, we reproduce the dualism that sets humanity and nature at opposite poles. We thereby leave ourselves little hope of discovering what an ethical, sustainable, honorable human place in nature might actually look like.

Worse: to the extent that we live in an urban-industrial civilization but at the same time pretend to ourselves that our real home is in the wilderness, to just that extent we give ourselves permission to evade responsibility for the lives we actually lead. We inhabit civilization while holding some part of ourselves—what we imagine to be the most precious part—aloof from its entanglements. We work our nine-to-five jobs in its institutions, we eat its food, we drive its cars (not least to reach the wilderness), we benefit from the intricate and all too invisible networks with which it shelters us, all the while pretending that these things are not an essential part of who we are. By imagining that our true home is in the wilderness, we forgive ourselves the homes we actually inhabit. In its flight from history, in its siren song of escape, in its reproduction of the dangerous dualism that sets human beings outside of nature—in all of these ways, wilderness poses a serious threat to responsible environmentalism at the end of the twentieth century.

By now I hope it is clear that my criticism in this essay is not directed at wild nature per se, or even at efforts to set aside large tracts of wild land, but rather at the specific habits of thinking that flow from this complex cultural construction called wilderness. It is not the things we label as wilderness that are the problem—for nonhuman nature and large tracts of the natural world do deserve protection—but rather what we ourselves mean when we use the label. Lest one doubt how pervasive these habits of thought actually are in contemporary environmentalism, let me list some of the places where wilderness serves as the ideological underpinning for environmental concerns that might otherwise seem quite remote from it. Defenders of biological diversity, for instance, although sometimes appealing to more utilitarian concerns, often point to "untouched" ecosystems as the best and richest repositories of the undiscovered species we must certainly try to protect. Although at first blush an apparently more "scientific" concept than wilderness, biological diversity in fact invokes many of the same sacred values, which is why organizations like the Nature Conservancy have been so quick to employ it as an alternative to the seemingly fuzzier and more problematic concept of wilderness. There is a paradox here, of course. To the extent that biological diversity (indeed, even wilderness itself) is likely to survive in the future only by the most vigilant and self-conscious management of the ecosystems that sustain it, the ideology of wilderness is potentially in direct conflict with the very thing it encourages us to protect. (26) The most striking instances of this have revolved around "endangered species," which serve as vulnerable symbols of biological diversity while at the same time standing as surrogates for wilderness itself. The terms of the Endangered Species Act in the United States have often meant that those hoping to defend pristine wilderness have had to rely on a single endangered species like the spotted owl to gain legal standing for their case—thereby making the full power of the sacred land inhere in a single numinous organism whose habitat then becomes the object of intense debate about appropriate management and use. (27) The ease with which antienvironmental forces like the wise-use movement have attacked such single-species preservation efforts suggests the vulnerability of strategies like these.

Perhaps partly because our own conflicts over such places and organisms have become so messy, the convergence of wilderness values with concerns about biological diversity and endangered species has helped produce a deep fascination for remote ecosystems, where it is easier to imagine that nature might somehow be "left alone" to flourish by its own pristine devices. The classic example is the tropical rain forest, which since the 1970s has become the most powerful modern icon of unfallen, sacred land—a veritable Garden of Eden—for many Americans and Europeans. And yet protecting the rain forest in the eyes of First World environmentalists all too often means protecting it from the people who live there. Those who seek to preserve such "wilderness" from the activities of native peoples run the risk of reproducing the same tragedy—being forceably removed from an ancient home—that befell American Indians. Third World countries face massive environmental problems and deep social conflicts, but these are not likely to be solved by a cultural myth that encourages us to "preserve" peopleless landscapes that have not existed in such places for millennia. At its worst, as environmentalists are beginning to realize, exporting American notions of wilderness in this way can become an unthinking and self-defeating form of cultural imperialism. (28)

Perhaps the most suggestive example of the way that wilderness thinking can underpin other environmental concerns has emerged in the recent debate about "global change." In 1989 the journalist Bill McKibben published a book entitled *The End of Nature*, in which he argued that the prospect of global climate change as a result of unintentional human manipulation of the atmosphere means that nature as we once knew it no longer exists. (29) Whereas earlier generations inhabited a natural world that remained more or less unaffected by their actions, our own generation is uniquely different. We and our children will henceforth live in a biosphere completely altered by our own activity, a planet in which the human and the natural can no longer be distinguished, because the one has overwhelmed the other. In McKibben's view, nature has died, and we are responsible for killing it. "The planet," he declares, "is utterly different now." (30)

But such a perspective is possible only if we accept the wilderness premise that nature, to be natural, must also be pristine—remote from humanity and untouched by our common past. In fact, everything we know about environmental history suggests that people have been manipulating the natural world on various scales for as long as we have a record of their passing. Moreover, we have unassailable evidence that many of the environmental changes we now face also occurred quite apart from human intervention at one time or another in the earth's past. (31) The point is not that our current problems are trivial, or that our devastating effects on the earth's ecosystems should be accepted as inevitable or "natural." It is rather that we seem unlikely to make much progress in solving these problems if we hold up to ourselves as the mirror of nature a wilderness we ourselves cannot inhabit.

To do so is merely to take to a logical extreme the paradox that was built into wilderness from the beginning: if nature dies because we enter it, then the only way to save nature is to kill ourselves. The absurdity of this proposition flows from the underlying dualism it expresses. Not only does it ascribe greater power to humanity that we in fact possess—physical and biological nature will surely survive in some form or another long after we ourselves have gone the way of all flesh—but in the end it offers us little more than a self-defeating counsel of despair. The tautology gives us no way out: if wild nature is the only thing worth saving, and if our mere presence destroys it, then the sole solution to our own unnaturalness, the only way to protect sacred wilderness from profane humanity, would seem to be suicide. It is not a proposition that seems likely to produce very positive or practical results.

And yet radical environmentalists and deep ecologists all too frequently come close to accepting this premise as a first principle. When they express, for instance, the popular notion that our environmental problems began with the invention of agriculture, they push the human fall from natural grace so far back into the past that all of civilized history becomes a tale of ecological declension. Earth First! founder Dave Foreman captures the familiar parable succinctly when he writes,

> Before agriculture was midwifed in the Middle East, humans were in the wilderness. We had no concept of "wilderness" because everything was wilderness and we were a part of it. But with irrigation ditches, crop surpluses, and permanent villages, we became apart from the natural world... Between the wilderness that created us and the civilization created by us grew an ever-widening rift. (32)

In this view the farm becomes the first and most important battlefield in the long war against wild nature, and all else follows in its wake. From such a starting place, it is hard not to reach the conclusion that the only way human beings can hope to live naturally on earth is to follow the hunter-gatherers back into a wilderness Eden and abandon virtually everything that civilization has given us. It may indeed turn out that civilization will end in ecological collapse or nuclear disaster, whereupon one might expect to find any human survivors returning to a way of life closer to that celebrated by Foreman and his followers. For most of us, though, such a debacle would be cause for regret, a sign that humanity had failed to fulfill its own promise and failed to honor its own highest values—including those of the deep ecologists.

In offering wilderness as the ultimate hunter-gatherer alternative to civilization, Foreman reproduces an extreme but still easily recognizable version of the myth of frontier primitivism. When he writes of his fellow Earth Firsters that "we believe we must return to being animal, to glorying in our sweat, hormones, tears, and blood" and that "we struggle against the modern compulsion to become dull, passionless androids," he is following in the footsteps of Owen Wister. (33) Although his arguments give primacy to defending biodiversity and the autonomy of wild nature, his prose becomes most passionate when he speaks of preserving "the wilderness experience." His own ideal "Big Outside" bears an uncanny resemblance to that of the frontier myth: wide open spaces and virgin land with no trails, no signs, no facilities, no maps, no guides, no rescues, no modern equipment. Tellingly, it is a land where hardy travelers can support themselves by hunting with "primitive weapons (bow and arrow, atlatl, knife, sharp rock)." (34) Foreman claims that "the primary value of wilderness is not as a proving ground for young Huck Finns and Annie Oakleys," but his heart is with Huck and Annie all the same. He admits that "preserving a quality wilderness experience for the human visitor, letting her or him flex Paleolithic muscles or seek visions, remains a tremendously important secondary purpose." (35) Just so does Teddy Roosevelt's rough rider live on in the greener garb of a new age.

However much one may be attracted to such a vision, it entails problematic consequences. For one, it makes wilderness the locus for an epic struggle between malign civilization and benign nature, compared with which all other social, political, and moral concerns seem trivial. Foreman writes, "The preservation of wildness and native diversity is the most important issue. Issues directly affecting only humans pale in comparison." (36) Presumably so do any environmental problems whose victims are mainly people, for such problems usually surface in landscapes that have already "fallen" and are no longer wild. This would seem to exclude from the radical environmentalist agenda problems of occupational health and safety in industrial settings, problems of toxic waste exposure on "unnatural" urban and agricultural sites, problems of poor children poisoned by lead exposure in the inner city, problems of famine and poverty and human suffering in the "overpopulated" places of the earth—problems, in short, of environmental justice. If we set too high a stock on wilderness, too many other corners of the earth become less than natural and too many other people become less than human, thereby giving us permission not to care much about their suffering or their fate.

It is no accident that these supposedly inconsequential environmental problems affect mainly poor people, for the long affiliation between wilderness and wealth means that the only poor people who count when wilderness is the issue are hunter-gatherers, who presumably do not consider themselves to be poor in the first place. The dualism at the heart of wilderness encourages its advocates to conceive of its protection as a crude conflict between the "human" and the "nonhuman"—or, more often, between those who value the nonhuman and those who do not. This in turn tempts one to ignore crucial differences among humans and the complex cultural and historical reasons why different peoples may feel very differently about the meaning of wilderness.

Why, for instance, is the "wilderness experience" so often conceived as a form of recreation best enjoyed by those whose class privileges give them the time and resources to leave their jobs behind and "get away from it all?" Why does the protection of wilderness so often seem to pit urban recreationists against rural people who actually earn their living from the land (excepting those who sell goods and services to the tourists themselves)? Why in the debates about pristine natural areas are "primitive" peoples idealized, even sentimentalized, until the moment they do something unprimitive, modern, and unnatural, and thereby fall from environmental grace? What are the consequences of a wilderness ideology that devalues productive labor and the very concrete knowledge that comes from working the land with one's own hands? (37) All of these questions imply conflicts among different groups of people, conflicts that are obscured behind the deceptive clarity of "human" vs. "nonhuman." If in answering these knotty questions we resort to so simplistic an opposition, we are almost certain to ignore the very subtleties and complexities we need to understand.

But the most troubling cultural baggage that accompanies the celebration of wilderness has less to do with remote rain forests and peoples than with the ways we think about ourselves—we American environmentalists who quite rightly worry about the future of the earth and the threats we pose to the natural world. Idealizing a distant wilderness too often means not idealizing the environment in which we actually live, the landscape that for better or worse we call home. Most of our most serious environmental problems start right here, at home, and if we are to solve those problems, we need an environmental ethic that will tell us as much about using nature as about not using it. The wilderness dualism tends to cast any use as abuse, and thereby denies us a middle ground in which responsible use and non-use might attain some kind of balanced, sustainable relationship. My own belief is that only by exploring this middle ground will we learn ways of imagining a better world for all of us: humans and nonhumans, rich people and poor, women and men, First Worlders and Third Worlders, white folks and people of color, consumers and producers—a world better for humanity in all of its diversity and for all the rest of nature too. The middle ground is where we actually live. It is where we—all of us, in our different places and ways—make our homes.

That is why, when I think of the times I myself have come closest to experiencing what I might call the sacred in nature, I often find myself remembering wild places much closer to home. I think, for instance, of a small pond near my house where water bubbles up from limestone springs to feed a series of pools that rarely freeze in winter and so play home to waterfowl that stay here for the protective warmth even on the coldest of winter days, gliding silently through streaming mists as the snow falls from gray February skies. I think of a November evening long ago when I found myself on a Wisconsin hilltop in rain and dense fog, only to have the setting sun break through the clouds to cast an otherworldly golden light on the misty farms and woodlands below, a scene so unexpected and joyous that I lingered past dusk so as not to miss any part of the gift that had come my way. And I think perhaps most especially of the blown-out, bankrupt farm in the sand country of central Wisconsin where Aldo Leopold and his family tried one of the first American experiments in ecological restoration, turning ravaged and infertile soil into carefully tended ground where the human and the nonhuman could exist side by side in relative harmony. What I celebrate about such places is not just their wildness, though that certainly is among their most important qualities; what I celebrate even more is that they remind us of the wildness in our own backyards, of the nature that is all around us if only we have eyes to see it.

Indeed, my principal objection to wilderness is that it may teach us to be dismissive or even contemptuous of such humble places and experiences. Without our quite realizing it, wilderness tends to privilege some parts of nature at the expense of others. Most of us, I suspect, still follow the conventions of the romantic sublime in finding the mountaintop more glorious than the plains, the ancient forest nobler than the grasslands, the mighty canyon more inspiring than the humble marsh. Even John Muir, in arguing against those who sought to dam his beloved Hetch Hetchy valley in the Sierra Nevada, argued for alternative dam sites in the gentler valleys of the foothills—a preference that had nothing to do with nature and everything with the cultural traditions of the sublime. (38) Just as problematically, our frontier traditions have encouraged Americans to define "true" wilderness as requiring very large tracts of roadless land—what Dave Foreman calls "The Big Outside." Leaving aside the legitimate empirical question in conservation biology of how large a tract of land must be before a given species can reproduce on it, the emphasis on big wilderness reflects a romantic frontier belief that one hasn't really gotten away from civilization unless one can go for days at a time without encountering another human being. By teaching us to fetishize sublime places and wide open country, these peculiarly American ways of thinking about wilderness encourage us to adopt too high a standard for what counts as "natural." If it isn't hundreds of square miles big, if it doesn't give us God's eye views or grand vistas, if it doesn't permit us the illusion that we are alone on the planet, then it really isn't natural. It's too small, too plain, or too crowded to be authentically wild.

In critiquing wilderness as I have done in this essay, I'm forced to confront my own deep ambivalence about its meaning for modern environmentalism. On the one hand, one of my own most important environmental ethics is that people should always be conscious that they are part of the natural world, inextricably tied to the ecological systems that sustain their lives. Any way of looking at nature that encourages us to believe we are separate from nature—as wilderness tends to do—is likely to reinforce environmentally irresponsible behavior. On the other band, I also think it no less crucial for us to recognize and honor nonhuman nature as a world we did not create, a world with its own independent, nonhuman reasons for being as it is. The autonomy of nonhuman nature seems to me an indispensable corrective to human arrogance. Any way of looking at nature that helps us remember—as wilderness also tends to do—that the interests of people are not necessarily identical to those of every other creature or of the earth itself is likely to foster responsible behavior. To the extent that wilderness has served as an important vehicle for articulating deep mom values regarding our obligations and responsibilities to the nonhuman world, I would not want to jettison the contributions it has made to our culture's ways of thinking about nature.

C

If the core problem of wilderness is that it distances us too much from the very things it teaches us to value, then the question we must ask is what it can tell us about home, the place where we actually live. How can we take the positive values we associate with wilderness and bring them closer to home? I think the answer to this question will come by broadening our sense of the otherness that wilderness seeks to define and protect. In reminding us of the world we did not make, wilderness can teach profound feelings of humility and respect as we confront our fellow beings and the earth itself. Feelings like these argue for the importance of self-awareness and self criticism as we exercise our own ability to transform the world around us, helping us set responsible limits to human mastery—which without such limits too easily becomes human hubris.

Wilderness is the place where, symbolically at least, we try to withhold our power to dominate. Wallace Stegner once wrote of

> the special human mark, the special record of human passage, that distinguishes man from all other species. It is rare enough among men, impossible to any other form of life. It is simply the deliberate and chosen refusal to make any marks at all...We are the most dangerous species of life on the planet, and every other species, even the earth itself, has cause to fear our power to exterminate. But we are also the only species which, when it chooses to do so, will go to great effort to save what it might destroy. (39)

The myth of wilderness, which Stegner knowingly reproduces in these remarks, is that we can somehow leave nature untouched by our passage. By now it should be clear that this for the most part is an illusion. But Stegner's deeper message then becomes all the more compelling. If living in history means that we cannot help leaving marks on a fallen world, then the dilemma we face is to decide what kinds of marks we wish to leave. It is just here that our cultural traditions of wilderness remain so important. In the broadest sense, wilderness teaches us to ask whether the Other must always bend to our will, and, if not, under what circumstances it should be allowed to flourish without our intervention. This is surely a question worth asking about everything we do, and not just about the natural world.

When we visit a wilderness area, we find ourselves surrounded by plants and animals and physical landscapes whose otherness compels our attention. In forcing us to acknowledge that they are not of our making, that they have little or no need of our continued existence, they recall for us a creation far greater than our own. In the wilderness, we need no reminder that a tree has its own reasons for being, quite apart from us. The same is less true in the gardens we plant and tend ourselves: there it is far easier to forget the otherness of the tree. (40) Indeed, one could almost measure wilderness by the extent to which our recognition of its otherness requires a conscious, willed act on our part. The romantic legacy means that wilderness is more a state of mind than a fact of nature, and the state of mind that today most defines wilderness is wonder. The striking power of the wild is that wonder in the face of it requires no act of will, but forces itself upon us—as an expression of the nonhuman world experienced through the lens of our cultural history—as proof that ours is not the only presence in the universe.

Wilderness gets us into trouble only if we imagine that this experience of wonder and otherness is limited to the remote corners of the planet, or that it somehow depends on pristine landscapes we ourselves do not inhabit. Nothing could be more misleading. The tree in the garden is in reality no less other, no less worthy of our wonder and respect, than the tree in an ancient forest that has never known an ax or a saw—even though the tree in the forest reflects a more intricate web of ecological relationships. The tree in the garden could easily have sprung from the same seed as the tree in the forest, and we can claim only its location and perhaps its form as our own. Both trees stand apart from us; both share our common world. The special power of the tree in the wilderness is to remind us of this fact. It can teach us to recognize the wildness we did not see in the tree we planted in our own backyard. By seeing the otherness in that which is most unfamiliar, we can learn to see it too in that which at first seemed merely ordinary. If wilderness can do this—if it can help us perceive and respect a nature we had forgotten to recognize as natural—then it will become part of the solution to our environmental dilemmas rather than part of the problem.

This will only happen, however, if we abandon the dualism that sees the tree in the garden as artificial—completely fallen and unnatural—and the tree in the wilderness as natural—completely pristine and wild. Both trees in some ultimate sense are wild; both in a practical sense now depend on our management and care. We are responsible for both, even though we can claim credit for neither. Our challenge is to stop thinking of such things according to set of bipolar moral scales in which the human and the nonhuman, the unnatural and the natural, the fallen and the unfallen, serve as our conceptual map for understanding and valuing the world. Instead, we need to embrace the full continuum of a natural landscape that is also cultural, in which the city, the suburb, the pastoral, and the wild each has its proper place, which we permit ourselves to celebrate without needlessly denigrating the others. We need to honor the Other within and the Other next door as much as we do the exotic Other that lives far away—a lesson that applies as much to people as it does to (other) natural things. In particular, we need to discover a common middle ground in which all of these things, from the city to the wilderness, can somehow be encompassed in the word "home." Home, after all, is the place where finally we make our living. It is the place for which we take responsibility, the place we try to sustain so we can pass on what is best in it (and in ourselves) to our children. (41)

The task of making a home in nature is what Wendell Berry has called "the forever unfinished lifework of our species." "The only thing we have to preserve nature with" he writes, "is culture; the only thing we have to preserve wildness with is domesticity." (42) Calling a place home inevitably means that we will use the nature we find in it, for there can be no escape from manipulating and working and even killing some parts of nature to make our home. But if we acknowledge the autonomy and otherness of the things and creatures around us—an autonomy our culture has taught us to label with the word "wild"—then we will at least think carefully about the uses to which we put them, and even ask if we should use them at all. just so can we still join Thoreau in declaring that "in Wildness is the preservation of the World," for wildness (as opposed to wilderness) can be found anywhere: in the seemingly tame fields and woodlots of Massachusetts, in the cracks of a Manhattan sidewalk, even in the cells of our own bodies. As Gary Snyder has wisely said, "A person with a clear heart and open mind can experience the wilderness anywhere on earth. It is a quality of one's own consciousness. The planet is a wild place and always will be." (43) To think ourselves capable of causing "the end of nature" is an act of great hubris, for it means forgetting the wildness that dwells everywhere within and around us.

Learning to honor the wild—learning to remember and acknowledge the autonomy of the other—means striving for critical self-consciousness in all of our actions. It means the deep reflection and respect must accompany each act of use, and means too that we must always consider the possibility of non-use. It means looking at the part of nature we intend to turn toward our own ends and asking whether we can use it again and again and again—sustainably—without its being diminished in the process. It means never imagining that we can flee into a mythical wilderness to escape history and the obligation to take responsibility for our own actions that history inescapably entails. Most of all, it means practicing remembrance and gratitude, for thanksgiving is the simplest and most basic of ways for us to recollect the nature, the culture, and the history that have come together to make the world as we know it. If wildness can stop being (just) out there and start being (also) in here, if it can start being as humane as it is natural, then perhaps we can get on with the unending task of struggling to live rightly in the world—not just in the garden, not just in the wilderness, but in the home that encompasses them both. ■

Notes

1. Henry David Thoreau, "Walking," *The Works of Thoreau*, ed. Henry S. Canby (Boston, Massachusetts: Houghton Mifflin, 1937), p. 672.
2. *Oxford English Dictionary*, s.v. "wilderness"; see also Roderick Nash, *Wilderness and the American Mind*, 3rd ed. (New Haven, Connecticut: Yale Univ. Press, 1982), pp. 1–22; and Max Oelsehlaeger, *The Idea of Wilderness: From Prehistory to the Age of Ecology* (New Haven, Connecticut: Yale Univ. Press, 1991).
3. Exodus 32:1–35, KJV.
4. Exodus 14:3, KJV.
5. Mark 1:12–13, KJV; see also Matthew 4:1–11; Luke 4:1–13
6. John Milton, "Paradise Lost," *John Milton: Complete Poems and Major Prose*, ed. Merritt Y. Hughes (New York: Odyssey Press, 1957), pp. 280–81, lines 131–42
7. I have discussed this theme at length in "Landscapes of Abundance and Scarcity," in Clyde Milner et al., eds., *Oxford History of the American West* (New York: Oxford Univ. Press, 1994), pp. 603–37. The classic work on the Puritan "city on a hill" in colonial New England is Perry Miller, *Errand into the Wilderness* (Cambridge, Massachusetts: Harvard Univ. Press, 1956).
8. John Muir, My First Summer in the Sierra (1911), reprinted in John Muir: *The Eight Wilderness Discovery Books* (London, England: Diadem; Seattle, Washington: Mountaineers, 1992), P. 211.
9. Alfred Route, *National Parks: The American Experience*, 2nd ed. (Lincoln: Univ. of Nebraska Press, 1987)

10. John Muir, The Yosemite (1912), reprinted in *John Muir: Eight Wilderness Discovery Books*, P. 715.
11. Scholarly work on the sublime is extensive. Among the most important studies are Samuel Monk, *The Sublime: A Study of Critical Theories in XVIII Century England* (New York: Modern Language Association, 1935); Basil Willey, *The Eighteenth-Century Background: Studies on the Idea of Nature in the Thought of the Period* (London, England: Chattus and Windus, 1949); Marjorie Hope Nicolson, *Mountain Gloom and Mountain Glory: The Development of the Aesthetics of the Infinite* (Ithaca, New York: Cornell Univ. Press, 1959); Thomas Weiskel, *The Romantic Sublime: Studies in the Structure and Psychology of Transcendence* (Baltimore, Maryland: Johns Hopkins Univ. Press, 1976); Barbara Novak, *Nature and Culture: American Landscape Painting, 1825–1875* (New York: Oxford Univ. Press, 1980).
12. The classic works are Immanuel Kant, *Observations on the Feeling of the Beautiful and Sublime* (1764), trans. John T. Goldthwait (Berkeley: Univ. of California Press, 1960); Edmund Burke, *A Philosophical Enquiry into the Origin of Our Ideas of the Sublime and Beautiful*, ed. James T. Boulton (1958; Notre Dame, Indiana: Univ. of Notre Dame Press, 1968); William Gilpin, *Three Essays: On Picturesque Beauty; on Picturesque Travel; and on Sketching Landscape* (London, England, 1803)
13. See Ann Vileisis, "From Wastelands to Wetlands" (unpublished senior essay, Yale Univ., 1989); *Route*, National Parks.
14. William Wordsworth, "The Prelude," bk. 6, in Thomas Hutchinson, ed., *The Poetical Works of Wordsworth* (London, England: Oxford Univ. Press, 1936), p. 536.
15. Henry David Thoreau, *The Maine Woods* (1864), in Henry David Thoreau (New York: Library of America, 1985), pp. 640–41.
16. Exodus 16:10, KJV.
17. John Muir, *My First Summer in the Sierra*, p. 238. Part of the difference between these descriptions may reflect the landscapes the three authors were describing. In his essay, "Reinventing Common Nature: Yosemite and Mount Rushmore—A Meandering Tale of a Double Nature," Kenneth Olwig notes that early American travelers experienced Yosemite as much through the aesthetic tropes of the pastoral as through those of the sublime. The ease with which Muir celebrated the gentle divinity of the Sierra Nevada had much to do with the pastoral qualities of the landscape he described. See Olwig, "Reinventing Common Nature: Yosemite and Mount Rushmore—A Meandering Tale of a Double Nature," *Uncommon Ground: Toward Reinventing Nature*, ed. William Cronon (New York: W. W. Norton & Co, 1995), PP 379–408.
18. Frederick Jackson Turner, *The Frontier in American History* (New York: Henry Holt, 1920), pp. 37–38.
19. Richard Slotkin has made this observation the linchpin of his comparison between Turner and Theodore Roosevelt. See Slotkin, *Gunfighter Nation: The Myth of the Frontier in Twentieth-Century America* (New York: Atheneum, 1992), pp. 29–62.

C

20. Owen Wister, *The Virginian: A Horseman of the Plains* (New York: Macmillan, 1902), pp. viii–ix.
21. Theodore Roosevelt, *Ranch Life and the Hunting Trail* (1888; New York: Century, 1899), p. 100.
22. Wister, Virginian, p. x.
23. On the many problems with this view, see William M. Denevan, "The Pristine Myth: The Landscape of the Americas in 1492," *Annals of the Association of American Geographers* 82 (1992): 369–85
24. Louis Warren, "The Hunter's Came: Poachers, Conservationists, and Twentieth-Century America" (Ph.D. diss., Yale University, 1994).
25. Wilderness also lies at the foundation of the Clementsian ecological concept of the climax. See Michael Barbour, "Ecological Fragmentation in the Fifties" in Cronon, Uncommon Ground, pp. 233–55, and William Cronon, "Introduction: In Search of Nature," in Cronon, *Uncommon Ground*, pp. 23–56.
26. On the many paradoxes of having to manage wilderness in order to maintain the appearance of an unmanaged landscape, see John C. Hendee et al., *Wilderness Management*, USDA Forest Service Miscellaneous Publication No. 1365 (Washington, D.C.: Government Printing Office, 1978).
27. See James Proctor, "Whose Nature?: The Contested Moral Terrain of Ancient Forests," in Cronon, *Uncommon Ground*, pp. 269–97
28. See Candace Slater, "Amazonia as Edenic Narrative," in Cronon, *Uncommon Ground*, pp. 114–31. This argument has been powerfully made by Ramachandra Cuba, "Radical American Environmentalism: A Third World Critique," *Environmental Ethics* 11 (1989): 71–83
29. Bill McKibben, *The End of Nature* (New York: Random House, 1989).
30. McKibben, *The End of Nature*, p. 49
31. Even comparable extinction rates have occurred before, though we surely would not want to emulate the Cretaceous-Tertiary boundary extinctions as a model for responsible manipulation of the biosphere!
32. Dave Foreman, *Confessions of an Eco-Warrior* (New York: Harmony Books, 1991, p. 69 (italics in original)). For a sampling of other writings by followers of deep ecology and/or Earth First!, see Michael Tobias, ed., *Deep Ecology* (San Diego, California: Avant Books, 1984); Bill Devall and George Sessions, *Deep Ecology: Living as if Nature Mattered* (Salt Lake City, Utah: Gibbs Smith, 1985); Michael Tobias, *After Eden: History, Ecology, and Conscience* (San Diego, California: Avant Books, 1985); Dave Foreman and Bill Haywood, eds., *Ecodefense: A Field Guide to Monkey Wrenching*, 2nd ed. (Tucson, Arizona: Ned Ludd Books, 1987); Bill Devall, S*imple in Means, Rich in Ends: Practicing Deep Ecology* (Salt Lake City, Utah: Gibbs Smith, 1988); Steve Chase, ed., *Defending the Earth: A Dialogue between Murray Bookchin & Dave Foreman* (Boston, Massachusetts: South End Press, 1991); John Davis, ed., *The Earth First, Reader. Ten Years of Radical Environmentalism* (Salt Lake City, Utah: Gibbs Smith, 1991); Bill Devall, *Living Richly in an Age of Limits: Using Deep Ecology for an Abundant Life* (Salt Lake, City, Utah: Gibbs Smith, 1993); Michael E. Zimmerman et al., eds., E*nvironmental*

Philosophy: From Animal Rights to Radical Ecology (Englewood Cliffs, New Jersey: Prentice-Hall, 1993). A useful survey of the different factions of radical environmentalism can be found in Carolyn Merchant, *Radical Ecology: The Search for a Livable World* (New York: Routledge, 1992). For a very interesting critique of this literature (first published in the anarchist newspaper Fifth Estate), see George Bradford, *How Deep is Deep Ecology?* (Ojai, California: Times Change Press, 1989).

33. Foreman, *Confessions of an Eco-Warrior*, P. 34.
34. Foreman, *Confessions of an Eco-Warrior*, p. 65. See also Dave Foreman and Howie Wolke, *The Big Outside: A Descriptive Inventory of the Big Wilderness Areas of the U.S.* (Tucson, Arizona: Ned Ludd Books, 1989).
35. Foreman, *Confessions of an Eco-Warrior*, p. 63
36. Foreman, *Confessions of an Eco-Warrior*, p. 27
37. See Richard White, "'Are You an Environmentalist or Do You Work for a Living?': Work and Nature," in Cronon, *Uncommon Ground*, pp. 171–85. Compare its analysis of environmental knowledge through work with Jennifer Price's analysis of environmental knowledge through consumption. It is not much of an exaggeration to say that the wilderness experience is essentially consumerist in its impulses.
38. Compare with Muir, Yosemite, in *John Muir: Eight Wilderness Discovery Books*, p. 714
39. Wallace Stegner, ed., *This Is Dinosaur: Echo Park Country and Its Magic Rivers* (New York: Knopf, 1955), P. 17 (italics in original).
40. Katherine Hayles helped me see the importance of this argument.
41. Analogous arguments can be found in John Brinckerhoff Jackson, "Beyond Wilderness," *A Sense of Place, a Sense of Time* (New Haven, Connecticut: Yale Univ. Press, 1994), pp. 71–91, and in the wonderful collection of essays by Michael Pollan, *Second Nature: A Gardener's Education* (New York: Atlantic Monthly Press, 1991).
42. Wendell Berry, *Home Economics* (San Francisco, California: North Point, 1987), pp. 138, 143.
43. Gary Snyder, quoted in *New York Times*, "Week in Review," 18 September 1994, p. 6.

C

AUTHOR PROFILE

William Cronon (born September 11, 1954) is an environmental historian who works to understand the relationship between humans and the nonhuman world. In particular, he is interested in how our view of history shapes how we understand the world and the decisions we make about it: better histories, he argues, will lead to better environmentalist practices. Much of Cronon's work focuses on the history of the American West, as seen in *Under an Open Sky: Rethinking America's Western Past* (1992) and *Uncommon Ground: Rethinking the Human Place in Nature* (1995). "The Trouble with Wilderness" was originally published in *The New York Times* and has been reprinted widely. The article generated controversy among traditional environmentalists for attacking highly valued concepts like "wilderness" and "nature." For this many saw Cronon as attacking environmentalism in general and betraying academic environmental studies in particular. Cronon, however, asserts that environmental scholars also have a responsibility to public activism and that environmentalist goals can only be met if all citizens have access to current environmental thought. Cronon currently is a Research Professor of History, Geography, and Environmental studies at the University of Wisconsin–Madison. He is working on a history of Portage, Wisconsin, spanning the end of the last Ice Age to the present.

The War Photo No One Would Publish

By Torie Rose DeGhett

When Kenneth Jarecke photographed an Iraqi man burned alive, he thought it would change the way Americans saw the Gulf War. But the media wouldn't run the picture.

The Iraqi soldier died attempting to pull himself up over the dashboard of his truck. The flames engulfed his vehicle and incinerated his body, turning him to dusty ash and blackened bone. In a photograph taken soon afterward, the soldier's hand reaches out of the shattered windshield, which frames his face and chest. The colors and textures of his hand and shoulders look like those of the scorched and rusted metal around him. Fire has destroyed most of his features, leaving behind a skeletal face, fixed in a final rictus. He stares without eyes.

On February 28, 1991, Kenneth Jarecke stood in front of the charred man, parked amid the carbonized bodies of his fellow soldiers, and photographed him. At one point, before he died this dramatic mid-retreat death, the soldier had had a name. He'd fought in Saddam Hussein's army and had a rank and an assignment and a unit. He might have been devoted to the dictator who sent him to occupy Kuwait and fight the Americans. Or he might have been an unlucky young man with no prospects, recruited off the streets of Baghdad.

Jarecke took the picture just before a ceasefire officially ended Operation Desert Storm—the U.S.-led military action that drove Saddam Hussein and his troops out of Kuwait, which they had annexed and occupied the previous August. The image and its anonymous subject might have come to symbolize the Gulf War. Instead, it went unpublished in the United States, not because of military obstruction but because of editorial choices.

It's hard to calculate the consequences of a photograph's absence. But sanitized images of warfare, *The Atlantic*'s Conor Friedersdorf argues, make it "easier…to accept bloodless language" such as 1991 references to "surgical strikes" or modern-day terminology like "kinetic warfare." The Vietnam War, in contrast, was notable for its catalog of chilling and iconic war photography. Some images, like Ron Haeberle's pictures of the My Lai massacre, were initially kept from the public, but other violent images—Nick Ut's scene of child napalm victims and Eddie Adams's photo of a Vietcong man's execution—won Pulitzer Prizes and had a tremendous impact on the outcome of the war.

Not every gruesome photo reveals an important truth about conflict and combat. Last month, *The New York Times* decided—for valid ethical reasons—to remove images of dead passengers from an online story about Flight MH-17 in Ukraine and replace them with photos of mechanical wreckage. Sometimes though, omitting an image means shielding the public from the messy, imprecise consequences of a war—making the coverage incomplete, and even deceptive.

In the case of the charred Iraqi soldier, the hypnotizing and awful photograph ran against the popular myth of the Gulf War as a "video-game war"—a conflict made humane through precision bombing and night-vision equipment. By deciding not to publish it, *Time* magazine and the Associated Press denied the public the opportunity to confront this unknown enemy and consider his excruciating final moments.

The image was not entirely lost. *The Observer* in the United Kingdom and *Libération* in France both published it after the American media refused. Many months later, the photo also appeared in *American Photo*, where it stoked some controversy, but came too late to have a significant impact. All of this surprised the photographer, who had assumed the media would be only too happy to challenge the popular narrative of a clean, uncomplicated war. "When you have an image that disproves that myth," he says today, "then you think it's going to be widely published."

1992 © Kenneth Jarecke (Contact Press Images)

"He was fighting to save his life to the very end, till he was completely burned up," Jarecke says of the man he photographed. "He was trying to get out of that truck."

"Let me say up front that I don't like the press," one Air Force officer declared, starting a January 1991 press briefing on a blunt note. The military's bitterness toward the media was in no small part a legacy of the Vietnam coverage decades before. By the time the Gulf War started, the Pentagon had developed access policies that drew on press restrictions used in the U.S. wars in Grenada and Panama in the 1980s. Under this so-called "pool" system, the military grouped print, TV, and radio reporters together with cameramen and photojournalists and sent these small teams on orchestrated press junkets, supervised by Public Affairs Officers (PAOs) who kept a close watch on their charges.

By the time Operation Desert Storm began in mid-January 1991, Kenneth Jarecke had decided he no longer wanted to be a combat photographer—a profession, he says, that "dominates your life." But after Saddam Hussein's invasion of Kuwait in August 1990, Jarecke developed a low opinion of the photojournalism coming out of Desert Shield, the pre-war operation to build up troops and equipment in the Gulf. "It was one picture after another of a sunset with camels and a tank," he says. War was approaching and Jarecke says he saw a clear need for a different kind of coverage. He felt he could fill that void.

After the U.N.'s January 15, 1991 deadline for Iraq's withdrawal from Kuwait came and went, Jarecke, now certain he should go, convinced *Time* magazine to send him to Saudi Arabia. He packed up his cameras and shipped out from Andrews Air Force Base on January 17—the first day of the aerial bombing campaign against Iraq.

Out in the field with the troops, Jarecke recalls, "anybody could challenge you," however absurdly and without reason. He remembers straying 30 feet away from his PAO and having a soldier bark at him, "What are you doing?" Jarecke retorted, "What do you *mean* what am I doing?"

Recounting the scene two decades later, Jarecke still sounds exasperated. "Some first lieutenant telling me, you know, where I'm gonna stand. *In the middle of the desert.*"

As the war picked up in early February, PAOs accompanied Jarecke and several other journalists as they attached to the Army XVIII Airborne Corps and spent two weeks at the Saudi-Iraqi border doing next to nothing. That didn't mean nothing was happening—just that they lacked access to the action.

During the same period, military photojournalist Lee Corkran was embedding with the U.S. Air Force's 614th Tactical Fighter Squadron in Doha, Qatar, and capturing their aerial bombing campaigns. He was there to take pictures for the Pentagon to use as it saw fit—not primarily for media use. In his images, pilots look over their shoulders to check on other planes. Bombs hang off the jets' wings, their sharp-edged darkness contrasting with the soft colors of the clouds and desert below. In the distance, the curvature of the earth is visible. On missions, Corkran's plane would often flip upside down at high speed as the pilots dodged missiles, leaving silvery streaks in the sky. Gravitational forces multiplied the weight of his cameras—so much so that if he had ever needed to eject from the plane, his equipment could have snapped his neck. This was the air war that comprised most of the combat mission in the Gulf that winter.

The scenes Corkran witnessed weren't just off-limits to Jarecke; they were also invisible to viewers in the United States, despite the rise of 24-hour reporting during the conflict. Gulf War television coverage, as Ken Burns wrote at the time, felt cinematic and often sensational, with "distracting theatrics" and "pounding new theme music," as if "the war itself might be a wholly owned subsidiary of television."

Some of the most widely seen images of the air war were shot not by photographers, but rather by unmanned cameras attached to planes and laser-guided bombs. Grainy shots and video footage of the roofs of targeted buildings, moments before impact, became a visual signature of a war that was deeply associated with phrases like "smart bombs" and "surgical strike." The images were taken at an altitude that erased the human presence on the ground. They were black-and-white shots, some with bluish or greenish casts. One from February 1991, published in the photo book *In The Eye of Desert Storm* by the now-defunct Sygma photo agency, showed a bridge that was being used as an Iraqi supply route. In another, black plumes of smoke from French bombs blanketed an Iraqi Republican Guard base like ink blots. None of them looked especially violent.

The hardware-focused coverage of the war removed the empathy that Jarecke says is crucial in photography, particularly photography that's meant to document death and violence. "A photographer without empathy," he remarks, "is just taking up space that could be better used."

In late February, during the war's final hours, Jarecke and the rest of his press pool drove across the desert, each of them taking turns behind the wheel. They had been awake for several days straight. "We had no idea where we were. We were in a convoy," Jarecke recalls. He dozed off.

When he woke up, they had parked and the sun was about to rise. It was almost 6 o'clock in the morning. The group received word that a ceasefire was a few hours away, and Jarecke remembers another member of his pool cajoling the press officer into abandoning the convoy and heading toward Kuwait City.

The group figured they were in southern Iraq, somewhere in the desert about 70 miles away from Kuwait City. They began driving toward Kuwait, hitting Highway 8 and stopping to take pictures and record video footage. They came upon a jarring scene: burned-out Iraqi military convoys and incinerated corpses. Jarecke sat in the truck, alone with Patrick Hermanson, a public affairs officer. He moved to get out of the vehicle with his cameras.

Hermanson found the idea of photographing the scene distasteful. When I asked him about the conversation, he recalled asking Jarecke, "What do you need to take a picture of that for?" Implicit in his question was a judgment: There was something dishonorable about photographing the dead.

"I'm not interested in it either," Jarecke recalls replying. He told the officer that he didn't want his mother to see his name next to photographs of corpses. "But if I don't take pictures like these, people like my mom will think war is what they see in movies." As Hermanson remembers, Jarecke added, "It's what I came here to do. It's what I have to do."

"He let me go," Jarecke recounts. "He didn't try to stop me. He could have stopped me because it was technically not allowed under the rules of the pool. But he didn't stop me and I walked over there."

More than two decades later, Hermanson notes that Jarecke's resulting picture was "pretty special." He doesn't need to see the photograph to resurrect the scene in his mind. "It's seared into my memory," he says, "as if it happened yesterday."

The incinerated man stared back at Jarecke through the camera's viewfinder, his blackened arm reaching over the edge of the truck's windshield. Jarecke recalls that he could "see clearly how precious life was to this guy, because he was fighting for it. He was fighting to save his life to the very end, till he was completely burned up. He was trying to get out of that truck."

He wrote later that year in *American Photo* magazine that he "wasn't thinking at all about what was there; if I had thought about how horrific the guy looked I wouldn't have been able to make the picture." Instead, he maintained his emotional remove by attending to the more prosaic and technical elements of photography. He kept himself steady; he concentrated on the focus. The sun shone in through the rear of the destroyed truck and backlit his subject. Another burned body lay directly in front of the vehicle, blocking a close-up shot, so Jarecke used the full 200mm zoom lens on his Canon EOS-1.

In his other shots of the same scene, it is apparent that the soldier could never have survived, even if he had pulled himself up out of the driver's seat and through the window. The desert sand around the truck is scorched. Bodies are piled behind the vehicle, indistinguishable from one another. A lone, burned man lies face down in front of the truck, everything incinerated except the soles of his bare feet. In another photograph, a man lies spread-eagle on the sand, his body burned to the point of disintegration, but his face mostly intact and oddly serene. A dress shoe lies next to his body.

The group continued on across the desert, passing through more stretches of highway littered with the same fire-ravaged bodies and vehicles. Jarecke and his pool were possibly the first members of the Western media to come across these scenes, which appeared along what eventually became known as the Highway of Death, sometimes referred to as the Road to Hell.

The retreating Iraqi soldiers had been trapped. They were frozen in a traffic jam, blocked off by the Americans, by Mutla Ridge, by a minefield. Some fled on foot; the rest were strafed by American planes that swooped overhead, passing again and again to destroy all the vehicles. Milk vans, fire trucks, limousines, and one bulldozer appeared in the wreckage alongside armored cars and trucks, and T-55 and T-72 tanks. Most vehicles held fully loaded, but rusting, Kalashnikov variants. According to descriptions from reporters like *The New York Times*' R.W. Apple and the *Observer*'s Colin Smith, amid the plastic mines, grenades, ammunition, and gas masks, a quadruple-barreled anti-aircraft gun stood crewless and still pointing skyward. Personal items, like a photograph of a child's birthday party and broken crayons, littered the ground beside weapons and body parts. The body count never seems to have been determined, although the BBC puts it in the "thousands."

"In one truck," wrote Colin Smith in a March 3 dispatch for the *Observer*, "the radio had been knocked out of the dashboard but was still wired up and faintly picking up some plaintive Arabic air which sounded so utterly forlorn I thought at first it must be a cry for help."

Following the February 28 ceasefire that ended Desert Storm, Jarecke's film roll with the image of the incinerated soldier reached the Joint Information Bureau in Dhahran, Saudi Arabia, where the military coordinated and corralled the press, and where pool editors received and filed stories and photographs. At that point, with the operation over, the photograph would not have needed to pass through a security screening, says Maryanne Golon, who was the on-site photo editor for *Time* in Saudi Arabia and is now director of photography for *The Washington Post*. Despite the obviously shocking content, she tells me she reacted like an editor in work mode. She selected it, without debate or controversy among the pool editors, to be scanned and transmitted. The image made its way back to the editors' offices in New York City.

Jarecke also made his way from Saudi Arabia to New York. Passing through Heathrow Airport on a layover, he bought a copy of the March 3 edition of the *Observer*. He opened it to find his photograph on page 9, printed at the top across eight columns under the heading, "The real face of war."

That weekend in March, when the *Observer*'s editors made the final decision to print the image, every magazine in North America made the opposite choice. Jarecke's photograph did not even appear on the desks of most U.S. newspaper editors (the exception being *The New York Times*, which had a photo wire service subscription but nonetheless declined to publish the image). The photograph was entirely absent from American media until far past the time when it was relevant to ground reporting from Iraq and Kuwait. Golon says she wasn't surprised by this, even though she'd chosen to transmit it to the American press. "I didn't think there was any chance they'd publish it," she says.

Apart from the *Observer*, the only major news outlet to run the Iraqi soldier's photograph at the time was the Parisian news daily *Libération*, which ran it on March 4. Both newspapers refrained from putting the image on the front page, though they ran it prominently inside. But Aidan Sullivan, the pictures editor for the British *Sunday Times*, told the *British Journal of Photography* on March 14 that he had opted instead for a wide shot of the carnage: a desert highway littered with rubble. He challenged the *Observer*: "We would have thought our readers could work out that a lot of people had died in those vehicles. Do you have to show it to them?"

"There were 1,400 [Iraqi soldiers] in that convoy, and every picture transmitted until that one came, two days after the event, was of debris, bits of equipment," Tony McGrath, the *Observer*'s pictures editor, was quoted as saying in the same article. "No human involvement in it at all; it could have been a scrapyard. That was some dreadful censorship."

The media took it upon themselves to "do what the military censorship did not do," says Robert Pledge, the head of the Contact Press Images photojournalism agency that has represented Jarecke since the 1980s. The night they received the image, Pledge tells me, editors at the Associated Press' New York City offices pulled the photo entirely from the wire service, keeping it off the desks of virtually all of America's newspaper editors. It is unknown precisely how, why, or by whom the AP's decision was handed down.

Vincent Alabiso, who at the time was the executive photo editor for the AP, later distanced himself from the wire service's decision. In 2003, he admitted to *American Journalism Review* that the photograph ought to have gone out on the wire and argued that such a photo would today.

Yet the AP's reaction was repeated at *Time* and *Life*. Both magazines briefly considered the photo, unofficially referred to as "Crispy," for publication. The photo departments even drew up layout plans. *Time*, which had sent Jarecke to the Gulf in the first place, planned for the image to accompany a story about the Highway of Death.

"We fought like crazy to get our editors to let us publish that picture," former photo director Michele Stephenson tells me. As she recalls, Henry Muller, the managing editor, told her, "*Time* is a family magazine." And the image was, when it came down to it, just too disturbing for the outlet to publish. It was, to her recollection, the only instance during the Gulf War where the photo department fought but failed to get an image into print.

James Gaines, the managing editor of *Life*, took responsibility for the ultimate decision not to run Jarecke's image in his own magazine's pages, despite photo director Peter Howe's push to give it a double-page spread. "We thought that this was the stuff of nightmares," Gaines told Ian Buchanan of the *British Journal of Photography* in March 1991. "We have a fairly substantial number of children who read *Life* magazine," he added. Even so, the photograph was published later that month in one of *Life*'s special issues devoted to the Gulf War—not typical reading material for the elementary-school set.

Stella Kramer, who worked as a freelance photo editor for *Life* on four special-edition issues on the Gulf War, tells me that the decision to not publish Jarecke's photo was less about protecting readers than preserving the dominant narrative of the good, clean war. Flipping through 23-year-old issues, Kramer expresses clear distaste at the editorial quality of what she helped to create. The magazines "were very sanitized," she says. "So, that's why these issues are all basically just propaganda." She points out the picture on the cover of the February 25 issue: a young blond boy dwarfed by the American flag he's holding. "As far as Americans were concerned," she remarks, "nobody ever died."

"If pictures tell stories," Lee Corkran tells me, "the story should have a point. So if the point is the utter annihilation of people who were in retreat and all the charred bodies...if that's your point, then that's true. And so be it. I mean, war is ugly. It's hideous." To Corkran, who was awarded the Bronze Star for his Gulf War combat photography, pictures like Jarecke's tell important stories about the effects of American and allied airpower. Even Patrick Hermanson, the public affairs officer who originally protested the idea of taking pictures of the scene, now says the media should not have censored the photo.

The U.S. military has now abandoned the pool system it used in 1990 and 1991, and the Internet has changed the way photos reach the public. Even if the AP did refuse to send out a photo, online outlets would certainly run it, and no managing editor would be able to prevent it from being shared across various social platforms, or being the subject of extensive op-ed and blog commentary. If anything, today's controversies often center on the vast abundance of disturbing photographs, and the difficulty of putting them in a meaningful context.

Some have argued that showing bloodshed and trauma repeatedly and sensationally can dull emotional understanding. But never showing these images in the first place guarantees that such an understanding will never develop. "Try to imagine, if only for a moment, what your intellectual, political, and ethical world would be like if you had never seen a photograph," author Susie Linfield asks in *The Cruel Radiance*, her book on photography and political violence. Photos like Jarecke's not only show that bombs drop on real people; they also make the public feel accountable. As David Carr wrote in *The New York Times* in 2003, war photography has "an ability not just to offend the viewer, but to implicate him or her as well."

As an angry 28-year-old Jarecke wrote in *American Photo* in 1991: "If we're big enough to fight a war, we should be big enough to look at it." ■

AUTHOR PROFILE

Torie Rose DeGhett is a freelance journalist who writes about foreign affairs and global politics. Her work has appeared in *The Atlantic*, *The Guardian*, *Foreign Policy*, *The Awl*, *The LA Review of Books*, and *Guernica*. She has written about foreign affairs and global politics, and is a recent graduate of the MA program at Columbia University's Graduate School of Journalism.

Principles of Environmental Justice

Delegates to the First National People of Color Environmental Leadership Summit held on October 24–27, 1991, in Washington, D.C., drafted and adopted 17 principles of Environmental Justice. Since then, The Principles have served as a defining document for the growing grassroots movement for environmental justice.

WE, THE PEOPLE OF COLOR, gathered together at this multinational People of Color Environmental Leadership Summit, to begin to build a national and international movement of all peoples of color to fight the destruction and taking of our lands and communities, do hereby re-establish our spiritual interdependence to the sacredness of our Mother Earth; to respect and celebrate each of our cultures, languages and beliefs about the natural world and our roles in healing ourselves; to ensure environmental justice; to promote economic alternatives which would contribute to the development of environmentally safe livelihoods; and, to secure our political, economic and cultural liberation that has been denied for over 500 years of colonization and oppression, resulting in the poisoning of our communities and land and the genocide of our peoples, do affirm and adopt these Principles of Environmental Justice:

1. **Environmental Justice** affirms the sacredness of Mother Earth, ecological unity and the interdependence of all species, and the right to be free from ecological destruction.
2. **Environmental Justice** demands that public policy be based on mutual respect and justice for all peoples, free from any form of discrimination or bias.
3. **Environmental Justice** mandates the right to ethical, balanced and responsible uses of land and renewable resources in the interest of a sustainable planet for humans and other living things.
4. **Environmental Justice** calls for universal protection from nuclear testing, extraction, production and disposal of toxic/hazardous wastes and poisons and nuclear testing that threaten the fundamental right to clean air, land, water, and food.
5. **Environmental Justice** affirms the fundamental right to political, economic, cultural and environmental self-determination of all peoples.
6. **Environmental Justice** demands the cessation of the production of all toxins, hazardous wastes, and radioactive materials, and that all past and current producers be held strictly accountable to the people for detoxification and the containment at the point of production.
7. **Environmental Justice** demands the right to participate as equal partners at every level of decision-making, including needs assessment, planning, implementation, enforcement and evaluation.

8. **Environmental Justice** affirms the right of all workers to a safe and healthy work environment without being forced to choose between an unsafe livelihood and unemployment. It also affirms the right of those who work at home to be free from environmental hazards.

9. **Environmental Justice** protects the right of victims of environmental injustice to receive full compensation and reparations for damages as well as quality health care.

10. **Environmental Justice** considers governmental acts of environmental injustice a violation of international law, the Universal Declaration On Human Rights, and the United Nations Convention on Genocide.

11. **Environmental Justice** must recognize a special legal and natural relationship of Native Peoples to the U.S. government through treaties, agreements, compacts, and covenants affirming sovereignty and self-determination.

12. **Environmental Justice** affirms the need for urban and rural ecological policies to clean up and rebuild our cities and rural areas in balance with nature, honoring the cultural integrity of all our communities, and provided fair access for all to the full range of resources.

13. **Environmental Justice** calls for the strict enforcement of principles of informed consent, and a halt to the testing of experimental reproductive and medical procedures and vaccinations on people of color.

14. **Environmental Justice** opposes the destructive operations of multi-national corporations.

15. **Environmental Justice** opposes military occupation, repression and exploitation of lands, peoples and cultures, and other life forms.

16. **Environmental Justice** calls for the education of present and future generations which emphasizes social and environmental issues, based on our experience and an appreciation of our diverse cultural perspectives.

17. **Environmental Justice** requires that we, as individuals, make personal and consumer choices to consume as little of Mother Earth's resources and to produce as little waste as possible; and make the conscious decision to challenge and reprioritize our lifestyles to ensure the health of the natural world for present and future generations. ■

AUTHOR PROFILE

As grassroots organizations began challenging America's largest environmental groups about the racism inherent in their platforms, activists Charles Lee, Benjamin Chavis, Richard Moore, Pat Bryant, Dana Alston, Donna Chavis, and Robert Bullard planned the First National People of Color Environmental Leadership Summit. It was held in Washington, D.C. in October of 1991. The summit sought to address concerns that "mainstream" environmentalist movements failed to recognize historic environmental efforts led by native people and people of color. These movements also overlooked the disproportionate amounts of toxicity, denial of access to land, and other environmental injustices experienced by people of color. 700 activists and observers attended the summit, and the result was an environmental justice platform that recognized that the social and economic experiences of people of color are inseparable from their experiences of the environment. Fair environmental policy, the delegates argued, must necessarily include awareness of race, class, and gender. The "Principles of Environmental Justice" created at this conference were adopted by many grassroots environmental movements as well by President Bill Clinton's 1994 executive order on the environment, and continue to influence environmental justice thinking today.

Living Like Weasels

By Annie Dillard

I

A weasel is wild. Who knows what he thinks? He sleeps in his underground den, his tail draped over his nose. Sometimes he lives in his den for two days without leaving. Outside, he stalks rabbits, mice, muskrats, and birds, killing more bodies than he can eat warm, and often dragging the carcasses home. Obedient to instinct, he bites his prey at the neck, either splitting the jugular vein at the throat or crunching the brain at the base of the skull, and he does not let go. One naturalist refused to kill a weasel who was socketed into his hand deeply as a rattlesnake. The man could in no way pry the tiny weasel off, and he had to walk half a mile to water, the weasel dangling from his palm, and soak him off like a stubborn label.

And once, says Ernest Thompson Seton—once, a man shot an eagle out of the sky. He examined the eagle and found the dry skull of a weasel fixed by the jaws to his throat. The supposition is that the eagle had pounced on the weasel and the weasel swiveled and bit as instinct taught him, tooth to neck, and nearly won. I would like to have seen that eagle from the air a few weeks or months before he was shot: was the whole weasel still attached to his feathered throat, a fur pendant? Or did the eagle eat what he could reach, gutting the living weasel with his talons before his breast, bending his beak, cleaning the beautiful airborne bones?

II

I have been reading about weasels because I saw one last week. I startled a weasel who startled me, and we exchanged a long glance.

Twenty minutes from my house, through the woods by the quarry and across the highway, is Hollins Pond, a remarkable piece of shallowness, where I like to go at sunset and sit on a tree trunk. Hollins Pond is also called Murray's Pond; it covers two acres of bottomland near Tinker Creek with six inches of water and six thousand lily pads. In winter, brown-and-white steers stand in the middle of it, merely dampening their hooves; from the distant shore they look like miracle itself, complete with miracle's nonchalance. Now, in summer, the steers are gone. The water lilies have blossomed and spread to a green horizontal plane that is terra firma to plodding blackbirds, and tremulous ceiling to black leeches, crayfish, and carp.

This is, mind you, suburbia. It is a five-minute walk in three directions to rows of houses, though none is visible here. There's a 55-mph highway at one end of the pond, and a nesting pair of wood ducks at the other. Under every bush is a muskrat hole or a beer can. The far end is an alternating series of fields and woods, fields and woods, threaded everywhere with motorcycle tracks—in whose bare clay wild turtles lay eggs.

So, I had crossed the highway, stepped over two low barbed-wire fences, and traced the motorcycle path in all gratitude through the wild rose and poison ivy of the pond's shoreline up into high grassy fields. Then I cut down through the woods to the mossy fallen tree where I sit. This tree is excellent. It makes a dry, upholstered bench at the upper, marshy end of the pond, a plush jetty raised from the thorny shore between a shallow blue body of water and a deep blue body of sky.

The sun had just set. I was relaxed on the tree trunk, ensconced in the lap of lichen, watching the lily pads at my feet tremble and part dreamily over the thrusting path of a carp. A yellow bird appeared to my right and flew behind me. It caught my eye; I swiveled around—and the next instant, inexplicably, I was looking down at a weasel, who was looking up at me.

III

Weasel! I'd never seen one wild before. He was ten inches long, thin as a curve, a muscled ribbon, brown as fruitwood, soft-furred, alert. His face was fierce, small and pointed as a lizard's; he would have made a good arrowhead. There was just a dot of chin, maybe two brown hairs' worth, and then the pure white fur began that spread down his underside. He had two black eyes I didn't see, any more than you see a window.

The weasel was stunned into stillness as he was emerging from beneath an enormous shaggy wild rose bush four feet away. I was stunned into stillness twisted backward on the tree trunk. Our eyes locked, and someone threw away the key.

Our look was as if two lovers, or deadly enemies, met unexpectedly on an overgrown path when each had been thinking of something else: a clearing blow to the gut. It was also a bright blow to the brain, or a sudden beating of brains, with all the charge and intimate grate of rubbed balloons. It emptied our lungs. It felled the forest, moved the fields, and drained the pond; the world dismantled and tumbled into that black hole of eyes. If you and I looked at each other that way, our skulls would split and drop to our shoulders. But we don't. We keep our skulls. So.

He disappeared. This was only last week, and already I don't remember what shattered the enchantment. I think I blinked, I think I retrieved my brain from the weasel's brain, and tried to memorize what I was seeing, and the weasel felt the yank of separation, the careening splash-down into real life and the urgent current of instinct. He vanished under the wild rose. I waited motionless, my mind suddenly full of data and my spirit with pleadings, but he didn't return.

Please do not tell me about "approach-avoidance conflicts." I tell you I've been in that weasel's brain for sixty seconds, and he was in mine. Brains are private places, muttering through unique and secret tapes—but the weasel and I both plugged into another tape simultaneously, for a sweet and shocking time. Can I help it if it was a blank?

What goes on in his brain the rest of the time? What does a weasel think about? He won't say. His journal is tracks in clay, a spray of feathers, mouse blood and bone: uncollected, unconnected, loose leaf, and blown.

IV

I would like to learn, or remember, how to live. I come to Hollins Pond not so much to learn how to live as, frankly, to forget about it. That is, I don't think I can learn from a wild animal how to live in particular—shall I suck warm blood, hold my tail high, walk with my footprints precisely over the prints of my hands?—but I might learn something of mindlessness, something of the purity of living in the physical sense and the dignity of living without bias or motive. The weasel lives in necessity and we live in choice, hating necessity and dying at the last ignobly in its talons. I would like to live as I should, as the weasel lives as he should. And I suspect that for me the way is like the weasel's: open to time and death painlessly, noticing everything, remembering nothing, choosing the given with a fierce and pointed will.

V

I missed my chance. I should have gone for the throat. I should have lunged for that streak of white under the weasel's chin and held on, held on through mud and into the wild rose, held on for a dearer life. We could live under the wild rose wild as weasels, mute and uncomprehending. I could very calmly go wild. I could live two days in the den, curled, leaning on mouse fur, sniffing bird bones, blinking, licking, breathing musk, my hair tangled in the roots of grasses. Down is a good place to go, where the mind is single. Down is out, out of your ever-loving mind and back to your careless senses. I remember muteness as a prolonged and giddy fast, where every moment is a feast of utterance received. Time and events are merely poured, unremarked, and ingested directly, like blood pulsed into my gut through a jugular vein. Could two live that way? Could two live under the wild rose, and explore by the pond, so that the smooth mind of each is as everywhere present to the other, and as received and as unchallenged, as falling snow?

We could, you know. We can live any way we want. People take vows of poverty, chastity, and obedience—even of silence—by choice. The thing is to stalk your calling in a certain skilled and supple way, to locate the most tender and live spot and plug into that pulse. This is yielding, not fighting. A weasel doesn't "attack" anything; a weasel lives as he's meant to, yielding at every moment to the perfect freedom of single necessity.

VI

I think it would be well, and proper, and obedient, and pure, to grasp your one necessity and not let it go, to dangle from it limp wherever it takes you. Then even death, where you're going no matter how you live, cannot you part. Seize it and let it seize you up aloft even, till your eyes burn out and drop; let your musky flesh fall off in shreds, and let your very bones unhinge and scatter, loosened over fields, over fields and woods, lightly, thoughtless, from any height at all, from as high as eagles. ■

AUTHOR PROFILE

Annie Dillard (born 1945) is a graduate of Hollins College and the author of numerous works of creative nonfiction, poetry, memoirs, narrative essays, and stories. Her works include *Pilgrim at Tinker Creek,The Writing Life* (1989), *Living by Fiction* (1982), and *An American Childhood.* Dillard is the recipient of two Pulitzer Prizes for general nonfiction and of grants from the National Endowment for the Arts, the MacArthur Foundation, and the Guggenheim Foundation.

Learning to Read and Write

By Frederick Douglass

I lived in Master Hugh's family about seven years. During this time, I succeeded in learning to read and write. In accomplishing this, I was compelled to resort to various stratagems. I had no regular teacher. My mistress, who had kindly commenced to instruct me, had, in compliance with the advice and direction of her husband, not only ceased to instruct, but had set her face against my being instructed by anyone else. It is due, however, to my mistress to say of her, that she did not adopt this course of treatment immediately. She at first lacked the depravity indispensable to shutting me up in mental darkness. It was at least necessary for her to have some training in the exercise of irresponsible power, to make her equal to the task of treating me as though I were a brute.

My mistress was, as I have said, a kind and tender-hearted woman; and in the simplicity of her soul she commenced, when I first went to live with her, to treat me as she supposed one human being ought to treat another. In entering upon the duties of a slaveholder, she did not seem to perceive that I sustained to her the relation of a mere chattel, and that for her to treat me as a human being was not only wrong, but dangerously so. Slavery proved as injurious to her as it did to me. When I went there, she was a pious, warm, and tender-hearted woman. There was no sorrow or suffering for which she had not a tear. She had bread for the hungry, clothes for the naked, and comfort for every mourner that came within her reach. Slavery soon proved its ability to divest her of these heavenly qualities. Under its influence, the tender heart became stone, and the lamb-like disposition gave way to one of tiger-like fierceness. The first step in her downward course was in her ceasing to instruct me. She now commenced to practice her husband's precepts. She finally became even more violent in her opposition than her husband himself. She was not satisfied with simply doing as well as he had commanded; she seemed anxious to do better. Nothing seemed to make her more angry than to see me with a newspaper. She seemed to think that here lay the danger. I have had her rush at me with a face made all up of fury, and snatch from me a newspaper, in a manner that fully revealed her apprehension. She was an apt woman; and a little experience soon demonstrated, to her satisfaction, that education and slavery were incompatible with each other.

From this time I was most narrowly watched. If I was in a separate room any considerable length of time, I was sure to be suspected of having a book, and was at once called to give an account of myself. All this, however, was too late. The first step had been taken. Mistress, in teaching me the alphabet, had given me the inch, and no precaution could prevent me from taking the ell.

The plan which I adopted, and the one by which I was most successful, was that of making friends of all the little white boys whom I met in the street. As many of these as I could, I converted into teachers. With their kindly aid, obtained at different times and in different places, I finally succeeded in learning to read. When I was sent to errands, I always took my book with me, and by doing one part of my errand quickly, I found time to get a lesson before my return. I used also to carry bread with me, enough of which was always in the house, and to which I was always welcome; for I was much better off in this regard than many of the poor white children in our neighborhood. This bread I used to bestow upon the hungry little urchins, who, in return, would give me that more valuable bread of knowledge. I am strongly tempted to give the names of two or three of those little boys, as a testimonial of the gratitude and affection I bear them; but prudence forbids—not that it would injure me,—but it might embarrass them; for it is almost an unpardonable offense to teach slaves to read in this Christian country. It is enough to say of the dear little fellows, that they lived on Philpot Street, very near Durgin and Bailey's shipyard. I used to talk this matter of slavery over with them. I would sometimes say to them, I wished I could be as free as they would be when they got to be men. "You will be free as soon as you are twenty-one, but I am a slave for life! Have not I as good a right to be free as you have?" These words used to trouble them; they would express for me the liveliest sympathy, and console me with the hope that something would occur by which I might be free.

I was now about twelve-years-old, and the thought of being a slave for life began to bear heavily upon my heart. Just about this time, I got hold of a book entitled "The Columbian Orator." Every opportunity I got, I used to read this book. Among much of other interesting matter, I found in it a dialogue between a master and his slave. The slave was represented as having run away from his master three times. The dialogue represented the conversation which took place between them, when the slave was retaken the third time. In this dialogue, the whole argument in behalf of slavery was brought forward by the master, all of which was disposed of by the slave. The slave was made to say some very smart as, well as impressive things in reply to his master—things which had the desired though unexpected effect; for the conversation resulted in the voluntary emancipation of the slave on the part of the master.

In the same book, I met with one of Sheridan's mighty speeches on and in behalf of Catholic emancipation. These were choice documents to me. I read them over and over again with unabated interest. They gave tongue to interesting thoughts of my own soul, which had frequently flashed through my mind, and died away for want of utterance. The moral which I gained from the dialogue was the power of truth over the conscience of even a slaveholder. What I got from Sheridan was a bold denunciation of slavery, and a powerful vindication of human rights. The reading of these documents enabled me to utter my thoughts, and to meet the arguments brought forward to sustain slavery; but while they relieved me of one difficulty, they brought on another even more painful than the one of which I was relieved. The more I read, the more I was led to abhor and detest my enslavers. I could regard them in no other light than a band of successful robbers, who had left their homes, and gone to Africa, and stolen us from our homes, and in a strange land reduced us to slavery. I loathed them as being the meanest as well as the most wicked of men. As I read and contemplated the subject, behold that very discontentment which Master Hugh had predicted would follow my learning to read had already come, to torment and sting my soul to unutterable anguish. As I writhed under it, I would at times feel that learning to read had been a curse rather than a blessing. It had given me a view of my wretched condition, without the remedy. It opened my eyes to the horrible pit, but to no ladder upon which to get out. In moments of agony, I envied my fellow-slaves for their stupidity. I have often wished myself a beast. I preferred the condition of the meanest reptile to my own. Anything, no matter what, to get rid of thinking! It was this everlasting thinking of my condition that tormented me. There was no getting rid of it. It was pressed upon me by every object within sight or hearing, animate or inanimate. The silver trump of freedom had roused my soul to eternal wakefulness. Freedom now appeared, to disappear no more forever. It was heard in every sound, and seen in every thing. It was ever present to torment me with a sense of my wretched condition. I saw nothing without seeing it, I heard nothing without hearing it, and felt nothing without feeling it. It looked from every star, it smiled in every calm, breathed in every wind, and moved in every storm.

I often found myself regretting my own existence, and wishing myself dead; and but for the hope of being free, I have no doubt but that I should have killed myself, or done something for which I should have been killed. While in this state of mind, I was eager to hear anyone speak of slavery. I was a ready listener. Every little while, I could hear something about the abolitionists. It was some time before I found what the word meant. It was always used in such connections as to make it an interesting word to me. If a slave ran away and succeeded in getting clear, or if a slave killed his master, set fire to a barn, or did anything very wrong in the mind of a slaveholder, it was spoken of as the fruit of abolition. Hearing the word in this connection very often, I set about learning what it meant. The dictionary afforded me little or no help. I found it was "the act of abolishing"; but then I did not know what was to be abolished. Here I was perplexed. I did not dare to ask anyone about its meaning, for I was satisfied that it was something they wanted me to know very little about. After a patient waiting, I got one of our city papers, containing an account of the number of petitions from the North, praying for the abolition of slavery in the District of Columbia, and of the slave trade between the States. From this time I understood the words abolition and abolitionist, and always drew near when that word was spoken, expecting to hear something of importance to myself and fellow-slaves. The light broke in upon me by degrees. I went one day down on the wharf of Mr. Waters; and seeing two Irishmen unloading a scow of stone, I went, unasked, and helped them. When we had finished, one of them came to me and asked me if I were a slave. I told him I was. He asked, "Are ye a slave for life?" I told him that I was. The good Irishman seemed to be deeply affected by the statement. He said to the other that it was a pity so fine a little fellow as myself should be a slave for life. He said it was a shame to hold me. They both advised me to run away to the North; that I should find friends there, and that I should be free. I pretended not to be interested in what they said, and treated them as if I did not understand them; for I feared they might be treacherous. White men have been known to encourage slaves to escape, and then, to get the reward, catch them and return them to their masters. I was afraid that these seemingly good men might use me so; but I nevertheless remembered their advice, and from that time I resolved to run away. I looked forward to a time at which it would be safe for me to escape. I was too young to think of doing so immediately; besides, I wished to learn how to write, as I might have occasion to write my own pass. I consoled myself with the hope that I should one day find a good chance. Meanwhile, I would learn to write.

The idea as to how I might learn to write was suggested to me by being in Durgin and Bailey's ship-yard, and frequently seeing the ship carpenters, after hewing, and getting a piece of timber ready for use, write on the timber the name of that part of the ship for which it was intended. When a piece of timber was intended for the larboard side, it would be marked thus—"L." When apiece was for the starboard side, it would be marked thus—S.F." A piece for the larboard side forward, would be marked thus—"L.F." When apiece was for starboard side forward, it would be marked thus—"S.F." For larboard aft, it would be marked thus—"L.A." For starboard aft, it would be marked thus—"S.A." I soon learned the names of these letters, and for what they were intended when placed upon a piece of timber in the shipyard. I immediately commenced copying them, and in a short time was able to make the four letters named. After that, when I met with any boy who I knew could write, I would tell him I could write as well as he. The next word would be, "I don't believe you. Let me see you try it." I would then make the letters which I had been so fortunate as to learn, and ask him to beat that. In this way I got a good many lessons in writing, which it is quite possible I should never have gotten in any other way. During this time, my copy-book was the board fence, brick wall, and pavement; my pen and ink was a lump of chalk. With these, I learned mainly how to write. I then commenced and continued copying the Italics in Webster's Spelling Book, until I could make them all without looking in the book. By this time, my little Master Thomas had gone to school, and learned how to write, and had written over a number of copy-books. These had been brought home, and shown to some of our near neighbors, and then laid aside. My mistress used to go to class meeting at the Wilk Street meeting-house every Monday afternoon, and leave me to take care of the house. When left thus, I used to spend the time in writing in the spaces left in master Thomas's copy-book, copying what he had written. I continued to do this until I could write a hand very similar to that of Master Thomas. Thus, after a long, tedious effort for years, I finally succeeded in learning how to write. ■

D

AUTHOR PROFILE

Frederick Douglass (1818–1895) was an American abolitionist, advocate for women's rights, internationally acclaimed author, and orator. Douglass was born to slavery in Maryland. At the age of twenty he escaped to the North, and henceforth devoted himself to writing and speaking against the institution of slavery, despite considerable risks to his liberty and personal safety. His autobiographies, written in three parts between 1845 and 1881, are classic contributions to the abolitionist cause and to American autobiographical writing. "Learning to Read and Write" is excerpted from *The Narrative of the Life of Frederick Douglass, An American Slave*, originally published in 1845.

What We Hunger For

By Roxane Gay

All too often, representations of a woman's strength overlook the cost of that strength, where it rises from, and how it is called upon when needed most.

The Hunger Games, released in 2008, is the first book in a trilogy by Suzanne Collins. *Catching Fire* and *Mockingjay*, the next two books, were released in 2009 and 2010. The franchise was an instant success. More than 2.9 million copies of the books are in print. There are more than twenty foreign editions. *The Hunger Games* was on the *New York Times* bestseller list for one hundred weeks. There are special editions. There is merchandise, including a Katniss Barbie, which Katniss would absolutely hate. In March 2012, the movie was released and earned nearly $460 million worldwide.

The series tells the story about a young woman, Katniss Everdeen, who doesn't know her own strength until she is confronted by her need for that strength. She is a tough young woman who is forced to become even stronger in circumstances that might otherwise break her. She is a young woman who has no choice but to fight for survival—for herself, her family, her people.

I have found myself inexplicably drawn to these books, the complex world Collins has created, and the people she has placed in that world.

I am not the kind of person who becomes so invested in a book or movie or television show that my interest becomes a hobby or intense obsession, one where I start to declare allegiances or otherwise demonstrate a serious level of commitment to something fictional I had no hand in creating.

Or, I didn't used to be that kind of person.

Let me be clear: Team Peeta. I cannot fathom how one could be on any other team. Gale? I can barely acknowledge him. Peeta, on the other hand, is everything. He frosts things and bakes bread and is unconditional and unwavering in his love, and also he is very, very strong. He can throw a sack of flour, is what I am saying. Peeta is a place of solace and hope, and he is a good kisser.

In December 2011, I didn't know much about *The Hunger Games*. Given my abiding interest in pop culture, I'm not sure how I missed the books. Then a friend suggested that *The Hunger Games* would be a great book to teach in my novel-writing class, so I decided to check it out.

I do most of my leisure reading at the gym. I hate exercise. Yes, it's good for you and weight loss and whatever, but normally, I work out and want to die. I knew I was in love with *The Hunger Games* when I did not want to get off the treadmill. The book captivated me. I wanted to stay in the world Collins created. More than that, *The Hunger Games* moved me. There was so much at stake, so much drama, and it was all so intriguing, so hypnotizing, so intense and dark. I particularly appreciated what the book got right about strength and endurance, suffering and survival. I found myself gasping and hissing and even bursting into tears, more than once. I looked insane but I did not care. I was completely without shame.

After finishing *The Hunger Games*, I quickly read the next two books in the trilogy—my obsession, at this point, was raging and white hot. I was so invested I couldn't stop talking about the books. I daydreamed about Katniss, Peeta, and, I suppose, sometimes Gale, as well as the other compelling characters—Cinna, Rue, Thresh, Haymitch, Finnick, Annie. I wanted the best for these characters even when all seemed hopeless, was hopeless.

This obsession intensified well before I realized the first movie would be realized. That development took things to a whole new level.

I started counting down to the movie well before opening day. I could hardly contain myself. I attended the midnight showing even though I had to teach the next (same) morning. I warned my gentleman friend that he couldn't mock me for how I reacted during the movie because I knew I was going to get close to the rapture and didn't want to be judged. I live in a small town, so I expected that there wouldn't be many people attending the midnight opening, but AMC screened *The Hunger Games* on all ten screens and every screening was sold out. My friends and I joked that we were probably some of the oldest people in the auditorium. It was no small relief when we saw some silver-haired folk among us.

As we waited, the teenagers and tweens chattered energetically about the books and the casting and whatever else young people talk about these days. Nearly all of them were staring at electronic devices. I thought, *Don't they have school tomorrow?* The movie began, and I held my breath. I had so many expectations, and I didn't want those expectations, those hopes, destroyed by Hollywood, a known killer of dreams.

I was not disappointed. I had *feelings* throughout the movie, true, mad, deep *feelings*. Had I been alone, I would have embarrassed myself with vulgar displays of enthusiasm. At times I wanted to spontaneously break into applause to celebrate the thrill of seeing the book I've read so many times playing out twenty feet high. There was just so much to look at—the set design, the costumes, the glittery cast. The movie was almost cerebral and meticulously faithful to the book when it needed to be. The production values were impeccable with only a few missteps (whatever the hell was going on with Katniss's flaming outfits, for example). The actors acquitted themselves well. I became even more fervently a member of Team Peeta. I left the movie thrilled with the overall experience of the movie.

As a critic, I recognize the flaws, I do, but *The Hunger Games* is not a movie I am able to watch as a critic. The story means too much to me.

The Hunger Games books are not perfect. While the writing is engaging and well paced, the quality of the prose weakens with each successive book. Many of the secondary characters aren't well developed, and at times the plot strains credulity. The third book is rather rushed, and some of Collins's choices feel almost gratuitous, particularly with regard to the characters she chose to kill off. The complete erasure of sexuality is problematic. Intimacy is conveyed through a great deal of kissing to the point that it becomes laughable. It is disturbing that within the world of the Hunger Games, it is perfectly acceptable for teenagers to kill one another and die or otherwise suffer in really violent ways, but it is not at all acceptable for them to explore their sexuality.

I was struck, consistently, by the sheer brutality, and yet the undeniable heart of the story, of the characters, of my dearest Peeta and his devotion for Katniss, and how toward the end, even when it seemed hopeless, they found their way to each other. The books' imperfections are easily forgiven because the best parts of the books are the truest—that sometimes, the one you love best is the one who has always been right by your side, even when you didn't notice.

I am fascinated by strength in women.

People tend to think I'm strong. I'm not. And yet. I identify with Katniss because throughout the trilogy, the people around Katniss expect her to be strong and she does her best to meet those expectations, even when it costs her a great deal.

I come from a loving, tight-knit, imperfect but great family. My parents have always been involved in my life even when I pushed them away. I have wanted for little. One of my biggest weaknesses, one that has always shamed me, is that I have always been lonely. I've struggled to make friends because I can be socially awkward, because I'm weird, because I live in my head. When I was young, we moved around a lot, so there was rarely any time to get to know a new place, let alone new people. Loneliness was the one familiar thing, making me this bottomless pit of need, open and gaping and desperate for anything to fill me up.

I should not be this way but I am.

When I was in middle school, when I was young—old enough to like a boy but young enough to have no clue what that meant—there was a boy who I thought was my boyfriend and who said he was my boyfriend but who also completely ignored me at school. It's a sad, silly story lots of girls know. It was fine because when we were together, he made me feel like he could fill my gaping void. He was terrible, but he was also charming and persuasive. I was nerdy and friendless, all lanky limbs and crazy hair, and he was beautiful and popular. I accepted the state of affairs between us.

When we were together, he'd tell me what he wanted to do to me. He wasn't asking my permission. I was not an unwilling participant. I was not a willing participant. I felt nothing one way or the other. I wanted him to love me. I wanted to make him happy. If doing things to my body made him happy, I would let him do anything to my body. My body was nothing to me. It was just meat and bones around that void he filled by touching me. Technically we didn't have sex, but we did everything else. The more I gave, the more he took. At school, he continued to look right through me. I was dying but I was happy. I was happy because he was happy, because if I gave enough, he might love me. As an adult, I don't understand how I allowed him to treat me like that. I don't understand how he could be so terrible. I don't understand how desperately I wanted to sacrifice myself. I was young.

I was always a good girl. I was a straight-A student, top of my class. I did as I was told. I was polite to my elders. I was good to my siblings. I went to church. It was very easy to hide how very bad I was becoming from my family, from everyone. Being good is the best way to be bad.

It never crossed my mind to say no or that I should say no, that I could say no. He started pressuring me to have sex. I didn't say no but I didn't say yes and I did not want to say yes. I wanted to say no but could not because I would lose him. I would be nothing again.

One day we were riding our bikes in the woods. About a mile deep, there was an abandoned hunting cabin often used by teenagers to do the things teenagers do when they're hiding out in the woods. It was disgusting—small, a dirt floor littered with empty beer cans and used condom wrappers and discarded cigarette packs. There was a small bench. The glass in the windows was broken, brown with age. Several of his friends from school were there. I didn't know them well, had mostly seen them in the halls. They were all popular, handsome. They would never have reason to know a girl like me, quiet, shy, awkward.

I did not understand, not at first. I was very naïve despite what I thought I knew. Once I realized what was going on, I assumed this boy wanted me to give his friends blow jobs. I did not want to do that, to share what I thought was private between this boy and me, but I would have. I could have, if only to make him happy. I told him I wanted us to leave, to continue on our bike ride. I did that. I did try to save myself. I did understand I was not safe. They were all so much bigger and I finally felt something. I felt fear but I didn't know how to say no. I tried to leave, to run out of that cabin, but they grabbed me just past the threshold. I screamed. I opened my mouth and I screamed and my voice echoed through the woods and no one came for me. Not one person heard me. We were too far deep.

The boy I thought was my boyfriend pushed me to the ground. He took my clothes off, and I lay there with no body to speak of, just a flat board of skin and girl bones. I tried to cover myself with my arms but I couldn't, not really. The boys stared at me while they drank beer and laughed and said things I didn't understand because I knew things but I knew nothing about what a group of boys could do to kill a girl.

I was a good girl who went to church. I had faith. I believed in God back then, so I prayed. I prayed for God to save me because I could not save me. I whispered Our Father because it was the only prayer I knew by heart. I begged God to change those boys' minds. He didn't. And then I did say no, I found my voice, and it didn't matter and I wasted my first love, my first everything, on a boy who thought so very little of me.

They kept me there for hours. It was as bad as you might expect. The repercussions linger. I walked home alone, pushing my stupid bike, hating myself for thinking this boy loved me. I was a good girl, so that's what my parents saw when I came home a completely different person and went to my room and tried to pull myself together well enough to be the girl everyone knew. I had to hide what happened because I didn't want to get in trouble, because my parents were strict, because you're not allowed to have sex before marriage, because I was a good girl, so that's what I did. I swallowed the truth, which only made the gaping void of need inside me yawn wider.

Just because you survive something does not mean you are strong.

The worst of it was going to school the next day. I didn't want to but I had no choice. I was a good girl. I went to French class and sat in the second-to-last row. It was uncomfortable in every way. Just as class was about to begin, the boy behind me grabbed my shoulder and I felt a surge of adrenaline, then terror. He stood and leaned into me. He said, "You're a slut," and everyone heard and they snickered. Everyone started calling me a slut. When the teacher came in and stood at the front of the room, she looked at me differently. If she could have, she would have called me a slut too. I was mortified and trapped. I sat perfectly still and tried to concentrate, but all I could hear was the hiss of the word "slut." That shame was one of the worst things I have ever known. "Slut" was my name for the rest of the school year because those boys went and told a very different story about what happened in the woods.

In June 2011, Meghan Cox Gurdon wrote, in the *Wall Street Journal*, about how Young Adult fiction has taken too dark a turn, has unnecessarily exposed young readers to complex, difficult situations before they are mature enough to make sense of those situations. She wrote,

> If books show us the world, teen fiction can be like a ball of funhouse mirrors, constantly reflecting back hideously distorted portrayals of what life is. There are of course exceptions, but a careless young reader—or one who seeks out depravity—will find himself surrounded by images not of joy or beauty but of damage, brutality and losses of the most horrendous kinds.

She is correct in noting that there is darkness in some Young Adult fiction, but she largely ignores the diversity of the genre and the countless titles that aren't grounded in damage, brutality, or loss. More troubling, though, is the suggestion that somehow reality should be sanitized for teen readers.

The critical response to Gurdon's article was swift and passionate from writers and readers alike. Sherman Alexie wrote, "There are millions of teens who read because they are sad and lonely and enraged. They read because they live in an often-terrible world. They read because they believe, despite the callow protestations of certain adults, that books—especially the dark and dangerous ones—will save them."

I learned a long time ago that life introduces young people to situations they are in no way prepared for, even good girls, lucky girls who want for nothing. Sometimes, when you least expect it, you become the girl in the woods. You lose your name because another one is forced on you. You think you are alone until you find books about girls like you. Salvation is certainly among the reasons I read. Reading and writing have always pulled me out of the darkest experiences of my life. Stories have given me a place in which to lose myself. They have allowed me to remember. They have allowed me to forget. They have allowed me to imagine different endings and better possible worlds.

Perhaps I loved the Hunger Games trilogy because the books were, in their own way, a fairy tale and I am always, always in search of a fairy tale.

As I read the Hunger Games series, I thought of Gurdon's article because I was struck, more than once, by the intensity of the traumas the characters were put through, the relentlessness of that trauma, and the visible effects. At times, I thought, *This is too much*, but I know something of the world now, and there are rarely limits to suffering. In this trilogy, suffering has few limits, and suffering has consequences that, all too often, we forget when narratives neatly imply that everything turns out okay, when narratives imply that *it gets better* without demonstrating what it takes to get to better. In the Hunger Games, it takes everything.

My love for these books, at its purest, is not really about Peeta or anything silly and girly. I love that a young woman character is fierce and strong but human in ways I find believable, relatable. Katniss is clearly a heroine, but a heroine with *issues*. She intrigues me because she never seems to know her own strength. She isn't blandly insecure the way girls are often forced to be in fiction. She is brave but flawed. She is a heroine, but she is also a girl who loves two boys and can't choose which boy she loves more. She is not sure she is up to the task of leading a revolution, but she does her best, even as she doubts herself.

Katniss endures the unendurable. She is damaged and it shows. At times, it might seem like her suffering is gratuitous, but life often presents unendurable circumstances people manage to survive. Only the details differ. The Hunger Games trilogy is dark and brutal, but in the end, the books also offer hope—for a better world and a better people and, for one woman, a better life, a life she can share with a man who understands her strength and doesn't expect her to compromise that strength, a man who can hold her weak places and love her through the darkest of her memories, the worst of her damage. Of course I love the Hunger Games. The trilogy offers the tempered hope that everyone who survives something unendurable hungers for. ■

AUTHOR PROFILE

Roxane Gay has a PhD in rhetoric and technical communication from Michigan Technological University and is currently a professor of English at Purdue University. She has written a novel, *An Untamed State* (2014), a collection of short stories, *Ayiti* (2011), and a wealth of nonfiction essays. Her shorter works have been included in the 2014 edition of *Best American Mystery Stories* and the 2012 editions of *Best American Short Stories* and *Best Sex Writing*. "What We Hunger For" was published in her newest collection of essays, *Bad Feminist* (2014).

From Sombreros to *Sincronizadas*

Authenticity, Ethnicity, and the Mexican Restaurant Industry

By Marie Sarita Gaytán

While scholars agree that performances of authenticity and ethnicity express social relations and reveal the socially constructed character of identity, we know little about how these interactions contribute to the politics of everyday life. By engaging in participant observation, drawing on open-ended interviews, and analyzing the content of available data regarding restaurant culture, the author argues that the accomplishment of Mexican authenticity is a social construction. However, despite its socially created qualities, the author contends that performances of authenticity and ethnicity affect not only how individuals understand each other, but illustrate the challenges faced by different groups of people in the commercial production and consumption of identity.

Keywords: authenticity; consumption; ethnicity; representation; restaurants

Examining how individuals negotiate the social world and make sense of their experiences reveals not only how people understand each other, but illustrates how they view themselves in relation to those with whom they interact. Authenticity, as an index of these encounters, provides the opportunity to determine and communicate one's place as an individual in an increasingly global marketplace. While the search for authenticity highlights the desire for "genuine" forms of expression, it also calls attention to concerns regarding the interpretation and negotiation of contemporary consumer life. In a world where soft drinks are marketed as "the real thing" (Handler 1986, 6) and restaurants are named "The Authentic Café" (Halter 2000, 19), consumption serves as a means through which authenticity becomes a measure of the quality, efficacy, and legitimacy of one's experience in a particular setting.

Despite its fabricated character (Peterson 1997), performances of authenticity influence how people identify with and become involved in real world social, political, and cultural arrangements (Bauman and Briggs 1990). Central to these arrangements is the ability to enact distinction (Bourdieu 1984) and recognize difference (Bell and Valentine 1997). MacCannell (1973), for instance, noted that tourists consistently sought to enter the back regions of their destinations in an attempt to encounter how people different from themselves authentically lived. Like tourists, customers of "ethnic" restaurants also desire backstage (Goffman 1959) experiences and the "illusion of authenticity" when participating in different culinary traditions (Lu and Fine 1995, 541). These traditions are often linked to the meanings that people attach to their own ethnic identities (Tuchman and Levine 1992; Waters 1990) and the ethnic identities of others (Gabaccia 1998; Nenga 2003). As a measure of symbolic ethnicity (Gans 1979), authenticity contributes to the process, performance, and preservation of culture.

While scholars agree that performances of authenticity and ethnicity express social relations and demonstrate the socially constructed character of identity, we know little about how these interactions shape the politics of everyday life. By engaging in participant observation in Mexican restaurants, drawing on open-ended interviews with owners, managers, customers, and reviewers of Mexican restaurants, and considering the content of a range of available literature (i.e., restaurant industry reports, articles, and books) related to restaurant culture, I argue that the accomplishment of Mexican authenticity, whether maintained by Mexican owners or performed by large restaurant chains, is a social construction. However, despite its socially created qualities, performances of authenticity and ethnicity affect not only how individuals understand each other, but illustrate the challenges faced by different groups of people in the commercial production and consumption of identity. Focusing on the consequences and contradictions that are generated through different claims to authenticity, I examine the salience of ethnicity in day-to-day situations and explore the dynamics of cultural production.

Consuming Authenticity and Ethnicity

One of the first public nationwide debates over authenticity and Mexican food began in 1972 when Diana Kennedy, a British national, published *The Cuisines of Mexico*. Kennedy distinguished what she labeled authentic "interior Mexican food" from the "mixed plates" found at Mexican restaurants in the United States (Walsh 2004, 121). Referring to Americanized versions of food as *Tex-Mex*, a name previously used to describe food that was a combination of Texan and Mexican cuisine, Kennedy called for greater awareness of authentic Mexican cooking. Her insistence on authentic Mexican food and condemnation of inauthentic hybrid dishes was so influential that restaurants began to describe their food as "interior Mexican" in an attempt to follow the purist trend toward the authentic Mexican recipes included in her collection (Kennedy 1972, 121). She has even earned respect in Mexico where she was awarded the Order of the Aztec Eagle, the Mexican government's highest honor bestowed on foreigners, for her international promotion of Mexican food. As the accolades and esteem conferred on Diana Kennedy illustrate, matters of authenticity are not limited to the maintenance of a particular culinary tradition, but imply an attempt at the preservation of a greater cultural phenomenon—one that extends beyond the parameters of cuisine, and directs attention to representation, identity, and culture.

Scholars maintain that authenticity is a uniquely contemporary characteristic that affects individual selfhood and social relationships (Boorstin 1961, Handler 1986, Trilling 1971). According to Trilling (1971), the concept of authenticity signals a shift in how individuals relate to one another. Authenticity, as he put it, "...[is] part of the moral slang of our day [that] points to the peculiar nature of our fallen condition, our anxiety over the credibility of existence and of individual existences" (p. 93). Likewise, Boorstin (1961) in his work on the changing nature of the American news media, expressed concern over the presentation of authenticity and the significance of illusion or "the menace of unreality" (p. 240). Troubled by the growing trend to replace authentic events, scripts, and stories with inauthentic ones, occurrences of "pseudo-events" interfered with the ability to determine spontaneity; they obscured an underlying "reality," and promoted other pseudo-events. For example, the use of stereotypes, "stirred an irrational and undiscriminating hunger for fancier, more varied items" (pp. 38–39). As a form of pseudo-event, stereotypes "whetted the appetite" for pre-determined images as opposed to spontaneous proceedings (p. 39). Therefore, the spread of inauthentic pseudo-events is not only dangerous to society at large, but is detrimental to individuals' abilities to understand their roles in these encounters. From this perspective, authenticity is a modern cultural construct that sustains the assumption of a "true" experience or occasion. In addition, this position holds that authenticity is a common means through which individuals interpret their roles and the roles of others in a variety of social contexts (Goffman 1959; Grazian 2003; MacCannell 1973; Peterson 1997).

Focusing on the culture of country music, Peterson (1997) described how audiences anticipated certain types of performances that exemplified the genre's values. To gain notoriety, musicians were implicitly required to abide by a set of specific pre-existing standards to fulfill the expectations of their fans. The extent to which performers had to live up to consumers' ideas about different encounters demonstrates the political relevance of representation in the production and reproduction of culture. Similarly, Grazian (2004) documented how consumer desire, as an influential set of social forces, operated in Chicago blues clubs. For example, he found that cultural myths pertaining to white audiences' longing for black musicians and employees was so powerful that many venues employed black men exclusively as a means to create the impression of an authentic ambience. In the space of the blues club, registers of race and ethnicity served as key signifiers in the presentation of authentic cultural displays.

Performances of "ethnic" authenticity are generally seen as highlighting "genuine" characteristics, customs, and traditions of specific groups of people (Hobsbawm and Ranger 1983). When probed about the personal meanings attached to their ethnic identities, Waters' (1990) informants agreed that "having" an ethnicity made them feel special and provided them the opportunity to take part in a host of traditions such as eating "ethnic" food. Some confusion was apparent, such as one woman who explained that she celebrated her Irish heritage by eating sauerkraut. Misappropriations aside, consuming particular food was tantamount to displaying cultural pride. The decision to eat certain types of "ethnic" cuisine symbolizes a form of self expression, but can also delineate a boundary between "the collective self and the other" (Ohnuki-Tierney 1993, 3). Consequently, dining preferences may represent a positive attachment to one's culture and denote discrimination against others.

Goldman (1992), in her research on cooking and colonialism, maintains that accounts of cultural authority in texts such as cookbooks, memoirs, and novels illustrate the conscious and unconscious presence of "the self." In her estimation, the insistence on authentic cuisine not only implies the existence of inauthentic food, but reveals the ubiquity of self-assertions that affirm and appropriate the cultural expressions of people from different ethnic backgrounds. Hence, making claims to authenticity is capable of signaling an array of implicit and explicit power relations. Further developing the link between politics and authenticity, Abarca (2004) explains that the "gastronomical desire" for planned or genuine authenticity, while always rooted in cultural and socio-economic assumptions, "carries real colonizing attitudes and implications" that too easily essentialize certain ethnic groups (p. 18). As a result, assertions of authentic "ethnic" food espouse romantic ideas about the people who are typically associated with certain cuisines. Such processes stifle creative expression while at the same time reproduce the notion that some groups of people are more "exotic" and "ethnic" than others. Weary of the unquestioned ideals of cultural authenticity, Abarca contends that consumers should be more critical of the practices by which "our rather ordinary words and common phrases" influence how people from particular backgrounds are perceived (p. 19).

These findings point to the importance of authenticity and ethnicity not just as measures of the legitimacy of a specific cultural experience, but as concepts through which a variety of commonplace ideas are generated. What is more, performances of authenticity and ethnicity sustain commonly held beliefs about particular cultures, places, and people. Therefore, it is essential to examine, in greater detail, how notions of authenticity and ethnicity are negotiated by actors themselves in the very locations where such interactions take place. While research suggests that a diverse range of relations are expressed when individuals make claims about authenticity, few studies address how these interactions unfold and influence the production of culture. As a result, I pay close attention to the social conditions under which such assertions order the terms of representation and contribute to the politics of everyday life.

Exploring the Culture of Mexican Restaurants

Restaurants provide an empirically rich point of entry for observing interpersonal exchanges as part and parcel of the creation, enactment, and reproduction of symbolic meaning (Fine 1996; Finkelstein 1989; Spang 2000). As unique sites for observing "public ethnicity" (Lu and Fine 1995, 536), restaurants bring together social actors as participants and spectators in performances of culture. From September 2000 through June 2001, I became a participant observer in Mexican restaurants in Amherst, Northampton; Springfield, Massachusetts; and Hartford, Connecticut.[1] Additionally, I conducted interviews with customers, reviewers, owners, and managers of these restaurants. To gather a wide range of materials concerning the social relations of Mexican restaurants, I collected copies of flyers, menus, web pages, restaurant industry reports, restaurant reviews, and take-out containers. Thus, this project draws on participant observation, open-ended interviews, and content analysis to examine the culture of Mexican restaurants.

The towns of Amherst and Northampton are located approximately 90 miles west of Boston in the Pioneer Valley, and are small communities with a primarily Anglo-American population. In contrast, Springfield, Massachusetts, and Hartford, Connecticut are larger urban centers with a more ethnically diverse population.[2] These cities are located within a 25 and 45 minute drive from the Pioneer Valley. When this research was carried out, none of these locations had a large Mexican or Mexican-American population, and therefore restaurants catered to a non-Mexican clientele.[3] In each of these restaurants, I spent time observing the daily routines of management, employees, and customers. While some of the restaurants were open for breakfast, I generally conducted my fieldwork during the lunch and dinnertime hours. With my notebook in hand, I recorded the décor, layout, and atmosphere of each restaurant while sipping a coffee, enjoying a beer, or eating a meal—indeed, becoming a participant observer in Mexican restaurants was quite a savory experience.

With the help of my colleagues who were personally acquainted with several restaurant owners, I began compiling a list of potential informants. After conducting my first interview, I drew on the guidelines of snowball sampling by asking each restaurateur for the names and phone numbers of people they knew who owned or managed Mexican restaurants. I also searched the Internet and the Yellow Pages to locate restaurants outside of the Pioneer Valley. Aside from the management at Taco Bell who invoked "company policy" by not talking to anyone about their restaurants, arranging interviews with owners and managers of Mexican restaurants was fairly straightforward.

In total, I interviewed eight owners and managers of Mexican restaurants (two women and six men). These interviews were conducted face-to-face and included open-ended questions. They lasted from 1 to 2 hours, were tape recorded, and then transcribed. My conversations with customers of Mexican restaurants (12 women, 7 men) lasted from 15 minutes to an hour and were collected in restaurants and coffee shops in the towns of Amherst and Northampton. I approached people as they ordered, ate, and left the various establishments. Initially I was nervous about making contact with people in such an informal manner, but folks were quite eager to share their ideas about Mexican restaurants. Equally enthusiastic to talk to me were restaurant reviewers. My three interviews with restaurant reviewers (three women) took place after I contacted area newspapers that published restaurant reviews. In one case, a newspaper editor would not reveal the "true" name of its reviewer because he wanted to protect the reviewer's anonymity. Of the three interviews, one was conducted face-to-face and two were carried out over the telephone.

Unlike my experiences with customers and restaurant reviewers, establishing rapport with owners and managers of Mexican restaurants was more complicated than I expected. For instance, several were concerned about what my project was trying to "prove." Despite assuring them that my project was exploratory, and therefore not intent on confirming a particular thesis, on finishing interviews I was frequently re-questioned about what my "real" motives were for studying local Mexican restaurants. I suspect that some people thought that I was a restaurant reviewer determined to critique the authenticity of their cuisine. Others were eager to talk about their restaurants in relation to the local restaurant scene. Interestingly, in these cases conversations generally took place in both English and Spanish. To be sure, talking to me in Spanish served as a means to affirm their authenticity as Mexican owners and managers of Mexican restaurants, while it also operated as a way to test, or to authenticate, my intentions as a researcher.

Catering Mexican Authenticity

Sipping hot chocolate in the subterranean dining room of a local coffee shop, Adrian, a restaurant reviewer whose career in journalism spanned over 20 years, revealed "I like it authentic, real, from back home, the motherland." Although she had only recently acquired the position of senior food writer, Adrian was adamant about the importance of a reviewer's ability to accurately evaluate the authenticity of a restaurant's cuisine. When she was unable to gauge a restaurant's authenticity, Adrian brought along friends or colleagues to assist her. Such was the case when she reviewed an Argentinean restaurant. In her words, "I decided to take a friend from Chile with me to gauge how authentic it was. Everyone spoke Spanish, they were all from Argentina." Similarly, Catherine, a reviewer whom I talked to by telephone, explained how she intuitively knew when a restaurant was authentic by observing the rapport an owner established with customers. As she put it, "The owner is cooking, takes his time. The restaurant is full of warmth, of something that is common, that is family…If you and I are eating here, then we're family."

Adrian and Catherine's observations suggest that authenticity is an important measure in determining the quality of a dining experience. However, their responses also show that evaluating a restaurant's authenticity requires more than just an appraisal of a restaurant's menu, recipes, or ingredients. Specifically, a restaurant's atmosphere is vital to an assessment of authenticity. Like reviewers, customers described the ambiance of a restaurant in terms of people and not décor. Frequently commenting on the presence or absence of "Hispanic" or "Mexican" employees, the ability to interact with Spanish-speaking employees was a central means by which many assessed their experiences. One customer recognized that a particular Mexican restaurant was authentic because she could "order in Spanish and the order was given back in Spanish," while another stated that when "all the cooks [were] Hispanic," he could more readily determine if some restaurants were more authentic than others. Customers and reviewers also looked for other cues. As a customer put it, "When you see Mexicans eating there it gives you the feeling that it's authentic and not just yuppies eating burritos and sipping margaritas," while a reviewer noted that she knew a restaurant was authentic because labor activist César Chavez dined there when he used to visit the area.

Customers were more likely to describe a restaurant's atmosphere as "not quite Mexican" when college students worked in the dining room. For example, one remarked that because she could not speak Spanish to the person working at the register, this contributed to a "very Noho" (an abbreviated version of Northampton) atmosphere that affected her ability to "escape that we're in New England." Much like Grazian's (2004) observations in blues clubs, the presence of employees from different ethnic backgrounds allowed customers and reviewers to distinguish between experiences that were "authentically Mexican" and those that were not. Despite the fact that the vast majority of Spanish-speaking staff were from El Salvador, customers and reviewers did not question the possibility that their interactions were not with "authentic" Mexican employees.

Although customers and reviewers readily acknowledged the importance of authenticity, they were uncritical of the cuisine or atmosphere offered at the local Mexican restaurants that they considered "inauthentic." In one case, a reviewer observed, "They make no pretense of serving traditional Mexican fare…it's more whimsical and Americanized than loyal to any particular ethnic cuisine," while a customer remarked, "No, it's not authentic Mexican, but they don't claim to be." Even when a restaurant was unsuccessful at maintaining an authentic décor, reviewers still expressed confidence in making determinations about its authenticity. Such was the case with Jennifer, who explained that despite a restaurant's Formica tables and plastic chairs, she could still recognize "something real about the cuisine." Taken together, customers and reviewers' comments imply that there is more than one way to achieve authenticity and to evaluate those accomplishments. In addition, their responses suggest that there is something about *how* particular claims of authenticity are expressed that contributes to their assessment of their experiences. Turning to presentations of authenticity and ethnicity in Mexican restaurants, I examine the production of identity and the conditions of representation.

Commemorative Authenticity: "It's Got a Mexican Soul...and That Says a Lot"

Maintaining loyalty to tradition was central to how Enrique organized the overall layout of his restaurant. For instance, he labeled menu entrées "*comida de la gente*" (food of the people), and adorned the windows of his restaurant with decals that read "*hecho en Mexico*" (made in Mexico) and "*viva la raza*!" (a rallying cry made famous during the Chicano Rights Movement of the 1960s). Describing what he called an "essence," Enrique elaborated,

> For me, when I think about Mexican food I think about what kind of food you find at Mexican kitchens at home, not so much at a restaurant. It's more like what I would find at a *quinceañera* (cotillion), what I would find at a *boda* (wedding).

According to Enrique, the "essence" of authentic Mexican food is linked to cultural celebrations such as *quinceañeras* and weddings. While unable to fully replicate these environments within the context of his restaurant, he is able to offer his customers Mexican "home-style" cooking that celebrates Mexican identity by both challenging and reinforcing people's perceptions of what and when "real" Mexican food is consumed.

Differentiating himself from his competition, he described how his restaurant, Los Cabos, stood out from the other local offerings:

> If you go to that restaurant, what it does is takes a variety of ethnic foods, wraps them into a large flour tortilla and calls it a burrito. So what you have is a stirfried chicken burrito with roasted bell peppers, mushrooms, and yogurt, you know? [That] has nothing to do with what my *Tía* (aunt) Ana serves.

As he saw it, the use of unconventional burrito ingredients symbolized a departure from traditional food preparation.

Expressing his disappointment at the alterations restaurateurs commonly made to accommodate people's perceptions of Mexican food, Enrique detailed his refusal to compromise the traditional names of his menu items. In one case he challenged people's ideas about quesadillas:

> It would be easy for me to sell the quesadilla with your choice of flour or corn tortillas. Instead, what I say is let's call the flour tortillas with cheese inside for what they are, *sincronizadas*. Sin-chro-neez-ahh-dah [in an American English accent], well, that's made with flour tortillas. That's the difference so one day when they [his primarily Anglo clientele] go to Mexico, they're not shocked that their quesadilla isn't made with a flour tortilla, and they'll know what a *sincronizada* is.

Enrique's resistance against mainstream ideas about Mexican cuisine in general, and the local versions of Mexican food in particular, manifested not only in his menu, but also in the advertising and décor of his restaurant. When Los Cabos first opened, a college newspaper published a lukewarm review that praised the cuisine but commented extensively on its ambiance and "lack of Mexican charm." Recounting the incident, Enrique, clearly bothered by the remark explained:

> There's no *sombreros*, *zarapes*, or *piñatas*...it has a Mexican soul and you know that says a lot. It's not salt it isn't pepper, it's not nice tile or a beautiful chair. There's a spirit about it only those who are very proud of what Mexican is or how it should be represented can get it.

Symbols such as sombreros, *zarapes*, and piñatas, as Enrique put it, presented a limited version of Mexican identity, one that neglected to consider the "huge history of great art" produced and appreciated by Mexicans on both sides of the U.S.-Mexican border. In his estimation, stereotypical imagery could not contend with the "soul" and "spirit" fostered by presenting a commemorative approach to Mexican culture. With ads stating "*Evite el estereotipo*!" (avoid the stereotype), "Mexican food that Mexicans would want to eat," and "Mexican food like you've never had it in New England," Enrique actively engaged his customers in a political and cultural relationship that invoked authenticity as a significant and essential aspect of ethnic identity. Additionally, Enrique's comments suggest that even in commemorative versions of authenticity, consumers' preconceived ideas about how specific people create "charm" produce conflict when challenges are presented that extend the possibilities of available ethnic representations.

Loyalty to tradition was also a theme that emerged when I spoke with Ricardo, a restaurateur who recently moved to New England. Working collaboratively with his seven brothers, their first restaurant, Las Rosas, was named after their mother, and subsequent restaurants were named after other family members. This kind of environment, Ricardo explained, "emphasizes that we are family and that people can tell we are family and that people will feel like part of our family." Serving food typical of their home state of Jalisco, Mexico, they are accustomed to altering preparation styles and levels of spiciness to suit local palates. Even with such changes, Ricardo maintained:

> Our food is yes, really Mexican…It's authentic in the way that if you go to Mexico, to our hometown…well, it's a little different there, more spicy. Yes, it is authentic, but with a style from this side of the border.

According to this statement, while Ricardo asserts that his restaurant is "really Mexican," it is only authentic in comparison with Mexican food served within the United States. Claiming that although his restaurant is "the most Mexican in the area," Ricardo states that in order for it to be "truly" authentic, it would also need:

> …four or five small tables. Why? Because the woman of the house, the mother, the grandmother are really the ones who are going to cook. But if you go to a big restaurant like in Mexico City, there isn't anything that Mexican, it's more commercial. So, of all the restaurants here, I believe this is the most authentic.

Just above, Ricardo implies that authentic Mexican food is unavailable at "big" restaurants in large cities; instead, it comes from a kitchen where food is prepared by "the woman of the house." Ricardo's description of a mother or grandmother preparing food in a kitchen as a measure of an authentic dining experience is ironic, especially when considering that no women were employed in his restaurant. Moreover, his restaurant's dining area accommodates 60 customers while the bar area seats 25 customers—a far greater number than the "four or five small tables" he identifies. However, this does not stop Ricardo from promoting an authentic "family-style" experience so "that people will feel like part of our family." While he concedes that the food he serves is not entirely authentic, he presents it if it were. Ricardo reveals that Mexican food does not have to be authentic to *appear* authentic. Moreover, his comments suggest that performances of Mexican identity are inextricable from assumptions about class, gender, and family even in commemorative representations of ethnicity.

David, originally from New Mexico, opened his restaurant because "the area needed an authentic, traditional-type Mexican restaurant." Emphasizing the importance of preserving his family's recipes, David was interested in reaching-out to the community "to hand-down a tradition or share a tradition to the people of New England from the Southwest." Seeing his restaurant as representing Mexican culture, David explained the differences between his menu and that of a large Mexican chain restaurant located nearby:

> …a taco is a taco [but] it's what you put inside your taco [that] makes it different. Burritos are an American invention, there's no such thing as burritos in Mexico and the only reason that I serve them is because people love them.

Other alterations that David made to his menu included the addition of quesadillas and taquitos because "people kept requesting them." Décor was less relevant in David's opinion, especially when it came to displaying his heritage, "It's not important in a sense because really and truly I'm a Mexican-American, and the food I serve is traditional Mexican and New Mexican home-style cooking." In David's estimation, his Mexican-American background qualified him to represent authentic Mexican and New Mexican food. David's performance of authenticity, like that of Enrique and Ricardo's, is informed by claims that are unavailable to non-Mexican restaurateurs—in this case, tradition, family, and ethnic heritage rooted in Mexican culture.

As a social construction, authenticity generates a unique set of contradictions for those owners and managers who situate themselves as representatives of a specific collective identity. While they are able to display personal values associated with their presentation of ethnic heritage, they must also make concessions to fulfill certain customer expectations. In their research on the presentation of "ethnic" authenticity, Lu and Fine (1995) observed that the owners of Chinese restaurants often made changes to their cuisine to suite the "standards of the American palate" (p. 540). These alterations were based on aesthetic values linked to cultural discourses and the cost of particular food ingredients. Customers desired the "illusion of authenticity" regardless of modifications pertaining to the use of spices, methods of preparation, and styles of service (p. 541). Invoking innovative and adaptive measures, owners and chefs of Chinese restaurants cooked according to tradition even when adhering to customer preferences. Similarly, Ferraro (2002) found that the owners of Mexican restaurants in Los Angeles, California, used various names to describe menu items as a way to display their observance of authentic culinary styles and methods of preparation. According to this research, abiding by the guidelines of authenticity is an important and complicated endeavor that requires a combination of flexibility, foresight, and strategy. More importantly, however, these studies suggest that there are unique challenges for owners and chefs of "ethnic" restaurants whose performances of authenticity convey values that uphold the integrity of a particular culture.

In spite of the use of strategic measures in the presentation of authenticity, many restaurateurs were hesitant when it came to making menu alterations, and continued their ambitions to broaden customer's ideas about Mexican food and Mexican culture. This is fittingly exemplified in Enrique's discussion about serving tortilla chips:

> That's why for the longest time we never served chips in our restaurant. The essence of the fact of that's not how we start our food, it's not with a basket of chips. The only reason we serve a basket of chips in our restaurant is to break that in-between time when the food is waiting, but it is not something special.

Enrique intentionally excluded tortilla chips from his menu, but later compromised and offered them because of consistent customer demand. On his menu, tortilla chips were listed as *totopos*—a name that he insisted more accurately reflected the custom of consuming fried tortillas, and not as "something special" to "home-made" Mexican cuisine. Still not entirely comfortable with his addition of a menu item that he did not interpret as authentically Mexican, Enrique added:

> Americans can't take it as an essence like if they go over to my house, they'll get a basket of chips. That's not what my sister Veronica does when she first gets home, fries the tortillas for the chips, you know?

In commemorative presentations of authenticity, ethnicity is depicted as both challenging and conforming to a dominant set of ideas that portray identity as fixed, stable, and recognizable. For example, when Enrique displays Chicano/Latino artwork throughout his restaurant, he sees this decision as a symbolic act that expands his customers' knowledge of Mexican and Chicano heritage. Despite Enrique's desire to influence his customers' ideas about the diversity of Mexican culture, his strategies were unable to communicate a "different way of looking at Mexican food" because of expectations that he explained were put forth by "the standards of *lo gringo*" (that of American or non-Hispanic origin).

These types of struggles, as Gray (2004, p. xv) points out, call attention to the relationship of representations to "actual structural positions, social practices, cultural meanings, and the complex constellation of power" in which performances of authenticity take place. For members of historically marginalized communities, consumption is a key site where they are able to construct an identity that manages, contests, and extends common cultural categorizations that reproduce both oppositional *and* conventional representations (Kates and Belk 2001). However, as these owners' responses suggest, despite attempts to affirmatively represent their traditions or present their own versions of authenticity, they are often unable to disrupt mainstream ideas of what is and what is not "authentic." When established sets of expectations are challenged (e.g., not offering tortilla chips), these efforts conflict with customer demand and desire—both shaped by long standing social forces that impose market-oriented notions of authenticity that cater to "unreal" events over "real" ones (Boorstin 1961).

Hybrid Inauthenticity: "The Superbowl and Salsa are Synonymous"

Doug, an Anglo restaurateur, had the "burrito concept" in mind for several years before opening his restaurant. Living in a college town, he explained that a "burrito joint" was an appropriate addition to the area's other "ethnic" restaurants. He described his restaurant's food as follows:

> It's Mexican-American, well, more American than anything else, what we do as I see it. Sort of like pizza. We produce the Americanized version of something that's supposedly Mexican, and, in a way, authentic, but for the most part, it's an Americanized version of some foreign food like Chinese food that ends up appealing to the palate of people in this country, like fried rice, 'cause it's more American than anything else.

Remarking that the burrito is both "Mexican-American" and "more American than anything else," Doug is able to distinguish his restaurant's burritos from more "traditional" burritos. His observations are based on a distinction between different types of ingredients:

> Most of what's out there for a Mexican burrito has got a lot of fatty stuff in it. Like a lot of people perceive refried beans as made with lard, and they are, for the most part. We don't use refried beans, in fact, we don't use pinto beans. Predominantly we use black beans because they are more appealing to a broader market than pinto beans.

Ironically, part of Doug's success in the Mexican restaurant industry is a result of the perception that Mexican food is unhealthy. Capitalizing on what he calls the "burrito trend," he explains, "as an Americanized version of food, it [the burrito] fits into a nice classification system that's somehow there for whatever reason." Indeed, this "classification system" works to his benefit, even when it comes to the preparation of his restaurant's tacos:

> Our taco is really no more than a burrito than anything else. We call it a taco because it's smaller than the burrito and that was an arbitrary decision that seemed to make intuitive sense to our customers, and so that's what we called it.

Relying on an "arbitrary" decision to create tacos as similar, yet smaller versions of their burritos, reveals an approach to authenticity that adjusts to customer demand through a hybrid preparation and production of Mexican cuisine, one that in this case presents tacos as a different version of burritos. As he sees it, his customers are aware that they are not eating "truly authentic" Mexican food, but are instead consuming "healthy" and "funky" Mexican food. Even when it comes to the salsa, for Doug, "it's an illustration of something Americanized, and now, salsa's our thing. The Super Bowl and salsa are synonymous."

During our interview, I inquired about an El Salvadoran flag propped in a corner of the large indoor menu situated above the open kitchen. Explaining that the majority of his employees were El Salvadoran immigrants, he described how their input with regard to music and recipes was reflected throughout his restaurant. For example, one employee suggested the creation of an El Salvadoran burrito made with ingredients she cooked with in her own kitchen. Doug remarked, "I tried it, and liked it. It's a simple recipe and we adopted it and it was a sorta ethnic thing to have as an option...we've never really taken it off of the menu." As a "sorta ethnic" option, the inclusion of an El Salvadoran burrito reflects the hybrid inauthenticity through which Doug presents and markets his restaurant.

Sara, originally from California, described her style of cooking as "yuppified" and distinct from the food prepared by her Mexican mother. When referring to her menu, she stated, "I stay away from traditional Mexican food that I love because I've created this type of very quick, fresh food."

G

Emphasizing that her menu does not reflect a traditional or authentic Mexican fare, she explained her interest in flavors and spices that parallel those found in Mexico:

> I've found this similarity with Asian food and Mexican food. There's a very big similarity with the freshness and the produce such as tomatoes, squashes, all the salsas. The cooking techniques are also very similar to say, Southeast Asian food, which I love, and it's very accessible to the common palate.

Discovering a link between cross-ethnic cooking styles, Sara builds on similarities which accentuate the seasonings used in different cuisines. For instance, in many of her dishes she adds peanut sauce for a "Thai flavor" and feta cheese for a "Mediterranean flavor." When describing the combination of ingredients, she elaborates on a hybrid culinary approach, "When I first opened, people weren't used to experiencing a Thai chicken burrito with a rice and bean burrito. I've been able to slowly bring in different things and mix them all up." Like Doug, Sara refrains from making any claims to traditional Mexican cooking.

Doug and Sara's customers, while identifying their restaurants as serving Mexican cuisine, take notice of their hybrid inauthentic approach. Able to distinguish the differences from more traditional fares, customers and reviewers shared a range of comments about their restaurants specifically:

> It feels hippie-like. You sit on tree stumps and the menu isn't wildly Mexican. Chicken-cilantro salad doesn't strike me as Mexican, or their Cajun-fish taco.

> Yeah, they have pickled cabbage in one of their burritos. They've got the salsas going on. It's multi-ethnic, packed into a Mexican style.

> It's a gourmet burrito place; they've glamorized it into something not traditional.

> If you're looking for authentic Mexican food, don't come here. However, if you want Americanized Mexican food that's much better/cheaper than Taco Bell, this place is great.

> I'm from California, so I know what authentic Mexican food is like…and it's not anything like La Fiesta restaurant.

These remarks show that customers and reviewers carefully evaluate the extent to which the cuisine they consume abides by a standard of authenticity that adheres to particular aesthetics, menu items, and ingredients.

According to Tuchman and Levine (1992), the inevitable "naturalness" of products related to specific ethnic traditions is often associated with the created character of ethnicity. Examining the internal logic of "ethnic" cultural invention, they show how "eating Chinese" became a New York Jewish custom that reflected articulations of self-identity. In some cases, Chinese food provided a "biographical continuity" for different generations of New York Jews through the linking of cultural themes and fond memories when dining in Chinese restaurants (p. 401). As they put it, socially constructed cultural differences are "…social facts, enduring and real in their consequences, yet malleable to reinterpretation by future generations" (p. 401). In the context of performances of authenticity, these social facts symbolize innovative cultural representations and reveal the potential for diverse meanings of "eating ethnic."

While Mexican culinary culture is central to Doug and Sara's advertising, décor, and menu, they do not make assertions of Mexican authenticity. In its place, they emphasize qualities such as "freshness" and "alternative" methods of food preparation. Through the use of hybrid inauthenticity, their restaurants highlight the vitality of different styles of cooking and observe the unique contributions (e.g., ingredients and seasonings) of a variety of cultures (e.g., El Salvadoran and Thai). More importantly, however, they respect the role and maintain the integrity of Mexican cultural forms. In other words, instead of appropriating small parts of Mexican culture in a piecemeal fashion, Doug and Sarah's restaurants honor Mexican ethnicity by drawing on it as the primary means to create something new (El Salvadoran burrito and Thai chicken burrito). Hence, implementing a hybrid inauthentic approach is a valuable method of honoring tradition even as it departs from tradition in its pristine form.

G

Americanized Authenticity: "Now You Can't Do Mexican"

James, the manager of a popular international Mexican restaurant chain, began his career at El Torito,[4] a California-based corporation. When I asked James why there were no El Torito restaurants in New England, he explained that New Englanders were not "ready for that type of Mexican food." Conversely, the chain he currently managed would not be well received in California, "because it's too Americanized; we haven't been brought up on Mexican food like people in California, not to mention produce availability year round; that kind of drives the menu." From James's perspective, because of their different degrees of exposure to Mexican food, customers in California and New England diverged in their Mexican food preferences. His restaurant is "too Americanized" for Californian palates, but sufficiently "Americanized" for New England palates. Comparing the restaurant chain he manages now to his experiences at El Torito, he explained:

> In recent years we've gotten a little more traditional than we used to be. Well, El Torito, it's more authentic. We took on some of El Torito's ways. Like we have a certain salsa, have gone to thicker corn tortillas, which are way better than our old ones used to be, way more authentic, you know.

In moving toward the "more authentic" ways of El Torito, James's menu offered foods such as "traditional nachos," "fajita pizza," and a "Buffalo chicken sandwich" served on a "Mexican-style bun."

James remarked that it was important for his restaurant to "try to become everything" to reach a wider customer base. As a result, the menu evolved to satisfy consumer trends:

> We have ribs, grilled burritos, so a bit of the Tex-Mex has melded into our menu as a necessity to compete with Chili's...Now you can't do Mexican. I think you have to offer other food to capture that one of four people that doesn't eat Mexican food.

Again and again, James emphasized the need to "capture" potential customers who do not normally eat Mexican food. To accomplish this, the restaurant must adhere to an "Americanized" menu. As he sees it, people who do not normally eat Mexican food "think it's hot, spicy; they think that's the only way you can get Mexican food. I compare it to Italian food, it's very flavorful, but not everything's hot." James' description of people's perceptions of Mexican food as spicy or hot, in combination with his comparison with Italian food, corresponds to those values put forth by large corporations, whereby Mexican food is marketed as "familiar" as opposed to distinct in and of itself.

Down the road from James's restaurant, Daniella, a manager of another chain restaurant, told me the story of the Mexican vaquero:

> The name [of the restaurant] is based on the Mexican vaquero, who is the Mexican cowboy. If you look at the front of the menu it gives you the story of the Mexican vaquero—so our mood is based on food that you cook on the range, the Mexican range.

The restaurant's mood, as she explained, was vital to its theme. With its Mexican vaquero logo, Daniella's restaurant is able to offer a wide range of both "Mexican cowboyish stuff," and "authentic cowboy stuff." For example, menu items include "campfire queso," "portabello fajitas," and a "border T-bone steak." To maintain an "authentic atmosphere," Daniella's restaurant must "readapt those philosophies [pertaining to traditional Mexican cuisine] to go along with the guests, the customers. It has been changed to where you can't go on without your theme, it [the restaurant] just won't survive."

The image of the Mexican cowboy worked well with the restaurant's theme. For instance, offering selections such as "smoked barbeque ribs" and "mesquite-grilled salmon," the restaurant's menu contributed to ideas about "traditional Mexican favorites" through the inclusion of nontraditional Mexican entrees.

According to Daniella, creating a comfortable atmosphere is also a big part of the restaurant's success:

> Atmosphere has a lot to do with people's perceptions. They walk in here and they already have a preconceived notion [of how the food will taste] by how clean our restaurant is, by what they are looking at. If they walked in here [and saw] four walls painted white, with no Mexican music on, with 1970s music, or whatever the case may be, they aren't going to feel that homey comfort. I'm sitting by the campfire range eating Mexican food, it's huge.

Apparently Daniella's "guests" appreciate the atmosphere of the restaurant: "we get it on comment cards all the time; the atmosphere is awesome, it's warm, it's cozy, you feel like you're sitting in Mexico, you know, it's authentic."

Elaborately decorated with giant saddles, colorful blankets, and rustic lanterns, the dining area stood out from the cordoned-off bar area that was adorned with neon-lights, large screen televisions, and life-size beer advertisements. Daniella explained:

> Well, we try to keep it all the same flare, you know. We don't have that Mexican bar-type atmosphere because you can't generate business out of that. It has to be functional as well, so it's not as authentic in the bar area as it is out here.

G

According to Daniella, although customers enjoy eating in a Mexican atmosphere, they do not enjoy drinking in one. The "authentic" dining area and the "not as authentic" bar area fittingly capture a corporate approach to "ethnic" dining: ethnic, but not *too* ethnic, authentic, but not *too* authentic.

Like James, Daniella expressed concern about those people who do not normally eat Mexican food:

> Down South, they don't need to have a Porterhouse steak [on the menu]. People in the Northeast don't know Mexican food, so there are many people who are like, 'I don't know Mexican food, I will not go there.' But now we have a lot to offer people, food that isn't Mexican.

In a large-scale industry study titled "Riding the U.S. Ethnic Food Tide," consultants suggested that "A company must understand how cuisines will develop, identify the opportunities, and capture them before others do" (Promar International 1998, 2). However, before they do so, companies ought to consider the implications of authenticity. As a different industry publication advised:

> ...presenting a mass American market[5] with rigorously authentic products is not only impossible, but inadvisable. Unless you're talking specifically to the heart of an ethnic community, you don't want to offer truly authentic ethnic...it's just too unfamiliar to the wider group. (Decker 2003, 113)

From this perspective, the maintenance of familiarity, such as the atmosphere, cuisine, and mood of a restaurant should suitably follow tastes of the "American market." Moreover, "successful" authentic "ethnic" products:

> will respect that spectrum's boundaries, sticking close to traditional cuisines that reflect American tastes. Once a product goes past the line of comfort and accessibility...it will not be seen as a real choice. It will be seen as something that is not convenient and not comfortable. And then it becomes foreign again. (pp. 113–114)

In her article "Eating the Other: Desire and Resistance," hooks (1992) explores the commodification of racial "otherness." Looking specifically at desire through the lens of race, she shows how discourses and practices successfully promote the enjoyment of racial difference as a "new delight, more intense, more satisfying than normal ways of doing and feeling" (p. 21). Concerned with cultural arrangements that celebrate ethnicity as "a spice, [a] seasoning that can liven up the dull dish that is mainstream white culture," hooks describes the unconscious as a site of contestation where capitalism, patriarchy, and colonialism continue to re-inscribe relational hierarchies (p. 21). As she sees it, this type of longing is deeply embedded in ideas of white superiority and the West's crisis with its own identity— both rooted in the learned libidinal aspiration to dominate. Shaping a large-scale restaurant chain according to the desires of an "American market" situates ethnicity not as a central expression of heritage or culture, but instead as "a spice" that accommodates the "desires" of an Anglo customer base whose consumption practices are considered hierarchically distinct.

Adhering to the logic of an "American market" systematically fails to recognize non-Anglo individuals as consumers of "ethnic" cuisine. With structures of exclusion built into the commercial organization of ethnic restaurants, it is no surprise that attributes such as "comfort" and "accessibility" trump qualities of cultural uniqueness. In such circumstances, people who are not classified as "American" remain unrecognized for their participation in and contribution to social, economic, and cultural expressions of public consumption. If consumption is one "place" where scholars insist the terms of citizenship are put into practice (Dávila 2001; GarcíaCanclini 2001; McRobbie 1999), then those consumers who are not "mainstream Northern and Western European" are excluded from particular privileges of citizenship. These processes illustrate not only the limited value of cultural agency in large-scale marketing practices, but also reveal the limitations that hierarchies of exclusion place on different groups of people. Through the promotion of an Americanized authenticity, the vibrancy of cultural forms that celebrate identity and heritage are collapsed into narratives that emphasize similarity by staying "close to traditional cuisines that reflect American tastes" (Decker 2003, 114). In such arrangements, "authenticity itself becomes a hot commodity," fostering conditions that commemorate similarity as opposed to difference (Halter 2000, 18).

Fast-and-Easy Inauthenticity: "*Yo Quiero Un Taco*"

What the standardization of a formal Mexican cuisine did for the growth of the Mexican restaurant industry, mechanization did for the spread of the Mexican fast food market. Taco Bell, the most famous and successful of these outfits started in 1962, and serves 60 million people a week (Baldwin 1999). In his authorized biography, the founder of Taco Bell, Glen Bell, eager to capitalize on the fast food cultural transformation taking place throughout Southern California in the 1950s, described how ordering tacos at a full-service restaurant was a slow process, but that alterations to the method of preparation could speed-up production. After visiting several local Mexican restaurants, he experimented with wire baskets and stainless steel holders in an attempt to create an easily replicated taco shell. Together with a "taco slide" and "taco rail," Bell developed a taco production line, and introduced the first manufactured taco shell (Baldwin 1999, 64).

Each new restaurant was commemorated with grand opening "fiestas," and some included "Hispanic men in gold-embroidered jackets [playing] guitars and violins…Women wearing embroidered blouses, full skirts, and colorful woven belts [who] raised their arms, clicked castanets, and laughed as they danced" (p. 74). Bell and his business partners participated in numerous fiestas over the years. In keeping with the Mexican theme, Bell "felt a Taco Bell should look like a building that sold tacos; he asked Robert [his architect] to give the new restaurant a south-of-the-border look" (p. 100). Together with the original "Taco Bell boy," described as "a smiling Hispanic wearing a serape and sombrero," Bell had a product, a theme, and a mascot (p. 146).

In 1978, Taco Bell was purchased by PepsiCo, and expanded its locations worldwide. As it took on other multinational fast food competitors, Taco Bell's publicity and marketing strategy became increasingly more important. During the 1970s, the restaurant offered only four products, but in 1984 they unveiled a new approach by expanding their menu, and "convincing mainstream America that its Mexican fare is nourishing, fresh, All-American fast food, rather than some exotic, gastrointestinal question mark" (Paskowski 1984, 66). Lawrence Higby, then senior vice-president of marketing stated, "We're trying to bring together tastes and concepts that people who are not as familiar—or trustful—of Mexican can recognize as beef, cheese, and corn" (p. 66). In an attempt to accommodate shifting trends, Higby explained, "Sales of hamburgers are flat, and that whole category is mature. Mexican is the standout—and we're changing dramatically to capitalize on that" (p. 67). As a result, Taco Bell's advertising focused on presenting their products as "…comfortable, familiar food that can be shared, that this is food to be consumed just like you would a hamburger…" (p. 67). The goal of the new approach, according to Higby, was to help people "get over their uneasiness with Mexican food" (p. 67). One restaurant analyst explained the changes by describing the need to accommodate customers who "historically [have] been intimidated by Mexican food, linking it with Montezuma's revenge" (p. 68).

Taco Bell's campaign was successful, and the company continued to expand. In the early 1990s, they cut costs by preparing food outside of their restaurants, and unveiled a 59, 79, and 99-cent menu. During the first three quarters, the number of customer transactions increased 35 percent (Lev 1990), overall sales

G

grew 28 percent, and operating profits rose 36 percent (Weinstein 1991). That same year, sales in the Mexican restaurant industry increased by 10 percent, as compared with the 2 percent growth in the restaurant industry as a whole (Dawson 1991). By pushing prices down and marketing their products as "value menu" items, Taco Bell, together with its 3,700 restaurants, was the industry forerunner in linking cheapness to Mexican-ness.

Toward the end of the 1990s, sales started to dip, and the company sought a fresh campaign to curb the decline in earnings. Taco Bell hired a new advertising agency, and in 1998, Dinky the Chihuahua (a.k.a. Gidget) first barked "*Yo quiero Taco Bell*" on nationally distributed television commercials. Not even the advertising executives had foreseen how popular the ads would become. By the end of 1998, sales were up 9 percent, and the chain expected to sell 20 million plush-toy versions of the Chihuahua (Johnson 1999). As Taco Bell vice president Peter Stack remarked, "We're enjoying the highest awareness levels our advertising has ever generated…" (Johnson 1999, 1). Prompting more sales than campaigns featuring human celebrities such as basketball superstar Shaquille O'Neal, Dinky the Chihuahua, as Taco Bell president Peter Waller put it, was "critical" to their success, stating, "It happens maybe once in a lifetime that you get a nation talking about you" (Horovitz 1998, 1).

Taco Bell did indeed experience high awareness levels; however, not all of them were positive. Many national Latino groups expressed concern over a Spanish-speaking dog invoking the imagery of a variety of Latino icons such as Che Guevara (the Argentinean Marxist revolutionary) and Evita Perón (the celebrated former first lady of Argentina). Still others, like members of National Council of La Raza and the League of United Latin American Citizens (LULAC) were angered by the use of anthropomorphism—when human characteristics are assigned to animals. The employment of anthropomorphic advertising in reference to a specific ethnic group is often considered a base for the subsequent dehumanization of that population. Welquis Lopez, the vice chairman of the National Hispanic Republican Assembly stated, "Why can't they use something else?…Don't use an animal, because then you're treating us like we are part of an animal" (Estrada 1998, 38). Gabriel Cazares, a former Clearwater, Florida, mayor, and president of the Tampa chapter of LULAC, called for a nationwide boycott of Taco Bell explaining:

> I think it was an unfortunate commercial. I think that the use of a dog to depict Mexicans was very demeaning. If Taco Bell wanted to depict someone that would reflect Mexican culture, we have many live, two-legged artists, singers, dancers, musicians—some great people in America that could have been selected to give a testimonial for Taco Bell [and] say, "*yo quiero un taco*," and that wouldn't have been offensive. (http:www.latinousa.org/learning/ tacobell.html)

Santa Ana (1999) argues that the contemporary framing of American discourse on undocumented Latino immigrants is commonly communicated through the dominant metaphor "immigrants are animals" (p. 198). Looking specifically at print media texts pertaining to the 1994 California referendum, Proposition 187,[6] Santa Ana shows how these ideas are reflected in the media. As animals "to be lured, pitted, or baited," both proimmigration and anti-immigration supporters described immigrants in this fashion (p. 200). In his estimation, "The conceptual correspondence 'immigrants are animals' is racist. It belittles immigrants as it separates non-citizens and citizens, since it assigns them a less-than-human standing" (p. 216). When considering that everyday metaphors symbolize the "common-sense world-view of [their] target domain," the significance of such characterizations highlights the potential effects and far-reaching social implications in the establishment of conventional frames of reference (p. 192).

In light of a series of political legislation targeting the Latino community,[7] commercials starring a Spanish-accented dog pitching Mexican food, for some, was an unlikely coincidence. As Cazares remarked, "It comes at a time when Hispanics, especially Mexicans, suffer terribly from immigrant bashing. It just makes me feel like that this is another putdown to Mexicans" (Sullivan 1998, 5). However, not all Latinos or Latino groups responded as fervently as Lopez or Cazares. In fact, Belen Robles, the national president of LULAC, issued a press release denying reports that they had asked Taco Bell to stop running the commercials and stated that, as they saw it, the Chihuahua was not offensive to Latinos. In her words, "This is a non-issue for LULAC...We have many more substantive things to worry about...I seriously doubt they would intentionally air something that is offensive to the Hispanic community" (Reddick 1998, 1).

From the Taco Bell boy to Dinky the Chihuahua, Taco Bell's representation of fast-and-easy inauthenticity organizes ethnicity through the cultivation of contested meanings, adherence to sameness and safeness, and alignment with dominant dialogues of the time period. Through discourses of humor and harmlessness simultaneous messages are sent and received disguising "a more malevolent function" (Dubin 1987, 130). These transmissions draw on notions of familiarity that situate ethnicity through the lens of commonality, conformity, and comfort. Consequently, through the implementation of characters and characteristics that are easy to control, social statuses of inequality are replicated, unintended or otherwise, in the display of caricature and humor.

Conclusion

The contention that authenticity is a highly negotiated interaction that represents a romanticized representation of reality is by now a scholarly norm. Similarly, the notion that ethnicity is a socially constructed category that reflects a group's common origin and sense of unique collective solidarity, is also a widely accepted belief. Within the culture of the Mexican restaurant industry, the accomplishment of authenticity and ethnicity is a social construction, one that is produced by Mexicans and Mexican-Americans as much as it is scripted by marketing experts of large restaurant chains. However, in spite of its socially constructed character, practices of authenticity have real-world implications that illustrate the limits and constraints that less powerful populations face in the marketplace—especially when it comes to accessing the conditions that enable the production and consumption of their identities.

Mexican restaurants are important sites where ideas about Mexican culture are generated and maintained. While the restaurants in this study primarily catered to an Anglo customer base, future research should consider how authenticity is negotiated in Mexican restaurants that have a more diverse clientele. For instance, how does authenticity operate in Mexican restaurants in places like Chicago, Los Angeles, or San Antonio? Such a focus would enable a more detailed discussion of the politics of consumption in relation to cultural performance. Additionally, research that examines how performances of authenticity and ethnicity differ across cultures would provide a rich context for theorizing how representation operates as a form of power. Although ethnicity is one form of representation accomplished through authenticity, research that explores other taken-for-granted claims as they are negotiated by individuals in the locations where they are practiced is vital for gaining a greater understanding of the dynamics that influence the production of culture. Analyzing these types of social relations reveals the embeddedness of meaning-making practices in local contexts and highlights the construction of cultural ideals that enforce essentialist ideas about ethnicity (Lamont 2000).

Narratives of authenticity and ethnicity, as central to the commercial character of the "ethnic" food industry, forge structural and relational hierarchies that reproduce knowledge about particular groups of people. Rooted in anxieties related to the expansion of modern industrial society (Trilling 1971), and entrenched in the ongoing efforts to achieve equality (Abarca 2004), struggles over representation reflect the enduring political salience of identity. In the context of the oft-cited cliché, "you are what you eat," the consumption of different identities presents itself as a social and political practice of representation. Practices of representation, as Lipsitz (1994) reminds us, do not necessarily suggest relations of equal standing or mutual reciprocity, especially when participants in these dialogues "speak from positions of highly unequal access to power, opportunity, and life chances" (p. 4). For Mexicans, Mexican-Americans, and Chicanos, whose access to the legal and symbolic benefits of citizenship is consistently challenged, matters of representation yield powerful political and material outcomes. The next step, then, is to critique the dimensions of other seemingly neutral forms of representation so as to open new possibilities, strategies, and spaces for questioning existing social divisions and confronting continuing inequalities. ■

Notes

1. All informant and restaurant names are pseudonyms. In some cases I withhold citations to maintain confidentiality.

2. For instance, in 2000, Springfield's population was 56 percent white, 27 percent Latino, 21 percent Black, 1.9 percent Asian, and Hartford's population was 27.7 percent white, 40.4 percent Latino, 38.1 percent Black, and 1.6 percent Asian. In comparison, Amherst's population was 79.3 percent white and Northampton's population was 90 percent white (www.census.gov).

3. According to the U.S. Census Bureau (2000), individuals who identified as Mexican or Mexican-American comprised less than 1 percent of the inhabitants in each of these communities. The specific percentages of people who identified themselves as Mexican or Mexican-American include: Amherst, 0.5 percent; Northampton, 0.4 percent; Springfield, 0.4 percent; and Hartford, 0.8 percent (www.census.gov).
4. El Torito Inc. is an international Mexican restaurant chain that operates in the western and mid-western United States, Turkey, Japan, and the Middle East.
5. Decker characterizes the "American market" as consumers whose backgrounds are "mainstream Northern and Western European" (2003, 113).
6. Proposition 187 sought to restrict social services, health care, and education to undocumented immigrants.
7. In particular, California initiatives, Proposition 187 (1994), Proposition 209 (1995), and Proposition 227 (1999).

References

Abarca, M. 2004. Authentic or not, it's original. *Food and Foodways* 12 (1): 1–25.
Baldwin, D. L. 1999. *Taco titan: the Glen Bell story*. Arlington: Summit.
Bauman, R., and C. L. Briggs. 1990. Poetics and performance as critical perspectives on language and social life. *Annual Review of Anthropology* 19:59–88.
Bell, David, and Gill Valentine. 1997. *We are where we eat*. London: Routledge.
Boorstin, D. 1961. *The image: a guide to pseudo-events in America*. New York: Vintage.
Bourdieu, P. 1984. *Distinction: a social critique of the judgment of taste*. Cambridge: Harvard University Press.
Dávila, A. 2001. *Latinos Inc.: the marketing and making of a people*. Berkeley: University of California Press.
Dawson, B. M. 1991. Poco prices and mucho menu choices drive traffic jump. *Restaurants and Institutions* 24 (July): 111.
Decker, K. J. 2003. Expanding culinary horizons with dried mixes. *Food Product Design* (June): 106–130.
Dubin, S. 1987. Symbolic slavery: Black representations in popular culture. *Social Problems* 34 (2): 122–38.
Estrada, R. 1998. TV ads aren't as harmless as viewers think. *Rocky Mountain News*, April 27.
Ferraro, S. 2002. *Comida sin par*. Consumption of Mexican food in Los Angeles: "foodscapes" in a transnational consumer society. In *Food nations: selling taste in consumer societies,* ed. W. Belasco and P. Scranton, 194–219. New York and London: Routledge.
Fine, G. A. 1996. *Kitchens: a macro-interactionist approach to organizational life and culture*. Berkeley: University of California Press.

G

Finkelstein, J. 1989. *Dining out: a sociology of modern manners*. Cambridge: Polity.
Gabaccia, D. 1998. *We are what we eat: ethnic food and the making of Americans*. Cambridge: Harvard University Press.
Gans, H. 1979. Symbolic ethnicity: the future of ethnic groups and cultures in America. *Ethnic and Racial Studies* 2 (1): 1–20.
García-Canclini, N. 2001. *Consumers and citizens*, trans. G. Yudice. Minneapolis: University of Minnesota Press.
Goffman, E. 1959. *Presentation of self in everyday life*. New York: Doubleday.
Goldman, A. 1992. "I yam what I yam": cooking, culture, and colonialism. In *De/Colonizing the subject: the politics of gender in women's autobiography*, ed. S. Smith and J. Watson, 169–95. Minneapolis: University of Minnesota.
Gray, H. 2004. Introduction. In *Watching race: television and the struggle for blackness*, xiii–xxv. Minneapolis: University of Minnesota Press.
Grazian, D. 2003. *Blue Chicago: the search for authenticity in urban blues clubs*. Chicago: University of Chicago Press.
———. 2004. The production of popular music as a confidence game: the case of the Chicago blues. *Qualitative Sociology* 27 (2): 137–58.
Halter, M. 2000. *Shopping for identity: the marketing of ethnicity*. New York: Schocken.
Handler, R. 1986. Authenticity. *Anthropology today* 2 (1): 6–9.
hooks, b. 1992. Eating the other: desire and resistance. In *Black looks: race and representation*, 21–39. Boston: South End.
Horovitz, B. 1998. Taco Bell finds a dog's life quite fetching: a Chihuahua leaves a mark on society and takes a bite out of the fast-food competition. *USA Today*, October 22.
Johnson, G. 1999. Grooming an icon for the long haul: Taco Bell knows it has a gold mine in a tiny dog—the key is making it last. *Los Angeles Times*, February 18.
Kates, S. and R. Belk. 2001. The meaning of lesbian and gay pride day: resistance through consumption and resistance to consumption. *Journal of Contemporary Ethnography* 30 (4): 392–429.
Kennedy, D. 1972. *The cuisines of Mexico*. New York: Harper & Row.
Lamont, M. 2000. The future of cultural sociology: broadening our agenda. *Contemporary Sociology* 29 (4): 602–7.
Latino USA. Taco Bell and Latino stereotypes. Cited January 15, 2005. Available from http://www.latinousa.org/learning/tacobell.html.
Lev, M. 1990. Taco Bell finds price of success. *The New York Times*, December 17.
Lipsitz, G. 1994. *Dangerous crossroads: popular music, postmodernism and the poetics of place*. New York: Verso.
Lu, S., and G. A. Fine. 1995. The presentation of ethnic authenticity: Chinese food as a social accomplishment. *Sociological Quarterly* 36 (3): 535–53.
MacCannell, D. 1973. Staged authenticity: arrangements of social space in tourist settings. *American Journal of Sociology* 79 (3): 389–603.
McRobbie, A. 1999. *In the culture society: art, fashion and popular music*. London: Routledge.

Nenga, S. K. 2003. Social class and structures of feeling in women's childhood memories of clothing, food, and leisure. *Journal of Contemporary Ethnography* 32 (2): 167–99.
Ohnuki-Tierney, E. 1993. *Rice as self: Japanese identities through time*. Princeton: Princeton University Press.
Paskowski, M. 1984. Taco Bell targets mainstream America. *Marketing and Media Decisions* 19 (June): 66.
Peterson, R. 1997. *Creating country music: fabricating authenticity*. Chicago: University of Chicago Press.
Promar International. 1998. *Riding the U.S. ethnic food tide: strategies for food manufacturers into the new millennium*. The Strategic Consultant Series. Alexandria,VA: Promar International Publication.
Reddick, T. 1998. Hispanic league's national leader says "si" to Taco Bell's Dinky. *The Tampa Tribune*, March 30.
Santa Ana, O. 1999. Like an animal I was treated: anti-immigrant metaphor in U.S. public discourse. *Discourse and Society* 10 (2): 191–224.
Spang, R. 2000. *The invention of the restaurant: Paris and modern gastronomic culture*. Cambridge: Harvard University Press.
Sullivan, J. 1998. Hispanic leaders have beef supreme with Taco Bell. *Times-Picayune*, March 9.
Trilling, L. 1971. *Sincerity and authenticity*. Cambridge: Harvard University Press.
Tuchman G., and H. Levine. 1992. New York Jews and Chinese food: the social construction of an ethnic pattern. *Journal of Contemporary Ethnography* 22 (3): 382–407.
United States Census Bureau. 2000. Population and household economic topics. Available from http://www.census.gov/population/www/index.html.
Walsh, R. 2004. *The Tex-Mex cookbook: a history in recipes and photos*. New York: Bantam Dell.
Waters, M. 1990. *Ethnic options: choosing identities in America*. Berkeley: University of California Press.
Weinstein, J. 1991. Truth and consequences of fast-food value menus. *Restaurants and Institutions* 6 (February): 13.

G

AUTHOR PROFILE

Marie Sarita Gaytán is Assistant Professor of Sociology and Gender Studies at the University of Utah. Her many scholarly articles explore issues pertaining to race and ethnicity, gender and sexuality, Latin America, popular culture, and consumption. "From Sombreros to *Sincronizadas*: Authenticity, Ethnicity, and the Mexican Restaurant Industry" was first published in the *Journal of Contemporary Ethnography* in 2008. Her new book, *¡Tequila! Distilling the Spirit of Mexico* (2014), was released this winter from Stanford University Press.

A Supermarket in California

By Allen Ginsberg

What thoughts I have of you tonight Walt Whitman, for I walked down the sidestreets under the trees with a headache self-conscious looking at the full moon.

In my hungry fatigue, and shopping for images, I went into the neon fruit supermarket, dreaming of your enumerations!

What peaches and what penumbras! Whole families shopping at night! Aisles full of husbands! Wives in the avocados, babies in the tomatoes!—and you, Garcia Lorca, what were you doing down by the watermelons?

I saw you, Walt Whitman, childless, lonely old grubber, poking among the meats in the refrigerator and eyeing the grocery boys.

I heard you asking questions of each: Who killed the pork chops? What price bananas? Are you my Angel?

I wandered in and out of the brilliant stacks of cans following you, and followed in my imagination by the store detective.

We strode down the open corridors together in our solitary fancy tasting artichokes, possessing every frozen delicacy, and never passing the cashier.

Where are we going, Walt Whitman? The doors close in an hour. Which way does your beard point tonight?

(I touch your book and dream of our odyssey in the supermarket and feel absurd.)

Will we walk all night through solitary streets? The trees add shade to shade, lights out in the houses, we'll both be lonely.

Will we stroll dreaming of the lost America of love past blue automobiles in driveways, home to our silent cottage?

Ah, dear father, graybeard, lonely old courage-teacher, what America did you have when Charon quit poling his ferry and you got out on a smoking bank and stood watching the boat disappear on the black waters of Lethe?

Berkeley, 1955 ■

AUTHOR PROFILE

Allen Ginsberg (1926–1997) was one of the best-known Beat poets, who voluntarily inherited the poetic role and forms originally created by Walt Whitman: speaking for and to America. Though he began writing when he was quite young, Ginsberg's work as a poet really began in 1954 when he moved to San Francisco and met other Beat writers, such as Jack Kerouac and William Burroughs. It is here that Ginsberg wrote his most famous long poem, "Howl" (1956), a love song to the lives of people outcast by McCarthyism's conservative America. Over the course of his career, Ginsberg's countercultural work continued to challenge social norms, including class, sexuality, religion, and politics. Ginsberg died in 1997, leaving behind a large body of work that, like Whitman's before him, played a dominant role in shaping American literary culture. "A Supermarket in California" was published in Ginsberg's *Collected Poems 1947–1980*.

Visual Literacy

By Peter Goin

The illiterate of the future will be the person ignorant of the use of the camera as well as of the pen.

—Laszlo Moholy-Nagy, 1936, quoted in Traub 1982, 23

Whenever a camera shutter opens and closes, recording a latent image on film, a fiction is created. Yet the image, once developed and printed in positive form, presents to the uninformed an overwhelming conviction of fact. The accuracy and fine detail of photographs are persuasive; likenesses are preserved in gelatin silver surfaces with a facility rarely ever matched in, for example, traditional pre-nineteenth-century art and naturalist drawings. When the process of photography was introduced early in the nineteenth century, photographs were called "mirrors with a memory" and "faithful witnesses." Operators, as photographers were then called, were not considered artists; nor were photographs considered fine art. The camera obscura was interpreted by many early critics of the photographic practice as simply a tool assisting an artist or scientist in rendering proper form and perspective. The camera "machine" was a mechanical device that excluded the artist's hand, a clear argument reducing photography to mechanical reproduction, much as we think of a Xerox machine today.

William Henry Fox Talbot (1800–1877), scientist, mathematician, botanist, linguist, and inventor of an early photographic process, authored *The Pencil of Nature*, one of the first books to contain original photographs. Published in London in 1844, this volume consists of eighty pages in quarto format, with twenty-four mounted photographic images preceded by some remarks and a short history of the calotype (a negative process on paper, invented by Talbot). Talbot felt it was necessary to print this enjoinder: "The plates of the present work are impressed by the agency of Light alone, without any aid whatever from the artist's pencil. They are the sunpictures themselves, and not, as some persons have imagined, engravings in imitation" (1969, 5). Although he heralded the enormous potential of the photographic process across disciplines, Talbot could not foresee its importance as a means of expression, analysis, or insight. He understood only that the photograph's exactness made it a verifiable piece of visual evidence. He believed the photograph to be a copy of the memory of light, nothing more.

Unfortunately, this limited view of the potential of photography continues to this day. Although most social scientists, including geographers, use the photograph in some way, rarely do they rely on the metaphorical and lyrical elements within the image, instead depending on the photograph's common denominator—the presumed accuracy of reproduced "fact." Any viewer willing to briefly review many of the social science journals from the past decade will recognize and confirm that the photograph is only occasionally used as an integral element in either a textual essay or a visual one.

Challenging this belief, I chose reputable journals from a variety of social science disciplines, examined them, and compared the number of articles, number of photographs per article, and number of graphic illustrations, including maps, with how the photographs were used. How many photographs were used as facts? How many photographs were identified as fictional? (Virtually none.) How many photographs were used in an aesthetic context; how many were used in a visual essay in which the images were presented as elements in a sequence, unto themselves? How many photographs were reproduced in color or in black and white; and how many photographers were credited in the text or caption? Was the photographer given coauthor credit, where appropriate? Was the photographer or the image itself credited as an integral element of the thematic idea? These were just a few of the questions. The journals included the *American Political Science Review*, the *Environmental History Review*, the *Geographical Review*, the *Journal of Modern Literature*, and *Visual Anthropology*.

Obviously, this was not a comprehensive survey of all social science journals, and the period reviewed was the decade beginning in 1990.Yet as a sample, perhaps even a managed random sample, the results are informative. Understandably, maps are a dominant form of visual illustration. In many journals—those surveyed and others—photographs are used sparingly and often reprinted on less-than-ideal paper. Numerous but not all reproductions are of poor quality, including but not limited to out-of-focus areas, blocked low-lights, "muddy" appearance, and other similar technical distractions. Coauthor credit for a photographer was acknowledged, but only in 8 out of 120 articles that used photography. (Clearly, not all articles should include coauthor credit).

Some journals are predisposed to using photography, although I believe most, if not all, journals should consider a greater role for the photographic image. Almost no photographs in my sample are reproduced in color, principally due to cost considerations (according to sample interviews). Journals that discuss areas of mutual concern with photography, such as issues related to nature studies, geomorphology, environmental interpretation, or urban studies, use few—very few—original and contemporary photographers' work dealing with similar themes.

A secondary consideration in my review was an investigation of the depth of interdisciplinary involvement. Noticeably, the academic disciplines are still highly segregated. There are exceptions, of course, but the track record reflects underutilized and underrepresented potential for photographic collaboration. As a reader, you may notice these exceptions and recognize their merit; and if so, I hope you will encourage those writing in your field to take notice. One particular case involves the *Geographical Review* and its most recent editorial attempts to include and respect photographic contributions.

I have yet to find a social science researcher who does not use the photograph in some way. If we accept this assumption that photographs are frequently used to complement social science research, it is entirely valid to critique how they are used. I believe it is equally important to question not just how they are used but also, in those relevant cases where no visual evidence is offered, why they are not used. It is clear that the majority of photographs used in social science publishing are illustrative and subordinate to the written text. In the spring of 1991 Roderick

Nash—the author *Wilderness and the American Mind* (1967)—told the Water in the West group of photographers meeting in Reno, Nevada, that the photograph should be a "visual rest," a pleasing pause offsetting complicated (read "textual") ideas. This from a man who has participated in several major photo-essay publications (Nash 1970; Collins and Nash 1978).

If a photograph is an illustration, then by virtue of that definition the photograph becomes supportive rather than creative, endorsing rather than original. According to Nash, the essential meaning of any article is not conveyed through the visual language; yet Nash himself relies heavily on photographic "evidence." In this scenario, the photograph is placed by its proprietor in a secondary and arguably subordinate role. The "illustration" is an *example* of the idea rather than an *expression* of the idea itself. Where photographs are perceived and understood to be primary evidence, intrinsically establishing a hierarchical relationship, the significance of the image changes as its context is defined. In these cases, the author perceives the photograph as raw material subject to the scholarly interpretation of the social scientist. As a consequence the author explains, defines, and interprets the photograph in the written text. Jay Ruby, editor of *Visual Anthropology*, once told me that a photograph is meaningless until a "scholar" renders it meaningful. I assume he meant that photographs are primarily objects of evidence.

So has the photograph become the visual equivalent of the "other," denied its own voice and metaphoric significance? Clearly, in this process the photograph's semantics are recontextualized. New (and written) text is added, and although I am not saying that this is inherently or inevitably wrong, it does alter the context and ultimately the meaning of the photograph. For example, the original photographer's point of view (conceptual rather than literal) may be neglected. Issues that focus on the anthropological use of the term *voice* are commonly underemphasized or deemphasized. Often, the emotional content of a photograph is sublimated in favor of a factual (verifiable) reading of information. It is not the complex point of view of the photographer that maintains meaning, as an example, but the author's focus on the facts of landscape, building, vehicle, or individual. The photograph is therefore deconstructed, and its potential significance is reduced or at the very least altered. Also, the rich evolution of the visual language of photography defaults to the "Talbot Position." The rich lyrical impact of a photograph may be neglected, however benignly, in favor of describing changing skylines, patterns of dress, automobile design, or many other appropriations of visual "fact."

At a recent symposium sponsored by the National Park Service and the Center of the American West at the University of Colorado, Boulder, a portrait of a prominent early-twentieth-century anthropologist was presented as cropped so that the aboriginal skulls, placed clinically on a long table next to the subject, would not be visually evident. Obviously, the intent of the Park Service was to obliquely respect native requests for the repatriation of remains, to not offend, to avoid controversy. The caption did not mention the cropping, nor did the body of the text in the brochure indicate the specific politics of representation. What is truthful and what is fact intersect at the point where the integrity—and implied meaning—of the photograph is questioned.

Photography is a visual language that survives by constantly adapting; interpreting photographs is exactly what I encourage. However, the photograph is more than the sum of the facts contained therein. A significant difference exists between "talking about" or analyzing a photograph and assuming that a photograph is principally, objectively, or verifiably accurate. A consequence of singularly literal interpretations of visual information implies that, in some cases, rejected patterns of pictorial representation are accepted without question. Imagine, for a moment, what would happen if a social scientist began to write articles in Middle English (the antiquated manuscript style common in the twelfth to the fifteenth centuries). Photography changes, constantly. Reading a nineteenth-century photograph made, say, by an itinerant colonial photographer in India provides much more information than just how that scene appeared at that time and place. Even the technology of photography has changed, and these technologies offer metaphoric opportunities—then and now.

Consider a parallel example for cartographers: Within the grid system, what if we continued to presume that linear distance was unaffected by topography? What if cultural definitions of spatial environments were arbitrarily assumed to be equal in all regions of the globe? The visual language of photography, which includes elements of light, angle, scale, diagonal line, motion, hue, saturation, tone, value, frame of reference, among many, many others, incorporates syntactic order.

It is a fundamental lesson for students of the arts that form can convey psychological meaning. Our students learn the fundamental lesson of photographic practice—that photography is a visual language employing syntactic rules and significance. At the very least, I believe we need more informative articles about photography relating to understanding pictorial form presented within social science journals. Lest we ignore the complicated subtext of visual imagery, we may be condemned to fulfill Moholy-Nagy's prediction.

Consider the example of beauty. Within the fine arts, beauty is continually being redefined; within the social science use of photography, beauty has become mostly mannered, neglected, or decorative. The concept of beauty, which includes the distinction between the sublime and the decorative, differences between emotive, demotive, and connotative meaning(s), just as cursory examples, may arguably be problematic and complex. Clearly, the debate over interpreting beauty is inevitably and necessarily evident, even by its absence, in pictorial representation. To acquiesce and deny the role of "contested aesthetics" by presumed "objectivity" or "documentation" does not eliminate beauty; acquiescence has its own politics.

From my perspective as a teacher, author, and photographer, among other roles, a "best general view" that incorporates the prevailing vernacular interpretation of beauty may be banal. Postcard hues and saturation are familiar, perhaps even pleasing in that expected kind of way, but these values do not reflect the expanding technical and conceptual choices in pictorial representation. Many photographers work in color; yet their work is reproduced in black and white. Yes, I know, color reproduction is expensive. Perhaps if we removed all the adjectives from a novel or descriptive phrases from an academic journal we could cut costs as well. The popular expectation of what a photograph should be-pleasing to the eye, visually balanced, descriptive, accurate-is not necessarily or obviously consistent with the elevated level of academic discourse expected within social science journals. Expect from your authors the same level of discourse visually and textually.

Two things are happening. First, the photograph has been defined in a very limited way simply according to its ability to "faithfully" record light on a solid surface. Secondly, the semantics of the photograph are rarely acknowledged. Additionally, the photograph is almost never understood or presented as an idea unto itself. Although social scientists are commonly armed with cameras and may produce competent photographs, there is only scant evidence that prevailing conventions of pictorial representation are understood or even challenged. The myth of objectivity is hardly debated, much less the complexity of a photograph's construction and context. The paradox is omnipresent: Photographs *are* documents at one level of the visual spectrum. Yet the photograph is a constructed illusion woven within a cultural frame of reference and point of view. Within any photograph the subject may become a symbol that can transcend its own appearance. At the same time, the politics of representation cannot be ignored. *How* the subject is represented is as important as the subject itself. *In what relationship with other photographs* was the appropriated image intended? *For whom* was the photograph intended? The photographer may have acted as a participant, been an observer, or acted directorially to create a scene that would otherwise not exist. The photographer may have made an image while operating under a cultural frame of reference that is either obsolete or modified in some manner. The original caption may have been removed, possibly affecting the meaning of the original document.

In short, the photograph is a complicated visual phenomenon that appears elementary (factual). True, a photograph often reveals a great deal more information than its maker ever intended. Even family snapshots can reveal dysfunction through the culture of posing and body language. For example, a few psychiatrists believe that by viewing family photographs manic depression can be recognized, if not firmly diagnosed. Ansel Adams's photographs of the drama of pristine nature are commonly thought to be "calendar art," yet his oeuvre endorses a philosophical and activist environmental stance. And have many authors employing Adams's photographs acknowledged his manipulation of the scene—both at the site and within the darkroom—for pictorial/aesthetic benefit? The anthropological photographs of Edward Curtis are complicated because of his assumptions about the "noble savage." Curtis adopted his research methods from the biological sciences, stressing observation, recording, and classification. However, it is important to remember that the facts observed were carefully constructed. Photographs displace time and space. Photographs "frame" the view, creating boundaries and visual emphases that are unique to the process. The specific moment becomes emblematic of the whole. And the combination of aesthetic sensitivity with scientific fidelity creates a problem in reading the appropriate "context." And don't forget that the addition of text may change the meaning of the photograph. "Meaning" is historically and culturally determined.

Gregory Bateson (1904–1980), an influential philosopher and anthropologist, stated in *Mind and Nature* that many of our cultural premises are obsolete (1979). He specifically identified the "anti-aesthetic assumption, borrowed from the emphasis which Bacon, Locke, and Newton long ago gave to the physical sciences...that all phenomena (including the mental) can and shall be studied and *evaluated* in quantitative terms" (1979, 235; emphasis in the original). The categorical separation between photography as science and photography as art prevent the interdisciplinary synthesis of statistical analysis and visual assumptions, of topographical detail and visceral response, or bar graphs/trends and beauty, to name just a few possible combinations. Where do the social sciences recognize the significance of secular spirit or aesthetics in their analysis? A geomorphologist once told me that a rainbow cannot reflect any secular spiritualism because it can be explained in scientific terms. Can we truly understand a sense of place without thinking about light memory? Regardless of the clinical explanation of the properties of refraction, it is clear to me, and hopefully to you, that rainbows are tremendously important in artists'—in all of our—emotional understanding of specific places.

This essay is about the relationship of *fact* and *truth*. The photograph is perceived to be fact. According to the scientific method, facts can and should be verifiable. And photographs contain elements—such as optical accuracy—reminiscent of fact. Truth and fact, though, are not the same. Truths are culturally derived and do not depend on the same standard of "objectivity." Truths imply wisdom and discovery, human emotion and shared values. We know that a photograph can represent a fact. But a photograph can also represent a truth that transcends fact.

Every time a latent image is recorded on film, I noted at the beginning of this essay, a fiction is created. The fact of light on film is heavily contextualized, so much so that the photograph becomes a fiction. The simple and elegant rectangle is a window through which we view...already context is being defined. A photograph is perhaps a universal paradox, because inherent in the medium of photography is the potential for truth in the presence of both fact and fiction. This inherent contradiction contributes to the magical illusion of photography. Photography—a universally accessible medium—has dramatically altered our sense of history and ourselves, and has created an optical paradigm for the twenty-first century. To continue to rely on the photograph simply as fact denies all of us the tremendous potential still ahead. ■

G

Further Reading

Bateson, G. 1979. *Mind and Nature: A Necessary Unity*. New York: Dutton.

Collins, R. O., and R. Nash. 1978. *The Big Drops: Ten Legendary Rapids*. San Francisco: Sierra Club.

Curtis, E. S. 1907–1930. *The North American Indian, Being a Series of Volumes Picturing and Describing the Indians of the United States, and Alaska*. Edited by F. W. Hodge. 20 vols. Seattle, Wash.: E. S. Curtis; Cambridge, Mass.: The University Press.

———. 1915. *In the Land of the Head-Hunters*. Yonkers-on-Hudson, N.Y.: World Book Co.

———. 1976. *Edward Sheriff Curtis: Visions of a Vanishing Race*. Text by F. C. Graybill and V. Boesen. Photographs prepared by J.–A. du Lac. New York: Crowell.

Dawson, R., M. Webb, and P. Goin. 2000. *A Doubtful River*. Reno: University of Nevada Press.

Goin, P. 1987. *Tracing the Line: A Photographic Survey of the Mexican-American Border*. Reno: Library, University of Nevada.

———. 1991. *Nuclear Landscapes*. Baltimore, Md.: Johns Hopkins University Press.

———. 1992. *Stopping Time: A Rephotographic Survey of Lake Tahoe*. Essays by C. E. Raymond and R. E. Blesse. Albuquerque: University of New Mexico Press.

———. 1996. *Humanature*. Austin: University of Texas Press.

———, ed. 1992. *Arid Waters: Photographs from the Water in the West Project*. Text by E. Manchester. Reno: University of Nevada Press.

Nash, R. 1982. *Wilderness and the American Mind*. 3d ed. New Haven, Conn.: Yale University Press.

———, ed. 1970. *Grand Canyon of the Living Colorado*. Photos and journal by Ernest Braun. San Francisco: Sierra Club.

Riebsame, W. E., ed. 1997. *Atlas of the New West: Portrait of a Changing Region*. New York: W. W. Norton.

Talbot, W. H. F. 1969 [1844–1846]. *The Pencil of Nature*. New York: Da Capo Press.

Traub, C. 1982. Photographic Education Comes of Age. In *The New Vision: Forty Years of Photography at the Institute of Design*, edited by C. Traub, 23–72. Millerton, N.Y.: Aperture.

AUTHOR PROFILE

Peter Goin (born 1951) is a photographer and author known for his innovative work in landscape photography and videography. He is the author and editor of many texts on visual culture, including a book titled *Nuclear Landscapes* (1991), which presented photographs of abandoned nuclear test sites. Goin was nominated for an Emmy for a 1993 documentary about the Burning Man festival. His photography has been exhibited at museums throughout the country. Goin is currently a professor of photography and visual art at the University of Nevada at Reno, where he leads horseback field workshops through the Sierra Nevada and Ruby mountain ranges.

Why Women Aren't Welcome on the Internet

By Amanda Hess

January 06, 2014 • 3:00 a.m.

"Ignore the barrage of violent threats and harassing messages that confront you online every day." That's what women are told. But these relentless messages are an assault on women's careers, their psychological bandwidth, and their freedom to live online. We have been thinking about Internet harassment all wrong.

I was 12 hours into a summer vacation in Palm Springs when my phone hummed to life, buzzing twice next to me in the dark of my hotel room. I squinted at the screen. It was 5:30 a.m., and a friend was texting me from the opposite coast. "Amanda, this twitter account. Freaking out over here," she wrote. "There is a twitter account that seems to have been set up for the purpose of making death threats to you."

I dragged myself out of bed and opened my laptop. A few hours earlier, someone going by the username "headlessfemalepig" had sent me seven tweets. "I see you are physically not very attractive. Figured," the first said. Then: "You suck a lot of drunk and drug fucked guys cocks." As a female journalist who writes about sex (among other things), none of this feedback was particularly out of the ordinary. But this guy took it to another level: "I am 36 years old, I did 12 years for 'manslaughter,' I killed a woman, like you, who decided to make fun of guys cocks." And then: "Happy to say we live in the same state. Im looking you up, and when I find you, im going to rape you and remove your head." There was more, but the final tweet summed it up: "You are going to die and I am the one who is going to kill you. I promise you this."

H

My fingers paused over the keyboard. I felt disoriented and terrified. Then embarrassed for being scared, and, finally, pissed. On the one hand, it seemed unlikely that I'd soon be defiled and decapitated at the hands of a serial rapist-murderer. On the other hand, headlessfemalepig was clearly a deranged individual with a bizarre fixation on me. I picked up my phone and dialed 911.

Two hours later, a Palm Springs police officer lumbered up the steps to my hotel room, paused on the outdoor threshold, and began questioning me in a steady clip. I wheeled through the relevant background information: I am a journalist; I live in Los Angeles; sometimes, people don't like what I write about women, relationships, or sexuality; this was not the first time that someone had responded to my work by threatening to rape and kill me. The cop anchored his hands on his belt, looked me in the eye, and said, "What is Twitter?"

Staring up at him in the blazing sun, the best answer I could come up with was, "It's like an e-mail, but it's public." What I didn't articulate is that Twitter is the place where I laugh, whine, work, schmooze, procrastinate, and flirt. It sits in my back pocket wherever I go and lies next to me when I fall asleep. And since I first started writing in 2007, it's become just one of the many online spaces where men come to tell me to get out.

The examples are too numerous to recount, but like any good journalist, I keep a running file documenting the most deranged cases. There was the local cable viewer who hunted down my email address after a television appearance to tell me I was "the ugliest woman he had ever seen." And the group of visitors to a "men's rights" site who pored over photographs of me and a prominent feminist activist, then discussed how they'd "spend the night with" us. ("Put em both in a gimp mask and tied to each other 69 so the bitches can't talk or move and go round the world, any old port in a storm, any old hole," one decided.) And the anonymous commenter who weighed in on one of my articles: "Amanda, I'll fucking rape you. How does that feel?"

None of this makes me exceptional. It just makes me a woman with an Internet connection. Here's just a sampling of the noxious online commentary directed at other women in recent years. To Alyssa Royse, a sex and relationships blogger, for saying that she hated *The Dark Knight*: "you are clearly retarded, i hope someone shoots then rapes you." To Kathy Sierra, a technology writer, for blogging about software, coding, and design: "i hope someone slits your throat and cums down your gob." To Lindy West, a writer at the women's website Jezebel, for critiquing a comedian's rape joke: "I just want to rape her with a traffic cone." To Rebecca Watson, an atheist commentator, for blogging about sexism in the skeptic community: "If I lived in Boston I'd put a bullet in your brain." To Catherine Mayer, a journalist at *Time* magazine, for no particular reason: "A BOMB HAS BEEN PLACED OUTSIDE YOUR HOME. IT WILL GO OFF AT EXACTLY 10:47 PM ON A TIMER AND TRIGGER DESTROYING EVERYTHING."

A woman doesn't even need to occupy a professional writing perch at a prominent platform to become a target. According to a 2005 report by the Pew Research Center, which has been tracking the online lives of Americans for more than a decade, women and men have been logging on in equal numbers since 2000, but the vilest communications are still disproportionately lobbed at women. We are more likely to report being stalked and harassed on the Internet—of the 3,787 people who reported harassing incidents from 2000 to 2012 to the volunteer organization Working to Halt Online Abuse, 72.5 percent were female. Sometimes, the abuse can get physical: A Pew survey reported that 5 percent of women who used the Internet said "something happened online" that led them into "physical danger." And it starts young: Teenage girls are significantly more likely to be cyberbullied than boys. Just appearing as a woman online, it seems, can be enough to inspire abuse. In 2006, researchers from the University of Maryland set up a bunch of fake online accounts and then dispatched them into chat rooms. Accounts with feminine usernames incurred an average of 100 sexually explicit or threatening messages a day. Masculine names received 3.7.

There are three federal laws that apply to cyberstalking cases; the first was passed in 1934 to address harassment through the mail, via telegram, and over the telephone, six decades after Alexander Graham Bell's invention. Since the initial passage of the Violence Against Women Act, in 1994, amendments to the law have gradually updated it to apply to new technologies and to stiffen penalties against those who use them to abuse. Thirty-four states have cyberstalking laws on the books; most have expanded long-standing laws against stalking and criminal threats to prosecute crimes carried out online.

But making quick and sick threats has become so easy that many say the abuse has proliferated to the point of meaninglessness, and that expressing alarm is foolish. Reporters who take death threats seriously "often give the impression that this is some kind of shocking event for which we should pity the 'victims,'" my colleague Jim Pagels wrote in *Slate* this fall, "but anyone who's spent 10 minutes online knows that these assertions are entirely toothless." On Twitter, he added, "When there's no precedent for physical harm, it's only baseless fear mongering." My friend Jen Doll wrote, at the *Atlantic Wire*, "It seems like that old 'ignoring' tactic your mom taught you could work out to everyone's benefit....These people are bullying, or hope to bully. Which means we shouldn't take the bait." In the epilogue to her book *The End of Men*, Hanna Rosin—an editor at *Slate*—argued that harassment of women online could be seen as a cause for celebration. It shows just how far we've come. Many women on the Internet "are in positions of influence, widely published and widely read; if they sniff out misogyny, I have no doubt they will gleefully skewer the responsible sexist in one of many available online outlets, and get results."

So women who are harassed online are expected to either get over ourselves or feel flattered in response to the threats made against us. We have the choice to keep quiet or respond "gleefully."

But no matter how hard we attempt to ignore it, this type of gendered harassment—and the sheer volume of it—has severe implications for women's status on the Internet. Threats of rape, death, and stalking can overpower our emotional bandwidth, take up our time, and cost us money through legal fees, online protection services, and missed wages. I've spent countless hours over the past four years logging the online activity of one particularly committed cyberstalker, just in case. And as the Internet becomes increasingly central to the human experience, the ability of women to live and work freely online will be shaped, and too often limited, by the technology companies that host these threats, the constellation of local and federal law enforcement officers who investigate them, and the popular commentators who dismiss them—all arenas that remain dominated by men, many of whom have little personal understanding of what women face online every day.

This summer, Caroline Criado-Perez became the English-speaking Internet's most famous recipient of online threats after she petitioned the British government to put more female faces on its bank notes. (When the Bank of England announced its intentions to replace social reformer Elizabeth Fry with Winston Churchill on the £5 note, Criado-Perez made the modest suggestion that the bank make an effort to feature at least one woman who is not the Queen on any of its currency.) Rape and death threats amassed on her Twitter feed too quickly to count, bearing messages like "I will rape you tomorrow at 9 p.m ... Shall we meet near your house?"

Then, something interesting happened. Instead of logging off, Criado-Perez retweeted the threats, blasting them out to her Twitter followers. She called up police and hounded Twitter for a response. Journalists around the world started writing about the threats. As more and more people heard the story, Criado-Perez's follower count skyrocketed to near 25,000. Her supporters joined in urging British police and Twitter executives to respond.

Under the glare of international criticism, the police and the company spent the next few weeks passing the buck back and forth. Andy Trotter, a communications adviser for the British police, announced that it was Twitter's responsibility to crack down on the messages. Though Britain criminalizes a broader category of offensive speech than the U.S. does, the sheer volume of threats would be too difficult for "a hard-pressed police service" to investigate, Trotter said. Police "don't want to be in this arena." It diverts their attention from "dealing with something else."

Meanwhile, Twitter issued a blanket statement saying that victims like Criado-Perez could fill out an online form for each abusive tweet; when Criado-Perez supporters hounded Mark Luckie, the company's manager of journalism and news, for a response, he briefly shielded his account, saying that the attention had become "abusive." Twitter's official recommendation to victims of abuse puts the ball squarely in law enforcement's court: "If an interaction has gone beyond the point of name calling and you feel as though you may be in danger," it says, "contact your local authorities so they can accurately assess the validity of the threat and help you resolve the issue offline."

In the weeks after the flare-up, Scotland Yard confirmed the arrest of three men. Twitter—in response to several online petitions calling for action—hastened the rollout of a "report abuse" button that allows users to flag offensive material. And Criado-Perez went on receiving threats. Some real person out there—or rather, hundreds of them—still liked the idea of seeing her raped and killed.

The Internet is a global network, but when you pick up the phone to report an online threat, whether you are in London or Palm Springs, you end up face-to-face with a cop who patrols a comparatively puny jurisdiction. And your cop will probably be a man: According to the U.S. Bureau of Justice Statistics, in 2008, only 6.5 percent of state police officers and 19 percent of FBI agents were women. The numbers get smaller in smaller agencies. And in many locales, police work is still a largely analog affair: 911 calls are immediately routed to the local police force; the closest officer is dispatched to respond; he takes notes with pen and paper.

After Criado-Perez received her hundreds of threats, she says she got conflicting instructions from police on how to report the crimes, and was forced to repeatedly "trawl" through the vile messages to preserve the evidence. "I can just about cope with threats," she wrote on Twitter. "What I can't cope with after that is the victim-blaming, the patronising, and the police record-keeping." Last year, the American atheist blogger Rebecca Watson wrote about her experience calling a series of local and national law enforcement agencies after a man launched a website threatening to kill her. "Because I knew what town [he] lived in, I called his local police department. They told me there was nothing they could do and that I'd have to make a report with my local police department," Watson wrote later. "[I] finally got through to someone who told me that there was nothing they could do but take a report in case one day [he] followed through on his threats, at which point they'd have a pretty good lead."

The first time I reported an online rape threat to police, in 2009, the officer dispatched to my home asked, "Why would anyone bother to do something like that?" and declined to file a report. In Palm Springs, the officer who came to my room said, "This guy could be sitting in a basement in Nebraska for all we know." That my stalker had said that he lived in my state, and had plans to seek me out at home, was dismissed as just another online ruse.

Of course, some people are investigated and prosecuted for cyberstalking. In 2009, a Florida college student named Patrick Macchione met a girl at school, then threatened to kill her on Twitter, terrorized her with lewd videos posted to YouTube, and made hundreds of calls to her phone. Though his victim filed a restraining order, cops only sprang into action after a county sheriff stopped him for loitering, then reportedly found a video camera in his backpack containing disturbing recordings about his victim. The sheriff's department later worked with the state attorney's office to convict Macchione on 19 counts, one of which was cyberstalking (he successfully appealed that count on grounds that the law hadn't been enacted when he was arrested); Macchione was sentenced to four years in prison. Consider also a recent high-profile case of cyberstalking investigated by the FBI. In the midst of her affair with General David Petraeus, biographer Paula Broadwell allegedly created an anonymous email account for the purpose of sending harassing notes to Florida socialite Jill Kelley. Kelley reported them to the FBI, which sniffed out Broadwell's identity via the account's location-based metadata and obtained a warrant to monitor her email activity.

In theory, appealing to a higher jurisdiction can yield better results. "Local law enforcement will often look the other way," says Dr. Sameer Hinduja, a criminology professor at Florida Atlantic University and co-director of the Cyberbullying Research Center. "They don't have the resources or the personnel to investigate those crimes." County, state, or federal agencies at least have the support to be more responsive: "Usually they have a computer crimes unit, savvy personnel who are familiar with these cases, and established relationships with social media companies so they can quickly send a subpoena to help with the investigation," Hinduja says.

But in my experience and those of my colleagues, these larger law enforcement agencies have little capacity or drive to investigate threats as well. Despite his pattern of abusive online behavior, Macchione was ultimately arrested for an unrelated physical crime. When I called the FBI over headlessfemalepig's threats, a representative told me an agent would get in touch if the bureau was interested in pursuing the case; nobody did. And when Rebecca Watson reported the threats targeted at her to the FBI, she initially connected with a sympathetic agent—but the agent later expressed trouble opening Watson's file of screenshots of the threats, and soon stopped replying to her emails. The Broadwell investigation was an uncommon, and possibly unprecedented, exercise for the agency. As University of Wisconsin-Eau Claire criminal justice professor Justin Patchin told *Wired* at the time: "I'm not aware of any case when the FBI has gotten involved in a case of online harassment."

After I received my most recent round of threats, I asked Jessica Valenti, a prominent feminist writer (and the founder of the blog Feministing), who's been repeatedly targeted with online threats, for her advice, and then I asked her to share her story. "It's not really one story. This has happened a number of times over the past seven years," she told me. When rape and death threats first started pouring into her inbox, she vacated her apartment for a week, changed her bank accounts, and got a new cell number. When the next wave of threats came, she got in touch with law enforcement officials, who warned her that though the men emailing her were unlikely to follow through on their threats, the level of vitriol indicated that she should be vigilant for a far less identifiable threat: silent "hunters" who lurk behind the tweeting "hollerers." The FBI advised Valenti to leave her home until the threats blew over, to never walk outside of her apartment alone, and to keep aware of any cars or men who might show up repeatedly outside her door. "It was totally impossible advice," she says. "You have to be paranoid about everything. You can't just not be in a public place."

And we can't simply be offline either. When *Time* journalist Catherine Mayer reported the bomb threat lodged against her, the officers she spoke to—who thought usernames were secret codes and didn't seem to know what an IP address was—advised her to unplug. "Not one of the officers I've encountered uses Twitter or understands why anyone would wish to do so," she later wrote. "The officers were unanimous in advising me to take a break from Twitter, assuming, as many people do, that Twitter is at best a time-wasting narcotic."

All of these online offenses are enough to make a woman *want* to click away from Twitter, shut her laptop, and power down her phone. Sometimes, we do withdraw: Pew found that from 2000 to 2005, the percentage of Internet users who participate in online chats and discussion groups dropped from 28 percent to 17 percent, "entirely because of women's fall off in participation." But for many women, steering clear of the Internet isn't an option. We use our devices to find supportive communities, make a living, and construct safety nets. For a woman like me, who lives alone, the Internet isn't a fun diversion—it is a necessary resource for work and interfacing with friends, family, and, sometimes, law enforcement officers in an effort to feel safer from both online and offline violence.

The Polish sociologist Zygmunt Bauman draws a distinction between "tourists" and "vagabonds" in the modern economy. Privileged tourists move about the world "on purpose," to seek "new experience" as "the joys of the familiar wear off." Disempowered vagabonds relocate because they have to, pushed and pulled through mean streets where they could never hope to settle down. On the Internet, men are tourists and women are vagabonds. "Telling a woman to shut her laptop is like saying, 'Eh! Just stop seeing your family,'" says Nathan Jurgenson, a social media sociologist (and a friend) at the University of Maryland.

What does a tourist look like? In 2012, Gawker unmasked "Violentacrez," an anonymous member of the online community Reddit who was infamous for posting creepy photographs of underage women and creating or moderating subcommunities on the site with names like "chokeabitch" and "rapebait." Violentacrez turned out to be a Texas computer programmer named Michael Brusch, who displayed an exceedingly casual attitude toward his online hobbies. "I do my job, go home, watch TV, and go on the Internet. I just like riling people up in my spare time," he told Adrian Chen, the Gawker reporter who outed him. "People take things way too seriously around here."

Abusers tend to operate anonymously, or under pseudonyms. But the women they target often write on professional platforms, under their given names, and in the context of their real lives. Victims don't have the luxury of separating themselves from the crime. When it comes to online threats, "one person is feeling the reality of the Internet very viscerally: the person who is being threatened," says Jurgenson. "It's a lot easier for the person who made the threat—and the person who is investigating the threat—to believe that what's happening on the Internet isn't real."

When authorities treat the Internet as a fantasyland, it has profound effects on the investigation and prosecution of online threats. Criminal threat laws largely require that victims feel tangible, immediate, and sustained fear. In my home state of California, a threat must be "unequivocal, unconditional, immediate, and specific" and convey a "gravity of purpose and an immediate prospect of execution of the threat" to be considered a crime. If police don't know whether the harasser lives next door or out in Nebraska, it's easier for them to categorize the threat as non-immediate. When they treat a threat as a boyish hoax, the implication is that the threat ceases to be a criminal offense.

So the victim faces a psychological dilemma: How should she understand her own fear? Should she, as many advise, dismiss an online threat as a silly game, and not bother to inform the cops that someone may want to—ha, ha—rape and kill her? Or should she dutifully report every threat to police, who may well dismiss her concerns? When I received my most recent rape and death threats, one friend told me that I should rest assured that the anonymous tweeter was unlikely to take any physical action against me in real life; another noted that my stalker seemed like the type of person who would fashion a coat from my skin, and urged me to take any action necessary to land the stalker in jail.

Danielle Citron, a University of Maryland law professor who focuses on Internet threats, charted the popular response to Internet death and rape threats in a 2009 paper published in the *Michigan Law Review*. She found that Internet harassment is routinely dismissed as "harmless locker-room talk," perpetrators as "juvenile pranksters," and victims as "overly sensitive complainers." Weighing in on one online harassment case, in an interview on National Public Radio, journalist David Margolick called the threats "juvenile, immature, and obnoxious, but that is all they are…frivolous frat-boy rants."

Of course, the frat house has never been a particularly safe space for women. I've been threatened online, but I have also been harassed on the street, groped on the subway, followed home from the 7-Eleven, pinned down on a bed by a drunk boyfriend, and raped on a date. Even if I sign off Twitter, a threat could still be waiting on my stoop.

Today, a legion of anonymous harassers are free to play their "games" and "pranks" under pseudonymous screen names, but for the women they target, the attacks only compound the real fear, discomfort, and stress we experience in our daily lives.

If American police forces are overwhelmingly male, the technology companies that have created the architecture of the online world are, famously, even more so. In 2010, according to the information services firm CB Insights, 92 percent of the founders of fledgling Internet companies were male; 86 percent of their founding teams were exclusively male. While the number of women working across the sciences is generally increasing, the percentage of women working in computer sciences peaked in 2000 and is now on the decline. In 2012, the Bureau of Labor Statistics found, women made up just 22.5 percent of American computer programmers and 19.7 percent of software developers. In a 2012 study of 400 California companies, researchers at the University of California-Davis found that just seven percent of the highest-paid executives at Silicon Valley companies were women.

When Twitter announced its initial public offering in October, its filings listed an all-male board. Vijaya Gadde, Twitter's general counsel, was the only woman among its executive officers. When Vivek Wadhwa, a fellow at Stanford's Rock Center for Corporate Governance, suggested that the gender imbalance on Twitter's board was an issue of "elite arrogance" and "male chauvinistic thinking," Twitter CEO Dick Costolo responded with a joking tweet, calling Wadhwa "the Carrot Top of academic sources."

Most executives aren't intentionally boxing women out. But the decisions these men make have serious implications for billions of people. The gender imbalance in their companies compromises their ability to understand the lives of half their users.

Twitter "has a history of saying 'too bad, so sad'" when confronted with concerns about harassment on its platform, says Citron, the University of Maryland law professor who studies the emerging legal implications of online abuse against women. The culture of the platform has typically prioritized freewheeling discussion over zealous speech policing. Unlike Facebook, Twitter doesn't require people to register accounts under their real names. Users are free to enjoy the frivolity—and the protection—that anonymous speech provides. If a user runs afoul of Twitter's terms of service, he's free to create a new account under a fresh handle. And the Communications Decency Act of 1996 protects platforms like Twitter from being held legally responsible for what individuals say on the site.

The advent of the "report abuse" button is a development Citron finds "very heartening." Allowing people to block an abuser's account helps women avoid having to be faced with vile and abusive tweets. But our problems can't all be solved with the click of a button. In some cases, the report abuse button is just a virtual Band-Aid for a potentially dangerous real-world problem. It can undermine women by erasing the trail of digital evidence. And it does nothing to prevent these same abusers from opening a new account and continuing their crimes.

When I received those seven tweets in Palm Springs, a well-meaning friend reported them as abusive through Twitter's system, hoping that action on the platform's end would help further my case. A few hours later, the tweets were erased from the site without comment (or communication with me). Headlessfemalepig's Twitter feed was replaced with a page noting that the account had been suspended. Luckily, I had taken screenshots of the tweets, but to the cops working with a limited understanding of the platform, their sudden disappearance only confused the issue. The detective assigned to my case asked me to send him links pointing to where the messages lived online—but absent a subpoena of Twitter's records, they were gone from law enforcement's view. If someone had reported the threats before I got a chance to see them, I might not even have been able to indicate their existence at all. Without a proper investigation, I am incapable of knowing whether headlessfemalepig is a one-time offender or the serial stalker who has followed me for many years. Meanwhile, nothing's stopping headlessfemalepig from continuing to tweet away under a new name.

It shouldn't be Twitter's responsibility to hunt down and sanction criminals who use its service—that's what cops are (supposedly) for. Twitter has to balance its interests in addressing abusive behavior with its interests in protecting our private information (or that of, say, political dissidents), which means keeping a tight lid on users' IP addresses and refusing to offer up deleted material to civilians. When I asked how Twitter balances those demands, Nu Wexler, who leads public policy communications for the company, pointed me to a chart published by the Electronic Frontier Foundation—an advocacy group dedicated to defending the free speech and privacy rights of Internet users—that illustrates the platform's "commitment to user privacy." The chart, titled "Who Has Your Back: Which Companies Help Protect Your Data From the Government?," awards Twitter high marks for fighting for users' privacy rights in court and publishing a transparency report about government data requests.

A high score awarded by the Electronic Frontier Foundation communicates to users that their Internet activity will be safe from overreaching government snoops—and post–Edward Snowden, that concern is more justified than ever. But in some cases, the impulse to protect our privacy can interfere with the law's ability to protect us when we're harassed. Last year, the Electronic Frontier Foundation came out against an amendment to the Violence Against Women Act. Until recently, the law criminalized abusive, threatening, and harassing speech conveyed over a telephone line, provided the abuser placed the call; the new law, passed in March, applies to any electronic harassment targeted at a specific person, whether it's made over the telephone or by another means. Critics of the legislation pulled out the trope that the Internet is less real than other means of communication. As the Foundation put it, "a person is free to disregard something said on Twitter in a way far different than a person who is held in constant fear of the persistent ringing of a telephone intruding in their home."

The Electronic Frontier Foundation—and the tech companies that benefit from its ratings—are undoubtedly committed to fighting government First Amendment abuses. But when they focus their efforts on stemming the spread of anti-harassment laws from outdated media, like landline telephones, to modern means like Twitter, their efforts act like a thumb on the scale, favoring some democratic values at the expense of others. "Silicon Valley has the power to shape society to conform to its values, which prioritize openness and connectivity," Jurgenson says. "But why are engineers in California getting to decide what constitutes harassment for people all around the world?"

Tech companies are, of course, fully aware that they need a broad base of users to flourish as billion-dollar businesses. Today women have the bargaining power to draft successful petitions calling for "report abuse" buttons, but our corporate influence is limited, and alternative venues for action are few. Local police departments "have no money," Jurgenson says, and "it feels unlikely that the government is going to do more any time soon, so we're forced to put more pressure on Twitter." And while an organized user base can influence the decisions of a public, image-conscious company like Twitter, many platforms—like the dedicated "revenge porn" sites that have proliferated on the Web—don't need to appease women to stay popular. "I call this the myth of the market," Citron says. "There's definitely a desire for anti-social behavior. There are eyeballs. And there are users who are providing the content. The market isn't self-correcting, and it's not going to make this go away."

In a 2009 paper in the *Boston University Law Review*, Citron proposed a new way of framing the legal problem of harassment on the Internet: She argued that online abuse constitutes "discrimination in women's employment opportunities" that ought to be better addressed by the U.S. government itself. Title VII of the Civil Rights Act of 1964, which outlawed discrimination based on race, religion, or gender, was swiftly applied to members of the Ku Klux Klan, who hid behind hoods to harass and intimidate black Louisianians from voting and pursuing work. Anonymous online harassment, Citron argued, similarly discourages women from "writing and earning a living online" on the basis of their gender. "It interferes with their professional lives. It raises their vulnerability to offline sexual violence. It brands them as incompetent workers and inferior sexual objects. The harassment causes considerable emotional distress."

On the Internet, women are overpowered and devalued. We don't always think about our online lives in those terms—after all, our days are filled with work to do, friends to keep up with, Netflix to watch. But when anonymous harassers come along—saying they would like to rape us, or cut off our heads, or scrutinize our bodies in public, or shame us for our sexual habits—they serve to remind us in ways both big and small that we can't be at ease online. It is precisely the banality of Internet harassment, University of Miami law professor Mary Anne Franks has argued, that makes it "both so effective and so harmful, especially as a form of discrimination."

The personal and professional costs of that discrimination manifest themselves in very real ways. Jessica Valenti says she has stopped promoting her speaking events publicly, enlisted security for her public appearances, signed up for a service to periodically scrub the Web of her private information, invested in a post-office box, and begun periodically culling her Facebook friend list in an attempt to filter out readers with ulterior motives. Those efforts require a clear investment of money and time, but the emotional fallout is less directly quantifiable. "When people say you should be raped and killed for years on end, it takes a toll on your soul," she says. Whenever a male stranger approaches her at a public event, "the hairs on the back of my neck stand up." Every time we call the police, head to court to file a civil protection order, or get sucked into a mental hole by the threats that have been made against us, zeroes drop from our annual incomes. Says Jurgenson, "It's a monetary penalty for being a woman."

Citron has planted the seed of an emerging debate over the possibility of applying civil rights laws to ensure equal opportunities for women on the Internet. "There's no silver bullet for addressing this problem," Citron says. But existing legislation has laid the groundwork for potential future reforms. Federal civil rights law can punish "force or threat[s] of force" that interfere with a person's employment on the basis of race, religion, or national origin. That protection, though, doesn't currently extend to threats targeted at a person's gender. However, other parts of the Civil Rights Act frame workplace sexual harassment as discriminatory, and requires employers to implement policies to both prevent and remedy discrimination in the office. And Title IX of the Education Amendments of 1972 puts the onus on educational institutions to take action against discrimination toward women. Because Internet harassment affects the employment and educational opportunities of women, laws could conceivably be amended to allow women to bring claims against individuals.

But it's hard to get there from here. As Citron notes, the Internet is not a school or a workplace, but a vast and diffuse universe that often lacks any clear locus of accountability. Even if online threats are considered a civil rights violation, who would we sue? Anonymous tweeters lack the institutional affiliation to make monetary claims worthwhile. And there is the mobbing problem: One person can send just one horrible tweet, but then many others may pile on. A single vicious tweet may not clear the hurdle of discriminatory harassment (or repetitive abuse). And while a mob of individuals each lobbing a few attacks clearly looks and feels like harassment, there is no organized group to take legal action against. Bringing separate claims against individual abusers would be laborious, expensive, and unlikely to reap financial benefits. At the same time, amending the Communications Decency Act to put the onus on Internet platforms to police themselves could have a serious chilling effect on all types of speech, discriminatory or otherwise.

Citron admits that passing new civil rights legislation that applies to a new venue—the Internet—is a potentially Sisyphean task. But she says that by expanding existing civil rights laws to recognize the gendered nature of Internet threats, lawmakers could put more pressure on law enforcement agencies to take those crimes seriously. "We have the tools already," Citron says. "Do we use them? Not really." Prosecuting online threats as bias-motivated crimes would mean that offenders would face stronger penalties, law enforcement agencies would be better incentivized to investigate these higher-level crimes—and hopefully, the Internet's legions of anonymous abusers would begin to see the downside of mouthing off.

Our laws have always found a way to address new harms while balancing longstanding rights, even if they do it very slowly. Opponents of the Civil Rights Act of 1964 characterized its workplace protections as unconstitutional and bad for business. Before workplace sexual harassment was reframed as discriminatory under Title VII, it was written off as harmless flirting. When Title IX was first proposed to address gender discrimination in education, a Senate discussion on the issue ended in laughter when one senator cracked a co-ed football joke. Until domestic violence became a national policy priority, abuse was dismissed as a lovers' quarrel. Today's harmless jokes and undue burdens are tomorrow's civil rights agenda.

My serial cyberstalker began following me in 2009. I was on the staff of an alt-weekly when a mini-controversy flared up on a blog. One of the blog's writers had developed a pattern of airing his rape fantasies on the site; I interviewed him and the site's other contributors and published a story. Then I started receiving rape threats of my own. Their author posted a photo of me on his blog and wrote, "Oh, sure, you might say she's pretty. Or you might say she looks sweet or innocent. But don't let looks fool you. This woman is pure evil." (To some harassers, you're physically not very attractive; to others, you're beautiful.) "I thought I'd describe her on my blog as 'rape-worthy,' but ultimately decided against it," he added. "Oops! I've committed another thought crime!"

In the comments section below the article, threats popped up under a dozen fake names and several phony IP addresses—which usually point to a device's precise location, but can be easily faked if you have the right software. "Amanda, I'll fucking rape you," one said. "How's that feel? Like that? What's my IP address, bitch?" On his Twitter account, my stalker wrote that he planned to buy a gun—apparently intending to defend his First Amendment rights by exercising the Second.

Then, one night when my boyfriend and I were in our apartment, my cell phone started ringing incessantly. I received a series of voicemails, escalating in tone from a stern "You cut the shit right fucking now" to a slurred "You fucking dyke … I will fuck you up." For the first time ever, I called the police. When an officer arrived at my house, I described the pattern of abuse. He expressed befuddlement at the "virtual" crime, handed me his card, and told me to call if anyone came to my house—but he declined to take a report.

Without police support, I opted to file a civil protection order in family court. I posted a photograph of my stalker at my office's front desk. When the local sheriff's department failed to serve him court papers, I paid $100 for a private investigator to get the job done. It took me five visits to court, waiting for my case to be called up while sitting quietly across the aisle from him in the gallery as dozens of other local citizens told a domestic violence judge about the boyfriends and fathers and ex-wives who had threatened and abused them. These people were seeking protection from crowbar-wielding exes and gun-flashing acquaintances—more real crimes the justice system had failed to prosecute. By the time the judge finally called up my protection order for review, I had missed a half-dozen days of work pursuing the case. I was lucky to have a full-time job and an understanding boss—even if he didn't understand the threats on the same level I did. And because my case was filed under new anti-stalking protections—protections designed for cases like mine, in which I was harassed by someone I didn't have a personal relationship with—I was lucky to get a court-appointed lawyer, too. Most victims don't.

My harasser finally acquiesced to the protection order when my lawyer showed him that we knew the blog comments were coming from his computer—he had made a valiant attempt to obscure his comments, but he'd slipped up in a couple of instances, and we could prove the rape threats were his. When the judge approved the order, she instructed my harasser that he was not allowed to contact me in any way—not by email, Twitter, phone, blog comment, or by hiring a hot air balloon to float over my house with a message, she said. And he had to stay at least 100 feet away from me at all times. The restraining order would last one year.

Soon after the order expired, he sent an email to my new workplace. Every once in a while, he re-establishes contact. Last summer, he waded into the comments section of an article I wrote about sex website creator Cindy Gallop, to say, "I would not sacrifice the physiological pleasure of ejaculating inside the woman for a lesser psychological pleasure.... There is a reason it feels better to do it the right way and you don't see others in the ape world practicing this behavior." A few months later, he reached out via LinkedIn. ("Your stalker would like to add you to his professional network.") A few days before I received the threats in Palm Springs, he sent me a link via Twitter to a story he wrote about another woman who had been abused online. Occasionally, he sends his tweets directly my way—a little reminder that his "game" is back on.

It's been four years, but I still carry the case files with me. I record every tweet he sends me in a Word document, forward his emails to a dedicated account, and then print them out to ensure I'll have them ready for police in analog form if he ever threatens me again (or worse). Whenever I have business travel to the city where he lives, I cart my old protection order along, even though the words are beginning to blur after a dozen photocopies. The stacks of paper are filed neatly in my apartment. My anxieties are harder to organize. ■

AUTHOR PROFILE

Amanda Hess is a prominent journalist who reports on gender, teenagers, technology, Hollywood, sex, and sexuality. Her work has appeared in the *Los Angeles Times*, the *Columbia Journalism Review*, *Al Jazeera*, *NYTimes.com*, *Slate*, *Details*, *The Village Voice*, *Wired*, *Elle.com*, and *Nylon*. She is the co-founder and editor of *TOMORROW* magazine, which explores emerging trends and movements that are reshaping our world. Additionally, she is a contributor to the *Book of Jezebel*, an illustrated book of things important to modern women, and has appeared on CNN and *All Things Considered*. Her article, "Why Women Aren't Welcome on the Internet," was originally published by *Pacific Standard Magazine* and received a Sidney Award recognizing outstanding socially conscious journalism.

What's in a Package

By Thomas Hine

When you put yourself behind a shopping cart, the world changes. You become an active consumer, and you are moving through environments—the supermarket, the discount store, the warehouse club, the home center—that have been made for you.

During the thirty minutes you spend on an average trip to the supermarket, about thirty thousand different products vie to win your attention and ultimately to make you believe in their promise. When the door opens, automatically, before you, you enter an arena where your emotions and your appetites are in play, and a walk down the aisle is an exercise in self-definition. Are you a good parent, a good provider? Do you have time to do all you think you should, and would you be interested in a shortcut? Are you worried about your health and that of those you love? Do you care about the environment? Do you appreciate the finer things in life? Is your life what you would like it to be? Are you enjoying what you've accomplished? Wouldn't you really like something chocolate?

Few experiences in contemporary life offer the visual intensity of a Safeway, a Krogers, a Pathmark, or a Piggly Wiggly. No marketplace in the world—not Marrakesh or Calcutta or Hong Kong—offers so many different goods with such focused salesmanship as your neighborhood supermarket, where you're exposed to a thousand different products a minute. No wonder it's tiring to shop.

There are, however, some major differences between the supermarket and a traditional marketplace. The cacophony of a traditional market has given way to programmed, innocuous music, punctuated by enthusiastically intoned commercials. A stroll through a traditional market offers an array of sensuous aromas; if you are conscious of smelling something in a supermarket, there is a problem. The life and death matter of eating, expressed in traditional markets by the sale of vegetables with stems and roots and by hanging animal carcasses, is purged from the supermarket, where food is processed somewhere else, or at least trimmed out of sight.

But the most fundamental difference between a traditional market and the places through which you push your cart is that in a modern retail setting nearly all the selling is done without people. The product is totally dissociated from the personality of any particular person selling it—with the possible exception of those who appear in its advertising. The supermarket purges sociability, which slows down sales. It allows manufacturers to control the way they present their products to the world. It replaces people with packages.

Packages are an inescapable part of modern life. They are omnipresent and invisible, deplored and ignored. During most of your waking moments, there are one or more packages within your field of vision. Packages are so ubiquitous that they slip beneath conscious notice, though many packages are designed so that people will respond to them even if they're not paying attention.

Once you being pushing the shopping cart, it matters little whether you are in a supermarket, discount store, or a warehouse club. The important thing is that you are among packages: expressive packages intended to engage your emotions, ingenious packages that make a product useful, informative packages that help you understand what you want and what you're getting. Historically, packages are what made self-service retailing possible, and in turn such stores increased the number and variety of items people buy. Now a world without packages is unimaginable.

Packages lead multiple lives. They preserve and protect, allowing people to make use of things that were produced far away, or a while ago. And they are potently expressive. They assure that an item arrives unspoiled, and they help those who use the item feel good about it.

We share our homes with hundreds of packages, mostly in the bathroom and kitchen, the most intimate, body-centered rooms of the house. Some packages—a perfume flacon, a ketchup bottle, a candy wrapper, a beer can—serve as permanent landmarks in people's lives that outlast homes, careers, or spouses. But packages embody change, not just in their age-old promise that their contents are new and improved, but in their attempt to respond to changing tastes and achieve new standards of convenience. Packages record changing hairstyles and changing lifestyles. Even social policy of closures testify to the fragility of the social contract, and the susceptibility of the great mass of people to the destructive acts of a very few. It was a mark of rising environmental consciousness when containers recently began to make a novel promise: "less packaging."

For manufacturers, packaging is the crucial final payoff to a marketing campaign. Sophisticated packaging is one of the chief ways people find the confidence to buy. It can also give a powerful image to products and commodities that are in themselves characterless. In many cases, the shopper has been prepared for the shopping experience by lush, colorful print advertisements, thirty-second television minidramas, radio jingles, and coupon promotions. But the package makes the final sales pitch, seals the commitment, and gets itself placed in the shopping cart. Advertising leads consumers to temptation. Packaging is the temptation. In many cases it is what makes the product possible.

But the package is also useful to the shopper. It is a tool for simplifying and speeding decisions. Packages promise, and usually deliver, predictability. One reason you don't think about packages is that you don't need to. The candy bar, the aspirin, the baking powder, or the beer in the old familiar package may, at times, be touted as new and improved, but it will rarely be very different.

You put the package into your cart, or not, usually without really having focused on the particular product or its many alternatives. But sometimes you do examine the package. You read the label carefully, looking at what the product promises, what it contains, what it warns. You might even look on your dressing table, or you might think about whether someone might have tampered with it or whether it can be easily recycled. The possibility of such scrutiny is one of the things that make each detail of the package so important.

The environment through which you push your shopping cart is extraordinary because of the amount of attention that has been paid to the packages that line the shelves. Most contemporary environments are landscapes of inattention. In housing developments, malls, highways, office buildings, even furniture, design ideas are few and spread very thin. At the supermarket, each box and jar, stand-up pouch and squeeze bottle, each can and bag and tube and spray has been very carefully considered. Designers have worked and reworked the design on their computers and tested mock-ups on the store shelves. Refinements are measured in millimeters.

All sorts of retail establishments have been redefined by packaging. Drugs and cosmetics were among the earliest packaged products, and most drugstores now resemble small supermarkets. Liquor makers use packaging to add a veneer of style to the intrinsic allure of intoxication, and some sell their bottle rather than the drink. It is no accident that vodka, the most characterless of spirits, has the highest-profile packages. The local gas station sells sandwiches and soft drinks rather than tires and motor oil, and in turn, automotive products have been attractively repackaged for sales at supermarkets, warehouse clubs, and home centers.

With its thousands of images and messages, the supermarket is as visually dense, if not as beautiful, as a Gothic cathedral. It is as complex and as predatory as a tropical rain forest. It is more than a person can possibly take in during an ordinary half-hour shopping trip. No wonder a significant percentage of people who need to wear eyeglasses don't wear them when they're shopping, and some researchers have spoken of the trancelike state that pushing a cart through this environment induces. The paradox here is that the visual intensity that overwhelms shoppers is precisely the thing that makes the design of packages so crucial. Just because you're not looking at a package doesn't mean you don't see it. Most of the time, you see far more than a container and a label. You see a personality, an attitude toward life, perhaps even a set of beliefs.

The shopper's encounter with the product on the shelf is, however, only the beginning of the emotional life cycle of the package. The package is very important in the moment when the shopper recognizes it either as an old friend or a new temptation. Once the product is brought home, the package seems to disappear, as the quality or usefulness of the product it contains becomes paramount. But in fact, many packages are still selling even at home, enticing those who have bought them to take them out of the cupboard, the closet, or the refrigerator and consume their contents. Then once the product has been used up, and the package is empty, it becomes suddenly visible once more. This time, though, it is trash that must be discarded or recycled. This instant disposal is the time when people are most aware of packages. It is a negative moment, like the end of a love affair, and what's left seems to be a horrid waste.

The forces driving package design are not primarily aesthetic. Market researchers have conducted surveys of consumer wants and needs, and consultants have studied photographs of families' kitchen cupboards and medicine chests to get a sense of how products are used. Test subjects have been tied into pieces of heavy apparatus that measure their eye movement, their blood pressure or body temperature, when subjected to different packages. Psychologists get people to talk about the packages in order to get a sense of their innermost feelings about what they want. Government regulators and private health and safety advocates worry over package design and try to make it truthful. Stock-market analysts worry about how companies are managing their "brand-equity," that combination of perceived value and consumer loyalty that is expressed in advertising but embodied in packaging. The retailer is paying attention to the packages in order to weed out the ones that don't sell or aren't sufficiently profitable. The use of supermarket scanners generates information on the profitability of every cubic inch of the store. Space on the supermarket shelf is some of the most valuable real estate in the world, and there are always plenty of new packaged products vying for display.

Packaging performs a series of disparate tasks. It protects its contents from contamination and spoilage. It makes it easier to transport and store goods. It provides uniform measuring of contents. By allowing brands to be created and standardized, it makes advertising meaningful and large-scale distribution possible. Special kinds of packages, with dispensing caps, sprays, and other convenience features, make products more usable. Packages serve as symbols both of their contents and of a way of life. And just as they can very powerfully communicate the satisfaction a product offers, they are equally potent symbols of wastefulness once the product is gone.

Most people use dozens of packages each day and discard hundreds of them each year. The growth of mandatory recycling programs has made people increasingly aware of packages, which account in the United States for about forty-three million tons, or just under 30 percent of all refuse discarded. While forty-three million tons of stuff is hardly insignificant, repeated surveys have shown that the public perceives that far more than 30 percent—indeed, nearly all—their garbage consists of packaging. This perception creates a political problem for the packaging industry, but it also demonstrates the power of packaging. It is symbolic. It creates an emotional relationship. Bone and wasted food (thirteen million tons), grass clippings and yard waste (thirty-one million tons), or even magazines and newspapers (fourteen million tons) do not feel as wasteful as empty vessels that once contained so much promise.

Packaging is a cultural phenomenon, which means that it works differently in different cultures. The United States has been a good market for packages since it was first settled and has been an important innovator of packaging technology and culture. Moreover, American packaging is part of an international culture of modernity and consumption. At its deepest level, the culture of American packaging deals with the issue of surviving among strangers in a new world. This is an emotion with which anyone who has been touched by modernity can identify. In lives buffeted by change, people seek the safety and reassurance that packaged products offer. American packaging, which has always sought to appeal to large numbers of diverse people, travels better than that of most cultures.

But the similar appearance of supermarkets throughout the world should not be interpreted as the evidence of a single, global consumer culture. In fact, most companies that do business internationally redesign their packages for each market. This is done partly to satisfy local regulations and adapt to available products and technologies. But the principal reason is that people in different places have different expectations and make different uses of packaging.

The United States and Japan, the world's two leading industrial powers, have almost opposite approaches to packaging. Japan's is far more elaborate than America's, and it is shaped by rituals of respect and centuries-old traditions of wrapping and presentation. Packaging is explicitly recognized as an expression of culture in Japan and largely ignored in America. Japanese packaging is designed to be appreciated; American packaging is calculated to be unthinkingly accepted.

Foods that only Japanese eat—even relatively humble ones like refrigerated prepared fish cakes—have wrappings that resemble handmade paper or leaves. Even modestly priced refrigerated fish cakes have beautiful wrappings in which traditional design accommodates a scannable bar code. Such products look Japanese and are unambiguously intended to do so. Products that are foreign such as coffee, look foreign, even to the point of having only Roman lettering and no Japanese lettering on the can. American and European companies are sometimes able to sell their packages in Japan virtually unchanged, because their foreignness is part of their selling power. But Japanese exporters hire designers in each country to repackage their products. Americans—whose culture is defined not by refinements and distinctions but by inclusiveness—want to think about the product itself, not its cultural origins.

We speak glibly about global villages and international markets, but problems with packages reveal some unexpected cultural boundaries. Why are Canadians willing to drink milk out of flexible plastic pouches that fit into reusable plastic holders, while residents of the United States are believed to be so resistant to the idea that they have not even been given the opportunity to do so? Why do Japanese consumers prefer packages that contain two tennis balls and view the standard U.S. pack of three to be cheap and undesirable? Why do Germans insist on highly detailed technical specifications on packages of videotape, while Americans don't? Why do Swedes think that blue is masculine, while the Dutch see the color as feminine? The answers lie in unquestioned habits and deep-seated imagery, a culture of containing, adorning, and understanding that no sharp marketer can change overnight.

There is probably no other field in which designs that are almost a century old—Wrigley's gum, Campbell's soup, Hershey's chocolate bar—remain in production only subtly changed and are understood to be extremely valuable corporate assets. Yet the culture of packaging, defined by what people are buying and selling every day, keeps evolving, and the role nostalgia plays is very small.

For example, the tall, glass Heinz ketchup bottle has helped define the American refrigerator skyline for most of the twentieth century (even though it is generally unnecessary to refrigerate ketchup). Moreover, it provides the tables of diners and coffee shops with a vertical accent and a token of hospitality, the same qualities projected by candles and vases of flowers in more upscale eateries. The bottle has remained a fixture of American life, even though it has always been a nuisance to pour the thick ketchup through the little hole. It seemed not to matter that you have to shake and shake the bottle, impotently, until far too much ketchup comes out in one great scarlet plop. Heinz experimented for years with wide-necked jars and other sorts of bottles, but they never caught on.

Then in 1992 a survey of consumers indicated that more Americans believed that the plastic squeeze bottle is a better package for ketchup than the glass bottle. The survey did not offer any explanations for this change of preference, which has been evolving for many years as older people for whom the tall bottle is an icon became a less important part of the sample. Could it be that the difficulty of using the tall bottle suddenly became evident to those born after 1960? Perhaps the tall bottle holds too little ketchup. There is a clear trend toward buying things in larger containers, in part because lightweight plastics have made them less costly for manufacturers to ship and easier for consumers to use. This has happened even as the number of people in an average American household has been getting smaller. But houses, like packages, have been getting larger. Culture moves in mysterious ways.

The tall ketchup bottle is still preferred by almost half of consumers, so it is not going to disappear anytime soon. And the squeeze bottle does contain visual echoes of the old bottle. It is certainly not a radical departure. In Japan, ketchup and mayonnaise are sold in cellophane-wrapped plastic bladders that would certainly send Americans into severe culture shock. Still, the tall bottle's loss of absolute authority is a significant change. And its ultimate disappearance would represent a larger change in most people's visual environment than would the razing of nearly any landmark building.

But although some package designs are pleasantly evocative of another time, and a few appear to be unchanging icons in a turbulent world, the reason they still exist is because they still work. Inertia has historically played a role in creating commercial icons. Until quite recently, it was time-consuming and expensive to make new printing plates or to vary the shape or material of a container. Now computerized graphics and rapidly developing technology in the package-manufacturing industries make a packaging change easier than in the past, and a lot cheaper to change than advertising, which seems a far more evanescent medium. There is no constituency of curators or preservationists to protect the endangered package. If a gum wrapper manages to survive nearly unchanged for ninety years, it's not because any expert has determined that it is an important cultural expression. Rather, it's because it still helps sell a lot of gum.

So far, we've been discussing packaging in its most literal sense: designed containers that protect and promote products. Such containers have served as the models for larger types of packaging, such as chain restaurants, supermarkets, theme parks, and festival marketplaces...Still, it is impossible to ignore a broader conception of packaging that is one of the preoccupations of our time. This concerns the ways in which people construct and present their personalities, the ways in which ideas are presented and diffused, the ways in which political candidates are selected and public policies formulated. We must all worry about packaging ourselves and everything we do, because we believe that nobody has time to really pay attention.

Packaging strives at once to offer excitement and reassurance. It promises something newer and better, but not necessarily different. When we talk about a tourist destination, or even a presidential contender, being packaged, that's not really a metaphor. The same projection of intensified ordinariness, the same combination of titillation and reassurance, are used for laundry detergents, theme parks, and candidates alike.

The imperative to package is unavoidable in a society in which people have been encouraged to see themselves as consumers not merely of toothpaste and automobiles, but of such imponderables as lifestyle, government, and health. The marketplace of ideas is not an agora, where people haggle, posture, clash, and come to terms with one another. Rather, it has become a supermarket, where values, aspirations, dreams, and predictions are presented with great sophistication. The individual can choose to buy them, or leave them on the shelf.

In such a packaged culture, the consumer seems to be king. But people cannot be consumers all the time. If nothing else, they must do something to earn the money that allows them to consume. This, in turn, pressures people to package themselves in order to survive. The early 1990s brought economic recession and shrinking opportunities to all the countries of the developed world. Like products fighting for their space on the shelf, individuals have had to re-create, or at least represent, themselves in order to seem both desirable and safe. Moreover, many jobs have been reconceived to depersonalize individuals and to make them part of a packaged service experience.

These phenomena have their own history. For decades, people have spoken of writing resumes in order to package themselves for a specific opportunity. Thomas J. Watson Jr., longtime chairman of IBM, justified his company's famously conservative and inflexible dress code—dark suits, white shirts, and rep ties for all male employees—as "self-packaging," analogous to the celebrated product design, corporate imagery, and packaging done for the company by Elliot Noyes and Paul Rand. You can question whether IBM's employees were packaging themselves or forced into a box by their employer. Still, anyone who has ever dressed for success was doing a packaging job.

Since the 1950s, there have been discussions of packaging a candidate to respond to what voters are telling the pollsters who perform the same tasks as market researchers do for soap or shampoo. More recently, such discussions have dominated American political journalism. The packaged candidate, so he and his handlers hope, projects a message that, like a Diet Pepsi, is stimulating without being threatening. Like a Weight Watchers frozen dessert bar, the candidate's contradictions must be glazed over and, ultimately, comforting. Aspects of the candidate that are confusing or viewed as extraneous are removed, just as stems and sinew are removed from packaged foods. The package is intended to protect the candidate; dirt won't stick. The candidate is uncontaminated, though at a slight remove from the consumer-voter.

People profess to be troubled by this sort of packaging. When we say a person or an experience is "packaged," we are complaining of a sense of excessive calculation and a lack of authenticity. Such a fear of unreality is at least a century old; it arose along with industrialization and rapid communication. Now that the world is more competitive, and we all believe we have less time to consider things, the craft of being instantaneously appealing has taken on more and more importance. We might say, cynically, that the person who appears "packaged" simply doesn't have good packaging.

Still, the sense of uneasiness about encountering packaged people in a packaged world is real, and it shouldn't be dismissed. Indeed, it is a theme of contemporary life, equally evident in politics, entertainment, and the supermarket. Moreover, public uneasiness about the phenomenon of packaging is compounded by confusion over a loss of iconic packages and personalities.

Producers of packaged products have probably never been as nervous as they became during the first half of the 1990s. Many of the world's most famous brands were involved in the merger mania of the 1980s, which produced debt-ridden companies that couldn't afford to wait for results either from their managers or their marketing strategies. At the same time, the feeling was that it was far too risky to produce something really new. The characteristic response was the line extension—"dry" beer, "lite" mayonnaise, "ultra" detergent. New packages have been appearing at a rapid pace, only to be changed whenever a manager gets nervous or a retailer loses patience.

The same skittishness is evident in the projection of public personalities as the clear, if synthetic, images of a few decades ago have lost their sharpness and broken into a spectrum of weaker, reflected apparitions. Marilyn Monroe, for example, had an image that was, Jayne Mansfield notwithstanding, unique and well defined. She was luscious as a Hershey's bar, shapely as a Coke bottle. But in a world where Coke can be sugar free, caffeine free, and cherry flavored (and Pepsi can be clear!), just one image isn't enough for a superstar. Madonna is available as Marilyn or as a brunette, a Catholic schoolgirl, or a bondage devotee. Who knows what brand extension will come next? Likewise, John F. Kennedy and Elvis Presley had clear, carefully projected images. But Bill Clinton is defined largely by evoking memories of both. As our commercial civilization seems to have lost the power to amuse or convince us in new and exciting ways, formerly potent packages are recycled and devalued. That has left the door open for such phenomena as generic cigarettes, President's Choice cola, and H. Ross Perot.

This cultural and personal packaging both fascinates and infuriates. There is something liberating in its promise of aggressive self-creation, and something terrifying in its implication that everything must be subject to the ruthless discipline of the marketplace. People are at once passive consumers of their culture and aggressive packagers of themselves, which can be a stressful and lonely combination. ■

AUTHOR PROFILE

Thomas Hine (born 1946) is a writer and cultural historian. Originally from suburban Massachusetts, he grew up in Connecticut and earned his BA at Yale in 1969. He was the architecture and design critic for the *Philadelphia Inquirer* from 1973–1996 and returned in 2014 to write a bi-weekly column on art museum exhibitions. He has published six books on American design, culture, and shifting attitudes toward consumer society. He frequently contributes to periodicals such as *Atlantic Monthly, The Magazine Antiques*, and *Philadelphia Magazine* and has been a guest lecturer at Yale, Syracuse, Drexel, and Michigan State University. "What's in a Package" is a chapter from *The Total Package: The Secret History and Hidden Meanings of Boxes, Bottles, Cans and Other Persuasive Containers* (1995).

H

Introduction

From *Teaching to Transgress*

By bell hooks

In the weeks before the English Department at Oberlin College was about to decide whether or not I would be granted tenure, I was haunted by dreams of running away—of disappearing—yes, even of dying. These dreams were not a response to fear that I would not be granted tenure. They were a response to the reality that I *would* be granted tenure. I was afraid that I *would* be trapped in the academy forever.

Instead of feeling elated when I received tenure, I fell into a deep, life-threatening depression. Since everyone around me believed that I should be relieved, thrilled, proud, I felt "guilty" about my "real" feelings and could not share them with anyone. The lecture circuit took me to sunny California and the New Age world of my sister's house in Laguna Beach where I was able to chill out for a month. When I shared my feelings with my sister (she's a therapist), she reassured me that they were entirely appropriate because, she said, "You never wanted to be a teacher. Since we were little, all you ever wanted to do was write." She was right. It was always assumed by everyone else that I would become a teacher. In the apartheid South, black girls from working-class backgrounds had three career choices. We could marry. We could work as maids. We could become school teachers. And since, according to the sexist thinking of the time, men did not really desire "smart" women, it was assumed that signs of intelligence sealed one's fate. From grade school on, I was destined to become a teacher.

But the dream of becoming a writer was always present within me. From childhood, I believed that I would teach *and* write. Writing would be the serious work, teaching would be the not-so-serious-I-need-to-make-a-living "job." Writing, I believed then, was all about private longing and personal glory, but teaching was about service, giving back to one's community. For black folks teaching—educating—was fundamentally political because it was rooted in antiracist struggle. Indeed, my all-black grade schools became the location where I experienced learning as revolution.

Almost all our teachers at Booker T. Washington were black women. They were committed to nurturing intellect so that we could become scholars, thinkers, and cultural workers—black folks who used our "minds." We learned early that our devotion to learning, to a life of the mind, was a counter-hegemonic act, a fundamental way to resist every strategy of white racist colonization. Though they did not define or articulate these practices in theoretical terms, my teachers were enacting a revolutionary pedagogy of resistance that was profoundly anticolonial. Within these segregated schools, black children who were deemed exceptional, gifted, were given special care. Teachers worked with and for us to ensure that we would fulfill our intellectual destiny and by so doing uplift the race. My teachers were on a mission.

To fulfill that mission, my teachers made sure they "knew" us. They knew our parents, our economic status, where we worshipped, what our homes were like, and how we were treated in the family. I went to school at a historical moment where I was being taught by the same teachers who had taught my mother, her sisters, and brothers. My effort and ability to learn was always contextualized within the framework of generational family experience. Certain behaviors, gestures, habits of being were traced back.

Attending school then was sheer joy. I loved being a student. I loved learning. School was the place of ecstasy—pleasure and danger. To be changed by ideas was pure pleasure. But to learn ideas that ran counter to values and beliefs learned at home was to place oneself at risk, to enter the danger zone. Home was the place where I was forced to conform to someone else's image of who and what I should be. School was the place where I could forget that self and, through ideas, reinvent myself.

School changed utterly with racial integration. Gone was the messianic zeal to transform our minds and beings that had characterized teachers and their pedagogical practices in our all-black schools. Knowledge was suddenly about information only. It had no relation to how one lived, behaved. It was no longer connected to antiracist struggle. Bussed to white schools, we soon learned that obedience, and not a zealous will to learn, was what was expected of us. Too much eagerness to learn could easily be seen as a threat to white authority.

When we entered racist, desegregated, white schools we left a world where teachers believed that to educate black children rightly would require a political commitment. Now, we were mainly taught by white teachers whose lessons reinforced racist stereotypes. For black children, education was no longer about the practice of freedom. Realizing this, I lost my love of school. The classroom was no longer a place of pleasure or ecstasy. School was still a political place, since we were always having to counter white racist assumptions that we were genetically inferior, never as capable as white peers, even unable to learn. Yet, the politics were no longer counter-hegemonic. We were always and only responding and reacting to white folks.

That shift from beloved, all-black schools to white schools where black students were always seen as interlopers, as not really belonging, taught me the difference between education as the practice of freedom and education that merely strives to reinforce domination. The rare white teacher who dared to resist, who would not allow racist biases to determine how we were taught, sustained the belief that learning at its most powerful could indeed liberate. A few black teachers had joined us in the desegregation process. And, although it was more difficult, they continued to nurture black students even as their efforts were constrained by the suspicion they were favoring their own race.

Despite intensely negative experiences, I graduated from school still believing that education was enabling, that it enhanced our capacity to be free. When I began undergraduate work at Stanford University, I was enthralled with the process of becoming an insurgent black intellectual. It surprised and shocked me to sit in classes where professors were not excited about teaching, where they did not seem to have a clue that education was about the practice of freedom. During college, the primary lesson was reinforced: we were to learn obedience to authority.

In graduate school the classroom became a place I hated, a place where I struggled to claim and maintain the right to be an independent thinker. The university and the classroom began to feel more like a prison, a place of punishment and confinement rather than a place of promise and possibility. I wrote my first book during those undergraduate years, even though it was not published until years later. I was writing; but more importantly I was preparing to become a teacher.

Accepting the teaching profession as my destiny, I was tormented by the classroom reality I had known both as an undergraduate and a graduate student. The vast majority of our professors lacked basic communication skills, they were not self-actualized, and they often used the classroom to enact rituals of control that were about domination and the unjust exercise of power. In these settings I learned a lot about the kind of teacher I did not want to become.

In graduate school I found that I was often bored in classes. The banking system of education (based on the assumption that memorizing information and regurgitating it represented gaining knowledge that could be deposited, stored and used at a later date) did not interest me. I wanted to become a critical thinker. Yet that longing was often seen as a threat to authority. Individual white male students who were seen as "exceptional," were often allowed to chart their intellectual journeys, but the rest of us (and particularly those from marginal groups) were always expected to conform. Nonconformity on our part was viewed with suspicion, as empty gestures of defiance aimed at masking inferiority or substandard work. In those days, those of us from marginal groups who were allowed to enter prestigious, predominantly white colleges were made to feel that we were there not to learn but to prove that we were the equal of whites. We were there to prove this by showing how well we could become clones of our peers. As we constantly confronted biases, an undercurrent of stress diminished our learning experience.

My reaction to this stress and to the ever-present boredom and apathy that pervaded my classes was to imagine ways that teaching and the learning experience could be different. When I discovered the work of the Brazilian thinker Paulo Freire, my first introduction to critical pedagogy, I found a mentor and a guide, someone who understood that learning could be liberatory. With his teachings and my growing understanding of the ways in which the education I had received in all-black Southern schools had been empowering, I began to develop a blueprint for my own pedagogical practice. Already deeply engaged with feminist thinking, I had no difficulty bringing that critique to Freire's work. Significantly, I felt that this mentor and guide, whom I had never seen in the flesh, would encourage and support my challenge to his ideas if he was truly committed to education as the practice of freedom. At the same time, I used his pedagogical paradigms to critique the limitations of feminist classrooms.

During my undergraduate and graduate school years, only white women professors were involved in developing Women's Studies programs. And even though I taught my first class as a graduate student on black women writers from a feminist perspective, it was in the context of a Black Studies program. At that time, I found, white women professors were not eager to nurture any interest in feminist thinking and scholarship on the part of black female students if that interest included critical challenge. Yet their lack of interest did not discourage me from involvement with feminist ideas or participation in the feminist classroom. Those classrooms were the one space where pedagogical practices were interrogated, where it was assumed that the knowledge offered students would empower them to be better scholars, to live more fully in the world beyond academe. The feminist classroom was the one space where students could raise critical questions about pedagogical process. These critiques were not always encouraged or well received, but they were allowed. That small acceptance of critical interrogation was a crucial challenge inviting us as students to think seriously about pedagogy in relation to the practice of freedom.

When I entered my first undergraduate classroom to teach, I relied on the example of those inspired black women teachers in my grade school, on Freire's work, and on feminist thinking about radical pedagogy. I longed passionately to teach differently from the way I had been taught since high school. The first paradigm that shaped my pedagogy was the idea that the classroom should be an exciting place, never boring. And if boredom should prevail, then pedagogical strategies were needed that would intervene, alter, even disrupt the atmosphere. Neither Freire's work nor feminist pedagogy examined the notion of pleasure in the classroom. The idea that learning should be exciting, sometimes even "fun," was the subject of critical discussion by educators writing about pedagogical practices in grade schools, and sometimes even high schools. But there seemed to be no interest among either traditional or radical educators in discussing the role of excitement in higher education.

Excitement in higher education was viewed as potentially disruptive of the atmosphere of seriousness assumed to be essential to the learning process. To enter classroom settings in colleges and universities with the will to share the desire to encourage excitement, was to transgress. Not only did it require movement beyond accepted boundaries, but excitement could not be generated without a full recognition of the fact that there could never be an absolute set agenda governing teaching practices. Agendas had to be flexible, had to allow for spontaneous shifts in direction. Students had to be seen in their particularity as individuals (I drew on the strategies my grade-school teachers used to get to know us) and interacted with according to their needs (here Freire was useful). Critical reflection on my experience as a student in unexciting classrooms enabled me not only to imagine that the classroom could be exciting but that this excitement could co-exist with and even stimulate serious intellectual and/or academic engagement.

But excitement about ideas was not sufficient to create an exciting learning process. As a classroom community, our capacity to generate excitement is deeply affected by our interest in one another, in hearing one another's voices, in recognizing one another's presence. Since the vast majority of students learn through conservative, traditional educational practices and concern themselves only with the presence of the professor, any radical pedagogy must insist that everyone's presence is acknowledged. That insistence cannot be simply stated. It has to be demonstrated through pedagogical practices. To begin, the professor must genuinely *value* everyone's presence. There must be an ongoing recognition that everyone influences the classroom dynamic, that everyone contributes.

These contributions are resources. Used constructively they enhance the capacity of any class to create an open learning community. Often before this process can begin there has to be some deconstruction of the traditional notion that only the professor is responsible for classroom dynamics. That responsibility is relative to status. Indeed, the professor will always be more responsible because the larger institutional structures will always ensure that accountability for what happens in the classroom rests with the teacher. It is rare that any professor, no matter how eloquent a lecturer, can generate through his or her actions enough excitement to create an exciting classroom. Excitement is generated through collective effort.

Seeing the classroom always as a communal place enhances the likelihood of collective effort in creating and sustaining a learning community. One semester, I had a very difficult class, one that completely failed on the communal level. Throughout the term, I thought that the major drawback inhibiting the development of a learning community was that the class was scheduled in the early morning, before nine. Almost always between a third and a half of the class was not fully awake. This, coupled with the tensions of "differences," was impossible to overcome. Every now and then we had an exciting session, but mostly it was a dull class. I came to hate this class so much that I had a tremendous fear that I would not awaken to attend it; the night before (despite alarm clocks, wake-up calls, and the experiential knowledge that I had never forgotten to attend class) I still could not sleep. Rather than making me arrive sleepy, I tended to arrive wired, full of an energy few students mirrored.

Time was just one of the factors that prevented this class from becoming a learning community. For reasons I cannot explain it was also full of "resisting" students who did not want to learn new pedagogical processes, who did not want to be in a classroom that differed in any way from the norm. To these students, transgressing boundaries was frightening. And though they were not the majority, their spirit of rigid resistance seemed always to be more powerful than any will to intellectual openness and pleasure in learning. More than any other class I had taught, this one compelled me to abandon the sense that the professor could, by sheer strength of will and desire, make the classroom an exciting, learning community.

Before this class, I considered that *Teaching to Transgress: Education as the Practice of Freedom* would be a book of essays mostly directed to teachers. After the class ended, I began writing with the understanding that I was speaking to and with both students and professors. The scholarly field of writing on critical pedagogy and/or feminist pedagogy continues to be primarily a discourse engaged by white women and men. Freire, too, in conversation with me, as in much of his written work, has always acknowledged that he occupies the location of white maleness, particularly in this country. But the work of various thinkers on radical pedagogy (I use this term to include critical and/or feminist perspectives) has in recent years truly included a recognition of differences—those determined by class, race, sexual practice, nationality, and so on. Yet this movement forward does not seem to coincide with any significant increase in black or other nonwhite voices joining discussions about radical pedagogical practices.

My pedagogical practices have emerged from the mutually illuminating interplay of anticolonial, critical, and feminist pedagogies. This complex and unique blending of multiple perspectives has been an engaging and powerful standpoint from which to work. Expanding beyond boundaries, it has made it possible for me to imagine and enact pedagogical practices that engage directly both the concern for interrogating biases in curricula that reinscribe systems of domination (such as racism and sexism) while simultaneously providing new ways to teach diverse groups of students.

• • • • • • • • • • • • • •

Teaching is a performative act. And it is that aspect of our work that offers the space for change, invention, spontaneous shifts, that can serve as a catalyst drawing out the unique elements in each classroom. To embrace the performative aspect of teaching we are compelled to engage "audiences," to consider issues of reciprocity. Teachers are not performers in the traditional sense of the word in that our work is not meant to be a spectacle. Yet it is meant to serve as a catalyst that calls everyone to become more and more engaged, to become active participants in learning.

Just as the way we perform changes, so should our sense of "voice." In our everyday lives we speak differently to diverse audiences. We communicate best by choosing that way of speaking that is informed by the particularity and uniqueness of whom we are speaking to and with. In keeping with this spirit, these essays do not all sound alike. They reflect my effort to use language in ways that speak to specific contexts, as well as my desire to communicate with a diverse audience. To teach in varied communities not only our paradigms must shift but also the way we think, write, speak. The engaged voice must never be fixed and absolute but always changing, always evolving in dialogue with a world beyond itself.

These essays reflect my experience of critical discussions with teachers, students, and individuals who have entered my classes to observe. Multilayered, then, these essays are meant to stand as testimony, bearing witness to education as the practice of freedom. Long before a public ever recognized me as a thinker or writer, I was recognized in the classroom by students—seen by them as a teacher who worked hard to create a dynamic learning experience for all of us. Nowadays, I am recognized more for insurgent intellectual practice. Indeed, the academic public that I encounter at my lectures always shows surprise when I speak intimately and deeply about the classroom. That public seemed particularly surprised when I said that I was working on a collection of essays about teaching. This surprise is a sad reminder of the way teaching is seen as a duller, less valuable aspect of the academic profession. This perspective on teaching is a common one. Yet it must be challenged if we are to meet the needs of our students, if we are to restore to education and the classroom excitement about ideas and the will to learn.

There is a serious crisis in education. Students often do not want to learn and teachers do not want to teach. More than ever before in the recent history of this nation, educators are compelled to confront the biases that have shaped teaching practices in our society and to create new ways of knowing, different strategies for the sharing of knowledge. We cannot address this crisis if progressive critical thinkers and social critics act as though teaching is not a subject worthy of our regard.

The classroom remains the most radical space of possibility in the academy. For years it has been a place where education has been undermined by teachers and students alike who seek to use it as a platform for opportunistic concerns rather than as a place to learn. With these essays, I add my voice to the collective call for renewal and rejuvenation in our teaching practices. Urging all of us to open our minds and hearts so that we can know beyond the boundaries of what is acceptable, so that we can think and rethink, so that we can create new visions, I celebrate teaching that enables transgressions—a movement against and beyond boundaries. It is that movement which makes education the practice of freedom. ■

AUTHOR PROFILE

bell hooks (born 1952) is a teacher, an author, and a renowned critical theorist and activist. *Teaching to Transgress* is hooks' first book dedicated primarily to education. hooks lived through desegregation in the south, during which she was removed from an African-American school and placed in a desegregated, predominantly white school. Here she saw the difference between institutionalized schooling and the schooling of her youth, which she described as nurturing and engaging. hooks would later be profoundly influenced by Brazilian educational specialist Paulo Freire, who described much of modern schooling as oriented around a "banking model," where students were expected to simply passively receive and retain knowledge.

hooks went on to build on Freire's theories in her own writing on education and social justice. Her own career as a writer has spanned a wide range of fields, including the study of gender and sexuality, African-American studies, American Literature, and Appalachian studies. In 2004 hooks became a distinguished Professor in Residence of Appalachian studies at the Berea College Loyal Jones Appalachian Center. Of her own early life in Appalachia hooks writes, "While I do not claim an identity as Appalachian, I do claim a solidarity, a sense of belonging, that makes me one with the Appalachian past of my ancestors, black, Native American, white, all 'people of one blood' who made homeplace in isolated landscapes where they could invent themselves, where they could savor a taste of freedom."

Why Doctors Need Stories

By Peter D. Kramer

A few weeks ago, I received an email from the Danish psychiatrist Per Bech that had an unexpected attachment: a story about a patient. I have been writing a book about antidepressants—how well they work and how we know. Dr. Bech is an innovator in clinical psychometrics, the science of measuring change in conditions like depression. Generally, he forwards material about statistics.

Now he had shared a recently published case vignette. It concerned a man hospitalized at age 30 in 1954 for what today we call severe panic attacks. The treatment, which included "narcoanalysis" (interviewing aided by a "truth serum"), afforded no relief. On discharge, the man turned to alcohol. Later, when sober again, he endured increasing phobias, depression and social isolation.

Four decades later, in 1995, suicidal thoughts brought this anxious man back into the psychiatric system, at age 70. For the first time, he was put on an antidepressant, Zoloft. Six weeks out, both the panic attacks and the depression were gone. He resumed work, entered into a social life and remained well for the next 19 years—until his death.

If the narrative was striking, so was its inclusion in a medical journal. In the past 20 years, clinical vignettes have lost their standing. For a variety of reasons, including a heightened awareness of medical error and a focus on cost cutting, we have entered an era in which a narrow, demanding version of evidence-based medicine prevails. As a writer who likes to tell stories, I've been made painfully aware of the shift. The inclusion of a single anecdote in a research overview can lead to a reprimand, for reliance on storytelling.

My own view is that we need storytelling in medicine, need it for any number of reasons.

Repeatedly, I have been surprised by the impact that even lightly sketched case histories can have on readers. In my book "Listening to Prozac," I wrote about personality and how it might change on medication. "Should You Leave?" concerned theories of intimacy. Readers, however, often used the books for a different purpose: identifying depression. Regularly, I received—and still receive—phone calls: "My husband is just like—" one or another figure from a clinical example. For a decade and more, public health campaigns had circulated symptom lists meant to get people to recognize mood disorders, and still there remained a role for narrative to complete the job.

Other readers wrote to say that they'd recognized themselves. Seeing that they were not alone gave them hope. Encouragement is another benefit of case description, familiar to us in this age of memoir.

But vignettes can do more than illustrate and reassure. They convey what doctors see and hear, and those reports can set a research agenda.

Consider my experience prescribing Prozac. When it was introduced, certain of my patients, as they recovered from their depression or obsessionality, made note of personality effects. These patients said that, in responding to treatment, they had become "myself at last" or "better than baseline"—often, less socially withdrawn. I presented these examples first in essays for psychiatrists and then in my book, where I surrounded the narrative material with accounts of research. (Findings in cell biology, animal ethology and personality theory suggested that such antidepressants, which altered the way the brain handled serotonin, might increase assertiveness.)

My loosely buttressed descriptions—and colleagues' similar observations—led in time to controlled trials that confirmed the "better than well" phenomenon. (One study of depressed patients found that Paxil drastically decreased their "neuroticism," or emotional instability. Patients who became "better than well" appeared to gain extra protection from further bouts of mood disorder.) But doctors had not waited for controlled trials. In advance, the better-than-well hypothesis had served as a tentative fact. Treating depression, colleagues looked out for personality change, even aimed for it. Because clinical observations often do pan out, they serve as low-level evidence—especially if they jibe with what basic science suggests is likely.

To be sure, this approach, giving weight to the combination of doctors' experience and biological plausibility, stands somewhat in conflict with the principles of evidence-based medicine. The movement's manifesto, published in the Journal of the American Medical Association in 1992, proclaimed a new era that would see near-exclusive reliance on systematic clinical research—the direct assessment of treatments in patients. But even the manifesto conceded that less formal expertise would remain important in areas of practice that had not been subject to high-level testing.

That concession covers much of the territory. Making decisions about prescribing, often I exhaust the guidance that trials can give—and then I consult experts who tell me about this case and that outcome. Practicing psychotherapy, I employ methods that will never be subject to formal assessment. Among my teachers I number colleagues I know only through their descriptions of patient encounters. One psychoanalyst, Hellmuth Kaiser, imparted his wisdom through a fictional case portrayed in a stage play. I follow his precepts daily, hourly.

I have long felt isolated in this position, embracing stories, which is why I warm to the possibility that the vignette is making a comeback. This summer, Oxford University Press began publishing a journal devoted to case reports. And this month, in an unusual move, the New England Journal of Medicine, the field's bellwether, opened an issue with a case history involving a troubled mother, daughter and grandson. The contributors write: "Data are important, of course, but numbers sometimes imply an order to what is happening that can be misleading. Stories are better at capturing a different type of 'big picture.'"

Stories capture small pictures, too. I'm thinking of the anxious older man given Zoloft. That narrative has power. As Dr. Bech and his co-author, Lone Lindberg, point out, spontaneous recovery from panic and depression late in life is rare. (Even those who put great stock in placebo pills don't imagine that they do much for conditions that are severe and chronic.) The degree of transformation in the Danish patient is impressive. So is the length of observation. No formal research can offer a 40-year lead-in or a 19-year follow-up. Few studies report on both symptoms and social progress. Research reduces information about many people; vignette retains the texture of life in one of its forms.

How far should stories inform practice? Faced with an elderly patient who was anxious, withdrawn and never medicated, a well-read doctor might weigh many potential sources of guidance, this vignette among them. Often the knowledge that informs clinical decisions emerges, like a pointillist image, from the coalescence of scattered information.

Here is where I want to venture a radical statement about the worth of anecdote. Beyond its roles as illustration, affirmation, hypothesis-builder and low-level guidance for practice, storytelling can act as a modest counterbalance to a straitened understanding of evidence.

Take psychotherapy. Most of the research into its efficacy concerns cognitive behavioral therapy, or C.B.T., the treatment that teaches patients to moderate their habitual maladaptive thoughts. The reasons for this concentration are historical and temperamental. C.B.T. is rooted in a branch of psychology devoted to research, and the school of therapy attracts students who favor the practical and systematic over the spontaneous and poetic. There are no trials of existential psychotherapy.

But where the comparison has been made—primarily in the treatment of depression—C.B.T. does not outperform alternative approaches. (The alternatives tested are mostly distant derivatives of psychoanalysis.) And detailed research suggests that where C.B.T. works, specific techniques are not the reason. Studies of the components of therapy find that it is factors common to all schools, like the practitioner's commitment and the alliance with the patient, that do the job.

If we weigh "evidence" by the pound or the page, we risk moving toward a monoculture of C.B.T., a result I would consider unfortunate, since there are many ways to influence people for the better. Here's where case description shines. We hear the existential psychoanalyst Leston Havens describe his use of imitative statements, exclamations by the therapist that seem to come from within the patient: "What *is* one supposed to do?" For me, Dr. Havens's approach—sitting beside the patient metaphorically and looking outward, hand-crafting interventions on the spot—carries what I call psychological plausibility. The vignette corresponds to a convincing account of how people change.

It has been my hope that, while we wait for conclusive science, stories will preserve diversity in our theories of mind. For 17 years, starting in the 1980s, I ran a psychotherapy seminar for psychiatry residents. As readings, I assigned only case vignettes, trusting that one or another would speak to each trainee.

My recent reading of outcome trials of antidepressants has strengthened my suspicion that the line between research and storytelling can be fuzzy. In psychiatry—and the same is true throughout medicine—randomized trials are rarely large enough to provide guidance on their own. Statisticians amalgamate many studies through a technique called meta-analysis. The first step of the process, deciding which data to include, colors the findings. On occasion, the design of a meta-analysis stacks the deck for or against a treatment. The resulting charts are polemical. Effectively, the numbers are narrative.

Because so little evidence stands on its own, incorporating research results into clinical practice requires discernment. Thoughtful doctors consider data, accompanying narrative, plausibility and, yes, clinical anecdote in their decision making. To put the same matter differently, evidence-based medicine, properly enacted, is judgment-based medicine in which randomized trials, carefully assessed, are given their due.

I don't think that psychiatry—or, again, medicine in general—need be apologetic about this state of affairs. Our substantial formal findings require integration. The danger is in pretending otherwise. It would be unfortunate if psychiatry moved fully—prematurely—to squeeze the art out of its science. And it would be unfortunate if we marginalized the case vignette. We need storytelling, to set us in the clinical moment, remind us of the variety of human experience and enrich our judgment. ■

AUTHOR PROFILE

Peter D. Kramer (born October 22, 1948) is a psychiatrist and author. His controversial book *Listening to Prozac* (1994) was a *New York Times* bestseller. Kramer studied at Harvard and the University of London. He lives in Providence, Rhode Island, where he continues to practice psychiatry.

Natural-Born Liars

By David Livingstone Smith

Why Do We Lie, and Why Are We So Good At It? Because It Works

Deception runs like a red thread throughout all of human history. It sustains literature, from Homer's wily Odysseus to the biggest pop novels of today. Go to a movie, and odds are that the plot will revolve around deceit in some shape or form. Perhaps we find such stories so enthralling because lying pervades human life. Lying is a skill that wells up from deep within us, and we use it with abandon. As the great American observer Mark Twain wrote more than a century ago: "Everybody lies…every day, every hour, awake, asleep, in his dreams, in his joy, in his mourning. If he keeps his tongue still his hands, his feet, his eyes, his attitude will convey deception." Deceit is fundamental to the human condition.

Research supports Twain's conviction. One good example was a study conducted in 2002 by psychologist Robert S. Feldman of the University of Massachusetts Amherst. Feldman secretly videotaped students who were asked to talk with a stranger. He later had the students analyze their tapes and tally the number of lies they had told. A whopping 60 percent admitted to lying at least once during 10 minutes of conversation, and the group averaged 2.9 untruths in that time period. The transgressions ranged from intentional exaggeration to flat-out fibs. Interestingly, men and women lied with equal frequency; however, Feldman found that women were more likely to lie to make the stranger feel good, whereas men lied most often to make themselves look better.

In another study a decade earlier by David Knox and Caroline Schacht, both now at East Carolina University, 92 percent of college students confessed that they had lied to a current or previous sexual partner, which left the husband-and-wife research team wondering whether the remaining 8 percent were lying. And whereas it has long been known that men are prone to lie about the number of their sexual conquests, recent research shows that women tend to under-represent their degree of sexual experience. When asked to fill out questionnaires on personal sexual behavior and attitudes, women wired to a dummy polygraph machine reported having had twice as many lovers as those who were not, showing that the women who were not wired were less honest. It's all too ironic that the investigators had to deceive subjects to get them to tell the truth about their lies.

These references are just a few of the many examples of lying that pepper the scientific record. And yet research on deception is almost always focused on lying in the narrowest sense—literally saying things that aren't true. But our fetish extends far beyond verbal falsification. We lie by omission and through the subtleties of spin. We engage in myriad forms of nonverbal deception, too: we use makeup, hairpieces, cosmetic surgery, clothing and other forms of adornment to disguise our true appearance, and we apply artificial fragrances to misrepresent our body odors. We cry crocodile tears, fake orgasms and flash phony "have a nice day" smiles. Out-and-out verbal lies are just a small part of the vast tapestry of human deceit.

L

The obvious question raised by all of this accounting is: Why do we lie so readily? The answer: because it works.

The Homo sapiens who are best able to lie have an edge over their counterparts in a relentless struggle for the reproductive success that drives the engine of evolution. As humans, we must fit into a close-knit social system to succeed, yet our primary aim is still to look out for ourselves above all others. Lying helps. And lying to ourselves—a talent built into our brains—helps us accept our fraudulent behavior.

Passport to Success

If this bald truth makes any one of us feel uncomfortable, we can take some solace in knowing we are not the only species to exploit the lie. Plants and animals communicate with one another by sounds, ritualistic displays, colors, airborne chemicals and other methods, and biologists once naively assumed that the sole function of these communication systems was to transmit accurate information. But the more we have learned, the more obvious it has become that nonhuman species put a lot of effort into sending inaccurate messages.

The mirror orchid, for example, displays beautiful blue blossoms that are dead ringers for female wasps. The flower also manufactures a chemical cocktail that simulates the pheromones released by females to attract mates. These visual and olfactory cues keep hapless male wasps on the flower long enough to ensure that a hefty load of pollen is clinging to their bodies by the time they fly off to try their luck with another orchid in disguise. Of course, the orchid does not "intend" to deceive the wasp. Its fakery is built into its physical design, because over the course of history plants that had this capability were more readily able to pass on their genes than those that did not. Other creatures deploy equally deceptive strategies. When approached by an erstwhile predator, the harmless hog-nosed snake flattens its head, spreads out a cobralike hood and, hissing menacingly, pretends to strike with maniacal aggression, all the while keeping its mouth discreetly closed.

These cases and others show that nature favors deception because it provides survival advantages. The tricks become increasingly sophisticated the closer we get to Homo sapiens on the evolutionary chain. Consider an incident between Mel and Paul:

> Mel dug furiously with her bare hands to extract the large succulent corm from the rock-hard Ethiopian ground. It was the dry season and food was scarce. Corms are edible bulbs somewhat like onions and are a staple during these long, hard months. Little Paul sat nearby and surreptitiously observed Mel's labors. Paul's mother was out of sight; she had left him to play in the grass, but he knew she would remain within earshot in case he needed her. Just as Mel managed, with a final pull, to yank her prize out of the earth, Paul let out an ear-splitting cry that shattered the peace of the savannah. His mother rushed to him. Heart pounding and adrenaline pumping, she burst upon the scene and quickly sized up the situation: Mel

> had obviously harassed her darling child. Shrieking, she stormed after the bewildered Mel, who dropped the corm and fled. Paul's scheme was complete. After a furtive glance to make sure nobody was looking, he scurried over to the corm, picked up his prize and began to eat. The trick worked so well that he used it several more times before anyone wised up.

The actors in this real-life drama were not people. They were Chacma baboons, described in a 1987 article by primatologists Richard W. Byrne and Andrew Whiten of the University of St. Andrews in Scotland for New Scientist magazine and later recounted in Byrne's 1995 book The Thinking Ape (Oxford University Press). In 1983 Byrne and Whiten began noticing deceptive tactics among the mountain baboons in Drakensberg, South Africa. Catarrhine primates, the group that includes the Old World monkeys, apes and ourselves, are all able to tactically dupe members of their own species. The deceptiveness is not built into their appearance, as with the mirror orchid, nor is it encapsulated in rigid behavioral routines like those of the hog-nosed snake. The primates' repertoires are calculated, flexible and exquisitely sensitive to shifting social contexts.

Byrne and Whiten catalogued many such observations, and these became the basis for their celebrated Machiavellian intelligence hypothesis, which states that the extraordinary explosion of intelligence in primate evolution was prompted by the need to master ever more sophisticated forms of social trickery and manipulation. Primates had to get smart to keep up with the snowballing development of social gamesmanship.

The Machiavellian intelligence hypothesis suggests that social complexity propelled our ancestors to become progressively more intelligent and increasingly adept at wheeling, dealing, bluffing and conniving. That means human beings are natural-born liars. And in line with other evolutionary trends, our talent for dissembling dwarfs that of our nearest relatives by several orders of magnitude.

The complex choreography of social gamesmanship remains central to our lives today. The best deceivers continue to reap advantages denied to their more honest or less competent peers. Lying helps us facilitate social interactions, manipulate others and make friends.

There is even a correlation between social popularity and deceptive skill. We falsify our résumés to get jobs, plagiarize essays to boost grade-point averages and pull the wool over the eyes of potential sexual partners to lure them into bed. Research shows that liars are often better able to get jobs and attract members of the opposite sex into relationships. Several years later Feldman demonstrated that the adolescents who are most popular in their schools are also better at fooling their peers. Lying continues to work. Although it would be self-defeating to lie all the time (remember the fate of the boy who cried, "Wolf!"), lying often and well remains a passport to social, professional and economic success.

L

Fooling Ourselves

Ironically, the primary reasons we are so good at lying to others is that we are good at lying to ourselves. There is a strange asymmetry in how we apportion dishonesty. Although we are often ready to accuse others of deceiving us, we are astonishingly oblivious to our own duplicity. Experiences of being a victim of deception are burned indelibly into our memories, but our own prevarications slip off our tongues so easily that we often do not notice them for what they are.

The strange phenomenon of self-deception has perplexed philosophers and psychologists for more than 2,000 years. On the face of it, the idea that a person can con oneself seems as nonsensical as cheating at solitaire or embezzling money from one's own bank account. But the paradoxical character of self-deception flows from the idea, formalized by French polymath René Descartes in the 17th century, that human minds are transparent to their owners and that introspection yields an accurate understanding of our own mental life. As natural as this perspective is to most of us, it turns out to be deeply misguided.

If we hope to understand self-deception, we need to draw on a more scientifically sound conception of how the mind works. The brain comprises a number of functional systems. The system responsible for cognition—the thinking part of the brain—is somewhat distinct from the system that produces conscious experiences. The relation between the two systems can be thought of as similar to the relation between the processor and monitor of a personal computer. The work takes place in the processor; the monitor does nothing but display information the processor transfers to it. By the same token, the brain's cognitive systems do the thinking, whereas consciousness displays the information that it has received. Consciousness plays a less important role in cognition than previously expected.

This general picture is supported by a great deal of experimental evidence. Some of the most remarkable and widely discussed studies were conducted several decades ago by neuroscientist Benjamin Libet, now professor emeritus at the University of California at San Diego. In one experiment, Libet placed subjects in front of a button and a rapidly moving clock and asked them to press the button whenever they wished and to note the time, as displayed on the clock, the moment they felt an impulse to press the button. Libet also attached electrodes over the motor cortex, which controls movement, in each of his subjects to monitor the electrical tension that mounts as the brain prepares to initiate an action. He found that our brains begin to prepare for action just over a third of a second before we consciously decide to act. In other words, despite appearances, it is not the conscious mind that decides to perform an action: the decision is made unconsciously. Although our consciousness likes to take the credit (so to speak), it is merely informed of unconscious decisions after the fact. This study and others like it suggest that we are systematically deluded about the role consciousness plays in our lives. Strange as it may seem, consciousness may not do anything except display the results of unconscious cognition.

This general model of the mind, supported by various experiments beyond Libet's, gives us exactly what we need to resolve the paradox of self-deception—at least in theory. We are able to deceive ourselves by invoking the equivalent of a cognitive filter between unconscious cognition and conscious awareness. The filter preempts information before it reaches consciousness, preventing selected thoughts from proliferating along the neural pathways to awareness.

Solving the Pinocchio Problem

But why would we filter information? Considered from a biological perspective, this notion presents a problem. The idea that we have an evolved tendency to deprive ourselves of information sounds wildly implausible, self-defeating and biologically disadvantageous. But once again we can find a clue from Mark Twain, who bequeathed to us an amazingly insightful explanation. "When a person cannot deceive himself," he wrote, "the chances are against his being able to deceive other people." Self-deception is advantageous because it helps us lie to others more convincingly. Concealing the truth from ourselves conceals it from others.

In the early 1970s biologist Robert L. Trivers, now at Rutgers University, put scientific flesh on Twain's insight. Trivers made the case that our flair for self-deception might be a solution to an adaptive problem that repeatedly faced ancestral humans when they attempted to deceive one another. Deception can be a risky business. In the tribal, hunter-gatherer bands that were presumably the standard social environment in which our hominid ancestors lived, being caught red-handed in an act of deception could result in social ostracism or banishment from the community, to become hyena bait. Because our ancestors were socially savvy, highly intelligent primates, there came a point when they became aware of these dangers and learned to be self-conscious liars.

This awareness created a brand-new problem. Uncomfortable, jittery liars are bad liars. Like Pinocchio, they give themselves away by involuntary, nonverbal behaviors. A good deal of experimental evidence indicates that humans are remarkably adept at making inferences about one another's mental states on the basis of even minimal exposure to nonverbal information. As Freud once commented, "No mortal can keep a secret. If his lips are silent, he chatters with his fingertips; betrayal oozes out of him at every pore." In an effort to quell our rising anxiety, we may automatically raise the pitch of our voice, blush, break out into the proverbial cold sweat, scratch our nose or make small movements with our feet as though barely squelching an impulse to flee.

Alternatively, we may attempt to rigidly control the tone of our voice and, in an effort to suppress telltale stray movements, raise suspicion by our stiff, wooden bearing. In any case, we sabotage our own efforts to deceive. Nowadays a used-car salesman can hide his shifty eyes behind dark sunglasses, but this cover was not available during the Pleistocene epoch. Some other solution was required.

Natural selection appears to have cracked the Pinocchio problem by endowing us with the ability to lie to ourselves. Fooling ourselves allows us to selfishly manipulate others around us while remaining conveniently innocent of our own shady agendas.

If this is right, self-deception took root in the human mind as a tool for social manipulation. As Trivers noted, biologists propose that the overriding function of self-deception is the more fluid deception of others. Self-deception helps us ensnare other people more effectively. It enables us to lie sincerely, to lie without knowing that we are lying. There is no longer any need to put on an act, to pretend that we are telling the truth. Indeed, a self-deceived person is actually telling the truth to the best of his or her knowledge, and believing one's own story makes it all the more persuasive.

Although Trivers's thesis is difficult to test, it has gained wide currency as the only biologically realistic explanation of self-deception as an adaptive feature of the human mind. The view also fits very well with a good deal of work on the evolutionary roots of social behavior that has been supported empirically.

Of course, self-deception is not always so absolute. We are sometimes aware that we are willing dupes in our own con game, stubbornly refusing to explicitly articulate to ourselves just what we are up to. We know that the stories we tell ourselves do not jibe with our behavior, or they fail to mesh with physical signs such as a thumping heart or sweaty palms that betray our emotional states. For example, the students described earlier, who admitted their lies when watching themselves on videotape, knew they were lying at times, and most likely they did not stop themselves because they were not disturbed by this behavior.

At other times, however, we are happily unaware that we are pulling the wool over our own eyes. A biological perspective helps us understand why the cognitive gears of self-deception engage so smoothly and silently. They cleverly and imperceptibly embroil us in performances that are so skillfully crafted that the act gives every indication of complete sincerity, even to the actors themselves. ■

Further Reading

On the Decay of the Art of Lying. Mark Twain in *The Stolen White Elephant, Etc.* James R. Osgood and Company, 1882.

The Thinking Primate's Guide to Deception. Richard W. Byrne and Andrew A. Whiten In *New Scientist*, No. 1589, pages 54–57; December 3, 1987.

Who Lies? Deborah A. Kashy and Bella M. DePaulo in *Journal of Personality and Social Psychology*, Vol. 70, No. 5, pages 1037–1051; 1996.

Natural Selection and Social Theory: Selected Papers of Robert Trivers. Robert Trivers. Oxford University Press, 2002.

AUTHOR PROFILE

David Livingstone Smith (born 1953) teaches philosophy at the University of New England. He studied at the University of London, and is the cofounder of the New England Institute for Cognitive Science and Evolutionary Studies. His primary research interest is the intersection between human evolution, psychology, and the philosophy of mind. His books include *Why We Lie: The Evolutionary Roots of Deception and the Unconscious* (2004), *The Most Dangerous Animal: Human Nature and the Origins of War* (2007), and *Less Than Human: Why We Demean, Enslave, and Exterminate Others* (2011).

The Essay, an Exercise in Doubt

By Phillip Lopate

I am an essayist, for better or worse. I don't suppose many young people dream of becoming essayists. Even as nerdy and bookish a child as I was fantasized about entering the lists of fiction and poetry, those more glamorous, noble genres on which Nobels, Pulitzers and National Book Awards are annually bestowed. So if Freud was right in saying that we can be truly happy only when our childhood ambitions are fulfilled, then I must be content to be merely content.

I like the freedom that comes with lowered expectations. In the area of literary nonfiction, memoirs attract much more attention than essay collections, which are published in a modest, quasi-invisible manner, in keeping with anticipated lower sales. But despite periodic warnings of the essay's demise, the stuff does continue to be published; if anything, the essay has experienced a slight resurgence of late. I wonder if that may be because it is attuned to the current mood, speaks to the present moment. At bottom, we are deeply unsure and divided, and the essay feasts on doubt.

Ever since Michel de Montaigne, the founder of the modern essay, gave as a motto his befuddled "What do I know?" and put forth a vision of humanity as mentally wavering and inconstant, the essay has become a meadow inviting contradiction, paradox, irresolution and self-doubt. The essay's job is to track consciousness; if you are fully aware of your mind you will find your thoughts doubling back, registering little peeps of ambivalence or disbelief.

According to Theodor Adorno, the iron law of the essay is heresy. What is heresy if not the expression of contrarian doubt about communal pieties or orthodox positions? This is sometimes called "critical thinking," an ostensible goal of education in a democracy. But since such thinking often rocks the boat, we may find it less than supported in school settings. Typically, the exercise of doubt is something an individual has to cultivate on his or her own, in private, before summoning the courage to air it, say, in an essay.

Recently, with fiercely increased competition for admission to the better colleges, the "common app" essay has become an obsessive focus on the part of high school administrators, parents and students. This part of the college application requires each applicant to file a personal statement, a prose reflection conveying individual sensibility, experience or worldview.

Tutors advertise on lampposts for after-school courses to prep the college aspirant for the most seductive, winning common app. (I am delighted to see this career path opening for indigent essayists.) The problem is that, more often than not, the applicant is expected to put forward a confident presentation of self that is more like an advertisement, a smooth civic-minded con job, circumventing the essay's gift for candid, robust self-doubt.

When my daughter Lily, now a college freshman, was applying to schools, she wrote what I thought was a perfect common app essay about her mixed attraction to the idea of melancholy. Her high school counselor, while conceding it was well written, forced her to abandon it because it might give schools the wrong impression that she was a "downer." Earlier, Lily, whom I had encouraged to wear her ambivalence proudly, was reproved by teachers for writing papers that failed to support one side of a debate, instead arguing the validity of both positions.

I got it that they wanted her to sharpen her rhetorical ability. Argumentation is a good skill to have, but the real argument should be with oneself. Especially when it comes to the development of young writers, it is crucial to nudge them past that self-righteous inveighing, that shrill, defensive one-track that is deadly for personal essays or memoirs, and encourage a more polyphonic, playful approach. That may be why a classic essay technique is to stage an inner debate by thinking against oneself.

Doubt is my boon companion, the faithful St. Bernard ever at my side. Whether writing essays or just going about daily life, I am constantly second-guessing myself. My mind is filled with "yes, buts," "so whats?" and other skeptical rejoinders. I am forever monitoring myself for traces of folly, insensitivity, arrogance, false humility, cruelty, stupidity, immaturity and, guess what, I keep finding examples. Age has not made me wiser, except maybe in retrospect. My wife sometimes complains that I will never admit I am wrong. Of course I do–granted, less than I should, but it's not just because I am stubborn and hate to concede a point in the heat of argument. The main reason is that a part of me always assumes I'm wrong and at fault, to some extent; this is so obvious to me that it needn't bear stating. In any case, I often forget to say it aloud. But I certainly think it.

Strangely enough, doubt need not impede action. If you really become friends with your doubt, you can go ahead and take risks, knowing you will be questioning yourself at every turn, no matter what. It is part of living, a healthy evolutionary adaptation, I would imagine. The mistake is in trying to tune out your doubts. Accept them as a necessary (or at least unavoidable) soundtrack.

The only danger, then, is becoming smug about one's capacity for doubt–the essayist's occupational hazard, to which I periodically succumb. I have found the exercise of doubt to be an enormous help in writing essays, because it lets me start out with the knowledge that I may very well not achieve perfection on the page. Then I can forgive myself in advance for falling short of the mark, and get on with it. ■

AUTHOR PROFILE

Phillip Lopate (born 1943) is a writer, teacher, and Guggenheim fellowship recipient. Lopate writes in a wide range of genres, including fiction, poetry, novellas, memoir, criticism, and biography. His collected personal essays include *Bachelorhood* (1981), which was given a Texas Institute of Letters award, and *Portrait of My Body* (1996), which received a PEN Best Essay Book of the Year award. Lopate's shorter works have appeared in *The Best American Short Stories, The Best American Essays, The Paris Review, Harper's,* and *New York Times.* Lopate is the director of Columbia University's nonfiction graduate program.

A 21st-Century Education

By Joseph Marolla

In September 1966, I attended a mid-sized research university as an entering first-year student. I was filled with the usual initial feelings: excitement, anxiety, and anticipation. Earlier that summer, I had received my course schedule, so I knew I would be enrolled in a composition class, a foreign language class, a "finite" math class, a world history class, and a biology class. Over the next two years, I would enroll in similar classes in totally different content areas. Classes of 300 to 500 students were rather typical even in 1966. For the first time in my academic life, I would learn the value of multiple-choice tests and the techniques one could use to survive them. But more than anything else, I would learn that navigating an undergraduate curriculum was nothing more than determining the number of boxes that needed to be checked and then choosing courses that would result in an X in those boxes.

The problem was this experience did not match any of my expectations regarding what college would be like. I had naively expected that college was a place where intellectual curiosity would be supported, if not required. I had anticipated having serious conversations with other students and faculty, conversations that would have political and ideological content (after all, the Vietnam War had a full hold on the country at the time). I saw college as a time when discussions both inside and outside of class would explore the biggest questions of our time and maybe for all time. But none of this actually happened. Instead, we guys talked about girls, beer, and maybe our favorite sport teams or idols. I put part of the responsibility for this lack of connection or engagement on myself and my friends. Most of us had cruised through high school and were more than willing to take the same attitude toward college. Little did I realize that, for most of the 20th century, higher education had been moving away from broad and general courses toward a more technical, segmented, and bureaucratized education for the masses, and that this process would accelerate after WWII and the baby boom generation.

As someone trained in sociology, it seems to me perfectly reasonable to divide the labor of teaching into smaller and smaller units so that expertise can be achieved and passed on in any particular area of content. It also seems reasonable to bureaucratize the process if the goal is efficiency. The problem is that this segmentation has resulted in insulated departments whose primary stake is in claiming a particular content area and/or perspective. Each department justifies its existence based on its ability to claim sole authority over a particular perspective or type of content. This process has worked well to protect the viability and stability of many departments and their faculty but has done little to ensure an integrated education for the students. In fact, in most universities, students and their particular needs are not really part of this equation, and no one specifically is responsible for the key competencies and skill areas that are necessary to survival and success in today's very competitive marketplace.

However well or poorly the educational system functioned in the past, I, along with many others, am making the claim that there is a complete mismatch between today's entering college students and the goal of educating them for the 21st century. As many leaders in higher education have noted, many of today's college students are qualified to enter the system, but they are not ready to take full advantage of all its opportunities. Furthermore, while a college education has been an advantage in the marketplace for many decades, it has not always been the passport to a life of financial security versus one of desperation. Today's high school graduates can expect to earn 1.3 million dollars less than the average college graduate. Success in the academic world is no longer a luxury but rather defines one's life chances.

So, what changes are in the air that can move us into a new century of higher education opportunities for our students? Every major educational organization has been discussing student-centered, learning-centered, and learner-centered classrooms for many years. In fact, Barr and Tagg's seminal article, written in 1995, "From Teaching to Learning: A New Paradigm for Undergraduate Education," spelled out the problem and possible solutions long before many of us were aware of the primary issues. But we became sidetracked with arguments over what content was primary and essential to a generally educated person in the 21st century.

Many academics and employers are saying, regardless of the content, we need people who can communicate, think, work with others, and understand the emerging significance of the digital world. It is time we integrated such skill development into our curriculum and made these skills a priority for all those teaching our students, while making the university a place where the mind should be allowed and encouraged to explore ideas previously outside the parameters of one's world.

Here at Virginia Commonwealth University, we have declared a pledge to all our students and their parents. We will provide all our entering first-year students the opportunity to work on a highly valued skill set from the moment they enter the institution until they leave in their senior year. Furthermore, we will do this with full-time faculty who have as their primary goal furthering the learning of each and every student regardless of his or her entering skill level. We cannot guarantee the success of our students, but we can guarantee that substantial resources and faculty will be put in place to maximize the likelihood of our students' being successful. This pledge is called the VCU Compact and we began implementing it in Fall 2006.

Our first initiative was the creation of the University College, which houses all first-year advising and learning support programs such as tutoring and the Writing Center, first-year programs, and the Core Curriculum. The University College has been a huge success from almost any level of measurement. Students now know where they need to go to get help for almost any learning-related issue. With more than 32,000 students in attendance, it could be very difficult to maintain close contact with all our students. As our first-year students come through the door, we want them to feel they can talk to someone honestly and openly and receive the type of help and support a friend or mentor would give them. All our first-year students are assigned to advisors who are housed in University College and trained to assist the students in their curriculum choices as well as choices that may affect their lives after college.

The second initiative was the establishment of a Summer Reading Program for all entering students. We had a number of objectives in mind, but foremost were raising the level of expectations for all entering students, engaging the students in both a social and intellectual exercise, and incorporating the entire university in a collective experience. The program has been successful beyond our wildest dreams. Each year we think we cannot top the previous year but each year the program and the participation continue to grow.

The Summer Reading text is one of the foundational readings in the first semester of Focused Inquiry. Focused Inquiry was the third major initiative—a two-semester sequence required of all first-year students. Focused Inquiry I–II is a year-long class with a maximum enrollment of 22. The class targets six skill areas that we feel form the foundation of college success as well as success after college: oral communication, written communication, critical thinking, information fluency, ethical and civic responsibility, and quantitative literacy. The students remain in the same small class for two semesters, becoming a learning community guided by one faculty member. The faculty members were hired specifically to teach these classes, and they fully appreciate that the success of their students' learning is the key to the entire program. They work together as a team and constantly collaborate to improve the overall learning environment for the students. By the end of their first year, all the students learn to appreciate the efforts of their teachers and develop long-term bonds with classmates whom they have gotten to know through their writing and work together. It is a very special part of the VCU experience.

Our fourth major initiative was the creation of our Core Curriculum. For the first time in 40 years, VCU has an agreement to provide students with a common curriculum regardless of their chosen major. The Core Curriculum consists of 21 credits and includes the Focused Inquiry course sequence (UNIV 111, 112), Inquiry and the Craft of Argument (UNIV 200), a quantitative literacy course, and three learning-centered courses in science, social science, and the humanities. Integrated in all these courses are the skill areas of the VCU Compact. Each course must include learning objectives in at least three of the areas. The final component of the Core is a capstone or senior experience within the major. This experience must reintegrate one or more of the skill areas as an expression of the student's chosen major. The Core is supplemented with general education requirements that vary within each school and/or college.

In the end, we envision an education in which students are well aware of the meaning and intent of their coursework while they also experience the joy of making significant progress in each of the designated skill areas. Learning and changing should be a stimulating and rewarding experience. We feel this program is designed to achieve both those goals and much more. ■

AUTHOR PROFILE

Joseph Marolla earned his BA in English at the University of Rhode Island, an MA in sociology at the University of Rhode Island, and a PhD in sociology from the University of Denver. His research interests are varied and include change in higher education, deviant behavior, and the sociology of sport. He joined the faculty at Virginia Commonwealth University in 1975, became chairperson of the sociology/anthropology department in 1992, and was named Vice Provost for Instruction in 2006. Upon his retirement in 2013, he received the President's Award of Excellence and was named Professor Emeritus.

The Egg and the Sperm

How Science Has Constructed a Romance Based on Stereotypical Male–Female Roles

By Emily Martin

The theory of the human body is always a part of a world picture...The theory of the human body is always a part of a *fantasy*.

—James Hillman, *The Myth of Analysis*[1]

As an anthropologist, I am intrigued by the possibility that culture shapes how biological scientists describe what they discover about the natural world. If this were so, we would be learning about more than the natural world in high school biology class; we would be learning about cultural beliefs and practices as if they were part of nature. In the course of my research I realized that the picture of egg and sperm drawn in popular as well as scientific accounts of reproductive biology relies on stereotypes central to our cultural definitions of male and female. The stereotypes imply not only that female biological processes are less worthy than their male counterparts but also that women are less worthy than men. Part of my goal in writing this article is to shine a bright light on the gender stereotypes hidden within the scientific language of biology. Exposed in such a light, I hope they will lose much of their power to harm us.

Egg and sperm: A scientific fairy tale

At a fundamental level, all major scientific textbooks depict male and female reproductive organs as systems for the production of valuable substances, such as eggs and sperm.[2] In the case of women, the monthly cycle is described as being designed to produce eggs and prepare a suitable place for them to be fertilized and grown—all to the end of making babies. But the enthusiasm ends there. By extolling the female cycle as a productive enterprise, menstruation must necessarily be viewed as a failure. Medical texts describe menstruation as the "debris" of the uterine lining, the result of necrosis, or death of tissue. The descriptions imply that a system has gone awry, making products of no use, not to specification, unsalable, wasted, scrap. An illustration in a widely used medical text shows menstruation as

---

Portions of this article were presented as the 1987 Becker Lecture, Cornell University. I am grateful for the many suggestions and ideas I received on this occasion. For especially pertinent help with my arguments and data I thank Richard Cone, Kevin Whaley, Sharon Stephens, Barbara Duden, Susanne Kuechler, Lorna Rhodes, and Scott Gilbert. The article was strengthened and clarified by the comments of the anonymous *Signs* reviewers as well as the superb editorial skills of Amy Gage.

1 James Hillman, *The Myth of Analysis* (Evanston, Ill.: Northwestern University Press, 1972), 220.

2 The textbooks I consulted are the main ones used in classes for undergraduate premedical students or medical students (or those held on reserve in the library for these classes) during the past few years at Johns Hopkins University. These texts are widely used at other universities in the country as well.

a chaotic disintegration of form, complementing the many texts that describe it as "ceasing," "dying," "losing," "denuding," "expelling."[3]

Male reproductive physiology is evaluated quite differently. One of the texts that sees menstruation as failed production employs a sort of breathless prose when it describes the maturation of sperm: "The mechanisms which guide the remarkable cellular transformation from spermatid to mature sperm remain uncertain...Perhaps the most amazing characteristic of spermatogenesis is its sheer magnitude: the normal human male may manufacture several hundred million sperm per day."[4] In the classic text *Medical Physiology*, edited by Vernon Mountcastle, the male/female, productive/destructive comparison is more explicit: "Whereas the female *sheds* only a single gamete each month, the seminiferous tubules *produce* hundreds of millions of sperm each day" (emphasis mine).[5] The female author of another text marvels at the length of the microscopic seminiferous tubules, which, if uncoiled and placed end to end, "would span almost one-third of a mile!" She writes, "In an adult male these structures produce millions of sperm cells each day." Later she asks, "How is this feat accomplished?"[6] None of these texts expresses such intense enthusiasm for any female processes. It is surely no accident that the "remarkable" process of making sperm involves precisely what, in the medical view, menstruation does not: production of something deemed valuable.[7]

One could argue that menstruation and spermatogenesis are not analogous processes and, therefore, should not be expected to elicit the same kind of response. The proper female analogy to spermatogenesis, biologically, is ovulation. Yet ovulation does not merit enthusiasm in these texts either. Textbook descriptions stress that all of the ovarian follicles containing ova are already present at birth. Far from being *produced*, as sperm are, they merely sit on the shelf, slowly degenerating and aging like overstocked inventory: "At birth, normal human ovaries contain an estimated one million follicles [each], and no new ones appear after birth. Thus, in marked contrast to the male, the newborn female already has all the germ cells she will ever have. Only a few, perhaps 400, are destined to reach full maturity during her active productive life. All the others degenerate at some point in their development so that few, if any, remain by the time she reaches menopause at approximately 50 years of age."[8] Note the "marked contrast" that this description sets up between male and female: the male, who continuously produces fresh germ cells, and the female, who has stockpiled germ cells by birth and is faced with their degeneration.

Nor are the female organs spared such vivid descriptions. One scientist writes in a newspaper article that a woman's ovaries become old and worn out

[3] Arthur C. Guyton, *Physiology of the Human Body*, 6th ed. (Philadelphia: Saunders College Publishing, 1984), 624.

[4] Arthur J. Vander, James H. Sherman, and Dorothy S. Luciano, *Human Physiology: The Mechanisms of Body Function*, 3d ed. (New York: McGraw Hill, 1980), 483–84.

[5] Vernon B. Mountcastle, *Medical Physiology*, 14th ed. (London: Mosby, 1980), 2:1624.

[6] Eldra Pearl Solomon, *Human Anatomy and Physiology* (New York: CBS College Publishing, 1983), 678.

[7] For elaboration, see Emily Martin, *The Woman in the Body: A Cultural Analysis of Reproduction* (Boston: Beacon, 1987), 27–53.

[8] Vander, Sherman, and Luciano, 568.

from ripening eggs every month, even though the woman herself is still relatively young: "When you look through a laparoscope…at an ovary that has been through hundreds of cycles, even in a superbly healthy American female, you see a scarred, battered organ."[9]

To avoid the negative connotations that some people associate with the female reproductive system, scientists could begin to describe male and female processes as homologous. They might credit females with "producing" mature ova one at a time, as they're needed each month, and describe males as having to face problems of degenerating germ cells. This degeneration would occur throughout life among spermatogonia, the undifferentiated germ cells in the testes that are the long-lived, dormant precursors of sperm.

But the texts have an almost dogged insistence on casting female processes in a negative light. The texts celebrate sperm production because it is continuous from puberty to senescence, while they portray egg production as inferior because it is finished at birth. This makes the female seem unproductive, but some texts will also insist that it is she who is wasteful.[10] In a section heading for *Molecular Biology of the Cell*, a best-selling text, we are told that "Oogenesis is wasteful." The text goes on to emphasize that of the seven million oogonia, or egg germ cells, in the female embryo, most degenerate in the ovary. Of those that do go on to become oocytes, or eggs, many also degenerate, so that at birth only two million eggs remain in the ovaries. Degeneration continues throughout a woman's life: by puberty 300,000 eggs remain, and only a few are present by menopause. "During the 40 or so years of a woman's reproductive life, only 400 to 500 eggs will have been released;' the authors write. "All the rest will have degenerated. It is still a mystery why so many eggs are formed only to die in the ovaries."[11]

The real mystery is why the male's vast production of sperm is not seen as wasteful.[12] Assuming that a man "produces" 100 million (108) sperm per day (a

[9] Melvin Konner, "Childbearing and Age," *New York Times Magazine* (December 27, 1987), 22–23, esp. 22.

[10] I have found but one exception to the opinion that the female is wasteful: "Smallpox being the nasty disease it is, one might expect nature to have designed antibody molecules with combining sites that specifically recognize the epitopes on smallpox virus. Nature differs from technology, however: it thinks nothing of wastefulness. (For example, rather than improving the chance that a spermatozoon will meet an egg cell, nature finds it easier to produce millions of spermatozoa.)" (Niels Kaj Jerne, "The Immune System," *Scientific American* 229, no. 1 [July 1973]: 53). Thanks to a *Signs* reviewer for bringing this reference to my attention.

[11] Bruce Alberts et al., *Molecular Biology of the Cell* (New York: Garland, 1983), 795.

[12] In her essay "Have Only Men Evolved?" (in *Discovering Reality: Feminist Perspectives on Epistemology, Metaphysics, Methodology, and Philosophy of Science*, ed. Sandra Harding and Merrill B. Hintikka [Dordrecht: Reidel, 1983], 45–69, esp. 60–61), Ruth Hubbard points out that sociobiologists have said the female invests more energy than the male in the production of her large gametes, claiming that this explains why the female provides parental care. Hubbard questions whether it "really takes more 'energy' to generate the one or relatively few eggs than the large excess of sperms required to achieve fertilization." For further critique of how the greater size of eggs is interpreted in sociobiology, see Donna Haraway, "Investment Strategies for the Evolving Portfolio of Primate Females," in *Body/Politics*, ed. Mary Jacobus, Evelyn Fox Keller, and Sally Shuttleworth (New York: Routledge, 1990), 155–56.

conservative estimate) during an average reproductive life of sixty years, he would produce well over two trillion sperm in his lifetime. Assuming that a woman "ripens" one egg per lunar month, or thirteen per year, over the course of her forty-year reproductive life, she would total five hundred eggs in her lifetime. But the word "waste" implies an excess, too much produced. Assuming two or three offspring, for every baby a woman produces, she wastes only around two hundred eggs. For every baby a man produces, he wastes more than one trillion (10^{12}) sperm.

How is it that positive images are denied to the bodies of women? A look at language—in this case, scientific language—provides the first clue. Take the egg and the sperm.[13] It is remarkable how "femininely" the egg behaves and how "masculinely" the sperm.[14] The egg is seen as large and passive.[15] It does not *move* or *journey*, but passively "is transported," "is swept,"[16] or even "drifts"[17] along the fallopian tube. In utter contrast, sperm are small, "streamlined,"[18] and invariably active. They "deliver" their genes to the egg, "activate the developmental program of the egg;"[19] and have a "velocity" that is often remarked upon.[20] Their tails are "strong" and efficiently powered.[21] Together with the forces of ejaculation, they can "propel the semen into the deepest recesses of the vagina."[22] For this they need "energy," "fuel,"[23] so that with a "whiplashlike motion and strong lurches"[24] they can "burrow through the egg coat"[25] and "penetrate" it.[26]

At its extreme, the age-old relationship of the egg and the sperm takes on a royal or religious patina. The egg coat, its protective barrier, is sometimes called

---

[13] The sources I used for this article provide compelling information on interactions among sperm. Lack of space prevents me from taking up this theme here, but the elements include competition, hierarchy, and sacrifice. For a newspaper report, see Malcolm W. Browne, "Some Thoughts on Self Sacrifice," *New York Times* (July 5, 1988), C6. For a literary rendition, see John Barth, "Night-Sea Journey," in his *Lost in the Funhouse* (Garden City, N.Y.: Doubleday, 1968), 3–13.

[14] See Carol Delaney, "The Meaning of Paternity and the Virgin Birth Debate," *Man* 21, no. 3 (September 1986): 494–513. She discusses the difference between this scientific view that women contribute genetic material to the fetus and the claim of long-standing Western folk theories that the origin and identity of the fetus comes from the male, as in the metaphor of planting a seed in soil.

[15] For a suggested direct link between human behavior and purportedly passive eggs and active sperm, see Erik H. Erikson, "Inner and Outer Space: Reflections on Womanhood," *Daedalus* 93, no. 2 (Spring 1964): 582–606, esp. 591.

[16] Guyton (n. 3 above), 619; and Mountcastle (n. 5 above), 1609.

[17] Jonathan Miller and David Pelham, *The Facts of Life* (New York: Viking Penguin, 1984), 5.

[18] Alberts et al., 796.

[19] Ibid., 796.

[20] See, e.g., William F. Ganong, *Review of Medical Physiology*, 7th ed. (Los Altos, Calif.: Lange Medical Publications, 1975), 322.

[21] Alberts et al. (n. 11 above), 796.

[22] Guyton, 615.

[23] Solomon (n. 6 above), 683.

[24] Vander, Sherman, and Luciano (n. 4 above), 4th ed. (1985), 580.

[25] Alberts et al., 796.

[26] All biology texts quoted above use the word "penetrate."

its "vestments," a term usually reserved for sacred, religious dress. The egg is said to have a "corona,"[27] a crown, and to be accompanied by "attendant cells."[28] It is holy, set apart and above, the queen to the sperm's king. The egg is also passive, which means it must depend on sperm for rescue. Gerald Schatten and Helen Schatten liken the egg's role to that of Sleeping Beauty: "a dormant bride awaiting her mate's magic kiss, which instills the spirit that brings her to life."[29] Sperm, by contrast, have a "mission,"[30] which is to "move through the female genital tract in quest of the ovum."[31] One popular account has it that the sperm carry out a "perilous journey" into the "warm darkness," where some fall away "exhausted." "Survivors" "assault" the egg, the successful candidates "surrounding the prize."[32] Part of the urgency of this journey, in more scientific terms, is that "once released from the supportive environment of the ovary, an egg will die within hours unless rescued by a sperm."[33] The wording stresses the fragility and dependency of the egg, even though the same text acknowledges elsewhere that sperm also live for only a few hours.[34]

In 1948, in a book remarkable for its early insights into these matters, Ruth Herschberger argued that female reproductive organs are seen as biologically interdependent, while male organs are viewed as autonomous, operating independently and in isolation:

> At present the functional is stressed only in connection with women: it is in them that ovaries, tubes, uterus, and vagina have endless interdependence. In the male, reproduction would seem to involve "organs" only.
>
> Yet the sperm, just as much as the egg, is dependent on a great many related processes. There are secretions which mitigate the urine in the urethra before ejaculation, to protect the sperm. There is the reflex shutting off of the bladder connection, the provision of prostatic secretions, and various types of muscular propulsion. The sperm is no more independent of its milieu than the egg, and yet from a wish that it were, biologists have lent their support to the notion that the human female, beginning with the egg, is congenitally more dependent than the male.[35]

---

[27] Solomon, 700.

[28] A. Beldecos et al., "The Importance of Feminist Critique for Contemporary Cell Biology," *Hypatia* 3, no. 1 (Spring 1988): 61–76.

[29] Gerald Schatten and Helen Schatten, "The Energetic Egg," *Medical World News* 23 (January 23, 1984): 51–53, esp. 51.

[30] Alberts et al., 796.

[31] Guyton (n. 3 above), 613.

[32] Miller and Pelham (n. 17 above), 7.

[33] Alberts et al. (n. 11 above), 804.

[34] Ibid., 801.

[35] Ruth Herschberger, *Adam's Rib* (New York: Pelligrini & Cudahy, 1948), esp. 84. I am indebted to Ruth Hubbard for telling me about Herschberger's work, although at a point when this paper was already in draft form.

Bringing out another aspect of the sperm's autonomy, an article in the journal *Cell* has the sperm making an "existential decision" to penetrate the egg: "Sperm are cells with a limited behavioral repertoire, one that is directed toward fertilizing eggs. To execute the decision to abandon the haploid state, sperm swim to an egg and there acquire the ability to effect membrane fusion."[36] Is this a corporate manager's version of the sperm's activities—"executing decisions" while fraught with dismay over difficult options that bring with them very high risk?

There is another way that sperm, despite their small size, can be made to loom in importance over the egg. In a collection of scientific papers, an electron micrograph of an enormous egg and tiny sperm is titled "A Portrait of the Sperm."[37] This is a little like showing a photo of a dog and calling it a picture of the fleas. Granted, microscopic sperm are harder to photograph than eggs, which are just large enough to see with the naked eye. But surely the use of the term "portrait," a word associated with the powerful and wealthy, is significant. Eggs have only micrographs or pictures, not portraits.

One depiction of sperm as weak and timid, instead of strong and powerful—the only such representation in western civilization, so far as I know—occurs in Woody Allen's movie *Everything You Always Wanted To Know About Sex* *But Were Afraid to Ask*. Allen, playing the part of an apprehensive sperm inside a man's testicles, is scared of the man's approaching orgasm. He is reluctant to launch himself into the darkness, afraid of contraceptive devices, afraid of winding up on the ceiling if the man masturbates.

The more common picture—egg as damsel in distress, shielded only by her sacred garments; sperm as heroic warrior to the rescue—cannot be proved to be dictated by the biology of these events. While the "facts" of biology may not *always* be constructed in cultural terms, I would argue that in this case they are. The degree of metaphorical content in these descriptions, the extent to which differences between egg and sperm are emphasized, and the parallels between cultural stereotypes of male and female behavior and the character of egg and sperm all point to this conclusion.

New research, old imagery

As new understandings of egg and sperm emerge, textbook gender imagery is being revised. But the new research, far from escaping the stereotypical representations of egg and sperm, simply replicates elements of textbook gender imagery in a different form. The persistence of this imagery calls to mind what Ludwik Fleck termed "the self-contained" nature of scientific thought. As he described it, "the interaction between what is already known, what remains to be learned, and those who are to apprehend it, go to ensure harmony within the system. But at the same time they also preserve the harmony of illusions, which is quite secure within the confines of a given thought style."[38] We need to understand the way in which the

---

36 Bennett M. Shapiro. "The Existential Decision of a Sperm," *Cell* 49, no. 3 (May 1987): 293–94, esp. 293.

37 Lennart Nilsson, "A Portrait of the Sperm," in *The Functional Anatomy of the Spermatozoan*, ed. Bjorn A. Afzelius (New York: Pergamon, 1975), 79–82.

38 Ludwik Fleck, *Genesis and Development of a Scientific Fact*, ed. Thaddeus J. Trenn and Robert K. Merton (Chicago: University of Chicago Press, 1979), 38.

cultural content in scientific descriptions changes as biological discoveries unfold, and whether that cultural content is solidly entrenched or easily changed.

In all of the texts quoted above, sperm are described as penetrating the egg, and specific substances on a sperm's head are described as binding to the egg. Recently, this description of events was rewritten in a biophysics lab at Johns Hopkins University—transforming the egg from the passive to the active party.[39]

Prior to this research, it was thought that the zona, the inner vestments of the egg, formed an impenetrable barrier. Sperm overcame the barrier by mechanically burrowing through, thrashing their tails and slowly working their way along. Later research showed that the sperm released digestive enzymes that chemically broke down the zona; thus, scientists presumed that the sperm used mechanical *and* chemical means to get through to the egg.

In this recent investigation, the researchers began to ask questions about the mechanical force of the sperm's tail. (The lab's goal was to develop a contraceptive that worked topically on sperm.) They discovered, to their great surprise, that the forward thrust of sperm is extremely weak, which contradicts the assumption that sperm are forceful penetrators.[40] Rather than thrusting forward, the sperm's head was now seen to move mostly back and forth. The sideways motion of the sperm's tail makes the head move sideways with a force that is ten times stronger than its forward movement. So even if the overall force of the sperm were strong enough to mechanically break the zona, most of its force would be directed sideways rather than forward. In fact, its strongest tendency, by tenfold, is to escape by attempting to pry itself off the egg. Sperm, then, must be exceptionally efficient at *escaping* from any cell surface they contact. And the surface of the egg must be designed to trap the sperm and prevent their escape. Otherwise, few if any sperm would reach the egg.

The researchers at Johns Hopkins concluded that the sperm and egg stick together because of adhesive molecules on the surfaces of each. The egg traps the sperm and adheres to it so tightly that the sperm's head is forced to lie flat against the surface of the zona, a little bit, they told me, "like Br'er Rabbit getting more and more stuck to tar baby the more he wriggles." The trapped sperm continues to wiggle ineffectually side to side. The mechanical force of its tail is so weak that a sperm cannot break even one chemical bond. This is where the digestive enzymes released by the sperm come in. If they start to soften the zona just at the tip of the sperm and the sides remain stuck, then the weak, flailing sperm can get oriented in the right direction and make it through the zona—provided that its bonds to the zona dissolve as it moves in.

Although this new version of the saga of the egg and the sperm broke through cultural expectations, the researchers who made the discovery continued to write papers and abstracts as if the sperm were the active party who attacks,

---

[39] Jay M. Baltz carried out the research I describe when he was a graduate student in the Thomas C. Jenkins Department of Biophysics at Johns Hopkins University.

[40] Far less is known about the physiology of sperm than comparable female substances, which some feminists claim is no accident. Greater scientific scrutiny of female reproduction has long enabled the burden of birth control to be placed on women. In this case, the researchers' discovery did not depend on development of any new technology. The experiments made use of glass pipettes, a manometer, and a simple microscope, all of which have been available for more than one hundred years.

binds, penetrates, and enters the egg. The only difference was that sperm were now seen as performing these actions weakly.[41] Not until August 1987, more than three years after the findings described above, did these researchers reconceptualize the process to give the egg a more active role. They began to describe the zona as an aggressive sperm catcher, covered with adhesive molecules that can capture a sperm with a single bond and clasp it to the zona's surface.[42] In the words of their published account: "The innermost vestment, the *zona pellucida*, is a glycoprotein shell, which captures and tethers the sperm before they penetrate it…The sperm is captured at the initial contact between the sperm tip and the *zona*…Since the thrust [of the sperm] is much smaller than the force needed to break a single affinity bond, the first bond made upon the tip-first meeting of the sperm and *zona* can result in the capture of the sperm."[43]

Experiments in another lab reveal similar patterns of data interpretation. Gerald Schatten and Helen Schatten set out to show that, contrary to conventional wisdom, the "egg is not merely a large, yolk-filled sphere into which the sperm burrows to endow new life. Rather, recent research suggests the almost heretical view that sperm and egg are mutually active partners."[44] This sounds like a departure from the stereotypical textbook view, but further reading reveals Schatten and Schatten's conformity to the aggressive-sperm metaphor. They describe how "the sperm and egg first touch when, from the tip of the sperm's triangular head, a long, thin filament shoots out and harpoons the egg." Then we learn that "remarkably, the harpoon is not so much fired as assembled at great speed, molecule by molecule, from a pool of protein stored in a specialized region called the acrosome. The filament may grow as much as twenty times longer than the sperm head itself before its tip reaches the egg and sticks."[45] Why not call this "making a bridge" or "throwing out a line" rather than firing a harpoon? Harpoons pierce prey and injure or kill them, while this filament only sticks. And why not focus, as the Hopkins lab did, on the stickiness of the egg, rather than the stickiness of the sperm?[46] Later in the article, the Schattens replicate the common view of the sperm's perilous journey into the warm darkness of the vagina, this time for

[41] Jay Baltz and Richard A. Cone, "What Force Is Needed to Tether a Sperm?" (abstract for Society for the Study of Reproduction, 1985), and "Flagellar Torque on the Head Determines the Force Needed to Tether a Sperm" (abstract for Biophysical Society, 1986).

[42] Jay M. Baltz, David F. Katz, and Richard A. Cone, "The Mechanics of the Sperm-Egg Interaction at the Zona Pellucida," *Biophysical Journal* 54, no. 4 (October 1988): 643–54. Lab members were somewhat familiar with work on metaphors in the biology of female reproduction. Richard Cone, who runs the lab, is my husband, and he talked with them about my earlier research on the subject from time to time. Even though my current research focuses on biological imagery and I heard about the lab's work from my husband every day, I myself did not recognize the role of imagery in the sperm research until many weeks after the period of research and writing I describe. Therefore, I assume that any awareness the lab members may have had about how underlying metaphor might be guiding this particular research was fairly inchoate.

[43] Ibid., 643, 650.

[44] Schatten and Schatten (n. 29 above), 51.

[45] Ibid., 52.

[46] Surprisingly, in an article intended for a general audience, the authors do not point out that these are sea urchin sperm and note that human sperm do not shoot out filaments at all.

the purpose of explaining its journey into the egg itself: "[The sperm] still has an arduous journey ahead. It must penetrate farther into the egg's huge sphere of cytoplasm and somehow locate the nucleus, so that the two cells' chromosomes can fuse. The sperm dives down into the cytoplasm, its tail beating. But it is soon interrupted by the sudden and swift migration of the egg nucleus, which rushes toward the sperm with a velocity triple that of the movement of chromosomes during cell division, crossing the entire egg in about a minute."[47]

Like Schatten and Schatten and the biophysicists at Johns Hopkins, another researcher has recently made discoveries that seem to point to a more interactive view of the relationship of egg and sperm. This work, which Paul Wassarman conducted on the sperm and eggs of mice, focuses on identifying the specific molecules in the egg coat (the zona pellucida) that are involved in egg-sperm interaction. At first glance, his descriptions seem to fit the model of an egalitarian relationship. Male and female gametes "recognize one another," and "interactions…take place between sperm and egg."[48] But the article in *Scientific American* in which those descriptions appear begins with a vignette that presages the dominant motif of their presentation: "It has been more than a century since Hermann Fol, a Swiss zoologist, peered into his microscope and became the first person to see a sperm penetrate an egg, fertilize it and form the first cell of a new embryo."[49] This portrayal of the sperm as the active party—the one that *penetrates* and *fertilizes* the egg and *produces* the embryo—is not cited as an example of an earlier, now outmoded view. In fact, the author reiterates the point later in the article: "Many sperm can bind to and penetrate the zona pellucida, or outer coat, of an unfertilized mouse egg, but only one sperm will eventually fuse with the thin plasma membrane surrounding the egg proper (*inner sphere*), fertilizing the egg and giving rise to a new embryo."[50]

The imagery of sperm as aggressor is particularly startling in this case: the main discovery being reported is isolation of a particular molecule *on the egg coat* that plays an important role in fertilization! Wassarman's choice of language sustains the picture. He calls the molecule that has been isolated, ZP3, a "sperm receptor." By allocating the passive, waiting role to the egg, Wassarman can continue to describe the sperm as the actor, the one that makes it all happen: "The basic process begins when many sperm first attach loosely and then bind tenaciously to receptors on the surface of the egg's thick outer coat, the zona pellucida. Each sperm, which has a large number of egg-binding proteins on its surface, binds to many sperm receptors on the egg. More specifically, a site on each of the egg-binding proteins fits a complementary site on a sperm receptor, much as a key fits a lock."[51] With the sperm designated as the "key" and the egg the "lock," it is obvious which one acts and which one is acted upon. Could this imagery not be reversed, letting the sperm (the lock) wait until the egg produces the key? Or

---

[47] Schatten and Schatten, 53.

[48] Paul M. Wassarman, "Fertilization in Mammals," *Scientific American* 259, no. 6 (December 1988): 78–84, esp. 78, 84.

[49] Ibid., 78.

[50] Ibid., 79.

[51] Ibid., 78.

could we speak of two halves of a locket matching, and regard the matching itself as the action that initiates the fertilization?

It is as if Wassarman were determined to make the egg the receiving partner. Usually in biological research, the *protein* member of the pair of binding molecules is called the receptor, and physically it has a pocket in it rather like a lock. As the diagrams that illustrate Wassarman's article show, the molecules on the sperm are proteins and have "pockets." The small, mobile molecules that fit into these pockets are called ligands. As shown in the diagrams, ZP3 on the egg is a polymer of "keys"; many small knobs stick out. Typically, molecules on the sperm would be called receptors and molecules on the egg would be called ligands. But Wassarman chose to name ZP3 on the egg the receptor and to create a new term, "the egg-binding protein," for the molecule on the sperm that otherwise would have been called the receptor.[52]

Wassarman does credit the egg coat with having more functions than those of a sperm receptor. While he notes that "the zona pellucida has at times been viewed by investigators as a nuisance, a barrier to sperm and hence an impediment to fertilization," his new research reveals that the egg coat "serves as a sophisticated biological security system that screens incoming sperm, selects only those compatible with fertilization and development, prepares sperm for fusion with the egg and later protects the resulting embryo from polyspermy [a lethal condition caused by fusion of more than one sperm with a single egg]."[53] Although this description gives the egg an active role, that role is drawn in stereotypically feminine terms. The egg *selects* an appropriate mate, *prepares* him for fusion, and then *protects* the resulting offspring from harm. This is courtship and mating behavior as seen through the eyes of a sociobiologist: woman as the hard-to-get prize, who, following union with the chosen one, becomes woman as servant and mother.

And Wassarman does not quit there. In a review article for *Science*, he outlines the "chronology of fertilization."[54] Near the end of the article are two subject headings. One is "Sperm Penetration," in which Wassarman describes how the chemical dissolving of the zona pellucida combines with the "substantial propulsive force generated by sperm." The next heading is "Sperm-Egg Fusion." This section details what happens inside the zona after a sperm "penetrates" it. Sperm "can make contact with, adhere to, and fuse with (that is, fertilize) an egg."[55] Wassarman's word choice, again, is astonishingly skewed in favor of the sperm's activity, for in the next breath he says that sperm *lose* all motility upon fusion with the egg's surface. In mouse and sea urchin eggs, the sperm enters at the *egg's* volition, according to Wassarman' s description: "Once fused with egg plasma membrane [the surface of the egg], how does a sperm enter the egg? The surface of both mouse and sea urchin eggs is covered with thousands of plasma membrane-bound

[52] Since receptor molecules are relatively immotile and the ligands that bind to them relatively motile, one might imagine the egg being called the receptor and the sperm the ligand. But the molecules in question on egg and sperm are immotile molecules. It is the sperm as a cell that has motility, and the egg as a cell that has relative immotility.

[53] Wassarman, 78–79.

[54] Paul M. Wassarman, "The Biology and Chemistry of Fertilization," *Science* 235, no. 4788 (January 30, 1987): 553–60, esp. 554.

[55] Ibid., 557.

projections, called microvilli [tiny "hairs"]. Evidence in sea urchins suggests that, after membrane fusion, a group of elongated microvilli cluster tightly around and interdigitate over the sperm head. As these microvilli are resorbed, the sperm is drawn into the egg. Therefore, sperm motility, which ceases at the time of fusion in both sea urchins and mice, is not required for sperm entry."[56] The section called "Sperm Penetration" more logically would be followed by a section called "The Egg Envelops," rather than "SpermEgg Fusion." This would give a parallel—and more accurate—sense that both the egg and the sperm initiate action.

Another way that Wassarman makes less of the egg's activity is by describing components of the egg but referring to the sperm as a whole entity. Deborah Gordon has described such an approach as "atomism" ("the part is independent of and primordial to the whole") and identified it as one of the "tenacious assumptions" of Western science and medicine.[57] Wassarman employs atomism to his advantage. When he refers to processes going on within sperm, he consistently returns to descriptions that remind us from whence these activities came: they are part of sperm that penetrate an egg or generate propulsive force. When he refers to processes going on within eggs, he stops there. As a result, any active role he grants them appears to be assigned to the parts of the egg, and not to the egg itself. In the quote above, it is the microvilli that actively cluster around the sperm. In another example, "the driving force for engulfment of a fused sperm comes from a region of cytoplasm just beneath an egg's plasma membrane."[58]

Social implications: Thinking beyond

All three of these revisionist accounts of egg and sperm cannot seem to escape the hierarchical imagery of older accounts. Even though each new account gives the egg a larger and more active role, taken together they bring into play another cultural stereo type: woman as a dangerous and aggressive threat. In the Johns Hopkins lab's revised model, the egg ends up as the female aggressor who "captures and tethers" the sperm with her sticky zona, rather like a spider lying in wait in her web.[59] The Schatten lab has the egg's nucleus "interrupt" the sperm's dive with a "sudden and swift" rush by which she "clasps the sperm and guides its nucleus to the center."[60] Wassarman's description of the surface of the egg "covered with thousands of plasma membrane-bound projections, called microvilli" that reach out and clasp the sperm adds to the spiderlike imagery.[61]

These images grant the egg an active role but at the cost of appearing disturbingly aggressive. Images of woman as dangerous and aggressive, the femme fatale

---

[56] Ibid., 557–58. This finding throws into question Schatten and Schatten's description (n. 29 above) of the sperm, its tail beating, diving down into the egg.

[57] Deborah R. Gordon, "Tenacious Assumptions in Western Medicine," in *Bio-medicine Examined*, ed. Margaret Lock and Deborah Gordon (Dordrecht: Kluwer, 1988), 19–56, esp. 26.

[58] Wassarman, "The Biology and Chemistry of Fertilization," 558.

[59] Baltz, Katz, and Cone (n. 42 above), 643, 650.

[60] Schatten and Schatten, 53.

[61] Wassarman, "The Biology and Chemistry of Fertilization," 557.

who victimizes men, are widespread in Western literature and culture.[62] More specific is the connection of spider imagery with the idea of an engulfing, devouring mother.[63] New data did not lead scientists to eliminate gender stereotypes in their descriptions of egg and sperm. Instead, scientists simply began to describe egg and sperm in different, but no less damaging, terms.

Can we envision a less stereotypical view? Biology itself provides another model that could be applied to the egg and the sperm. The cybernetic model—with its feedback loops, flexible adaptation to change, coordination of the parts within a whole, evolution over time, and changing response to the environment—is common in genetics, endocrinology, and ecology and has a growing influence in medicine in general.[64] This model has the potential to shift our imagery from the negative, in which the female reproductive system is castigated both for not producing eggs after birth and for producing (and thus wasting) too many eggs overall, to something more positive. The female reproductive system could be seen as responding to the environment (pregnancy or menopause), adjusting to monthly changes (menstruation), and flexibly changing from reproductivity after puberty to nonreproductivity later in life. The sperm and egg's interaction could also be described in cybernetic terms. J. F. Hartman's research in reproductive biology demonstrated fifteen years ago that if an egg is killed by being pricked with a needle, live sperm cannot get through the zona.[65] Clearly, this evidence shows that the egg and sperm *do* interact on more mutual terms, making biology's refusal to portray them that way all the more disturbing.

We would do well to be aware, however, that cybernetic imagery is hardly neutral. In the past, cybernetic models have played an important part in the imposition of social control. These models inherently provide a way of thinking about a "field" of interacting components. Once the field can be seen, it can become the object of new forms of knowledge, which in turn can allow new forms of social control to be exerted over the components of the field. During the 1950s, for example, medicine began to recognize the psychosocial *environment* of the patient: the patient's family and its psychodynamics. Professions such as social work began to focus on this new environment, and the resulting knowledge became one way to further control the patient. Patients began to be seen not as isolated, individual bodies, but as psychosocial entities located in an "ecological" system: management of "the patient's psychology was a new entree to patient control."[66]

---

[62] Mary Ellman, *Thinking about Women* (New York: Harcourt Brace Jovanovich, 1968), 140; Nina Auerbach, *Woman and the Demon* (Cambridge, Mass.: Harvard University Press, 1982), esp. 186.

[63] Kenneth Alan Adams, "Arachnophobia: Love American Style," *Journal of Psychoanalytic Anthropology* 4, no. 2 (1981): 157–97.

[64] William Ray Arney and Bernard Bergen, *Medicine and the Management of Living* (Chicago: University of Chicago Press, 1984).

[65] J. F. Hartman, R. B. Gwatkin, and C. F. Hutchison, "Early Contact Interactions between Mammalian Gametes In Vitro," *Proceedings of the National Academy of Sciences* (U.S.) 69, no. 10 (1972): 2767–69.

[66] Arney and Bergen, 68.

The models that biologists use to describe their data can have important social effects. During the nineteenth century, the social and natural sciences strongly influenced each other: the social ideas of Malthus about how to avoid the natural increase of the poor inspired Darwin's *Origin of Species*.[67] Once the *Origin* stood as a description of the natural world, complete with competition and market struggles, it could be reimported into social science as social Darwinism, in order to justify the social order of the time. What we are seeing now is similar: the importation of cultural ideas about passive females and heroic males into the "personalities" of gametes. This amounts to the "implanting of social imagery on representations of nature so as to lay a firm basis for reimporting exactly that same imagery as natural explanations of social phenomena."[68]

Further research would show us exactly what social effects are being wrought from the biological imagery of egg and sperm. At the very least, the imagery keeps alive some of the hoariest old stereotypes about weak damsels in distress and their strong male rescuers. That these stereotypes are now being written in at the level of the *cell* constitutes a powerful move to make them seem so natural as to be beyond alteration.

The stereotypical imagery might also encourage people to imagine that what results from the interaction of egg and sperm—a fertilized egg—is the result of deliberate "human" action at the cellular level. Whatever the intentions of the human couple, in this microscopic "culture" a cellular "bride" (or femme fatale) and a cellular "groom" (her victim) make a cellular baby. Rosalind Petchesky points out that through visual representations such as sonograms, we are given "*images* of younger and younger, and tinier and tinier, fetuses being 'saved.'" This leads to "the point of visibility being 'pushed back' *indefinitely*."[69] Endowing egg and sperm with intentional action, a key aspect of personhood in our culture, lays the foundation for the point of viability being pushed back to the moment of fertilization. This will likely lead to greater acceptance of technological developments and new forms of scrutiny and manipulation, for the benefit of these inner "persons": court-ordered restrictions on a pregnant woman's activities in order to protect her fetus, fetal surgery, amniocentesis, and rescinding of abortion rights, to name but a few examples.[70]

Even if we succeed in substituting more egalitarian, interactive metaphors to describe the activities of egg and sperm, and manage to avoid the pitfalls of cybernetic models, we would still be guilty of endowing cellular entities with personhood. More crucial, then, than what *kinds* of personalities we bestow on cells is the very fact that we are doing it at all. This process could ultimately have the most disturbing social consequences.

---

[67] Ruth Hubbard, "Have Only Men Evolved?" (n. 12 above), 51–52.

[68] David Harvey, personal communication, November 1989.

[69] Rosalind Petchesky, "Fetal Images: The Power of Visual Culture in the Politics of Reproduction," *Feminist Studies* 13, no. 2 (Summer 1987): 263–92, esp. 272.

[70] Rita Arditti, Renate Klein, and Shelley Minden, *Test-Tube Women* (London: Pandora, 1984); Ellen Goodman, "Whose Right to Life?" *Baltimore Sun* (November 17, 1987); Tamar Lewin, "Courts Acting to Force Care of the Unborn," *New York Times* (November 23, 1987), A1 and B10; Susan Irwin and Brigitte Jordan, "Knowledge, Practice, and Power: Court Ordered Cesarean Sections," *Medical Anthropology Quarterly* 1, no. 3 (September 1987): 319–34.

One clear feminist challenge is to wake up sleeping metaphors in science, particularly those involved in descriptions of the egg and the sperm. Although the literary convention is to call such metaphors "dead," they are not so much dead as sleeping, hidden within the scientific content of texts—and all the more powerful for it.[71] Waking up such metaphors, by becoming aware of when we are projecting cultural imagery onto what we study, will improve our ability to investigate and understand nature. Waking up such metaphors, by becoming aware of their implications, will rob them of their power to naturalize our social conventions about gender.

Department of Anthropology
Johns Hopkins University ■

AUTHOR PROFILE

Emily Martin (born November 7, 1944) is a professor of socio-cultural anthropology at New York University. She received her PhD from Cornell University in 1971. Her research examines the anthropology of science from a feminist perspective. She has been the recipient of a Guggenheim fellowship, is the founding editor of the general interest magazine *Anthropology Now* sponsored by the American Ethnological Association, and co-organizes The Psyences Project, which brings clinicians into dialogue with academics around common interests in mind and brain. Martin is currently conducting ethnographic research on a new project that involves the history of the human subject in experimental psychology. Her book *Bipolar Expeditions* was the winner of the 2009 Diana Forsythe prize for the best book of feminist anthropological research on work, science, and technology. Martin published "The Sperm and the Egg" in 1991 in the journal *Signs*.

[71] Thanks to Elizabeth Fee and David Spain, who in February 1989 and April 1989, respectively, made points related to this.

On Truth and Lying in a Non-Moral Sense

By Friedrich Nietzsche

N

I

In some remote corner of the universe, flickering in the light of the countless solar systems into which it had been poured, there was once a planet on which clever animals invented cognition. It was the most arrogant and most mendacious minute in the 'history of the world'; but a minute was all it was. After nature had drawn just a few more breaths the planet froze and the clever animals had to die. Someone could invent a fable like this and yet they would still not have given a satisfactory illustration of just how pitiful, how insubstantial and transitory, how purposeless and arbitrary the human intellect looks within nature; there were eternities during which it did not exist; and when it has disappeared again, nothing will have happened. For this intellect has no further mission that might extend beyond the bounds of human life. Rather, the intellect is human, and only its own possessor and progenitor regards it with such pathos, as if it housed the axis around which the entire world revolved. But if we could communicate with a midge we would hear that it too floats through the air with the very same pathos, feeling that it too contains within itself the flying centre of this world. There is nothing in nature so despicable and mean that would not immediately swell up like a balloon from just one little puff of that force of cognition; and just as every bearer of burdens wants to be admired, so the proudest man of all, the philosopher, wants to see, on all sides, the eyes of the universe trained, as through telescopes, on his thoughts and deeds.

It is odd that the intellect can produce this effect, since it is nothing other than an aid supplied to the most unfortunate, most delicate and most transient of beings so as to detain them for a minute within existence; otherwise, without this supplement, they would have every reason to flee existence as quickly as did Lessing's infant son.[1] The arrogance inherent in cognition and feeling casts a blinding fog over the eyes and senses of human beings, and because it contains within itself the most flattering evaluation of cognition it deceives them about the value of existence. Its most general effect is deception—but each of its separate effects also has something of the same character.

As a means for the preservation of the individual, the intellect shows its greatest strengths in dissimulation, since this is the means to preserve those weaker, less robust individuals who, by nature, are denied horns or the sharp fangs of a

1 Lessing's first and only son died immediately after birth, followed soon after by his mother. This drew from Lessing the comment: 'Was it good sense that they had to pull him into the world with iron tongs, or that he noticed the filth so quickly? Was it not good sense that he took the first opportunity to leave it again?' (Letter to Eschenburg, 10 January 1778).

beast of prey with which to wage the struggle for existence. This art of dissimulation reaches its peak in humankind, where deception, flattery, lying and cheating, speaking behind the backs of others, keeping up appearances,[2] living in borrowed finery, wearing masks, the drapery of convention, play-acting for the benefit of others and oneself—in short, the constant fluttering of human beings around the one flame of vanity is so much the rule and the law that there is virtually nothing which defies understanding so much as the fact that an honest and pure drive towards truth should ever have emerged in them. They are deeply immersed in illusions and dream-images; their eyes merely glide across the surface of things and see 'forms'; nowhere does their perception lead into truth; instead it is content to receive stimuli and, as it were, to play with its fingers on the back of things. What is more, human beings allow themselves to be lied to in dreams every night of their lives, without their moral sense ever seeking to prevent this happening, whereas it is said that some people have even eliminated snoring by will-power. What do human beings really know about themselves? Are they even capable of perceiving themselves in their entirety just once, stretched out as in an illuminated glass case? Does nature not remain silent about almost everything, even about our bodies, banishing and enclosing us within a proud, illusory consciousness, far away from the twists and turns of the bowels, the rapid flow of the blood stream and the complicated tremblings of the nerve-fibres? Nature has thrown away the key, and woe betide fateful curiosity should it ever succeed in peering through a crack in the chamber of consciousness, out and down into the depths, and thus gain an intimation of the fact that humanity, in the indifference of its ignorance, rests on the pitiless, the greedy, the insatiable, the murderous—clinging in dreams, as it were, to the back of a tiger. Given this constellation, where on earth can the drive to truth possibly have come from?

Insofar as the individual wishes to preserve himself in relation to other individuals, in the state of nature he mostly used his intellect for concealment and dissimulation; however, because necessity and boredom also lead men to want to live in societies and herds, they need a peace treaty, and so they endeavour to eliminate from their world at least the crudest forms of the *bellum omnium contra omnes*.[3] In the wake of this peace treaty, however, comes something which looks like the first step towards the acquisition of that mysterious drive for truth. For that which is to count as 'truth' from this point onwards now becomes fixed, i.e. a way of designating things is invented which has the same validity and force everywhere, and the legislation of language also produces the first laws of truth, for the contrast between truth and lying comes into existence here for the first time: the liar uses the valid tokens of designation—words—to make the unreal appear to be real; he says, for example, 'I am rich', whereas the correct designation for this condition would be, precisely, 'poor'. He misuses the established conventions by arbitrarily switching or even inverting the names for things. If he does this in a manner that is selfish and otherwise harmful, society will no longer trust him and

[2] The verb Nietzsche uses is *repräsentieren*. This means keeping up a show in public, representing one's family, country, or social group before the eyes of the world.

[3] 'war of all against all': phrase associated with Thomas Hobbes' description of the state of nature before the institution of political authority (cf. Hobbes, *De cive* I.12 and *Leviathan*, chapter XIII).

therefore exclude him from its ranks. Human beings do not so much flee from being tricked as from being harmed by being tricked. Even on this level they do not hate deception but rather the damaging, inimical consequences of certain species of deception. Truth, too, is only desired by human beings in a similarly limited sense. They desire the pleasant, life-preserving consequences of truth; they are indifferent to pure knowledge if it has no consequences, but they are actually hostile towards truths which may be harmful and destructive. And, besides, what is the status of those conventions of language? Are they perhaps products of knowledge, of the sense of truth? Is there a perfect match between things and their designations? Is language the full and adequate expression of all realities?

Only through forgetfulness could human beings ever entertain the illusion that they possess truth to the degree described above. If they will not content themselves with truth in the form of tautology, i.e. with empty husks, they will for ever exchange illusions for truth. What is a word? The copy of a nervous stimulation in sounds. To infer from the fact of the nervous stimulation that there exists a cause outside us is already the result of applying the principle of sufficient reason wrongly. If truth alone had been decisive in the genesis of language, if the viewpoint of certainty had been decisive in creating designations, how could we possibly be permitted to say, 'The stone is hard', as if 'hard' were something known to us in some other way, and not merely as an entirely subjective stimulus? We divide things up by gender, describing a tree as masculine and a plant as feminine[4]—how arbitrary these translations are! How far they have flown beyond the canon of certainty! We speak of a snake; the designation captures only its twisting movements and thus could equally well apply to a worm. How arbitrarily these borders are drawn, how one-sided the preference for this or that property of a thing! When different languages are set alongside one another it becomes clear that, where words are concerned, what matters is never truth, never the full and adequate expression;[5] otherwise there would not be so many languages. The 'thing-in-itself' (which would be, precisely, pure truth, truth without consequences) is impossible for even the creator of language to grasp, and indeed this is not at all desirable. He designates only the relations of things to human beings, and in order to express them he avails himself of the boldest metaphors. The stimulation of a nerve is first translated into an image: first metaphor! The image is then imitated by a sound: second metaphor! And each time there is a complete leap from one sphere into the heart of another, new sphere. One can conceive of a profoundly deaf human being who has never experienced sound or music; just as such a person will gaze in astonishment at the Chladnian sound-figures in sand,[6] find their cause in the vibration of a string, and swear that he must now know what men call sound—this is precisely what happens to all of us with language. We believe that when we

---

4 'Tree' is masculine in German (*der Baum*) and 'plant' (*die Pflanze*) is feminine.

5 Nietzsche uses the term *adäquat* which indicates that the meaning of something is fully conveyed by a word or expression; English 'adequate' alone does not convey this sense completely.

6 The vibration of a string can create figures in the sand (in an appropriately constructed sand-box) which give a visual representation of that which the human ear perceives as a tone. The term comes from the name of the physicist Ernst Chladni, whose experiments demonstrated the effect.

speak of trees, colours, snow, and flowers, we have knowledge of the things themselves, and yet we possess only metaphors of things which in no way correspond to the original entities. Just as the musical sound appears as a figure in the sand, so the mysterious 'X' of the thing-in-itself appears first as a nervous stimulus, then as an image, and finally as an articulated sound. At all events, things do not proceed logically when language comes into being, and the entire material in and with which the man of truth, the researcher, the philosopher, works and builds, stems, if not from cloud-cuckoo land, then certainly not from the essence of things.

Let us consider in particular how concepts are formed; each word immediately becomes a concept, not by virtue of the fact that it is intended to serve as a memory (say) of the unique, utterly individualized, primary experience to which it owes its existence, but because at the same time it must fit countless other, more or less similar cases, i.e. cases which, strictly speaking, are never equivalent, and thus nothing other than nonequivalent cases. Every concept comes into being by making equivalent that which is non-equivalent. Just as it is certain that no leaf is ever exactly the same as any other leaf, it is equally certain that the concept 'leaf' is formed by dropping these individual differences arbitrarily, by forgetting those features which differentiate one thing from another, so that the concept then gives rise to the notion that something other than leaves exists in nature, something which would be 'leaf', a primal form, say, from which all leaves were woven, drawn, delineated, dyed, curled, painted—but by a clumsy pair of hands, so that no single example turned out to be a faithful, correct, and reliable copy of the primal form. We call a man honest; we ask, 'Why did he act so honestly today?' Our answer is usually: 'Because of his honesty.' Honesty!—yet again, this means that the leaf is the cause of the leaves. We have no knowledge of an essential quality which might be called honesty, but we do know of numerous individualized and hence nonequivalent actions which we equate with each other by omitting what is unlike, and which we now designate as honest actions; finally we formulate from them a *qualitas occulta*[7] with the name 'honesty'.

Like form, a concept is produced by overlooking what is individual and real, whereas nature knows neither forms nor concepts and hence no species, but only an 'X' which is inaccessible to us and indefinable by us. For the opposition we make between individual and species is also anthropomorphic and does not stem from the essence of things, although we equally do not dare to say that it does *not* correspond to the essence of things, since that would be a dogmatic assertion and, as such, just as incapable of being proved as its opposite.

What, then, is truth? A mobile army of metaphors, metonymies, anthropomorphisms, in short a sum of human relations which have been subjected to poetic and rhetorical intensification, translation, and decoration, and which, after they have been in use for a long time, strike a people as firmly established, canonical, and binding; truths are illusions of which we have forgotten that they are illusions, metaphors which have become worn by frequent use and have lost all sensuous vigour, coins which, having lost their stamp, are now regarded as metal and no longer as coins. Yet we still do not know where the drive to truth comes from, for so far we have only heard about the obligation to be truthful

[7] Hidden property.

which society imposes in order to exist, i.e. the obligation to use the customary metaphors, or, to put it in moral terms, the obligation to lie in accordance with firmly established convention, to lie *en masse* and in a style that is binding for all. Now, it is true that human beings forget that this is how things are; thus they lie unconsciously in the way we have described, and in accordance with centuries-old habits—and precisely *because of this unconsciousness*, precisely because of this forgetting, they arrive at the feeling of truth. The feeling that one is obliged to describe one thing as red, another as cold, and a third as dumb, prompts a moral impulse which pertains to truth; from its opposite, the liar whom no one trusts and all exclude, human beings demonstrate to themselves just how honourable, confidence-inspiring and useful truth is. As creatures of *reason*, human beings now make their actions subject to the rule of abstractions; they no longer tolerate being swept away by sudden impressions and sensuous perceptions; they now generalize all these impressions first, turning them into cooler, less colourful concepts in order to harness the vehicle of their lives and actions to them. Everything which distinguishes human beings from animals depends on this ability to sublimate sensuous metaphors into a schema, in other words, to dissolve an image into a concept. This is because something becomes possible in the realm of these schemata which could never be achieved in the realm of those sensuous first impressions, namely the construction of a pyramidal order based on castes and degrees, the creation of a new world of laws, privileges, subordinations, definitions of borders, which now confronts the other, sensuously perceived world as something firmer, more general, more familiar, more human, and hence as something regulatory and imperative. Whereas every metaphor standing for a sensuous perception is individual and unique and is therefore always able to escape classification, the great edifice of concepts exhibits the rigid regularity of a Roman *columbarium*,[8] while logic breathes out that air of severity and coolness which is peculiar to mathematics. Anyone who has been touched by that cool breath will scarcely believe that concepts too, which are as bony and eight-cornered as a dice and just as capable of being shifted around, are only the left-over *residue of a metaphor*, and that the illusion produced by the artistic translation of a nervous stimulus into images is, if not the mother, then at least the grandmother of each and every concept. Within this conceptual game of dice, however, 'truth' means using each die in accordance with its designation, counting its spots precisely, forming correct classifications, and never offending against the order of castes nor against the sequence of classes of rank. Just as the Romans and the Etruscans divided up the sky with rigid mathematical lines and confined a god in a space which they had thus delimited as in a *templum*, all peoples have just such a mathematically divided firmament of concepts above them, and they understand the demand of truth to mean that the god of every concept is to be sought only in *his* sphere. Here one can certainly admire humanity as a mighty architectural genius who succeeds in erecting the infinitely complicated cathedral of concepts on moving foundations, or even, one might say, on flowing water; admittedly, in order to rest on such foundations, it has to be like a thing constructed from cobwebs, so delicate that it can be carried off on the waves and yet so firm as not to be blown apart by the wind. By these

[8] Originally a dovecot, then a catacomb with niches at regular intervals for urns containing the ashes of the dead.

standards the human being is an architectural genius who is far superior to the bee; the latter builds with wax which she gathers from nature, whereas the human being builds with the far more delicate material of concepts which he must first manufacture from himself. In this he is to be much admired—but just not for his impulse to truth, to the pure cognition of things. If someone hides something behind a bush, looks for it in the same place and then finds it there, his seeking and finding is nothing much to boast about; but this is exactly how things are as far as the seeking and finding of 'truth' within the territory of reason is concerned. If I create the definition of a mammal and then, having inspected a camel, declare, 'Behold, a mammal', then a truth has certainly been brought to light, but it is of limited value, by which I mean that it is anthropomorphic through and through and contains not a single point which could be said to be 'true in itself', really and in a generally valid sense, regardless of mankind. Anyone who researches for truths of that kind is basically only seeking the metamorphosis of the world in human beings; he strives for an understanding of the world as something which is similar in kind to humanity, and what he gains by his efforts is at best a feeling of assimilation. Rather as the astrologer studies the stars in the service of human beings and in relation to humanity's happiness and suffering, this type of researcher regards the whole world as linked to humankind, as the infinitely refracted echo of an original sound, that of humanity, and as the multiple copy of a single, original image, that of humanity. His procedure is to measure all things against man, and in doing so he takes as his point of departure the erroneous belief that he has these things directly before him, as pure objects. Thus, forgetting that the original metaphors of perception were indeed metaphors, he takes them for the things themselves.

Only by forgetting this primitive world of metaphor, only by virtue of the fact that a mass of images, which originally flowed in a hot, liquid stream from the primal power of the human imagination, has become hard and rigid, only because of the invincible faith that *this* sun, *this* window, this table is a truth in itself—in short only because man forgets himself as a subject, and indeed as *an artistically creative* subject, does he live with some degree of peace, security, and consistency; if he could escape for just a moment from the prison walls of this faith, it would mean the end of his 'consciousness of self'.[9] He even has to make an effort to admit to himself that insects or birds perceive a quite different world from that of human beings, and that the question as to which of these two perceptions of the world is the more correct is quite meaningless, since this would require them to be measured by the criterion of the *correct perception*, i.e. by a *nonexistent* criterion. But generally it seems to me that the correct perception—which would mean the full and adequate expression of an object in the subject—is something contradictory and impossible; for between two absolutely different spheres, such as subject and object are, there is no causality, no correctness, no expression, but at most an *aesthetic* way of relating, by which I mean an allusive transference, a stammering translation into a quite different language. For which purpose a middle sphere and mediating force is certainly required which can freely invent and freely create poetry. The word appearance (*Erscheinung*) contains many

[9] The word Nietzsche uses here—*Selbstbewußtstein*—could also mean 'self-confidence'.

seductions, and for this reason I avoid using it as far as possible; for it is not true that the essence of things appears in the empirical world. A painter who has no hands and who wished to express in song the image hovering before him will still reveal more through this substitution of one sphere for another than the empirical world betrays of the essence of things. Even the relation of a nervous stimulus to the image produced thereby is inherently not a necessary relationship; but when that same image has been produced millions of times and has been passed down through many generations of humanity, indeed eventually appears in the whole of humanity as a consequence of the same occasion, it finally acquires the same significance for all human beings, as if it were the only necessary image and as if that relation of the original nervous stimulus to the image produced were a relation of strict causality—in exactly the same way as a dream, if repeated eternally, would be felt and judged entirely as reality. But the fact that a metaphor becomes hard and rigid is absolutely no guarantee of the necessity and exclusive justification of that metaphor.

Anyone who is at home in such considerations will certainly have felt a deep mistrust of this kind of idealism when once he has become clearly convinced of the eternal consistency, ubiquitousness and infallibility of the laws of nature; he will then conclude that everything, as far as we can penetrate, whether to the heights of the telescopic world or the depths of the microscopic world, is so sure, so elaborated, so endless, so much in conformity to laws, and so free of lacunae, that science will be able to mine these shafts successfully for ever, and that everything found there will be in agreement and without self-contradiction. How little all of this resembles a product of the imagination, for if it were such a thing, the illusion and the unreality would be bound to be detectable somewhere. The first thing to be said against this view is this: if each of us still had a different kind of sensuous perception, if we ourselves could only perceive things as, variously, a bird, a worm, or a plant does, or if one of us were to see a stimulus as red, a second person were to see the same stimulus as blue, while a third were even to hear it as a sound, nobody would ever speak of nature as something conforming to laws; rather they would take it to be nothing other than a highly subjective formation. Consequently, what is a law of nature for us at all? It is not known to us in itself but only in its effects, i.e. in its relations to other laws of nature which are in turn known to us only as relations. Thus, all these relations refer only to one another, and they are utterly incomprehensible to us in their essential nature; the only things we really know about them are things which we bring to bear on them: time and space, in other words, relations of succession and number. But everything which is wonderful and which elicits our astonishment at precisely these laws of nature, everything which demands explanation of us and could seduce us into being suspicious of idealism, is attributable precisely and exclusively to the rigour and universal validity of the representations of time and space. But these we produce within ourselves and from ourselves with the same necessity as a spider spins; if we are forced to comprehend all things under these forms alone, then it is no longer wonderful that what we comprehend in all these things is actually nothing other than these very forms; for all of them must exhibit the laws of number, and number is precisely that which is most astonishing about things. All the conformity to laws which we find so imposing in the orbits of the stars and chemical processes is basically identical with those qualities which we ourselves bring to bear on things, so that what we find imposing is our own activity. Of course the consequence of this is that the artistic production of metaphor, with which every sensation begins within us, already presupposes those forms, and is thus executed in them; only from the stability of these original forms can one explain how it is possible for an edifice of concepts to be constituted in its turn from the metaphors themselves. For this conceptual edifice is an imitation of the relations of time, space, and number on the foundations of metaphor.

2

Originally, as we have seen, it is *language* which works on building the edifice of concepts; later it is *science*. Just as the bee simultaneously builds the cells of its comb and fills them with honey, so science works unceasingly at that great *columbarium* of concepts, the burial site of perceptions, builds ever-new, ever-higher tiers, supports, cleans, renews the old cells, and strives above all to fill that framework which towers up to vast heights, and to fit into it in an orderly way the whole empirical world, i.e. the anthropomorphic world. If even the man of action binds his life to reason and its concepts, so as not to be swept away and lose himself, the researcher builds his hut close by the tower of science so that he can lend a hand with the building and find protection for himself beneath its already existing bulwarks. And he has need of protection, for there exist fearful powers which constantly press in on him and which confront scientific truth with 'truths' of quite another kind, on shields emblazoned with the most multifarious emblems.

That drive to form metaphors, that fundamental human drive which cannot be left out of consideration for even a second without also leaving out human beings themselves, is in truth not defeated, indeed hardly even tamed, by the process whereby a regular and rigid new world is built from its own sublimated products—concepts—in order to imprison it in a fortress. The drive seeks out a channel and a new area for its activity, and finds it in myth and in art generally. It constantly confuses the cells and the classifications of concepts by setting up new translations, metaphors, metonymies; it constantly manifests the desire to shape the given world of the waking human being in ways which are just as multiform, irregular, inconsequential, incoherent, charming and ever-new, as things are in the world of dream. Actually the waking human being is only clear about the fact that he is awake thanks to the rigid and regular web of concepts, and for that reason he sometimes comes to believe that he is dreaming if once that web of concepts is torn apart by art. Pascal is right to maintain that if the same dream were to come to us every night we would occupy ourselves with it just as much as we do with the things we see every day: 'If an artisan could be sure to dream each night for a full twelve hours that he was a king,' says Pascal, 'I believe he would be just as happy as a king who dreamt for twelve hours each night that he was an artisan.'[10] Thanks to the constantly effective miracle assumed by myth, the waking day of a people who are stimulated by myth, as the ancient Greeks were, does indeed resemble dream more than it does the day of a thinker whose mind has been sobered by science. If, one day, any tree may speak as a nymph, or if a god can carry

[10] *Pensées* VI. 386.

off virgins in the guise of a bull, if the goddess Athene herself is suddenly seen riding on a beautiful chariot in the company of Pisistratus through the market-places of Athens[11]—and that was what the honest Athenian believed—then anything is possible at any time, as it is in dream, and the whole of nature cavorts around men as if it were just a masquerade of the gods who are merely having fun by deceiving men in every shape and form.

But human beings themselves have an unconquerable urge to let themselves be deceived, and they are as if enchanted with happiness when the bard recites epic fairy-tales as if they were true, or when the actor in a play acts the king more regally than reality shows him to be. The intellect, that master of pretence, is free and absolved of its usual slavery for as long as it can deceive without *doing harm*, and it celebrates its Saturnalian festivals when it does so; at no time is it richer, more luxuriant, more proud, skilful, and bold. Full of creative contentment, it jumbles up metaphors and shifts the boundary stones of abstraction, describing a river, for example, as a moving road that carries men to destinations to which they normally walk. The intellect has now cast off the mark of servitude; whereas it normally labours, with dull-spirited industry, to show to some poor individual who lusts after life the road and the tools he needs, and rides out in search of spoils and booty for its master, here the intellect has become the master itself and is permitted to wipe the expression of neediness from its face. Whatever the intellect now does, all of it, compared with what it did before, bears the mark of pretence, just as what it did before bore the mark of distortion. It copies human life, but it takes it to be something good and appears to be fairly content with it. That vast assembly of beams and boards to which needy man clings, thereby saving himself on his journey through life, is used by the liberated intellect as a mere climbing frame and plaything on which to perform its most reckless tricks; and when it smashes this framework, jumbles it up and ironically re-assembles it, pairing the most unlike things and dividing those things which are closest to one another, it reveals the fact that it does not require those makeshift aids of neediness, and that it is now guided, not by concepts but by intuitions. No regular way leads from these intuitions into the land of the ghostly schemata and abstractions; words are not made for them; man is struck dumb when he sees them, or he will speak only in forbidden metaphors and unheard-of combinations of concepts so that, by at least demolishing and deriding the old conceptual barriers, he may do creative justice to the impression made on him by the mighty, present intuition.

There are epochs in which the man of reason and the man of intuition stand side by side, the one fearful of intuition, the other filled with scorn for abstraction, the latter as unreasonable as the former is unartistic. They both desire to rule over life; the one by his knowledge of how to cope with the chief calamities of life by providing for the future, by prudence and regularity, the other by being an 'exuberant hero'[12] who does not see those calamities and who only acknowledges life as real when it is disguised as beauty and appearance. Where the man of intuition, as was once the case in ancient Greece, wields his weapons more mightily and victoriously than his contrary, a culture can take shape, given favourable conditions, and the rule of art over life can become established; all the expressions

[11] Herodotus I. 60.

[12] Phrase used of Siegfried in Wagner's *Götterdämmerung* (act III).

of a life lived thus are accompanied by pretence, by the denial of neediness, by the radiance of metaphorical visions, and indeed generally by the immediacy of deception. Neither the house, nor the gait, nor the clothing, nor the pitcher of clay gives any hint that these things were invented by neediness; it seems as if all of them were intended to express sublime happiness and Olympian cloudlessness and, as it were, a playing with earnest things. Whereas the man who is guided by concepts and abstractions only succeeds thereby in warding off misfortune, is unable to compel the abstractions themselves to yield him happiness, and strives merely to be as free as possible of pain, the man of intuition, standing in the midst of a culture, reaps directly from his intuitions not just protection from harm but also a constant stream of brightness, a lightening of the spirit, redemption, and release. Of course, *when* he suffers, he suffers more severely; indeed he suffers more frequently because he does not know how to learn from experience and keeps on falling into the very same trap time after time. When he is suffering he is just as unreasonable as he is when happy, he shouts out loudly and knows no solace. How differently the same misfortune is endured by the stoic who has learned from experience and who governs himself by means of concepts! This man, who otherwise seeks only honesty, truth, freedom from illusions, and protection from the onslaughts of things which might distract him, now performs, in the midst of misfortune, a masterpiece of pretence, just as the other did in the midst of happiness: he does not wear a twitching, mobile, human face, but rather a mask, as it were, with its features in dignified equilibrium; he does not shout, nor does he even change his tone of voice. If a veritable storm-cloud empties itself on his head, he wraps himself in his cloak and slowly walks away from under it. ■

AUTHOR PROFILE

Friedrich Nietzsche (1844–1900) was a German philologist and philosopher. Nietzsche saw himself as a "cultural physician," who diagnosed the symptoms produced in the individual by constricting social forces such as religion, morality, philosophy, and science. Arguing that humans should embrace their inherent creativity, he championed ideas such as perspectivism and the übermensch. Although Nietzsche never achieved popularity during his life, he has greatly influenced movements in continental philosophy, including existentialism and post-modernism. Written in 1873, Nietzsche's "On Truth and Lying in a Non-Moral Sense" is interpreted by scholars to be either a work that is a cornerstone to understanding his philosophy or an early writing that reveals little about his complex philosophical arguments.

Big Data on Campus

By Marc Parry

Campuses are places of intuition and serendipity: a professor senses confusion on a student's face and repeats his point; a student majors in psychology after a roommate takes a course; two freshmen meet on the quad and eventually become husband and wife. Now imagine hard data substituting for happenstance.

As Katye Allisone, a freshman at Arizona State University, hunkers down in a computer lab for an 8:35 a.m. math class, the Web-based course watches her back. Answers, scores, pace, click paths—it hoovers up information, like Google. But rather than personalizing search results, data shape Ms. Allisone's class according to her understanding of the material.

With 72,000 students, A.S.U. is both the country's largest public university and a hotbed of data-driven experiments. One core effort is a degree-monitoring system that keeps tabs on how students are doing in their majors. Stray off-course and a student may have to switch fields.

And while not exactly matchmaking, Arizona State takes an interest in students' social lives, too. Its Facebook app mines profiles to suggest friends. One classmate shares eight things in common with Ms. Allisone, who "likes" education, photography and tattoos. Researchers are even trying to figure out social ties based on anonymized data culled from swipes of ID cards around the Tempe campus.

This is college life, quantified.

Data mining hinges on one reality about life on the Web: what you do there leaves behind a trail of digital breadcrumbs. Companies scoop those up to tailor services, like the matchmaking of eHarmony or the book recommendations of Amazon. Now colleges, eager to get students out the door more efficiently, are awakening to the opportunities of so-called Big Data.

The new breed of software can predict how well students will do before they even set foot in the classroom. It recommends courses, Netflix-style, based on students' academic records.

Data diggers hope to improve an education system in which professors often fly blind. That's a particular problem in introductory-level courses, says Carol A. Twigg, president of the National Center for Academic Transformation. "The typical class, the professor rattles on in front of the class," she says. "They give a midterm exam. Half the kids fail. Half the kids drop out. And they have no idea what's going on with their students."

As more of this technology comes online, it raises new tensions. What role does a professor play when an algorithm recommends the next lesson? If colleges can predict failure, should they steer students away from challenges? When paths are so tailored, do campuses cease to be places of exploration?

"We don't want to turn into just eHarmony," says Michael Zimmer, assistant professor in the School of Information Studies at the University of Wisconsin, Milwaukee, where he studies ethical dimensions of new technology. "I'm worried that we're taking both the richness and the serendipitous aspect of courses and professors and majors—and all the things that are supposed to be university life—and instead translating it into 18 variables that spit out, 'This is your best fit. So go over here.' "

Alert! You Are Off-Track

Ever since childhood, Rikki Eriven has felt certain of the career that would fit her best: working with animals. Specifically, large animals. The soft-spoken freshman smiles as she recalls the episode of "Animal Planet" that kindled this interest, the one about zoo specialists who treat rhinos, hippos and giraffes. So when Ms. Eriven arrived at Arizona State last fall, she put her plan in motion by picking biological sciences as her major.

But things didn't go according to plan. She felt overwhelmed. She dropped a class. She did poorly in biology (after experiencing problems, she says, with the clicker device used to answer multiple-choice questions in class). Ms. Eriven began seeing ominous alerts in her e-mail in-box and online student portal. "Off-track," they warned. "It told me that I had to seek eAdvising," she says. "And I was, like, eAdvising?"

Yes, eAdvising. Universities see such technology as one answer to a big challenge. On average, only 31 percent of students at public colleges get their bachelor's degree within four years, and 56 percent graduate within six years. Such statistics have come under greater scrutiny as parents and politicians demand accountability from colleges. Tennessee, for example, doles out higher education dollars in part by measuring how effective an institution is at graduating students.

Yet some students show up with ambitions that bear no relation to their skills. Or parents push them into a major that doesn't interest them. Or they feel like shoppers in a cereal aisle, confounded by the choices.

At Arizona State, which has more than 250 majors, the old system let students explore without much structure. A student could major in engineering to please his parents, only to pack his schedule with "Chinese Thought" and music, says Elizabeth D. Capaldi, the provost. No longer. Technology has redrawn the road map.

Under Arizona State's eAdvisor system—in use from 2008–9 and based on a similar effort at the University of Florida—students must pick a major freshman year and follow a plan that lays out when to take key courses. (Students can still study broadly, by choosing from five "exploratory" majors, like "arts and humanities" or "science and engineering," and staying in them for 45 credits.) If they fail to sign up for a key course or do well enough, the computer cracks a whip, marking them "off-track." Wander off-track two semesters in a row, and a student may have to change majors.

If that sounds harsh, there's a rationale: One way to ensure that students will reach the finish line is to quickly figure out if they've selected a suitable track. So the A.S.U. system front-loads key courses. For example, to succeed in psychology, a student must perform well in statistics.

"Kids who major in psych put that off, because they don't want to take statistics," Ms. Capaldi says. "They want to know: Does their boyfriend love them? Are they nuts? They take all those courses, then they hit statistics and they say: 'Oh,

God, I can't do this. I can't do experimental design.' And so they're in the wrong major. By putting those courses first, you can see if a student is going to succeed in that major early." Arizona State's retention rate rose to 84 percent from 77 percent in recent years, a change Ms. Capaldi credits largely to eAdvisor.

For students who run off-track, the outcome can sting. Ms. Eriven was shocked to learn she would have to change her major after the system flagged her. She cried, called her mother, and recalibrated her plans. In a meeting with an adviser, she detailed her interests. She likes science. She is family-oriented, interested in music, and good at writing. The adviser suggested a few possible majors, including psychology, family and human development, and creative writing.

Writing. It would involve only a couple of classes each semester. She could still take science and, hopefully, switch back to biology. So that's what she chose. "I didn't really have, like, a backup plan," Ms. Eriven says.

But what if you could rewind this story and shape a student's path before reaching such a crossroads?

You Will Pass (or Not)

When Adam Lange began working full time at Rio Salado College in 2008, he was still an undergraduate at nearby Arizona State, a 22-year-old computer science major with a budding obsession with data. Over time, that obsession would shape the learning experience for thousands of students—and drive his fiancée bonkers.

Mr. Lange's idea of fun is converting his home into a surveillance lab. He outfitted his cat Sammy, who has an eating disorder, with a device that is read by a scanner every time the cat cranes his neck over the bowl. Mr. Lange monitors the logs and feeds Sammy a treat if he hasn't eaten. He also rigged a webcam next to his fish tank, logging the coordinates of his Betta fish several times a second to find out what common paths it takes and how far it travels (90 feet in one hour!).

At Rio Salado, a community college with about 70,000 students, 43,000 of them online, Mr. Lange got excited about the behavioral data students leave behind: the vast wake of clicks captured by software that runs Web courses. Records of when they logged in, opened a syllabus, turned in homework—all of it just sitting there. Could you mine it to model patterns of students who succeeded in the past? Use that to identify current ones likely to fail? And then help those students? Many educators are now asking similar questions.

Mr. Lange and his colleagues had found that by the eighth day of class they could predict, with 70 percent accuracy, whether a student would score a "C" or better. Mr. Lange built a system, rolled out in 2009, that sent professors frequently updated alerts about how well each student was predicted to do, based on their course performance and online behavior.

To Mr. Lange, the underlying math doesn't differ much from what he might deploy in his fish espionage. Say the Betta makes two consecutive movements side to side, and then swims upward 85 percent of the time. In the future, if the fish moves left and then right, Mr. Lange can say with confidence that he'll then swim up. Similarly, Rio Salado knows from its database that students who handed in late assignments and didn't log in frequently often fail or withdraw from a course.

So the software is more likely to throw up a red flag for current students with those characteristics.

"There's a predictability about the fish," says Mr. Lange, now 26 and working for Ellucian, a higher-education software company. "The same concept applies to students."

The software can help the individual professor identify students who may need extra help. But Rio Salado's experiments with more formal intervention strategies have yielded mixed results. And in a cautionary tale about technical glitches, the college began sharing grade predictions with students last summer to encourage those lagging behind to step up, but it had to shut the alerts down in the spring. Revisions to courses had skewed calculations, and some predictions were found to be inaccurate over a period of about five days. An internal analysis found no increase in the number of students dropping classes. An improved system is promised for fall.

You May Also Like...

Austin Peay State, a midsize university about 45 minutes northwest of Nashville, takes the algorithmic approach to higher education one step further. Before students register for classes, a robot adviser assesses their profiles and nudges them to pick courses in which they're likely to succeed.

The project is the work of Tristan Denley, a programmer turned math professor turned provost. Mr. Denley's software borrows a page from Netflix. It melds each student's transcript with thousands of past students' grades and standardized test scores to make suggestions for every student. When students log into their online portal, they see 10 "Course Suggestions for You" ranked on a five-star scale. For, say, a health and human performance major, kinesiology might get five stars (as the next class needed for her major). Physics might also top the list (to satisfy a science requirement in the core curriculum).

Behind those recommendations is a complex algorithm, but the basics are simple enough. Degree requirements figure in the calculations. So do classes that can be used in many programs, like freshman writing. And it bumps up courses for which a student might have a talent, by mining their records—grades, high school grade-point average, ACT scores—and those of others who walked this path before.

"We're steering students toward the classes where they are predicted to make better grades," Mr. Denley says. The predictions, he adds, are within about half a letter grade, on average.

The prediction process is more subtle than getting a suggestion to watch "Goodfellas" because you liked "The Godfather." Take the hypothetical health major encouraged to take physics. The software sifts through a database of hundreds of thousands of grades other students have received. It analyzes the historical data to figure out how much weight to assign each piece of the health major's own academic record in forecasting how she will do in a particular course. Success in math is heavily predictive of success in physics, for example. So if her transcript and ACT score indicate a history of doing well in math, physics would likely be recommended over biology, though both satisfy the same core science requirement.

Mr. Denley points to a spate of recent books by behavioral economists, all with a common theme: When presented with many options and little information, people find it difficult to make wise choices. The same goes for college students trying to construct a schedule, he says. They know they must take a social science class, but they don't know the implications of taking political science vs. psychology vs. economics. They choose based on course descriptions or to avoid having to wake up for an 8 a.m. class on Monday. Every year, students in Tennessee lose their state scholarships because they fall a hair short of the G.P.A. cutoff, Mr. Denley says, a financial swing that "massively changes their likelihood of graduating."

"When students do indeed take the courses that are recommended to them, they actually do substantially better," he says. And take them they do. Last fall, 45 percent of classes on student schedules were from top-10 recommendations, 57 percent from their top 15. Though these systems are in their infancy, the concept is taking hold. Three other Tennessee colleges have adopted Mr. Denley's software, and some institutions outside the state are developing their own spins on the idea.

Some express concerns about deferring such important decisions to algorithms, which have already come to dictate—and limit—so much of what we see and do online. Mr. Zimmer, the Milwaukee information-studies professor, sees the value in preventing students from going down paths that may frustrate them or cause them to quit college. But as higher education gets more efficient, he fears the loss of the unanticipated discovery.

"It's the same as if you're worried about whether or not Google or Amazon are going to present you with alternative topics, or only the topics that fit your history," he says. "We hope the role of a university is to make sure people are exposed to diverse things and challenged."

In Class: Direction Through Data

At Arizona State, algorithms figure in course content, too. Thousands of A.S.U. students now take math courses through a system that mines performance and behavioral data, building a profile on each user and delivering recommendations about what learning activity they should do next. The system, created by the start-up company Knewton, has given the university a fresh way of addressing the continuous problem of students being unprepared for college math. But it also offers a glimpse into what many more students will experience as teaching increasingly shifts from textbooks and lectures that feed the same structure of information to a class of 300, regardless of individual expertise, to machines that study their users' learning patterns and adapt to them.

That excites some educators. George Siemens, a data-mining expert at the Canadian distance-learning university Athabasca, calls the traditional approach an inefficient model "that generates a fair degree of dropouts."

Knewton dismantles that model. Ms. Allisone's 8:35 a.m. class is not a lecture. Although students are supposed to show up at a fixed time, and an instructor is there to work with them, the action is on screen. Knewton allows Ms. Allisone to skip past some concepts she gets, like factors and multiples. When she struggles with inverting linear functions, the software provides more online tutoring. Two students who complete the same lesson might see different recommendations as to what to do next, based on their proficiency.

As the company develops and works with more data and content—major universities like University of Nevada, Las Vegas, are adopting its technology, as is the publishing giant Pearson—it will tailor instruction more finely. What time of day does a student best learn math? What materials and delivery styles most engage the student? Say you have the same concept explained in a video, in a textbook-like format and in Socratic steps. Knewton will associate a student's "engagement metrics" with those styles and use that to help determine the next step.

But what sounds flashy may be based, at least in part, on flawed assumptions, warns Richard E. Clark, professor of educational psychology and technology at the University of Southern California. He says there is no evidence that there are "visual" learners who benefit from video over text, as Knewton implies. Studies, he says, have shown that "learning styles" are not effective for shaping instruction.

The broader problem with data mining, as Mr. Clark sees it, is that it is seldom done right. Data analysts often make "questionable assumptions" about the meaning of keystrokes, he says. They assume students who are spending the most time on some learning material are most interested in that content, for example. "That assumption may be true when people choose to watch Netflix movies but is not at all the case in many university courses where few choices are available," Mr. Clark says.

Meanwhile, dismantling old models leaves both professors and students adjusting to new roles.

Suzanne Galayda, an Arizona State math instructor, finds it takes longer to penetrate the wall of computer screens and build rapport with students. In her remedial class, they start off feeling uncomfortable asking questions. But even as software elbows her off center stage, it also helps her play her part with far more information—so much data about what students do, and when, that it sometimes surprises them.

"Students don't realize that we're watching them in these classes," she says.

Ms. Galayda can monitor their progress. In her cubicle on a recent Monday, she sees the intimacies of students' study routines—or lack of them—from the last activity they worked on to how many tries they made at each end-of-lesson quiz. For one crammer, the system registers 57 attempts on multiple quizzes in seven days. Pulling back to the big picture, a chart shows 15 students falling behind (in red) and 17 on schedule (in green).

On Wednesday, Ms. Galayda rubs her hands with satisfaction. The bar is mostly green. Mostly. When class meets, she taps her nails on the hard drive of Carolina Beltran's computer. "You were working on it at 4 a.m.," the instructor tells the student.

"Yeah, I mean, like, I sleep. My sleeping schedule is weird," Ms. Beltran stammers.

Arizona State's initial results look promising. Of the more than 2,000 students who took the Knewton-based remedial course this past year, 75 percent completed it, up from an average of 64 percent in recent years.

In Ms. Galayda's experience, students "either love it or hate it."

Ms. Allisone raves: "I learned more in this semester than I have in a year in high school." She praises the clarity and concision of the system's instructional videos, contrasting that with the many teachers who "have issues communicating correctly."

But another freshman, a health sciences major who requested anonymity because she did poorly for two semesters, recalls a downward slide that began when she started falling a couple of lessons behind. That scared her at first, until she talked to her peers. Some were six lessons behind. Twelve, even. How bad could two be? She didn't sweat it. As she juggled social life, work and other classes, math fell through the cracks. She ended up having to retake the course, a case study in the danger of giving self-paced classes to freshmen.

"I like lecture better," she says. "I'm not used to teaching myself. So it was a huge adjustment."

The Social Network

These experiments are only the beginning. Colleges will likely dig deeper into the data at their disposal, touching more and more aspects of student life. Already, some researchers are eyeing the next frontier: social life.

Research shows that social ties can influence academic success. If students are more integrated into campus life, they're more likely to stay in school. If a friend drops out, they're more likely to as well.

"If the university could model, at a high level, the social network of the college, that would be a very useful data layer," says Matt Pittinsky, who co-founded Blackboard, a company that provides a platform for online classes, and later became an assistant research professor in the sociology program at Arizona State. A university might reach out to a student "who is not showing evidence of social integration," Mr. Pittinsky says, pointing out extracurricular activities and communities that might tie them more deeply to the institution.

Working with computer scientists, Mr. Pittinsky started an academic research project that tiptoes toward a better understanding of social connections. The research team's raw material: anonymous logs from swipes made with Arizona State ID cards. When students use these cards, be it to buy food on campus or access the fitness center, the transaction gets recorded. The question that struck Mr. Pittinsky was whether or not you could infer social ties from those trails.

Say two students swipe within 5 or 10 seconds of each other at different times of day in different contexts. Are they more likely to be friends? And can you predict attrition by pinpointing changes in how a student uses a campus? Say someone goes to Starbucks at 2 p.m. every day before 2:15 p.m. class. Then stops. "If that happens three weeks in a row," Mr. Pittinsky says, "and we're not seeing log-ins into Blackboard, and maybe you've made a request at the registrar to have your transcript sent somewhere, there ought to be an adviser with a really big red flashing light saying, reach out to this student."

The prospect of card-swipe surveillance discomforts Mr. Zimmer. He worries authorities might misuse location data to do things like track foreign students or instigators of a student protest.

But the broader issue of privacy hangs over even less Orwellian efforts to collect and monitor personal data. In his own courses, Mr. Zimmer includes a disclaimer on his syllabus disclosing what he can see through Milwaukee's online-learning platform, including "the dates and times individual students access the system, what pages a student has viewed, the duration of visits, and the IP address of the computer used to access the course Web site."

For his part, Mr. Pittinsky stresses that the card-swipe research is "very focused on the ability to protect anonymity."

As for students, they've never been too fond of adults meddling on Facebook, let alone getting all Big Brother with card swipes. "Creeping on us" is how Ms. Allisone describes the card-swipe project. Ms. Allisone has managed to keep one aspect of her life—she hopes to transfer—from any "creeping." But that, too, may change.

Arizona State monitors requests for transcripts to be sent elsewhere, according to Ms. Capaldi, the provost. "Which," she says, "is kind of sneaky." ■

AUTHOR PROFILE

Marc Parry is a senior reporter at *The Chronicle of Higher Education*, covering research in the humanities and social sciences. His article, "Big Data on Campus," appeared in the *New York Times* on July 18, 2012 in conjunction with *The Chronicle*. Parry currently writes about people and debates shaping the world of ideas on the "ideas beat." Before moving to the ideas beat, he covered technology for *The Chronicle*, reporting on subjects like distraction, data-mining, online education, privacy, and copyright. Parry co-wrote a report about the Gates Foundation's influence on higher education, which earned an investigative reporting award from the Education Writers Association. Parry has worked as a reporter for daily newspapers in Massachusetts and New York. He studied literature at University of Michigan and journalism at Columbia University.

Waśicuia ya he? Do you speak English?

By Delphine Red Shirt

I did not learn how to write a composition in English until I left the government school and entered seventh grade at a small school run by nuns from the Notre Dame order. I discovered that despite their shortcomings, the nuns brought people, volunteers, to the school, who were intent on teaching. There, at the school with its simple white buildings closely nestled in a small valley, I learned to read, write, and finally how to converse in English.

I learned to read properly in a program at the school, which they called a "reading lab." The lab was actually a trailer house that was equipped with small reading booths, where there were no books, only strips of film in darkened reading booths where we were required after every reading session to answer a set of comprehension questions. While there, I watched sentences flow at a speed which I controlled and therefore could read. I could not rewind or review before answering the questions at the end of the session. I started slowly, reading at a speed that allowed me to answer the questions correctly. I enjoyed the darkened room, the quiet trailer, and the chance to learn without someone looking over my shoulder.

I remember one girl in my class who was fond of bypassing all the work. She showed me where the answers were one day when she lingered behind to point out the answer sheets in a file hidden at the end of a cabinet. I think she did it because she wanted to be my friend. We were friends all through high school. I tried to look past her shortcomings, particularly her inclination to cheat. In those early years, I seemed to have accepted people as what they were more readily than I do now. I continued painstakingly, and many times erroneously, to learn to read properly. I forced myself to try to comprehend the language I did not speak at home, the language I felt self-conscious speaking, the language I will never fully comprehend.

I learned more at that small school run by the nuns and volunteers than I learned at the government school, where I entered in the fourth grade and stayed through sixth grade. The government school, which had all the modern conveniences that the small Catholic school didn't have, seemed, by comparison, to be massive, sterile, and empty in an inexplicable way. It had desks, chairs, blackboards, and books, but it lacked something which I was not able to pinpoint until I met the nuns and teachers at the Catholic school. It had all the trappings of a school, but it did not educate the way the Catholic school did, with heart and feeling for the children in it.

The government school was worlds away from the bright classrooms I left behind in rural Nebraska. There were no sweet-smelling teachers in rouge who hung snowflakes and valentines in the windows. There was no daily reminder to "Put on your thinking cap," and no daily practice with reading or writing. There were no libraries or music classes. Instead, at the government school we had teachers who were past retirement and who fell asleep in the classroom, teachers who were

R

more eager to keep order in the classroom than to teach. They were more eager to put you in your place and gladly shunned you after school. I do not remember having one conversation with any of my teachers at the government school. What I did learn, I still carry with me. I learned shame there, as they pulled our hair and checked it for lice. I learned silence there, as I stood in line and watched the teacher pull a girl's hair to keep her in line. I learned fighting there, as we channeled our energy the wrong way, for we took our frustrations out on one another. There was no positive regard or positive reinforcement, only suspicion and mistrust.

Despite it all, I had a favorite teacher in that school run by the Bureau of Indian Affairs. This teacher, a black man or *ha sapa*, as the people called him, 'skin that is black,' was considered a *wašicu*, a 'black "white" man'. He seemed to belong to that category of "white man," and Kah-kah said that in all his mannerisms, this person, the "black man," seemed closer to the wašicu than anyone else on the reservation. He was the first and only black person I remember seeing in my early life. My world back then was only Lakota and wašicu. It was said that at one time, the black teacher had brought a wife, a son, and a daughter to the reservation. They left, but he stayed. I know how he must have felt as the only black man in our midst; for many years I was the only "Indian" in the classroom in rural Nebraska.

I liked him because he was my first teacher on the reservation, and my first year there I celebrated the whole year. I celebrated because it was the first time in my life that I was not the only "Indian" in the classroom. All the girls and all the boys were just like me. They had hair, skin, and eyes that were the same color as mine. They spoke English as I did, some better than others. I looked at my friends, cousins, and other children at the school with happy eyes. They were kids who had families like mine, who lived in houses like mine, *miye sé*, meaning 'just like me'. I finally belonged somewhere.

This soon gave way to the realization, even as a young child, that a prison is a prison, no matter how pleasant it may seem, and I know that I soon realized that while we lived within the confines of the reservation, we were all under the constant eye and supervision of a benevolent but neglectful government. I soon realized that the isolation we all felt made us despair silently and that it drove some adults to alcohol and others to insanity. We children, at least, had the school to distract us; for the adults there was nothing, day after day. My father didn't stay on the reservation, and in that he was like other fathers, and some mothers. They had nothing there; only the patient ones, the old ones, the children, and those who clung to the old ways could find comfort in the land, the language, and the occasional powwow or dance celebrating some event. For anyone else, the reservation and its schools were a black hole in which your energy is eventually drained. By the time I left the government school in seventh grade, I was a shadow of the happy little girl who had gone skipping out to play at recess in fourth grade. I had become silent and belligerent, but I did not despair.

I had known freedom outside the reservation, and I knew that if I just bided my time, I could someday leave and find something more. I was ready for something to restore me. I wanted to grow stronger, to replenish my spirit, which I knew was on the wane. I could go forward at that critical age, or I could succumb to what others, who were in the same place I was, did. Some tried suicide, others tried alcohol, and still others dropped out of the government schools and followed their parents somewhere, to Denver or Minneapolis, to get away from that demoralizing place called the government school. I was one of those kids who didn't play a sport in school, but I wish I had. I needed to vent my energy in some way. My way was as always in the realm of thought, and perhaps books would have offered me solace. But we had no library; music and art would have consoled me, but they didn't offer those things at that school.

The only music I remember in the government school came from the kindergarten classroom where a senile teacher often sang. Her favorite song was from the *Wizard of Oz*. She would sing, "Somewhere over the rainbow, blue birds fly." When I hear that song, I can still see the tall gray-haired woman in kindergarten who, perhaps because she was somewhat senile, was the happiest person on the teaching staff. She would sing as she wandered from her classroom to the principal's office. When she wasn't singing, she was fond of napping.

The other person who loved music was our fourth grade teacher, the large black man whose baritone voice rang out, "Nobody knows the trouble I've seen. Nobody knows but Jesus." We played tricks on him. We knew that he would not punish us in any way, that he was the only one who seemed to have a sense of humor, so we played harmless tricks on him. One of our favorite tricks was to have someone stand behind him when he sang one of his favorite songs, which was often. He would stop whatever he was doing and lean back in his desk chair, close his eyes, and break into song. We would have someone creep up behind him and have that person pretend to shine the bald spot on the back of his head with the chalkboard eraser, keeping time to the song he was singing. He would always catch on after a few stanzas of his song, when he opened his eyes and saw us all giggling. He would reach behind him to grab whoever was there. His singing seemed to break the monotony of the long days we spent at our desks. He seemed to know that if he sang, we listened and joined in, by being playful in our own way. I liked him because he allowed us to be kids in the classroom.

There were many things that my old school in Nebraska had that I missed at the government school I attended on the reservation. I missed the smell of new books that seemed a natural part of my life in my old school; the clear sound of the triangle when the music teacher played a note to get our attention for music class; the Friday afternoon art class when we could bring bubble gum to class and chew it while we worked unhurried and unsupervised on some art project. Somewhere between my old school and my new one, someone had made the judgment that books, music, and art were no longer important, but I knew they were and I missed them. I remember the year my older brother gave me a pad of drawing paper and charcoal for my birthday. I was already in junior high, but, I felt as if I was back in that sunny classroom in Nebraska, in first grade, when I took a large blank sheet of paper and a new box of crayons and sat down to create something. I don't remember that same freedom in any classroom in the government school.

In contrast, my first year at the Catholic school, I listened to Haydn, Bach, and Mozart. The volunteer the nuns hired at fifty dollars a month plus room and board brought out an ancient record player and played classical music while she had us rest our heads on our desks. I remember "Poppa Haydn" the best. I was in seventh grade at the school, an adolescent ready and able to learn, despite what the government school though I could or could not learn, what I should or should not be exposed to, what freedom I should or should not be given, even with a simple box of crayons and a blank piece of art paper.

My teacher, a balding woman in her thirties, brought new things to us: she brought books and music—but not art. Her specialties were books, music, and composition. I wrote my first short story for her. I wrote about a ghetto where a young boy died when he broke his promise to his mother to stay away from drugs. The last words he spoke were to his mother, to whom he said, "I'm sorry I broke my promise." The story was called "Broken Promise." I remember it because I wrote it after I had pilfered my older brother's book about a boy growing up in a ghetto and had read it in secret.

It was a time when I was like an empty vessel, ready to hold whatever was poured into me. It was also a time when I realized that I had the power to pour into myself those things that I thought were interesting and new. I "borrowed" my brother's books whenever I could. I read about Hiroshima in secret, suffering nightmares about my skin melting like butter and not being able to die before it happened. It was a time during which I covered my ears when I heard the nightly news because I didn't want to hear the body counts of how many died in Vietnam that day. It was a fearful time, to be in seventh grade, in knee highs and dresses that were one inch below the knee, and feel that the world I read about in my "stolen" books was much more interesting but terrifying than my own.

It was there at that school, in that small valley with the large cottonwood, apple orchards, and statues of the Virgin Mary, that I found the freedom to enjoy all the things in which I have always felt a certain solace: especially books, but also music and art. I was now able to learn, finally to read and write well; *Owagahniġe*, meaning 'I understood'. I also learned how to converse with my teachers in a playful way. The teachers I was exposed to at the Catholic school were not government employees; they were real people. They came to the school to volunteer their talents for the grace of their church, and they were real.

In my second year there, I was finally given a teacher who was an artist. He became my mentor, my substitute for my older brother, who no longer had time for me. My brother had married his high school girlfriend, and they both went away to college. I needed someone to replace him, and this teacher who had come all the way from the East Coast, from Schenectady, New York, with his young child and wife, became the perfect replacement. In secret he called me *wanahca*, meaning 'flower or blossom', and he tended to me like a careful gardener, just like my older brother had done in his own way.

My teacher-friend taught me many things, but one of the most important things I learned was from watching him, how he vented his creative energy. I remember well how he seemed to have a deep well within him from which he drew the sweetest water. He was able to go off alone and come back with something he created, something beautiful and admirable, whether it was a simple watercolor, a poem, a story, or a piece of dry wood that he had cleaned and varnished. In whatever way he chose to give expression to his creative tendencies, he always produced something tangible to give or share. He gave me many things, but the most important thing that he gave me was time, the time he spent talking to me.

I liked sitting in his living room and swapping stories with him. He listened well. No matter when I showed up at his door, he would sit down with me and we would talk. The house he and his wife and small child lived in had two bedrooms and a large kitchen and living room combination. They had one couch, an armchair, and a kitchen table and four chairs, which was all that could fit in the small space. The things he seemed to cherish the most in his living space were his books and his music—there were stacks of books and records everywhere. To me, he seemed rich in the things he had, and I have tried to imitate him in what I fill my house with today.

I know now that the most important thing he taught me, neither of us had known then. He taught me in his direct and honest way how to converse in English. He spent time with me, time that up until then no other *waśicu*, or 'English-speaking person', had. I admired that in him, his acceptance of others who were different. He insisted that we were not so different, the Lakota and the Irish-Catholic. He had been to Ireland, the Ireland that James Joyce had written about. He even made a list of the similarities between what happened to the "Indians" in America and to the Irish in Ireland. He talked about concepts like oppression, things about which I had not heard before. It was not until after he had died, many years later, that I understood what he had told me about his people and mine. I often wish that I could go back to his living room, back to that time, only with the knowledge and understanding that I have now, and have a real conversation with him.

I remember the nuns who ran the school. The women, some of whom had been orphans before coming to the convent, had turned to the church to give them families. They cooked wholesome foods, taught literature, and celebrated the mass among themselves without the Pope looking over their shoulders. I liked their clear minds, practical nature, and calm faith. I respected them, and deep inside I wanted to be one, to have that freedom to be what they were—teachers, cooks, administrators, or whatever it seemed they wanted to be. I liked their mass, a celebration of faith that didn't require you to speak in tongues or dance in the spirit. I liked the quietness of their beautiful church, and the way the priest broke the bread and you had to say, "Lord I am not worthy to receive you, but only say the word and I shall be healed."

I did not always like them. I remember a time before I went to school there, the time my cousin and I went to see them. I remember the face of the nun in the doorway. Her bright, clear, white complexion and red cheeks. Her head covered and her eyes peering through her wire glasses. I remember my cousin knocking on the door and waiting expectantly. I stood behind her, feeling somewhat apprehensive. I was never sure whether I would stand there long enough to be seen or run and hide before they answered the door. My cousin, who was my age, waited very confidently and patiently. Her patience was a source of comfort for me. We were best friends. I was her opposite—flighty and ready to laugh or giggle at the drop of a hat, or run at the sight of a strange dog. She, on the other hand, always maintained a quiet and calm demeanor, her face expressionless. We looked alike, everyone said. I didn't think so. We both had long hair. We were both thin and sometimes we both seemed thoughtful, but our faces were different. Her Lakotaness was real, mine a mixture of French and Indian. My chin was too pointed and my eyes too expressive.

The day we knocked on the nun's door, my cousin was there at the bidding of an older woman, a relative who was indigent. Her husband had asked her to leave their home, and she did, leaving behind a son. She lived here here and there, all alone and always looking hungry, perhaps like Iktomi. I feared somewhere in the back of my mind that I might tum out like her. She stood waiting behind a tall cottonwood tree, hiding. The woman had asked my cousin to ask the nuns for some food, to tell them that we were hungry. We were supposed to say not only that we were hungry but to ask specifically for a "cheese sandwich." I hated cheese sandwiches.

When one of the nuns answered the door, she looked at us. "Yes?" she asked expectantly. I stepped back one step, and my cousin began to speak. "May we have a cheese san-witch?" she asked. I turned red and suddenly felt hot and uncomfortable. I didn't want a cheese sandwich. I wanted to know what was inside the convent. They were mysterious to me, the nuns and the priests that we called *sapų* or 'they that wear black'. I was not Catholic. I had been baptized as an infant by the *ska ų*, meaning 'they that wear white', the Episcopalians. I knew nothing about the nuns. I was curious, and I wanted to know. I would have my chance a few years later to see exactly what was in that convent, but that day when I stood at the door, it was the first time in my life that I had the opportunity to see a nun up close. I was surprised at how young she seemed, how impatient and human she seemed when she abruptly said, "just a minute," and went back inside. Within a few minutes she came back out with two cold cheese sandwiches. She handed them to us without hesitating and was ready to close the door. My cousin took them and turned away after saying "thank you." I stood there, as if I had seen a ghost. I waited for something terrible to happen to me, but nothing did. I had just encountered something that I had not expected. She was just as human as any of us, that nun who answered that door. "Next time, why don't you cook for them," she said loudly to the woman who stood hiding behind us somewhere. It occurred to me years later that had I felt confident in my ability to speak English, I would have told the nun about her, the woman who had us beg for cheese sandwiches for her. I would have asked the nun whether she felt it was appropriate for a Christian to tell someone who obviously had no food and was hungry to cook for herself. I wanted to pull the nun out of that door, away from that large white house called a "convent," down the neatly graveled road to the place that the woman lived, to the places we all lived. I wanted to show her what it was like out there where we lived, where for some of us, American cheese and white bread were a luxury beyond words. I stood looking at the door after she closed it and left, and I wondered how I could tell her those things, how I could communicate so that she would know the things I wanted her to know, the things I thought she should know about us. "I could not speak English," back then. "*Waṡicuia owakihi ṡni*." ■

AUTHOR PROFILE

Delphine Red Shirt (born 1957), a member of the Oglala Lakota nation, spent her early childhood near the Pine Ridge Indian Reservation in Nebraska. She did her undergraduate studies at Regis College in Denver in accounting and history, and received her Master of Arts in Liberal Studies in Creative Writing from Weslyan University. She received her PhD in American Indian Studies from the University of Arizona in 2013. Red Shirt has served as a visiting lecturer for Connecticut College and at Yale University, where she also served as an advisor to Native students. Red Shirt has been a freelance writer and syndicated columnist for *Indian Country Today*, the *Lakota Nation Journal*, and the *Native Sun News*. She is the author of *Bead on an Ant Hill* (1997), where "Waśicuia ya he? Do you speak English?" was first published, and *Turtle Lung Woman's Grandaughter* (2002). Red Shirt has served in the United States Marine Corps and on the United Nations Committee on the International Decade of the World's Indigenous People.

Love on the March

Reflections on the gay community's political progress—and its future.

By Alex Ross

I. The Change

The week after Barack Obama was first elected President, I attended a music festival at Arizona State University, in Tempe. Because Veterans Day was the following Tuesday, it was a party weekend at the school, and thousands of students swarmed the main strip. The central event of the festival ran long, and around midnight I went with another participant, the writer and filmmaker Paul Festa, in search of somewhere to eat. The only place we could find was a Jack in the Box.

We gave our orders at the drive-through window. A car was idling there, with several college students inside. Moments later, a second car roared the wrong way up the drive-through lane and screeched to a halt. A visibly drunk young man, tall and blond, wearing a standard collegiate uniform of T-shirt over long-sleeved T and jeans, lurched out, shouting, "Some whore called me a faggot!" The cashier handed Paul a strawberry milkshake. Paul and I are both gay; we traded uneasy glances while the guy carried on.

"My parents raised me right," the blond guy hollered at the students in the second car, who turned out to be his friends. "And I'm proud of who I am." Paul and I looked at each other again, now in amazement.

A beefy, sour-faced guy wearing a backward baseball cap came around the corner. This, evidently, was the person who had called the blond a faggot. "I'm going to beat you up," the newcomer shouted. A friend was trailing behind him.

Like most gay men, I have been called a faggot a few times. I've seen friends talk back to homophobes. But I'd never witnessed anything like this: it had a weird theatrical intensity, as if the young man were being goaded by an offstage director.

"How dare you?" he yelled. "Our forefathers came to this country to escape from their religions and be free. How dare you, asshole! Don't you know this is the land of equal opportunity? Go back to fucking Connecticut with your two cars and a garage!"

The beefy guy wilted in the face of this semi-coherent invective. He shrugged at his friend, and they started to walk off.

The blond guy stumbled after them for a minute or two, bellowing, "In this country, I can marry ANYONE I WANT! Because there's CHANGE in this country now!"

Even after his opponents had disappeared, he continued ranting, his face lit with euphoric rage. He had become a little scary, this one-man Stonewall riot. Eventually, his friends calmed him down, and they left.

I am forty-four years old, and I have lived through a startling transformation in the status of gay men and women in the United States. Around the time I was born, homosexual acts were illegal in every state but Illinois. Lesbians and gays were barred from serving in the federal government. There were no openly gay politicians. A few closeted homosexuals occupied positions of power, but they tended to make things more miserable for their kind. Even in the liberal press, homosexuality drew scorn: in *The New York Review of Books*, Philip Roth denounced the "ghastly pansy rhetoric" of Edward Albee, and a *Time* cover story dismissed the gay world as a "pathetic little second-rate substitute for reality, a pitiable flight from life." David Reuben's 1969 best-seller, "Everything You Always Wanted to Know About Sex (But Were Afraid to Ask)"—a book I remember perusing shakily at the library—advised that "if a homosexual who wants to renounce homosexuality finds a psychiatrist who knows how to cure homosexuality, he has every chance of becoming a happy, well-adjusted heterosexual."

By the mid-eighties, when I was beginning to come to terms with my sexuality, a few gay people held political office, many states had dropped long-standing laws criminalizing sodomy, and sundry celebrities had come out. (The tennis champion Martina Navratilova did so, memorably, in 1981.) But anti-gay crusades on the religious right threatened to roll back this progress. In 1986, the Supreme Court, upholding Georgia's sodomy law, dismissed the notion of constitutional protection for gay sexuality as "at best, facetious." AIDS was killing thousands of gay men each year. The initial response of the Reagan Administration—and of the mainstream media—is well summarized by a Larry Speakes press briefing in October, 1982:

> Q: Larry, does the President have any reaction to the announcement [from] the Centers for Disease Control in Atlanta that AIDS is now an epidemic and have over 600 cases?
>
> MR. SPEAKES: What's AIDS?
>
> Q: Over a third of them have died. It's known as "gay plague." (*Laughter.*) No, it is. I mean it's a pretty serious thing that one in every three people that get this have died. And I wondered if the President is aware of it?
>
> MR. SPEAKES: I don't have it. Do you? (*Laughter.*)

By the time Reagan first spoke at length about AIDS, in May, 1987, the death toll in the U.S. had surpassed twenty thousand. What I remember most about my first sexual experience is the fear.

Today, gay people of a certain age may feel as though they had stepped out of a lavender time machine. That's the sensation that hit me when I watched the young man in Tempe shout down a homophobe in the name of the President-elect. Gay marriage is legal in six states and in Washington, D.C. Gays can serve in the military without hiding their sexuality. We've seen openly gay judges, congresspeople, mayors (including a four-term mayor of Tempe), movie stars, and talk-show hosts. Gay film and TV characters are almost annoyingly ubiquitous. The Supreme Court, which finally annulled sodomy laws in 2003, is set to begin examining the marriage issue. And the 2012 campaign has shown that Republicans no longer see the gays as a reliable wedge issue: although Mitt Romney opposes same-sex marriage, he has barely mentioned it this fall. If thirty-two people were to die today in a mass murder at a gay bar, both Obama and Romney would presumably express sympathy for the victims—more than any official in New Orleans did when, back in 1973, an arsonist set fire to the Upstairs Lounge.

Gay life in America is hardly carefree, especially outside certain Zip Codes in the big cities. Although the religious right has a weaker grip on politics than it once did, it can still chill the air: in August, hundreds of thousands across the country lined up to buy chicken sandwiches in support of Chick-fil-A, whose nonprofit foundation has given millions of dollars to anti-gay groups. (Fast food: the final battleground.) Still, gay rights have made such rapid progress that there is an urge to look back and assess what has happened. Several new books offer different perspectives on the tectonic shifts of recent decades. Linda Hirshman, in "Victory: The Triumphant Gay Revolution," delivers a vivid history of a movement that was invented, out of nothing, circa 1950. David Halperin, a leading figure in queer-studies scholarship, sounds a more wistful tone in "How to Be Gay," celebrating the sharp-elbowed camp culture that many now consider obsolete. And Bishop Gene Robinson, in "God Believes in Love: Straight Talk About Gay Marriage," imagines a future in which the prohibitions of Judeo-Christian scripture have receded.

One fashionable explanation for the turnabout credits popular culture: out-and-proud celebrities and gay-friendly sitcoms have made straight Americans more comfortable with their other-minded neighbors. When, in May, Vice-President Joe Biden declared his support for gay marriage, prompting Obama to do the same, he said, "Things really begin to change…when the social culture changes. I think 'Will & Grace' probably did more to educate the American public than almost anything anybody's ever done so far." Not that long ago, though, Hollywood was regularly portraying gays and lesbians as flouncing sissies, pathetic suicide cases, and serial killers; Vito Russo documented that practice in his 1981 book, "The Celluloid Closet." A decade later, I joined a demonstration, organized by the San Francisco chapter of Queer Nation, against the movie "Basic Instinct," which was being filmed in the city, and whose plot featured homicidal lesbians. My activist career ended there, but the protest, and others like it, made headway. Belatedly, Hollywood stopped teaching America to fear homosexuality. The entertainment industry, far from leading the way, caught up with a new social reality.

Three-dimensional people are more persuasive than two-dimensional ones, as Biden surely knows. In the end, the big change likely came about because, each year, a few thousand more gay people make the awkward announcement to their families and friends, supplanting images from the folklore of disgust. My primary political moment happened when I wrote long, lugubrious letters to my closest friends, finally revealing the rest of me. In one, I came out in a footnote on the seventh page, amid pompous but heartfelt quotations from Wallace Stevens: "The greatest poverty is not to live / In a physical world, to feel that one's desire / Is too difficult to tell from despair." Harvey Milk always said that this was how the revolution would happen: one lonely kid at a time.

II. The Rise of Gay Politics

Although the formerly unspeakable practices associated with homosexuality are older than recorded history, the notion of a distinct gay identity is a relatively recent invention. Not until the nineteenth century did anyone have the idea of dividing humanity neatly into those who desire their own sex and those who desire the other. Before then, confusion reigned. Gay sex acts were forbidden almost everywhere, but punishment was inconsistent. Between 1786 and 1873, there were only twenty prosecutions for sodomy in New York. George Chauncey, in his classic 1994 book, "Gay New York," evokes a loosey-goosey metropolis at the turn of the last century, in which single men from all classes of society could amuse themselves with fairies—flamboyant, often cross-dressing men, who played the passive role in sex—when girls weren't readily available. Lesbian relationships could flourish under the cover of Boston marriages: socially acceptable alliances between unmarried women, so named for the charged friendship between Olive Chancellor and Verena Tarrant, in Henry James's "The Bostonians."

The American gay movement drew inspiration from Germany, where, in 1867, a renegade legal scholar named Karl Heinrich Ulrichs went before the Congress of German Jurists, in Munich, to plead for the repeal of sodomy laws. He was shouted down, but by the end of the century Magnus Hirschfeld had established the first gay-rights organization, in Berlin. In Chicago, in 1924, a German immigrant named Henry Gerber, who had studied Hirschfeld's organization, founded a Society for Human Rights. It was quickly stymied by the police, with the press shuddering at the existence of a "strange sex cult." Even so, gay subcultures were surreptitiously thriving in large cities. At the end of the twenties, gay life became almost chic in New York, with curiosity-seekers attending drag balls, Mae West parading gay friends, and the cabaret star Jean Malin presiding over a "pansy craze" in midtown. ("I'd rather be Spanish than mannish," Malin sang.)

The first creaking open of the closet led to a colossal shove of repression. Chauncey's book gives a queasy sense of a progressive society suddenly grinding in reverse: it seems as though the public-spiritedness of the Depression and the Second World War era required certain individuals to be expelled as scapegoats. New York passed laws against cross-dressing, onstage representations of homosexuals, and gatherings of gays in clubs. Police could close a bar if they heard men talking in high-pitched voices. In the thirties, the Motion Picture Production Code banned any hint of homosexuality. Leading psychiatrists, abandoning Freud's relatively nonjudgmental position, described homosexuals as "sexual psychopaths." There were experiments in electric and pharmacological shock treatment, hormone injection, castration, and lobotomy. One site of such remedies, Atascadero State Hospital, in California, later became known as "Dachau for queers."

The hysteria reached its climax in the fifties, when politicians seized on the idea that lesbians and gays were a security risk. Senator Joseph McCarthy set off the witch-hunt when he noted the presence of homosexuals on his infamous list of Communists at the State Department. In 1953, President Dwight Eisenhower signed Executive Order 10450, which banned, among other things, "sexual perversion" in government; the historian David Johnson estimates that some five thousand gay people lost their jobs as a result. In an episode loosely dramatized in the novel and film "Advise and Consent," Senator Lester Hunt, of Wyoming, killed himself after Styles Bridges, a senator from New Hampshire, threatened to expose Hunt's son as a homosexual. Bridges still has a highway named after him.

Despite the noxious atmosphere, a more forthright gay culture emerged. In fact, the inquisition may have only hastened the process. The question lobbed at prospective soldiers during the Second World War—"Are you homosexual?"—raised consciousness rather than suppressing it. (Wait, *am* I?) G.I.s who carried the stigma of the "blue discharge," for homosexual behavior, had nothing to lose by living openly. Lesbians were emboldened by the shakeup of gender roles in the era of Rosie the Riveter and Eleanor Roosevelt. "I venture to predict that there will be a time in the future when gay folk will be accepted as part of regular society," Edith Eyde wrote in the pioneering magazine *Vice Versa*, which she distributed via carbon copies. And a few literary figures came out: before Gore Vidal and Truman Capote, there was the poet Robert Duncan, who, in his 1944 essay "The Homosexual in Society," asked liberals to "recognize homosexuals as equals."

The first durable gay organization, the Mattachine Society, arose in 1951. It was the brainchild of Harry Hay, a cross-dressing Southern Californian who went to high school with John Cage and taught music classes at the People's Educational Center, in Los Angeles. Hirshman, in "Victory," delights in the fact that Hay took inspiration from the writings of the virulently homophobic Stalin, and in particular from Stalin's definition of nationhood as a "community of language, territory, economic life, and psychological make-up manifested in a community of culture." Hay decided on these grounds that there should also be a gay nation; he took the name Mattachine from Renaissance bands of dancers dressed as fools. Hay's radicalism soon caused internal discord, and the Mattachines moved in a less confrontational direction. In public appearances, they made a point of looking respectable, wearing coats and ties. Members of the Daughters of Bilitis, a like-minded lesbian organization, were urged to abandon mannish clothes.

The way the gay-rights story is usually told, things got moving only in 1969, when a fed-up phalanx of bull dykes, drag queens, and street youths rioted at the Stonewall Inn, in the West Village. One advantage of Hirshman's book—breezily written, but kinetic in its storytelling—is that it honors the activism of the pre-Stonewall era, when any public exposure required considerable courage. Political and legal advances, such as a 1958 Supreme Court decision ruling that the gay magazine *ONE* was not obscene material, were modest but hard won. Hirshman also highlights the work of Glide Memorial Church, a liberal Methodist congregation in San Francisco. When police intimidated attendees at a gay ball on New Year's Eve, in 1964, ministers denounced the incident as "the most lavish display of police harassment known in recent times."

The leader of the Mattachines in Washington, D.C., was Frank Kameny, an astronomer and an Army veteran who had lost his government job during the gay purges of the fifties. In the early sixties, he began sending the Mattachine newsletter to the office of J. Edgar Hoover, the head of the Federal Bureau of Investigation. As F.B.I. files reveal, an agent informed Kameny that Hoover wished to be removed from the mailing list. Kameny replied that he would put the matter to his board, and his associate added that the director was welcome to attend the next Mattachine convention. The mailings continued, and the Mattachines' veiled taunt of the most feared man in Washington went unanswered. "It is time to open the closet door and let in the fresh air and the sunshine," Kameny said, in 1968. More than any other activist of his generation, he insisted that gay people had to declare themselves openly. He died last year, at the age of eighty-six; his home is now on the National Register of Historic Places.

The tumult of the sixties allowed the next generation of lesbians and gays to drop the façade of politesse: "black power" bred "fag power" and "dyke power." But leaders of the left did not rush to embrace the latest insurgent minority. Betty Friedan viewed lesbians as a "lavender menace"; Tom Hayden made homosexuals feel unwelcome in Students for a Democratic Society. Hirshman argues that gay groups were actually fortunate in their isolation. "The more inclusive [a movement] becomes of other identities," she writes, "the weaker it gets." Avoiding, to some extent, the groupthink and the infighting that can plague minority coalitions, the gay-rights movement kept barrelling single-mindedly ahead and, in an astonishingly short period of time, moved from social oblivion to the moral high ground.

The most important consequence of Stonewall was the gay-pride parade that marked the first anniversary of the uprising. Amid the sexual carnival of the seventies, gay life started to look fun rather than fearful. Politics followed suit. Activists became expert manipulators of a sensation-seeking media: the technique of the "zap," of the out-of-the-blue protest, was used to good effect, notably at the 1971 meeting of the American Psychiatric Association. When demonstrators began protesting aversion therapy and other "cures," one attendee shouted, "Faggot! Get out of here!" Suddenly, the psychiatrists looked crazier than their patients. The classification of homosexuality as a mental disorder was scrapped two years later.

AIDS, the dominant event in modern gay history, initially threatened to restore the Dark Ages. Much of the country believed that people with the disease should be quarantined, and William F. Buckley proposed tattooing their arms and buttocks. Yet Hirshman discerns a "terrible political payoff" in the reaction to the crisis. Within a few years, the spectacle of so much raw emotion—lovers grieving, families and friends in mourning, the disciplined rage of Larry Kramer and ACT UP—had humanized a population commonly depicted as soulless narcissists. Gallup polls hint at the persuasive power of ACT UP and of the AIDS Quilt, which was displayed on the Washington Mall, in 1987, and then began touring the country. In 1988, fifty-seven per cent thought that gay sex should be illegal; in a single year, the number dropped to thirty-six per cent.

The catastrophe of AIDS also helped to inspire the quest for gay marriage. So much illness and death underscored agonizing inequalities: lovers lacked the right to visit each other in the hospital or to oversee funeral arrangements. The next gay generation tended to emphasize monogamy over promiscuity, at least in theory. In 1993, Andrew Sullivan, then the editor of *The New Republic*, wrote a widely noticed essay called "The Politics of Homosexuality," proposing that the movement focus on two issues: same-sex marriage and gays in the military. He argued that fighting for those goals would confer a dignity and a nobility that could not easily be won by other political means.

In the nineties, talk of gay marriage sounded kooky and futuristic, like something out of a left-wing version of "The Jetsons." In the elections of 2004, when measures against gay marriage passed in eleven states, the campaign appeared to have backfired. Over time, though, the concerted emphasis on marriage and the military generated increasingly potent political imagery: elderly gay men pleading for recognition of their decades-long relationships, lesbian ex-officers testifying with military terseness. The ennobling effect that Sullivan had predicted came to pass. I felt it in 2005, when my partner, Jonathan Lisecki, and I spontaneously got married during a trip to Toronto. When you get married, your relationship is taken more seriously by those around you; when you are also gay, the sense of public affirmation goes strikingly deep. Friends reacted as if we had done something vaguely heroic. I realized, as with coming out, that personal gestures ripple outward into politics.

However long it takes for a real victory to be certified—no matter what happens on Election Day, it will be too early to unfurl a "Mission Accomplished" banner—the once ragtag march of lovers has acquired an air of inevitability. Edith Eyde's prophecy is almost fulfilled: gays are more or less regular folk. All the same, many who came out during the Stonewall era are wondering what will be lost as the community sheds its pariah status. They are baffled by the latter-day cult of marriage and the military—emblems of Eisenhower's America that the Stonewall generation joyfully rejected. The gay world is confronting a question with which Jews, African-Americans, and other marginalized groups have long been familiar: the price of assimilation.

III. The Fall of Gay Culture

In March, 2000, David Halperin, an English professor at the University of Michigan, was preparing to teach a class called "How to Be Gay: Male Homosexuality and Initiation." The idea was to explore how gay men define themselves, not in terms of sex but in terms of taste. Halperin wanted to anatomize the motley array of cultural activities that had come to be associated with gay-male life: musical theatre, grand opera, cabaret, Bette Davis and Joan Crawford movies, and various other artifacts gathered under the problematic name "camp." When *National Review* got hold of Halperin's class description, there was predictable hysteria on the right, along with some sniggering in the gay press. One side saw evidence of a dangerous recruiting drive; the other, a pedantic inquiry into the screamingly obvious. The University of Michigan held fast, and Halperin taught the class for several years. His book of the same title begins with an account of the brouhaha, and then delivers a summary—exhaustive, discursive, at times frustrating, but always absorbing—of what he learned from it all.

In "How to Be Gay," Halperin speaks of avoiding academic jargon and addressing the general reader. While he doesn't quite stick to that—anyone unfamiliar with the intricate work of the literary scholar Eve Kosofsky Sedgwick will stumble over the phrase "the epistemology of the closet"—much of the book is straightforward in style. It is focussed almost entirely on the male experience, although similar debates have unfolded over the seeming decline of butch style in lesbian culture. The chief virtue of the book is its unblinking concentration on an issue that has seldom been treated in depth: gay men's shame about their past, their urge to wish it away. Halperin, who came of age during the heyday of gay liberation, in the seventies, writes:

> Gay men my age prided themselves on their generational difference. We were dimly aware that for a lot of gay men ten or twenty years older than us, being gay had something to do with liking Broadway musicals, or listening to show tunes or torch songs or Judy Garland, or playing the piano,

> wearing fluffy sweaters, drinking cocktails, smoking cigarettes, and calling each other "girlfriend."...From my youthful perspective, which aspired fervently to qualify as "liberated," those old queens were sad remnants from a bygone era of sexual repression—victims of self-hatred, internalized homophobia, social isolation, and state terror. (It did not occur to me at the time that some lingering self-hatred or internalized homophobia of my own might be responsible for the righteous aversion I felt to *their* self-hatred and homophobia, or what I took to be such.)

Later, Halperin had second thoughts about his rejection of the gay past. A boyfriend tutored him in the "cultural curriculum," and he surrendered to its quaint charms. This account will ring true for many readers: the same history keeps repeating. Circa 1990, when I came out, the macho gay culture of the seventies seemed abject, the Judy Garland business antediluvian. I wanted very much not to be *that* kind of gay. The new thing was to dress in faded T-shirts and listen to indie rock. When I was working at a gay-oriented video store, I scandalized fellow-workers by revealing that I had never seen "The Wizard of Oz." At that time, I wanted to activate a sexual existence but otherwise remain the same person. I found, though, that living the life of a guy who "just happens to be gay," as the phrase goes, can be lonely. Coming out doesn't make you at home in the world; nor, certainly, does sex. You need bonds beyond sex: a community, a culture, a shared set of obsessions.

How can someone be gay without having seen "Mildred Pierce" or "The Wizard of Oz"? To answer that, you first have to know what such movies have to do with being gay. Halperin observes, as others have before him, that gay boys often display stereotypical tastes long before sex enters the picture. As he points out, sexuality is the area where gay men differ *least* from straight men: the male in heat is a uniform animal. Gay taste is something more singular, probably linked to incipient feelings of dissimilarity from one's peers. This alienation can happen in class, or in the locker room, or at a friend's house when straight porn is unveiled. However these experiences unfold, they have a lasting impact, equivalent to a trauma with no visible cause. One common response is preëmptive withdrawal. The boy buries himself in some obscure aesthetic pursuit. One self-help book calls it "velvet rage." My ignorance of "The Wizard of Oz" didn't save me from becoming a typical case: at the age of ten, I developed a peculiar predilection for Austro-German symphonies.

Of course, a love for Golden Age movies or interior design is not necessarily a telltale sign. Plenty of straight kids flee from the locker room to the Drama Club, and plenty of gay kids thrive at sports. Yet the anecdotal evidence for the early onset of gay taste is vast. In retrospect, my mania for Beethoven may have been a way of forestalling a reckoning with my sexuality: rather than commit myself, I disappeared into a fleshless realm. Halperin sees another dimension to this kind of engagement—a willful resistance to the male-adolescent herd, a form of quasi-political dissidence. It's a heady idea to attribute political motives to gay children, but Halperin is on to something. The fanatical twelve-year-old aesthete displays something like cultural disobedience.

The trickiest component of gay-male culture is the role of women in its midst. Feminist critics have long detected misogynist mockery in drag acts and in gay men's howling response to melodramatic scenes that were not intended to be funny, such as Joan Crawford's verbal annihilation of her aloof, ingrate daughter in "Mildred Pierce." Halperin, like many before him, sees a more complex identification at work. Crawford maintains a flawlessly high pitch as she gyrates between "feminine glamour" and "feminine abjection," and the typical gay male viewer may feel at home at both extremes: so many gay kids work at presenting a perfected surface to the world, and so many are hounded by the fear that some grotesque exposure will tear it down.

At the same time, the plunge into abjection can be liberating—"the politics of emotion," Halperin calls it, of "losing it," of "righteous, triumphant fury." (That young man at the Jack in the Box, despite his frat-boy affect, had a Joan Crawford quality.) Furthermore, as the feminist theorist Judith Butler has argued, these extravagant diva turns, and, more particularly, the drag acts that perpetuate them, reveal the artificiality of conventional gender roles, the "hyperbolic status of the norm itself." As Halperin puts it, "every identity is a role or an act." It's just that straight-male performance is granted instant authenticity. Super Bowl Sunday, seen from a certain angle, is a pageant as intricate and contrived as the annual invasion of the drag queens on Fire Island.

Having plausibly defined gay culture, Halperin ponders its fate. Its demise has been prophesied many times, often with eagerness: already in 1944, Robert Duncan sounds fed up with the rites of camp. In the nineties, there was a vogue for the phrase "post-gay," signifying life outside the ghetto, and in 2005 Andrew Sullivan announced the "end of gay culture." Yet, like Sarah Bernhardt, camp always seems to be coming around for one more farewell tour. Chris Colfer, the fearlessly swishy young actor who has become the star of "Glee," has revived the cult of Judy and Babs for the post-millennial generation. Curiously, Halperin doesn't mention "Glee," but he says that his gay students lap up all that antiquated lore, effortlessly unravelling its codes. He also notes that the gay audience tends to lose interest when coded messages give way to explicitly affirmative ones. Lady Gaga tried to write a new gay anthem with "Born This Way," yet the song failed to ignite the clubs and bars as "Poker Face" had before it. Subtext is sexier.

In the straight world, meanwhile, the mortal fear of being mistaken for gay is weakening. Halperin could have added a chapter on the semiotics of "Call Me Maybe," the pop ditty by Carly Rae Jepsen that became a monster hit this past summer, thanks in part to YouTube videos where everyone from Justin Bieber to Colin Powell was seen singing along. The official video gave the song a queer vibe from the outset: the singer sees a half-naked young man mowing the lawn, requests a possible telephone connection, and then discovers, to her dismay, that he prefers his own kind. (His "Call me" pantomime to another guy is more than a bit camp.) The most popular of the lip-synch videos features members of the Harvard baseball team, in all their macho splendor. Such gayish cavorting would have been unthinkable a generation ago. Likewise, you knew that the days of Don't Ask, Don't Tell were numbered when soldiers stationed in war zones uploaded videos of themselves prancing suggestively to Ke$ha's "Blah Blah Blah" and other dance hits. At certain moments, straight people can seem gayer than the gays.

This is especially noticeable when—as Halperin writes, in his acidulous final chapter—gay people are "preening themselves on their dullness, commonness, averageness." He also laments the rise of online hookup sites, which, he says, are erasing the messy diversity of gay bars. "Sometimes I think homosexuality is wasted on gay people," Halperin says, with what I take to be a Bette Davis scowl. Other academic writers have inveighed against the New Gay Normalcy. The most influential of them is the Yale professor Michael Warner, whose 1999 book, "The Trouble with Normal," attacks the constraints of straight and gay marriage alike, celebrating instead porn stores, sex clubs, cruising grounds, and other sites of what he calls "the queer ethos." These scholars also maintain that imagery of wholesome relationships and talk of the power of the "gay dollar" signal a collusion with social conservatism, with market capitalism, even with an imperial American foreign policy.

As a married gay man with three cats, I'm chastened by this critique of domesticity, but I'm not entirely swayed by it. The queer ethos has its own confinements, its own essentialism: the implication is that anyone who goes in for marriage is betraying the bohemian essence of gayness. Both sides of the debate tend to reduce the dizzying variety of gay lives to an ideal condition: either you're prowling the bars or you're gardening in the Berkshires. It is possible to do both, or, perhaps, to transition gently from one to the other as time goes by. There are riddles of love and lust that ideology will never solve.

Still, Halperin is right to defend the old rituals and the lingo and body language that go with them. Those who fit the classic stereotypes—the ones who get called queer, faggot, pansy, sissy—have been abused in one society after another, whatever the prevailing attitude toward same-sex acts. The insult "*magnus cinaedus*"—essentially, "big fag"—can be found on the walls of Pompeii. Sadly, gay men are capable of using such language against one another. A Web site devoted to culling obnoxious messages from gay hookup sites includes the following: "Don't be gay," "No fats or fems," "If you have a broken wrist keep movin'." Fleeing stereotypes, gay men too often fall into a deeper conformity—the rigid choreography of the average male.

So long live camp, and all the other cultural pursuits that gay people have traditionally embraced. Perhaps the historic devotion to theatre, opera, high fashion, and other venerable disciplines will wither away, but it seems likely that many gay kids will still feel the trauma of difference and go on seeking refuge in artier spheres. Halperin speaks of a "tension between egalitarian ethics and hierarchical aesthetics" in gay taste; he sees it as a snobbery not of class but of knowledge, open to all who can hold their own. It stands in opposition to a society that joins egalitarian aesthetics—the notion that the perfect cultural product appeals to all—to an economic system whose inequalities become more glaring by the day. Gay culture's long memory, its arch sympathy for fading worlds, is a check against the razing of the past.

IV. Jesus and the Centurion

To read through the seismographic record of the gay movement, with its sudden waves of repression and its equally abrupt forward leaps, is to confront the unpredictable dynamics of bigotry. In the fifties, the prejudice seemed monolithic, yet its effects were arbitrary, destroying some lives and leaving others untouched. A man fired from the State Department blows his brains out on the corner of Twenty-first Street and Virginia Avenue; Truman Capote swans across late-night TV. Intolerance has a way of dissolving in one place and becoming feral in another. In large cities, being gay has never been easier; in some devout small towns, it may never have been harder. As American gays chatter of victory, their Iranian counterparts inhabit a medieval world of floggings and public hangings.

An elemental question kept crossing my mind as I browsed dozens of volumes of gay history and theory: Why has this small part of the population caused such vexation across the centuries? What inspires such profound contempt, contempt that is inscribed in the texts of several world religions? I grew up in the Greek Orthodox church, serving for a time as an altar boy, and attended an Episcopalian high school. Although I don't recall hearing denunciations of homosexuality in either place, I certainly became aware of the most vehemently anti-gay passages in the Christian tradition, and they both scared and mystified me. St. Thomas Aquinas could be found saying that the "sin against nature" was among the gravest of offenses, because it entails "the corruption of the principle on which the rest depend." The response is disproportionate, as if Aquinas were carpet-bombing an elusive target. There is much evil under the sun, and Rosie O'Donnell's gay-family cruise is not the prime cause of it.

The retreat of anti-gay feeling in the secular West probably has much to do with the realization that homosexuality is not a choice, a "life style," but, rather, a life. I knew I was gay before I consciously met a gay person; I came out before I had sex. No life style drew me in; if anything, the life style kept me away. Recent scientific research has presented murky evidence of a genetic basis for homosexuality. The neuroscientist Simon LeVay, in his 2010 book, "Gay, Straight, and the Reason Why," informs me that the third interstitial nucleus of my anterior hypothalamus is probably smaller than it is in most straight men. If, indeed, gay people are born this way, as Lady Gaga avers, it becomes a little harder to call them sinners or beat them up.

Yet most gay historians resist any depiction of homosexuality as a fixed category transcending time. Ever since Michel Foucault published the first volume of his "History of Sexuality," in 1976, sexual identity has often been portrayed as a "social construction," as the jargon goes. David Halperin made his name as a Foucauldian; his 1990 book, "One Hundred Years of Homosexuality," shows in ripe detail how the mores of ancient Greece differed from our own. Same-sex acts were considered normal within set bounds: an adult male could impose himself on boys, foreigners, or slaves, but to submit to another of equal status was shameful. It appears that countless Greeks indulged in such behavior not because they were genetically distinct but because so many others were doing it. Aspects of that old regime persist in prisons, in same-sex schools, and in societies where women are segregated from men. In Kandahar, for example, Pashtun men make a cult of teen-age boys. Even if genetics predict certain desires, social forces can transform them.

If, as Halperin and others insist, it is nonsense to speak of a gay-straight dichotomy in Greco-Roman times, it is also nonsense to insert the word "homosexuality" into the Old and New Testaments, as some modern translations do. Bishop Gene Robinson's "God Believes in Love," a slender book that carries blurbs from Barack Obama and Desmond Tutu, makes this point repeatedly. Robinson is the gay Episcopal priest who helped to set off a semi-schism in the Anglican Church when he was elected Bishop of New Hampshire, in 2003. He opens his essay with familiar tales of a confused childhood and early adulthood, but says that his struggles never caused a crisis of faith. Rather, he came to believe that by hiding his sexuality he was being untruthful to God.

When Robinson examines Biblical passages that condemn gay acts, he emphasizes, in social-constructionist fashion, gaps between ancient and modern practices. St. Paul, in the Letter to the Romans, inveighs against all manner of fornicators, including men and women who act "against nature." Elsewhere, Paul employs the word *arsenokoitai*, which he evidently coined: "man-liers" would be a literal translation. In all likelihood, Paul was talking about attachments between older men and boys, since those were the most prevalent same-sex pairings in his time. He almost certainly did not have in mind anything like, say, the twenty-seven-year relationship between the late astronaut Sally Ride and her partner, Tam O'Shaughnessy. Robinson asks, "Do we really want to base our condemnation of an entire group of people on a shaky translation of an unknowable Greek word?"

Paul's vague strictures hardened into dogma in the early Christian era. St. John Chrysostom reached the dire conclusion that sodomy was worse than murder: "The murderer dissevers the soul from the body, but [the sodomite] ruins the soul with the body…For I should not only say that thou hast become a woman, but that thou hast lost thy manhood." The problem with gay sex, in other words, is that it undermines the dominance of the male. Ironically, the Greeks and the Romans followed the same logic in censuring effeminate males. The pagan and Christian worlds had more in common than the church fathers might have liked to admit—especially when you look at the persistence of pedophilia in the priesthood. Jesus Christ did not speak the same hierarchical language. Why did Mosaic law allow men to divorce their wives while women could not divorce their husbands? "Because of the hardness of your hearts."

Jesus is famously silent on the subject of same-sex love. "If homosexuality is such a heinous sin against God, why does Jesus himself never refer to it?" Robinson writes. "Why no mention of an issue now causing entire churches to split?" This silence has not stopped some on the Christian right from locating an objection to gay marriage in Jesus' disquisition on divorce: "He which made them at the beginning made them male and female.…What therefore God hath joined together, let not man put asunder." Here is the source of the slogan "God made Adam and Eve, not Adam and Steve." But the context for Jesus' statement points up an underlying hypocrisy in the history of homophobia. The American divorce rate climbed steeply in the first part of the twentieth century, hitting an early peak in 1945. In this same period, homophobia intensified into official policy. The two developments may not be unrelated: a largely Christian nation, having abandoned Jesus' teachings on divorce, reinforced its moral credentials at the expense of a friendless minority.

R

In one story from the New Testament, Jesus' silence becomes almost conspicuous. This is from the Book of Matthew:

> And when Jesus was entered into Capernaum, there came unto him a centurion, beseeching him,
>
> And saying, Lord, my servant [*pais*] lieth at home sick of the palsy, grievously tormented.
>
> And Jesus saith unto him, I will come and heal him.
>
> The centurion answered and said, Lord, I am not worthy that thou shouldest come under my roof: but speak the word only, and my servant shall be healed.
>
> For I am a man under authority, having soldiers under me: and I say to this *man*, Go, and he goeth; and to another, Come, and he cometh; and to my servant, Do this, and he doeth *it*.
>
> When Jesus heard *it*, he marvelled, and said to them that followed, Verily I say unto you, I have not found so great faith, no, not in Israel.

An interpretive battle has broken out over this passage, on account of the use of *pais*. The centurion is effectively saying "my boy," and some pro-gay theologians have jumped to the conclusion that the relationship was sexual, and that Jesus implicitly blessed the union. From what is known of the private lives of centurions, the speculation is not outrageous; in Plato's Symposium and many other sources, a *pais* is a boy beloved by an older man. Then again, it's perfectly possible that, as conservative commentators insist, this boy is nothing more than a servant; the word *pais* is entirely ambiguous. What's striking is that Jesus shows no interest in resolving the ambiguity. He asks nothing about the relationship. His eye is elsewhere. Only the centurion's faith matters.

Imprecations from the religious right notwithstanding, houses of worship are thronged with gay people. A few years ago, an evangelical pollster discovered, to his surprise, that sixty per cent of lesbians and gays considered faith to be "very important" in their lives. In a few cases, they have rescued churches struggling to find a following; a Methodist church in Columbus, Ohio, recently reported that attendance had more than doubled after it made a point of welcoming gay parishioners. The influx may have to do with the lingering fragility of many gay lives, their proximity to danger and disorder. Even now, the unleashing of pent-up desires in adulthood can cause a degree of chaos with which many socially sheltered straight people are unfamiliar. Presbyterians, Episcopalians, Lutherans, and Unitarians, among other denominations, have recognized this yearning for refuge; the Web site gaychurch.org lists seven thousand "gay-affirming" churches.

Of course, not every church will respond in kind. It may be, as John Cardinal O'Connor once intoned, that the Catholic Church will be teaching that homosexuality is a sin "until the end of time." Recent history suggests, however, that change can happen blindingly fast. I knew as much when, earlier this year, I found myself standing in the chapel at my high school, addressing a meeting of the school's Gay-Straight Alliance. The existence of such a group was staggering enough; then, there was the fact that the gathering was held in a religious space. I struggled for words, not only because I felt like a visitor from the time of the Mattachine Society—the faces in front of me betrayed little of the dread I once experienced—but also because I was standing in front of an image of Christ on the Cross. I fought off the ancient sense of not belonging, here or anywhere. Eventually, I stammered out something along the lines of what Robinson states crisply in his book: nothing in Jesus' teachings prevents the recognition of devoted gay relationships. Indeed, Robinson's title flatly suggests that God wishes it so. Linda Hirshman, in "Victory," says that the gay movement conquered a fortress of hatred on the strength of its "moral certainty." That certainty is rooted in the conviction that abiding love cannot be a sin.

I can't define my current spiritual beliefs with any coherence, but I keep a pocket edition of the King James Bible at my desk. These days, I pick it up not only to absorb the grandeur of the language—King James was a man of discriminating taste—but to wrestle with what it says. Perhaps because it is again a political season, with the rights of gay people up for a vote and under legal review, I read the story of Jesus and the centurion as a parable about the workings of compassion in the corridors of power: the centurion's pity for one under his command, Jesus' pity for an unseen stranger. Those in power feel invisible restrictions on their freedom to act; even when they mean to do good, they lose their nerve in the face of a hard-hearted world. Sometimes, though, all they need to do is speak the word. ■

AUTHOR PROFILE

Alex Ross (born 1968) is an American music critic and essayist. He received a degree in English from Harvard in 1990 and became a music critic for *The New York Times* shorty after graduation while also contributing to publications such as *The New Republic*, *Slate*, and the *London Review of Books*. He started writing for *The New Yorker* in 1993 and became a staff writer in 1996. His work since has focused on music, literature, twentieth-century history, and gay culture. His first book, *The Rest Is Noise: Listening to the Twentieth Century* (2007), a cultural history of music since 1900, received widespread praise in the U.S., winning a National Book Critics Circle Award and a finalist citation for the Pulitzer Prize in general nonfiction. "Love on the March" appeared in the November 12, 2012 issue of *The New Yorker*.

Who Deserves What?/Aristotle

From *Justice: What's the Right Thing to Do?*

By Michael Sandel

Callie Smartt was a popular freshman cheerleader at Andrews High School in West Texas. The fact that she had cerebral palsy and moved about in a wheelchair didn't dampen the enthusiasm she inspired among the football players and fans by her spirited presence on the sidelines at junior varsity games. But at the end of the season, Callie was kicked off the squad.[1]

At the urging of some other cheerleaders and their parents, school officials told Callie that, to make the squad the next year, she would have to try out like everyone else, in a rigorous gymnastic routine involving splits and tumbles. The head cheerleader's father led the opposition to Callie's inclusion on the cheerleading team. He claimed he was concerned for her safety. But Callie's mother suspected the opposition was motivated by resentment of the acclaim Callie received.

Callie's story raises two questions. One is a question of fairness. Should she be required to do gymnastics in order to qualify as a cheerleader, or is this requirement unfair, given her disability? One way of answering this question would be to invoke the principle of nondiscrimination: Provided she can perform well in the role, Callie should not be excluded from cheerleading simply because, through no fault of her own, she lacks the physical ability to perform gymnastic routines.

But the nondiscrimination principle isn't much help, because it begs the question at the heart of the controversy: What does it mean to perform well in the role of cheerleader? Callie's opponents claim that to be a good cheerleader you must be able to do tumbles and splits. That, after all, is how cheerleaders traditionally excite the crowd. Callie's supporters would say this confuses the purpose of cheerleading with one way of achieving it. The real point of cheerleading is to inspire school spirit and energize the fans. When Callie roars up and down the sidelines in her wheelchair, waving her pom-poms and flashing her smile, she does well what cheerleaders are supposed to do—fire up the crowd. So in order to decide what the qualifications should be, we have to decide what's essential to cheerleading, and what's merely incidental.

The second question raised by Callie's story is about resentment. What kind of resentment might motivate the head cheerleader's father? Why is he bothered by the presence of Callie on the squad? It can't be fear that Callie's inclusion deprives his daughter of a place; she's already on the team. Nor is it the simple envy he might feel toward a girl who outshines his daughter at gymnastic routines, which Callie, of course, does not.

Here is my hunch: his resentment probably reflects a sense that Callie is being accorded an honor she doesn't deserve, in a way that mocks the pride he takes in his daughter's cheerleading prowess. If great cheerleading is something that can be done from a wheelchair, then the honor accorded those who excel at tumbles and splits is depreciated to some degree.

If Callie should be a cheerleader because she displays, despite her disability, the virtues appropriate to the role, her claim does pose a certain threat to the honor accorded the other cheerleaders. The gymnastic skills they display no longer appear essential to excellence in cheerleading, only one way among others of rousing the crowd. Ungenerous though he was, the father of the head cheerleader correctly grasped what was at stake. A social practice once taken as fixed in its purpose and in the honors it bestowed was now, thanks to Callie, redefined. She had shown that there's more than one way to be a cheerleader.

Notice the connection between the first question, about fairness, and the second, about honor and resentment. In order to determine a fair way to allocate cheerleading positions, we need to determine the nature and purpose of cheerleading. Otherwise, we have no way of saying what qualities are essential to it. But determining the essence of cheerleading can be controversial, because it embroils us in arguments about what qualities are worthy of honor. What counts as the purpose of cheerleading depends partly on what virtues you think deserve recognition and reward.

As this episode shows, social practices such as cheerleading have not only an instrumental purpose (cheering on the team) but also an honorific, or exemplary, purpose (celebrating certain excellences and virtues). In choosing its cheerleaders, the high school not only promotes school spirit but also makes a statement about the qualities it hopes students will admire and emulate. This explains why the dispute was so intense. It also explains what is otherwise puzzling—how those already on the team (and their parents) could feel they had a personal stake in the debate over Callie's eligibility. These parents wanted cheerleading to honor the traditional cheerleader virtues their daughters possessed.

S

Justice, Telos, and Honor

Seen in this way, the dustup over cheerleaders in West Texas is a short course in Aristotle's theory of justice. Central to Aristotle's political philosophy are two ideas, both present in the argument over Callie:

1. Justice is teleological. Defining rights requires us to figure out the *telos* (the purpose, end, or essential nature) of the social practice in question.
2. Justice is honorific. To reason about the telos of a practice—or to argue about it—is, at least in part, to reason or argue about what virtues it should honor and reward.

The key to understanding Aristotle's ethics and politics is to see the force of these two considerations, and the relation between them.

Modern theories of justice try to separate questions of fairness and rights from arguments about honor, virtue, and moral desert. They seek principles of justice that are neutral among ends, and enable people to choose and pursue their ends for themselves. Aristotle (384–322 B.C.) does not think justice can be neutral in this way. He believes that debates about justice are, unavoidably, debates about honor, virtue, and the nature of the good life.

Seeing why Aristotle thinks justice and the good life must be connected will help us see what's at stake in the effort to separate them.

For Aristotle, justice means giving people what they deserve, giving each person his or her due. But what is a person due? What are the relevant grounds of merit or desert? That depends on what's being distributed. Justice involves two factors: "things, and the persons to whom things are assigned." And in general we say that "persons who are equal should have assigned to them equal things."[2]

But here there arises a difficult question: Equals in what respect? That depends on what we're distributing—and on the virtues relevant to those things.

Suppose we're distributing flutes. Who should get the best ones? Aristotle's answer: the best flute players.

Justice discriminates according to merit, according to the relevant excellence. And in the case of flute playing, the relevant merit is the ability to play well. It would be unjust to discriminate on any other basis, such as wealth, or nobility of birth, or physical beauty, or chance (a lottery).

> Birth and beauty may be greater goods than ability to play the flute, and those who possess them may, upon balance, surpass the flute-player more in these qualities than he surpasses them in his flute-playing; but the fact remains that he is the man who ought to get the better supply of flutes.[3]

There is something funny about comparing excellences across vastly disparate dimensions. It may not even make sense to ask, "Am I more handsome than she is a good lacrosse player?" Or, "Was Babe Ruth a greater baseball player than Shakespeare was a playwright?" Questions such as these may make sense only as parlor games. Aristotle's point is that, in distributing flutes, we should not look for the richest or best-looking or even the best person overall. We should look for the best flute player.

This idea is perfectly familiar. Many orchestras conduct auditions behind a screen, so that the quality of the music can be judged without bias or distraction. Less familiar is Aristotle's reason. The most obvious reason for giving the best flutes to the best flute players is that doing so will produce the best music, making us listeners better off. But this is not Aristotle's reason. He thinks the best flutes should go to the best flute players because that's what flutes are *for*—to be played well.

The purpose of flutes is to produce excellent music. Those who can best realize this purpose ought to have the best ones.

Now it's also true that giving the best instruments to the best musicians will have the welcome effect of producing the best music, which everyone will enjoy—producing the greatest happiness for the greatest number. But it's important to see that Aristotle's reason goes beyond this utilitarian consideration.

His way of reasoning from the purpose of a good to the proper allocation of the good is an instance of teleological reasoning. (*Teleological* comes from the Greek word telos, which means purpose, end, or goal.) Aristotle claims that in order to determine the just distribution of a good, we have to inquire into the telos, or purpose, of the good being distributed.

Teleological Thinking: Tennis Courts and Winnie-the-Pooh

Teleological reasoning may seem a strange way to think about justice, but it does have a certain plausibility. Suppose you have to decide how to allocate use of the best tennis courts on a college campus. You might give priority to those who can pay the most for them, by setting a high fee. Or you might give priority to campus big shots—the president of the college, say, or the Nobel Prize–winning scientists. But suppose two renowned scientists were playing a rather indifferent tennis game, barely getting the ball over the net, and the varsity tennis team came along, wanting to use the court. Wouldn't you say that the scientists should move to a lesser court so that the varsity players could use the best one? And wouldn't your reason be that excellent tennis players can make the best use of the best courts, which are wasted on mediocre players?

Or suppose a Stradivarius violin is for up sale, and a wealthy collector outbids Itzhak Perlman for it. The collector wants to display the violin in his living room. Wouldn't we regard this as something of a loss, perhaps even an injustice—not because we think the auction is unfair, but because the outcome is unfitting? Lying behind this reaction may be the (teleological) thought that a Stradivarius is meant to be played, not displayed.

In the ancient world, teleological thinking was more prevalent than it is today. Plato and Aristotle thought that fire rose because it was reaching for the sky, its natural home, and that stones fell because they were striving to get closer to the earth, where they belonged. Nature was seen as having a meaningful order. To understand nature, and our place in it, was to grasp its purpose, its essential meaning.

With the advent of modern science, nature ceased to be seen as a meaningful order. Instead, it came to be understood mechanistically, governed by the laws of physics. To explain natural phenomena in terms of purposes, meanings, and ends was now considered naïve and anthropomorphic. Despite this shift, the temptation to see the world as teleologically ordered, as a purposeful whole, is not wholly absent. It persists, especially in children, who have to be educated out of seeing the world in this way. I noticed this when my children were very young, and I read them the book *Winnie-the-Pooh*, by A. A. Milne. The story evokes a childlike view of nature as enchanted, animated by meaning and purpose.

Early in the book, Winnie-the-Pooh is walking in the forest and comes to a large oak tree. From the top of the tree, "there came a loud buzzing-noise."

> Winnie-the-Pooh sat down at the foot of the tree, put his head between his paws and began to think.
>
> First of all he said to himself: "That buzzing-noise means something. You don't get a buzzing-noise like that, just buzzing and buzzing, without its meaning something. If there's a buzzing-noise, somebody's making a buzzing-noise, and the only reason for making a buzzing-noise that *I* know of is because you're a bee."
>
> Then he thought another long time, and said: "And the only reason for being a bee that *I* know of is making honey."
>
> And then he got up, and said: "And the only reason for making honey is so as *I* can eat it." So he began to climb the tree.[4]

Pooh's childlike line of thought about the bees is a good example of teleological reasoning. By the time we are adults, most of us outgrow this way of viewing the natural world, seeing it as charming but quaint. And having rejected teleological thinking in science, we are also inclined to reject it in politics and morals. But it is not easy to dispense with teleological reasoning in thinking about social institutions and political practices. Today, no scientist reads Aristotle's works on biology or physics and takes them seriously. But students of ethics and politics continue to read and ponder Aristotle's moral and political philosophy.

What's the Telos of a University?

The debate over affirmative action can be recast in terms that echo Aristotle's account of flutes. We begin by seeking just criteria of distribution: Who has a right to be admitted? In addressing this question, we find ourselves asking (at least implicitly), "What is the purpose, or telos, of a university?"

As is often the case, the telos is not obvious but contestable. Some say universities are for the sake of promoting scholarly excellence, and that academic promise should be the sole criterion of admission. Others say universities also exist to serve certain civic purposes, and that the ability to become a leader in a diverse society, for example, should be among the criteria of admission. Sorting out the telos of a university seems essential to determining the proper criteria of admission. This brings out the teleological aspect of justice in university admissions.

Closely connected to the debate about a university's purpose is a question about honor: What virtues or excellences do universities properly honor and reward? Those who believe that universities exist to celebrate and reward scholarly excellence alone are likely to reject affirmative action, whereas those who believe universities also exist to promote certain civic ideals may well embrace it.

That arguments about universities—and cheerleaders and flutes—naturally proceed in this way bears out Aristotle's point: Arguments about justice and rights are often arguments about the purpose, or telos, of a social institution, which in turn reflect competing notions of the virtues the institution should honor and reward.

What can we do if people disagree about the telos, or purpose, of the activity in question? Is it possible to reason about the telos of a social institution, or is the purpose of a university, say, simply whatever the founding authority or governing board declared it to be?

Aristotle believes that it is possible to reason about the purpose of social institutions. Their essential nature is not fixed once and for all, but neither is it simply a matter of opinion. (If the purpose of Harvard College were simply determined by the intention of its founders, then its primary purpose would still be the training of Congregationalist ministers.)

How, then, can we reason about the purpose of a social practice in the face of disagreement? And how do notions of honor and virtue come into play? Aristotle offers his most sustained answer to these questions in his discussion of politics.

What's the Purpose of Politics?

When we discuss distributive justice these days, we are concerned mainly with the distribution of income, wealth, and opportunities. For Aristotle, distributive justice was not mainly about money but about offices and honors. Who should have the right to rule? How should political authority be distributed?

At first glance, the answer seems obvious—equally, of course. One person, one vote. Any other way would be discriminatory. But Aristotle reminds us that all theories of distributive justice discriminate. The question is: Which discriminations are just? And the answer depends on the purpose of the activity in question.

So, before we can say how political rights and authority should be distributed, we have to inquire into the purpose, or telos, of politics. We have to ask, "What is political association *for*?"

This may seem an unanswerable question. Different political communities care about different things. It's one thing to argue about the purpose of a flute, or a university. Notwithstanding the room for disagreement at the margins, their purposes are more or less circumscribed. The purpose of a flute has something to do with making music; the purpose of a university has something to do with education. But can we really determine the purpose or goal of political activity as such?

These days, we don't think of politics as such as having some particular, substantive end, but as being open to the various ends that citizens may espouse. Isn't that why we have elections—so that people can choose, at any given moment, what purposes and ends they want collectively to pursue? To attribute some purpose or end to political community in advance would seem to preempt the right of citizens to decide for themselves. It would also risk imposing values not everyone shares. Our reluctance to invest politics with a determinate telos, or end, reflects a concern for individual freedom. We view politics as a procedure that enables persons to choose their ends for themselves.

S

Aristotle doesn't see it this way. For Aristotle, the purpose of politics is not to set up a framework of rights that is neutral among ends. It is to form good citizens and to cultivate good character.

> [A]ny polis which is truly so called, and is not merely one in name, must devote itself to the end of encouraging goodness. Otherwise, a political association sinks into a mere alliance...Otherwise, too, law becomes a mere covenant..."a guarantor of men's rights against one another"—instead of being, as it should be, a rule of life such as will make the members of a polis good and just.[5]

Aristotle criticizes what he takes to be the two major claimants to political authority—oligarchs and democrats. Each has a claim, he says, but only a partial claim. The oligarchs maintain that they, the wealthy, should rule. The democrats maintain that free birth should be the sole criterion of citizenship and political authority. But both groups exaggerate their claims, because both misconstrue the purpose of political community.

The oligarchs are wrong because political community isn't only about protecting property or promoting economic prosperity. If it were only about those things, then property owners would deserve the greatest share of political authority. For their part, the democrats are wrong because political community isn't only about giving the majority its way. By *democrats*, Aristotle means what we would call majoritarians. He rejects the notion that the purpose of politics is to satisfy the preferences of the majority.

Both sides overlook the highest end of political association, which for Aristotle is to cultivate the virtue of citizens. The end of the state is not "to provide an alliance for mutual defence...or to ease economic exchange and promote economic intercourse."[6] For Aristotle, politics is about something higher. It's about learning how to live a good life. The purpose of politics is nothing less than to enable people to develop their distinctive human capacities and virtues—to deliberate about the common good, to acquire practical judgment, to share in self-government, to care for the fate of the community as a whole.

Aristotle acknowledges the usefulness of other, lesser forms of association, such as defense pacts and free trade agreements. But he insists that associations of this kind don't amount to true political communities. Why not? Because their ends are limited. Organizations such as NATO and NAFTA and the WTO are concerned only with security or economic exchange; they don't constitute a shared way of life that shapes the character of the participants. And the same can be said of a city or a state concerned only with security and trade and that is indifferent to the moral and civic education of its members. "If the spirit of their intercourse were still the same after their coming together as it had been when they were living apart," Aristotle writes, their association can't really be considered a polis, or political community.[7]

"A polis is not an association for residence on a common site, or for the sake of preventing mutual injustice and easing exchange." While these conditions are necessary to a polis, they are not sufficient. "The end and purpose of a polis is the good life, and the institutions of social life are means to that end."[8]

If the political community exists to promote the good life, what are the implications for the distribution of offices and honors? As with flutes, so with politics: Aristotle reasons from the purpose of the good to the appropriate way of distributing it. "Those who contribute most to an association of this character" are those who excel in civic virtue, those who are best at deliberating about the common good. Those who are greatest in civic excellence—not the wealthiest, or the most numerous, or the most handsome—are the ones who merit the greatest share of political recognition and influence.[9]

Since the end of politics is the good life, the highest offices and honors should go to people, such as Pericles, who are greatest in civic virtue and best at identifying the common good. Property holders should have their say. Majoritarian considerations should matter some. But the greatest influence should go to those with the qualities of character and judgment to decide if and when and how to go to war with Sparta.

The reason people such as Pericles (and Abraham Lincoln) should hold the highest offices and honors is not simply that they will enact wise policies, making everyone better off. It is also that political community exists, at least in part, to honor and reward civic virtue. According public recognition to those who display civic excellence serves the educative role of the good city. Here again, we see how the teleological and honorific aspects of justice go together.

Can You Be a Good Person if You Don't Participate in Politics?

If Aristotle is right that the end of politics is the good life, it's easy to conclude that those who display the greatest civic virtue merit the highest offices and honors. But is he right that politics is for the sake of the good life? This is, at best, a controversial claim. These days, we generally view politics as a necessary evil, not an essential feature of the good life. When we think of politics, we think of compromise, posturing, special interests, corruption. Even idealistic uses of politics—as an instrument of social justice, as a way to make the world a better place—cast politics as a means to an end, one calling among others, not as an essential aspect of the human good.

Why, then, does Aristotle think that participating in politics is somehow essential to living a good life? Why can't we live perfectly good, virtuous lives without politics?

The answer lies in our nature. Only by living in a polis and participating in politics do we fully realize our nature as human beings. Aristotle sees us as beings "meant for political association, in a higher degree than bees or other gregarious animals." The reason he gives is this: Nature makes nothing in vain, and human beings, unlike other animals, are furnished with the faculty of language. Other animals can make sounds, and sounds can indicate pleasure and pain. But language, a distinctly human capacity, isn't just for registering pleasure and pain. It's about declaring what is just and what is unjust, and distinguishing right from wrong. We don't grasp these things silently, and then put words to them; language is the medium through which we discern and deliberate about the good.[10]

Only in political association, Aristotle claims, can we exercise our distinctly human capacity for language, for only in a polis do we deliberate with others about justice and injustice and the nature of the good life. "We thus see that the polis exists by nature and that it is prior to the individual," he writes in Book I of *The Politics*.[11] By *prior* , he means prior in function, or purpose, not chronologically prior. Individuals, families, and clans existed before cities did; but only in the polis are we able to realize our nature. We are not self-sufficient when we are isolated, because we can't yet develop our capacity for language and moral deliberation.

> The man who is isolated—who is unable to share in the benefits of political association, or has no need to share because he is already self-sufficient—is no part of the polis, and must therefore be either a beast or a god.[12]

So we only fulfill our nature when we exercise our faculty of language, which requires in turn that we deliberate with others about right and wrong, good and evil, justice and injustice.

But why, you might wonder, can we exercise this capacity for language and deliberation only in politics? Why can't we do it in families, clans, or clubs? To answer this question, we need to consider the account of virtue and the good life that Aristotle presents in the *Nicomachean Ethics*. Although this work is primarily about moral philosophy, it shows how acquiring virtue is bound up with being a citizen.

The moral life aims at happiness, but by *happiness* Aristotle doesn't mean what the utilitarians mean—maximizing the balance of pleasure over pain. The virtuous person is someone who takes pleasure and pain in the right things. If someone takes pleasure in watching dog fights, for example, we consider this a vice to be overcome, not a true source of happiness. Moral excellence does not consist in aggregating pleasures and pains but in aligning them, so that we delight in noble things and take pain in base ones. Happiness is not a state of mind but a way of being, "an activity of the soul in accordance with virtue."[13]

But why is it necessary to live in a polis to live a virtuous life? Why can't we learn sound moral principles at home, or in a philosophy class, or by reading a book about ethics—and then apply them as needed? Aristotle says we don't become virtuous that way. "Moral virtue comes about as a result of habit." It's the kind of thing we learn by doing. "The virtues we get by first exercising them, as also happens in the case of the arts as well."[14]

Learning by Doing

In this respect, becoming virtuous is like learning to play the flute. No one learns how to play a musical instrument by reading a book or listening to a lecture. You have to practice. And it helps to listen to accomplished musicians, and hear how they play. You can't become a violinist without fiddling. So it is with moral virtue: "we become just by doing just acts, temperate by doing temperate acts, brave by doing brave acts."[15]

It is similar with other practices and skills, such as cooking. Many cookbooks are published, but no one becomes a great chef simply by reading them. You have to do lots of cooking. Joke telling is another example. You don't become a comedian by reading joke books and collecting funny stories. Nor could you simply learn the principles of comedy. You have to practice—the pacing, timing, gestures, and tone—and watch Jack Benny, or Johnny Carson, or Eddie Murphy, or Robin Williams.

If moral virtue is something we learn by doing, we have somehow to develop the right habits in the first place. For Aristotle, this is the primary purpose of law—to cultivate the habits that lead to good character. "Legislators make the citizens good by forming habits in them, and this is the wish of every legislator, and those who do not effect it miss their mark, and it is in this that a good constitution differs from a bad one." Moral education is less about promulgating rules than forming habits and shaping character. "It makes no small difference... whether we form habits of one kind or of another from our very youth; it makes a very great difference, or rather *all* the difference."[16]

Aristotle's emphasis on habit does not mean he considers moral virtue a form of rote behavior. Habit is the first step in moral education. But if all goes well, the habit eventually takes, and we come to seethe point of it. The etiquette columnist Judith Martin (aka "Miss Manners") once bemoaned the lost habit of writing thank-you letters. Nowadays we assume that feelings trump manners, she observed; as long as you feel grateful, you don't need to bother with such formalities. Miss Manners disagrees: "I think, to the contrary, that it is safer to hope that practicing proper behavior eventually encourages virtuous feeling; that if you write enough thank-you letters, you may actually feel a flicker of gratitude."[17]

That's how Aristotle conceives moral virtue. Being steeped in virtuous behavior helps us acquire the disposition to act virtuously.

It is common to think that acting morally means acting according to a precept or a rule. But Aristotle thinks this misses a distinctive feature of moral virtue. You could be equipped with the right rule and still not know how or when to apply it. Moral education is about learning to discern the particular features of situations that call for this rule rather than that one. "Matters concerned with conduct and questions of what is good for us have no fixity, any more than matters of health...The agents themselves must in each case consider what is appropriate to the occasion, as happens also in the art of medicine or of navigation."[18]

The only general thing that can be said about moral virtue, Aristotle tells us, is that it consists of a mean between extremes. But he readily concedes that this generality doesn't get us very far, because discerning the mean in any given situation is not easy. The challenge is to do the right thing "to the right person, to the right extent, at the right time, with the right motive, and in the right way."[19]

This means that habit, however essential, can't be the whole of moral virtue. New situations always arise, and we need to know which habit is appropriate under the circumstances. Moral virtue therefore requires judgment, a kind of knowledge Aristotle calls "practical wisdom." Unlike scientific knowledge, which concerns "things that are universal and necessary,"[20] practical wisdom is about how to act. It must "recognize the particulars; for it is practical, and practice is concerned with particulars."[21] Aristotle defines practical wisdom as "a reasoned and true state of capacity to act with regard to the human good."[22]

Practical wisdom is a moral virtue with political implications. People with practical wisdom can deliberate well about what is good, not only for themselves but for their fellow citizens, and for human beings in general. Deliberation is not philosophizing, because it attends to what is changeable and particular. It is oriented to action in the here and now. But it is more than calculation. It seeks to identify the highest human good attainable under the circumstances.[23]

S

Politics and the Good Life

We can now see more clearly why, for Aristotle, politics is not one calling among others, but is essential to the good life. First, the laws of the polis inculcate good habits, form good character, and set us on the way to civic virtue. Second, the life of the citizen enables us to exercise capacities for deliberation and practical wisdom that would otherwise lie dormant. This is not the kind of thing we can do at home. We can sit on the sidelines and wonder what policies we would favor if we had to decide. But this is not the same as sharing in significant action and bearing responsibility for the fate of the community as a whole. We become good at deliberating only by entering the arena, weighing the alternatives, arguing our case, ruling and being ruled—in short, by being citizens.

Aristotle's vision of citizenship is more elevated and strenuous than ours. For him, politics is not economics by other means. Its purpose is higher than maximizing utility or providing fair rules for the pursuit of individual interests. It is, instead, an expression of our nature, an occasion for the unfolding of our human capacities, an essential aspect of the good life.

Aristotle's Defense of Slavery

Not everyone was included in the citizenship Aristotle celebrated. Women were ineligible, as were slaves. According to Aristotle, their natures did not suit them to be citizens. We now see such exclusion as an obvious injustice. It's worth recalling that these injustices persisted for more than two thousand years after Aristotle wrote. Slavery was not abolished in the United States until 1865, and women won the right to vote only in 1920. Still, the historic persistence of these injustices does not exonerate Aristotle for accepting them.

In the case of slavery, Aristotle not only accepted it but offered a philosophical justification. It's worth examining his defense of slavery to see what light it sheds on his political theory as a whole. Some see in Aristotle's argument for slavery a defect in teleological thinking as such; others see it as misguided application of such thinking, beclouded by the prejudices of his time.

I don't think Aristotle's defense of slavery reveals a flaw that condemns his political theory as a whole. But it's important to see the force of that thoroughgoing claim.

For Aristotle, justice is a matter of fit. To allocate rights is to look for the telos of social institutions, and to fit persons to the roles that suit them, the roles that enable them to realize their nature. Giving persons their due means giving them the offices and honors they deserve and the social roles that accord with their nature.

Modern political theories are uneasy with the notion of fit. Liberal theories of justice, from Kant to Rawls, worry that teleological conceptions are at odds with freedom. For them, justice is not about fit but about choice. To allocate rights is not to fit people to roles that suit their nature; it is to let people choose their roles for themselves.

From this point of view, the notions of telos and fit are suspect, even dangerous. Who is to say what role is fitting for me, or appropriate to my nature? If I'm not free to choose my social role for myself, I might well be forced into a role against my will. So the notion of fit can easily slide into slavery, if those in power decide that a certain group is somehow suited for a subordinate role.

Prompted by this worry, liberal political theory argues that social roles should be allocated by choice, not fit. Rather than fit people to roles we think will suit their nature, we should enable people to choose their roles for themselves. Slavery is wrong, in this view, because it coerces people into roles they have not chosen. The solution is to reject an ethic of telos and fit in favor of an ethic of choice and consent.

But this conclusion is too quick. Aristotle's defense of slavery is no proof against teleological thinking. On the contrary, Aristotle's own theory of justice provides ample resources for a critique of his views on slavery. In fact, his notion of justice as fit is more morally demanding, and potentially more critical of existing allocations of work, than theories based on choice and consent. To see how this is so, let's examine Aristotle's argument.

For slavery to be just, according to Aristotle, two conditions must be met: it must be necessary, and it must be natural. Slavery is necessary, Aristotle argues, because someone must look after the household chores if citizens are to spend time in the assembly deliberating about the common good. The polis requires a division of labor. Unless we invent machines that could take care of all menial tasks, some people have to attend to the necessities of life so that others can be free to participate in politics.

So Aristotle concludes that slavery is necessary. But necessity is not enough. For Slavery to be just, it must also be the case that certain persons are suited by their nature to perform this role.[24] So Aristotle asks if there are "persons for whom slavery is the better and just condition, or whether the reverse is the case and all slavery is contrary to nature."[25] Unless there are such people, the political and economic need for slaves is not enough to justify slavery.

Aristotle concludes that such people exist. Some people are born to be slaves. They differ from ordinary people in the same way that the body differs from the soul. Such people "are by nature slaves, and it is better for them…to be ruled by a master."[26]

"A man is thus by nature a slave if he is capable of becoming (and this is the reason why he also actually becomes) the property of another, and if he participates in reason to the extent of apprehending it in another, though destitute of it himself.[27]

"[J]ust as some are by nature free, so others are by nature slaves, and for these latter the condition of slavery is both beneficial and just."[28]

Aristotle seems to sense something questionable in the claim he is making, because he quickly qualifies it: "But it is easy to see that those who hold an opposite view are also in a way correct."[29] Looking at slavery as it existed in the Athens of his day, Aristotle had to admit that the critics had a point. Many slaves found themselves in that condition for a purely contingent reason: they were formerly free people who had been captured in war. Their status as slaves had nothing to do with their being fit for the role. For them, slavery was not natural, but the result of bad luck. By Aristotle's own standard, their slavery is unjust: "Not all those who are actually slaves, or actually freemen, are natural slaves or natural freemen."[30]

How can you tell who is fit to be a slave? Aristotle asks. In principle, you would have to see who, if anyone, flourishes as a slave, and who chafes in the role or tries to flee. The need for force is a good indication that the slave in question is not suited to the role.[31] For Aristotle, coercion is a sign of injustice, not because consent legitimates all roles, but because the need for force suggests an unnatural fit. Those who are cast in a role consistent with their nature don't need to be forced.

S

For liberal political theory, slavery is unjust because it is coercive. For teleological theories, slavery is unjust because it is at odds with our nature; coercion is a symptom of the injustice, not the source of it. It is perfectly possible to explain, within the ethic of telos and fit, the injustice of slavery, and Aristotle goes some way (though not all the way) toward doing so.

The ethic of telos and fit actually sets a more demanding moral standard for justice in the workplace than does the liberal ethic of choice and consent.[32] Consider a repetitive, dangerous job, such as working long hours on an assembly line in a chicken processing plant. Is this form of labor just or unjust?

For the libertarian, the answer would depend on whether the workers had freely exchanged their labor for a wage: if they did, the work is just. For Rawls, the arrangement would be just only if the free exchange of labor took place against fair background conditions. For Aristotle, even consent against fair background conditions is not sufficient; for the work to be just, it has to be suited to the nature of the workers who perform it. Some jobs fail this test. They are so dangerous, repetitive, and deadening as to be unfit for human beings. In those cases, justice requires that the work be reorganized to accord with our nature. Otherwise, the job is unjust in the same way that slavery is.

Casey Martin's Golf Cart

Casey Martin was a professional golfer with a bad leg. Due to a circulatory disorder, walking the course caused Martin considerable pain and posed a serious risk of hemorrhaging and fracture. Despite his disability, Martin had always excelled at the sport. He played on Stanford's championship team while in college, then turned pro.

Martin asked the PGA (Professional Golfers' Association) for permission to use a golf cart during tournaments. The PGA turned him down, citing its rule prohibiting carts in top professional tournaments. Martin took his case to court. He argued that the Americans with Disabilities Act (1990) required reasonable accommodations for people with disabilities, provided the change did not "fundamentally alter the nature" of the activity.[33]

Some of the biggest names in golf testified in the case. Arnold Palmer, Jack Nicklaus, and Ken Venturi all defended the ban on carts. They argued that fatigue is an important factor in tournament golf, and that riding rather than walking would give Martin an unfair advantage.

The case went to the United States Supreme Court, where the justices found themselves wrestling with what seemed to one a silly question, at once beneath their dignity and beyond their expertise: "Is someone riding around a golf course from shot to shot *really* a golfer?"[34]

In fact, however, the case raised a question of justice in classic Aristotelian form: In order to decide whether Martin had a right to a golf cart, the Court had to determine the essential nature of the activity in question. Was walking the course essential to golf, or merely incidental? If, as the PGA claimed, walking was an essential aspect of the sport, then to let Martin ride in a cart would "fundamentally alter the nature" of the game. To resolve the question about rights, the court had to determine the telos, or essential nature, of the game.

The Court ruled 7-2 that Martin had a right to use a golf cart. Justice John Paul Stevens, writing for the majority, analyzed the history of golf and concluded that the use of carts was not inconsistent with the fundamental character of the game. "From early on, the essence of the game has been shot-making-using clubs to cause a ball to progress from the teeing ground to a hole some distance away with as few strokes as possible."[35] As for the claim that walking tests the physical stamina of golfers, Stevens cited testimony by a physiology professor who calculated that only about five hundred calories were expended in walking eighteen holes, "nutritionally less than a Big Mac."[36] Because golf is "a low intensity activity, fatigue from the game is primarily a psychological phenomenon in which stress and motivation are the key ingredients."[37] The Court concluded that accommodating Martin's disability by letting him ride in a cart would not fundamentally alter the game or give him an unfair advantage.

Justice Antonin Scalia disagreed. In a spirited dissent, he rejected the notion that the Court could determine the essential nature of golf. His point was not simply that judges lack the authority or competence to decide the question. He challenged the Aristotelian premise underlying the Court's opinion—that it is possible to reason about the telos, or essential nature of a game:

> To say that something is "essential" is ordinarily to say that it is necessary to the achievement of a certain object. But since it is the very nature of a game to have no object except amusement (that is what distinguishes games from productive activity), it is quite impossible to say that any of a game's arbitrary rules is "essential."[38]

Since the rules of golf "are (as in all games) entirely arbitrary," Scalia wrote, there is no basis for critically assessing the rules laid down by the PGA. If the fans don't like them, "they can withdraw their patronage." But no one can say that this or that rule is irrelevant to the skills that golf is meant to test.

Scalia's argument is questionable on several grounds. First, it disparages sports. No real fan would speak of sports that way—as governed by totally arbitrary rules and having no real object or point. If people really believed that the rules of their favorite sport were arbitrary rather than designed to call forth and celebrate certain skills and talents worth admiring, it would be hard for them to care about the outcome of the game. Sport would fade into spectacle, a source of amusement rather than a subject of appreciation.

Second, it's perfectly possible to argue the merits of different rules, and to ask whether they improve or corrupt the game. These arguments take place all the time—on radio call-in shows and among those who govern the game. Consider the debate over the designated-hitter rule in baseball. Some say it improves the game by enabling the best hitters to bat, sparing weak-hitting pitchers the ordeal. Others say it damages the game by overemphasizing hitting and removing complex elements of strategy. Each position rests on a certain conception of what baseball at its best is all about: What skills does it test, what talents and virtues does it celebrate and reward? The debate over the designated-hitter rule is ultimately a debate about the telos of baseball—just as the debate over affirmative action is a debate about the purpose of the university.

Finally, Scalia, by denying that golf has a telos, misses altogether the honorific aspect of the dispute. What, after all, was the four-year saga over the golf cart really about? On the surface, it was an argument about fairness. The PGA and the golfing greats claimed that allowing Martin to ride would give him an unfair advantage; Martin replied that, given his disability, the cart would simply level the playing field.

If fairness were the only thing at stake, however, there is an easy and obvious solution: let all golfers use carts in the tournaments. If everyone can ride, the fairness objection disappears. But this solution was anathema to professional golf, even more unthinkable than making an exception for Casey Martin. Why? Because the dispute was less about fairness than about honor and recognition—specifically the desire of the PGA and top golfers that their sport be recognized and respected as an athletic event.

Let me put the point as delicately as possible: Golfers are somewhat sensitive about the status of their game. It involves no running or jumping, and the ball stands still. No one doubts that golf is a demanding game of skill. But the honor and recognition accorded great golfers depends on their sport being seen as a physically demanding athletic competition. If the game at which they excel can be played while riding in a cart, their recognition as athletes could be questioned or diminished. This may explain the vehemence with which some professional golfers opposed Casey Martin's bid for a cart. Here is Tom Kite, a twenty-five-year veteran of the PGA Tour, in an op-ed piece in *The New York Times*:

> It seems to me that those who support Casey Martin's right to use a cart are ignoring the fact that we are talking about a competitive sport...We are talking about an athletic event. And anyone who doesn't think professional golf is an athletic sport simply hasn't been there or done that.[39]

Whoever is right about the essential nature of golf, the federal case over Casey Martin's cart offers a vivid illustration of Aristotle's theory of justice. Debates about justice and rights are often, unavoidably, debates about the purpose of social institutions, the goods they allocate, and the virtues they honor and reward. Despite our best attempts to make law neutral on such questions, it may not be possible to say what's just without arguing about the nature of the good life. ■

Notes

1. Callie Smartt's story was reported in Sue Anne Pressley, "A 'Safety' Blitz," *Washington Post*, November 12, 1996, pp. A1, A8 . The analysis I present here draws on Michael J. Sandel, "Honor and Resentment," *The New Republic*, December 23, 1996, p. 27; reprinted in Michael J. Sandel, *Public Philosophy: Essays on Morality in Politics* (Cambridge, Mass.: Harvard University Press, 2005), pp. 97–100.
2. Aristotle, *The Politics*, edited and translated by Ernest Barker (New York: Oxford University Press, 1946), Book III, chap. xii [1282b].
3. Ibid.
4. A. A. Milne, *Winnie-the-Pooh* (1926; New York: Dutton Children's Books, 1988), pp. 5–6.
5. Aristotle, *The Politics*, Book III, chap. ix [1280b].
6. Ibid. [1280a].
7. Ibid. [1280b].
8. Ibid.
9. Ibid., [1281a]; Book III, chap. xii [1282b].
10. Ibid., Book I, chap. ii [1253a].
11. Ibid.
12. Ibid.
13. Aristotle, *Nicomachean Ethics*, translated by David Ross (New York: Oxford University Press, 1925), Book II, chap. 3 [1104b].
14. Ibid., Book II, chap. 1 [1103a].
15. Ibid. [1103a–1103b].
16. Ibid. [1003b].
17. Judith Martin, "The Pursuit of Politeness," *The New Republic*, August 6, 1984, p. 29.
18. Aristotle, *Nicomachean Ethics*, Book II, chap. 2 [1104a].
19. Ibid., Book II, chap. 9 [1109a].
20. Ibid., Book VI, chap. 6 [1140b].
21. Ibid., Book VI, chap. 7 [1141b].
22. Ibid., Book VI, chap. 5 [1140b].
23. Ibid., Book VI, chap. 7 [1141b].
24. I am indebted here to the illuminating discussion in Bernard Williams, *Shame and Necessity* (Berkeley: University of California Press, 1993), pp. 103–29.
25. Aristotle, *The Politics*, Book I, chap. v [1254a].
26. Ibid. [1254b].
27. Ibid. [1254b].

28. Ibid. (1255a].
29. Ibid., Book I, chap. vi [1254b].
30. Ibid. (1255b].
31. Ibid., Book I, chap. iii [1253b).
32. For an illuminating discussion of this point, see Russell Muirhead, *Just Work* (Cambridge, Mass.: Harvard University Press, 2004).
33. *PGA Tour v. Martin*, 532 U.S. 661 (2001).
34. Ibid., Justice Scalia dissent, at 700.
35. Ibid., Justice Stevens opinion, at 682.
36. Ibid., at 687.
37. Ibid.
38. Ibid., Justice Scalia dissent, at 701.
39. Tom Kite, "Keep the PGA on Foot," *New York Times*, February 2, 1998.

AUTHOR PROFILE

Michael J. Sandel (born March 5, 1953) is the Anne T. and Robert M. Bass Professor of Government at Harvard University, where he has taught political philosophy since 1980. Sandel graduated from Brandeis University in 1975 with a degree in politics and received his doctorate in 1981 from Oxford University where he was a Rhodes Scholar. His recent book, *What Money Can't Buy: The Moral Limits of Markets*, takes on one of the biggest ethical questions of our time: What should be the role of money and markets in our society? A recipient of the Harvard-Radcliffe Phi Beta Kappa Teaching Prize, he was recognized by the American Political Science Association in 2008 for a career of excellence in teaching. He has been a visiting professor at the Sorbonne, delivered the Tanner Lectures on Human Values at Oxford University, and in 2009 delivered the BBC Reith Lectures. In 2010, *China Newsweek* named him the "most influential foreign figure of the year" in China. Sandel served on the President's Council on Bioethics from 2002–2005.

The Key

From *Persepolis*

By Marjane Satrapi

I AGREED WITH MY MOTHER. I TOO TRIED TO THINK ONLY OF LIFE. HOWEVER, IT WASN'T ALWAYS EASY: AT SCHOOL, THEY LINED US UP TWICE A DAY TO MOURN THE WAR DEAD. THEY PUT ON FUNERAL MARCHES, AND WE HAD TO BEAT OUR BREASTS.

"Girls of iran"

AFTER A LITTLE WHILE, NO ONE TOOK THE TORTURE SESSIONS SERIOUSLY ANYMORE. AS FOR ME, I IMMEDIATELY STARTED MAKING FUN OF THEM.
THE MARTYRS! THE MARTYRS!
KILL ME!
SATRAPI! WHAT ARE YOU DOING ON THE GROUND?
I'M SUFFERING, CAN'T YOU SEE?
EVERY SITUATION OFFERED AN OPPORTUNITY FOR LAUGHS: LIKE WHEN WE HAD TO KNIT WINTER HOODS FOR THE SOLDIERS...
STOP THAT! OR I'LL CALL THE PRINCIPAL!!
...OR WHEN WE HAD TO DECORATE THE CLASSROOM FOR THE ANNIVERSARY OF THE REVOLUTION...
WHAT ARE THESE GAR-LANDS?
TOILET PAPER??
YOU'RE AS WORTHLESS AS YOUR DECORATIONS! YOU'RE WORTHLESS!! YOU HEAR ME?! WORTHLESS!!!...
POOPOO
WHO SAID THAT? WHO WAS IT? DOES SHE HAVE THE COURAGE TO STAND UP? IF NOT, YOU'LL ALL BE PUNISHED! WELL? WHO WAS IT??!!?
WE WERE COMPLETELY UNITED.
YOU'RE ALL SUSPENDED FOR A WEEK!

I THINK THAT THE REASON WE WERE SO REBELLIOUS WAS THAT OUR GENERATION HAD KNOWN SECULAR SCHOOLS. OBVIOUSLY, THEY CALLED OUR PARENTS IN.
YOUR CHILDREN HAVE NO RESPECT FOR ANYTHING. NO SELF-CONTROL! THE BASIS OF EDUCATION COMES FROM THE FAMILY!
STOP RIGHT THERE. YOU'RE SAYING THAT WE DON'T KNOW HOW TO EDUCATE OUR CHILDREN?
LISTEN, WE'RE AT WAR. A LOT OF CHILDREN DON'T EVEN HAVE SCHOOL THESE DAYS. YOURS HAVE A RARE OPPORTUNITY. SO YOU SHOULD MAKE SURE THEY'RE WELL-BEHAVED!
WELL-BEHAVED? SO THEY CAN HIT THEMSELVES TWICE A DAY??
SO THEY CAN BE COVERED FROM HEAD TO TOE?
SO THAT THEY CAN BE FORBIDDEN TO PLAY LIKE THE KIDS THEY ARE??
OH!
ANYWAY, THAT'S HOW IT IS! EITHER THEY OBEY THE LAW, OR THEY'RE EXPELLED!!
AND MAKE SURE THEY WEAR THEIR VEILS CORRECTLY...
IF HAIR IS AS STIMULATING AS YOU SAY, THEN YOU NEED TO SHAVE YOUR MUSTACHE!
MY FATHER ACTUALLY SAID THAT.

GIRLS HAD TO MAKE WINTER HOODS FOR THE SOLDIERS, BUT BOYS HAD TO PREPARE TO BECOME SOLDIERS.
HI MRS. NASRINE. YOU DON'T LOOK WELL.
MRS. NASRINE WAS OUR MAID.
SO, TELL ME, WHAT'S WRONG?
YOU OK?
NO, MY CHILD. I'M NOT OK.
YOU SEE THIS?
IT'S A PLASTIC KEY PAINTED GOLD.
THEY GAVE THIS TO MY SON AT SCHOOL. THEY TOLD THE BOYS THAT IF THEY WENT TO WAR AND WERE LUCKY ENOUGH TO DIE, THIS KEY WOULD GET THEM INTO HEAVEN.
MY GOD!
IT'S OK, CRY, LET YOURSELF GO.
I'LL MAKE SOME TEA.
I'VE SUFFERED SO MUCH. I RAISED MY FIVE KIDS WITH THE WATER OF MY TEARS, NOW THEY WANT TO TRADE THIS KEY FOR MY OLDEST SON...
ALL MY LIFE, I'VE BEEN FAITHFUL TO THE RELIGION. IF IT'S COME TO THIS... WELL, I CAN'T BELIEVE IN ANYTHING ANYMORE...
AND THE CHILD, WHAT DOES HE SAY?

THEY TOLD HIM THAT IN PARADISE THERE WILL BE PLENTY OF FOOD, WOMEN AND HOUSES MADE OF GOLD AND DIAMONDS.
WOMEN?
YEAH. WELL, HE'S FOURTEEN YEARS OLD. THAT'S EXCITING.
BRING HIM HERE, I'LL TALK TO HIM.
WELL, I'M OFF TO SCHOOL.
ON THE WAY, I THOUGHT OF MY COUSIN PEYMAN. HE WAS ALSO FOURTEEN.
WHEN I GOT BACK FROM SCHOOL...
LISTEN, CHILD, THOSE ARE JUST MADE-UP STORIES! WHAT HELL? WHAT PARADISE?
HI!
LISTEN INSTEAD OF STUFFING YOUR FACE!
THINK ABOUT WHEN YOU'RE GROWN UP. YOU WILL GO TO COLLEGE. YOU'LL BECOME SOMEBODY.
I'LL MARRY HER!
YOU IDIOT!
STOP, IT'S NO BIG DEAL!
WHAP!
I'M GOING TO MY ROOM.
HEY! PEYMAN?...WHAT?... NEXT WEEK YOU'RE HAVING A PARTY?...I'LL ASK MY MOM.
TELL ME, AT SCHOOL, DID THEY GIVE YOU THE KEYS TO PARADISE?
KEYS TO WHAT?

MOM, PEYMAN INVITED ME TO A PARTY. CAN I GO?
DING DONG
OOOH! SHAHAB!
HEY!
HI!
SHAHAB WAS ANOTHER COUSIN. HE HADN'T BEEN LUCKY: THE WAR STARTED JUST AS HE BEGAN HIS MILITARY SERVICE. THEY SENT HIM TO THE FRONT RIGHT AWAY.
I'M ON LEAVE.
COME IN, COME IN. I'LL MAKE SOME TEA.
I WAS JUST TALKING TO MY MAID. SHE SAID THEY'RE RECRUITING CHILDREN FOR THE FRONT. REALLY!!?
IT'S AWFUL. EVERY DAY I SEE BUSES FULL OF KIDS ARRIVING.
SHIT, YOU SEE THAT?
THEY COME FROM THE POOR AREAS, YOU CAN TELL...FIRST THEY CONVINCE THEM THAT THE AFTERLIFE IS EVEN BETTER THAN DISNEYLAND, THEN THEY PUT THEM IN A TRANCE WITH ALL THEIR SONGS...
IT'S NUTS! THEY HYPNOTIZE THEM AND JUST TOSS THEM INTO BATTLE. ABSOLUTE CARNAGE.

* there is always talk about struggles w/ women, while this article talks about the struggle of yong men.

AUTHOR PROFILE

Marjane Satrapi (born November 22, 1969) is an internationally acclaimed writer, illustrator, painter, and filmmaker. She is best known for her autobiographical graphic novel, *Persepolis*, from which "The Key" was excerpted. In *Persepolis* (published in multiple volumes from 2000 to 2003), Satrapi describes her experiences growing up in a liberal, wealthy family in Tehran during the Iranian revolution. The graphic novel traces her dismay at the growing fundamentalism and violence of the Revolution, the experiences of her family and community during this period, and her struggles as a young adult living in exile in Europe. Satrapi co-directed and co-wrote an animated adaptation of *Perselopis*, released in 2007, which was nominated for the Academy Award for Best Animated Feature and won the Jury Prize at the Cannes Film Festival.

Has Feminism Changed Science?

By Londa Schiebinger

Feminism has brought some remarkable changes to science. Who could have predicted just a decade ago that the chief scientist at NASA would be a woman or that the president of the foremost association of Japanese physicists would be a woman? Who would have expected to see *Science*, the premier science journal in the United States, debating whether a "female style" exists in science or the famous French physicist Marie Curie, once shunned by the prestigious Parisian Académie des Sciences, exhumed and reburied in the Pantheon, the resting place of such national heroes as Voltaire, Rousseau, and Hugo?

The current "science wars," as the unfortunate tussles between scientists and their critics are called, offer a certain measure of the successes of feminism in science. I was shocked to read in Paul Gross and Norman Levitt's *Higher Superstition* that "the only widespread, *obvious* discrimination today is against white males" (1994, 110), but I was more surprised by the depth of our agreement. Feminists and some of our most vocal opponents now agree that women should have a fair chance at careers, inside and outside academia. We agree that the "record of science, until recently, is—in its social aspect—tarnished by gender-based exclusions." We agree further that "baseless paradigms" in medicine and the behavioral sciences have been pretexts for subordinating women. "All this," Gross and Levitt claim, "is beyond dispute and generally recognized" (110). From a historical point of view, this depth of agreement marks an extraordinary change for women, who were admitted to American and European universities only about a century ago, to graduate programs even more recently, and who were told as late as 1950 that women simply need not apply for professorships in biochemistry. By this measure, we have all become feminists.

One area of disagreement remains, however, and here Gross and Levitt speak for many in proclaiming that "there are as yet no examples" of feminists uncovering sexism in the substance of science—as opposed to women merely being excluded from this or that area of inquiry. More than a decade ago when I wrote a review essay on gender and science for *Signs*, one of my purposes was to highlight feminist critiques that revealed "gender distortions" in science (Schiebinger 1987). Providing concrete examples of the multifarious ways that regimes of inequality produced and reproduced gender in the substance of science was an important project in 1987. Today, I want to highlight a different question: Has feminism changed science? After being in business for nearly two decades, what new insights, directions, and priorities have feminists—men or women—brought to the sciences?

Let me offer the examples of two sciences in which gender studies have made deep and lasting impressions: medicine and primatology. The late 1980s saw mainstream biomedicine's great awakening to women's health concerns. Feminists began to shower infamy upon several influential medical studies that omitted women completely—notably the 1982 "Physicians Health Study of Aspirin and Cardiovascular Disease" performed on 22,071 male physicians and 0 women and the "Multiple Risk Factor Intervention Trial" studying coronary heart disease in 15,000 men and 0 women. Even in studies where women were included, the male body typically represented the normal human; the female body has traditionally been studied as a deviation from that norm (Rosser 1994).

Beginning in the late 1980s, feminist reform in publicly funded biomedical research in the United States was pushed forward through strong measures taken by the federal government. In 1986 the National Institutes of Health (NIH) initiated a requirement that medical research include female subjects where appropriate, and in 1991 distinctively female health concerns began to be addressed by the fourteen-year $625 million Women's Health Initiative. The 1990 founding of the NIH Office of Research on Women's Health represented a triumph for feminism. Between 1990 and 1994, the U.S. Congress enacted no fewer than twenty-five pieces of legislation to improve the health of American women. While many feminists argue that these reforms in clinical and biomedical medicine have retained too narrow a focus on disease management, few deny the importance of the reforms undertaken within NIH (see Fee and Krieger 1994; Ruzek, Olesen, and Clarke 1997).

Similarly, primatology has undergone a sea change with respect to gender. The composition of the profession has changed dramatically from the 1960s, when American women received no Ph.D.s, to today, when they receive 78 percent of Ph.D.s in primatology granted each year.[1] But more important have been the changes in the content of the science. In primatology, as in medicine, the majority of feminist changes to date have come from reevaluations of stereotypical attitudes toward both males and females. Only in the 1960s did primatologists begin questioning stereotypes of male aggression and dominance and begin looking seriously at female behavior. They began studying the significance of female bonding through matrilineal networks and analyzing female sexual assertiveness, female social strategies, female cognitive skills, and female competition. Today, in a turnabout from the 1960s, conventional wisdom on baboons recognizes that females provide social stability, while males move from group to group. Changes in primatology have been so foundational that at least one mainstream primatologist, Linda Fedigan (1997), has pronounced it a feminist science.

Of course, feminist interventions have not occurred uniformly across all of the sciences. A lack of gender neutrality can be documented in the social, medical, and life sciences, where research objects are sexed or easily imagined to have sex and gender. The physical sciences, however, have by and large resisted feminist analysis (for a number of historically specific reasons that I have discussed elsewhere [Schiebinger 1999]). Here I turn to a different question: In the instances where positive change in science has resulted from a critical awareness of gender, what has brought success?

There is a pressing need to dispel the myth that currently has a stranglehold on many feminists and nonfeminists alike—that is, the myth that women qua

[1] I thank Trudy Turner and Linda Fedigan for these numbers. See also Fedigan 1994.

women are changing science, that women have been the primary architects of foundational disciplinary changes. The question of who or what might create beneficial change in science has been confused by Americans' distrust of feminism. For many, *feminism* is still a dirty word, even among those who support the advancement of professional careers for women. Especially within the sciences, people seem to prefer to discuss *women* rather than *feminism*. This refusal to acknowledge politics—to call a feminist a feminist—has led to a simple equating of women entering the profession with change in science. Many women scientists, however, have no desire to rock the boat, and women who consider themselves "old boys" often become the darlings of conservatives.

People often conflate the terms *women*, *gender*, *female*, *feminine*, and *feminist*. These terms, of course, have distinct meanings. A woman is a specific individual; *gender* denotes power relations between the sexes and includes men as much as it does women; *female* designates biological sex; *feminine* refers to idealized mannerisms and behaviors of women in a particular time and place; and *feminist* defines a political outlook or agenda. Emphasizing women as the crucial element in the process of change within the sciences overlooks the hard-won successes of twenty years of academic women's studies, the role of feminist men, and much else. Introducing new questions and directions into the natural sciences requires long years of training in a discipline, sustained attention to gender studies and feminist theory, the support of universities and agencies that provide funding for such work, the existence of departments that recognize that work as tenurable, and so forth.

There is no firm starting point—no Archimedean point—that, once established, will ensure progressive reform, unless it is a critical understanding of the problem, which is in large part already available. Feminists have tended to make a distinction between getting women into science and changing knowledge. Getting women in is generally considered the easier of the two tasks. However, both require tools of gender analysis. Both are institutional *and* intellectual problems. Bringing feminism successfully into science will require difficult battles and a complex process of political and social change. Science departments cannot solve the problems themselves because the problems are deeply cultural. That does not, however, let them off the hook. Change must occur in many areas: conceptions of knowledge and research priorities, domestic relations, attitudes in schools, university structures, classroom practices, the relationship between home life and the professions, and the relationships between different nations and cultures.

Government programs are also important supports in this ongoing process. Bernadine Healy a former head of NIH, put it simply: "Let's face it, the way to get scientists to move into a certain area is to fund that area" (*Science* 1995, 773). In the United States, advances in women's health research have been reinforced by laws requiring that grant applications include female participants in medical research. Similar efforts could be made to foster feminism in science nationwide. In Congress, the Morella Commission has called for a full review of women in science, and a federal bill proposed in 1993 would set up a seventeen-member commission to study the problems women face entering and succeeding in technical professions. No action has yet been taken (the two bills are still in committee); nonetheless, the groundwork for action has been laid. In Europe, the European Union set up a new commission in the spring of 1998 to oversee efforts to improve the status of women in European science.

These projects marry research on women and gender to government initiatives, a kind of mission-oriented science that is well precedented. The U.S. Manhattan Project was government-directed science aimed at securing national defense, and the Apollo Program to land men on the moon, the attempt to build, launch, and operate a space station, and the costly Human Genome Project are all examples of mission-oriented government science. Governments might launch a "Feminist Science and Engineering Initiative" aimed at analyzing gender in the content of the sciences and securing equality for women in science and technical fields. Such initiatives should be collaborative efforts joining the expertise of scientists and humanists. ■

References

Fedigan, Linda. 1994. "Science and the Successful Female: Why There Are So Many Women Primatologists." *American Anthropologist* 96:10–20.

———. 1997. "Is Primatology a Feminist Science?" In *Women in Human Evolution*, ed. Lori D. Hager, 56–75. London: Routledge.

Fee, Elizabeth, and Nancy Krieger, eds. 1994. *Women's Health, Politics, and Power: Essays on Sex/Gender, Medicine, and Public Health*. Amityville, N.Y.: Baywood.

Gross, Paul, and Norman Levitt. 1994. *Higher Superstition: The Academic Left and Its Quarrels with Science*. Baltimore: Johns Hopkins University Press.

Rosser, Sue V. 1994. *Women's Health—Missing from U.S. Medicine*. Bloomington: Indiana University Press.

Ruzek, Sheryl Burt, Virginia L. Olesen, and Adele Clarke, eds. 1997. *Women's Health: Complexities and Differences*. Columbus: Ohio State University Press.

Science. 1995. *Science* 269 (August 11): 773.

Schiebinger, Londa. 1987. "The History and Philosophy of Women in Science: A Review Essay." *Signs: Journal of Women in Culture and Society* 12(2):305–32.

———. 1999. *Has Feminism Changed Science?* Cambridge, Mass.: Harvard University Press.

AUTHOR PROFILE

Londa Schiebinger is a Professor of History of Science at Stanford University and a member of the American Academy of Arts and Sciences. She was educated at Harvard and specializes in the intersection of gender and science. She has authored and edited thirteen books, including *The Mind Has No Sex?: Women in the Origins of Modern Science* (1989), *Nature's Body: Gender in the Making of Modern Science* (1993), and *Has Feminism Changed Science?* (1999). Schiebinger currently directs Stanford's Gendered Innovations in Science, Health & Medicine, Engineering, and Environment project. The project was presented to the European Parliament in July 2013.

The Drowning Child and the Expanding Circle

By Peter Singer

To challenge my students to think about the ethics of what we owe to people in need, I ask them to imagine that their route to the university takes them past a shallow pond. One morning, I say to them, you notice a child has fallen in and appears to be drowning. To wade in and pull the child out would be easy, but it will mean that you get your clothes wet and muddy, and by the time you go home and change you will have missed your first class.

I then ask the students: do you have any obligation to rescue the child? Unanimously, the students say they do. The importance of saving a child so far outweighs the cost of getting one's clothes muddy and missing a class, that they refuse to consider it any kind of excuse for not saving the child. Does it make a difference, I ask, that there are other people walking past the pond who would equally be able to rescue the child but are not doing so? No, the students reply, the fact that others are not doing what they ought to do is no reason why I should not do what I ought to do.

Once we are all clear about our obligations to rescue the drowning child in front of us, I ask: would it make any difference if the child were far away, in another country perhaps, but similarly in danger of death, and equally within your means to save, at no great cost—and absolutely no danger—to yourself? Virtually all agree that distance and nationality make no moral difference to the situation. I then point out that we are all in that situation of the person passing the shallow pond: we can all save lives of people, both children and adults, who would otherwise die, and we can do so at a very small cost to us: the cost of a new CD, a shirt or a night out at a restaurant or concert, can mean the difference between life and death to more than one person somewhere in the world—and overseas aid agencies like Oxfam overcome the problem of acting at a distance.

At this point the students raise various practical difficulties. Can we be sure that our donation will really get to the people who need it? Doesn't most aid get swallowed up in administrative costs, or waste, or downright corruption? Isn't the real problem the growing world population, and is there any point in saving lives until the problem has been solved? These questions can all be answered: but I also point out that even if a substantial proportion of our donations were wasted, the cost to us of making the donation is so small, compared to the benefits that it provides when it, or some of it, does get through to those who need our help, that we would still be saving lives at a small cost to ourselves—even if aid organizations were much less efficient than they actually are.

I am always struck by how few students challenge the underlying ethics of the idea that we ought to save the lives of strangers when we can do so at relatively little cost to ourselves. At the end of the nineteenth century W.H. Lecky wrote of human concern as an expanding circle which begins with the individual, then embraces the family and "soon the circle... includes first a class, then a nation, then a coalition of nations, then all humanity, and finally, its influence is felt in the dealings of man [sic] with the animal world." On this basis the overwhelming majority of my students seem to be already in the penultimate stage—at least—of Lecky's expanding circle. There is, of course, for many students and for various reasons a gap between acknowledging what we ought to do, and doing it; but I shall come back to that issue shortly.

Our century is the first in which it has been possible to speak of global responsibility and a global community. For most of human history we could affect the people in our village, or perhaps in a large city, but even a powerful king could not conquer far beyond the borders of his kingdom. When Hadrian ruled the Roman Empire, his realm covered most of the 'known' world, but today when I board a jet in London leaving what used to be one of the far-flung outposts of the Roman Empire, I pass over its opposite boundary before I am even halfway to Singapore, let alone to my home in Australia. Moreover, no matter what the extent of the empire, the time required for communications and transport meant that there was simply no way in which people could make any difference to the victims of floods, wars, or massacres taking place on the other side of the globe. By the time anyone had heard of the events and responded, the victims were dead or had survived without assistance. "Charity begins at home" made sense, because it was only "at home"—or at least in your own town—that you could be confident that your charity would make any difference.

Instant communications and jet transport have changed all that. A television audience of two billion people can now watch hungry children beg for food in an area struck by famine, or they can see refugees streaming across the border in search of a safe place away from those they fear will kill them. Most of that huge audience also have the means to help people they are seeing on their screens. Each one of us can pull out a credit card and phone in a donation to an aid organization which can, in a few days, fly in people who can begin distributing food and medical supplies. Collectively, it is also within the capacity of the United Nations—with the support of major powers—to put troops on the ground to protect those who are in danger of becoming victims of genocide.

Our capacity to affect what is happening, anywhere in the world, is one way in which we are living in an era of global responsibility. But there is also another way that offers an even more dramatic contrast with the past. The atmosphere and the oceans seemed, until recently, to be elements of nature totally unaffected by the puny activities of human beings. Now we know that our use of chlorofluorocarbons has damaged the ozone shield; our emission of carbon dioxide is changing the climate of the entire planet in unpredictable ways and raising the level of the sea; and fishing fleets are scouring the oceans, depleting fish populations that once seemed limitless to a point from which they may never recover. In these ways the actions of consumers in Los Angeles can cause skin cancer among Australians, inundate the lands of peasants in Bangladesh, and force Thai villagers who could once earn a living by fishing to work in the factories of Bangkok.

In these circumstances the need for a global ethic is inescapable. Is it nevertheless a vain hope? Here are some reasons why it may not be.

We live in a time when many people experience their lives as empty and lacking in fulfilment. The decline of religion and the collapse of communism have left but the ideology of the free market whose only message is: consume, and work hard so you can earn money to consume more. Yet even those who do reasonably well in this race for material goods do not find that they are satisfied with their way of life. We now have good scientific evidence for what philosophers have said throughout the ages: once we have enough to satisfy our basic needs, gaining more wealth does not bring us more happiness.

Consider the life of Ivan Boesky, the multimillionaire Wall Street dealer who in 1986 pleaded guilty to insider trading. Why did Boesky get involved in criminal activities when he already had more money than he could ever spend? Six years after the insider-trading scandal broke, Boesky's estranged wife Seema spoke about her husband's motives in an interview with Barbara Walters for the American ABC Network's *20/20* program. Walters asked whether Boesky was a man who craved luxury. Seema Boesky thought not, pointing out that he worked around the clock, seven days a week, and never took a day off to enjoy his money. She then recalled that when in 1982 *Forbes* magazine first listed Boesky among the wealthiest people in the US, he was upset. She assumed he disliked the publicity and made some remark to that effect. Boesky replied: "That's not what's upsetting me. We're no-one. We're nowhere. We're at the bottom of the list and I promise you I won't shame you like that again. We will not remain at the bottom of that list."

We must free ourselves from this absurd conception of success. Not only does it fail to bring happiness even to those who, like Boesky, do extraordinarily well in the competitive struggle; it also sets a social standard that is a recipe for global injustice and environmental disaster. We cannot continue to see our goal as acquiring more and more wealth, or as consuming more and more goodies, and leaving behind us an even larger heap of waste.

We tend to see ethics as opposed to self-interest; we assume that those who make fortunes from insider trading are successfully following self-interest—as long as they don't get caught—and ignoring ethics. We think that it is in our interest to take a more senior better-paid position with another company, even though it means that we are helping to manufacture or promote a product that does no good at all, or is environmentally damaging. On the other hand, those who pass up opportunities to rise in their career because of ethical "scruples" about the nature of the work, or who give away their wealth to good causes, are thought to be sacrificing their own interest in order to obey the dictates of ethics.

Many will say that it is naive to believe that people could shift from a life based on consumption, or on getting on top of the corporate ladder, to one that is more ethical in its fundamental direction. But such a shift would answer a palpable need. Today the assertion that life is meaningless no longer comes from existentialist philosophers who treat it as a shocking discovery: it comes from bored adolescents for whom it is a truism. Perhaps it is the central place of self-interest, and the way in which we conceive of our own interest, that is to blame here. The pursuit of self-interest, as standardly conceived, is a life without any meaning beyond our own pleasure or individual satisfaction. Such a life is often a self-defeating enterprise. The ancients knew of the "paradox of hedonism," according to which the more explicitly we pursue our desire for pleasure, the more elusive we will find its satisfaction. There is no reason to believe that human nature has changed so dramatically as to render the ancient wisdom inapplicable.

Here ethics offer a solution. An ethical life is one in which we identify ourselves with other, larger, goals, thereby giving meaning to our lives. The view that there is harmony between ethics and enlightened self-interest is an ancient one, now often scorned. Cynicism is more fashionable than idealism. But such hopes are not groundless, and there are substantial elements of truth in the ancient view that an ethically reflective life is also a good life for the person leading it. Never has it been so urgent that the reasons for accepting this view should be widely understood.

In a society in which the narrow pursuit of material self-interest is the norm, the shift to an ethical stance is more radical than many people realize. In comparison with the needs of people going short of food in Rwanda, the desire to sample the wines of Australia's best vineyards pales into insignificance. An ethical approach to life does not forbid having fun or enjoying food and wine, but it changes our sense of priorities. The effort and expense put into fashion, the endless search for more and more refined gastronomic pleasures, the added expense that marks out the luxury-car market—all these become disproportionate to people who can shift perspective long enough to put themselves in the position of others affected by their actions. If the circle of ethics really does expand, and a higher ethical consciousness spreads, it will fundamentally change the society in which we live. ■

S

AUTHOR PROFILE

Peter Singer (born 1946) is an Australian specialist in the field of ethics and an early proponent of the animal liberation movement. Singer is a professor of bioethics at the Center for Human Values in Princeton University. The Council of Australian Humanist Societies named him the Australian Humanist of the Year in 1994. Singer is probably best known for his 1975 book *Animal Liberation*, which was a groundbreaking work in the evolution of ideas about animal rights. Currently Singer is editing a collection of essays, *Does Anything Really Matter? Parfit on Objectivity*, focused on the work of Derek Parfit. In response, Parfit is authoring a text entitled *On What Matters*. "The Drowning Child and the Expanding Circle" originally appeared in Issue 289 of *The New Internationalist* in April 1997.

Poor Teeth

By Sarah Smarsh

I am bone of the bone of them that live in trailer homes. I grew up next to Tiffany 'Pennsatucky' Doggett, the hostile former drug addict from the prison TV drama *Orange Is the New Black*. I know her by her teeth.

Pennsatucky—a scrappy slip of a woman menacing, beating and proselytising to fellow inmates—stole the show during the first season of the Netflix prison series. But amid an ensemble cast of similarly riveting, dangerous characters, it was her grey, jagged teeth that shocked viewers into repulsed fixation. She was the villain among villains, a monster that fans loved to hate; 'Pennsatucky teeth' became a pejorative in social media.

Actress Taryn Manning's gnarly, prosthetic teeth startled viewers because, by and large, poor characters in TV and film are played by actors whose whitened, straightened, veneered smiles aren't covered up. It's hard to think of characters besides Pennsatucky through whom heinous teeth convey rather than lampoon the physicality of the poor. The first that comes to mind is the derelict serial killer in a movie actually called *Monster* (2003); as with Manning, Charlize Theron's Oscar-winning transformation generated astonishment with fake teeth.

In my life, Pennsatucky and her teeth are entirely familiar. She's the slurring aunt who passed out in our farm's swimming pool while babysitting me, and later stole my mom's wedding band to buy the drugs that dug grooves in her cheeks. She's the step-parent whose brain, organs and teeth corroded over the years and now lives in a mobile-home park with my construction-worker dad.

But Pennsatucky's teeth aren't just 'meth teeth.' They are the teeth of poor folk, of the young grandma who helped to raise me and for decades worked from diner to factory line to a desk job as a probation officer for the county court system in Wichita, Kansas. She was just 35 when I was born, so I knew her as a radiant thing; at the downtown courthouse, where I tagged along—babysitters are expensive—attorneys turned flirtatious near her green eyes, long limbs and shiny, natural-blonde bob. Then at night, in her farmhouse or the tiny brick house we fixed up in a rough Wichita neighbourhood, I watched her take out her teeth, scrub them with a rough brush, and drop them into a cup of water with a fizzy tablet.

'Brush your teeth and don't eat too much candy,' she'd tell me. 'You don't want to end up like Grandma.' She'd widen her eyes and pop her dentures forward so that they bulged from her lips, sending me giggling. In the early 1970s, a dentist had pried every one of her teeth, too far gone or too expensive to save, from her 20-something skull. She's 69 now and has worn false teeth for more than 40 years.

'I had bad teeth all my life. They were straight and looked OK, but I always had toothaches,' she tells me when I ask how she ended up with dentures. As I was growing up, the story fluctuated—she was in a car accident, her natural teeth just fell out, and so on. 'I was excited to have them, knowing I would never have another toothache. Now I think it was pretty stupid, but at the time it was really painful, and I thought I was doing the right thing.'

More than 126 million people in the US—nearly half the population—had no dental coverage in 2012, according to the US National Association of Dental Plans. In 2007, the *New York State Dental Journal* reported that while only one-tenth of general physician costs were paid out of pocket, nearly half of all dental costs were settled directly by patients. This reflects spending by the uninsured but also those sharing costs with coverage providers; most plans cover routine cleanings but leave patients to pay for 20 to 50 per cent of fillings, crowns and other big-ticket visits. For those who can't afford to pay that difference, treatment is delayed and teeth continue to degrade.

But expense isn't the only barrier to dental care. Those on Medicaid find that few dentists participate in the programme due to its low payout. And more than 45 million people in the US live in areas, often rural or impoverished, with dentist shortages, according to the US Department of Health and Human Services. Medicare, as a general rule, doesn't include dental.

In the past year, the Affordable Care Act, or 'ObamaCare', has changed many lives for the better—mine included. But its omission of dental coverage, a result of political compromise, is a dangerous, absurd compartmentalisation of health care, as though teeth are apart from and less important than the rest of the body.

About a decade ago, at the age of 50, my dad almost died when infection from an abscessed tooth poisoned his blood and nearly stopped his heart. He has never had dental insurance and has seen a dentist only a handful of times when some malady became unbearable. In 2009, according to the US Agency for Healthcare Research and Quality, dental issues caused about 936,000 emergency-room visits and almost 13,000 inpatient hospital stays. Many of these patients had low incomes and dental coverage that restricted care to emergencies or wasn't accepted by accessible dentists.

'I notice people's teeth because mine are so bad,' Dad tells me during a break from a side job renovating a fraternity house. He has long been the handsome object of crushes, but his teeth have become increasingly askew with time, one of his eye teeth now ragged and long like a rabbit's for lack of a carrot to file it down. 'Nutrition affects teeth, right?'

I point out that Gatorade, which he favours when he splurges on a bottled beverage, is full of sugar. But it wasn't sugar, heaps of which are sucked down daily by the middle and upper classes, that guided his and my grandma's dental fates. And it wasn't meth. It was lack of insurance, lack of knowledge, lack of good nutrition—poverties into which much of the country was born.

My family's distress over our teeth—what food might hurt or save them, whether having them pulled was a mistake—reveals the psychological hell of having poor teeth in a rich, capitalist country: the underprivileged are priced out of the dental-treatment system yet perversely held responsible for their dental condition. It's a familiar trick in the privatisation-happy US—like, say, underfunding public education and then criticising the institution for struggling. Often, bad teeth are blamed solely on the habits and choices of their owners, and for the poor therein lies an undue shaming.

'Don't get fooled by those mangled teeth she sports on camera!' says the ABC News host introducing the woman who plays Pennsatucky. 'Taryn Manning is one beautiful and talented actress.' This suggestion that bad teeth and talent, in particular, are mutually exclusive betrays our broad, unexamined bigotry toward those long known, tellingly, as 'white trash.' It's become less acceptable in recent decades to make racist or sexist statements, but blatant classism generally goes unchecked. See the hugely successful blog People of Walmart that, through submitted photographs, viciously ridicules people who look like contemporary US poverty: the elastic waistbands and jutting stomachs of diabetic obesity, the wheelchairs and oxygen tanks of gout and emphysema.

Upper-class supremacy is nothing new. A hundred years ago, the US Eugenics Records Office not only targeted racial minorities but 'sought to demonstrate scientifically that large numbers of rural poor whites were genetic defectives,' as the sociologist Matt Wray explains in his book *Not Quite White: White Trash and the Boundaries of Whiteness* (2006). The historian and civil rights activist W E B du Bois, an African American, wrote in his autobiography *Dusk of Dawn* (1940) that, growing up in Massachusetts in the 1870s, 'the racial angle was more clearly defined against the Irish than against me. It was a matter of income and ancestry more than colour.' Martin Luther King, Jr made similar observations and was organising a poor-people's march on Washington at the time of his murder in 1968.

Such marginalisation can make you either demonise the system that shuns you or spurn it as something you never needed anyway. When I was a kid and no one in the family had medical or dental insurance, Dad pointed out that those industries were criminal—a sweeping analysis that, whether accurate or not, suggested we were too principled to support the racket rather than too poor to afford it.

My baby teeth were straight and white, and I wasn't obese—an epidemic among poor kids that hadn't yet taken hold in the 1980s—but I had plenty of 'tells': crooked bangs, trimmed at home with sewing shears; a paper grocery sack carrying my supplies on the first day of school while other kids wore unicorn backpacks; a near-constant case of ringworm infection (I kept a jar of ointment on my nightstand year-round); the smell of cigarette smoke on my clothes, just as cigarettes were falling out of favour with the middle and upper classes; sometimes, ill-fitting clothes, as when the second-grade teacher I revered looked at my older cousin's shirt sagging off my shoulder and said: 'Tell your mother to send you to school in clothes that fit you.' In fifth grade, a girl noticed my generic, plastic-smelling, too-pointy boots—a Kmart version of the black leather lace-ups that were in fashion—and for weeks hounded me before and after school, kicking dirt on my shins and calling me Pippi Longstocking.

I had moments of cool clothes and good haircuts, too, and I was a confident child who earned friends and accolades. But I still think of the boy who handed me a dessert cup from his lunch box every day when a mix-up in the free-lunch programme left me without a meal card for months.

Common throughout those years was a pulsing throb in my gums, a shock wave up a root when biting down, a headache that agitated me in classrooms. While they looked OK, my baby teeth were cavity-ridden. Maybe it was the soy formula in my bottle when they were growing in, or the sugary cereals to which my brain later turned for dopamine production in a difficult home. Maybe it was because our water supply, whether from a rural well or the Wichita municipal system, wasn't fluoridated. But richer teeth faced the same challenges. The primary reason my mouth hurt was lack of money.

Once, around third grade, an upper molar that had menaced beyond all—the worst toothache I ever had—finally rotted so thoroughly that it cracked in half while still in my jaw. Mom took me to the dentist, somehow. The pain was tremendous, he explained, because the pulpy nerve at the tooth's centre was exposed. He pulled from my skull the greyed tooth, cracked perfectly down the middle, and let me take it home. For years, I kept the two pieces in a tiny jewellery box, sometimes taking them out and joining them like interlocking sides of the heart-shaped friendship necklaces I coveted.

Around that time, I had my jaw X-rayed for the first time. The results were grim.

'You might as well start saving for braces right now,' my mom recalls the dentist saying. We were at the outset of a post-divorce period that would include much moving and a slew of partial-coverage dental insurance plans: employer-based, which would be cancelled with Mom's regular job switches, and variations on state-funded, poor-kid programmes in between. Each time the policy changed, Mom had to find a new dentist who would accept our coverage. Then we'd ride out a waiting period before scheduling a cleaning or filling. My dental records were often lost in this shuffle, as was the case with my general health files in doctors' offices and school districts—I got a new round of shots just about every year for lack of immunisation records on file.

S

There would, of course, be no saving for braces.

It took years to find out whether the X-raying dentist's pessimistic prediction would come true. My baby teeth were slow to fall out, their replacements slow to grow in. But at some point came the unequivocal, surprising verdict: my teeth grew in straight.

I don't just mean straight enough. I mean 99th-percentile straight. I mean dentists call hygienists over to take a look.

'Doesn't she have pretty teeth?' they say, my mouth under hot lamps. 'Are you sure you didn't have braces? But you whiten them, right?'

I shake my head no and in the dentist's chair tingle with the bliss of gratitude. That my environment and genes somehow conspired to shake out a bright, orderly smile is a blessing I can't explain. But I can tell you what preserved the blessing: me.

When a health teacher said brush your teeth twice a day, I brushed my teeth twice a day. When a TV commercial imparted that dentists recommend flossing daily, I flossed daily. A college room-mate once remarked on the fervour of my dental regimen. After boozy nights, when other kids were passing out, I held on, stumbled to the bathroom and squeezed paste onto a brush. However tired, however drunk, I scrubbed every side of every tooth, uncoiled a waxed string and threaded it into sacred spaces.

Poor teeth, I knew, beget not just shame but more poorness: people with bad teeth have a harder time getting jobs and other opportunities. People without jobs are poor. Poor people can't access dentistry—and so goes the cycle.

If Pennsatucky ever gets out of poverty, it will be thanks in part to a prison-yard fight in the season-one finale, when the upper-class protagonist knocks out her nasty grill; early in the second season, her rotten gums nearly toothless, she blackmails the warden into a new set of teeth. Upon incarceration, Pennsatucky traded meth for 'born-again' religious fanaticism, but her new teeth are a harbinger of a more substantive rebirth. If the eyes are the soul's windows, its door is the mouth—the fence across which pass food, drink, words, our very breath.

Privileged America, ever striving for organic purity, judges harshly the mouths that chew orange Doritos, drink yellow Mountain Dew, breathe with a sawdust rattle, carry a lower lip's worth of brown chaw, use dirty words and bad grammar. When Pennsatucky gets out of prison, she'll need respect, rehabilitation, employment. To that end, for all her praying and testifying, Pennsatucky's pearly gates might be her pearly, albeit prosthetic, whites. She cries with joy in a prison van on the way to get them, and later shows off with an over-the-top smile during laundry duty.

'You're acting a little, like, retarded,' an envious inmate tells her.

'I'm not retarded,' she says. 'I got new teeth!'

When I was a young adult, I learnt I'd been born without wisdom teeth. The dentist told me I was 'evolutionarily advanced' since human beings, no longer in the business of tearing raw flesh from mastodon bones, don't need so many teeth now. So many TV shows, bad jokes and bucktoothed hillbilly costumes in Halloween aisles had suggested that my place of origin made me 'backwards', primitive and uncivilised, that the dentist's comment struck me deeply, just as in fourth grade when I read the word 'genius' in a school psychologist's evaluation notes to my mother and wept on the sidewalk.

Having straddled a class divide and been wrongly stereotyped on both sides of it, throughout my life I've found peace in the places and things that don't evaluate my status: nature, animals, art, books. 'I sit with Shakespeare,' wrote du Bois in *The Souls of Black Folk* (1903), 'and he winces not.' Social disadvantage and hazard engender what he called 'double consciousness', the ever-present awareness of more than one self. For du Bois, his most challenging two-ness in the wake of slavery was to be educated and black—a tension of socialisation still at work, to be sure, as President Barack Obama's raw first memoir attests. Today, for me and millions of people in the US living on one side of a historic income gap, the defining double consciousness is to be educated and poor.

The latter, for many of those who suffered losses after the economic collapse of 2008, is a terrifying new identity, its horror projected on to Pennsatucky's serrated mouth and hard to reconcile with the Americans they thought they were. But in my academic and professional 'climbing', I learnt early and often that one doesn't leave a place, class or culture and enter another, but rather holds the privilege and burden of many narratives simultaneously.

Friends who know my background sometimes kid me when I'm drunk and misconjugate a verb or slip into a drawl, or when, thoroughly sober, I reveal a gross blind spot in the realm of book-learning (if, say, the question involves whatever one learns in sixth grade, most of which I spent playing in red dirt outside a two-room schoolhouse near the Oklahoma state line). They smile at the pleasure I take in scoring solid furniture from yard sales or, once, for expressing delight over a tiny cast-iron skillet, a miniature version of the pan my grandma once used to fight a drunken stepfather off her mother. I enjoy the kidding and feel appreciated when they recognise the true clichés that weave my story.

But here's the thing: wealthy people use cast-iron skillets and bad grammar, too. It's just not their narrative and thus passes without remark. I've observed fellow journalists, the same ones who made trailer-park tornado survivors famous for a loose grip on the past participle, edit dumb-sounding quotes by city commissioners to suit the speaker's stature. And while I took the education I wasn't given through libraries, encyclopedias and my former stepfather's *New Yorker* subscription, plenty of members of the middle and upper classes refuse or lack the ability to seize the opportunities handed them. It can be useful to acknowledge the cultural forces that carve us, or edifying to indulge in the tropes of our assigned narratives, but true distinctions of character, intelligence, talent and skill exist at the level of the individual, not of the class—or the ethnicity, the gender, the sexual orientation, the religion and so on. To claim otherwise, as we've discovered across time and countless persecutions of our own doing, is at best an insult and at worst an excuse for enslavement and genocide.

In Thomas Harris's best-selling crime-novel series, the FBI consults the imprisoned serial killer and mastermind psychiatrist Hannibal Lecter in its search for 'the Tooth Fairy', a family-slayer who bites his victims with dentures made from a mould of his grandmother's distorted, razor-sharp teeth. Years after that manhunt, the FBI again turns to Lecter for help; this time, the refined sociopath—a former philharmonic orchestra board member and mannerly purveyor of his victims' flesh—finds it more interesting to analyse the agent than the latest case.

S

'You know what you look like to me, with your good bag and your cheap shoes?' he asks the young agent Clarice Starling—who comes from the same place as Pennsatucky but whose intellect, health, grit and ambition, presumably, landed her on the right side of the prison bars. 'You look like a rube. A well-scrubbed, hustling rube with a little taste. Good nutrition's given you some length of bone, but you're not more than one generation from poor white trash, are you, Agent Starling? And that accent you've tried so desperately to shed: pure West Virginia. What is your father, dear? Is he a coal miner?'

Lecter's condescending soliloquy from a cell decorated with sketches of the Duomo cathedral in Florence—a place Starling surely hadn't heard of when she left her family sheep farm for the FBI Academy at Quantico—hits home but doesn't derail her. His most famous line—the aggressive posturing about fava beans and good Italian wine—happens when Starling sends a psychological evaluation through the glass and tells him to look at his damn self. We should do the same in the US, where the liberal proponents of Occupy Wall Street are often the same people who think Southerners are inbred and Walmart shoppers slovenly miscreants with no social awareness.

A century ago, du Bois wrote: 'The problem of the 20th century is the problem of the colour line.' The problem of the 21st century is that of the class line. For the American Dream to put its money where its mouth is, we need not just laws ensuring, say, universal dental care, but individual awareness of the judgments we pass on people whose teeth—or clothes, waist lines, grocery carts, or limps—represent our worst nightmares. ■

AUTHOR PROFILE

Sarah Smarsh is a journalist, speaker, and educator. She holds an MFA in nonfiction from Columbia University, has reported for *Harper's* and *The Guardian*, and has taught journalism and creative writing at Washburn University, Columbia University, and Ottawa University. Smarsh is an avid researcher on the life and culture of the state of Kansas; she is a fellow of the Center for Kansas Studies and works closely with the Kansas Humanities Council and the Kansas Arts Commission.

Miss Adele Amidst the Corsets

By Zadie Smith

Well, that's that," Miss Dee Pendency said, and Miss Adele, looking back over her shoulder, saw that it was. The strip of hooks had separated entirely from the rest of the corset. Dee held up the two halves, her big red slash mouth pulling in opposite directions.

"Least you can say it died in battle. Doing its duty."

"Bitch, I'm on in ten minutes."

"*When an irresistible force like your ass...*"

"Don't sing."

"*Meets an old immovable corset like this... You can bet as sure as you liiiiiive!*"

"It's your fault. You pulled too hard."

"*Something's gotta give, something's gotta give, SOMETHING'S GOTTA GIVE.*"

"You pulled too hard."

"Pulling's not your problem." Dee lifted her bony, white Midwestern leg up onto the counter, in preparation to put on a thigh-high. With a heel she indicated Miss Adele's mountainous box of chicken and rice: "Real talk, baby."

Miss Adele sat down on a grubby velvet stool before a mirror edged with blown-out bulbs. She was thickening and sagging in all the same ways, in all the same places, as her father. Plus it was midwinter: her skin was ashy. She felt like some once-valuable piece of mahogany furniture lightly dusted with cocaine. This final battle with her corset had set her wig askew. She was forty-six years old.

"Lend me yours."

"Good idea. You can wear it on your arm."

And tired to death, as the Italians say—tired to *death*. Especially sick of these kids, these "millennials," or whatever they were calling themselves. Always on. No backstage to any of them—only front of house. Wouldn't know a sincere, sisterly friendship if it kicked down the dressing-room door and sat on their faces.

Miss Adele stood up, untaped, put a furry deerstalker on her head, and switched to her comfortable shoes. She removed her cape. Maybe stop with the cape? Recently she had only to catch herself in the mirror at a bad angle, and there was Daddy, in his robes.

"The thing about undergarments," Dee said, "is they can only do so much with the cards they've been dealt. Sorta like Obama?"

"Stop talking."

Miss Adele zipped herself into a cumbersome floor-length padded coat, tested—so the label claimed—by climate scientists in the Arctic.

"Looking swell, Miss Adele."

"Am I trying to impress somebody? Tell Jake I went home."

"He's out front—tell him yourself!"

"I'm heading this way."

"You know what they say about choosing between your ass and your face?"

Miss Adele put her shoulder to the fire door and heaved it open. She caught the punch line in the ice-cold stairwell.

"You should definitely choose one of those at some point."

Aside from the nights she worked, Miss Adele tried not to mess much with the East Side. She'd had the same sunny rentcontrolled studio apartment on Tenth Avenue and Twenty-Third since '93, and loved the way the West Side communicated with the water and the light, loved the fancy galleries and the big anonymous condos, the High Line funded by bankers and celebrities, the sensation of clarity and wealth. She read the real estate section of the *Times* with a kind of religious humility: the news of a thirty-four-million-dollar townhouse implied the existence of a mighty being, out there somewhere, yet beyond her imagining. But down here? Depressing. Even worse in the daylight. Crappy old buildings higgledy-piggledy on top of each other, ugly students, shitty pizza joints, delis, tattoo parlors. Nothing bored Miss Adele more than ancient queens waxing lyrical about the good old bad old days. At least the bankers never tried to rape you at knifepoint or sold you bad acid. And then once you got past the Village, everything stopped making sense. Fuck these little streets with their dumbass names! Even the logistics of googling her location—remove gloves, put on glasses, find the phone—were too much to contemplate in a polar vortex. Instead, Miss Adele stalked violently up and down Rivington, cutting her eyes at any soul who dared look up. At the curb she stepped over a frigid pool of yellow fluid, three paper plates frozen within it. What a dump! Let the city pull down everything under East Sixth, rebuild, number it, make it logical, pack in the fancy hotels—not just one or two but a whole bunch of them. Don't half gentrify—follow through. Stop preserving all this old shit. Miss Adele had a right to her opinions. Thirty years in a city gives you the right. And now that she was, at long last, no longer beautiful, her opinions were all she had. They were all she had left to give to people. Whenever her disappointing twin brother, Devin, deigned to call her from his three-kids-and-a-Labradoodle, goofy-sweater wearing, golf-playing, liberal-Negro-wet-dream-of-a-Palm-Springs-fantasy existence, Miss Adele made a point of gathering up all her hard-won opinions and giving them to him good. "I wish he could've been mayor forever. FOR-EVAH. I wish he was my boyfriend. I wish he was my daddy." Or : "They should frack the hell out of this whole state. We'll get rich, secede from the rest of you dope-smoking, debt-ridden assholes. You the ones dragging us all down." Her brother accused Miss Adele of turning rightward in old age. It would be more accurate to say that she was done with all forms of drama—politics included. That's what she liked about gentrification, in fact: gets rid of all the drama.

And who was left, anyway, to get dramatic about? The beloved was gone, and so were all the people she had used, over the years, as substitutes for the beloved. Every kid who'd ever called her gorgeous had already moved to Brooklyn, Jersey, Fire Island, Provincetown, San Francisco, or the grave. This simplified matters. Work, paycheck, apartment, the various lifestyle sections of the *Times*, Turner Classic Movies, Nancy Grace, bed. Boom. Maybe a little *Downton*. You needn't put your face on to watch *Downton*. That was her routine, and disruptions to it—like having to haul ass across town to buy a new corset—were rare. Sweet Jesus, this cold! Unable to feel her toes, she stopped a shivering young couple in the street. British tourists, as it turned out; clueless, nudging each other and beaming up at her Adam's apple with delight, like she was in their guidebook, right next to the Magnolia Bakery and the Naked Cowboy. They had a map, but without her glasses it was useless. They had no idea where they were. "Sorry! Stay warm!" they cried, and hurried off, giggling into their North Face jackets. Miss Adele tried to remember that her new thing was that she positively liked all the tourists and missed Bloomberg and loved Midtown and the Central Park nags and all the Prada stores and *The Lion King* and lining up for cupcakes wherever they happened to be located. She gave those British kids her most winning smile. Sashayed round the corner in her fur-cuffed Chelsea boots with the discreet heel. Once out of sight, though, it all fell apart; the smile, the straightness of her spine, everything. Even if you don't mess with it—even when it's not seven below—it's a tough city. New York just expects so much from a girl—acts like it can't stand even the *idea* of a wasted talent or opportunity. And Miss Adele had been around. Rome says: enjoy me. London: survive me. New York: gimme all you got. What a thrilling proposition! The chance to be "all that you might be." Such a thrill—until it becomes a burden. To put a face on—to put a self on—this had once been, for Miss Adele, pure delight. And part of the pleasure had been precisely this: the buying of things. She used to love buying things! Lived for it! Now it felt like effort, now if she never bought another damn thing again she wouldn't even—

Clinton Corset Emporium. No awning, just a piece of cardboard stuck in the window. As Miss Adele entered, a bell tinkled overhead—an actual bell, on a catch wire—and she found herself in a long narrow room—a hallway really—with a counter down the left-hand side and a curtained-off cubicle at the far end, for privacy. Bras and corsets were everywhere, piled on top of each other in anonymous white cardboard boxes, towering up to the ceiling. They seemed to form the very walls of the place.

"Good afternoon," said Miss Adele, daintily removing her gloves, finger by finger. "I am looking for a corset."

A radio was on; talk radio—incredibly loud. Some AM channel bringing the latest from a distant land, where the people talk from the back of their throats. One of those Eastern-y, Russian-y places. Miss Adele was no linguist, and no geographer. She unzipped her coat, made a noise in the back of her own throat, and looked pointedly at the presumed owner of the joint. He sat slumped behind the counter, listening to this radio with a tragic twist to his face, like one of those sad-sack cab drivers you see hunched over the wheel, permanently tuned in to the bad news from back home. And what the point of that was, Miss Adele would never understand. Turn that shit down! Keep your eyes on the road! Lord knows, the day Miss Adele stepped out of the state of Florida was pretty much the last day that godforsaken spot ever crossed her mind.

Could he even see her? He was angled away, his head resting in one hand. Looked to be about Miss Adele's age, but further gone: bloated face, about sixty pounds overweight, bearded, religious type, wholly absorbed by this radio of his. Meanwhile, somewhere back there, behind the curtain, Miss Adele could make out two women talking:

S

"Because she thinks Lycra is the answer to everything. Why you don't speak to the nice lady? She's trying to help you. She just turned fourteen."

"So she's still growing. We gotta consider that. Wendy—can you grab me a Brava 32B ?"

A slip of an Asian girl appeared from behind the curtain, proceeded straight to the counter and vanished below it. Miss Adele turned back to the owner. He had his fists stacked like one potato, two potato—upon which he rested his chin—and his head tilted in apparent appreciation of what Miss Adele would later describe as "the ranting"—for did it not penetrate every corner of that space? Was it not difficult to ignore? She felt she had not so much entered a shop as some stranger's spittle-filled mouth. RAGE AND RIGHTEOUSNESS, cried this radio—in whatever words it used—RIGHTEOUSNESS AND RAGE. Miss Adele crossed her arms in front of her chest, like a shield. Not this voice—not today. Not any day—not for Miss Adele. And though she had learned, over two decades, that there was nowhere on earth entirely safe from the voices of rage and righteousness—not even the new New York—still Miss Adele had taken great care to organize her life in such a way that her encounters with them were as few as possible. (On Sundays, she did her groceries in a cutoff T-shirt that read THOU SHALT.) As a child, of course, she had been fully immersed—dunked in the local water—with her daddy's hand on the back of her head, with his blessing in her ear. But she'd leaped out of that shallow channel the first moment she was able.

"A corset," she repeated, and raised her spectacular eyebrows. "Could somebody help me?"

"WENDY," yelled the voice behind the curtain, "could you see to our customer?"

The shopgirl sprung up, like a jack-in-the-box, clutching a stepladder to her chest.

"Looking for Brava!" shouted the girl over the radio, turned her back on Miss Adele, opened the stepladder, and began to climb it. Meanwhile, the owner shouted something at the woman behind the curtain, and the woman, adopting his tongue, shouted something back.

"It is customary, in retail—" Miss Adele began.

"Sorry—one minute;' said the girl, came down with a box underarm, dashed right past Miss Adele, and disappeared once more behind the curtain.

Miss Adele took a deep breath. She stepped back from the counter, pulled her deerstalker off her head, and tucked a purple bang behind her ear. Sweat prickled her face for the first time in weeks. She was considering turning on her heel and making that little bell shake till it fell off its goddamn string when the curtain opened and a mousy girl emerged, with her mother's arm around her. They were neither of them great beauties. The girl had a pissy look on her face and moved with an angry slouch, like a prisoner, whereas you could see the mother was at least trying to keep things civilized. The mother looked beat—and too young to have a teenager. Or maybe she was the exact right age. Devin's kids were teenagers. Miss Adele was almost as old as the president. None of this made any sense, and yet you were still expected to accept it, and carry on, as if it were the most natural process in the world.

"Because they're not like hands and feet," a warm and lively voice explained, from behind the curtain. "They grow independently."

"Thank you so much for your advice, Mrs. Alexander," said the mother, the way you talk to a priest through a screen. "The trouble is this thickness here. All the women in our family got it, unfortunately. Curved rib cage."

"But actually, you know—it's inneresting—it's a totally different curve from you to her. Did you realize that?"

The curtain opened. The man looked up sharply. He was otherwise engaged, struggling with the antennae of his radio to banish the static, but he paused a moment to launch a little invective in the direction of a lanky, wasp-waisted woman in her early fifties, with a long, humane face—dimpled, self-amused—and an impressive mass of thick chestnut hair.

"Two birds, two stones," said Mrs. Alexander, ignoring her husband, "that's the way we do it here. Everybody needs something different. That's what the big stores won't do for you. Individual attention. Mrs. Berman, can I give you a tip?" The young mother looked up at the long-necked Mrs. Alexander, a duck admiring a swan. "Keep it on all the time. Listen to me, I know of what I speak. I'm wearing mine right now, I wear it every day. In my day they gave it to you when you walked out of the hospital!"

"Well, you look amazing."

"Smoke and mirrors. Now, all you need is to make sure the straps are fixed right like I showed you." She turned to the sulky daughter and put a fingertip on each of the child's misaligned shoulders. "You're a lady now, a beautiful young lady, you—" Here again she was interrupted from behind the counter, a sharp exchange of mysterious phrases, in which—to Miss Adele's satisfaction—the wife appeared to get the final word. Mrs. Alexander took a cleansing breath and continued: "So you gotta hold yourself like a lady. Right?" She lifted the child's chin and placed her hand for a moment on her cheek. "Right?" The child straightened up despite herself. See, some people are trying to ease your passage through this world—so ran Miss Adele's opinion—while others want to block you at every turn. Think of poor Mama, taking folk round those god-awful foreclosures, helping a family to see the good life that might yet be lived there—that had just as much chance of sprouting from a swamp in the middle of nowhere as anyplace else. That kind of instinctive, unthinking care. If only Miss Adele had been a simple little fixer-upper, her mother might have loved her unconditionally! Now that Miss Adele had grown into the clothes of middle-aged women, she noticed a new feeling of affinity toward them, far deeper than she had ever felt for young women, back when she could still fit into the hot pants of a showgirl. She walked through the city struck by middle-aged women and the men they had freely chosen, strange unions of the soft and the hard. In shops, in restaurants, in line at the CVS. She always had the same question. Why in God's name are you still married to this asshole? Lady, your children are grown. You have your own credit cards. You're the one with life force. Can't you see he's just wallpaper? It's not 1850. This is New York. Run, baby, run!

"Who's waiting? How can I help you?"

Mother and daughter duck followed the shopgirl to the counter to settle up. The radio, after a brief pause, made its way afresh up the scale of outrage. And Miss Adele? Miss Adele turned like a flower to the sun.

"Well, I need a new corset. A strong one."

Mrs. Alexander beamed: "Come right this way."

Together, they stepped into the changing area. But as Miss Adele reached to pull the curtain closed behind them both—separating the ladies from the assholes—a look passed between wife and husband and Mrs. Alexander caught the shabby red velvet swathe in her hand, a little higher up than Miss Adele had, and held it open.

"Wait—let me get Wendy in here." An invisible lasso, thought Miss Adele. He throws it and you go wherever you're yanked. "You'll be all right? The curtain's for modesty. You modest?"

Oh, she had a way about her. Her face expressed emotion in layers: elevated, ironic eyebrows, mournful violet eyes, and sly, elastic mouth. Miss Adele could have learned a lot from a face like that. A face straight out of an old movie. But which one, in particular?

"You're a funny lady."

"A life like mine, you have to laugh—Marcus, please, one minute—" He was barking at her, still—practically insisting, perhaps, that she *stop talking to that schwarze*, which prompted Mrs. Alexander to lean out of the changing room to say something very like: *What is wrong with you? Can't you see I'm busy here?* On the radio, strange atonal music replaced the ranting; Mrs. Alexander stopped to listen to it, and frowned. She turned back to her new friend and confidante, Miss Adele. "Is it okay if I don't measure you personally? Wendy can do it in a moment. I've just got to deal with—but listen, if you're in a hurry, don't panic, our eyes, they're like hands."

"Can I just show you what I had?"

Miss Adele unzipped her handbag and pulled out the ruin.

"Oh! You're breaking my heart! From here?"

"I don't remember. Maybe ten years ago?"

"Makes sense, we don't sell these any more. Ten years is ten years. Time for a change. What's it to go under? Strapless? Short? Long?"

"Everything. I'm trying to hide some of this."

"You and the rest of the world. Well, that's my job." She leaned over and put her lips just a little shy of Miss Adele's ear: "What you got up there? You can tell me. Flesh or feathers?"

"Not the former."

"Got it. WENDY! I need a Futura and a Queen Bee, corsets, front fastening, forty-six. Bring a forty-eight, too. Marcus—please. One *minute*. And bring the Paramount in, too! The crossover! Some people," she said, turning to Miss Adele, "you ask them these questions, they get offended. Everything offends them. Personally, I don't believe in 'political correctness.'" She articulated the phrase carefully, with great sincerity, as if she had recently coined it. "My mouth's too big. I gotta say what's on my mind! Now, when Wendy comes, take off everything to here and try each corset on at its tightest setting. If you want a defined middle, frankly it's going to hurt. But I'm guessing you know that already."

"Loretta Young," called Miss Adele to Mrs. Alexander's back. "You look like Loretta Young. Know who that is?"

"Do I know who Loretta Young is? Excuse me one minute, will you?"

Mrs. Alexander lifted her arms comically, to announce something to her husband, the only parts of which Miss Adele could fully comprehend were the triple repetition of the phrase "Loretta Young." In response, the husband made a noise somewhere between a sigh and a grunt.

"Do me a favor," said Mrs. Alexander, letting her arms drop and turning back to Miss Adele, "put it in writing, put it in the mail. He's a reader."

The curtain closed. But not entirely. An inch hung open and through it Miss Adele watched a silent movie—silent only in the sense that the gestures were everything. It was a marital drama, conducted in another language, but otherwise identical to all those she and Devin had watched as children, through a crack in the door of their parents' bedroom. God save Miss Adele from marriage! Appalled, fascinated, she watched the husband, making the eternal, noxious point in a tone Miss Adele could conjure in her sleep (*You bring shame upon this family*), and Mrs. Alexander, apparently objecting (*I've given my life to this family*); she watched as he became belligerent (*You should be ashamed*) and she grew sarcastic (*Ashamed of having a real job? You think I don't know what "pastoral care" means? Is that God's love you're giving to every woman in this town?*), their voices weaving in and out of the hellish noise on the radio, which had returned to ranting (*THOU SHALT NOT!*).

Miss Adele strained to separate the sounds into words she might google later. If only there was an app that translated the arguments of strangers! A lot of people would buy that app. Hadn't she just been reading in the *Times* about some woman who had earned eight hundred grand off such an app—just for having the idea for the app. You want to know what Miss Adele would do with eight hundred grand? Buy a studio down in Battery Park, and do nothing all day but watch the helicopters fly over the water. Stand at the floor-to-ceiling window, bathed in expensive light, wearing the kind of silk kimono that hides a multitude of sins.

Sweating with effort and anxiety, in her windowless Lower East Side cubicle, Miss Adele got stuck again at her midsection, which had become, somehow, Devin's midsection. Her fingers fumbled with the heavy-duty eyes and hooks. She found she was breathing heavily. ABOMINATION, yelled the radio. *Get it out of my store!* cried the man, in all likelihood. *Have mercy!* pleaded the woman, basically. No matter how she pulled, she simply could not contain herself. So much effort! She was making odd noises, grunts almost.

"Hey, you okay in there? "

"First doesn't work. About to try the second."

"No, don't do that. Wait. Wendy, get in there."

In a second, the girl was in front of her, and as close as anybody had been to Miss Adele's bare body in a long time. Without a word, a little hand reached out for the corset, took hold of one side of it and, with surprising strength, pulled it toward the other end until both sides met. The girl nodded, and this was Miss Adele's cue to hook the thing together while the girl squatted like a weight lifter and took a series of short, fierce breaths. Outside of the curtain, the argument had resumed.

S

"Breathe," said the girl.

"They always talk to each other like that?" asked Miss Adele. The girl looked up, uncomprehending.

"Okay now?"

"Sure. Thanks."

The girl left Miss Adele alone to examine her new silhouette. It was as good as it was going to get. She turned to the side and frowned at three days of chest stubble. She pulled her shirt over her head to see the clothed effect from the opposite angle, and in the transition got a fresh view of the husband, still berating Mrs. Alexander, though in a violent whisper. He had tried bellowing over the radio; now he would attempt to tunnel underneath it. Suddenly he looked up at Miss Adele—not as far as her eyes, but tracing, from the neck down, the contours of her body. RIGHTEOUSNESS, cried the radio, RIGHTEOUSNESS AND RAGE! Miss Adele felt like a nail being hammered into the floor. She grabbed the curtain and yanked it shut. She heard the husband end the conversation abruptly—as had been her own father's way—not with reason or persuasion, but with sheer volume. Above the door to the emporium the little bell rang.

"Molly! So good to see you! How're the kids? I'm just with a customer!" Mrs. Alexander's long pale fingers curled round the hem of the velvet. "May I?"

Miss Adele opened the curtain.

"Oh, it's good! See, you got shape now."

Miss Adele shrugged, dangerously close to tears: "It works."

"Marcus said it would. He can spot a corset size at forty paces, believe me. He's good for that at least. So, if that works, the other will work. Why not take both? Then you don't have to come back for another twenty years! It's a bargain." She turned to shout over her shoulder, "Molly, I'm right with you;' and threw open the curtain.

In the store there had appeared a gaggle of children, small and large, and two motherly looking women, who were greeting the husband and being greeted warmly in turn, smiled at, truly welcomed. Miss Adele picked up her enormous coat and began the process of re-weatherizing herself She observed Mrs. Alexander's husband as he reached over the counter to joke with two young children, ruffling their hair, teasing them, while his wife—whom she watched even more intently—stood smiling over the whole phony operation, as if all that had passed between him and her were nothing at all, some silly wrangle about the accounts or whatnot. Oh, Loretta Young. Whatever you need to tell yourself, honey. Family first! A phrase that sounded, to Miss Adele, so broad, so empty; one of those convenient pits into which folk will throw any and everything they can't deal with alone. A hole for cowards to hide in. Under its cover you could even have your hands round your wife's throat, you could have your terrified little boys cowering in a corner—yet when the bell rings, it's time for iced tea and "Family First!" with all those nice churchgoing ladies as your audience, and Mama's cakes, and smiles all round. *These are my sons, Devin and Darren.* Two shows a day for seventeen years .

"I'll be with you in one minute, Sarah! It's been so long! And look at these girls! They're really tall now!"

On the radio, music again replaced the voice—strange, rigid, unpleasant music, which seemed to Miss Adele to be entirely constructed from straight lines and corners. Between its boundaries, the vicious game restarted, husband and wife firing quick volleys back and forth, at the end of which he took the radio's old-fashioned dial between his fingers and turned it up. Finally Mrs. Alexander turned from him completely, smiled tightly at Miss Adele, and began packing her corsets back into their boxes.

"Sorry, but am I causing you some kind of issue?" asked Miss Adele, in her most discreet tone of voice. "I mean, between you and your…"

"You?" said Mrs. Alexander, and with so innocent a face Miss Adele was tempted to award her the Oscar right then and there, though it was only February. "How do you mean, issue?"

Miss Adele smiled.

"You should be on the stage. You could be my warm-up act."

"Oh, I doubt you need much warming. No, you don't pay me, you pay him." A small child ran by Mrs. Alexander with a pink bra on his head.

Without a word she lifted it, folded it in half, and tucked the straps neatly within the cups. "Kids. But you gotta have life. Otherwise the whole thing moves in one direction. You got kids?"

Miss Adele was so surprised, so utterly wrong-footed by this question, she found herself speaking the truth.

"My twin—he has kids. We're identical. I guess I feel like his kids are mine, too."

Mrs. Alexander put her hands on her tiny waist and shook her head.

"Now, that is *fascinating*. You know, I never thought of that before. Genetics is an amazing thing—amazing! If I wasn't in the corset business, I'm telling you, that would have been my line. Better luck next time, right?" She laughed sadly, and looked over at the counter. "He listens to his lectures all day, he's educated. I missed out on all that." She picked up the two corsets packed back into their boxes. "Okay, so—are we happy?"

Are *you* happy? Are you really happy, Loretta Young? Would you tell me if you weren't, Loretta Young, the Bishop's Wife? Oh, Loretta Young, Loretta Young! Would you tell anybody?

"Molly, don't say another word—I know exactly what you need. Nice meeting you," said Mrs. Alexander to Miss Adele, over her shoulder, as she took her new customer behind the curtain. "If you go over to my husband, he'll settle up. Have a good day."

Miss Adele approached the counter and placed her corsets upon it. She stared down a teenage girl leaning on the counter to her left, who now, remembering her manners, looked away and closed her mouth. Miss Adele returned her attention to the side of Mrs. Alexander's husband's head. He picked up the first box. He looked at it as if he'd never seen a corset box before. Slowly he wrote something down in a notepad in front of him. He picked up the second and repeated the procedure, but with even less haste. Then, without looking up, he pushed both boxes to his left, until they reached the hands of the shopgirl, Wendy.

"Forty-six fifty," said Wendy, though she didn't sound very sure. "Um…Mr. Alexander—is there discount on Paramount?"

He was in his own world. Wendy let a finger brush the boss's sleeve, and it was hard to tell if it was this—or something else—that caused him to now sit tall in his stool and thump a fist upon the counter, just like Daddy casting out the devil over breakfast, and start right back up shouting at his wife—some form of stinging question—repeated over and over, in that relentless way men have. Miss Adele strained to understand it. Something like: *You happy now?* Or: *Is this what you want?* And underneath, the unmistakable: *Can't you see he's unclean?*

"Hey, you," said Miss Adele, "Yes, you, sir. If I'm so disgusting to you? If I'm so beneath your contempt? Why're you taking my money? Huh? You're going to take my money? *My* money? Then, please: look me in the eye. Do me that favor, okay? Look me in the eye."

Very slowly a pair of profoundly blue eyes rose to meet Miss Adele's own green contacts. The blue was unexpected, like the inner markings of some otherwise unremarkable butterfly, and the black lashes were wet and long and trembling. His voice, too, was the opposite of his wife's, slow and deliberate, as if each word had been weighed against eternity before being chosen for use.

"You are speaking to me?"

"Yes, I'm speaking to you. I'm talking about customer service. Customer service. Ever hear of it? I am your customer. And I don't appreciate being treated like something you picked up on your shoe!"

The husband sighed and rubbed at his left eye.

"I don't understand—I say something to you? My wife, she says something to you?"

Miss Adele shifted her weight to her other hip and very briefly considered a retreat. It did sometimes happen, after all—she knew from experience—that is, when you spent a good amount of time alone—it did sometimes come to pass—when trying to decipher the signals of others—that sometimes you mistook—

"Listen, your wife is friendly—she's civilized, I ain't talking about your wife. I'm talking about *you*. Listening to your…whatever the hell that this—your *sermon*—blasting through this store. You may not think I'm godly, brother, and maybe I'm not, but I am in your store with good old-fashioned American money and I ask that you respect that and you respect me."

He began on his other eye, same routine.

"I see," he said, eventually.

"Excuse me?"

"You understand what is being said, on this radio?"

"*What?*"

"You speak this language that you hear on the radio?"

"I don't *need* to speak it to understand it. And why you got it turned up to eleven? I'm a customer—whatever's being said, I don't want to listen to that shit. I don't need a translation—I can hear the tone. And don't think I don't see the way you're looking at me. You want to tell your wife about that? When you were peeping at me through that curtain?"

"Now I'm looking at you?"

"Is there a problem?" said Mrs. Alexander. Her head came out from behind the curtain.

"I'm not an idiot, okay?" said Miss Adele.

The husband brought his hands together, somewhere between prayer and exasperation, and shook them at his wife as he spoke to her, over Miss Adele's head, and around her comprehension.

"Hey—talk in English. English! Don't disrespect me! Speak in English!"

"Let me translate for you: I am asking my wife what she did to upset you."

Miss Adele turned and saw Mrs. Alexander, clinging to herself and swaying, less like Loretta now, more like Vivien Leigh swearing on the red earth of Tara.

"I'm not talking about her!"

"Sir, was I not polite and friendly to you? Sir?"

"First up, I ain't no sir—you live in this city, use the right words for the right shit, okay?"

There was Miss Adele's temper, bad as ever. She'd always had it. Even before she was Miss Adele, when she was still little Darren Bailey, it had been a problem. Had a tendency to go off whenever she felt herself on uncertain ground, like a cheap rocket—the kind you could buy back home in the same store you bought a doughnut and a gun. Short fused and likely to explode in odd, unpredictable directions, hurting innocent bystanders—often women, for some reason. How many women had stood opposite Miss Adele with the exact same look on their faces as Mrs. Alexander wore right now? Starting with her mother and stretching way out to kingdom come. The only Judgment Day that had ever made sense to Miss Adele was the one where all the hurt and disappointed ladies form a line—a chorus line of hurt feelings—and one by one give you your pedigree, over and over, for all eternity.

S

"Was I rude to you?" asked Mrs. Alexander, the color rising in her face, "No, I was not. I live, I let live."

Miss Adele looked around at her audience. Everybody in the store had stopped what they were doing and fallen silent.

"I'm not talking to you. I'm trying to talk to this gentleman here. Could you turn off that radio so I can talk to you, please?"

"Okay," he said, "so maybe you leave now."

"Second of all," said Miss Adele, counting it out on her hand, though there was nothing to follow in the list, "contrary to appearances, and just as a point of information, I am not an Islamic person? I mean, I get it. Pale, long nose. But no. So you can hate me, fine—but you should know who you're hating and hate me for the right reasons. Because right now? You're hating in the wrong direction—you and your radio are wasting your hate. If you want to hate me, file it under N-word. As in African American. Yeah."

The husband frowned and held his beard in his hand.

"You are a very confused person. I don't care what you are. All such conversations are very boring to me, in fact."

"Oh, I'm *boring* you?"

"Honestly, yes. And you are also being rude. So now I ask politely: leave, please."

"Baby, I am out that door, believe me. But I am not leaving without my motherfucking corsets."

The husband slipped off his stool, finally, and stood up.

"You leave now, please."

"Now, who's gonna make me? 'Cause you can't touch me, right? That's one of your laws, right? I'm unclean, right? So who's gonna touch me? Miss Tiny Exploited Migrant Worker over here?"

"Hey, I'm international student! NYU!"

Et tu, Wendy? Miss Adele looked sadly at her would-be ally. Wendy was a whole foot taller now, thanks to the stepladder, and she was using the opportunity to point a finger in Miss Adele's face. Miss Adele was tired to death.

"Just give me my damn corsets."

"Sir, I'm sorry but you really have to leave now," said Mrs. Alexander, walking toward Miss Adele, her elegant arms wrapped around her itty-bitty waist. "There are minors in here, and your language is not appropriate."

"Y'all call me 'sir' one more time," said Adele, speaking to Mrs. Alexander, but still looking at the husband, "I'm gonna throw that radio right out that fucking window. And don't you be thinking I'm an anti-Semite or some shit..." Miss Adele faded. She had the out-of-body sense that she was watching herself on the big screen, at one of those screenings she used to attend, with the beloved boy, long dead, who'd adored shouting at the screen, back when young people still went to see old movies in a cinema. Oh, if that boy were alive! If he could see Miss Adele up on that screen right now! Wouldn't he be shouting at her performance—wouldn't he groan and cover his eyes! The way he had at Joan and Bette and Barbara, as they made their terrible life choices, all of them unalterable, no matter how loudly you shouted.

"It's a question," stated Miss Adele, "of simple politeness. Po-lite-ness." The husband shook his shaggy head and laughed, softly.

"See, you're trying to act like I'm crazy, but from the moment I stepped up in here, you been trying to make me feel like you don't want someone like me up in here—why you even denying it? You can't even look at me now! I know you hate black people. I know you hate homosexual people. You think I don't know that? I can look at you and know that."

"But you're wrong!" cried the wife.

"No, Eleanor," said the husband, putting out a hand to stop the wife continuing, "maybe she's a divinity. Maybe she sees into the hearts of men."

"You know what? It's obvious this lady can't speak for herself when you're around. I don't even want to talk about this another second. My money's on the counter. This is twenty-first-century New York. This is America. And I've paid for my goods. Give me my goods."

"Take your money and leave. I ask you politely. Before I call the police."

"I'm sure he'll go peacefully," predicted Mrs. Alexander, tearing the nail of her index finger between her teeth, but, instead, one more thing went wrong in Miss Adele's mind, and she grabbed those corsets right out of poor Wendy's hands, kicked the door of Clinton Corset Emporium wide open, and hightailed it down the freezing street, slipped on some ice and went down pretty much face-first.

After which, well, she had some regrets, sure, but there wasn't much else to do at that point but pick herself up and run, with a big, bleeding dramatic graze all along her left cheek, wig askew, surely looking to everyone she passed exactly like some Bellevue psychotic, a hot crazy mess, an old-school deviant from the fabled city of the past—except, every soul on these streets was a stranger to Miss Adele. They didn't have the context, didn't know a damn thing about where she was coming from, nor that she'd paid for her goods in full, in dirty green American dollars, and was only taking what was rightfully hers. ■

AUTHOR PROFILE

Zadie Smith (born 1975) is a novelist, essayist, and short story writer. Her first novel, *White Teeth* (2000), propelled her to literary fame and received esteemed awards such as the Orange Prize, the Whitbread Book Award, and the Guardian First Book Award. Although best known for exploring the complexities of racial identity in her work, Smith writes on a range of topics, including technology, reading, the writing process, and has even edited an anthology of sex writing. "Miss Adele Amidst the Corsets," runner-up for the 2014 BBC National Short Story Award, was published in the Spring 2014 issue of *The Paris Review*.

The Complexity of Identity: "Who Am I?"

By Beverly Daniel Tatum

The concept of identity is a complex one, shaped by individual characteristics, family dynamics, historical factors, and social and political contexts. Who am I? The answer depends in large part on who the world around me says I am. Who do my parents say I am? Who do my peers say I am? What message is reflected back to me in the faces and voices of my teachers, my neighbors, store clerks? What do I learn from the media about myself? How am I represented in the cultural images around me? Or am I missing from the picture altogether? As social scientist Charles Cooley pointed out long ago, other people are the mirror in which we see ourselves.[1]

This "looking glass self" is not a flat one-dimensional reflection, but multidimensional. How one's racial identity is experienced will be mediated by other dimensions of oneself: male or female; young or old; wealthy, middle-class, or poor; gay, lesbian, bisexual, transgender, or heterosexual; able-bodied or with disabilities; Christian, Muslim, Jewish, Buddhist, Hindu, or atheist…

What has my social context been? Was I surrounded by people like myself, or was I part of a minority in my community? Did I grow up speaking standard English at home or another language or dialect? Did I live in a rural county, an urban neighborhood, a sprawling suburb, or on a reservation? Who I am (or say I am) is a product of these and many other factors. Erik Erikson, the psychoanalytic theorist who coined the term *identity crisis*, introduced the notion that the social, cultural, and historical context is the ground in which individual identity is embedded. Acknowledging the complexity of identity as a concept, Erikson writes,

> We deal with a process "located" *in the core of the individual* and yet also *in the core of his communal culture*… In psychological terms, identity formation employs a process of simultaneous reflection and observation, a process taking place on all levels of mental functioning, by which the individual judges himself in the light of what he perceives to be the way in which others judge him in comparison to themselves and to a typology significant to them.[2]

Triggered by the biological changes associated with puberty, the maturation of cognitive abilities, and changing societal expectations, this process of simultaneous reflection and observation, the self-creation of one's identity, is commonly experienced in the United States and other Western societies during the period of adolescence.' Though the foundation of identity is laid in the experiences of childhood, younger children lack the physical and cognitive development needed to reflect on the self in this abstract way. The adolescent capacity for self-reflection (and resulting self-consciousness) allows one to ask, "Who am I now?" "Who was

I before?" "Who will I become?" The answers to these questions will influence choices about who one's romantic partners will be, what type of work one will do, where one will live, and what belief system one will embrace. Choices made in adolescence ripple throughout the lifespan.

Who Am I? Multiple Identities

Integrating one's past, present, and future into a cohesive, unified sense of self is a complex task that begins in adolescence and continues for a lifetime... The salience of particular aspects of our identity varies at different moments in our lives. The process of integrating the component parts of our self-definition is indeed a lifelong journey.

Which parts of our identity capture our attention first? While there are surely idiosyncratic responses to this question, a classroom exercise I regularly use with my psychology students reveals a telling pattern. I ask my students to complete the sentence, "I am ___________," using as many descriptors as they can think of in sixty seconds. All kinds of trait descriptions are used-friendly, shy, assertive, intelligent, honest, and so on—but over the years I have noticed something else. Students of color usually mention their racial or ethnic group: for instance. I am Black, Puerto Rican, Korean American. White students who have grown up in strong ethnic enclaves occasionally mention being Irish or Italian. But in general, White students rarely mention being White. When I use this exercise in coeducational settings, I notice a similar pattern in terms of gender, religion, and sexuality. Women usually mention being female, while men don't usually mention their maleness. Jewish students often say they are Jews. while mainline Protestants rarely mention their religious identification. A student who is comfortable revealing it publicly may mention being gay, lesbian, or bisexual. Though I know most of my students are heterosexual, it is very unusual for anyone to include their heterosexuality on their list.

T

Common across these examples is that in the areas where a person is a member of the dominant or advantaged social group, the category is usually not mentioned. That element of their identity is so taken for granted by them that it goes without comment. It is taken for granted by them because it is taken for granted by the dominant culture. In Eriksonian terms, their inner experience and outer circumstance are in harmony with me another, and the image reflected by others is similar to the image within. In the absence of dissonance, this dimension of identity escapes conscious attention.

The parts of our identity that *do* capture our attention are those that other people notice, and that reflect back to us. The aspect of identity that is the target of others' attention, and subsequently of our own, often is that which sets us apart as exceptional or "other" in their eyes. In my life I have been perceived as both. A precocious child who began to read at age three, I stood out among my peers because of my reading ability. This "gifted" dimension of my identity was regularly commented upon by teachers and classmates alike, and quickly became part of my self-definition. But I was also distinguished by being the only Black student in the class, an "other," a fact I grew increasingly aware of as I got older.

While there may be countless ways one might be defined as exceptional, there are at least seven categories of "otherness" commonly experienced in U.S. society.

People are commonly defined as other on the basis of race or ethnicity, gender, religion, sexual orientation, socioeconomic status, age, and physical or mental ability. Each of these categories has a form of oppression associated with it: racism, sexism, religious oppression/anti-Semitism,[4] heterosexism, classism, ageism, and ableism, respectively. In each case, there is a group considered dominant (systematically advantaged by the society because of group membership) and a group considered subordinate or targeted (systematically disadvantaged). When we think about our multiple identities, most of us will find that we are both dominant and targeted at the same time. But it is the targeted identities that hold our attention and the dominant identities that often go unexamined.

In her essay, "Age. Race. Class. and Sex: Women Redefining Difference," Audre Lorde captured the tensions between dominant and targeted identities coexisting in one individual. This self-described "forty-nine-year-old Black lesbian feminist socialist mother of two" wrote,

> Somewhere, on the edge of consciousness, there is what I call a *mythical norm*, which each one of us within our hearts knows "that is not me." In america, this norm is usually defined as white, thin, male, young, heterosexual, Christian, and financially secure. It is with this mythical norm that the trappings of power reside within society. Those of us who stand outside that power often identify one way in which we are different, and we assume that to be the primary cause of all oppression, forgetting other distortions around difference, some of which we ourselves may be practicing.[5]

Even as I focus on race and racism in my own writing and teaching, it is helpful to remind myself and my students of the other distortions around difference that I (and they) may be practicing. It is an especially useful way of generating empathy for our mutual learning process. If I am impatient with a White woman for not recognizing her White privilege, it may be useful for me to remember how much of my life I spent oblivious to the fact of the daily advantages I receive simply because I am heterosexual, or the ways in which I may take my class privilege for granted.

Domination and Subordination

It is also helpful to consider the commonality found in the experience of being dominant or subordinate even when the sources of dominance or subordination are different. Jean Baker Miller, author of *Toward a New Psychology of Women*, has identified some of these areas of commonality.[6]

Dominant groups, by definition, set the parameters within which the subordinates operate. The dominant group holds the power and authority in society relative to the subordinates and determines how that power and authority may be acceptably used. Whether it is reflected in determining who gets the best jobs, whose history will be taught in school, or whose relationships will be validated by society, the dominant group has the greatest influence in determining the structure of the society.

The relationship of the dominants to the subordinates is often one in which the targeted group is labeled as defective or substandard in significant ways. For example, Blacks have historically been characterized as less intelligent than Whites, and women have been viewed as less emotionally stable than men. The dominant group assigns roles to the subordinate that reflect the latter's devalued status, reserving the most highly valued roles in the society for themselves. Subordinates are usually said to be innately incapable of performing the preferred roles. To the extent that those in the target group internalize the images that the dominant group reflects back to them, they may find it difficult to believe in their own ability.

When a subordinate demonstrates positive qualities believed to be more characteristic of dominants, the individual is defined by dominants as an anomaly. Consider the following illustrative example. Following a presentation I gave to some educators, a White man approached me and told me how much he liked my ideas and how articulate I was. "You know," he concluded, "if I had had my eyes closed, I wouldn't have known it was a Black woman speaking." (I replied, "This is what a Black Woman sounds like.")

The dominant group is seen as the norm for humanity. Jean Baker Miller also asserts that inequitable social relations are seen as the model for "normal human relationships." Consequently, it remains perfectly acceptable in many circles to tell jokes that denigrate a particular group, to exclude subordinates from one's neighborhood or work setting, or to oppose initiatives that might change the power balance.

Miller points out that dominant groups generally do not like to be reminded of the existence of inequality. Because rationalizations have been created to justify the social arrangements, it is easy to believe everything is as it should be. Dominants "can avoid awareness because their explanation of the relationship becomes so well integrated in *other terms*; they can even believe both they and the subordinate group share the same interests and, to some extent, a common experience."[7]

The truth is that the dominants do not really know what the experiences of the subordinates is. In contrast, the subordinates are very well informed about the dominants. Even when firsthand experience is limited by social segregation, the number and variety of images of the dominant group available through television, magazines, books, and newspapers provide subordinates with plenty of information about the dominants. The dominant worldview has saturated the culture for all to learn. Even the Black or Latino child living in a segregated community can enter White homes of many kinds daily via the media. However, dominant access to information about the subordinates is often limited to stereotypical depictions of the "other." For example, there are many images of heterosexual relations on television, but very few images of gay or lesbian domestic partnerships beyond the caricatures of comedy shows. There are many images of White men and women in all forms of media, but relatively few portrayals of people of color.

Not only is there greater opportunity for the subordinates to learn about the dominants, there is also greater need. Social psychologist Susan Fiske writes, "It is a simple principle: People pay attention to those who can control their outcomes. In an effort to predict and possibly influence what is going to happen to them, people gather information about those with power."[8]

In a situation of unequal power, a subordinate group has to focus on survival. It becomes very important for subordinates to become highly attuned to the dominants as a way of protecting themselves. For example, women who have been battered by men often talk about the heightened sensitivity they develop to their partners' moods. Being able to anticipate and avoid the men's rage is important to survival.

Survival sometimes means not responding to oppressive behavior directly. To do so could result in physical harm to oneself, even death. In his essay "The Ethics of Living Jim Crow" Richard Wright describes eloquently the various strategies he learned to use to avoid the violence of Whites who would brutalize a Black person who did not "stay in his place."[9] Though it is tempting to think that the need for such strategies disappeared with Jim Crow laws, their legacy lives on in the frequent and sometimes fatal harassment Black men experience at the hands of White police officers.[10]

Because of the risks inherent in unequal relationships, subordinates often develop covert ways of resisting or undermining the power of the dominant group. As Miller points out, popular culture is full of folktales, jokes, and stories about how the subordinate—whether the woman, the peasant, or the sharecropper—outwitted the "boss."[11] In his essay "I Won't Learn from You," Herbert Kohl identifies one form of resistance, "not learning," demonstrated by targeted students who are too often seen by their dominant teachers as "others":

> Not-learning tends to take place when someone has to deal with unavoidable challenges to her or his personal and family loyalties, integrity, and identity. In such situations, there are forced choices and no apparent middle ground. To agree to learn from a stranger who does not respect your integrity causes a major loss of self. The only alternative is to not-learn and reject their wodd.[12]

The use of either strategy, attending very closely to the dominants or not attending at all, is costly to members of the targeted group. "Not-learning" may mean there are needed skills that are not acquired. Attending Closely to the dominant group may leave little time or energy to attend to one's self. Worse yet, the negative messages of the dominant group about the subordinates may be internalized, leading to self-doubt or, in its extreme form, self-hate. There are many examples of subordinates attempting to make themselves over in the image of the dominant group-Jewish people who want to change the Semitic look of their noses, Asians who have cosmetic surgery to alter the shapes of their eyes, Blacks who seek to lighten their skin with bleaching creams, women who want to smoke and drink "like a man." Whether one succumbs to the devaluing pressures of the dominant culture or successfully resists them, the fact is that dealing with oppressive systems from the underside, regardless of the strategy, is physically and psychologically taxing.

Breaking beyond the structural and psychological limitations imposed on one's group is possible, but not easy. To the extent that members of targeted groups do push societal limits—achieving unexpected success, protesting injustice, being "uppity"—by their actions they call the whole system into question.

Miller writes that they "expose the inequality, and throw into question the basis for its existence. And they will make the inherent conflict an open conflict. They will then have to bear the burden and take the risks that go with being defined as 'troublemakers.'"[13]

The history of subordinate groups is filled with so-called troublemakers, yet their names are often unknown. Preserving the record of those subordinates and their dominant allies who have challenged the status quo is usually of little interest to the dominant culture, but it is of great interest to subordinates who search for an empowering reflection in the societal mirror.

Many of us are both dominant and subordinate. As Audre Lorde said, from her vantage point as a Black lesbian, "there is no hierarchy of oppressions." The thread and threat of violence runs through all of the isms. There is a need to acknowledge each other's pain, even as we attend to our own.

For those readers who are in the dominant racial category, it may sometimes be difficult to take in what is being said by and about those who are targeted by racism. When the perspective of the subordinate is shared directly, an image is reflected to members of the dominant group that is disconcerting. To the extent that one can draw on one's own experience of subordination—as a young person, as a person with a disability, as someone who grew up poor, as a woman—it may be easier to make meaning of another targeted group's experience. For those readers who are targeted by racism and are angered by the obliviousness of Whites, it may be useful to attend to your experience of dominance where you may find it—as a heterosexual, as an able-bodied person, as a Christian, as a man—and consider what systems of privilege you may be overlooking. The task of resisting our own oppression does not relieve us of the responsibility of acknowledging our complicity in the oppression of others.

Our ongoing examination of who we are in our full humanity, embracing all of our identities, creates the possibility of building alliances that may ultimately free us all. ■

Notes

1. See C. Cooley, *Human Nature and the Social Order* (New York: Scribner, 1922). George H. Mead expanded on this idea in his book *Mind, Self, and Society* (Chicago: University of Chicago Press, 1934).
2. E. H. Erikson, *Identity, Youth, and Crisis* (New York: W. W. Norton, 1968), 22: emphasis in the original.
3. For a discussion of the Western biases in the concept of the self and individual identity, see A. Roland, "Identity, Self, and Individualism in a Multicultural Perspective," in E. P. Salett and D. R. Koslow, eds., *Race, Ethnicity, and Self: Identity in Multicultural Perspective* (Washington, D.C.: National MultiCultural Institute, 1994).
4. *Anti-Semitism* is a term commonly used to describe the oppression of Jewish people. However, other Semitic peoples (Arab Muslims, for example) are also subject to oppressive treatment on the basis of ethnicity as well as religion. For that reason, the terms *Jewish oppression* and *Arab oppression* are sometimes used to specify the particular form of oppression under discussion.

T

5. A. Lorde, "Age, Race, Class, and Sex: Women Redefining Difference," in P. S. Rothenberg, ed., *Race, Class, and Gender in the United States: An Integrated Study*, 3d ed. (New York: St. Martin's Press, 1995),446; emphasis in the original.
6. J. B. Miller, "Domination and Subordination," in *Toward a New Psychology of Women* (Boston: Beacon Press, 1976).
7. Ibid., 8; emphasis in the original.
8. S. T. Fiske, "Controlling Other People: The Impact of Power on Stereotyping," *American Psychologist* 48, no. 6 (1993), 621–28.
9. R. Wright, "The Ethics of Living Jim Crow" (1937), reprinted in P. S. Rothenberg, ed., *Race, Class, and Gender in the United States: An Integrated Study*, 3d ed. (New York: St. Martin's Press, 1995).
10. An article in the popular weekly magazine *People* chronicled the close encounters of famous black men with white police officers. Despite their fame, these men were treated as potential criminals. Highlighted in the article is the story of Johnny Gammage, who was beaten to death, by white police officers following a routine traffic stop in Pittsburgh. T. Fields-Meyer, "Under Suspicion," *People* (January 15,1996), 40–47.
11. Miller, "Domination and Subordination," p. 10.
12. H. Kohl, "I Won't Learn from You: Confronting Student Resistance," in *Rethinking Our Classrooms: Teaching for Equity and Justice* (Milwaukee: Rethinking Our Schools, 1994), 134.
13. Miller, "Domination and Subordination," 12.

AUTHOR PROFILE

Beverly Daniel Tatum (born 1954) is a clinical psychologist with an interest in race relations and identity. She received her BA in psychology from Wesleyan University, her MA and PhD in clinical psychology from University of Michigan, and an MA in Religious Studies from Hartford Seminary. She has been a faculty member at University of California in Santa Barbara and Westfield State University, served as a dean at Mount Holyoke College, and as president of Spellman College. Her major works include *Why Are All the Black Kids Sitting Together in the Cafeteria?: A Psychologist Explains the Development of Racial Identity* (1997), *Assimilation Blues: Black Families in a White Community* (2000), and *Can We Talk about Race?: And Other Conversations in an Era of School Resegregation* (2007). "The Complexity of Identity: 'Who Am I?'" comes from *Why Are The Black Kids Sitting Together in the Cafeteria?: A Psychologist Explains the Development of Racial Identity* (1997).

On the Decay of the Art of Lying

By Mark Twain [Samuel Clemens]

Essay, for discussion, read at a meeting of the historical and antiquarian club of hartford, and offered for the thirty-dollar prize.[*]

[*] Did not take the prize.

Observe, I do not mean to suggest that the *custom* of lying has suffered any decay or interruption—no, for the Lie, as a Virtue, A Principle, is eternal; the Lie, as a recreation, a solace, a refuge in time of need, the fourth Grace, the tenth Muse, man's best and surest friend, is immortal, and cannot perish from the earth while this club remains. My complaint simply concerns the decay of the *art* of lying. No high-minded man, no man of right feeling, can contemplate the lumbering and slovenly lying of the present day without grieving to see a noble art so prostituted. In this veteran presence I naturally enter upon this theme with diffidence; it is like an old maid trying to teach nursery matters to the mothers in Israel. It would not become to me to criticise you, gentlemen—who are nearly all my elders—and my superiors, in this thing—if I should here and there *seem* to do it, I trust it will in most cases be more in a spirit of admiration than fault-finding; indeed if this finest of the fine arts had everywhere received the attention, the encouragement, and conscientious practice and development which this club has devoted to it, I should not need to utter this lament, or shred a single tear. I do not say this to flatter: I say it in a spirit of just and appreciative recognition. [It had been my intention, at this point, to mention names and to give illustrative specimens, but indications observable about me admonished me to beware of the particulars and confine myself to generalities.]

No fact is more firmly established than that lying is a necessity of our circumstances—the deduction that it is then a Virtue goes without saying. No virtue can reach its highest usefulness without careful and diligent cultivation—therefore, it goes without saying that this one ought to be taught in the public schools—even in the newspapers. What chance has the ignorant uncultivated liar against the educated expert? What chance have I against Mr. Per—against a lawyer? *Judicious* lying is what the world needs. I sometimes think it were even better and safer not to lie at all than to lie injudiciously. An awkward, unscientific lie is often as ineffectual as the truth.

Now let us see what the philosophers say. Note that venerable proverb: Children and fools *always* speak the truth. The deduction is plain —adults and wise persons *never* speak it. Parkman, the historian, says, "The principle of truth may itself be carried into an absurdity." In another place in the same chapters he says, "The saying is old that truth should not be spoken at all times; and those whom a sick conscience worries into habitual violation of the maxim are imbeciles and nuisances." It is strong language, but true. None of us could *live* with an habitual truth-teller; but thank goodness none of us has to. An habitual truth-teller is simply an impossible creature; he does not exist; he never has existed. Of course there are people who *think* they never lie, but it is not so—and this ignorance is one of the very things that shame our so-called civilization. Everybody lies—every day; every hour; awake; asleep; in his dreams; in his joy; in his mourning; if he keeps his tongue still, his hands, his feet, his eyes, his attitude, will convey deception—and purposely. Even in sermons—but that is a platitude.

In a far country where I once lived the ladies used to go around paying calls, under the humane and kindly pretence of wanting to see each other; and when they returned home, they would cry out with a glad voice, saying, "We made sixteen calls and found fourteen of them out" —not meaning that they found out anything important against the fourteen—no, that was only a colloquial phrase to signify that they were not at home—and their manner of saying it expressed their lively satisfaction in that fact. Now their pretence of wanting to see the fourteen—and the other two whom they had been less lucky with—was that commonest and mildest form of lying which is sufficiently described as a deflection from the truth. Is it justifiable? Most certainly. It is beautiful, it is noble; for its object is, *not* to reap profit, but to convey a pleasure to the sixteen. The iron-souled truth-monger would plainly manifest, or even utter the fact that he didn't want to see those people—and he would be an ass, and inflict totally unnecessary pain. And next, those ladies in that far country—but never mind, they had a thousand pleasant ways of lying, that grew out of gentle impulses, and were a credit to their intelligence and an honor to their hearts. Let the particulars go.

The men in that far country were liars, every one. Their mere howdy-do was a lie, because *they* didn't care how you did, except they were undertakers. To the ordinary inquirer you lied in return; for you made no conscientious diagnostic of your case, but answered at random, and usually missed it considerably. You lied to the undertaker, and said your health was failing—a wholly commendable lie, since it cost you nothing and pleased the other man. If a stranger called and interrupted you, you said with your hearty tongue, "I'm glad to see you," and said with your heartier soul, "I wish you were with the cannibals and it was dinner-time." When he went, you said regretfully, "*Must* you go?" and followed it with a "Call again;" but you did no harm, for you did not deceive anybody nor inflict any hurt, whereas the truth would have made you both unhappy.

I think that all this courteous lying is a sweet and loving art, and should be cultivated. The highest perfection of politeness is only a beautiful edifice, built, from the base to the dome, of graceful and gilded forms of charitable and unselfish lying.

What I bemoan is the growing prevalence of the brutal truth. Let us do what we can to eradicate it. An injurious truth has no merit over an injurious lie. Neither should ever be uttered. The man who speaks an injurious truth lest his soul be not saved if he do otherwise, should reflect that that sort of a soul is not strictly worth saving. The man who tells a lie to help a poor devil out of trouble, is one of whom the angels doubtless say, "Lo, here is an heroic soul who casts his own welfare in jeopardy to succor his neighbor's; let us exalt this magnanimous liar."

An injurious lie is an uncommendable thing; and so, also, and in the same degree, is an injurious truth—a fact that is recognized by the law of libel.

Among other common lies, we have the *silent* lie—the deception which one conveys by simply keeping still and concealing the truth. Many obstinate truth-mongers indulge in this dissipation, imagining that if they *speak* no lie, they lie not at all. In that far country where I once lived, there was a lovely spirit, a lady whose impulses were always high and pure, and whose character answered to them. One day I was there at dinner, and remarked, in a general way, that we are all liars. She was amazed, and said, "Not *all*?" It was before "Pinafore's" time so I did not make the response which would naturally follow in our day, but frankly said, "Yes, *all*—we are all liars. There are no exceptions." She looked almost offended, "Why, do you include *me*?" "Certainly," I said. "I think you even rank as an expert." She said "Sh-'sh! the children!" So the subject was changed in deference to the children's presence, and we went on talking about other things. But as soon as the young people were out of the way, the lady came warmly back to the matter and said, "I have made a rule of my life to never tell a lie; and I have never departed from it in a single instance." I said, "I don't mean the least harm or disrespect, but really you have been lying like smoke ever since I've been sitting here. It has caused me a good deal of pain, because I'm not used to it." She required of me an instance—just a single instance. So I said—

"Well, here is the unfilled duplicate of the blank, which the Oakland hospital people sent to you by the hand of the sick-nurse when she came here to nurse your little nephew through his dangerous illness. This blank asks all manners of questions as to the conduct of that sick-nurse: 'Did she ever sleep on her watch? Did she ever forget to give the medicine?' and so forth and so on. You are warned to be very careful and explicit in your answers, for the welfare of the service requires that the nurses be promptly fined or otherwise punished for derelictions. You told me you were perfectly delighted with this nurse —that she had a thousand perfections and only one fault: you found you never could depend on her wrapping Johnny up half sufficiently while he waited in a chilly chair for her to rearrange the warm bed. You filled up the duplicate of this paper, and sent it back to the hospital by the hand of the nurse. How did you answer this question—'Was the nurse at any time guilty of a negligence which was likely to result in the patient's taking cold?' Come—everything is decided by a bet here in California: ten dollars to ten cents you lied when you answered that question." She said, "I didn't; *I left it blank!*" "Just so—you have told a *silent* lie; you have left it to be inferred that you had no fault to find in that matter." She said, "Oh, was that a lie? And *how* could I mention her one single fault, and she is so good?—It would have been cruel." I said, "One ought always to lie, when one can do good by it; your impulse was right, but your judgment was crude; this comes of unintelligent practice. Now observe the results of this inexpert deflection of yours. You know Mr. Jones's Willie is lying very low with scarlet-fever; well, your recommendation was so enthusiastic that that girl is there nursing him, and the worn-out family have all been trustingly sound asleep for the last fourteen hours, leaving their darling with full confidence in those fatal hands, because you, like young George Washington, have a reputa—However, if you are not going to have anything to do, I will come around to-morrow and we'll attend the funeral together, for, of course, you'll naturally feel a peculiar interest in Willie's case—as personal a one, in fact, as the undertaker."

But that was not all lost. Before I was half-way through she was in a carriage and making thirty miles an hour toward the Jones mansion to save what was left of Willie and tell all she knew about the deadly nurse. All of which was unnecessary, as Willie wasn't sick; I had been lying myself. But that same day, all the same, she sent a line to the hospital which filled up the neglected blank, and stated the *facts*, too, in the squarest possible manner.

Now, you see, this lady's fault was *not* in lying, but in lying injudiciously. She should have told the truth, *there*, and made it up to the nurse with a fraudulent compliment further along in the paper. She could have said, "In one respect this sick-nurse is perfection—when she is on the watch, she never snores." Almost any little pleasant lie would have taken the sting out of that troublesome but necessary expression of the truth.

Lying is universal—we *all* do it. Therefore, the wise thing is for us diligently to train ourselves to lie thoughtfully, judiciously; to lie with a good object, and not an evil one; to lie for others' advantage, and not our own; to lie healingly, charitably, humanely, not cruelly, hurtfully, maliciously; to lie gracefully and graciously, not awkwardly and clumsily; to lie firmly, frankly, squarely, with head erect, not haltingly, tortuously, with pusillanimous mien, as being ashamed of our high calling. Then shall we be rid of the rank and pestilent truth that is rotting the land; then shall we be great and good and beautiful, and worthy dwellers in a world where even benign Nature habitually lies, except when she promises execrable weather. Then—But am I but a new and feeble student in this gracious art; I cannot instruct *this* club.

Joking aside, I think there is much need of wise examination into what sorts of lies are best and wholesomest to be indulged, seeing we *must* all lie and we *do* all lie, and what sorts it may be best to avoid—and this is a thing which I feel I can confidently put into the hands of this experienced Club—a ripe body, who may be termed, in this regard, and without undue flattery, Old Masters. ■

AUTHOR PROFILE

Mark Twain (1835–1910) was the pen name of American author and humorist Samuel Clemens. He was born in Missouri and grew up along the Mississippi River. Twain wrote novels, travel books, essays, and short stories, but he is probably best known for works such as *The Adventures of Tom Sawyer* (1876) and *The Adventures of Huckleberry Finn* (1884). Twain was a sharp critic of Gilded Age politics, American imperialism, and the foibles of human nature. "On the Decay of the Art of Lying" was first read at a meeting of the Historical and Antiquarian Club of Hartford, where it was offered up for discussion and for thirty dollars in prize money. It did not win. Today the essay has been published in *Mark Twain: Collected Tales, Sketches, Speeches, and Essays, 1852–1890.*

You did not build the city of Richmond

By August Wade

September 21, 2014

The first time, I wasn't sure I read the shirt right. Maybe it was a Jefferson Starship reference, and it could be just that. But context matters and seeing two white students wearing VCU shirts with the words "We built this city" is frustrating, to say the least.

Don't misconstrue this as a direct attack of or on the student alumni association or individuals that choose to wear these shirts, but rather, an attack on the ethos, audacity and general historical ignorance permeating through some parts of VCU, both in reference to the institution and individuals. Undoubtedly, VCU functions as a strong addition to the city of Richmond, helping to boost the municipal economy by creating jobs, infrastructure projects and maintaining a student populace and their relevant needs (food, housing, etc.), but VCU didn't build this city; slaves and a system of slavery did.

It's crucial to remember that fact. Ignoring it allows us to live in an undeserved bliss, a kind of daze that allows wealthy interests to build parking lots over slave burial grounds and idolize Confederate military officers through numerous statutes.

The city of Richmond has an ugly history of racism, continued discrimination, class-based oppression, gentrification and other ills; I would not wish for VCU to take on that same history by allying itself with the message that a collective "we" built this city. This city, as well as this nation, was built on the genocide of Native Americans and the metaphysical destruction and enslavement of blacks. Layered onto that is Richmond's time as the capital of the Confederacy, an aggressive actor of the slave trade and a participant in disenfranchisement laws.

That's the foundation of the ground we walk on.

The achievements of black people in America, both modern day and enslaved, are routinely forgotten, especially by whites, as a matter of convenient ignorance. To live with eyes wide shut and to address issues of race by saying, "I'm colorblind" exclusively serves to perpetuate a status quo of misinformation. It is a sinful action that ignores and undermines truth to help people feel better. The past is not dead. History lives and acts upon us; even though we cannot see it, it influences us, changes us, exalts us, vilifies us and defines us.

Although it might be frustrating and difficult to accept, you didn't build that. Aside from the inhuman toil that created this country's structural foundation, a myriad of factors built this city, including but not limited to taxpayer money, honest labor, legislation, committees, grassroots organizations and petitions.

It would behoove certain members of our community to educate themselves on the history of Richmond before asserting VCU's dominance in the role of the construction of the city, whether the comment is meant metaphorically or otherwise. The city is a separate entity from VCU, and without Richmond, there would be no VCU. The fraudulent claim that "we built this city" downplays the city as a municipality and implies that Richmond is lucky to have us, when, indeed, it is we who are fortunate to have Richmond, a city underpinned by a shameful history, but working toward righting past wrongs and progressing itself into a thriving, truly diverse community. ■

Follow-up on "You did not build the city of Richmond"

By August Wade

September 26, 2014

In the column, "You did not build the city of Richmond," a few very vocal individuals insisted that my column was somehow petty and inaccurate because I stated that slaves built the city of Richmond.

To them, I offer no apology. I was and am correct. The truth of the matter is that enslaved blacks both physically and metaphorically built this city.

What I do need to do, however, is offer an extended elaboration and an unnecessary clarification: Slave labor did not exclusively physically construct the entirety of the city of Richmond.

I take offense to the shirts for two reasons: As a black person, I take offense because it embodies the ethos of white southerner historical negationist who, generally speaking, claim that "slavery wasn't so bad," (it was a genocide against black people that involved unwarranted executions, sexual abuse, slave breeding, the destruction of cultural identity, family displacement, inhuman living conditions and general dehumanizing practices, among other crimes) and that "the Confederacy wanted to get rid of slavery," (inaccurate for a number of reasons, but the fact that the Confederate vice president, Alexander Stephens, believed slavery was the ideological corner-stone of the Confederate government should speak volumes); as a current (and temporary) Richmond resident, I take offense because it's factually and metaphorically inaccurate.

When I say slaves built the city of Richmond, I am afraid I did not accurately articulate the truth as it should be known. In "Built by Blacks: African-American Architecture and Neighborhoods in Richmond," by Selden Richardson and Maurice Duke, the authors clearly state the role of slave labor in the construction of the city of Richmond: "Through their forced labor, African American slaves played a major role in shaping the physical appearance and moral structure of Richmond long before it was incorporate as a city in 1782…[They] furnished much of the unskilled labor that dug Richmond's canals, constructed buildings and manned the growing number of heavy industries. clustered along the banks of the James River."

Slaves built the city of Richmond, from before it was a city, thus making it viable to incorporate as a city, and metaphorically after they'd been forced to physically construct the city by acting as Richmond's economic engine.

To further emphasize the point on slavery's economic impact, Professor Midori Takagi states in her 1999 book "Rearing Wolves to Our Own Destruction: Slavery in Richmond, Virginia, 1782–1865," that "slave labor that made tobacco manufacturing (the backbone of Richmond's antebellum economy) a multimilliondollar industry by 1860 and greatly contributed to the growth of a range of other industries."

W

It is interest to note that Takagi also found urban slaves in Richmond "highly skilled workers. Richmond slaves were not ordinary field hands, but craftsmen, ironmakers, blacksmiths, tailors, and tobacco processors," showing that they weren't just the economic engineers that made the establishment of Richmond and the antebellum American economy functional, but were physically involved with the construction of the nation and the city.

These are the clear, plain facts: Slaves built Richmond and slavery built Richmond, directly through forced labor and indirectly, by being an economic force and industry.

Without the kidnapping and enslavement of blacks (who would later become African Americans) by white Europeans, and the white European-inflicted genocide of indigenous tribes (that are collectively and colloquially known as Native Americans), there would be no America as we know it today. There would be no plantations, no booming industrial economy, no White House, no United States of America.

I don't hate to say "I told you so."

As an aside, as we all know, slavery did exist in Africa and throughout the world before the Transatlantic slave trade began. That point has little to nothing to do with my column or claims. Just because something is the norm doesn't make it correct or somehow excusable. If, in a hypothetical world, the roles were reversed, I assure you my moral compass would be critical of my own people for their hypothetical role in inflicting a human and metaphysical genocide onto a people.

But that is entirely hypothetical and irrelevant to reality. The reality is that white Europeans enslaved, traded, murdered, mutilated, dehumanized and enacted a multi-generational genocide against persons of color and varying ethnicities throughout the globe for hundreds of years, the effects of which still reverberate today. That is the subject of history and reality. To in any way temper, detract or diminish that history in favor of the oppressors is racist, offensive and inexcusable.

Furthermore, and to that point, the fact that Irish people were also enslaved doesn't make the genocide against blacks any less significant, so much as it further highlights the inhumanity of white Europeans. While the subject of Irish enslavement is, in my opinion, under-discussed, it is not germane to the column for a number of reasons (additionally, historian Noel Ignatiev has written a fine book detailing how the Irish became white, conveniently titled "How the Irish Became White," by enacting violence against free blacks and supporting slavery). Anyone defending their beliefs regarding the treatment and status of enslaved blacks by highlighting the Irish or other white slaves is working in a false equivalency.

It seems generally agreed upon by commenters that the shirt is a bit silly, and I do understand why people would think me shallow for attacking a shirt (as a side note, an example of me being shallow or petty would be writing about my disdain for people riding Razor scooters around campus, something I did actually do). But it's not about the shirt. It's about the message, the arrogance and the ethos that created it.

As I have stated in previous columns throughout the years, VCU has and continues to be a driving force in the city of Richmond. What it has not done, however, is build or rebuild this city. This city has fostered VCU's growth, given VCU a structure and provided VCU a community to further the betterment of both university students and residents. Richmond is VCU's home, not the other way around. To assert otherwise, as the message on the shirts does, is yuppie egocentrism. It glorifies the temporary residents that VCU students often are at the expense of misaligning the truth for the sake of attractiveness and to profit. It's pseudo-revisionism, printed onto a T-shirt. "We helped revitalize this city" may not have the same ring to it, but at least it's honest and doesn't prize referentiality and profit over respect.

I'm not saying we should burn the shirts or that they're racist. Do wear the shirt, if you wish. It is your right as an American to do so and black foremothers and forefathers died so that you may have the right to do so.

If you do, remember what you're wearing is a bold-print lie, a disrespectful, offensive assertion and an ignorant statement to make. I'm saying they're disrespectful to Richmond's current residents and irreverent to the history of Richmond. I'm saying you know nothing about this city or this university. I'm saying you should be ashamed of yourself. ■

AUTHOR PROFILE

August Wade (VCU '15, English) came to Richmond, Virginia by way of Brooklyn, New York and completed his undergraduate degree in English at Virginia Commonwealth University. At the beginning of his senior year, he published the editorial, "You did not build this city," commenting on the racial politics of a T-shirt distributed by VCU student organization Students Today Alumni Tomorrow (STAT). The editorial set off a furious debate about race, history, and VCU's position in the city of Richmond. Wade followed up that editorial with subsequent pieces in both the *Commonwealth Times* and *Style Weekly*, in which he expanded his research and analysis. The original editorial was shared thousands of times on social media, and the controversy earned national media attention. Outside of his editorial work, Wade has written short (perpetually unfinished) stories, enjoys consulting people on their own writing, and looks forward to starting his own publication in the future.

Consider the Lobster

By David Foster Wallace

The enormous, pungent, and extremely well marketed Maine Lobster Festival is held every late July in the state's midcoast region, meaning the western side of Penobscot Bay, the nerve stem of Maine's lobster industry. What's called the midcoast runs from Owl's Head and Thomaston in the south to Belfast in the north. (Actually, it might extend all the way up to Bucksport, but we were never able to get farther north than Belfast on Route 1, whose summer traffic is, as you can imagine, unimaginable.) The region's two main communities are Camden, with its very old money and yachty harbor and five-star restaurants and phenomenal B&Bs, and Rockland, a serious old fishing town that hosts the Festival every summer in historic Harbor Park, right along the water.[1]

Tourism and lobster are the midcoast region's two main industries, and they're both warm-weather enterprises, and the Maine Lobster Festival represents less an intersection of the industries than a deliberate collision, joyful and lucrative and loud. The assigned subject of this article is the 56th Annual MLF, July 30 to August 3, 2003, whose official theme was "Lighthouses, Laughter, and Lobster." Total paid attendance was over 80,000, due partly to a national CNN spot in June during which a Senior Editor of a certain other epicurean magazine hailed the MLF as one of the best food-themed festivals in the world. 2003 Festival highlights: concerts by Lee Ann Womack and Orleans, annual Maine Sea Goddess beauty pageant, Saturday's big parade, Sunday's William G. Atwood Memorial Crate Race, annual Amateur Cooking Competition, carnival rides and midway attractions and food booths, and the MLF's Main Eating Tent, where something over 25,000 pounds of fresh-caught Maine lobster is consumed after preparation in the World's Largest Lobster Cooker near the grounds' north entrance. Also available are lobster rolls, lobster turnovers, lobster sauté, Down East lobster salad, lobster bisque, lobster ravioli, and deep-fried lobster dumplings. Lobster Thermidor is obtainable at a sit-down restaurant called The Black Pearl on Harbor Park's northwest wharf. A large all-pine booth sponsored by the Maine Lobster Promotion Council has free pamphlets with recipes, eating tips, and Lobster Fun Facts. The winner of Friday's Amateur Cooking Competition prepares Saffron Lobster Ramekins, the recipe for which is available for public downloading at www.mainelobsterfestival.com. There are lobster T-shirts and lobster bobblehead dolls and inflatable lobster pool toys and clamp-on lobster hats with big scarlet claws that wobble on springs. Your assigned correspondent saw it all, accompanied by one girlfriend and both his own parents—one of which parents was actually born and raised in Maine, albeit in the extreme northern inland part, which is potato country and a world away from the touristic midcoast.[2]

For practical purposes, everyone knows what a lobster is. As usual, though, there's much more to know than most of us care about—it's all a matter of what your interests are. Taxonomically speaking, a lobster is a marine crustacean of the family Homaridae, characterized by five pairs of jointed legs, the first pair terminating in large pincerish claws used for subduing prey. Like many other species of benthic carnivore, lobsters are both hunters and scavengers. They have stalked eyes, gills on their legs, and antennae. There are dozens of different kinds worldwide, of which the relevant species here is the Maine lobster, *Homarus americanus*. The name "lobster" comes from the Old English *loppestre*, which is thought to be a corrupt form of the Latin word for locust combined with the Old English *loppe*, which meant spider.

Moreover, a crustacean is an aquatic arthropod of the class Crustacea, which comprises crabs, shrimp, barnacles, lobsters, and freshwater crayfish. All this is right there in the encyclopedia. And an arthropod is an invertebrate member of the phylum Arthropoda, which phylum covers insects, spiders, crustaceans, and centipedes/millipedes, all of whose main commonality, besides the absence of a centralized brain-spine assembly, is a chitinous exoskeleton composed of segments, to which appendages are articulated in pairs.

The point is that lobsters are basically giant sea-insects.[3] Like most arthropods, they date from the Jurassic period, biologically so much older than mammalia that they might as well be from another planet. And they are—particularly in their natural brown-green state, brandishing their claws like weapons and with thick antennae awhip—not nice to look at. And it's true that they are garbagemen of the sea, eaters of dead stuff,[4] although they'll also eat some live shellfish, certain kinds of injured fish, and sometimes each other.

But they are themselves good eating. Or so we think now. Up until sometime in the 1800s, though, lobster was literally low-class food, eaten only by the poor and institutionalized. Even in the harsh penal environment of early America, some colonies had laws against feeding lobsters to inmates more than once a week because it was thought to be cruel and unusual, like making people eat rats. One reason for their low status was how plentiful lobsters were in old New England. "Unbelievable abundance" is how one source describes the situation, including accounts of Plymouth pilgrims wading out and capturing all they wanted by hand, and of early Boston's seashore being littered with lobsters after hard storms—these latter were treated as a smelly nuisance and ground up for fertilizer. There is also the fact that premodern lobster was often cooked dead and then preserved, usually packed in salt or crude hermetic containers. Maine's earliest lobster industry was based around a dozen such seaside canneries in the 1840s, from which lobster was shipped as far away as California, in demand only because it was cheap and high in protein, basically chewable fuel.

Now, of course, lobster is posh, a delicacy, only a step or two down from caviar. The meat is richer and more substantial than most fish, its taste subtle compared to the marine-gaminess of mussels and clams. In the U.S. pop-food imagination, lobster is now the seafood analog to steak, with which it's so often twinned as Surf 'n' Turf on the really expensive part of the chain steak house menu.

In fact, one obvious project of the MLF, and of its omnipresently sponsorial Maine Lobster Promotion Council, is to counter the idea that lobster is unusually luxe or rich or unhealthy or expensive, suitable only for effete palates or the occasional blow-the-diet treat. It is emphasized over and over in presentations and pamphlets at the Festival that Maine lobster meat has fewer calories, less cholesterol, and less saturated fat than chicken.[5] And in the Main Eating Tent, you can get a "quarter" (industry shorthand for a 1‰-pound lobster), a 4-ounce cup of melted butter, a bag of chips, and a soft roll w/ butter-pat for around $12.00, which is only slightly more expensive than supper at McDonald's.

Be apprised, though, that the Main Eating Tent's suppers come in Styrofoam trays, and the soft drinks are iceless and flat, and the coffee is convenience-store coffee in yet more Styrofoam, and the utensils are plastic (there are none of the special long skinny forks for pushing out the tail meat, though a few savvy diners bring their own). Nor do they give you near enough napkins, considering how messy lobster is to eat, especially when you're squeezed onto benches alongside children of various ages and vastly different levels of fine-motor development—not to mention the people who've somehow smuggled in their own beer in enormous aisle-blocking coolers, or who all of a sudden produce their own plastic tablecloths and try to spread them over large portions of tables to try to reserve them (the tables) for their little groups. And so on. Any one example is no more than a petty inconvenience, of course, but the MLF turns out to be full of irksome little downers like this—see for instance the Main Stage's headliner shows, where it turns out that you have to pay $20 extra for a folding chair if you want to sit down; or the North Tent's mad scramble for the NyQuil-cup-size samples of finalists' entries handed out after the Cooking Competition; or the much-touted Maine Sea Goddess pageant finals, which turn out to be excruciatingly long and to consist mainly of endless thanks and tributes to local sponsors. What the Maine Lobster Festival really is is a midlevel county fair with a culinary hook, and in this respect it's not unlike Tidewater crab festivals, Midwest corn festivals, Texas chili festivals, etc., and shares with these venues the core paradox of all teeming commercial demotic events: It's not for everyone.[6] Nothing against the aforementioned euphoric Senior Editor, but I'd be surprised if she'd spent much time here in Harbor Park, watching people slap canal-zone mosquitoes as they eat deep-fried Twinkies and watch Professor Paddywhack, on six-foot stilts in a raincoat with plastic lobsters protruding from all directions on springs, terrify their children.

Lobster is essentially a summer food. This is because we now prefer our lobsters fresh, which means they have to be recently caught, which for both tactical and economic reasons takes place at depths of less than 25 fathoms. Lobsters tend to be hungriest and most active (i.e., most trappable) at summer water temperatures of 45–50°F. In the autumn, some Maine lobsters migrate out into deeper water, either for warmth or to avoid the heavy waves that pound New England's coast all winter. Some burrow into the bottom. They might hibernate; nobody's sure. Summer is also lobsters' molting season—specifically early- to mid-July. Chitinous arthropods grow by molting, rather the way people have to buy bigger clothes as they age and gain weight. Since lobsters can live to be over 100, they can also get to be quite large, as in 20 pounds or more—though truly senior lobsters are rare now, because New England's waters are so heavily trapped.[7] Anyway, hence the culinary distinction between hard- and soft-shell lobsters, the latter sometimes a.k.a. shedders. A soft-shell lobster is one that has recently molted. In midcoast restaurants, the summer menu often offers both kinds, with shedders being slightly cheaper even though they're easier to dismantle and the meat is allegedly sweeter. The reason for the discount is that a molting lobster uses a layer of seawater for insulation while its new shell is hardening, so there's slightly less actual meat when you crack open a shedder, plus a redolent gout of water that gets all over everything and can sometimes jet out lemonlike and catch a tablemate right in the eye. If it's winter or you're buying lobster someplace far from New England, on the other hand, you can almost bet that the lobster is a hard-shell, which for obvious reasons travel better.

As an à la carte entrée, lobster can be baked, broiled, steamed, grilled, sautéed, stir-fried, or microwaved. The most common method, though, is boiling. If you're someone who enjoys having lobster at home, this is probably the way you do it, since boiling is so easy. You need a large kettle w/ cover, which you fill about half full with water (the standard advice is that you want 2.5 quarts of water per lobster). Seawater is optimal, or you can add two tbsp salt per quart from the tap. It also helps to know how much your lobsters weigh. You get the water boiling, put in the lobsters one at a time, cover the kettle, and bring it back up to a boil. Then you bank the heat and let the kettle simmer—ten minutes for the first pound of lobster, then three minutes for each pound after that. (This is assuming you've got hard-shell lobsters, which, again, if you don't live between Boston and Halifax, is probably what you've got. For shedders, you're supposed to subtract three minutes from the total.) The reason the kettle's lobsters turn scarlet is that boiling somehow suppresses every pigment in their chitin but one. If you want an easy test of whether the lobsters are done, you try pulling on one of their antennae—if it comes out of the head with minimal effort, you're ready to eat.

A detail so obvious that most recipes don't even bother to mention it is that each lobster is supposed to be alive when you put it in the kettle. This is part of lobster's modern appeal: It's the freshest food there is. There's no decomposition between harvesting and eating. And not only do lobsters require no cleaning or dressing or plucking (though the mechanics of actually eating them are a different matter), but they're relatively easy for vendors to keep alive. They come up alive in the traps, are placed in containers of seawater, and can, so long as the water's aerated and the animals' claws are pegged or banded to keep them from tearing one another up under the stresses of captivity,[8] survive right up until they're boiled. Most of us have been in supermarkets or restaurants that feature tanks of live lobster, from which you can pick out your supper while it watches you point. And part of the overall spectacle of the Maine Lobster Festival is that you can see actual lobstermen's vessels docking at the wharves along the northeast grounds and unloading freshly caught product, which is transferred by hand or cart 100 yards to the great clear tanks stacked up around the Festival's cooker—which is, as mentioned, billed as the World's Largest Lobster Cooker and can process over 100 lobsters at a time for the Main Eating Tent.

So then here is a question that's all but unavoidable at the World's Largest Lobster Cooker, and may arise in kitchens across the U.S.: Is it all right to boil a sentient creature alive just for our gustatory pleasure? A related set of concerns: Is the previous question irksomely PC or sentimental? What does "all right" even mean in this context? Is it all just a matter of individual choice?

As you may or may not know, a certain well-known group called People for the Ethical Treatment of Animals thinks that the morality of lobster-boiling is not just a matter of individual conscience. In fact, one of the very first things we hear about the MLF...well, to set the scene: We're coming in by cab from the almost indescribably odd and rustic Knox County Airport[9] very late on the night before the Festival opens, sharing the cab with a wealthy political consultant who lives on Vinalhaven Island in the bay half the year (he's headed for the island ferry in Rockland). The consultant and cabdriver are responding to informal journalistic probes about how people who live in the midcoast region actually view the MLF, as in is the Festival just a big-dollar tourist thing or is it something local residents look forward to attending, take genuine civic pride in, etc. The cabdriver—who's in his seventies, one of apparently a whole platoon of retirees the cab company puts on to help with the summer rush, and wears a U.S.-flag lapel pin, and drives in what can only be called a very deliberate way—assures us that locals do endorse and enjoy the MLF, although he himself hasn't gone in years, and now come to think of it no one he and his wife know has, either. However, the demilocal consultant's been to recent Festivals a couple times (one gets the impression it was at his wife's behest), of which his most vivid impression was that "you have to line up for an ungodly long time to get your lobsters, and meanwhile there are all these ex-flower children coming up and down along the line handing out pamphlets that say the lobsters die in terrible pain and you shouldn't eat them."

And it turns out that the post-hippies of the consultant's recollection were activists from PETA. There were no PETA people in obvious view at the 2003 MLF,[10] but they've been conspicuous at many of the recent Festivals. Since at least the mid-1990s, articles in everything from *The Camden Herald* to *The New York Times* have described PETA urging boycotts of the MLF, often deploying celebrity spokespeople like Mary Tyler Moore for open letters and ads saying stuff like "Lobsters are extraordinarily sensitive" and "To me, eating a lobster is out of the question." More concrete is the oral testimony of Dick, our florid and extremely gregarious rental-car guy, to the effect that PETA's been around so much in recent years that a kind of brittlely tolerant homeostasis now obtains between the activists and the Festival's locals, e.g.: "We had some incidents a couple years ago. One lady took most of her clothes off and painted herself like a lobster, almost got herself arrested. But for the most part they're let alone. [Rapid series of small ambiguous laughs, which with Dick happens a lot.] They do their thing and we do our thing."

This whole interchange takes place on Route 1, 30 July, during a four-mile, 50-minute ride from the airport[11] to the dealership to sign car-rental papers. Several irreproducible segues down the road from the PETA anecdotes, Dick—whose son-in-law happens to be a professional lobsterman and one of the Main Eating Tent's regular suppliers—articulates what he and his family feel is the crucial mitigating factor in the whole morality-of-boiling-lobsters-alive issue: "There's a part of the brain in people and animals that lets us feel pain, and lobsters' brains don't have this part."

Besides the fact that it's incorrect in about 11 different ways, the main reason Dick's statement is interesting is that its thesis is more or less echoed by the Festival's own pronouncement on lobsters and pain, which is part of a Test Your Lobster IQ quiz that appears in the 2003 MLF program courtesy of the Maine Lobster Promotion Council: "The nervous system of a lobster is very simple, and is in fact most similar to the nervous system of the grasshopper. It is decentralized with no brain. There is no cerebral cortex, which in humans is the area of the brain that gives the experience of pain."

Though it sounds more sophisticated, a lot of the neurology in this latter claim is still either false or fuzzy. The human cerebral cortex is the brain-part that deals with higher faculties like reason, metaphysical self-awareness, language, etc. Pain reception is known to be part of a much older and more primitive system of nociceptors and prostaglandins that are managed by the brain stem and thalamus.[12] On the other hand, it is true that the cerebral cortex is involved in what's variously called suffering, distress, or the emotional experience of pain—i.e., experiencing painful stimuli as unpleasant, very unpleasant, unbearable, and so on.

Before we go any further, let's acknowledge that the questions of whether and how different kinds of animals feel pain, and of whether and why it might be justifiable to inflict pain on them in order to eat them, turn out to be extremely complex and difficult. And comparative neuroanatomy is only part of the problem. Since pain is a totally subjective mental experience, we do not have direct access to anyone or anything's pain but our own; and even just the principles by which we can infer that others experience pain and have a legitimate interest in not feeling pain involve hard-core philosophy—metaphysics, epistemology, value theory, ethics. The fact that even the most highly evolved nonhuman mammals can't use language to communicate with us about their subjective mental experience is only the first layer of additional complication in trying to extend our reasoning about pain and morality to animals. And everything gets progressively more abstract and convolved as we move farther and farther out from the higher-type mammals into cattle and swine and dogs and cats and rodents, and then birds and fish, and finally invertebrates like lobsters.

The more important point here, though, is that the whole animal-cruelty-and-eating issue is not just complex, it's also uncomfortable. It is, at any rate, uncomfortable for me, and for just about everyone I know who enjoys a variety of foods and yet does not want to see herself as cruel or unfeeling. As far as I can tell, my own main way of dealing with this conflict has been to avoid thinking about the whole unpleasant thing. I should add that it appears to me unlikely that many readers of *Gourmet* wish to think hard about it, either, or to be queried about the morality of their eating habits in the pages of a culinary monthly. Since, however, the assigned subject of this article is what it was like to attend the 2003 MLF, and thus to spend several days in the midst of a great mass of Americans all eating lobster, and thus to be more or less impelled to think hard about lobster and the experience of buying and eating lobster, it turns out that there is no honest way to avoid certain moral questions.

There are several reasons for this. For one thing, it's not just that lobsters get boiled alive, it's that you do it yourself—or at least it's done specifically for you, on-site.[13] As mentioned, the World's Largest Lobster Cooker, which is highlighted as an attraction in the Festival's program, is right out there on the MLF's north grounds for everyone to see. Try to imagine a Nebraska Beef Festival[14] at which part of the festivities is watching trucks pull up and the live cattle get driven down the ramp and slaughtered right there on the World's Largest Killing Floor or something—there's no way.

The intimacy of the whole thing is maximized at home, which of course is where most lobster gets prepared and eaten (although note already the semiconscious euphemism "prepared," which in the case of lobsters really means killing them right there in our kitchens). The basic scenario is that we come in from the store and make our little preparations like getting the kettle filled and boiling, and then we lift the lobsters out of the bag or whatever retail container they came home in ...whereupon some uncomfortable things start to happen. However stuporous the lobster is from the trip home, for instance, it tends to come alarmingly to life when placed in boiling water. If you're tilting it from a container into the steaming kettle, the lobster will sometimes try to cling to the container's sides or even to hook its claws over the kettle's rim like a person trying to keep from going over the edge of a roof. And worse is when the lobster's fully immersed. Even if you cover the kettle and turn away, you can usually hear the cover rattling and clanking as the lobster tries to push it off. Or the creature's claws scraping the sides of the kettle as it thrashes around. The lobster, in other words, behaves very much as you or I would behave if we were plunged into boiling water (with the obvious exception of screaming).[15] A blunter way to say this is that the lobster acts as if it's in terrible pain, causing some cooks to leave the kitchen altogether and to take one of those little lightweight plastic oven timers with them into another room and wait until the whole process is over.

There happen to be two main criteria that most ethicists agree on for determining whether a living creature has the capacity to suffer and so has genuine interests that it may or may not be our moral duty to consider.[16] One is how much of the neurological hardware required for pain-experience the animal comes equipped with—nociceptors, prostaglandins, neuronal opioid receptors, etc. The other criterion is whether the animal demonstrates behavior associated with pain. And it takes a lot of intellectual gymnastics and behaviorist hairsplitting not to see struggling, thrashing, and lid-clattering as just such pain-behavior. According to marine zoologists, it usually takes lobsters between 35 and 45 seconds to die in boiling water. (No source I could find talked about how long it takes them to die in superheated steam; one rather hopes it's faster.)

There are, of course, other fairly common ways to kill your lobster on-site and so achieve maximum freshness. Some cooks' practice is to drive a sharp heavy knife point-first into a spot just above the midpoint between the lobster's eyestalks (more or less where the Third Eye is in human foreheads). This is alleged either to kill the lobster instantly or to render it insensate—and is said at least to eliminate the cowardice involved in throwing a creature into boiling water and then fleeing the room. As far as I can tell from talking to proponents of the knife-in-the-head method, the idea is that it's more violent but ultimately more merciful, plus that a willingness to exert personal agency and accept responsibility for stabbing the lobster's head honors the lobster somehow and entitles one to eat it. (There's often a vague sort of Native American spirituality-of-the-hunt flavor to pro-knife arguments.) But the problem with the knife method is basic biology: Lobsters' nervous systems operate off not one but several ganglia, a.k.a. nerve bundles, which are sort of wired in series and distributed all along the lobster's underside, from stem to stern. And disabling only the frontal ganglion does not normally result in quick death or unconsciousness. Another alternative is to put the lobster in cold salt water and then very slowly bring it up to a full boil. Cooks who advocate this method are going mostly on the analogy to a frog, which can supposedly be kept from jumping out of a boiling pot by heating the water incrementally. In order to save a lot of research-summarizing, I'll simply assure you that the analogy between frogs and lobsters turns out not to hold.

Ultimately, the only certain virtues of the home-lobotomy and slow-heating methods are comparative, because there are even worse/crueler ways people prepare lobster. Time-thrifty cooks sometimes microwave them alive (usually after poking several extra vent holes in the carapace, which is a precaution most shellfish-microwavers learn about the hard way). Live dismemberment, on the other hand, is big in Europe: Some chefs cut the lobster in half before cooking; others like to tear off the claws and tail and toss only these parts in the pot.

And there's more unhappy news respecting suffering-criterion number one. Lobsters don't have much in the way of eyesight or hearing, but they do have an exquisite tactile sense, one facilitated by hundreds of thousands of tiny hairs that protrude through their carapace. "Thus," in the words of T.M. Prudden's industry classic *About Lobster*, "it is that although encased in what seems a solid, impenetrable armor, the lobster can receive stimuli and impressions from without as readily as if it possessed a soft and delicate skin." And lobsters do have nociceptors,[17] as well as invertebrate versions of the prostaglandins and major neurotransmitters via which our own brains register pain.

Lobsters do not, on the other hand, appear to have the equipment for making or absorbing natural opioids like endorphins and enkephalins, which are what more advanced nervous systems use to try to handle intense pain. From this fact, though, one could conclude either that lobsters are maybe even *more* vulnerable to pain, since they lack mammalian nervous systems' built-in analgesia, or, instead, that the absence of natural opioids implies an absence of the really intense pain-sensations that natural opioids are designed to mitigate. I for one can detect a marked upswing in mood as I contemplate this latter possibility: It could be that their lack of endorphin/enkephalin hardware means that lobsters' raw subjective experience of pain is so radically different from mammals' that it may not even deserve the term *pain*. Perhaps lobsters are more like those frontal-lobotomy patients one reads about who report experiencing pain in a totally different way than you and I. These patients evidently do feel physical pain, neurologically speaking, but don't dislike it—though neither do they like it; it's more that they feel it but don't feel anything *about* it—the point being that the pain is not distressing to them or something they want to get away from. Maybe lobsters, who are also without frontal lobes, are detached from the neurological-registration-of-injury-or-hazard we call pain in just the same way. There is, after all, a difference between (1) pain as a purely neurological event, and (2) actual suffering, which seems crucially to involve an emotional component, an awareness of pain as unpleasant, as something to fear/dislike/want to avoid.

Still, after all the abstract intellection, there remain the facts of the frantically clanking lid, the pathetic clinging to the edge of the pot. Standing at the stove, it is hard to deny in any meaningful way that this is a living creature experiencing pain and wishing to avoid/escape the painful experience. To my lay mind, the lobster's behavior in the kettle appears to be the expression of a *preference*; and it may

W

well be that an ability to form preferences is the decisive criterion for real suffering.[18] The logic of this (preference p suffering) relation may be easiest to see in the negative case. If you cut certain kinds of worms in half, the halves will often keep crawling around and going about their vermiform business as if nothing had happened. When we assert, based on their post-op behavior, that these worms appear not to be suffering, what we're really saying is that there's no sign that the worms know anything bad has happened or would *prefer* not to have gotten cut in half.

Lobsters, however, are known to exhibit preferences. Experiments have shown that they can detect changes of only a degree or two in water temperature; one reason for their complex migratory cycles (which can often cover 100-plus miles a year) is to pursue the temperatures they like best.[19] And, as mentioned, they're bottom-dwellers and do not like bright light: If a tank of food lobsters is out in the sunlight or a store's fluorescence, the lobsters will always congregate in whatever part is darkest. Fairly solitary in the ocean, they also clearly dislike the crowding that's part of their captivity in tanks, since (as also mentioned) one reason why lobsters' claws are banded on capture is to keep them from attacking one another under the stress of close-quarter storage.

In any event, at the Festival, standing by the bubbling tanks outside the World's Largest Lobster Cooker, watching the fresh-caught lobsters pile over one another, wave their hobbled claws impotently, huddle in the rear corners, or scrabble frantically back from the glass as you approach, it is difficult not to sense that they're unhappy, or frightened, even if it's some rudimentary version of these feelings … and, again, why does rudimentariness even enter into it? Why is a primitive, inarticulate form of suffering less urgent or uncomfortable for the person who's helping to inflict it by paying for the food it results in? I'm not trying to give you a PETA-like screed here—at least I don't think so. I'm trying, rather, to work out and articulate some of the troubling questions that arise amid all the laughter and saltation and community pride of the Maine Lobster Festival. The truth is that if you, the Festival attendee, permit yourself to think that lobsters can suffer and would rather not, the MLF can begin to take on aspects of something like a Roman circus or medieval torture-fest.

Does that comparison seem a bit much? If so, exactly why? Or what about this one: Is it not possible that future generations will regard our own present agribusiness and eating practices in much the same way we now view Nero's entertainments or Aztec sacrifices? My own immediate reaction is that such a comparison is hysterical, extreme—and yet the reason it seems extreme to me appears to be that I believe animals are less morally important than human beings;[20] and when it comes to defending such a belief, even to myself, I have to acknowledge that (a) I have an obvious selfish interest in this belief, since I like to eat certain kinds of animals and want to be able to keep doing it, and (b) I have not succeeded in working out any sort of personal ethical system in which the belief is truly defensible instead of just selfishly convenient.

Given this article's venue and my own lack of culinary sophistication, I'm curious about whether the reader can identify with any of these reactions and acknowledgments and discomforts. I am also concerned not to come off as shrill or preachy when what I really am is confused. Given the (possible) moral status and (very possible) physical suffering of the animals involved, what ethical convictions do gourmets evolve that allow them not just to eat but to savor and enjoy flesh-based viands (since of course refined *enjoyment*, rather than just ingestion, is the whole point of gastronomy)? And for those gourmets who'll have no truck with convictions or rationales and who regard stuff like the previous paragraph as just so much pointless navel-gazing, what makes it feel okay, inside, to dismiss the whole issue out of hand? That is, is their refusal to think about any of this the product of actual thought, or is it just that they don't want to think about it? Do they ever think about their reluctance to think about it? After all, isn't being extra aware and attentive and thoughtful about one's food and its overall context part of what distinguishes a real gourmet? Or is all the gourmet's extra attention and sensibility just supposed to be aesthetic, gustatory?

These last couple queries, though, while sincere, obviously involve much larger and more abstract questions about the connections (if any) between aesthetics and morality, and these questions lead straightaway into such deep and treacherous waters that it's probably best to stop the public discussion right here. There are limits to what even interested persons can ask of each other. ■

Footnotes

1. There's a comprehensive native apothegm: "Camden by the sea, Rockland by the smell."
2. N.B. All personally connected parties have made it clear from the start that they do not want to be talked about in this article.
3. Midcoasters' native term for a lobster is, in fact, "bug," as in "Come around on Sunday and we'll cook up some bugs."
4. Factoid: Lobster traps are usually baited with dead herring.
5. Of course, the common practice of dipping the lobster meat in melted butter torpedoes all these happy fat-specs, which none of the Council's promotional stuff ever mentions, any more than potato-industry PR talks about sour cream and bacon bits.
6. In truth, there's a great deal to be said about the differences between working-class Rockland and the heavily populist flavor of its Festival versus comfortable and elitist Camden with its expensive view and shops given entirely over to $200 sweaters and great rows of Victorian homes converted to upscale B&Bs. And about these differences as two sides of the great coin that is U.S. tourism. Very little of which will be said here, except to amplify the above-mentioned paradox and to reveal your assigned correspondent's own preferences. I confess that I have never understood why so many people's idea of a fun vacation is to don flip-flops and sunglasses and crawl through maddening traffic to loud hot crowded tourist venues in order to sample a "local flavor" that is by definition ruined by the presence of tourists. This may (as my Festival companions keep pointing out) all be a matter of personality and hardwired taste: The fact that I just do not like tourist venues means that I'll never understand their appeal and so am probably not the one to talk

W

about it (the supposed appeal). But, since this note will almost surely not survive magazine-editing anyway, here goes:

As I see it, it probably really is good for the soul to be a tourist, even if it's only once in a while. Not good for the soul in a refreshing or enlivening way, though, but rather in a grim, steely-eyed, let's-look-honestly-at-the-facts-and-find-some-way-to-deal-with-them way. My personal experience has not been that traveling around the country is broadening or relaxing, or that radical changes in place and context have a salutary effect, but rather that intranational tourism is radically constricting, and humbling in the hardest way—hostile to my fantasy of being a real individual, of living somehow outside and above it all. (Coming up is the part that my companions find especially unhappy and repellent, a sure way to spoil the fun of vacation travel:) To be a mass tourist, for me, is to become a pure late-date American: alien, ignorant, greedy for something you cannot ever have, disappointed in a way you can never admit. It is to spoil, by way of sheer ontology, the very unspoiledness you are there to experience. It is to impose yourself on places that in all noneconomic ways would be better, realer, without you. It is, in lines and gridlock and transaction after transaction, to confront a dimension of yourself that is as inescapable as it is painful: As a tourist, you become economically significant but existentially loathsome, an insect on a dead thing.

7. Datum: In a good year, the U.S. industry produces around 80 million pounds of lobster, and Maine accounts for more than half that total.
8. N.B. Similar reasoning underlies the practice of what's termed "debeaking" broiler chickens and brood hens in modern factory farms. Maximum commercial efficiency requires that enormous poultry populations be confined in unnaturally close quarters, under which conditions many birds go crazy and peck one another to death. As a purely observational side-note, be apprised that debeaking is usually an automated process and that the chickens receive no anesthetic. It's not clear to me whether most *Gourmet* readers know about debeaking, or about related practices like dehorning cattle in commercial feedlots, cropping swine's tails in factory hog farms to keep psychotically bored neighbors from chewing them off, and so forth. It so happens that your assigned correspondent knew almost nothing about standard meat-industry operations before starting work on this article.
9. The terminal used to be somebody's house, for example, and the lost-luggage-reporting room was clearly once a pantry.
10. It turned out that one Mr. William R. Rivas-Rivas, a high-ranking PETA official out of the group's Virginia headquarters, was indeed there this year, albeit solo, working the Festival's main and side entrances on Saturday, August 2, handing out pamphlets and adhesive stickers emblazoned with "Being Boiled Hurts," which is the tagline in most of PETA's published material about lobster. I learned that he'd been there only later, when speaking with Mr. Rivas-Rivas on the phone. I'm not sure how we missed seeing him *in situ* at the Festival, and I can't see much to do except apologize for the oversight—although it's also true that Saturday was the day of the

big MLF parade through Rockland, which basic journalistic responsibility seemed to require going to (and which, with all due respect, meant that Saturday was maybe not the best day for PETA to work the Harbor Park grounds, especially if it was going to be just one person for one day, since a lot of diehard MLF partisans were off-site watching the parade (which, again with no offense intended, was in truth kind of cheesy and boring, consisting mostly of slow homemade floats and various midcoast people waving at one another, and with an extremely annoying man dressed as Blackbeard ranging up and down the length of the crowd saying "Arrr" over and over and brandishing a plastic sword at people, etc.; plus it rained)).

11. The short version regarding why we were back at the airport after already arriving the previous night involves lost luggage and a miscommunication about where and what the local National Car Rental franchise was—Dick came out personally to the airport and got us, out of no evident motive but kindness. (He also talked nonstop the entire way, with a very distinctive speaking style that can be described only as manically laconic; the truth is that I now know more about this man than I do about some members of my own family.)
12. To elaborate by way of example: The common experience of accidentally touching a hot stove and yanking your hand back before you're even aware that anything's going on is explained by the fact that many of the processes by which we detect and avoid painful stimuli do not involve the cortex. In the case of the hand and stove, the brain is bypassed altogether; all the important neurochemical action takes place in the spine.
13. Morality-wise, let's concede that this cuts both ways. Lobster-eating is at least not abetted by the system of corporate factory farms that produces most beef, pork, and chicken. Because, if nothing else, of the way they're marketed and packaged for sale, we eat these latter meats without having to consider that they were once conscious, sentient creatures to whom horrible things were done. (N.B. PETA distributes a certain video—the title of which is being omitted as part of the elaborate editorial compromise by which this note appears at all—in which you can see just about everything meat-related you don't want to see or think about. (N.B. 2 Not that PETA's any sort of font of unspun truth. Like many partisans in complex moral disputes, the PETA people are fanatics, and a lot of their rhetoric seems simplistic and self-righteous. Personally, though, I have to say that I found this unnamed video both credible and deeply upsetting.))
14. Is it significant that "lobster," "fish," and "chicken" are our culture's words for both the animal and the meat, whereas most mammals seem to require euphemisms like "beef" and "pork" that help us separate the meat we eat from the living creature the meat once was? Is this evidence that some kind of deep unease about eating higher animals is endemic enough to show up in English usage, but that the unease diminishes as we move out of the mammalian order? (And is "lamb"/"lamb" the counterexample that sinks the whole theory, or are there special, biblico-historical reasons for that equivalence?)

W

15. There's a relevant populist myth about the high-pitched whistling sound that sometimes issues from a pot of boiling lobster. The sound is really vented steam from the layer of seawater between the lobster's flesh and its carapace (this is why shedders whistle more than hard-shells), but the pop version has it that the sound is the lobster's rabbitlike death scream. Lobsters communicate via pheromones in their urine and don't have anything close to the vocal equipment for screaming, but the myth's very persistent—which might, once again, point to a low-level cultural unease about the boiling thing.
16. "Interests" basically means strong and legitimate preferences, which obviously require some degree of consciousness, responsiveness to stimuli, etc. See, for instance, the utilitarian philosopher Peter Singer, whose 1974 *Animal Liberation* is more or less the bible of the modern animal-rights movement: "It would be nonsense to say that it was not in the interests of a stone to be kicked along the road by a schoolboy. A stone does not have interests because it cannot suffer. Nothing that we can do to it could possibly make any difference to its welfare. A mouse, on the other hand, does have an interest in not being kicked along the road, because it will suffer if it is."
17. This is the neurological term for special pain receptors that are (according to Jane A. Smith and Kenneth M. Boyd's *Lives in the Balance*) "sensitive to potentially damaging extremes of temperature, to mechanical forces, and to chemical substances which are released when body tissues are damaged."
18. "Preference" is maybe roughly synonymous with "interest," but it is a better term for our purposes because it's less abstractly philosophical—"preference" seems more personal, and it's the whole idea of a living creature's personal experience that's at issue.
19. Of course, the most common sort of counterargument here would begin by objecting that "like best" is really just a metaphor, and a misleadingly anthropomorphic one at that. The counterarguer would posit that the lobster seeks to maintain a certain optimal ambient temperature out of nothing but unconscious instinct (with a similar explanation for the low-light affinities about to be mentioned in the main text). The thrust of such a counterargument will be that the lobster's thrashings and clankings in the kettle express not unpreferred pain but involuntary reflexes, like your leg shooting out when the doctor hits your knee. Be advised that there are professional scientists, including many researchers who use animals in experiments, who hold to the view that nonhuman creatures have no real feelings at all, only "behaviors." Be further advised that this view has a long history that goes all the way back to Descartes, although its modern support comes mostly from behaviorist psychology.

    To these what-look-like-pain-are-really-only-reflexes counterarguments, however, there happen to be all sorts of scientific and pro-animal-rights countercounterarguments. And then further attempted rebuttals and redirects, and so on. Suffice to say that both the scientific and the philosophical arguments on either side of the animal-suffering issue are involved, abstruse, technical, often informed by self-interest or ideology, and in the end so totally inconclusive that as a practical matter, in the kitchen or restaurant, it all still seems to come down to individual conscience, going with (no pun) your gut.

20. Meaning a *lot* less important, apparently, since the moral comparison here is not the value of one human's life vs. the value of one animal's life, but rather the value of one animal's life vs. the value of one human's taste for a particular kind of protein. Even the most diehard carniphile will acknowledge that it's possible to live and eat well without consuming animals.

AUTHOR PROFILE

David Foster Wallace (1962–2008) was born in Ithaca, New York and studied English and philosophy at Amherst College. He earned an MFA in creative writing from the University of Arizona. He is best known for his 1996 novel *Infinite Jest* and was awarded a MacArthur Fellowship after its publication. His other novels are *The Broom of the System* (1987) and *The Pale King* (2011), which was published posthumously. He authored numerous books of nonfiction on a variety of subjects including politics, terrorism, sports, ethics, and special effects in film. He taught at Emerson College, Illinois State University, and Pomona College. His books have been adapted into plays, films, and an opera. "Consider the Lobster" was originally published in *Gourmet Magazine* in 2004.

We Aren't the World

By Ethan Watters

Joe Henrich and his colleagues are shaking the foundations of psychology and economics—and hoping to change the way social scientists think about human behavior and culture.

In the summer of 1995, a young graduate student in anthropology at UCLA named Joe Henrich traveled to Peru to carry out some fieldwork among the Machiguenga, an indigenous people who live north of Machu Picchu in the Amazon basin. The Machiguenga had traditionally been horticulturalists who lived in single-family, thatch-roofed houses in small hamlets composed of clusters of extended families. For sustenance, they relied on local game and produce from small-scale farming. They shared with their kin but rarely traded with outside groups.

While the setting was fairly typical for an anthropologist, Henrich's research was not. Rather than practice traditional ethnography, he decided to run a behavioral experiment that had been developed by economists. Henrich used a "game"—along the lines of the famous prisoner's dilemma—to see whether isolated cultures shared with the West the same basic instinct for fairness. In doing so, Henrich expected to confirm one of the foundational assumptions underlying such experiments, and indeed underpinning the entire fields of economics and psychology: that humans all share the same cognitive machinery—the same evolved rational and psychological hardwiring.

The test that Henrich introduced to the Machiguenga was called the ultimatum game. The rules are simple: in each game there are two players who remain anonymous to each other. The first player is given an amount of money, say $100, and told that he has to offer some of the cash, in an amount of his choosing, to the other subject. The second player can accept or refuse the split. But there's a hitch: players know that if the recipient refuses the offer, both leave empty-handed. North Americans, who are the most common subjects for such experiments, usually offer a 50-50 split when on the giving end. When on the receiving end, they show an eagerness to punish the other player for uneven splits at their own expense. In short, Americans show the tendency to be equitable with strangers—and to punish those who are not.

Among the Machiguenga, word quickly spread of the young, square-jawed visitor from America giving away money. The stakes Henrich used in the game with the Machiguenga were not insubstantial—roughly equivalent to the few days' wages they sometimes earned from episodic work with logging or oil companies. So Henrich had no problem finding volunteers. What he had great difficulty with, however, was explaining the rules, as the game struck the Machiguenga as deeply odd.

When he began to run the game it became immediately clear that Machiguengan behavior was dramatically different from that of the average North American. To begin with, the offers from the first player were much lower. In addition, when on the receiving end of the game, the Machiguenga rarely refused even the lowest possible amount. "It just seemed ridiculous to the Machiguenga that you would reject an offer of free money," says Henrich. "They just didn't understand why anyone would sacrifice money to punish someone who had the good luck of getting to play the other role in the game."

The potential implications of the unexpected results were quickly apparent to Henrich. He knew that a vast amount of scholarly literature in the social sciences—particularly in economics and psychology—relied on the ultimatum game and similar experiments. At the heart of most of that research was the implicit assumption that the results revealed evolved psychological traits common to all humans, never mind that the test subjects were nearly always from the industrialized West. Henrich realized that if the Machiguenga results stood up, and if similar differences could be measured across other populations, this assumption of universality would have to be challenged.

Henrich had thought he would be adding a small branch to an established tree of knowledge. It turned out he was sawing at the very trunk. He began to wonder: What other certainties about "human nature" in social science research would need to be reconsidered when tested across diverse populations?

Henrich soon landed a grant from the MacArthur Foundation to take his fairness games on the road. With the help of a dozen other colleagues he led a study of 14 other small-scale societies, in locales from Tanzania to Indonesia. Differences abounded in the behavior of both players in the ultimatum game. In no society did he find people who were purely selfish (that is, who always offered the lowest amount, and never refused a split), but average offers from place to place varied widely and, in some societies—ones where gift-giving is heavily used to curry favor or gain allegiance—the first player would often make overly generous offers in excess of 60 percent, and the second player would often reject them, behaviors almost never observed among Americans.

The research established Henrich as an up-and-coming scholar. In 2004, he was given the U.S. Presidential Early Career Award for young scientists at the White House. But his work also made him a controversial figure. When he presented his research to the anthropology department at the University of British Columbia during a job interview a year later, he recalls a hostile reception. Anthropology is the social science most interested in cultural differences, but the young scholar's methods of using games and statistics to test and compare cultures with the West seemed heavy-handed and invasive to some. "Professors from the anthropology department suggested it was a bad thing that I was doing," Henrich remembers. "The word 'unethical' came up."

So instead of toeing the line, he switched teams. A few well-placed people at the University of British Columbia saw great promise in Henrich's work and created a position for him, split between the economics department and the psychology department. It was in the psychology department that he found two kindred spirits in Steven Heine and Ara Norenzayan. Together the three set about writing a paper that they hoped would fundamentally challenge the way social scientists thought about human behavior, cognition, and culture.

A modern liberal arts education gives lots of lip service to the idea of cultural diversity. It's generally agreed that all of us see the world in ways that are sometimes socially and culturally constructed, that pluralism is good, and that ethnocentrism is bad. But beyond that the ideas get muddy. That we should welcome and celebrate people of all backgrounds seems obvious, but the implied corollary—

that people from different ethno-cultural origins have particular attributes that add spice to the body politic—becomes more problematic. To avoid stereotyping, it is rarely stated bluntly just exactly what those culturally derived qualities might be. Challenge liberal arts graduates on their appreciation of cultural diversity and you'll often find them retreating to the anodyne notion that under the skin everyone is really alike.

If you take a broad look at the social science curriculum of the last few decades, it becomes a little more clear why modern graduates are so unmoored. The last generation or two of undergraduates have largely been taught by a cohort of social scientists busily doing penance for the racism and Eurocentrism of their predecessors, albeit in different ways. Many anthropologists took to the navel gazing of postmodernism and swore off attempts at rationality and science, which were disparaged as weapons of cultural imperialism.

Economists and psychologists, for their part, did an end run around the issue with the convenient assumption that their job was to study the human mind stripped of culture. The human brain is genetically comparable around the globe, it was agreed, so human hardwiring for much behavior, perception, and cognition should be similarly universal. No need, in that case, to look beyond the convenient population of undergraduates for test subjects. A 2008 survey of the top six psychology journals dramatically shows how common that assumption was: more than 96 percent of the subjects tested in psychological studies from 2003 to 2007 were Westerners—with nearly 70 percent from the United States alone. Put another way: 96 percent of human subjects in these studies came from countries that represent only 12 percent of the world's population.

Henrich's work with the ultimatum game was an example of a small but growing countertrend in the social sciences, one in which researchers look straight at the question of how deeply culture shapes human cognition. His new colleagues in the psychology department, Heine and Norenzayan, were also part of this trend. Heine focused on the different ways people in Western and Eastern cultures perceived the world, reasoned, and understood themselves in relationship to others. Norenzayan's research focused on the ways religious belief influenced bonding and behavior. The three began to compile examples of cross-cultural research that, like Henrich's work with the Machiguenga, challenged long-held assumptions of human psychological universality.

Some of that research went back a generation. It was in the 1960s, for instance, that researchers discovered that aspects of visual perception were different from place to place. One of the classics of the literature, the Müller-Lyer illusion, showed that where you grew up would determine to what degree you would fall prey to the illusion that these two lines are different in length:

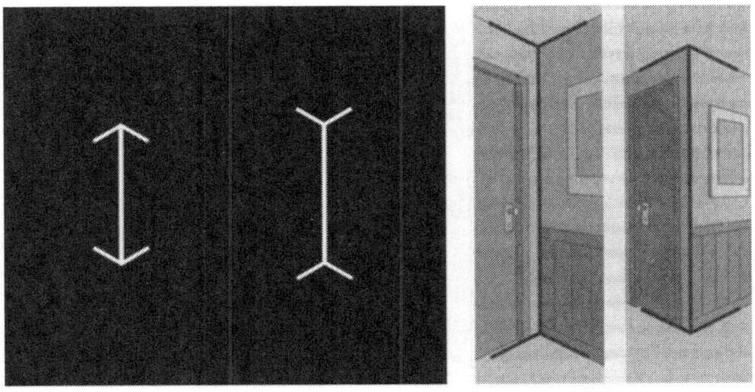

(A) (B) (C)

Researchers found that Americans perceive the line with the ends feathered outward (B) as being longer than the line with the arrow tips (A). San foragers of the Kalahari, on the other hand, were more likely to see the lines as they are: equal in length. Subjects from more than a dozen cultures were tested, and Americans were at the far end of the distribution—seeing the illusion more dramatically than all others.

More recently psychologists had challenged the universality of research done in the 1950s by pioneering social psychologist Solomon Asch. Asch had discovered that test subjects were often willing to make incorrect judgments on simple perception tests to conform with group pressure. When the test was performed across 17 societies, however, it turned out that group pressure had a range of influence. Americans were again at the far end of the scale, in this case showing the least tendency to conform to group belief.

As Heine, Norenzayan, and Henrich furthered their search, they began to find research suggesting wide cultural differences almost everywhere they looked: in spatial reasoning, the way we infer the motivations of others, categorization, moral reasoning, the boundaries between the self and others, and other arenas. These differences, they believed, were not genetic. The distinct ways Americans and Machiguengans played the ultimatum game, for instance, wasn't because they had differently evolved brains. Rather, Americans, without fully realizing it, were manifesting a psychological tendency shared with people in other industrialized countries that had been refined and handed down through thousands of generations in ever more complex market economies. When people are constantly doing business with strangers, it helps when they have the desire to go out of their way (with a lawsuit, a call to the Better Business Bureau, or a bad Yelp review) when they feel cheated. Because Machiguengan culture had a different history, their gut feeling about what was fair was distinctly their own. In the small-scale societies with a strong culture of gift-giving, yet another conception of fairness prevailed. There, generous financial offers were turned down because people's minds had been shaped by a cultural norm that taught them that the acceptance of generous gifts brought burdensome obligations. Our economies hadn't been shaped by our sense of fairness; it was the other way around.

The growing body of cross-cultural research that the three researchers were compiling suggested that the mind's capacity to mold itself to cultural and environmental settings was far greater than had been assumed. The most interesting thing about cultures may not be in the observable things they do—the rituals, eating preferences, codes of behavior, and the like—but in the way they mold our most fundamental conscious and unconscious thinking and perception.

For instance, the different ways people perceive the Müller-Lyer illusion likely reflects lifetimes spent in different physical environments. American children, for the most part, grow up in box-shaped rooms of varying dimensions. Surrounded by carpentered corners, visual perception adapts to this strange new environment (strange and new in terms of human history, that is) by learning to perceive converging lines in three dimensions.

When unconsciously translated in three dimensions, the line with the outward-feathered ends (C) appears farther away and the brain therefore judges it to be longer. The more time one spends in natural environments, where there are no carpentered corners, the less one sees the illusion.

As the three continued their work, they noticed something else that was remarkable: again and again one group of people appeared to be particularly unusual when compared to other populations—with perceptions, behaviors, and motivations that were almost always sliding down one end of the human bell curve.

In the end they titled their paper "The Weirdest People in the World?" By "weird" they meant both unusual and Western, Educated, Industrialized, Rich, and Democratic. It is not just our Western habits and cultural preferences that are different from the rest of the world, it appears. The very way we think about ourselves and others—and even the way we perceive reality—makes us distinct from other humans on the planet, not to mention from the vast majority of our ancestors. Among Westerners, the data showed that Americans were often the most unusual, leading the researchers to conclude that "American participants are exceptional even within the unusual population of Westerners—outliers among outliers."

Given the data, they concluded that social scientists could not possibly have picked a worse population from which to draw broad generalizations. Researchers had been doing the equivalent of studying penguins while believing that they were learning insights applicable to all birds.

Not long ago I met Henrich, Heine, and Norenzayan for dinner at a small French restaurant in Vancouver, British Columbia, to hear about the reception of their weird paper, which was published in the prestigious journal *Behavioral and Brain Sciences* in 2010. The trio of researchers are young—as professors go—good-humored family men. They recalled that they were nervous as the publication time approached. The paper basically suggested that much of what social scientists thought they knew about fundamental aspects of human cognition was likely only true of one small slice of humanity. They were making such a broadside challenge to whole libraries of research that they steeled themselves to the possibility of becoming outcasts in their own fields.

"We were scared," admitted Henrich. "We were warned that a lot of people were going to be upset."

"We were told we were going to get spit on," interjected Norenzayan.

"Yes," Henrich said. "That we'd go to conferences and no one was going to sit next to us at lunchtime."

Interestingly, they seemed much less concerned that they had used the pejorative acronym WEIRD to describe a significant slice of humanity, although they did admit that they could only have done so to describe their own group. "Really," said Henrich, "the only people we could have called weird are represented right here at this table."

Still, I had to wonder whether describing the Western mind, and the American mind in particular, as weird suggested that our cognition is not just different but somehow malformed or twisted. In their paper the trio pointed out cross-cultural studies that suggest that the "weird" Western mind is the most self-aggrandizing and egotistical on the planet: we are more likely to promote ourselves as individuals versus advancing as a group. WEIRD minds are also more analytic, possessing the tendency to telescope in on an object of interest rather than understanding that object in the context of what is around it.

The WEIRD mind also appears to be unique in terms of how it comes to understand and interact with the natural world. Studies show that Western urban children grow up so closed off in man-made environments that their brains never form a deep or complex connection to the natural world. While studying children from the U.S., researchers have suggested a developmental timeline for what is called "folkbiological reasoning." These studies posit that it is not until children are around 7 years old that they stop projecting human qualities onto animals and begin to understand that humans are one animal among many. Compared to Yucatec Maya communities in Mexico, however, Western urban children appear to be developmentally delayed in this regard. Children who grow up constantly interacting with the natural world are much less likely to anthropomorphize other living things into late childhood.

Given that people living in WEIRD societies don't routinely encounter or interact with animals other than humans or pets, it's not surprising that they end up with a rather cartoonish understanding of the natural world. "Indeed," the report concluded, "studying the cognitive development of folkbiology in urban children would seem the equivalent of studying 'normal' physical growth in malnourished children."

During our dinner, I admitted to Heine, Henrich, and Norenzayan that the idea that I can only perceive reality through a distorted cultural lens was unnerving. For me the notion raised all sorts of metaphysical questions: Is my thinking so strange that I have little hope of understanding people from other cultures? Can I mold my own psyche or the psyches of my children to be less WEIRD and more able to think like the rest of the world? If I did, would I be happier?

Henrich reacted with mild concern that I was taking this research so personally. He had not intended, he told me, for his work to be read as postmodern self-help advice. "I think we're really interested in these questions for the questions' sake," he said.

The three insisted that their goal was not to say that one culturally shaped psychology was better or worse than another—only that we'll never truly understand human behavior and cognition until we expand the sample pool beyond its current small slice of humanity. Despite these assurances, however, I found it hard not to read a message between the lines of their research. When they write, for example, that weird children develop their understanding of the natural world in a "culturally and experientially impoverished environment" and that they are in this way the equivalent of "malnourished children," it's difficult to see this as a good thing.

The turn that Henrich, Heine, and Norenzayan are asking social scientists to make is not an easy one: accounting for the influence of culture on cognition will be a herculean task. Cultures are not monolithic; they can be endlessly parsed. Ethnic backgrounds, religious beliefs, economic status, parenting styles, rural upbringing versus urban or suburban—there are hundreds of cultural differences that individually and in endless combinations influence our conceptions of fairness, how we categorize things, our method of judging and decision making, and our deeply held beliefs about the nature of the self, among other aspects of our psychological makeup.

We are just at the beginning of learning how these fine-grained cultural differences affect our thinking. Recent research has shown that people in "tight" cultures, those with strong norms and low tolerance for deviant behavior (think India, Malaysia, and Pakistan), develop higher impulse control and more self-monitoring abilities than those from other places. Men raised in the honor culture of the American South have been shown to experience much larger surges of testosterone after insults than do Northerners. Research published late last year suggested psychological differences at the city level too. Compared to San Franciscans, Bostonians' internal sense of self-worth is more dependent on community status and financial and educational achievement. "A cultural difference doesn't have to be big to be important," Norenzayan said. "We're not just talking about comparing New York yuppies to the Dani tribesmen of Papua New Guinea."

As Norenzayan sees it, the last few generations of psychologists have suffered from "physics envy," and they need to get over it. The job, experimental psychologists often assumed, was to push past the content of people's thoughts and see the underlying universal hardware at work. "This is a deeply flawed way of studying human nature," Norenzayan told me, "because the content of our thoughts and their process are intertwined." In other words, if human cognition is shaped by cultural ideas and behavior, it can't be studied without taking into account what those ideas and behaviors are and how they are different from place to place.

This new approach suggests the possibility of reverse-engineering psychological research: look at cultural content first; cognition and behavior second. Norenzayan's recent work on religious belief is perhaps the best example of the intellectual landscape that is now open for study. When Norenzayan became a student of psychology in 1994, four years after his family had moved from Lebanon to America, he was excited to study the effect of religion on human psychology. "I remember opening textbook after textbook and turning to the index and looking for the word 'religion,' " he told me, "Again and again the very word wouldn't be listed. This was shocking. How could psychology be the science of human behavior and have nothing to say about religion? Where I grew up you'd have to be in a coma not to notice the importance of religion on how people perceive themselves and the world around them."

Norenzayan became interested in how certain religious beliefs, handed down through generations, may have shaped human psychology to make possible the creation of large-scale societies. He has suggested that there may be a connection between the growth of religions that believe in "morally concerned deities"—that is, a god or gods who care if people are good or bad—and the evolution of large cities and nations. To be cooperative in large groups of relative strangers, in other words, might have required the shared belief that an all-powerful being was forever watching over your shoulder.

If religion was necessary in the development of large-scale societies, can large-scale societies survive without religion? Norenzayan points to parts of Scandinavia with atheist majorities that seem to be doing just fine. They may have climbed the ladder of religion and effectively kicked it away. Or perhaps, after a thousand years of religious belief, the idea of an unseen entity always watching your behavior remains in our culturally shaped thinking even after the belief in God dissipates or disappears.

Why, I asked Norenzayan, if religion might have been so central to human psychology, have researchers not delved into the topic? "Experimental psychologists are the weirdest of the weird," said Norenzayan. "They are almost the least religious academics, next to biologists. And because academics mostly talk amongst themselves, they could look around and say, 'No one who is important to me is religious, so this must not be very important.'" Indeed, almost every major theorist on human behavior in the last 100 years predicted that it was just a matter of time before religion was a vestige of the past. But the world persists in being a very religious place.

Henrich, Heine, and Norenzayan's fear of being ostracized after the publication of the WEIRD paper turned out to be misplaced. Response to the paper, both published and otherwise, has been nearly universally positive, with more than a few of their colleagues suggesting that the work will spark fundamental changes. "I have no doubt that this paper is going to change the social sciences," said Richard Nisbett, an eminent psychologist at the University of Michigan. "It just puts it all in one place and makes such a bold statement."

More remarkable still, after reading the paper, academics from other disciplines began to come forward with their own mea culpas. Commenting on the paper, two brain researchers from Northwestern University argued that the nascent field of neuroimaging had made the same mistake as psychologists, noting that 90 percent of neuroimaging studies were performed in Western countries. Researchers in motor development similarly suggested that their discipline's body of research ignored how different child-rearing practices around the world can dramatically influence states of development. Two psycholinguistics professors suggested that their colleagues had also made the same mistake: blithely assuming human homogeneity while focusing their research primarily on one rather small slice of humanity.

At its heart, the challenge of the WEIRD paper is not simply to the field of experimental human research (do more cross-cultural studies!); it is a challenge to our Western conception of human nature. For some time now, the most widely accepted answer to the question of why humans, among all animals, have so successfully adapted to environments across the globe is that we have big brains with the ability to learn, improvise, and problem-solve.

Henrich has challenged this "cognitive niche" hypothesis with the "cultural niche" hypothesis. He notes that the amount of knowledge in any culture is far greater than the capacity of individuals to learn or figure it all out on their own. He suggests that individuals tap that cultural storehouse of knowledge simply by mimicking (often unconsciously) the behavior and ways of thinking of those around them. We shape a tool in a certain manner, adhere to a food taboo, or think about fairness in a particular way, not because we individually have figured out that behavior's adaptive value, but because we instinctively trust our culture to show us the way. When Henrich asked Fijian women why they avoided certain potentially toxic fish during pregnancy and breastfeeding, he found that many didn't know or had fanciful reasons. Regardless of their personal understanding, by mimicking this culturally adaptive behavior they were protecting their offspring. The unique trick of human psychology, these researchers suggest, might be this: our big brains are evolved to let local culture lead us in life's dance.

The applications of this new way of looking at the human mind are still in the offing. Henrich suggests that his research about fairness might first be applied to anyone working in international relations or development. People are not "plug and play," as he puts it, and you cannot expect to drop a Western court system or form of government into another culture and expect it to work as it does back home. Those trying to use economic incentives to encourage sustainable land use will similarly need to understand local notions of fairness to have any chance of influencing behavior in predictable ways.

Because of our peculiarly Western way of thinking of ourselves as independent of others, this idea of the culturally shaped mind doesn't go down very easily. Perhaps the richest and most established vein of cultural psychology—that which compares Western and Eastern concepts of the self—goes to the heart of this problem. Heine has spent much of his career following the lead of a seminal paper published in 1991 by Hazel Rose Markus, of Stanford University, and Shinobu Kitayama, who is now at the University of Michigan. Markus and Kitayama suggested that different cultures foster strikingly different views of the self, particularly along one axis: some cultures regard the self as independent from others; others see the self as interdependent. The interdependent self—which is more the norm in East Asian countries, including Japan and China—connects itself with others in a social group and favors social harmony over self-expression. The independent self—which is most prominent in America—focuses on individual attributes and preferences and thinks of the self as existing apart from the group.

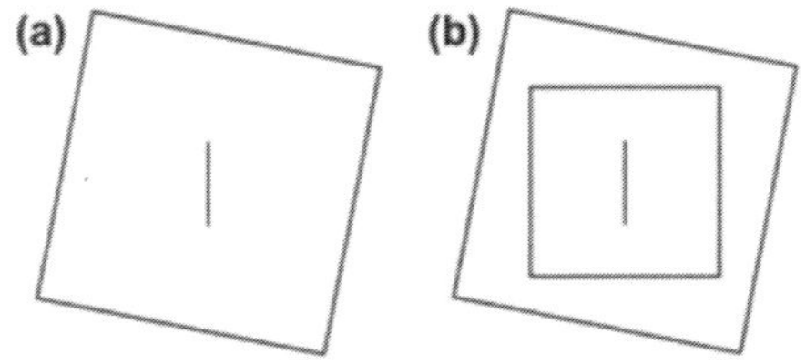

The classic "rod and frame" task: Is the line in the center vertical?

That we in the West develop brains that are wired to see ourselves as separate from others may also be connected to differences in how we reason, Heine argues. Unlike the vast majority of the world, Westerners (and Americans in particular) tend to reason analytically as opposed to holistically. That is, the American mind strives to figure out the world by taking it apart and examining its pieces. Show a Japanese and an American the same cartoon of an aquarium, and the American will remember details mostly about the moving fish while the Japanese observer will likely later be able to describe the seaweed, the bubbles, and other objects in the background. Shown another way, in a different test analytic Americans will do better on something called the "rod and frame" task, where one has to judge whether a line is vertical even though the frame around it is skewed. Americans see the line as apart from the frame, just as they see themselves as apart from the group.

Heine and others suggest that such differences may be the echoes of cultural activities and trends going back thousands of years. Whether you think of yourself as interdependent or independent may depend on whether your distant ancestors farmed rice (which required a great deal of shared labor and group cooperation) or herded animals (which rewarded individualism and aggression). Heine points to Nisbett at Michigan, who has argued that the analytic/holistic dichotomy in reasoning styles can be clearly seen, respectively, in Greek and Chinese philosophical writing dating back 2,500 years. These psychological trends and tendencies may echo down generations, hundreds of years after the activity or situation that brought them into existence has disappeared or fundamentally changed.

And here is the rub: the culturally shaped analytic/individualistic mind-sets may partly explain why Western researchers have so dramatically failed to take into account the interplay between culture and cognition. In the end, the goal of boiling down human psychology to hardwiring is not surprising given the type of mind that has been designing the studies. Taking an object (in this case the human mind) out of its context is, after all, what distinguishes the analytic reasoning style prevalent in the West. Similarly, we may have underestimated the impact of culture because the very ideas of being subject to the will of larger historical currents and of unconsciously mimicking the cognition of those around us challenges our Western conception of the self as independent and self-determined. The historical missteps of Western researchers, in other words, have been the predictable consequences of the WEIRD mind doing the thinking. ■

W

AUTHOR PROFILE

Ethan Watters is a journalist and author whose work explores trends in social psychology and psychiatry. His writing has appeared in *The New York Times, Mother Jones, Wired, Pacific Standard Magazine,* and *Esquire.* His books include *Urban Tribes: Are Friends the New Family?* (2004), and *Crazy Like Us: The Globalization of the American Psyche* (2010). Watters is a co-founder of the San Francisco Writers' Grotto, a workspace for writers, artists, and designers.

The Right to Your Opinion

By Jamie Whyte

"Know your rights!"

So we are advised by all sorts of well-meaners. When I was an undergraduate student, activists wanted me to know the rights that protected me against police harassment. Having dutifully learned them, I was disappointed never to encounter the expected harassment. Now I receive pamphlets telling me that I may have a right to various kinds of government assistance, including money. Alas, the result of inquiry is always the discovery that I don't qualify. As with cheap flights, conditions apply, and it seems that I am the citizen's equivalent of someone who wants to fly to Sydney at Christmas.

My poor return from knowing my rights shouldn't put you off. Knowing your rights is usually useful and we could all do better at it. How many British citizens are aware, for example, that they have a right to a good night's sleep? Well, they do.[1] In a few years, when my newborn daughter has finally got herself a decent job, I plan legal action against her. Learning your rights can also mean discovering that you do not really have rights you think you do. This can also be useful. Suppose, for example, that you thought you had a right to do to your body whatever you like, provided you injure no one else. Such a delusion could well land you in prison convicted of drug use or assault.[2]

In this spirit, my purpose here is to stop you from believing in another right that you do not really have, namely, the right to your own opinions.

Perhaps you don't believe you have this right; then I am sorry for being presumptuous. But, you would be the first person I have met who doesn't believe it. The slogan "You are entitled to your opinion" is so often repeated that it is near impossible for the brain of a modern Westerner not to have absorbed it.

Like many other views that have at times enjoyed universal assent, however, it isn't true. You don't really have a right to your own opinions. And the idea that you do, besides being false, is forever being invoked when it would be irrelevant even if it were true.

The Irrelevant Right

Before showing that this cliché is false, let's first be clear that its common use in discussion or debate really does amount to a fallacy. It is often used preemptively, when an assertion is prefaced with the acknowledgment that "Of course, you are entitled to your opinion, but..." Yet its more basic use, which the above acknowledgment is intended to preempt, is defensive.

---

[1] The right was confirmed by the European Court of Human Rights in October 2001. The court upheld the claim of people living in the flight path of Heathrow airport that early-morning flights violated this right to a good night's sleep.

[2] In December 1990 a group of men who, for the sake of pleasure, volunteered to have each other cut their genitals were convicted of various crimes, including actual bodily harm.

Jack has offered some opinion—that President Bush invaded Iraq to steal its oil, let's say—with which his friend Jill disagrees. Jill offers some reasons why Jack's opinion is wrong and after a few unsuccessful attempts at answering them, Jack petulantly retorts that he is entitled to his opinion.

The fallacy lies in Jack's assumption that this retort is somehow a satisfactory reply to Jill's objections, while, in fact, it is completely irrelevant. Jack and Jill disagreed about Bush's motivation for invading Iraq, and Jill gave reasons to believe that Jack was mistaken. She did not claim that he had no right to this mistaken view. By pointing out that he is entitled to his view, Jack has simply changed the subject from the original topic, the reason Iraq was invaded, to a discussion of his rights. For all it contributes to the invasion question, he may as well have pointed out that whales are warm-blooded or that in Spain it rains mainly on the plains.

As with most of our fallacies, once seen, it is obvious. Here is a simple way of putting it. If the opinions to which we are entitled might nevertheless be false, the entitlement cannot properly be invoked to settle a dispute. It adds no new information on the original matter; it does nothing to show that the opinion in question is true.

Interpreting the cliché to exclude the possibility of falsity—that is, to mean that we are entitled to have all our opinions be *true*—has two problems. First, it is ridiculous. Second, it does not in fact make the entitlement to an opinion relevant in deciding who is correct in any dispute. If Jack has a right to his true opinion then presumably Jill has a right to hers too. But then, since Jack and Jill disagree, one of them must be suffering a rights violation; one of them has a false belief. So, even if we had the right to true beliefs, that would only show that it is a right that is violated all the time, on precisely those occasions when our opinions are in fact false. In any dispute, to know whose right to a true belief is being violated we would first need to work out whose belief is false. That is, we would need to settle the *original* dispute—in the case of Jack and Jill, about President Bush's reason for invading Iraq. And a diversion on the matter of rights gets no one any closer to answering that question.

So, even on the strongest, and utterly incredible, interpretation of our opinion entitlement, it is irrelevant to anything else we might be debating. Why then is insisting on one's right to an opinion such a popular argumentative ploy?

In part, it is encouraged by an ambiguity in the word *entitlement*. It has a political or legal interpretation, by which we are all entitled to any opinion we might have, however groundless. But it also has an epistemic interpretation, that is, one related to, or concerned with, truth or knowledge. You are entitled to an opinion, in this epistemic sense, only when you have good reasons for holding it: evidence, sound arguments, and so on. Far from being universal, this epistemic entitlement is the kind you earn. It is like being entitled to boast, which depends on having done something worth boasting about.

So, the two senses of entitlement could not be further from each other. Yet it is too tempting to muddle them. The implied argument of the muddler runs as follows:

1. If someone is entitled to an opinion then her opinion is well-supported by evidence. (This is precisely what it means to be entitled to an opinion.)
2. I am entitled to my opinion (as is everyone in a democratic society).
3. Therefore, my opinion is well-supported by evidence.

This is a beautiful example of the fallacy of equivocation, i.e., slipping between different meanings of a word in an argument that would be valid only if the word were used with the same meaning throughout. (See the chapter "Equivocation.")

Once pointed out, it's easy to see that this confusion of the political with the epistemic notion of entitlement is a mistake. And though, strictly, that will do for the purposes of this book, I don't want to leave the matter here. Even if the cliché that we are entitled to our opinions is not employed in the truly egregious way so far discussed, it is part of a mindset that increasingly impedes the free flow of ideas and their robust assessment. Many people seem to feel that their opinions are somehow sacred, so that everyone else is obliged to handle them with great care. When confronted with counterarguments, they do not pause and wonder if they might be wrong after all. They take offense.

The culture of caution this attitude generates is a serious obstacle to those who wish to get at the truth. So it is important to strip away any bogus ideas that support the attitude, such as the idea that we all have a right to our own opinions.

Rights and Duties

To see that there is really nothing at all to this idea that we have a right to our opinions we need only understand one basic point about rights, namely, that rights entail duties. I don't mean to endorse the fashionable slogan, "No rights without responsibilities," which is supposed to justify policies whereby the government imposes good behavior conditions on the receipt of social welfare. I mean something much more fundamental about rights: they are *defined* by the duties to which they give rise.[3]

The law gives all citizens a right to life. Your right to life means that everyone else has a duty not to kill you. This is not something that a government may or may not decide to associate with your right to life; it *is* that right. A law that did not impose on others a duty not to kill you would fail to establish your right to life. Does your right to life mean that others have a duty to feed you, to house you, or to provide you with medical care? These are hotly debated questions, but no one doubts that the answers to these questions about others' duties are what define and delimit the right to life.

So when anyone claims a right, first ask which duties does this right impose on others; that will tell you what the right is supposed to be. And it also provides a good test for whether there is, or should be, any such right. It will often be clear

[3] For those interested in a fuller discussion of the connection between rights and duties, see P. Jones, *Rights* (Basingstoke, McMillan, 1994).

that no one really has the implied duties, or that it would be preposterous to claim they should.

Mary Robinson, in her former role as the United Nations High Commissioner for Human Rights, claimed that we have a human right to be healthy. Yet, without qualification it is difficult to know what she could possibly have meant. According to the World Health Organization:

> Health is a state of complete physical, mental and social well-being and not merely the absence of disease or infirmity.

Yet everyone ages and dies. And when they do, their physical, mental, and social well-being are less than complete. So the simple fact of human mortality means that everyone's right to be healthy is ultimately violated, and someone has failed to do his duty. But what could that duty be? To find a remedy for human mortality, presumably. But who could possibly bear this burden? Surely not each of us, who mostly know so little about the mechanics of human aging.

There is, of course, no unqualified human right to good health, any more than there is a human right to all those other things that it would be nice to have—such as long eyelashes and silk sheets—but which no one has a duty to provide. If she wanted to make sense of her claim, Mary Robinson should have started with the duties rather than the right. What duties does each of us have with respect to others' health or governments with respect to the health of their citizens? Then we would know what this right to good health is supposed to amount to.

Opinion Duties

What then are the duties that the right to your opinions might entail? What am I obliged to do to respect this right? Let's start from the boldest possible demands and work down to the more humble.

Does your right to your opinion oblige me to agree with you?

No. If only because that would be impossible to square with the universality of the right to an opinion. I, too, am entitled to my own opinion which might contradict yours. Then we can't both do our duty toward each other. And think of the practical implications. Everyone would have to change his mind every time he met someone with a different opinion, changing his religion, his politics, his car, his eating habits. Foreign vacations would become as life-changing as the brochures claim.

Does your right to your opinion oblige me to listen to you?

No. I haven't the time. Many people have many opinions on many matters. You cannot walk through the West End of London without hearing some enthusiast declaring his opinions on our savior Jesus or on the Zionist conspiracy or some other topic of pressing concern. Listening to them all is practically impossible and not therefore a duty.

Does your right to your opinion oblige me to let you keep it?

This is the closest to what I think most mean when they claim a right to their opinion. They do so at just that point in an argument when they would otherwise be forced to admit error and change their position. And this is also the weakest possible interpretation of the right and thus the most likely to pass the test.

Yet it is still too strong. We have no duty to let others keep their opinions. On the contrary, we often have a duty to try to change them. Take an obvious example. You are about to cross the street with a friend. A car is coming yet your friend still takes a stride into the road. Knowing that she is not suicidal, you infer that she is of the opinion that no cars are coming. Are you obliged to let her keep this opinion?

I say no. You ought to take every reasonable measure to change her opinion, perhaps by drawing her attention to the oncoming car, saying something like, "Look out, a car is coming." By so doing, you have not violated her rights. Indeed, she will probably thank you. On matter like whether or not a car is about to crush them, everybody is interested in believing the truth; they will take the correction of their errors as a favor. The same goes for any other topic. If someone is interested in believing the truth, then she will not take the presentation of contrary evidence and argument as some kind of injury.

It's just that, on some topics, many people are not really interested in believing the truth. They might prefer it if their opinion turns out to be true—that would be the icing on the cake—but truth is not too important. Most of my friends, though subscribing to no familiar religion, claim to believe in a "superior intelligence" or "something higher than us." Yet they will also cheerfully admit the absence of even a shred of evidence. Never mind. There is no cost in error, because the claim is so vague that is has no implications for action (unlike the case of the oncoming car). They just like believing it, perhaps because it would be nice if it were true, or because it helps them get along with their religious parents, or for some other reason.

But truth really is not the point, and it is most annoying to be pressed on the matter. And to register this, to make it clear that truth is neither here nor there, they declare, "I am entitled to my opinion." Once you hear these words, you should realize that it is simple rudeness to persist with the matter. You may be interested in whether or not their opinion is true, but take the hint, they aren't. ■

AUTHOR PROFILE

Jamie Whyte (born 1965) is a philosopher, political writer, and New Zealand political figure. After finishing as an undergraduate at the University of Auckland, he moved to the United Kingdom to attend St. John's College, Cambridge, for his PhD in philosophy. After completing his graduate studies, Whyte served as a research fellow and philosophy lecturer at Corpus Christi College. Since his career in academia, he has served as a management consultant in New York while also publishing four popular books: *Crimes Against Logic* (2004), *A Load of Blair* (2005), *Free Thoughts* (2012), and *Quack Policy* (2013). Whyte is a free-market advocate and proponent of classical liberalism, who once served as the leader of ACT New Zealand. "The Right to Your Opinion" is a chapter from his first book, *Crimes Against Logic* (2004).

Making Systems of Privilege Visible

By Stephanie M. Wildman with Adrienne D. Davis

The notion of privilege, although part of the consciousness of popular culture, has not been recognized in legal language and doctrine. This failure to acknowledge privilege, to make it visible in legal doctrine, creates a serious gap in legal reasoning, rendering us unable to address issues of systemic unfairness.

The invisibility of privilege strengthens the power it creates and maintains. The invisible cannot be combated, and as a result privilege is allowed to perpetuate, regenerate, and re-create itself. Privilege is systemic, not an occasional occurrence. Privilege is invisible only until looked for, but silence in the face of privilege sustains its invisibility.

Silence is the lack of sound and voice. Silence may result from a desire for quiet; it may signify intense mental concentration; it may also arise from oppression or fear. Whatever the reason, when there is silence, no criticism is expressed. What we do not say, what we do not talk about, allows the status quo to continue. To describe these unspoken systems means we need to use language. But even when we try to talk about privilege, the language we use inhibits our ability to perceive the systems of privilege that constitute the status quo.

How Language Veils the Existence of Systems of Privilege

Language contributes to the invisibility and regeneration of privilege. To begin the conversation about subordination, we sort ideas into categories such as race and gender. These words are part of a system of categorization that we use without thinking and that seems linguistically neutral. Race and gender are, after all, just words.

Yet when we learn that someone has had a child, our first question is usually "Is it a girl or a boy?" Why do we ask that, instead of something like "Are the mother and child healthy?" We ask, "Is it a girl or a boy?" according to philosopher Marilyn Frye, because we do not know how to relate to this new being without knowing its gender.[1] Imagine how long you could have a discussion "With or about someone without knowing her or his gender. We place people into these categories because our world is gendered.

Similarly, our world is also raced, and it is hard for us to avoid taking mental notes as to race. We use our language to categorize by race, particularly, if we are white, when that race is other than white. Marge Shultz has written of calling on a Latino student in her class.[2] She called him Mr. Martinez, but his name was Rodriguez. The class tensed up at her error; earlier that same day another professor had called him Mr. Hemindez, the name of the defendant in the criminal law case under discussion. Professor Shultz talked with her class, at its next session, about her error and how our thought processes lead us to categorize in order to think. She acknowledged how this process leads to stereotyping that causes pain to individuals. We all live in this raced and gendered world, inside these powerful categories, that make it hard to see each other as whole people.

W

But the problem does not stop with the general terms "race" and "gender." Each of these categories contains the images, like an entrance to a tunnel with many passages and arrows pointing down each possible path, of subcategories. Race is often defined as Black and white; sometimes it is defined as white and "of color." There are other races, and sometimes the categories are each listed, for example, as African American, Hispanic American, Asian American, Native American, and White American, if whiteness is mentioned at all. All these words, describing racial subcategories, seem neutral on their face, like equivalent tides. But however the subcategories are listed, however neutrally the words are expressed, these words mask a system of power, and that system privileges whiteness.

Gender, too, is a seemingly neutral category that leads us to imagine subcategories of male and female. A recent scientific article suggested that five genders might be a more accurate characterization of human anatomy, but there is a heavy systemic stake in our image of two genders.[3] The apparently neutral categories male and female mask the privileging of males that is part of the gender power system. Try to think of equivalent gendered tides, like king and queen, prince and princess, and you will quickly see that male and female are not equal titles in our cultural imagination.

Poet and social critic Adrienne Rich has written convincingly about the compulsory heterosexuality that is part of this gender power system.[4] Almost everywhere we look, heterosexuality is portrayed as the norm. In Olympic ice-skating and dancing, for example, a couple is defined as a man partnered with a woman.[5] Heterosexuality is privileged over any other relationship. The words we use, such as "marriage,"' "husband," and "wife," are not neutral, but convey this privileging of heterosexuality. What is amazing, says Rich, is that there are any lesbians or gay men at all.[6]

Our culture suppresses conversation about class privilege as well as race and gender privileges. Although we must have money or access to money to obtain human necessities such as food, clothing, and shelter, those fundamental needs are recognized only as an individual responsibility. The notion of privilege based on economic wealth is viewed as a radical, dangerous idea, or an idiosyncratic throwback to the past, conjuring up countries with monarchies, nobility, serfs, and peasants. Yet even the archaic vocabulary makes clear that no one wants to be categorized as a have-not. The economic power system is not invisible—everyone knows that money brings privilege. But the myth persists that all have access to that power through individual resourcefulness. This myth of potential economic equality supports the invisibility of the other power systems that prevent fulfillment of that ideal.

Other words we use to describe subordination also mask the operation of privilege. Increasingly, people use terms like "racism" and "sexism" to describe disparate treatment and the perpetuation of power. Yet this vocabulary of "isms" as a descriptive shorthand for undesirable, disadvantaging treatment creates several serious problems.

First, calling someone a racist individualizes the behavior and veils the fact that racism can occur only where it is culturally, socially, and legally supported. It lays the blame on the individual rather than the systemic forces that have shaped that individual and his or her society. White people know they do not want to be labeled racist; they become concerned "With how to avoid that label, rather than worrying about systemic racism and how to change it.

Second, the isms language focuses on the larger category, such as race, gender, sexual preference. Isms language suggests that within these larger categories two seemingly neutral halves exist, equal parts in a mirror. Thus Black and white, male and female, heterosexual and gay/lesbian appear, through the linguistic juxtaposition, as equivalent subparts. In fact, although the category does not take note of it, Blacks and whites, men and women, heterosexuals and gays/lesbians are not equivalently situated in society. Thus the way we think and talk about the categories and subcategories that underlie the isms allows us to consider them parallel parts, and obscures the pattern of domination and subordination "Within each classification.

Similarly, the syllable "isms" itself gives the illusion that all patterns of domination and subordination are the same and interchangeable. The language suggests that someone subordinated under one form of oppression would be similarly situated to another person subordinated under another form. Thus, a person subordinated under one form may feel no need to view himself/herself as a possible oppressor, or beneficiary of oppression, within a different form. For example, white women, having an ism that defines their condition—sexism—may not look at the way they are privileged by racism. They have defined themselves as one of the oppressed.

Finally, the focus on individual behavior, the seemingly neutral subparts of categories, and the apparent interchangeability underlying the vocabulary of isms all obscure the existence of systems of privilege and power. It is difficult to see and talk about how oppression operates when the vocabulary itself makes these systems of privilege invisible. "White supremacy" is associated with a lunatic fringe, not with the everyday life of well-meaning white citizens. "Racism" is defined by whites in terms of specific, discriminatory racist actions by others. The vocabulary allows us to talk about discrimination and oppression, but it hides the mechanism that makes that oppression possible and efficient. It also hides the existence of specific, identifiable beneficiaries of oppression, who are not always the actual perpetrators of discrimination. The use of isms language, or any focus on discrimination, masks the privileging that is created by these systems of power.

Thus the very vocabulary we use to talk about discrimination obfuscates these power systems and the privilege that is their natural companion. To remedy discrimination effectively we must make the power systems and the privileges they create visible and part of the discourse. To move toward a unified theory of the dynamics of subordination, we have to find a way to talk about privilege. When we discuss race, sex, and sexual orientation, each needs to be described as a power system that creates privileges in some people as well as disadvantages in others. Most of the literature has focused on disadvantage or discrimination, ignoring the element of privilege. To really talk about these issues, privilege must be made visible.

What Is Privilege?

What then is privilege? We all recognize its most blatant forms. "Men only admitted to this club." "We will not allow African Americans into that school." Blatant exercises of privilege certainly exist, but they are not what most people think of as our way of life. They are only the tip of the iceberg, however.

When we try to look at privilege we see several elements. First, the characteristics of the privileged group define the societal norm, often benefiting those in the privileged group. Second, privileged group members can rely on their privilege and avoid objecting to oppression. Both the conflation of privilege with the societal norm and the implicit option to ignore oppression mean that privilege is rarely seen by the holder of the privilege.

A. The Normalization of Privilege

The characteristics and attributes of those who are privileged group members are described as societal norms—as the way things are and as what is normal in society.[7] This normalization of privilege means that members of society are judged, and succeed or fail, measured against the characteristics that are held by those privileged. The privileged characteristic is the norm; those who stand outside are the aberrant or "alternative."

For example, a thirteen-year-old girl who aspires to be a major-league ballplayer can have only a low expectation of achieving that goal, no matter how superior a batter and fielder she is. Maleness is the foremost "qualification" of major-league baseball players. Similarly, those who legally are permitted to marry are heterosexual. A gay or lesbian couple prepared to make a life commitment, cannot cross the threshold of qualification to be married.

I had an example of being outside the norm recently when I was called to jury service. Jurors are expected to serve until 5 P.M. During that year, my family's life was set up so that I picked up my children after school at 2:40 and made sure that they got to various activities. If courtroom life were designed to privilege my needs, then there would have been an afternoon recess to honor children. But in this culture children's lives and the lives of their caretakers are the alternative or other, and we must conform to the norm.

Even as these child care needs were outside the norm, I was privileged economically to be able to meet my children's needs. What many would have described as mothering, not privilege—my ability to pick them up and be present in their after-school lives—was a benefit of my association with privilege.

Members of the privileged group gain many benefits by their affiliation with the dominant side of the power system. This affiliation with power is not identified as such; often it may be transformed into and presented as individual merit. Legacy admissions at elite colleges and professional schools are perceived to be merit-based, when this process of identification with power and transmutation into qualifications occurs. Achievements by members of the privileged group are viewed as the result of individual effort, rather than privilege…

B. Choosing Whether to Struggle Against Oppression

Members of privileged groups can opt out of snuggles against oppression if they choose. Often this privilege may be exercised by silence. At the same time that I was the outsider in jury service, I was also a privileged insider. During *voir dire*, each prospective juror was asked to introduce herself or himself. The plaintiff's and defendant's attorneys then asked additional questions. I watched the defense attorney, during voir dire, ask each Asian-looking male prospective juror if he spoke English. No one else was asked. The judge did nothing. The Asian American man sitting next to me smiled and flinched as he was asked the questions. I wondered how many times in his life he had been made to answer such a question. I considered beginning my own questioning by saying, "I'm Stephanie Wildman, I'm a professor of law, and yes, I speak English." I wanted to focus attention on the subordinating conduct of the attorney, but I did not. I exercised my white privilege by my silence. I exercised my privilege to opt out of engagement, even though this choice may not always be consciously made by someone with privilege.

Depending on the number of privileges someone has, she or he may experience the power of choosing the types of struggles in which to engage. Even this choice may be masked as an identification with oppression, thereby making the privilege that enables the choice invisible.

...Privilege is not visible to its holder; it is merely there, a part of the world, a way of life, simply the way things are. Others have a *lack*, an absence, a deficiency.

Systems of Privilege

Although different privileges bestow certain common characteristics (membership in the norm, the ability to choose whether to object to the power system, and the invisibility of its benefit), the form of a privilege may vary according to the power relationship that produces it. White privilege derives from the race power system of white supremacy. Male privilege[8] and heterosexual privilege result from the gender hierarchy.[9] Class privilege derives form an economic, wealth-based hierarchy.

Visualizing Privilege

For me the struggle to visualize privilege has most often taken the form of the struggle to see my white privilege. Even as I write about this struggle, I fear that my own racism will make things worse, causing me to do more harm than good. Some readers may be shocked to see a white person contritely acknowledge that she is racist. I do not say this with pride. I simply believe that no matter how hard I work at not being racist, I still am. Because part of racism is systemic, I benefit from the privilege that I am struggling to see.

White do not look at the world through a filter of racial awareness, even though whites are, of course, members of a race. The power to ignore race, when white is the race, is a privilege, a societal advantage. The term "racism/white supremacy" emphasizes the link between discriminatory racism and the privilege held by whites to ignore their own race.

As bell hooks explains, liberal whites do not see themselves as prejudiced or interested in domination through coercion, yet "they cannot recognize the ways their actions support and affirm the very structure of racist domination and oppression that they profess to wish to see eradicated."[10] The perpetuation of white supremacy is racist.

All whites are racist in this use of the term, because we benefit from systemic white privilege. Generally whites think of racism as voluntary, intentional conduct, done by horrible others. Whites spend a lot of time trying to convince ourselves and each other that we are not racist. A big step would be for whites to admit that we are racist and then to consider what to do about it.[11] ■

Notes

1. See Marilyn Frye, *The Politics of Reality: Essays in Feminist Theory* 19–34 (1983) (discussing sex marking, sex announcing, and the necessity to determine gender).
2. Angela Harris and Marge Shultz, "A(nother) Critique of Pure Reason": *Toward Civic Virtue in Legal Education*, 45 Stan. L. Rev. 1773, 1796 (1993).
3. Anne Fausto-Sterling, *The Five Sexes: Why Male and Female Are Not Enough*, Sciences, Mar./Apr. 1993. (Thanks to Gregg Bryan for calling my attention to this article.) See also Frye, supra note 1, at 25.
4. Adrienne Rich, *Compulsory Heterosexuality and Lesbian Existence*, in Blood, Bread, and Poetry, Selected Prose 1979–1985 (1986).
5. See Stephanie M. Wildman and Becky Wildman-Tobriner, *Sex Roles Iced Popular Team?* S.F. Chron., Feb. 25, 1994, at A23.
6. Rich, supra note 4, at 57 ("Heterosexuality has been both forcibly and subliminally imposed on women").
7. Richard Delgado and Jean Stefancic, *Pornography and Harm to Women: "No Empirical Evidence?"* 53 Ohio St. L. J. 1037 (1992) (describing this "way things are." Because the norm or reality is perceived as including these benefits, the privileges are not visible.)
8. Catharine A. MacKinnon, *Toward a Feminist Theory of the State* 224 (1989).
9. Sylvia Law, *Homosexuality and the Social Meaning of Gender*, 1988 Wis. L. Rev. 187, 197 (1988); Marc Fajer, *Can Two Real Men Eat Quiche Together? Storytelling, Gender-Role Stereotypes, and Legal Protection for Lesbians and Gay Men*, 46 U. Miami L. Rev. 511., 617 (1992). Both articles describe heterosexism as a form of gender oppression.
10. bell hooks, *overcoming white supremacy: a comment*, in Talking Back: Thinking Feminist, Thinking Black 113 (1989).
11. See also Jerome McCristal Culp Jr., *Water Buffalo and Diversity: Naming Names and Reclaiming the Racial Discourse*, 26 Conn. L. Rev. 209 (1993) (urging people to name racism as racism).

AUTHOR PROFILE

Stephanie M. Wildman is a professor emerita of the University of San Francisco's School of Law and the current Director for the Center of Social Justice and Public Service at Santa Clara University School of Law. She specializes in social justice, gender and sex discrimination, and property law.

Adrienne D. Davis is a Professor of Law and Vice Provost of Washington University. She specializes in gender and feminist legal theory as well as race, race reparations, and slavery. Davis has also created several academic programs dedicated to the intersection of race, gender, and culture. She is a founder and the current director of the Black Sexual Economies Project at Washington University's Center for the Interdisciplinary Study of Work and Social Capital.

Wildman and Davis have collaborated on several writing projects, including *Privilege Revealed: How Invisible Preference Undermines America* (1996), winner of the the Gustavus Myers Center for Human Rights's 1997 Outstanding Book Award.

Selection from "Saved"

From *The Autobiography of Malcolm X: As Told to Alex Haley*

By Malcolm X [El-Hajj Malik El-Shabazz]

It was because of my letters that I happened to stumble upon starting to acquire some kind of a homemade education.

I became increasingly frustrated—at not being able to express what I wanted to convey in letters that I wrote, especially those to Mr. Elijah Muhammad. In the street, I had been the most articulate hustler out there–I had commanded attention when I said something. But now, trying to write simple English, I not only wasn't articulate, I wasn't even functional. How would I sound writing in slang, the way I would *say* it, something such as, "Look, daddy, let me pull your coat about a cat, Elijah Muhammad—"

Many who today hear me somewhere in person, or on television, or those who read something I've said, will think I went to school far beyond the eighth grade. This impression is due entirely to my prison studies.

It had really begun back in the Charlestown Prison, when Bimbi first made me feel envy of his stock of knowledge. Bimbi had always taken charge of any conversations he was in, and I had tried to emulate him. But every book I picked up had few sentences which didn't contain anywhere from one to nearly all of the words that might as well have been in Chinese. When I just skipped those words, of course, I really ended up with little idea of what the book said. So I had come to the Norfolk Prison Colony still going through only book-reading motions. Pretty soon, I would have quit even these motions, unless I had received the motivation that I did.

I saw that the best thing I could do was get hold of a dictionary—to study, to learn some words. I was lucky enough to reason also that I should try to improve my penmanship. It was sad. I couldn't even write in a straight line. It was both ideas together that moved me to request a dictionary along with some tablets and pencils from the Norfolk Prison Colony school.

I spent two days just riffling uncertainly through the dictionary's pages. I'd never realized so many words existed! I didn't know *which* words I needed to learn. Finally, just to start some kind of action, I began copying.

In my slow, painstaking, ragged handwriting, I copied into my tablet everything printed on that first page, down to the punctuation marks.

I believe it took me a day. Then, aloud, I read back, to myself, everything I'd written on the tablet. Over and over, aloud, to myself, I read my own handwriting.

I woke up the next morning, thinking about those words—immensely proud to realize that not only had I written so much at one time, but I'd written words that I never knew were in the world. Moreover, with a little effort, I also could remember what many of these words meant. I reviewed the words whose meanings I didn't remember. Funny thing, from the dictionary first page right now, that "aardvark" springs to my mind. The dictionary had a picture of it, a long-tailed, long-eared, burrowing African mammal, which lives off termites caught by sticking out its tongue as an anteater does for ants.

I was so fascinated that I went on—I copied the dictionary's next page. And the same experience came when I studied that. With every succeeding page, I also learned of people and places and events from history. Actually the dictionary is like a miniature encyclopedia. Finally the dictionary's A section had filled a whole tablet—and I went on into the B's. That was the way I started copying what eventually became the entire dictionary. It went a lot faster after so much practice helped me to pick up handwriting speed. Between what I wrote in my tablet, and writing letters, during the rest of my time in prison I would guess I wrote a million words.

I suppose it was inevitable that as my word-base broadened, I could for the first time pick up a book and read and now begin to understand what the book was saying. Anyone who has read a great deal can imagine the new world that opened. Let me tell you something: from then until I left that prison, in every free moment I had, if I was not reading in the library, I was reading on my bunk. You couldn't have gotten me out of books with a wedge. Between Mr. Muhammad's teachings, my correspondence, my visitors,… and my reading of books, months passed without my even thinking about being imprisoned. In fact, up to then, I never had been so truly free in my life.

The Norfolk Prison Colony's library was in the school building. A variety of classes was taught there by instructors who came from such places as Harvard and Boston universities. The weekly debates between inmate teams were also held in the school building. You would be astonished to know how worked up convict debaters and audiences would get over subjects like "Should Babies Be Fed Milk?"

Available on the prison library's shelves were books on just about every general subject. Much of the big private collection that Parkhurst[1] had willed to the prison was still in crates and boxes in the back of the library—thousands of old books. Some of them looked ancient: covers faded, oldtime parchment-looking binding. Parkhurst…seemed to have been principally interested in history and religion. He had the money and the special interest to have a lot of books that you wouldn't have in a general circulation. Any college library would have been lucky to get that collection.

As you can imagine, especially in a prison where there was heavy emphasis on rehabilitation, an inmate was smiled upon if he demonstrated an unusually intense interest in books. There was a sizable number of well-read inmates, especially the popular debaters. Some were said by many to be practically walking encyclopedias. They were almost celebrities. No university would ask any student to devour literature as I did when this new world opened to me, of being able to read and *understand.*

I read more in my room than in the library itself. An inmate who was known to read a lot could check out more than the permitted maximum number of books. I preferred reading in the total isolation of my own room.

[1] Charles H. Parkhurst (1842–1933); American clergyman, reformer, and president of the Society for the Prevention of Crime.

When I had progressed to really serious reading, every night at about ten P.M. I would be outraged with the "lights out." It always seemed to catch me right in the middle of something engrossing.

Fortunately, right outside my door was a corridor light that cast a glow into my room. The glow was enough to read by, once my eyes adjusted to it. So when "lights out" came, I would sit on the floor where I could continue reading in that glow.

At one-hour intervals at night guards paced past every room. Each time I heard the approaching footsteps, I jumped into bed and feigned sleep. And as soon as the guard passed, I got back out of bed onto the floor area of that light-glow, where I would read for another fifty-eight minutes until the guard approached again. That went on until three or four every morning. Three or four hours of sleep a night was enough for me. Often in the years in the streets I had slept less than that.

The teachings of Mr. Muhammad stressed how history had been "whitened"—when white men had written history books, the black man simply had been left out. Mr. Muhammad couldn't have said anything that would have struck me much harder. I had never forgotten how when my class, me and all of those whites, had studied seventh-grade United States history back in Mason, the history of the Negro had been covered in one paragraph, and the teacher had gotten a big laugh with his joke, "Negroes' feet are so big that when they walk, they leave a hole in the ground."

This is one reason why Mr. Muhammad's teachings spread so swiftly all over the United States, among *all* Negroes, whether or not they became followers of Mr. Muhammad. The teachings ring true-to every Negro. You can hardly show me a black adult in America—or a white one, for that matter—who knows from the history books anything like the truth about the black man's role. In my own case, once I heard of the "glorious history of the black man," I took special pains to hunt in the library for books that would inform me on details about black history.

I can remember accurately the very first set of books that really impressed me. I have since bought that set of books and I have it at home for my children to read as they grow up. It's called *Wonders of the World.* It's full of pictures of archeological finds, statues that depict, usually, non-European people.

I found books like Will Durant's *Story of Civilization.* I read H. G. Wells' *Outline of History. Souls of Black Folk* by W. E. B. Du Bois gave me a glimpse into the black people's history before they came to this country. Carter G. Woodson's *Negro History* opened my eyes about black empires before the black slave was brought to the United States, and the early Negro struggles for freedom.

J. A. Rogers' three volumes of *Sex and Race* told about race-mixing before Christ's time; and Aesop being a black man who told fables; about Egypt's Pharaohs; about the great Coptic Christian Empire[2]; about Ethiopia, the earth's oldest continuous black civilization, as China is the oldest continuous civilization.

Mr. Muhammad's teaching about how the white man had been created led me to *Findings in Genetics*, by Gregor Mendel. (The dictionary's G section was where I had learned what "genetics" meant.) I really studied this book by the Austrian monk. Reading it over and over, especially certain sections, helped me to

2 A native Egyptian Christian church that retains elements of its African origins.

understand that if you started with a black man, a white man could be produced; but starting with a white man, you never could produce a black man—because the white chromosome is recessive. And since no one disputes that there was but one Original Man, the conclusion is clear.

During the last year or so, in the *New York Times*, Arnold Toynbeell used the word "bleached" in describing the white man. His words were: "White (i.e., bleached) human beings of North European origin…" Toynbee also referred to the European geographic area as only a peninsula of Asia. He said there was no such thing as Europe. And if you look at the globe, you will see for yourself that America is only an extension of Asia. (But at the same time Toynbee is among those who have helped to bleach history. He has written that Africa was the only continent that produced no history. He won't write that again. Every day now, the truth is coming to light.)

I never will forget how shocked I was when I began reading about slavery's total horror. It made such an impact upon me that it later became one of my favorite subjects when I became a minister of Mr. Muhammad's. The world's most monstrous crime, the sin and the blood on the white man's hands, are almost impossible to believe. Books like the one by Frederick Olmsted opened my eyes to the horrors suffered when the slave was landed in the United States. The European woman, Fanny Kemble, who had married a Southern white slaveowner, described how human beings were degraded. Of course I read *Uncle Tom's Cabin*. In fact, I believe that's the only novel I have ever read since I started serious reading.

Parkhurst's collection also contained some bound pamphlets of the Abolitionist Anti-Slavery Society of New England. I read descriptions of atrocities, saw those illustrations of black slave women tied up and flogged with whips; of black mothers watching their babies being dragged off, never to be seen by their mothers again; of dogs after slaves, and of the fugitive slave catchers, evil white men with whips and clubs and chains and guns. I read about the slave preacher Nat Turner, who put the fear of God into the white slave master. Nat Turner wasn't going around preaching pie-in-the-sky and "non-violent" freedom for the black man. There in Virginia one night in 1831, Nat and seven other slaves started out at his master's home and through the night they went from one plantation "big house" to the next, killing, until by the next morning 57 white people were dead and Nat had about 70 slaves following him. White people, terrified for their lives, fled from their homes, locked themselves up in public buildings, hid in the woods, and some even left the state. A small army of soldiers took two months to catch and hang Nat Turner. Somewhere I have read where Nat Turner's example is said to have inspired John Brown to invade Virginia and attack Harpers Ferry nearly thirty years later, with thirteen white men and five Negroes.

I read Herodotus, "the father of History," or, rather, I read about him. And I read the histories of various nations, which opened my eyes gradually, then wider and wider, to how the whole world's white men had indeed acted like devils, pillaging and raping and bleeding and draining the whole world's non-white people. I remember, for instance, books such as Will Durant's *The Story of Oriental Civilization*, and Mahatma Gandhi's accounts of the struggle to drive the British out of India.

Book after book showed me how the white man had brought upon the world's black, brown, red, and yellow peoples every variety of the suffering of exploitation. I saw how since the sixteenth century, the so-called "Christian trader" white man began to ply the seas in his lust for Asian and African empires, and plunder, and power. I read, I saw, how the white man never has gone among the non-white peoples bearing the Cross in the true manner and spirit of Christ's teachings—meek, humble, and Christlike.

I perceived, as I read, how the collective white man had been actually nothing but a piratical opportunist who used Faustian machinations[3] to make his own Christianity his initial wedge in criminal conquests. First, always "religiously," he branded "heathen" and "pagan" labels upon ancient non-white cultures and civilizations. The stage thus set, he then turned upon his non-white victims his weapons of war.

I read how, entering India—half a *billion* deeply religious brown people—the British white man, by 1759, through promises, trickery, and manipulations, controlled much of India through Great Britain's East India Company. The parasitical British administration kept tentacling out to half of the sub-continent. In 1857, some of the desperate people of India finally mutinied—and, excepting the African slave trade, nowhere has history recorded any more unnecessary bestial and ruthless human carnage than the British suppression of the non-white Indian people.

Over 115 million African blacks—close to the 1930's population of the United States-were murdered or enslaved during the slave trade. And I read how when the slave market was glutted, the cannibalistic white powers of Europe next carved up, as their colonies, the richest areas of the black continent. And Europe's chancelleries for the next century played a chess game of naked exploitation and power from Cape Horn to Cairo.

Ten guards and the warden couldn't have torn me out of those books. Not even Elijah Muhammad could have been more eloquent than those books were in providing indisputable proof that the collective white man had acted like a devil in virtually every contact he had with the world's collective non-white man. I listen today to the radio, and watch television, and read the headlines about the collective white man's fear and tension concerning China. When the white man professes ignorance about why the Chinese hate him so, my mind can't help flashing back to what I read, there in prison, about how the blood forebears of this same white man raped China at a time when China was trusting and helpless. Those original white "Christian traders" sent into China millions of pounds of opium. By 1839, so many of the Chinese were addicts that China's desperate government destroyed twenty thousand chests of opium. The first Opium war[4] was promptly declared by the white man. Imagine! Declaring *war* upon someone who objects to being narcotized! The Chinese were severely beaten, with Chinese-invented gunpowder.

The Treaty of Nanking made China pay the British white man for the destroyed opium; forced open China's major ports to British trade; forced China to abandon Hong Kong; fixed China's import tariffs so low that cheap British articles soon flooded in, maiming China's industrial development.

---

[3] Evil plots or schemes. Faust was a fictional character who sold his soul to the devil for knowledge and power.

[4] The "Opium War" of 1839–1842 was between Britain and China and ended when Hong Kong was handed over to Britain.

After a second Opium War, the Tientsin Treaties legalized the ravaging opium trade, legalized a British-French-American control of China's customs. China tried delaying that Treaty's ratification; Peking was looted and burned.

"Kill the foreign white devils!" was the 1901 Chinese war cry in the Boxer Rebellion.[5] Losing again, this time the Chinese were driven from Peking's choicest areas. The vicious, arrogant white man put up the famous signs, "Chinese and dogs not allowed."

Red China after World War II closed its doors to the Western white world. Massive Chinese agricultural, scientific, and industrial efforts are described in a book that *Life* magazine recently published. Some observers inside Red China have reported that the world never has known such a hate-white campaign as is now going on in this non-white country where, present birth-rates continuing, in fifty more years Chinese will be half the earth's population. And it seems that some Chinese chickens will soon come home to roost, with China's recent successful nuclear tests.

Let us face reality. We can see in the United Nations a new world order being shaped, along color lines—an alliance among the non-white nations. America's U.N. Ambassador Adlai Stevenson complained not long ago that in the United Nations "a skin game" was being played. He was right. He was facing reality. A "skin game" is being played. But Ambassador Stevenson sounded like Jesse James accusing the marshal of carrying a gun. Because who in the world's history ever has played a worse "skin game" than the white man?

Mr. Muhammad, to whom I was writing daily, had no idea of what a new world had opened up to me through my efforts to document his teachings in books.

When I discovered philosophy, I tried to touch all the landmarks of philosophical development. Gradually, I read most of the old philosophers, Occidental and Oriental. The Oriental philosophers were the ones I came to prefer; finally, my impression was that most Occidental philosophy had largely been borrowed from the Oriental thinkers. Socrates, for instance, traveled in Egypt. Some sources even say that Socrates was initiated into some of the Egyptian mysteries. Obviously Socrates got some of his wisdom among the East's wise men.

I have often reflected upon the new vistas that reading opened to me. I knew right there in prison that reading had changed forever the course of my life. As I see it today, the ability to read awoke inside me some long dormant craving to be mentally alive. I certainly wasn't seeking any degree, the way a college confers a status symbol upon its students. My homemade education gave me, with every additional book that I read, a little bit more sensitivity to the deafness, dumbness, and blindness that was afflicting the black race in America. Not long ago, an English writer telephoned me from London, asking questions. One was, "What's your alma mater?" I told him, "Books." You will never catch me with a free fifteen minutes in which I'm not studying something I feel might be able to help the black man.

Yesterday I spoke in London, and both ways on the plane across the Atlantic I was studying a document about how the United Nations proposes to insure the human rights of the oppressed minorities of the world. The American black man

[5] The Boxer Rebellion of 1898–1900. An uprising by members of a secret Chinese society who opposed foreign influence in Chinese affairs.

is the world's most shameful case of minority oppression. What makes the black man think of himself as only an internal United States issue is just a catch-phrase, two words, "civil rights." How is the black man going to get "civil rights" before first he wins his *human* rights? If the American black man will start thinking about his *human* rights, and then start thinking of himself as part of one of the world's great peoples, he will see he has a case for the United Nations.

I can't think of a better case! Four hundred years of black blood and sweat invested here in America, and the white man still has the black man begging for what every immigrant fresh off the ship can take for granted the minute he walks down the gangplank.

But I'm digressing. I told the Englishman that my alma mater was books, a good library. Every time I catch a plane, I have with me a book that I want to read—and that's a lot of books these days. If I weren't out here every day battling the white man, I could spend the rest of my life reading, just satisfying my curiosity—because you can hardly mention anything I'm not curious about. I don't think anybody ever got more out of going to prison than I did. In fact, prison enabled me to study far more intensively than I would have if my life had gone differently and I had attended some college. I imagine that one of the biggest troubles with colleges is there are too many distractions, too much panty-raiding, fraternities, and boola-boola and all of that. Where else but in a prison could I have attacked my ignorance by being able to study intensely sometimes as much as fifteen hours a day? ■

AUTHOR PROFILE

El-Hajj Malik El-Shabazz (1925–1965, best known as Malcolm X) was a writer, scholar, Muslim minister, and passionate spokesman for civil rights. Born Malcolm Little, he changed his name to Malcolm X in 1950 in rejection of the erasure of black identity that came from imposition of European names onto enslaved people. He joined the Nation of Islam in the 1940s, and underwent a second name change after his completion of the Hajj in the mid-1960s. "Saved" is excerpted from *The Autobiography of Malcolm X* (1965), an autobiographical text adapted by journalist Alex Haley from a series of interviews conducted between Haley and El-Shabazz. This passage tells the story of his self-education. Although he was an honors student in his youth, El-Shabazz left school after receiving discouragement from a teacher who believed advanced schooling was not appropriate for black youth. El-Shabazz often cited his real education as beginning in adulthood, outside the biases of the mainstream educational system. El-Shabazz was assassinated on February 21, 1965. Today he is regarded as an icon of the African-American civil rights movement.

STUDENT ESSAYS

There Must Be Something

By Jessica Schuler

1ST PLACE—NARRATIVE

Kneeling in a black dress with my palms folded, mimicking my father's that rested on the pulpit in front of us, I glanced around trying to catch my cousins' eyes, but they were all closed in prayer. Stubborn child that I was, I kept mine open and continued to peer about the church at all the sad, lowered heads. Finally everyone began to rise. Shaking my tiny feet, I glanced again at my father. He was looking very serious. I, however, was feeling very bored. The black dress began to stick to my back. The man standing at the front, one of my relatives, not that I really knew who he was, was speaking about how Grandma Wheeler was in "a better place now." I frowned; to my knowledge, Grandma Wheeler was in the ground. Later, more people stood and spoke. I learned that this "better place" everyone was referring to was heaven. My four-year old mind couldn't help but wander. I imagined the pearly gates and the angels sitting on clouds playing trumpets. Yes, I decided, that would be a better place than the ground.

I sat staring blankly at the screen. Never in my six (almost seven!) years of life had I seen a more depressing movie. Dogs should not die in movies, even if they are cartoons. He went to heaven, for sure, it's in the title "All Dogs Go to Heaven"; but he died. In the other room I heard my mother say, "If there was ever a man to go to hell…" I poked my head in and looked at the TV. A man was being escorted in a dark room by two men in black ski masks, he wore a noose around his neck. "Who is?" My mom turned around quickly and told me I shouldn't be watching this and she's sorry I heard that. I walked in and sat next to her. "Why does he have a rope?" She sighed and looked over at my father. He looked at me and said that the man was Saddam Hussein and he was being executed, meaning that he was going to die. "Oh no! Is anyone going to save him?" My mom put her arm around me and whispered, "No, this is a good thing. He's a very bad guy, he's killed a lot of innocent people." I quieted down and let my mom cover my eyes. What happened next wasn't something I wanted to see. After my mom went to bed, I stayed up with my dad. "What's hell?" He rubbed the little spot at the top of his nose, in between his eyes, something he did when I asked a question he didn't want to answer. "Hell is a place where bad people go after they die." Out came the classic "why?" question from my little lips. "It's a place for them to feel the pain they inflicted." I went to bed that night thinking about what that meant.

Finally. History, my favorite class of the day. Fourth grade meant Greek mythology, which to me meant fairytales for an entire hour. Miss Piro stood at the front of the room dressed in a tight black turtleneck and a long grey skirt. Around her neck she wore a long necklace with a skull charm that rested just above her naval. She had sitting beside her a sliced open pink fruit, overflowing with pink seeds. "Turn to page 56, if you please." I whipped out my *D'Aulalaires' Book of Greek Myths* and began rapidly flipping through the pages, excited to know what the fruit was and how Miss Piro's outfit corresponded with our lesson for the day. Written at the top of page 56 was one word, Hades. Miss Piro hopped off her desk where she had been perched and smiled at us. "Today we're going to learn about the Underworld." She continued the lesson, telling tales of how the Greeks would place a gold coin under the tongue of the deceased in order to grant them passage over the river Styx. Once across they would be allowed in one of the three planes of the Underworld. Most souls would be doomed to wander the lands of Hades forever rotting in the bleak dreariness. The wicked would be damned into the dark pits of Tartarus, to suffer and be tortured for their lives. However, a select few, the heroes and kings, would be destined for the golden fields of Elysium. The Underworld was ruled by Hades and his queen, Persephone, whom he had trapped by inviting her eat six pomegranate seeds, the food of the Underworld. "So there isn't just heaven and hell." I thought. That's just a religion, just as these myths are. Religion's nothing but fairytales we tell ourselves to understand the world we're living in. "So what comes next?"

I sat in the front of Mr. Thompson's seventh grade English class, completely turned around in my seat, explaining to my best friend, Caitlyn, just what she had missed in last night's reading. "So, basically, Faustus is this guy who makes a deal with the devil where he sells him his soul in exchange for power and knowledge. He obviously needed the knowledge or else he wouldn't have made the deal with the devil in the first place? Amiright? Anyways, he gets 24 years on Earth, and then he's damned to hell. The play's full of him missing opportunities to repent, probably meaning it's never too late to repent, but in the end he goes to hell. I don't personally buy it, but whatever." "What do you mean you don't buy it?" "I just don't really believe in the whole idea of heaven and hell as presented certain religions." "Why?" "I don't know, I guess I'm just not that religious." Behind her purple-rimmed glasses, Caitlyn's bright blue eyes grew a little darker. Her cheeks turned slightly redder and I saw her forehead crease. She looked so insulted; so shocked that anyone could possibly believe that there wasn't a heaven and hell. I grinned at her, "Are you alright?" "Fine." She snapped, then flipped open her own copy of Faustus. She didn't seem fine; she seemed personally offended by my own beliefs, something I thought I could discuss with her openly. As I turned back around in my seat and faced the blank chalkboard, I suddenly realized that my best friend was uninterested in the notion that there could be something else after death other than what the Bible dictated. My open minded, overwhelmingly liberal friend was a devout Catholic, who just realized her own best friend was anything but.

I sprinted up the stairs with my friend Allie hot on my heels, breath caught in our throats. We were sixteen years old and up until now had thought that ghosts only belonged in the horror films. We stopped at the top of the stairs and looked down towards the dark basement where a Ouija board I had just purchased from a flea market sat on the floor with two candles on either side. "You swear you weren't pushing it?" she screamed at me. Her eyes were still seeing the arrow trace the word GOODBYE written across the bottom of the Ouija board. "No! I've told you a hundred times! It works!" "How can it work?" It was my aunt who had first introduced me to the idea of owning a Ouija board. Ever since she told me about it over dinner at Silverado's, it was all I could think about. Ouija boards were the best way to communicate with the other side, that is until they got annoyed with the conversation. You would think that ghosts would just be waiting for another person to talk to and discuss their feelings with, but apparently that was not the case with this one. I sighed, adrenaline rush over. "We should go get the board." "Are you f-ing kidding me?" She still looked terrified. "The board said 'GOODBYE', that means the spirit left." We went back down and flipped on the light switch. With a single breath we blew out the candles and watched the smoke dance about until it dissolved into the air.

"First day of sophomore year." I smiled at myself in the mirror. "No longer freshmeat." "Jessica, I swear to God if you don't get your butt downstairs, we're leaving without you." I rolled my eyes, but snatched up my book bag and my already worn out copy of *Hamlet*. In the past year I had already read it three times and highlighted all my favorite passages. The beach over the summer had left the pages thinner and weaker, but I had decided earlier that I would try annotating it this time around, determined that pages were not so weak as to rip upon coming in contact with a pen. I was pretty far along already, but then again, Hamlet hadn't completely lost it quite yet. As I sat in my chemistry class after reviewing the syllabus and now with nothing to do, I pulled out the play and opened to where I had left off. I was on Hamlet's "To be or not to be" speech, arguably Shakespeare's most famous speech of all his plays. "To sleep, perchance to dream." I couldn't help but smile at the line. Dreaming while dead. It was a ridiculous thought. "For in this sleep of death, what dreams may come?" Maybe it wasn't that ridiculous. I started writing furiously on the opposite page in bright pink pen. "Wouldn't it be wonderful if death were just a never-ending sleep where we dream forevermore? If we are guilty then those dreams would be nightmares of crimes once committed. But if we were good we are allowed to dream peacefully for the remainder of eternity. Just a philosophy…" Everyone's idea of heaven is different, different things make different people happy. If your soul just dreamed, you would have your own personal heaven or hell and it would never fill up with other spirits. Maybe ghosts are just lucid dreamers. My Hamlet had become a sort of journal, something so special I could never possibly share its secrets.

I'm sitting here at my desk at two in the morning staring past my computer screen out the 18-story high window into the city thinking about how the city lights replace the stars in the sky and how there's a belief that when we die, our souls fly up through the black cloth that is our sky and break tiny holes to reach heaven and that is why we have stars. I look back at my bright computer screen, then over at my sleeping roommates. I'm on the last paragraph, the conclusion, probably my least favorite part of any paper. How can one write a conclusion that isn't a bookend? I look back out into the city then glance back up at the never-ending sea of black, thinking of how in such a huge universe where so many things are possible even among the tiniest of creatures; people can still sit content with their thoughts that there isn't an afterlife. The fact that so many people who have seen life's greatest miracles believe that afterwards it just ends is as unfathomable as the universe in which we live. There must be something.

The Perfectionist

By LaRissa Rogers

2ND PLACE—NARRATIVE

Upon seeing the painting for the first time at the age of seventeen, I was disturbed; it had an ugly edge and, despite the bright colors, an unsettling anger and violence seethed under its fractured surface. The boy in the painting did not become a man, but rather a skull with no body. The childlike drawings, scribblings, and letter printing could be mistaken for rubbish, but Basquiat transmuted human emotion into images that were not pretty, but profound and beautiful nevertheless the presence of the boy in the painting was expressed by absence. Basquiat changed contemporary standards for art: taking art off of the gallery wall and into the street, skewing traditional perspective with primitive scrawls, and ultimately, changing me.

I wasn't always inspired by messiness. When I was little, I hated getting my hands dirty. Sandboxes were too messy, play-dough smelled funny, and anything short of a clean line would set me on edge. I was a perfectionist; maybe I still am a little bit. Mentally, physically, spiritually, I wanted to achieve excellence, and failure conditioned my satisfaction. I wasn't able to admit the truth of that old saw—"nobody's perfect"—until I saw a giant beautiful mess of scribbles and shapes.

"Untitled, 1981" by Jean-Michel Basquiat is the opposite of what I would have considered "perfect" growing up. Angry and "childlike" to the uneducated eye, his work manifests the complexity of consciousness itself, the way we see things as ourselves and as our former selves. Beauty lies within chaos and imperfection; it builds on our past perceptions. In this painting, Basquiat taps into emotions that are not easily expressible, but this painting found a visual way to express the complex emotions I had felt but not been able to convey.

I always felt misunderstood and complicated, as if no one truly knew me. In eighth grade I started to become friends with the "popular pretty girls." Before I became part of their clique I envied their supposed perfection. They had glamorous big houses, nice clothes, and a perfect "Sisterhood of The Traveling Pants" type of friendship. So when I began to have lunch with them and get invited to their parties I felt honored. But I soon realized that their perfection that appealed to me originally was not perfection at all. They made fun of girls at the lunch table, calling them fat and pointing out their flaws. Most importantly certain people were not to be associated with because they dressed different, were not thin enough, did not have enough money or were not pretty enough. Soon, the morals that I had been taught from a young age began to waiver and I could no longer pretend to hide behind this fake persona to please my new supposed friends.

The combination of harsh and blurred lines in Basquiat's painting created a paradoxical effect that I could relate to. This one picture portrayed life, and the harsh lines showed the real self hiding behind my false front, but the blurred lines left the sense of ambiguity that is part of life. Like the painting, I was complex and had many layers. The colors, while disturbing, were honest, true, and direct. This one picture reflected life as a journey, with ups and downs, triumphs and failures, beauty and ugliness. The transformation of the boy into the skull was a visual reminder of how destructive and toxic perfectionism could be. Perfectionism not only tore down my self-esteem by convincing me I was never good enough, but it left with overwhelming feelings of anger and depression similar to the black and red accents of color in the painting. My thoughts and perception of myself stopped me from reaching my full potential, which could be directly related to the stitching of the skull within Basquiat's work. The stitching links everything together, the color, and the emotion into one. It's the backbone of not only the picture but in my case, what made me, me.

This painting made me realize the extent of damage that I was causing myself, and how oblivious I was to my own corrupted outlook. It was like a prophecy in a sense: if I stayed on the path I was on I would slowly decay and become a skeleton fragile and without flesh or depth. Basquiat was scared and trampled by the art world, confident as an artist, haunted by prejudice, he was always on a quest for the acknowledgement and appreciation of his own artistic expression, never quite accepted or appreciated for his brilliance. I felt the same, misunderstood.

I wanted to be perfect because I wanted to get good grades, have a lot of friends, and achieve success. But at the same time I loved and hated the idea of having to be perfect. I loved the idea of perfection because it is virtually programed into every human being to see it, but on the other hand perfection was stressful and impossibly difficult to achieve. This idea of my having to be perfect can be seen through an art assignment I was given in kindergarten. I was asked to paint a tree with leaves. The teacher gave the class an array of colors to use for the project, but in my mind none of the colors were good enough. Instead of using the colors given, I mixed my own fancy pastel colors and then and only then did I deem the colors "perfect." But, I also remember not being able to run the mile in gym class, and as I walked around the field praying to God that I wouldn't die I envied every pretty, thin, white girl who could. I remember being called fat and not feeling comfortable to sit at the desk, tie my own shoe, or change for gym class in front of my peers. I remember the tears and hatred that I inflicted onto myself for not being "perfect" in society's eyes. I wasn't thin, pretty, or confident because I wasn't able to reach this perfect physical state. I pretended to be happy, I pretended that I didn't cry myself to sleep, and I pretended that I didn't care what others thought of me. And because I wasn't perfect in those aspects I focused on being perfect in everything else that I did—down to my handwriting.

This one piece of artwork unsettled me because it was the simple truth with no sugar coating. It surprised me how honest Basquiat was able to be, but also simple and complex at the same time. Simple in the fact that his paintings were childlike and mimicked scribbles, but complex and highly sophisticated in the way that he was able to load context, emotion, information and meaning into one painting. His stripped down wordplay that is disguised by a top layer of scribbles combined with images suggest the human consciousness, and defines art in a way that had not been done before. By scribbling over his initial words it seemed as another way of reinforcing this idea of suffocation of not only the mind but the struggle between two choices, similarly to how I felt. Art embodies the reality of everyday life; imperfect and beautiful. The words act as a sword, cutting through the initial completion of the painting and unveiling its ugliness. The painting was a revelation, and made me examine myself. It felt as if the painting were a mirror reflecting my personal secrets back at me, forcing me to open my eyes and face reality. It showed me the beauty in imperfection.

After realizing that imperfection is beautiful I no longer worry about being perfect in everything I do. I am the beautiful intense colors in Basquiat's painting, and I am also the childlike scribblings. I have flaws and imperfections, but those imperfections complement the beauty in a way that intensifies its presence. Perfection is not universal, and even though it took me seventeen years and a disturbingly beautiful piece of artwork to realize that, perfection is not everything. Perfection is an ideal and cannot be reached, and there *is* beauty in imperfection.

The Commodification of the Human Genome

By Katharine Thompson

1ST PLACE—ANALYSIS

There is little argument over the importance of the Human Genome Project to better predict and treat illnesses and create a more efficient health care process. The applications of genetic research range from cancer prediction and prevention to life-saving treatments. However, for some, the obvious humanitarian benefits are not enough. Recent genetic research has been marked by intense competition between scientists to stake claims in this field and has led to an outbreak of gene patenting. Since the boom in genetic research sparked by the commencement of the Human Genome Project in 1990, approximately twenty percent of the human genome has been patented largely by pharmaceutical companies (Robertson 379, Rausch). Gene patenting makes genes that have been discovered the intellectual property of the scientist or the company that funded the scientist's research and creates a royalty system where the scientist or company profits from any research and treatment involving the gene (Robertson 380). As a result, the cost to perform genetic studies increases because researchers must pay to use any relevant patented genes, while the healthcare costs of tests and treatments for patients also drastically rises. Companies must work toward making a profit and that scientists must fulfill their innovative research goals, but it is important to balance their respective goals with the medical needs of patients and the furthering of scientific advancements. From these perspectives, the question emerges as to whether it is ethical for a company or individual to claim ownership of genetic information since anyone who has a genetic condition or that may be at risk of developing an illness linked to his or her genetics may be dependent on advancements in scientific research and access to medical treatments resulting from the patents. The ethical implications of gene patenting on the availability of healthcare and rewards for companies and researchers will be explored through the application of Sandel's "The Lost Art of Democratic Debate," Singer's "The Drowning Child and the Expanding Circle," and Asma's "The Myth of Universal Love."

First of all, we must consider what this means for the majority group that is involved— the general public who might need access to the medical care resulting from gene patents. According to Singer, "Our capacity to affect what is happening, anywhere in the world, is one way in which we are living in an era of global responsibility" (381). From this perspective, gene patenting is unjust because it privileges the few who discover the gene or can afford to study or test it and prevents the greatest many—the patients—from reaping the benefits of the research. Sandel would argue that the purpose of scientific research and the qualities worth honoring of these researchers must be established to formulate a response to the problem. He might find that the scientists involved in the discovery of genes deserve to be honored for their innovations and important contributions to research because without them we would not have discoveries that improve our quality of life. Asma would agree with Sandel that the establishment and continuations of the virtues that promote scientific discovery is most important but would sharply disagree with Singer's idea of "global responsibility" (381) because he believes that the "equal and impartial concern of all human beings" is impossible (Asma 12). In contrast to Sandel and Singer, Asma promotes "loyalty" for the "kith and kin," leading to the question of who among patients, fellow medical professionals, patent holders, and researchers deserves the priority of doctors (14).

In order to properly address this question, the different interpretations of the purpose of scientific research must be considered. As this question is adapted to different perspectives of the purpose of research and medical care, Sandel's ethical perspective shifts. If Sandel defined the purpose of scientific research as the resulting well-being of patients, doctors would hold the needs of patients above researchers and pharmaceutical companies. With this interpretation, we see Sandel's overall view shift to an anti-patent view and align with Singer while contrasting with Asma. This is because the function of research has changed from a commodity to a humanitarian act, which shifts Sandel's ethical assessment of the scientist's role. Singer would agree that the patent holders should not need an incentive to conduct research that could prevent disease and save the lives of their fellow men. He believes that the interest of the largest group of stakeholders—the patients—is the top priority because it has the potential for the greatest overall effect. As a result of this interpretation, Asma would believe that doctors experience enough enjoyment and satisfaction from their contribution to the betterment of patients' lives because they are their "kith and kin."

On the other hand, Sandel could also take on the view that the fundamental purpose of medical care and, in this case, genetic research is solely the gain of knowledge and understanding of the human genome. The scientist is no longer a humanitarian but is a vehicle for the understanding of nature's work. With this interpretation, Sandel would disagree with Singer's point that the patients' benefit is of utmost importance. Also, this shift of interpretation alters Asma's notion of loyalty because the health care officials, as members of the scientific community, would privilege the knowledge of the human genome over the well being of patients. In addition, as Sandel's purpose of scientific research becomes the simple understanding of nature rather than the improvement of health, thus Asma's concept of "kith and kin" is better served by the researchers whose mission it is to discover information. This is because the researchers, in this case, work toward understanding genetics rather than developing treatments and, therefore, satisfy the doctors' goals without the involvement of patients.

These different formulations of the purpose of scientific research demonstrate the fluidity of Sandel's ethical approach to gene patenting because each interpretation shifts what he believes should be done, and, simultaneously, alters Asma's definition of "kith and kin" insofar as doctor's loyalty changes from the patient to fellow researchers. Interestingly, the only approach that remains constant through both interpretations is Singer's because he always posits that the group most deserving of the doctor's loyalty is the group with the greatest majority—the patients.

Others, aligning with Asma's and Sandel's ideas, argue that the virtues of diligent medical research and the passion and dedication that the scientists poured into their discoveries warrants a tangible reward such as royalties from a patent. In order to address this topic, we must consider what the definition of a reward should be. Aligning himself with a thread of philosophical thought "throughout the ages," Singer sees the acquisition of wealth beyond our basic needs as detrimental to our happiness and well-being, finding that the intangible reward of personal satisfaction only arises through improving the lives of others (381). In contrast, Asma would define the reward as money and recognition and argue that health care officials—like all humans—are not capable of the constant altruistic motives that Singer demands. He states "Care is like sprint racing. It takes time—duration, energy, systemic warm-up and cool-down, practice, and a strange mixture of pleasure and pain" (14). This means that people must have a stake in the people that they care about because biologically, we do not have the strength or endurance to care for each person that we come in contact with. This is where the incentive comes in. Continuing Asma's sprinting metaphor, runners naturally run faster and with more drive when there is a prize to be won. In this context, that prize waiting at the finish line is made up of royalties from a patent. In this case, Asma would assert that patents are necessary to create the drive needed for significant scientific developments. Here, Asma and Singer are the ones who overlap in their concern for the welfare of the individual performing the act in their ethical approached to rewarding that individual. This emphasis differentiates them from Sandel because he is consistently concerned only with the function of the action performed by the individual and highlighting the resulting virtues of the actors.

However, as we all—even doctors—have the potential to become patients, the issue that we are most likely to care about is the cost of treatment under gene patents. In this case, it seems as though the application of patients as doctors' "kith and kin" seems most appropriate since it fits with Asma's assertion that "care is a limited resource" (14). In this case, cost is the largest obstacle to the improvement of patient care. All the royalty fees that researchers, pharmaceutical companies, and hospitals must pay to satisfy the legal constraints of the patents adds up and all ends up falling to the patient—again, putting the generation of profit at odds with the well-being of the patient. This brings us back to the scientist as the humanitarian or businessman. With Sandel's method of finding the purpose of research and tests, we can look at this situation in one of two ways. With the scientist as a humanitarian, his or her purpose is to provide the best care and outcome for the patient. Aligned with Singer's point of view, this means that the scientist asks for nothing in return for providing the information and technology crucial for the patient's health. This also aligns with Asma's view of patients as doctors' "kith and kin." However, the second view is from the scientist as a businessman which aligns with Asma's view that the purpose of research is to benefit the scientist who conducts it—therefore making the scientist the "kin" of the doctor. Both angles depend on the idea that health care officials cannot feel the necessary satisfaction and reward from a patient's good unless that patient is part of his or her "kith and kin." Ultimately, what we see here is that Asma's and Sandel's ideas can mold to fit with both interpretations of the scientists' roles as a businessman or humanitarian, whereas Singer would disagree strongly with the idea that the scientist should be seen as a businessman. Outside of his or her kin the scientist needs a more direct and tangible way of validating his or her accomplishments which—in our system—is money. In our current situation, researchers as doctors' kin seems to be the most accepted practice even though it has created a huge problem of affordability for genetic testing.

In order to create the best situation for all involved, as Singer demands, we must look at the effects that patents have on companies in addition to patients. This high cost does not necessarily create the intended benefit for researchers and pharmaceutical companies. This is because while one company may hold a patent and generate profit from one set of genes, another company might hold patents on other genes. If one company decides to do research on genes that are patented by another company, the first company must pay the other, cutting into profits. Since over 4,000 genes of the human genome are patented under different companies, many pharmaceutical companies feel the effects from both ends. Looking at this from Singer's point of view, the drawbacks of this system such as limited profit and the discouragement of sharing data far outweigh the potential benefits of widely available genetic information. In this context, gene patenting limits the goals of both parties—patients have a harder time affording the care that they need and the pharmaceutical companies have a harder time making a profit. With the way that this works out, no one seems to benefit. Singer's view that the greatest many are taken care of is unfulfilled because companies cannot do the necessary research to treat patients effectively; Asma is not satisfied because the pharmaceutical companies actually end up diminishing one another's success as kith and kin; and neither of Sandel's ethical viewpoints are satisfied because companies interfering which each other stifles research and the efficacy of patient care.

Ultimately, there is no easy solution. The abolition of patents will lead not only to a question regarding what to do with current patents, but also with incentivizing pharmaceutical companies and scientists to pour the same resources into the crucial research of genetics. On the other hand, keeping the patents will prevent the incentivized research from becoming truly effective. The clash of Singer's faith in human altruism, Asma's assertion that we must see a direct and tangible reward for our actions, and Sandel's quest to understand the purpose and reward the virtues that promote the fulfillment of that purpose just goes to show the multiple layers of this difficult issue. The only element that seems to remain constant is the selfish nature of humans. Once we find the best way to serve our selfish sides so that we improve the lives of others, the sooner we will find a solution to this complicated ethical problem.

Works Cited

Asma, Stephen. "The Myth of Universal Love." *Focused Inquiry Reader: Evolving Idea 2014–2015*. Ed. Department of Focused Inquiry. Plymouth, MI: Hayden-McNeil, 2014. 12–15. Print.

"Gene Patenting Pros and Cons." *HRF*. HealthResearchFunding.org, 1 Jan. 2014. Web. 11 Oct. 2014.

Rausch, Lawrence. "International Patenting Trends in Biotechnology: Genetic Engineering." *National Science Foundation*, 18 June 1999. Web. 11 Oct. 2014.

Robertson, Andrew. "The Role of DNA Patents in Genetic Test Innovation and Access." *Northwestern Journal of Technology and Intellectual Property*, 1 Mar. 2011. Web. 12 Oct. 2014.

Sandel, Michael. "The Lost art of Democratic Debate." TED, Feb. 2010. Web. 7 Oct. 2014.

Singer, Peter. "The Drowning Child and the Expanding Circle." *Focused Inquiry Reader: Evolving Idea 2014–2015*. Eds. Department of Focused Inquiry. Plymouth, MI: Hayden-McNeil, 2014. 380–383. Print.

Mystery of the FMF Fighters

By Karen Pak

2ND PLACE—ANALYSIS

The aroma of fresh Vanilla Hazelnut coffee awakened me from my tiring shift in the Police Detective Department in New York.

"Here, Karen," said Chief Tom as he handed me the coffee, "Go home and get some sleep, you've been at this case for hours now," he sighed.

"Rotten kids," I moaned.

Charlotte, the secretary, saw my distress and asked, "What's the case?"

"Some kids are going around town and targeting Feminist Majority Foundation members. They vandalize their home and properties. The members of the FMF are becoming more concerned as to what they'll do next and if it will progress to more serious crimes," I explained to her.

"Feminist Majority Foundation? What's that? " Charlotte asked.

"Let me show you this video that was just uploaded from the conference," I said as I clicked the television controller towards the television. It turned onto channel twelve with the head title, "FMF Conference 2014."

On the television, a woman speaker walked onto the podium in front of hundreds of people.

She announced, "Hello, my fellow strong powerful, women of our generation! I am the speaker to represent the Feminist Majority Foundation! We are here to promote equality and independency for women all around the world! Our organization believes that every woman should have the right to do whatever she wants with her body! Am I Right?! (Mission and Principles).

The crowd screamed, "YEAHHHH!"

The woman spoke again, "We don't need a man to tell us what to do! We also shouldn't be scared to be rape or be under violence! When I say we promote equality, I mean every aspect of equality for women like sexual orientation, race, age, rights, and pay! (Missions and Principles). Women in other countries like Afghanistan have to hide underneath their veils, head dresses, or burqas (Ali). How are they able to show their full potential as a woman in that kind of society? We have the ability to save women in distress from oppression in other countries! It's our responsibility to take action (Ali). So who's with me?!

The crowd began to roar again in unison.

"Basically, the FMF promotes equality and exhibits Western feminist views for women's freedom. Western feminism also includes characteristics like women being able to take birth control and abortions, suffrage, etc" (Mission and Principles). I clarified to Charlotte.

"Oh, I see. Well, there must be some motive behind those kids' actions right? Maybe you should do some background research on what their motives might be. I actually have a friend who's a Muslim scholar and could help you with that!" Charlotte exclaimed.

"Great! That would be really helpful. Tell your friend to meet me tomorrow at the Café at 12 am," I responded to her.

The next day, her friend met me at the Café, like I said, at 12 am sharp. We both took our spot in the booth tables.

"Hello, I've heard you've got a tricky case on your hands. My name is Caren Kaplan."

"Nice to meet you! My name is Karen too. Haha, yeah, I guess I do. So why do you think people would target such a positive organization like the FMF?" I questioned.

"Well, although they are trying to support a positive cause for women's equality, western feminism is not the only kind of ideology out there," Kaplan answered.

"What other kind of ideology would not agree with Western feminism?" I asked in confusion.

"Another type would be fundamentalism. Although feminism and fundamentalism both focus on the same concepts like the use of women's bodies, what women should value, and the identities women should take, I can assure you they both steer in opposite directions" (Kaplan 324), she replied.

"Oh, that's very interesting. How are they different?" I asked.

"Fundamentalism is more conservative as opposed to Western feminism which is exhibited in the United States. However, other Middle Eastern countries like Afghanistan follow under Islam fundamentalism (327). Western feminism is more for the individuality of women to make any rational decision they want and the equality of all aspects (327). Afghan women believe in Islam fundamentalism where the women take a role in the community which involves sacrificing individuality and more taking a sense of an identity from the role" (327), Kaplan explained.

"Oh yes. I've heard about the Taliban's rule in 1996 in Afghanistan where they were forced to wear certain clothing like the burqas and veils and inflicted strict rules that followed deadly punishments" (Salat), I added.

"The clothing women wore were forced by the Taliban; however, there were other significant symbolism and meaning behind it that did not involve the Taliban (330). My friend, Marie-Aimée Hélie-Lucas, even told me that women were thought to be sacred to the community which is why they are under so much protection and enforcement of laws. Women gave birth to valuable sons, which were raised by the women, to be 'warriors of Islam' (Hélie-Lucas 394). Women there also had to be escorted by a male relative everywhere they went and had to be fully clothed to reduce sexual harassment and sexuality" (Salvat), she stated.

"I have no idea that values of fundamentalism are so different to the familiar western feminism. I guess the perpetrators might have a different ideology. Is Islam fundamentalism denying women their rights then? To what extent should the US intrude? " I asked.

"I'm afraid I don't exactly know the answer to those questions. It sounds pretty controversial. I bet you could the perpetrators' view on that if you catch them," she said.

"Okay I will. Thank you!" I exclaimed.

"No problem! Glad I could help!" she said.

After understanding the difference between the ideologies, I began to pick the next place to find my next clue. I searched for fundamentalist groups around the city on the internet and, to my surprise, there was one right down the block.

I immediately changed and went to see for myself if there would be anyone who would know about the people targeting the FMF. I left my uniform to blend in seamlessly with the crowd.

I walked into the old building where the fundamentalist group was. I arrived just as they were about to start the event for the awareness of the foundations for fundamentalism throughout the city. As the leader was speaking, I noticed a couple of suspicious people in the back corner; they were not paying attention and planning something.

"Riffat, you meet us there in thirty minutes. Abida, don't forget to bring the goods," Russo whispered.

After the meeting, I discreetly followed them down two blocks. Eventually, I lost sight of them for a few seconds and they were gone.

Confused, I circled around the area, wondering how they could have disappeared in such a short amount of time. I was led to a dead end of a dirty alley, flanked by rusty fences. There was a note on the fence that read, "Nice Try."

"Guess, they're not as dumb as I thought, but now at least I know I'm on the right trail," I shrugged.

I asked the stores managers around the area if they have heard of the names Riffat and Abida.

One store manager said, "Oh, them? They come here almost every week to buy tape and other materials. They stay up pretty late. Check in that West Grace neighborhood."

"Perfect!" I thought. I decided to take a visit and patrol there that night. I parked the police car around the back of the neighborhood. Several hours passed; I glanced at my watch: three a.m. "Man, I'm not paid enough to do this," I yawned, until I heard a loud crack down the street that shook my body wide awake. I quickly ran to the scene and called for backup. Three people were hitting a mailbox with steel bats. I hollered in the dark, "STOP RIGHT THERE." Everyone else scattered, but I continued to run after one of them.

He took a quick glance behind and rammed into a street pole. "Thank god, I don't know if I could have run longer," I thought to myself. I quickly handcuffed him and took him down to the station and to our questioning room. I could already tell that the perpetrator had a sour attitude based on his beady stare and annoyed expression on his face.

"So what's your name, kid?"

"I don't have to tell you anything. I have my rights just like those women who think their rights are superior to everyone else's."

"What do you mean? The FMF? They're just trying to help," I unconfidently muttered.

"Not at all," he scoffed.

"What are you trying to say, kid?"

"Alright, stop calling me kid. I'm 18 years old. Fine, my name is Russo. Sure, the FMF is trying to promote equality, but do they even consider how the structure or fundamentals of certain societies are? The FMF thinks that the United

States has every right to take control of Afghanistan and implement *their* policies for a democracy and equality for women's rights. They think every country wants to be just like them. They're just advocating US imperialism in a different aspect. FMF thinks that Afghan women aren't free just because they have to wear veils and burqas, but don't even understand the religious aspect of their lives/meaning that it has..." (Russo).

Chief Tom knocked on the door as Russo was speaking and said, "Sorry to interrupt you, but I caught the other two for your case." Next to Tom was a girl named Riffat and boy named Abida who were at the meeting.

"Bring them in too," I commanded as I still kept my one eye on Russo.

"Riffat. Abida. Tell her what you guys think about the United States imposing Western feminism on Afghanistan and other countries that already have a set feminist view through their ideology of fundamentalism," Russo stated as he saw them come in.

"Of course, Western feminists need to understand other views/culture and stop trying to change Afghanistan into a society like theirs. The ideas of Western feminism do not correspond with their ideas of freedom and values into such an Islam community like Afghanistan. Western feminists are wrongfully putting Muslim countries in the media and perceiving it as if the religion of Islam is the "new enemy" (Hassan), Riffat explained.

"Not the mention, even in the Quran that they worship upon, makes it clearly obvious that men and women are equal" (Alijaz), Abida stated.

"For example, in the Quran, it states that "every man and women has the right to work" (Hassan) and states that each individual "should be treated with the utmost care" (Hassan), Riffat included.

"So you guys are arguing that the ideology of fundamentalism may appear like they're stripping away women's rights but they're not through the eyes of a Muslim woman in the community? It doesn't sound equal to me. Women being the ones to take care of the children while the men are the ones with the jobs. Women have to be escorted by a male relative when going out in public and have to cover themselves strictly" (Salvat), Tom and I argued against.

"But even though it may not look equal, they have different roles within the society that balances out and makes it equal. It is equal fundamentally, which is different from the Western feminists' view of equality that they don't understand" (Alijaz), they argued.

"I guess that's true...but what about the Taliban invading Afghanistan in 1996? Even though the structure of Afghanistan is like that, it wasn't to the point where women could not get adequate health care since they weren't allowed to be treated by a male doctor and the female doctors were not allowed to give health care (Salvat). They were also punished inhumanely by being stoned or beaten (Salvat). Are you guys saying that it's okay for the US to just leave countries like that where they are under a dictator and suffer traumatically?" I asked.

Riffat, Abida, and even Russo looked at each other slyly. Russo replied, "We mainly just focused on how the US viewed countries like Afghanistan in a hegemonic mentality of their views of feminism. We believe that the United States should not be involved with their implementation of their democratic views for feminism (Alijaz). However, Taliban claimed that their ideology was Islamic fundamentalism, but in fact their actions did not reflect upon that at all (Al-Marayati). I guess we can't really give you an answer. "

"I think I can answer that question," Jutta Joachim answered as she walked in with her heels clapping against the floor. "Sorry Karen, I walked in, I have been waiting outside to talk to you about the case, but I overheard these questions and couldn't stand still."

"Let me ask you guys something. So many countries in Africa, Middle East, and Asia have been practicing something called "female genital mutilation" where young teen girls get parts of the genital organs cut off without any anesthesia (Joachim). However, people who practice it say that it is supposed to 'affirm girls' femininity' (Joachim) and just is part of the culture. The after effects of the procedure are very serious too. They include complications with child birth, infections, and bleeding (Joachim). Do you think other countries should impede that even though it is part of their "culture"?

"Of course! That sounds painful and terrible! What if some girls don't want to proceed through that?" Abida uttered.

"Oh, I understand. That is exactly like the Afghanistan situation. Some of the Islamic ideology appeared to be mixed with the Taliban's motives. It's not the view of fundamentalism of Afghanistan that led to the mistreatment of women. It was the Taliban," I replied.

"Exactly. That is when other countries like the United States should intrude, " Joachim responded.

"I get it. The United States should only intrude with the sole motive to help a country under something that is a universal misconduct of the leader, not necessarily changing their original culture," Russo states.

"Perfect! That is exactly what I'm trying to explain to you guys! Pertaining to the aftermath of the Taliban's rule, even the President of the United States, Barack Obama, announced that the US supports the Afghan constitution in order for Afghanistan to recover from the Taliban's rule and ensure universal human rights to all, especially women" (R.E.A.L. Organization), Jutta Joachim said.

"But how could we have universal human rights for all when countries don't agree for certain concepts like the rights of women?" I questioned.

"That is a good point which is why Afghanistan has their own constitution that is different. It states that "no laws can be contrary to the beliefs and provisions of the sacred religion of Islam" (U.S State Department). However, in 2009, President Karzai removed some context of the constitution that could be misinterpreted of "restriction of women's right," (R.E.A.L Organization), Jutta Joachim argued.

"Okay, that's great! Afghanistan is on the road to recovery, not from the fundamentalist views, but from the oppression of the Taliban and continuing to preserve the rights of women and the people" Russo furthered.

"It's a good thing that the Taliban no longer rule Afghanistan," Abida declared.

I exclaimed, "I agree. Well, I think we've all learned something new today! America's view of Western feminism should not perceive that their views are superior to other views like Islamic fundamentalism in Afghanistan. In the eyes of Western feminism, Afghanistan may appear like they are taking away the rights of women but through the eyes of Islamic fundamentalism, it is equal (with the exception of the Taliban's dictation)."

Chief Tom points out, "and don't forget that the Islamic religion is not denying the women their rights. In addition, the ideal rights for women vary in different countries due to different ideologies and culture. Therefore, it is difficult to achieve universal rights for women that all countries will accommodate."

"Wow, that was a long, insightful discussion. Thank you for displaying another perspective and further our knowledge on international conflicts of women's rights!" Russo announced.

Abida said with a smile, "Yeah, I agree with Russo. It was interesting to learn more about feminism with the different effects and views it has on other countries."

Riffat, Abida, and Russo all shook our hands and thanked us some more.

As they were about to leave the station, Riffat affirmed, "Don't worry, we won't do anything to those FMF's houses again!"

I smiled and waved back to them. "Wait…they just got away with serious counts of vandalism!" I shouted as I came to reality.

I tried to chase after them but they were already gone.

"Rotten kids," I sighed.

Works Cited

Ali, Anisa J. "Establishing Transnational Feminist Solidarity in Academia and Activism: The Feminist Majority Foundation's Campaigns for Afghan Women." Thesis, University of Wisconsin-Madison, 2012. PDF.

Al-Marayati, Laila. "Afghanistan's Taliban: Not a valid interpretation of Islam." Muslim Women's League. *Muslim Women's League*, Nov. 1996. Web. 5 Nov. 2014.

Eijaz, Abida, and Rana Eiaz Ahmed. "Discourses of Feminism in the Perspective of Allama Iqbal and the West/ Les Discours du Feminisme Dans la Perspective D'Allama Iqbal et d'Occident." *Canadian Social Science*. 7.5 (2011): 190–97. PDF.

Hassan, Riffat. "Are Human Rights Compatible with Islam?." *The Religious Consultation on Population, Reproductive Health, and Ethnics*. ReligiousConsultation.org, n.d. Web. 5 Nov. 2014.

Hélie-Lucas, Marie-Aimée. "The Preferential Symbol for Islamic Identity: Women in Muslim Personal Laws." *Identity Politics & Women*. Ed. Valentine M. Moghadam. Boulder, Colorado: West View Press, 1994. 391–400. Print.

Kaplan, Caren, Norma Alarcon, and Minoo Moallem. *Between Woman and Nation*. Durham: Duke University Press, 1999. Print.

"Mission and Principles." *Feminist Majority Foundation Equality Around the World*. Feminist Majority Foundation, n.d. Web. 28 Oct. 2014.

R.E.A.L Organization, "Afghan Constitution, Women's Rights, and the Taliban." *Responsible For Equality and Liberty (R.E.A.L)*. RealCourage.org, 12 May 2010. Web. 5 Nov. 2014.

Russo, Ann. "The Feminist Majority Foundation's Campaign to Stop Gender Apartheid." *International Feminist Journal of Politics*, 8 (2006): 557–580. PDF.

Salvat, Joan. *The Taliban Legacy*. Filmakers Library, 2001. Filmakers Library Online. Film.

United States. U.S State Department. Bureau of Democracy, Human Rights, and Labor, "2013 Report on International Religious Freedom," US Dept of State, 28 July 2014. Web. 28 Oct. 2014.

"Women's Rights as Human Rights: The Case of Violence Against Women." From *Agenda Setting, the UN, and NGOs: Gender Violence and Reproductive Rights.* Jutta M. Joachim, ed. Washington D.C: Georgetown University Press, 2007. Print.

Ecotourism Is No Panacea—Yet

By Evan Tuten

1ST PLACE—ARGUMENT

Miles underground, a heart beats. A mass of scorching, red hot magma undulates, acting as the soul of one of the largest super volcanoes in the world. The magma gives life to Yellowstone National Park, heating the park's unique geothermal features. A stream of boiling water shoots out of a cavity in the ground. Each day, hundreds of people gather in Yellowstone National Park to watch nature's fountain, the geyser. One of these geysers, known as Old Faithful, has become an icon for the park, attracting traditional tourists and ecotourists alike.

Since its creation as America's first National Park, Yellowstone has been the destination for throngs of tourists each year. As reported by the National Park Service, Yellowstone has received more than 3 million visitors in the past year, making it one of the most attended parks in the United States. These visitors include thousands of ecotourists, who flock to the park each year in an attempt to make a positive effect on its wildlife and environment. The park and its surrounding areas rely primarily on the tourism industry as a source of revenue. Amanda Stronza of the Department of Recreation, Park and Tourism Sciences at Texas A&M University argues that ecotourism has grown to become a large segment the tourism industry over past decades, making it an important market for parks and other destinations to attract (6).

According to Costas Christ, Director of Ecotourism at Conservation International, "the basic tenets of ecotourism…[are] conserving nature and benefiting local communities" (ix). Ecotourists travel with the goal of having little to no negative environmental changes on the place they are visiting. An ecotourist could engage in hiking, camping, or simply viewing Old Faithful. Ecotourism includes any activity that appreciates and helps in protecting or conserving a natural area. The public's desire, or 'demand', to visit areas with vibrant natural beauty, like Yellowstone, promotes conservation because by creating a clear incentive to preserve and protect parkland. Demand for the park motivates its safekeeping. In addition, ecotourism ventures benefit the local community, more so than larger, nationally based companies. Essentially, ecotourism is an attempt to unite conservation efforts with the tourism industry.

However, ecotourism in Yellowstone National Park seems to have made little to no positive change in the area's environment. As a whole, tourism in the area has led to various instances of environmental degradation, some of which include pollution, geyser extinction, and changes in wildlife behavior. Ecotourism has not achieved its goal in the park, and has failed as an ethical and effective tool for conservation because of improperly applied services. Ecotourism's primary role as an industry, rather than as a method for environmental management, places it at an ethical crossroads. It must balance conservation with reasonable tourist accommodations. Failures in these accommodations can be seen in snowmobile use and overdevelopment around precious natural features. In fact, much of the environmental destruction that has been performed to help facilitate ecotourism cannot be undone.

At times, ecotourists' ideals come into conflict with Yellowstone's harsh natural conditions. National Park Service maps of Yellowstone illustrate that only one road in Yellowstone is open year-round. The majority of roads in Yellowstone are unplowable due to the large amount of snow the park receives each winter. Most destinations in the park, including Old Faithful, are unreachable by car in the winter, making snowmobiles the primary form of transport. For ecotourists wanting to travel moderate distances in the park during the winter, snowmobiles, as well as snowcoaches, are the only way to go. Use of snowmobiles in Yellowstone is convenient for ecotourists wanting to explore the wilderness, but is inconvenient for the environment. Snowmobiles are one of the leading causes of wintertime pollution in the park. George P. Ingersoll at the USGS found that "by-products of gasoline combustion such as ammonium and benzene [were] detected in snowpack samples [from Yellowstone]" (1). Ammonium contributes to soil acidification, and both chemicals can contaminate groundwater once the snow melts. The addition of these pollutants to Yellowstone's environment can disrupt the area's ecosystem. While the study found that "snowpack-sampling sites indicate that elevated emission levels in snow along highway corridors generally are dispersed into surrounding watersheds at concentrations below levels likely to threaten human or ecosystem health [,] localized, episodic acidification of aquatic ecosystem…may be possible" (22). Areas with high snowmobile traffic have the potential to pollute Yellowstone's lakes and streams. While the study does not take into account air pollution from snowmobiles, the possible water and snow pollution from the vehicles should be enough to discourage ecotourists from using them. Reliance on snowmobiles for ecotourists does not help their goal of conservation. A slightly better alternative to gas-powered snowmobiles would be the previously mentioned snowcoaches, which carry many people at a time, and can be seen as being similar to public transport. An even better solution would be cross country skiing, which would allow for a more organic visit to the park that would not create any pollution from fossil fuels.

One more substitute for gas-powered snowmobiles would be electric snowmobiles, which are still in development. However, electric snowmobiles would have similar problems that gas-powered snowmobiles have, in that both would negatively affect Yellowstone's ecology. Motorized human presence in backcountry and well-traveled areas of Yellowstone has caused various changes to wildlife behavior. In a report on wildlife response to snowmobile use, Craig McClure at the Yellowstone Center for Resources found that 25% of animals responded to "humans traveling in oversnow vehicles," with over "5% display[ing] alarm… and 1% fleeing from the area" (1). Although this does not seem like a substantial amount, a master's thesis by Amanda Hardy shows that mere exposure to motorized vehicles elevates the level of stress hormones on elk in the park. Ecotourists visiting Yellowstone in the winter have another reason not to use snowmobiles. Human presence on oversnow vehicles in wildlife habitats is bad for the animals living in it because it elevates their stress hormones and changes their behavioral patterns. Some ways to lessen the impact of ecotourist visitation on winter vehicles would be to reduce the size of wildlife viewing groups, and to not "[travel] into areas not generally traveled by humans in the winter" (McClure 11). Another fact to be considered can be found in an article in the *Journal of Park and Recreation Administration*, "winter use of YNP has grown significantly since snowmobiles were first permitted" (Davenport et al. 52). The convenience of snowmobile transportation makes Yellowstone a more attractive wintertime destination for tourists. Ending allowance of snowmobiles would curb the amount of pollutants from the machines while also lessening changes in wildlife behavior. This change would lead to a decrease in the number of visitors as well.

Ecotourists are also constrained by park infrastructure, which was designed with traditional tourists in mind, as well as practical considerations of the physical terrain of the park. One of Yellowstone's biggest draws are its geysers. In addition to being one of 5 geyser fields in the entire world, an article in *Yellowstone Science*, a publication devoted to Yellowstone's natural resources, states that the park contains "more [geysers] than any other geothermal region" (12). Yellowstone's plethora of geysers are precious and scarce natural features. Ecotourists visiting the park may not harm the geysers at all, but a lot of damage has already been done. While poorly documented, "development of tourist facilities…in thermal areas has undoubtedly damaged some features" (9). Raised pathways used for tourists to access the geothermal sites compress soil and alter drainage patterns, clogging geyser vents with sand and debris, leading to possible geyser extinction (15). Ecotourists using these access paths are second-handedly harming the natural features they come to see. Public "access to thermal features can create significant problems" (15). Development of these areas can help to keep visitors on a certain path, or certain distance away from an important environmental feature, but they can still negatively impact geysers a considerable amount. This creates the issue of balancing visitor wants with environmental needs. The only viable ecotourist response would be to view the geysers from afar, such as at home on their computer screen, until a more practical solution is found.

Even though ecotourism is supposed to help the environment, it mostly fails in this goal, and can even end up harming it instead. While ecotourism is more environmentally conscious than traditional tourism, some of the most basic ecotourist activities can still inflict harm on an ecosystem. Compiling information about the impact of hiking on flora, D. N. Cole at the Aldo Leopold Wilderness Research Institute, found that hikers can contribute to the abrasion of soil horizons, the bruising of vegetation, and soil compaction. This leads to a loss in species richness and reduced porosity in the soil, as well as an increased possibility of erosion and runoff (46). Even though these issues seem localized, evaluations of the impact of recreation on a larger scale have yet to be performed (56). Reminiscent of the butterfly effect, little actions can have large consequences. While their intentions to promote conservation make ecotourists seemingly a positive for a community, too much 'good' (e.g. visitors) can do much damage.

Conservation of natural areas is an important ethical issue. Hardin's tragedy of the commons is going full force in Yellowstone, and at other similar areas around the world. Meaningful environmental sites like Yellowstone must be protected and utilized in a sustainable manner. Ecotourism has a basis in conservation, but is currently characterized by "large numbers, short visits, and relatively passive orientation." (Davenport et al. 62). For there to be a significant change in the effects of ecotourism, visitors should come in small, environmentally manageable groups, and regardless of the duration of their stay in the park, should display an active role in conservation and environmental maintenance in the park. Passivity, and passive activities, such as hiking, especially on the part of ecotourists, does nothing to change the harms conventional tourism has already caused. A large-scale reorientation of this new kind of tourist has the potential to make huge, positive changes in Yellowstone's ecological landscape.

Works Cited

Christ, Costas. "Foreword." Foreword. *Environmental Impacts of Ecotourism*. Ed. Ralf Buckley. Vol. 2. Cambridge: CABI, 2004. ix–x. Ecotourism Book Ser. *ProQuest ebrary*. ebrary, Aug. 2004. Web. 2 Dec. 2014.

Cole, D. N. "Impacts of Hiking and Camping on Soils and Vegetation: a Review." *Environmental Impacts of Ecotourism*. Ed. Ralf Buckley. Vol. 2. Cambridge: CABI, 2004. 41–60. Ecotourism Book Ser. *ProQuest ebrary*. ebrary, Aug. 2004. Web. 2 Dec. 2014.

Davenport, Mae A., William T. Borrie, Wayne A. Freidmund, and Robert E. Manning. "Assessing the Relationship Between Desired Experiences and Support for Management Actions at Yellowstone National Park Using Multiple Methods." *Journal of Park and Recreation Administration* 20.3 (2002): 51–64. Web. 13 Nov. 2014.

Hardy, Amanda R. "Bison and Elk Responses to Winter Recreation in Yellowstone National Park." Thesis. Montana State University, 2001. *Snowmobileinfo.org*. American Council of Snowmobile Associations, 2001. Web. 2 Dec. 2014.

Ingersoll, George P. "Effects of Snowmobile Use on Snowpack Chemistry in Yellowstone National Park." *USGS Water-Resources Investigations Report* 99–4148 (1999): Web. 28 Oct. 2014.

United States. Department of the Interior. National Park Service. "Annual Park Recreation Visitation." Chart. *NPS Stats*. IRMA Data System. 2013. Web. 20 Nov. 2014.

———. "Yellowstone National Park Map." Map. *National Park Service*. US Department of the Interior, Feb. 2012. Web. 2 Dec. 2014.

Steingisser, Alethea, and W. Andrew Marcus. "Human Impacts on Geyser Basins." *Yellowstone Science*. Yellowstone Association for Natural Science, History, & Education, Jan. 2009. Web. 2 Dec. 2014.

Stronza, A. "The Bold Agenda of Ecotourism." *Ecotourism and Conservation in the Americas*. Eds. A. Stronza and W. H. Durham. Vol. 7. Cambridge: CABI, 2008. 3–17. Ecotourism Book Ser. *ProQuest ebrary*. ebrary, Aug. 2008. Web. 2 Dec. 2014.

McClure, Craig, Dan Reinhart, P.J. White, Mary Donovan, and Brian Teets. "Wildlife Responses to Motorized Winter Recreation in Yellowstone: 2009 Annual Report" *Yellowstone Center for Resources*. 18 Jun. 2009. Web. 28 Oct. 2014.

Emotions in Messages

By Maylin Sze

2ND PLACE—ARGUMENT

When I was in high school, I had a history teacher who would always end her sentences with an ellipsis. Throughout the year, I would occasionally email her about a question I had and she would reply with an ellipsis at the end of every sentence. I interpreted the ellipsis negatively; it made me feel as though I had asked an "obvious" question that I should have already known the answer to. Although she probably did not intend to make me feel that way, it definitely affected my relationship with her. The fact that even something as simple as "three periods in a row" can make a message so negative shows the importance of expressing emotions appropriately in non-face-to-face communication; without it, conflicts may erupt and lead to unhealthy relationships.

There are many ways to express emotions and tones in computer-mediated communication; one example is through the alteration of capitalization. A sentence in "all caps" typically symbolizes yelling, which can be interpreted as angry or aggressive. Even if the sender does not intend to give off the wrong attitude, the audience may interpret the capitalization as being hostile. Punctuation can also create a tone just as it does in traditional writing. Exclamation marks symbolize excitement or surprise; question marks end questions and can even symbolize confusion; ellipses can portray uncertainty and even awkwardness. Grammar, syntax, capitalization, and spelling can help create a unique and expressive style of writing. It is important for a writer to have a unique style of writing that differentiates himself or herself from everyone else. In non-face-to-face communication, a style of writing is like a voice; it is uncommon to meet two people with the same voice just as it is uncommon to meet two people with the same exact writing style. One familiar with text messaging can understand the irritation of having someone reply with one-word text messages. One-word messages can also be unintentionally rude since they're usually abrupt and blunt which can eventually sever the relationship between the sender and the receiver. Lastly, emoticons, which are facial expressions created by text, can also be used to bring forth emotions. Any of these can be used by itself or along with others to create a more influential effect. Given all of these ways, one can see the importance of being able to express emotions in non-face-to-face communication.

"As mediated interaction provides less bandwidth than face-to-face communication, the medium is assumed to diminish social presence, which renders communicators less salient to each other" (Peña and Hancock 96). Since non-face-to-face communication lacks social cues that help express certain emotions, emoticons have been created to help prevent misunderstandings, give messages a tone, help represent the sender "correctly," and play a role in the receiver's impression of the sender. A message without emoticons may be ambiguous, so adding emoticons can help direct a message's tone towards a path desired by the sender which allows for fewer misunderstandings. Emoticons also help with producing good impressions of the sender and leaving good impressions on the receivers which is an important aspect of healthy relationships. "Misinterpretations of the message can be prevented by the use of emoticons: a smiling emoticon may, for example, reduce the ambiguity of a message" (Ganster, Eimler, and Krämer 226). As one can see, emoticons can be extremely beneficial in non-face-to-face communication.

While there are many ways that emoticons can be advantageous, they can also be disadvantageous. Although emoticons are intended to make interpretation of emotions in text easier, some emoticons may be misinterpreted by certain people. When emoticons are misinterpreted, it defeats the original purpose of using them in the first place. Even capitalization can be misinterpreted. As stated earlier, "all caps" can represent yelling which can show rage and aggression; however, it can also be interpreted as excitement or surprise. Another drawback of emoticons is that they can have multiple different meanings which can cause confusion. For example, researcher Alecia Wolf states, "in some instances the emoticon :-Q means 'user smokes'; others define it as meaning 'tongue hanging out in nausea' or 'sticking out tongue'" (829). This can cause confusion among the receiver; thus, weakening the relationship between the sender and the receiver. Poor emoticon usage may lead to contradicting messages which can also be confusing. Finally, overuse of emoticons has been viewed to some as immature and unprofessional. Because people do not want to be labeled as "childish" for overusing emoticons, they might use less which can influence their ability to fully express themselves. Alecia Wolf points out "the following warning from The Hacker's Dictionary: 'Note for the newbie: overuse of the smiley is a mark of loserhood. More than one per paragraph is a fairly sure sign that you've gone over the line'" (829). Although being able to express oneself is no doubt important in maintaining healthy relationships, too much expressing can be a major "no-no." As one can see, emoticons are only beneficial if they are used properly.

Emoticon usage is definitely a double standard. Luor, Wu, Lu, and Tao argue that "some studies even showed that females are more intensive emoticon users than males" (891). It has been shown that women generally use more emoticons than men. However, women will not be seen as "overusing emoticons" even if they use a significantly higher amount than men. Interestingly enough, Luor, Wu, Lu, and Tao states that "Lee (2003) studied gender differences in instant messaging and found that men rarely used emoticons in conversations with other men, but used more emoticons when interacting with women," which shows that when males are communicating with females, they typically use more emoticons than when communicating with other males (891). This is probably because men try to express more emotions, "a quality historically reserved for women," to better relate with women since women are generally the more emotional gender; thus, better relationships will form (Wolf 829). Luor, Wu, Lu, and Tao quotes that "for women, there is no difference in the use of emoticons in relation to their interaction collaborator: they use the same amount of emoticons in conversing with men as they do with other women (Lee, 2003)" (891). So while males generally express fewer emotions when communicating with the same gender than with the opposite gender, females, on the other hand, generally use the same amount of emoticons when communicating with either gender. Studies by Alecia Wolf also show that "women most frequently use emoticons to express humor" while "men use emoticons most often to express teasing/sarcasm" (831). Researchers Luor, Wu, Tu, and Tao also agree that "women tend to use emoticons more frequently to communicate humor of solidarity, whereas men use them to display sarcasm" (891). These differences in how men and women use emoticons show that even the population as a whole has its own way of expressing emotions.

Gender isn't the only factor in which emoticon usage differs. Studies by Peña and Hancock have shown that there are also emoticon usage differences between online video game players. 'The most experienced participants exchanged significantly more positive and significantly fewer negative socioemotional messages than their less-experienced counterparts" (Peña and Hancock 105). Experienced players use more emoticons and are more likely to produce positive messages than less experienced users. This is probably because the experienced players are "especially dedicated members of their virtual group or clan' so they are more committed to the game; thus, they want to establish good relationships with their fellow online gamers 'to maintain cohesion and satisfaction within the virtual group" (Peña and Hancock 105). Experienced online game players use more than just emoticons to express themselves; they also incorporate abbreviations, "shared jargon," internet slang, and "expressions of tension release" such as "jokes and representations of laughter" in their messages to bring about a positive tone (Peña and Hancock 98, 103). Abbreviations such as AFK (away from keyboard) and TTYL (talk to you later) are commonly used in chatrooms and the like. Game jargon consists of vocabulary that is difficult for non-gamers to comprehend since such vocabulary is not used in everyday life. An example of "internet slang" is the word "newbie." The word "newbie" means "newcomer," but people also use it as "amateur" which can be offending in some cases. The slang word "newbie" can be used as an insult or as a joke. This can affect the relationships between online gamers and result in either close friendships or terrible relationships. All of these ways to express emotions in online gaming are so important that Peña and Hancock state "for example, in one study of Internet video game players, Yee (2001) reported that approximately half of the players rate their online gaming friendships as comparable to their offline friendships. Some players indicated that some of their online gaming friendships are actually better than their offline counterparts" (93). The fact that some people consider their online gaming friendships as equally important and some even better than their offline friendships show that by being able to express themselves through their messages, they have the opportunity to maintain healthy relationships with others.

As non-face-to-face ways of communication, such as text messaging and computer-mediated communication, have become increasingly popular in the past decade, it is important that there are many ways one can express oneself through their messages. Much communication, whether it be relating to education, work, and even recreational online gaming, is done without ever having to meet face-to-face. While messages lack verbal cues and body language that exists in face-to-face communication, many computer-mediated communication conventions have been introduced to counter this issue. The ability to express emotions, whether positive or negative, has a strong impact on the relationships between a sender and a receiver.

Works Cited

Gallagher, John. "The Emotion For Opening The Text Message." *Transformations: The Journal Of Inclusive Scholarship & Pedagogy* 22.2 (2011): 36–43. *Education Research Complete*. Web. 27 Oct. 2014.

Ganster, Tina, Sabrina C. Eimler, and Nicole C. Krämer. "Same Same But Different!? The Differential Influence Of Smilies And Emoticons On Person Perception." *Cyberpsychology, Behavior & Social Networking* 15.4 (2012): 226–230. *Academic Search Complete*. Web. 3 Nov. 2014.

Luor, Tainyi (Ted) and Wu, Ling-ling and Lu, Hsi-Peng and Tao, Yu-Hui. "The Effect of Emoticons in Simplex and Complex Task-oriented Communication: An Empirical Study of Instant Messaging". *Computers in Human Behavior* 26.5 (September 2010): 889–895. Web. 3 November 2014.

Peña, Jorge, and Jeffrey T. Hancock. "An Analysis Of Socioemotional And Task Communication In Online Multiplayer Video Games." *Communication Research* 33.1 (2006): 92–109. *Academic Search Complete*. Web. 5 November 2014.

Wolf, Alecia. "Emotional Expression Online: Gender Differences In Emoticon Use." *Cyberpsychology & Behavior* 3.5 (2000): 827–833. *Academic Search Complete*. Web. 28 Oct. 2014.

AUTHOR AND TITLE INDEX

AUTHOR AND TITLE INDEX

AUTHOR AND TITLE INDEX

Acknowledgments

(continued from page ii)

Michelle Alexander—"The Lockdown." From *The New Jim Crow: Mass Incarceration in the Age of Colorblindness*—Copyright © 2010, 2012 by Michelle Alexander. Reprinted by permission of The New Press. www.thenewpress.com.

Sherman Alexie—"Defending Walt Whitman." Reprinted from *The Summer of Black Widows*. © 1996 by Sherman Alexie, by permission of Hanging Loose Press.

Rachel Aviv—"Wrong Answer." Reprinted by permission © 2015 by Rachel Aviv. http://www.newyorker.com/magazine/2014/07/21/wrong-answer?mbid=social_tablet_e.

Daniel A. Bonevac—"Making Moral Arguments." From: *Today's Moral Issues*, 3e by Daniel Bonevac. Mountain View, Calif.: Mayfield Pub., 1999. Reproduced with permission of McGraw-Hill Education.

danah boyd and Kate Crawford—"Six Provocations for Big Data." Republished with permission of Taylor and Francis © 2011; permission conveyed through Copyright Clearance Center, Inc.

Octavia E. Butler—"Bloodchild." From *BloodChild and Other Stories*. Originally published in *Isaac Asimov's Science Fiction Magazine* (June 1984). Copyright © 1984, 1995 by Octavia E. Butler. Reprinted with the permission of The Permissions Company, Inc., on behalf of Seven Stories Press, www.sevenstories.com.

Ta-Nehisi Coates—"Acting French." Reprinted by permission © 2014 The Atlantic Media Co., as first published in *The Atlantic Magazine*. All rights reserved. Distributed by Tribune Content Agency, LLC.

William Cronon—"The Trouble with Wilderness; or, Getting Back to the Wrong Nature." From *Uncommon Ground*, edited by William Cronon. Copyright © 1995 by William Cronon. Used by permission of W. W. Norton & Company, Inc.

Torie Rose DeGhett—"The War Photo No One Would Publish." Reprinted by permission © 2014 The Atlantic Media Co., as first published in *The Atlantic Magazine*. All rights reserved. Distributed by Tribune Content Agency, LLC.

"Principles of Environmental Justice." Reprinted, by permission, from Proceedings: The First National People of Color Environmental Leadership Summit, Principles of Environmental Justice, October 1991, Charles Lee, ed., 1992. Copyright 1991 by United Church of Christ Commission for Racial Justice: New York (now Justice and Witness Ministries, a Covenanted Ministry of the United Church of Christ, Cleveland, Ohio).

Annie Dillard—"Living Like Weasels." From *Teaching a Stone to Talk: Expeditions and Encounters* by Annie Dillard. Copyright © 1982 by Annie Dillard. Reprinted by permission of HarperCollins Publishers.

ACKNOWLEDGMENTS

Frederick Douglass—"Learning to Read and Write." From *Narrative of the Life of Frederick Douglass, An American Slave*. Boston. Published at the Anti-Slavery Office, No. 25 Cornhill, 1845.

Roxane Gay—"What We Hunger For." From *Bad Feminist* by Roxane Gay. Copyright © 2014 by Roxane Gay. Reprinted by permission of HarperCollins Publishers.

Marie Sarita Gaytán—"From Sombreros to *Sincronizadas*." From "From Sombreros to *Sincronizadas*: Authenticity, Ethnicity, and the Mexican Restaurant Industry." From *Journal of Contemporary Ethnography*, vol. 37 no. 3; pp. 314–341, copyright © 2008 by SAGE Publications. Reprinted by Permission of SAGE Publications.

Allen Ginsberg—"A Supermarket in California." From *Collected Poems 1947–1980* by Allen Ginsberg. Copyright © 1955 by Allen Ginsberg. Reprinted by permission of HarperCollins Publishers.

Peter Goin—"Visual Literacy." Republished with permission of John Wiley & Sons, from *Geographical Review*, Peter Goin, Vol. 91, No. 1–2, pp. 363–369. © 2001; permission conveyed through Copyright Clearance Center, Inc.

Amanda Hess—"Why Women Aren't Welcome on the Internet." Republished with permission of *Pacific Standard*, © 2014; permission conveyed through Copyright Clearance Center, Inc.

Thomas Hine—"What's in a Package." From *The Total Package: The Secret History and Hidden Meanings of Boxes, Bottles, Cans, and Other Persuasive Containers* by Thomas Hine. Copyright © 1995 by Thomas Hine. Used by permission of Little, Brown and Company.

bell hooks—"Introduction." Reprinted by permission from hooks, bell. From *Teaching to Transgress*, Routledge (September 14, 1994); permission conveyed through Copyright Clearance Center, Inc.

Peter D. Kramer—"Why Doctors Need Stories." From *The New York Times*, October 19, 2014. © *The New York Times*. All rights reserved. Used by permission and protected by the Copyright Laws of the United States. The printing, copying, redistribution, or retransmission of this Content without express written permission is prohibited.

David Livingstone Smith—"Natural-Born Liars." Reproduced with permission. Copyright © 2005 Scientific American, Inc. All rights reserved.

Phillip Lopate—"The Essay, an Exercise in Doubt." From *The New York Times*, February 17, 2013. © *The New York Times*. All rights reserved. Used by permission and protected by the Copyright Laws of the United States. The printing, copying, redistribution, or retransmission of this Content without express written permission is prohibited.

Joseph Marolla—"A 21st-Century Education." Used by permission.

ACKNOWLEDGMENTS

Mark Twain [Samuel Clemens]—"On the Decay of the Art of Lying." A short essay written in 1880 for a meeting of the Historical and Antiquarian Club of Hartford, Connecticut. Twain published the text in *The Stolen White Elephant Etc.* (1882).

August Wade—"You did not build the city of Richmond." Reprinted by permission, © 2014.

August Wade—"Follow-up on 'You did not build the city of Richmond.'" Reprinted by permission, © 2014.

David Foster Wallace—"Consider the Lobster." Originally Published August 2004 in *Gourmet* magazine. Reprinted by permission of Hill Nadell Literary Agency.

Ethan Watters—"We Aren't the World." Republished with permission of *Pacific Standard*, © 2013; permission conveyed through Copyright Clearance Center, Inc.

Jamie Whyte—"The Right to Your Opinion." From *Crimes Against Logic* by Jamie Whyte. McGraw-Hill © 2005. Reprinted by the permission of Jamie Whyte.

Stephanie M. Wildman with Adrienne D. Davis—"Making Systems of Privilege Visible." Reprinted by permission from Stephanie M. Wildman with Adrienne D. Davis, "Language and Silence: Making Systems of Privilege Visible," 34 *Santa Clara L. Rev.* 881 © 1995. Another version of this essay is available in Stephanie M. Wildman with contributions by Margalynne Armstrong, Adrienne D. Davis, and Trina Grillo, *Privilege Revealed: How Invisible Preference Undermines America* (1996).

Malcolm X [El-Hajj Malik El-Shabazz]—"Selection from *Saved*." "Learning to Read" from *Autobiography of Malcolm X* by Malcolm X as told to Alex Haley, copyright © 1964 by Alex Haley and Malcolm X. Copyright © 1965 by Alex Haley and Betty Shabazz. Used by permission of Ballantine Books, an imprint of Random House, a division of Penguin Random House LLC. All rights reserved.